CONTENTS

According to the tourist importance of a place we give:
— the principal facts of local history;
— a description of "Main Sights";
— a description of "Additional Sights";
— under the title "Excursions", a choice of short or long walks radiating from the major centres.

Some figures...
Area : 301 262 Km²
Coastline : 7 456 Km
Population : 56 014 166 (1976)
Average Pop. density : 186/Km²

D1319476

PRINCIPAL SIGHTS

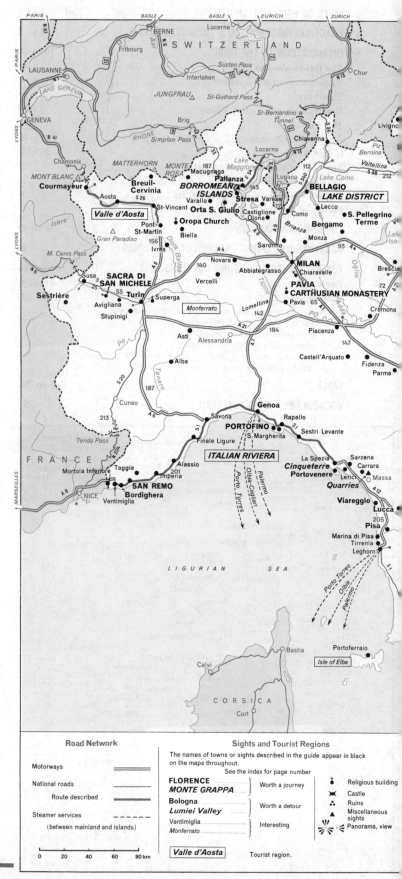

Road Network

Motorways

National roads

Route described

Steamer services
(between mainland and islands)

0   20   40   60   80 km

Valle d'Aosta   Tourist region.

Sights and Tourist Regions

The names of towns or sights described in the guide appear in black
on the maps throughout.
See the index for page number

FLORENCE *MONTE GRAPPA*	Worth a journey
Bologna *Lumiei Valley*	Worth a detour
Ventimiglia *Monferrato*	Interesting

✝ Religious building
⚔ Castle
∴ Ruins
▲ Miscellaneous sights
☀ Panorama, view

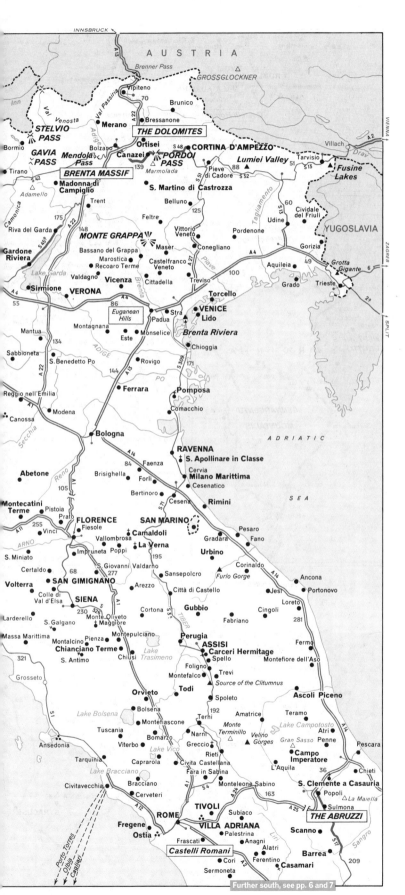

INNSBRUCK

AUSTRIA

Brenner Pass

GROSSGLOCKNER

Inn

Vipiteno

Brunico

Val Passiria

STELVIO
PASS

Merano

THE DOLOMITES

CORTINA D'AMPEZZO

Villach

VIENNA

Bormio

GAVIA
PASS

Mendola
Pass

Bolzano

Ortisei

PORDOI
PASS

Lumiei Valley

Tarvisio

Drav

Canazei

Marmolada

Pieve
di Cadore

Fusine
Lakes

Tirano

BRENTA MASSIF

Madonna di
Campiglio

Adamello

Trent

S. Martino di Castrozza

Belluno

YUGOSLAVIA

ZAGREB

Riva del Garda

Feltre

Cividale
del Friuli

Gardone
Riviera

MONTE GRAPPA

Bassano del Grappa

Maser

Vittorio
Veneto

Pordenone

Udine

Gorizia

Grotta
Gigante

Marostica

Castelfranco
Veneto

Conegliano

Aquileia

Trieste

Recoaro Terme

Valdagno

Vicenza

Cittadella

Treviso

Grado

SPLIT

Sirmione

VERONA

Torcello

Mantua

Euganean
Hills

Padua

Stra

VENICE
Lido

Montagnana

Este

Monselice

Brenta Riviera

Sabbioneta

S. Benedetto Po

Rovigo

Chioggia

ADIGE

PO

Reggio nell'Emilia

Ferrara

POMPOSA

Canossa

Modena

Comacchio

ADRIATIC

Bologna

RAVENNA

Abetone

Faenza

S. Apollinare in Classe

Brisighella

Forlì

Cervia

Milano Marittima

Bertinoro

Cesenatico

SEA

Montecatini
Terme

Pistoia

Prato

Cesena

Rimini

FLORENCE

SAN MARINO

Vinci

Fiesole

Pesaro

ARNO

Vallombrosa

Camaldoli

Gradara

Fano

Imphuneta

Poppi

La Verna

Urbino

S. Miniato

S. Giovanni Valdarno

Corinaldo

Ancona

Certaldo

SAN GIMIGNANO

Sansepolcro

Furlo Gorge

Volterra

Colle di
Val d'Elsa

Arezzo

Città di Castello

Jesi

Portonovo

SIENA

Cortona

Gubbio

Cingoli

Loreto

Larderello

Monte Oliveto
Maggiore

Fabriano

Massa Marittima

S. Galgano

Montepulciano

Perugia

Fermo

Montalcino

Pienza

ASSISI

Chianciano Terme

Chiusi

Lake
Trasimeno

Carceri Hermitage

Spello

Montefiore dell'Aso

S. Antimo

Foligno

Trevi

Grosseto

Orvieto

Montefalco

Source of the Clitumnus

Todi

Ascoli Piceno

Bolsena

Spoleto

Lake Bolsena

Montefiascone

Terni

Amatrice

Teramo

Tuscania

Bomarzo

Narni

Monte
Terminillo

Lake Campotosto

Atri

Viterbo

Lake Vico

Greccio

Velino
Gorges

Gran Sasso

Penne

Ansedonia

Caprarola

Rieti

Campo
Imperatore

Pescara

Tarquinia

Civita Castellana

L'Aquila

Chieti

Lake Bracciano

Fara in Sabina

Civitavecchia

Bracciano

Monteleone Sabino

S. Clemente a Casauria

Cerveteri

Popoli

La Maiella

ROME

TIVOLI

Subiaco

Sulmona

THE ABRUZZI

Fregene

VILLA ADRIANA

Palestrina

Scanno

Ostia

Frascati

Anagni

Alatri

Castelli Romani

Cori

Ferentino

Barrea

Casamari

Sermoneta

Further south, see pp. 6 and 7

5

PRINCIPAL SIGHTS

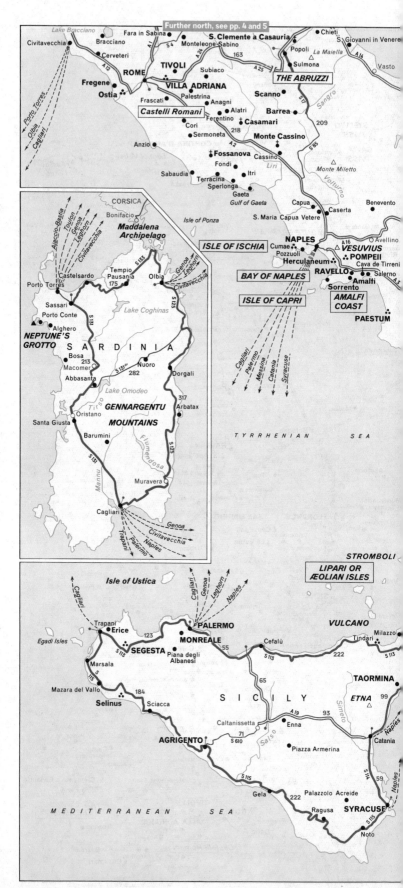

Further north, see pp. 4 and 5

Lake Bracciano
Civitavecchia
Bracciano
Fara in Sabina
Monteleone-Sabino
S. Clemente a Casauria
Chieti
S. Giovanni in Venere
Cerveteri
Popoli
La Maiella
Vasto
ROME
TIVOLI
Subiaco
Sulmona
THE ABRUZZI
Fregene
VILLA ADRIANA
Frascati
Palestrina
Anagni
Scanno
Sangro
Ostia
Castelli Romani
Alatri
Barrea
Cori
Ferentino
Casamari
Anzio
Sermoneta
Monte Cassino
Fossanova
Cassino
Monte Miletto
Fondi
Liri
Volturno
Sabaudia
Terracina
Itri
Sperlonga
Capua
Benevento
Gaeta
Gulf of Gaeta
Caserta
S. Maria Capua Vetere

CORSICA
Bonifacio
Isle of Ponza
NAPLES
VESUVIUS
Cumae
POMPEII
Maddalena Archipelago
ISLE OF ISCHIA
Pozzuoli
Herculaneum
Cava de Tirreni
RAVELLO
Salerno
Castelsardo
Tempio Pausania
Olbia
BAY OF NAPLES
Amalfi
Porto Torres
Sorrento
AMALFI COAST
ISLE OF CAPRI
Sassari
Lake Coghinas
PAESTUM
Porto Conte
Alghero
NEPTUNE'S GROTTO
S A R D I N I A
Bosa
Macomer
Nuoro
Abbasanta
Dorgali
Lake Omodeo
GENNARGENTU MOUNTAINS
Arbatax
Oristano
Santa Giusta
Barumini
T Y R R H E N I A N   S E A
Muravera
Cagliari
Genoa
Civitavecchia
Naples

STROMBOLI
LIPARI OR ÆOLIAN ISLES
Isle of Ustica
PALERMO
VULCANO
Milazzo
Trapani
Erice
MONREALE
Cefalù
Tindari
Egadi Isles
SEGESTA
Piana degli Albanesi
TAORMINA
Marsala
ETNA
Mazara del Vallo
S I C I L Y
Selinus
Sciacca
Caltanissetta
Enna
Catania
AGRIGENTO
Piazza Armerina
Gela
Palazzolo Acreide
Ragusa
SYRACUSE
M E D I T E R R A N E A N   S E A
Noto

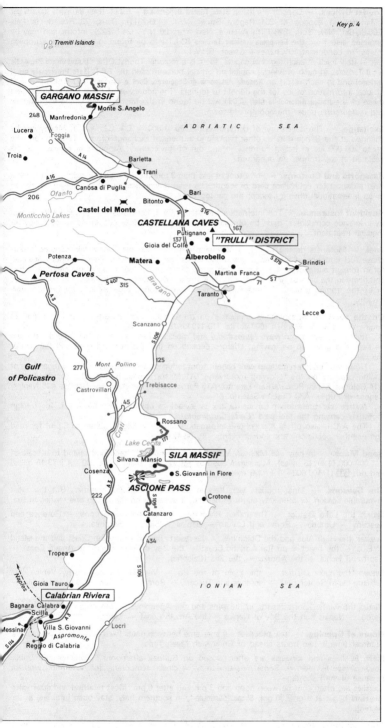

Key p. 4

Tremiti Islands

GARGANO MASSIF
337
Monte S. Angelo
248 Manfredonia
Lucera
Foggia
A 14
Troia
Barletta
Trani
A 16
Canosa di Puglia
206 *Ofanto*
Bari
Monticchio Lakes
Castel del Monte
Bitonto
S 16
CASTELLANA CAVES
167
Putignano
"TRULLI" DISTRICT
Gioia del Colle 137
Potenza
Matera
Alberobello
S 379
Brindisi
Pertosa Caves
S 407
315
Martina Franca 71 S 7
Taranto
A 3
Bradano
Lecce
Scanzano
S 106
125
Mont. Pollino
277
Gulf of Policastro
Trebisacce
Castrovillari
45
Crati
Rossano
5
Lake Cecita 177
Silvana Mansio
SILA MASSIF
Cosenza
S. Giovanni in Fiore
A 3
ASCIONE PASS
222
Crotone
S 108
Catanzaro
434
Tropea
S 106
Gioia Tauro
Naples
Calabrian Riviera
Bagnara Calabra
Scilla
Messina
Villa S. Giovanni
Locri
Aspromonte
S 114
Reggio di Calabria

ADRIATIC SEA

IONIAN SEA

The earthquake of 23 November 1980 and subsequent tremors damaged cities, towns and villages in southern Italy in the Naples, Salerno, Avellino and Potenza area.

ROAD MAPS

With this guide use the latest **Michelin maps:**

for the whole country,
Michelin map No. **988** *Italy-Switzerland at 1:1 000 000;*

for northern Italy,
Michelin maps Nos. **24 26 77** *at 1:200 000 and No.* **195** *at 1:100 000.*

7

PRACTICAL INFORMATION

Tourist Offices. — Consult the Italian State Tourist Department — E.N.I.T. (Ente Nazionale Italiano per il Turismo); in London at 201 Regent Street, W.I. (439-2311); Paris, 23 Rue de la paix (266-66-68); New York, 626 Fifth Avenue, New York 20 N.Y. (24 54822). Information may be obtained also from the **Compania Italiana Turismo** (C.I.T.) to be found in many large European towns; in London at 10 Charles II Street, S.W.I.

In Italy itself in each regional capital, there is a regional Tourist Office (**Assessorato Regionale per il Turismo**); in each provincial capital an official bureau called the **E.P.T. (Ente Provinciale per il Turismo)** and in each resort an **Azienda Autonoma di Soggiorno, Cura e Turismo (A.S.)** which is a kind of local information office for the benefit of tourists. The addresses of these tourist offices and those of the **Italian Automobile Club (A.C.I.)** will be found in the Michelin Red Guide Italia (hotels and restaurants) under the appropriate town.

Exchange. — The Italian unit of currency is the *lire:* 1 800 = £ 1; 825 = $ 1: Money can be changed at the Banca d'Italia, other banks and authorised exchange offices. Tourists can take up to 200 000 lire in Italian currency in and out of the country. Amounts in excess must be declared at the frontier on departure.

Passports and Customs. — For a tour of less than 3 months duration the visitor must have: a valid passport (or equivalent card of identity), a valid driving licence with an Italian translation or an international driving licence; the car log book.

Accident Insurance. — The International Insurance Card, known as the "Green Card", issued by insurance companies, must be obtained. It is advisable to take out an insurance Policy for medical treatment.

Fuel. — Motorists driving to Italy in a foreign registered car may on certain conditions purchase fuel coupons at reduced prices (issue temporarily suspended). These coupons are paid for in foreign currency and are issued (on presentation of car log book, identification and hire certificate in the case of hired cars) in the U.K. by the motoring organisations and the E.N.I.T., or by the frontier offices of the A.C.I. Apply to the motoring organisations for further information.

On the road. — Speed limits applicable on trunk roads and motorways are according to engine capacity: 80-90 km/h (600 cc) to 110-140 km/h (over 1 300 cc).

Italy has many motorways *(autostrade)* and most of these are toll roads; the ticket must be kept and given up on leaving; charges depend on the distances travelled and the size of the car.

However, foreign registered cars benefit from reduced rates (motorcycle rate) regardless of engine capacity on the following motorways: A1 Milan-Florence-Rome; A13 Bologna-Padua; A14 Bologna-Rimini-Pescara-Bari-Taranto; A15 Parma-La Spezia; A2 Rome-Naples; A16 Naples-Canosa di Puglia, A30 Caserta-Salerno.

A free car breakdown service (a tax is levied) is operated by the A.C.I. for foreign motorists carrying the fuel card *(Carta Carburante)*.

The A.C.I. also offers a telephone information service in English (8 am to 5 pm) for road and weather conditions and tourist events: ☏ 06-4212.

Road Maps. — In Italy use Michelin Main Road Map no. **988**, Italy/Switzerland to a scale of 1/1 000 000 (1 in/16 miles). Michelin Maps nos. **24**, **26**, **77** (scale 1/200 000 - 1 in/3.15 miles) and no. **195** (1/100 000 - 1 in/1.5 miles).

The Seasons. — Most tourists visit Italy in the late spring and summer. But the most favourable season for a holiday ought to depend, if possible, on the region one wishes to see.

Spring: the Lake District — The Italian Riviera — Venice and its environs — Florence and Tuscany — Umbria — Rome and Latium — Naples — Sicily — Sardinia.

Summer: the High Alps and the Dolomites — the resorts on the Tyrrhenian Coast and the Island of Elba — the beaches on the Adriatic Coast — the Bay of Naples and the Amalfi Coast — Capri and Ischia — the Abruzzi — the Sila (Calabria).

Autumn: the Lake District — the Plain of the Po — Venetia and particularly Venice (the "season" is in September) — Florence and Tuscany — Rome and Latium — Bari and Apulia — Sicily.

Winter: the winter sports resorts in the Alps and the Apennines — the Italian Riviera — Lake Garda — Naples and the Bay of Naples — the Amalfi Coast — Sicily.

Hours of Opening. — Italy practises summer time between dates fixed annually by parliament. Summer time is two hours ahead of Greenwich Mean Time.

Public buildings and **museums** are often closed on Sunday afternoons, Mondays and public holidays (see list below). Some museums may be closed temporarily for restoration work or because of staff shortage.
Churches are often shut between noon and 3 pm and after 6 pm. Most **theatrical** and **other entertainments** begin at 9 or 9.30 pm. **Shops**, particularly in southern Italy, stay open until late in the evening.

Principal Public Holidays. — 1 January, 25 April (Anniversary of the 1945 Liberation), 1 May, first Sunday in June, 15 August (Ferragosto) and 25 December. In addition each town celebrates the feast of its patron Saint.

Hotels and Restaurants. — To find a hotel or restaurant consult the current Michelin Red Guide Italia which is published yearly and lists establishments according to grade, comfort, location, amenities and prices.

Camping. — All you need do before pitching your tent is to ask the landowner's permission. There are also many equipped camping grounds in Italy.

Information should be obtained from the Federazione del Campeggio, Casella Postale 649, 50100 Firenze (Florence) ☏ 8878641. This organisation publishes a map of camping sites in Italy and a list of camping grounds which offer special rates to holders of the International Camping Card; it also publishes an annual, *Campeggi e villaggi turistici in Italia* in collaboration with the Italian Touring Club (T.C.I.).

A FEW CURRENT PRICES

	Cigarettes *(Esportazione)*	450 lire
	Cigarettes (American)	950-1 200 —
	Newspapers (foreign)	600 —
	Newspapers (Italian)	300 —
	Postage: letter, abroad	220 —
	Postage: postcard, abroad	150 —
	Bus, trolleybus and train (generally a fixed fare)	100-200 —
	Milan metro	200 —
	Attended car park	250-500 —
	Petrol (per litre)	685-700 —
	Oil (1 kg. can)	2 400-3 500 —
	Garage (for medium sized car for 1 night)	3 000-6 000 —

TOURIST EVENTS

DATE	PLACE	NATURE OF THE EVENT
February (Carnival)	Viareggio	Grand masked procession with allegorical and comic floats.
Last Friday of Carnival	Verona	Bacchanalian Carnival of the *Gnocco*.
1 April	San Marino	Investiture of the Regents of the Town *(see p 221)*.
Holy Week	Taranto	Grand Processions *(see p 233)*.
Easter Day	Sulmona	Feast of the *Madonna che scappa in Piazza* *(see p 233)*.
Easter Day (mid-day)	Florence	*Scoppio del Carro (see p 103)*.
1 May	Cagliari	Feast of St. Efisio *(see p 268)*.
First Saturday in May	Naples	Miracle of St Januarius *(see p 153)*.
7 and 8 May	Bari	Feast of St. Nicholas *(see p 58)*.
15 May	Gubbio	*Corsa dei Ceri (see p 121)*.
Last Sunday in May	Gubbio	*Palio,* or horse race, of the Arbaleta; shooting match on the Piazza della Signoria.
End of May	Taormina	Carnival with Sicilian costumes and floats.
End of May (or last two weeks in September)	Sassari	*Cavalcata Sarda (see p 271)*.
Ascension Day	Florence	Feast of the Crickets (sale of singing crickets — *see p 103)*.
Mid-June to mid-July	Spoleto	International Festival of Music, Drama and Dancing.
24 and 28 June	Florence	Ball game in 16C costume *(see p 103)*.
2 July	Siena	*Palio delle Contrade;* procession in 15C costume of representatives of the 17 quarters of the town. Horse race in the Piazza del Campo *(see p 226)*.
16 July	Naples	Feast of Santa Maria del Carmine (illumination of bell-tower).
Night of 3rd Saturday/ Sunday in July	Venice	Feast of the Redeemer at the Guidecca.
First Sunday in August	Ascoli Piceno	Feast of the Quintain *(see p 53)*.
14 August	Sassari	Procession of Candles *(see p 271)*.
16 August	Siena	*Padio delle Contrade (see p 226)*.
Second Sunday in September	Arezzo	The Saracen's Game on the Piazza Grande *(see p 52)*.
First Sunday in September	Venice	Historical regatta on the Grand Canal.
8 September	Naples	Feast of the Madonna of Piedigrotta.
7 September	Florence	Night festival of the *Rificoloni,* or lanterns *(see p 103)*.
8 September	Loreto	Feast of the Nativity of the Virgin *(see p 133)*.
Second and third Sundays in September	Foligno	Tilting at the Quintain (Carrousel — *see p 114)*.
Second Sunday in September	Sansepolcro	Cross-bow competition held in mediaeval costumes.
13 September	Lucca	*Luminara di Santa Croce (see p 134)*.
Third Sunday in September	Asti	*Palio* or horse race *(see p 57)*.
Last two weeks in September (or end of May)	Sassari	*Cavalcata Sarda (see p 271)*.
19 September	Naples	Miracle of St. Januarius *(see p 153)*.
1 October	San Marino	Investiture of the Regents of the Town *(see p 221)*.
10 December	Loreto	Feast of the Translation of the Holy House (Santa Casa — *see p 133)*.
End of December	Naples	Display of local cribs.

INTRODUCTION TO THE TOUR

From the time of the Gaulish leader Brennus (who invaded Italy and defeated a Roman army in 390 BC) to that of Napoleon (1769-1821), Italy exercised on the peoples of Europe a fascination which made it the theatre of many wars. Normans, Angevins, Valois, Germanic foot-soldiers, Napoleon's *grognards* (grousers) and the "Kaiserlicks" of Franz-Josef, Emperor of Austria-Hungary fought for the possession of this happy land.

Today peaceful armies of tourists set their feet in the steps of Du Bellay, Montaigne, Goethe, Chateaubriand, Stendhal, Byron, Shelley and innumerable artists who have come to drink from the spring of western civilisation.

Traditional Italy. — For many people, Italy, the mother of the arts, is a museum-country where the masterpieces born of Antiquity, Christian and humanist culture are preserved. Here are found the Greek temples of Sicily or Campania, which should be seen in the light of the setting sun; Etruscan burial grounds; the Roman Forum or dead cities now brought to light; basilicas glittering with mosaics; churches splendid with marble and sculpture, and museums housed in palaces with majestic façades where pictures and statues, often celebrated works of art, are brought together.

The Roman Catholic makes his pilgrimage to the sources of his faith. Rome, the cradle of Catholicism and seat of the Head of the Church, is the meeting-place of Catholics from all over the world who come to pray at the tomb of St. Peter and to venerate the places where the martyrs suffered.

Italy is also a landscape of pure and noble aspect, where orange trees blossom and where wheat, vines and olives, the classic trilogy of the Mediterranean countries, flourish. It is the Tuscan countryside, with its hills and valleys, laced with rows of cypresses and umbrella pines. It is the light bouquet of Chianti, the scents of the Borromean Islands, the warm brown brick of churches and mediaeval towers, the Baroque forms of cool fountains, the gondolas dancing on the Grand Canal.

A marvellous golden light bathes ancient cities, mountains, lakes and graceful bays; it purifies outlines, magnifies shapes and, by its brightness, brings joy to the heart.

Modern Italy. — In this land abounding in every type of beauty, the Italian lives and moves with perfect ease. Dark-haired, black-eyed, gesticulating, nimble and passionate, he is all movement and fantasy.

This overflowing vitality appears in many modern achievements that may surprise the visitor. Improvement of the soil, industrial complexes, nuclear power centres, dams, motorways and skyscrapers, characterise the fantastic economic development which has taken place after World War II, giving Italy a new look and belying the legend of the macaroni-eating, guitar-playing Italian. A new way of life has been created in the country.

THE ITALIAN WAY OF LIFE

There are two good places to watch the behaviour of Italians: one is a café terrace in the main square of a small town, which will give you a picture of public life; the other is the interior of a large church, where you may observe the bearing of different individuals.

The Passeggiata. — This evening walk takes place in the main squares of provincial towns or the main streets near them. Every evening, before dinner, the wives of prominent men, young men and smartly dressed girls go for a stroll. The men sit on the café terraces at the tables to watch the show. When they are prominent citizens you will hear them addressing one another by their titles, which are deeply respected in Italy: "dear *Ragioniere*" (Bachelor of Arts), "esteemed *Dottore*" (Doctor), "illustrious *Professore*" (Professor), "*Avvocato*" (Advocate), "*Ingegnere*" (Engineer), "*Direttore*" (Director), etc. Road-keepers and dustmen are often called *Capo* (Chief) because of the gold-braided caps they wear.

Religious Feeling. — The Catholic faith plays an important part in Italian life and still exercises considerable influence on civil and political events. In the churches you will notice how freely the congregation move about, as though they were in a public square, and their behaviour may seem to the uninitiated to lack respect for the holy place; but their piety is frequently shown when they go in pilgrimage, walk in procession, gather in reverend crowds, genuflect before altars and venerate chalices containing relics. During services a low murmuring provides a base drone to the liturgy.

Manners. — The Italians are courteous and friendly, always willing to render service: you should be cordial, too, and ready to make friends. Take care how you dress, for even humble people are nearly always neatly turned out. Do not walk about town in shorts and open-necked shirts; women must have their heads and arms covered when entering churches.

At Table. — Italian table manners are different from the English and there is nowhere better to observe them than in a restaurant. Note particularly — and try to imitate — the dexterity of Italians in eating spaghetti; do not chop up your spaghetti with a knife on the pretext that it is too long, take two strands on your fork and roll it round pivoting the fork in the bowl of your spoon and praying that it may not fall off into the *sugo* (sauce).

On the Road and in Town. — Make good use of your horn, do not race other cars and never lose your temper, even if another driver seems to pass you aggressively. You will have to be patient if you travel on the national highways as traffic is often slowed down by heavy lorries. It is wiser not to leave any valuables in your car and to lock it when you leave it. You should also be wary of exchange rates which are above average and of purchasing goods on sale at bargain prices.

*Join us in our never ending task
of keeping up to date.
Send us your comments
and suggestions, please.
Michelin Tyre Co Ltd
Tourism Department
81 Fulham Road, LONDON SW3 6RD*

APPEARANCE OF THE COUNTRY

Italy extends for 1 200 km - 745 miles — from north to south. It has 7 456 km - 4 632 miles — of coastline and juts like a pier into the Mediterranean between Greece and Spain. It is bounded by the Alpine range and by four inner seas: the Ligurian, Tyrrhenian, Ionian and Adriatic. It has an extraordinary variety of climate — wonderful sunlight effects — and topography and supported 56 014 166 inhabitants in 1976 on an area of 301 262 km² -139 087 sq miles.

Topography. — The Alps, which arose from the folding of the earth's crust in the Tertiary Era, form a gigantic barrier and a reservoir of electrical power. They consist mainly of shale, with a limestone fringe, the Pre-Alps. At the heads of deep valleys great passes communicate with France, Switzerland and Austria. These are, with France, the Tenda (1 871 m - 6 139 ft), the Mont Cenis (2 083 m - 6 837 ft) and the Little St. Bernard Passes (2 188 m -7 178 ft); with Switzerland, the Great St. Bernard (2 469 m - 8 101 ft), the Simplon (2 005 m - 6 578 ft), and the St. Gothard Passes (2 108 m - 6 916 ft); and with Austria, the Brenner Pass (1 374 m - 4 508 ft). The Mont Blanc and Tenda, the Great St. Bernard and San Bernardino road tunnels assure all the year round passage between Italy and France, and Italy and Switzerland.

The most famous peaks attract many mountaineers: at their head is the Mont Blanc Massif, whose 4 807 m - 15 771 ft — surpasses the 4 477 m - 14 688 ft — of the Matterhorn, the 4 634 m - 15 203 ft — of Monte Rosa, the 3 150 m - 10 336 ft — of the Cima Brenta and the 3 342 m - 10 964 ft of the Marmolada in the Dolomites.

The Apennines, a limestone range formed by a Tertiary fold running down into Sicily, are the backbone of the Italian Peninsula. The Gran Sasso, with its altitude of 2 914 m - 9 560 ft — is their highest point.

The face of Italy has been changed by volcanic eruptions. The volcanic massifs are sometimes embedded in the Apennines like the Sabine and Alban Hills (the latter being the Castelli Romani hills), sometimes detached from this chain, like the Euganean Hills. Some volcanoes are still active: Vesuvius and the Phlegrean Fields in the district of Naples, Etna in Sicily and Stromboli in the Lipari or Æolian Islands.

Climate. — This varies with latitude and altitude. The mountain climate is harsh and windy; the continental climate, in the Plain of the Po, runs to extremes, with biting cold in winter and torrid heat in summer; the Mediterranean climate, which covers most of Italy, is mild in winter and hot and dry in summer, but cooled by sea breezes. See the section on **the Seasons** (p 8).

THE REGIONS

The regions differ greatly and often show marked local peculiarities. The largest towns are: in the north, Milan, Turin, Genoa, Venice; in the centre, the capital, Rome and Florence; in the south, Naples and Palermo.

The Valle d'Aosta. — This great, deep furrow between the highest mountains in Europe, is watered by the Dora Baltea River whose tributaries form picturesque lateral valleys: the Valtournenche, Val di Gressoney, Val d'Ayas, Val Grisanche.

From Pont-St-Martin to Courmayeur the people still speak French, but Italianisation is proceeding rapidly. Towns and villages have kept their French names, and the region enjoys a certain degree of administrative autonomy.

A pastoral, mountain people, attached to their traditions, they live in chalets and rear their sheep. The valley's economy, however, depends primarily on its iron mines at Cogne and the tourism which has developed as a result of the construction of the Great St. Bernard and Mont Blanc Tunnels.

Aosta is the capital of the valley; Courmayeur and Breuil-Cervinia are large winter sports resorts.

Piedmont. — Piedmont, at the foot of the mountain range, has a landscape, a dialect, a history and a way of life similar to those of the nearer parts of France.

Piedmont consists mainly of the Plain of the Po, intersected with long rows of poplars, where grassland alternates with crops of wheat and rice. This last crop, introduced by Count Cavour (Italian statesman, 1810-1861), is concentrated in the districts of Vercelli and Novara (three-fifths of Italian production). The **Canavese district**, west of the lakes, specialises in the growth of hemp.

Southeast of Turin the gently rolling chalk hills of the **Monferrato** bear the well known Asti vines and produce the famous Gorgonzola cheese (in the Casale Monferrato region).

As regards industry, large hydro-electric power stations supply current for the textile factories of Biella, the metal, engineering and chemical works of Turin (motor-cars and tyres) and for food and paper production, etc.

Turin, on the Po, is rich in industries, a fashion centre, and the former capital of the dynasty of Savoy. It moulds the character of the typical Piedmontese, who is intelligent energetic and a remarkably gifted mechanic.

Lombardy. — This is the busiest region in Italy. With its quivering aspens, poplars and willows, it occupies the green Plain of the Po, between the Ticino and the Mincio. To the north the great lake valleys formed by glaciers give access to the Alpine passes.

Lombardy takes first place in the production of silk. In the **Brianza district**, rows of mulberry bushes divide the wheat and maize fields. Natural or artificial pastures have given birth to a modern milk products industry which makes, among others, the famous Gorgonzola cheese. Finally, in the **Lomellina district**, great areas are given over to rice growing.

Many towns are scattered over the countryside. Their bankers and traders spread the name of Lombards all over mediaeval and Renaissance Europe. Today Como is the centre of the silk industry, Bergamo has engineering and textile works, Brescia has developed its steel, chemical and engineering industries, while Mantua and Cremona live on agriculture and Pavia on its famous university and its sewing machines.

Milan is a thriving town with ultra-modern institutions connecting it with the whole world (the Milan Fair). As one of the most important commercial centres of Europe it specialises, in the surrounding suburbs, in such industries as textiles, petroleum, chemistry, metallurgy, engineering and food.

The Venetias. — There are three: Venetia proper, or Veneto; Venezia Giulia (Friuli — Venezia Giulia) — the plain of Friuli along the coast and Istria; and Venezia Tridentina (Trentino and Alto Adige).

Venetia (Veneto) comprises the basins formed by the Po and the Brenta. Near Verona, on the glaciary moraines of Lake Garda, a mild climate makes it possible to cultivate fruit trees, olives and especially vines of high quality (Bardolino, Valpolicella). The valleys which run up into the Pre-Alps use hydro-electric power in the locally established textile industries. Like Vicenza and Padua, Verona is an agricultural, commercial and industrial centre now that it has lost its strategic importance as the key to the Adige gap. The plain is rich in various crops: wheat, maize, mulberries, vines climbing among fruit trees and forage crops. But danger lurks in the rivers, whose changeable courses give rise to flooding.

The landscape is punctuated by two small volcanic groups: the Berici Montains south of Vicenza and the Euganean Hills near Padua. The slopes of these blackish heights carry vines, peach orchards and hot springs.

In the deltas of the Po (Polesina) and of the Adige lie impoverished, grandiose and desolate areas, subject to river floods but beginning to show profits after reclamation. Wheat and beet are grown on an industrial scale.

The coastline takes the form of lagoons (lido) separated from the sea by spits of sand pierced by gaps (porti). Venice, whose industries are growing (oil refineries, foundries, chemical industries at Mestre Marghera), is built on piles in one of these lagoons.

Friuli — Venezia Giulia prolongs Venetia to the east, and forms an administrative and culturally independent area. It is essentially a silk-spinning district, but vines and fruit trees also flourish there. Udine is a busy centre.

By way of the Trieste Riviera you will reach that port, the natural (and formerly the territorial) outlet of Austria, which trades with the Far East (Lloyd Triestino) and is still subject to a special statute.

The Trentino — Alto Adige is an area where race and language are partly Germanic and the region enjoys a certain degree of autonomy; it includes the Valleys of the Adige and the Isarco and the mountains surrounding them. The Adige Valley, at the southern exit from the Brenner Pass, has always been easy of access and much used for traffic. Though deep, it opens out towards the sunny south, and it is rich. Cereals grow on the floor of the valley, vines and fruit trees higher up, then come pastures (Merano has a well-known breed of horses). Bolzano and Trent where there is some industrial development, are the regional markets.

The **Dolomites** lie in the Trentino and in Venetia. Their eastern section is called the Cadore. The range is a limestone massif, much worn by erosion *(details p 92)*.

The **Carnic Alps**, a shale massif covered by forests of conifers and great pastures, lie farther east.

Emilia Romagna. — The plain skirting the Apennines derives its name from the Via Emilia, a straight Roman road that crosses it from Piacenza to Rimini; south of Bologna the district is known as Romagna. Its soil, which is intensively cultivated, is among the best in Italy .for wheat, barley and beet. The monotonous landscape consists of wide fields intersected at regular intervals by rows of mulberries and vines clinging to tall poles, maples or elms; so close do the vines cling that an Italian proverb has it: *"si amano come la vite e l'olmo"* (they love each other as do the vine and the elm). Other vines grow on the slopes of the Apennines.

The towns are strung out along the Via Emilia: the most important, Bologna, famous for its ancient university, and linked today by good roads with Tuscany, is a communications and industrial (steel, engineering, food) centre and a market for wheat and pigs.

(After photo by De Agostini)

A lake in the Dolomites

The region to the east of Ferrara through which runs the Po river is devoted to rice growing. To the south are the *valli* of Comacchio, great lagoons where fishermen catch eels at their spring and autumn migrations. Ravenna, which has been somewhat revived by its port and its oil refinery, was once the capital of the Western Roman Empire, and the chief town of Romagna before the creation of Emilia-Romagna, with Bologna as the chief town of the province.

Liguria. — Liguria, furrowed with deep, narrow valleys at right angles to the coast, had a maritime civilisation before the Roman Era. The steep slopes of the inner valleys are dotted with poor perched villages, watching over groves of chestnut or olive trees and cultivated terraces.

The rocky, indented coastline has few fish to offer but has enjoyed heavy coastwise traffic since the time of the Ligures (200 BC), facilitated by many small deep-water ports. The Roman Empire gave its present appearance to the country, with olive groves and vineyards, to which have been added vegetables, fruit (melons, peaches) and flowers grown on an industrial scale. The **Riviera di Ponente**, west of Genoa, is sunnier and more sheltered than the **Riviera di Levante** to the east, but the latter has a more luxuriant vegetation.

The chief towns are Imperia, Savona and Genoa (shipyards, oil terminal, thermo-electric power station) and La Spezia, the naval base and commercial port (thermo-electric power plant, steel industry).

Tuscany. — Mountains and hills with clean, graceful curves under a limpid light, plains, forests and vineyards join with the serenity of cypress and pine to make this country a temple of beauty. By some mysterious influence, sometimes called "the Tuscan miracle", this harmony has gifted the Tuscan people with great artistic sense and a deep love of liberty. Florence, the capital of Tuscany, is the crucible in which the Tuscan genius has been formed.

None the less, the province is composed of a variety of soils. On the sea, the Tuscan Archipelago, with the Island of Elba, mountainous and containing rich deposits of iron ore, faces a shore which is sometimes rocky (south of Leghorn), sometimes flat and sandy (Versi-

lia, Viareggio). North of the Arno the shining marble flanks of the **Apuan Alps** bask in the Carrara sunshine, while round Volterra the summits, white with sand and salt, crumble here and there, forming crevasses and cliffs known as *balze*.

In the heart of Tuscany the **Arno Basin** lies fertile and beautiful: festoons of vines and silvery olives come to meet fields of wheat, tobacco and maize; peppers, pumpkins and the famous Lucca beans grow among the mulberries. Alone on their mounds, old farms are ennobled by the fine shapes of pines or cypresses, standing out against a pale blue sky.

Southern Tuscany is a land of hills, soft and vine-clad in the Chianti district south of Florence, quiet and pastoral near Siena, dry and desolate round Monte Oliveto Maggiore, massive and mysterious in the metal-bearing mountains, marked by the white plumes of the *soffioni*, jets of steam from the bowels of the earth.

On the borders of Latium, **Maremma**, with its melancholy beauty, formerly a marshy district haunted by shepherds and bandits has now been reclaimed.

(After photo by del Duca)

Tuscan countryside

Umbria. — The gentle land where St. Francis lived is a country of hills, valleys and river basins, where the poplars raise their rustling heads to limpid skies. This is the Green Umbria of the Clitumnus (Clitunno) Valley, whose pastures were already famous in ancient times and were described in the poems of Giosuè Carducci (1835-1907). Umbria has two lakes, Trasimeno and Piediluco, and many rivers, including the Tiber. Mediaeval cities which succeeded Etruscan settlements overlook ravines and valleys: grim Gubbio, haughty Perugia, the capital of Umbria, Franciscan Assisi, Spello, Spoletto, etc. Others stand each in the centre of a plain, like Foligno and Terni, the great Italian arsenal.

The Marches. — So-called because they were formerly frontier provinces of the Frankish Empire and the papal domains, the Marches form a much sub-divided area between San Marino and Ascoli Piceno, where the parallel spurs of the Apennines run down into the Adriatic, forming a series of deep, narrow valleys. There is, however, a flat and rectilinear coastal belt dotted with beaches and canal-ports. The inhabitants of the Marches have a reputation for friendliness, piety and diligence. Apart from the capital, Ancona, a busy port, most of the old towns are built on commanding sites: among then Urbino and Loreto should be noted, one for its artistic atmosphere, the other for its venerated church.

Latium. — Lying between the Tyrrhenian Sea and the Apennines, from Tuscan Maremma to Gaèta, Latium, the cradle of Roman civilisation, borders a sandy coast whose seaports, such as Ostia, are now silted up. Civitavecchia today is the only modern port on the coastline. In the centre of Latium, Rome is mainly a residential city.

To the east and north, volcanic hills, whose craters contain lonely lakes, overlook the famous **Roman Campagna**, beloved by the writers and painters who have often described this great, desolate expanses, peopled by shepherds with their flocks and covered with aqueducts and ruins under a wondrous light. In the last few years these waste lands *(latifundia),* formerly hotbeds of malaria, have been revived: the drainage of the Pontine Marshes, in the Latina district south of Rome, is the most spectacular achievement in this field. Cassino (cars) is the most important industrial centre. A flourishing industrial area has developed round the atomic centre at Latina.

To the south is the distinctive Ciociaria. This region takes its name from the shoes *(ciocie),* which form part of the traditional costume. They have thick soles, and thongs which are wound round the calf of the leg. The beauty of the women and its folklore are renowned.

The Abruzzi. — Under its harsh climate, this is the part of the Apennines which most suggests a country of high mountains, grand and wild, with its Gran Sasso and Maiella Massifs. Narrow gorges, chalky mountain masses with slopes cut into sharp ridges, great empty, windy plateaux (the Cinquemiglia) and uninhabited forests attract nature lovers and enthusiasts for winter sports. A nature reserve in the Upper Sangro Valley gives protection to chamois, bears, etc. In basins sheltered from the wind are meadows and rich plantations (vines, almonds, olives) whose products are sent to market towns like L'Aquila and Sulmona or Avezzano, which lie near a great drained marsh bearing maize, tomatoes and beet as well as pasture. There is some industrial development in the Chieti-Pescara area.

Molise. — Molise extends south of the Abruzzi, with which it has many features in common: a mountainous relief, dark valleys and wild forests. The area is bordered on the west by the Maiella, on the east by the Adriatic. Agriculture forms the basis of the local economy.

Campania. — Campania forms a fertile crescent along the Bay of Naples. It owes its name to the Neapolitan countryside, which is enriched by volcanic soil. As a port for trade with the Americas, Naples has tended to become industrialised: it has engineering works, steel plants, oil refineries and food factories (macaroni and canning).

As for the Bay of Naples, its charm and its mystery stirred the imagination of the Ancients 1000 years before Christ. It was here that Ulysses, in the *Odyssey,* narrowly escaped the wiles of the sirens; here too, the ancients located the entrance to the Infernal Kingdom, terrified as they were by volcanic eruptions and the oppressive atmosphere of the Phlegrean (scorching) Fields and of Vesuvius.

The Romantic poets of the 19C would no longer recognise the coast between Pozzuoli and Castellamare, now covered with buildings and factories, but they would still be moved by the enchanting beauties of Posillipo and the Italian Sea, the Sorrento Peninsula with its flowering orange trees and the Islands of Capri, Ischia and Procida.

Apulia, Basilicata, Calabria. — These three provinces cover the foot of the Italian "boot". **Apulia,** on the east side, facing the Adriatic, is less poor than is commonly supposed. Agriculture is flourishing. The wooded but relatively barren promontory of Gargano is distinguished from the rest by its altitude and its position as spur of the coast.

South of Bari the vegetation, peculiar dwellings *(trulli)* resembling circular beehives of uncemented stone, and almost Oriental customs, characterise an unusual type of country.

Bari, the capital of Apulia, has regained the position it enjoyed at the time of the Crusades, thanks to its September fair and the traffic of its port with the Levant.

Basilicata, or Lucania, and **Calabria,** to the west and south, comprise differing types of country: the rocky *corniche* from the Gulf of Policastro to Reggio, the grim, grand mountains of the Sila Massif, with its vast mountain pastures and wide horizons, the great chestnut forests clothing the upper slopes, and finally the prosperous coastal plain along the Gulf of Taranto, rich in vines, citrus and olive trees. From the summits of the Aspromonte may be seen extensive views of the Adriactic and Tyrrhenian Seas, Sicily and the Lipari (Æolian) Islands.

Sardinia and Sicily. — Descriptions of these islands are given on pp 267 and 272.

(After photo by T.C.I.)

Church in Calabria

ECONOMY

At one time, Italy was mainly devoted to agriculture but in recent years there has been an astonishing industrial expansion taking place and the country now has modern installations.

The Italian economy which was in full expansion when the oil crisis struck is today one of the most advanced in Europe in spite of a strong recession in 1975. Though suffering a certain shortage of capital, aggravated by the almost total lack of coal and basic raw materials (iron), it has been able to get remarkable results from its hydro-electric resources and its subterranean heavy gas. A steadily growing population (nearly 57 million inhabitants in 1979) moreover keeps Italy supplied with plentiful labour.

AGRICULTURE

The agricultural sector has made every effort to improve traditional farming methods taking into account the relief (terrace cultivation in mountain areas), soil (clay, volcanic and marshy land), and climate of the different regions.

Italy is a land of contrasts with large numbers of small holdings following the redistribution of poor agricultural land, alongside large enterprises. Measures have been adopted on several fronts: mechanisation (in the Padua plain), single crop or mixed farming, use of fertilisers, drainage, irrigation, dams in low-lying plains as in the Po region, land reclamation and reaforestation to combat soil erosion.

Special Crops. — The Italians use the geographical situation of their country and its peculiar climate to produce unusual crops.

Rice. — This grain, which requires a great deal of water and heat for ripening, finds favourable soils in the Po Plain, which is saturated with water and can be flooded or drained at will by means of sluices and pumping stations.

After the ploughing by tractor, comes the spring sowing and the planting-out, formerly done by long lines of women workers, the *mondine*, wearing rice-straw hats and today done mostly mechanically. Once the rice has been harvested, husking and blanching or instead "parboiling", when the rice is baked whole, takes place.

The chief areas of production are Piedmont (Vercelli-Novara district), Lombardy (Lomellina), Venezia (the Po Plain) and Emilia-Romagna (Ferrara). Production in 1979 amounted to nearly 1 031 000 metric tons.

The Mulberry and Silk. — The silk industry was introduced into Sicily in the 12C and developed in Venetia and Lombardy. Annual production in 1978 totalled 181.5 metric tons of cocoon. Production of raw silk is now concentrated in Venetia.

In 1979 the Italian processing industry used over 31 000 metric tons of raw silk from the Far East. Spinning is concentrated in the districts of Como, Milan and Varese. Italy is the leading producer of raw silk and of spun or woven textiles. Nylon, rayon and other synthetic fibres compete strongly with natural silk.

Mediterranean Crops. — As in all Mediterranean countries, agriculture is dominated by wheat, vines and olives. As a basic crop wheat, hard (for *pasta*) and soft (for bread), amounted to 9 350 000 metric tons in 1978 (U.K.: 6 610 000 metric tons) while the vines produced 1 400 000 metric tons of table grapes and 10 000 000 metric tons of grapes for wine production. Italy is the second European producer of wheat after France and is the world's leading wine and olive oil producer. Olive production was 2 300 000 metric tons in 1978. Other important crops include maize at over 6 200 000 metric tons and citrus fruits at 2 800 000 metric tons. Italy is the world's leading orange and lemon producer (1 600 000 and almost 800 000 metric tons in 1978 respectively).

Cattle-breeding. — Livestock includes many sheep (approx. 9 million) bred mainly in Sardinia, while cattle are limited to 8 700 000 mostly in the Po Plain, goats 980 000 mainly in the south, donkeys and mules about 240 000 and horses more than 270 000 in 1978. Cattle-breeding aims equally at milk and meat production and has given birth to an important cheese industry making Italy one of the leading producers. Pig-breeding (approx. 9 million head) also plays a large part in Italian farming. (U.K.: sheep, 21 651 000; cattle, 13 493 000; pigs, 7 965 000).

SOURCES OF ENERGY

Italy is lacking in the traditional mineral sources of power.

Its production of coal (Sardinia) and lignite (Tuscany, Umbria, Lucania) is strictly limited. It therefore has to draw on its subterranean gases and its mountain torrents. The development of these sources of power is beneficial not only to Italy but to the whole of Europe. Atomic energy is of growing importance to the economy.

Oil and its Derivatives. — Production of petroleum is somewhat limited (1 478 000 metric tons yearly) but natural gas reached 14 000 million cubic metres in 1978 and production is increasing.

Prospecting continues throughout the country, especially off shore, in the Po Plain and in Sicily.

Gas is distributed by a network of pipelines more than 12 000 km - 7 452 miles — long. In a large part of Italy, methane, propane and butane are burnt in the factories. They are also used for domestic heating and to drive transport vehicles.

Italy has built large refineries and in the main is a net importer of crude oil (more than 109 million tons yearly).

Hydro-electric Power. — The hydro-electric power stations (over 2 000) and thermal power stations (over 500) produce about 170 000 million kWh. yearly.

In Italy there are few huge plants like those on the Rhine, or the Rhone, but a multitude of medium sized plants. Most of them (75 per cent) are in the Trentino-Alto Adige region, in Lombardy, Piedmont and Venetia. The Apennines are more difficult to develop because of the torrential nature of their rivers; none the less, the Terni-Tivoli area is fairly well supplied. In the south, especially in the Sila, several dams supply southern Italy and Sicily with electric current.

Nearly 60 per cent of this electricity is used by industry.

Atomic Energy. — Atomic research centres have been established at Ispra (Euratom), Saluggia, and Frascati. Industrial atomic power stations are to be found at Latina, Gargiliano north of Naples, Caorso east of Piacenza and Trino near Vercelli. Nuclear power stations are being developed.

INDUSTRY

Being poor in natural resources, Italy has turned to manufactures in which skilled labour counts for more than raw materials and also to the transformation industries.

Metallurgy. — Italy mined 1 868 000 metric tons of coal or lignite and pig iron production amounted to 353 000 metric tons in 1978. Sulphur output (523 000 metric tons) mainly from Sicilian mines and mercury production (140 000 metric tons) in Tuscany are in full expansion.

The tonnage of steel produced in 1978 reached 24 283 000 metric tons; output of rolled steel was nearly 20 000 000 metric tons and of cast iron amounted to 11 340 000 metric tons. The principal foundries are in Piedmont, Lombardy, Venetia and Liguria.

Engineering industries have profited from this expansion — the automobile industry particularly, followed by the sewing machine, the typewriter and the calculating machine industries in which Italy has specialised. Italy is the leading Common Market producer of electrical household appliances.

Motor Vehicles. — The car and motorcycle industries are amongst the largest and the most modern in Italy and account for a large share of world production. Production of motorcycles amounted to 1 216 500 units in 1978, the number of coaches and commercial vehicles exceeded 148 000 units and that of tractors 116 000 units. The number of cars leaving the factory reached 1 440 000 in 1977 (5th greatest producer in the world).

In 1944 the Italians invented the scooter; the best known manufacturers are Piaggio (Vespa) and Innocenti (Lambretta); the motorcycle manufacturers with the highest reputations are Guzzi, Gilera and MV.

The Motor-Car. — The principal Italian firm and one of the leaders in Europe is FIAT of Turin. In 1978, 42 per cent of production was exported. Some models are also produced with a boosted engine and stream-lined body. FIAT also produces coaches, tractors, lorries, rail cars and engineering vehicles as well as boat engines and aeroplanes. Lancia, also in Turin, produces meticulous and elegant cars. Alfa-Romeo, famous for its racing cars, manufactures small and medium sized cars in its Naples (Alfasud) factory. Autobianchi and Innocenti make low and medium powered cars.

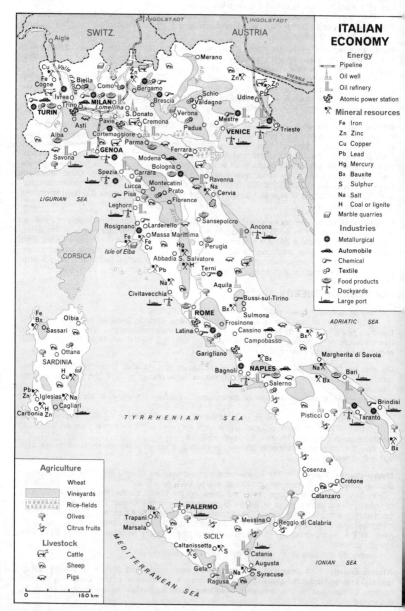

The Modena firms, Tomaso, Maserati and Ferrari, the latter directed by Enzo Ferrari, the Sorcerer of Modena, have devoted themselves to the production of sports and racing cars. The Lamborghini firm in Emilia also builds sports cars. The last of the Grand Prix races is held each year in September at Monza.

In the field of coachwork, the name of Pinin Farina, both as founder of the firm and as a designer who inspired new ideas in car design, is known the world over. (Farina himself died in 1966). Michelin, Pirelli, Ceat, Goodyear and Firestone share the Italian tyre market.

A native product: *pasta*. — This is the Italian national dish. It is made everywhere, but the factories producing the best known brands are in Tuscany, Emilia and the Campania. Hard wheat, water and sometimes milk, eggs and other ingredients enter into making *pasta*. These components are ground, mixed by machinery and then drawn out, moulded or rolled, according to the shape required, and automatically cut and dried. Some forms of spaghetti are up to a yard long. But the best *pasta* is *casalinga*, made at home by hand. Every housewife and working man has her or his special recipe, favourite kind of wheat and exact mixture. The port of Naples forwards some of this product to countries to which Italians have emigrated: France, Belgium, South America, Australia...

Textile Industry. — In this domain, apart from silk *(p 15)*, cotton and wool are also being produced at the rate of 288 500 spun tons and man-made fibres at the rate of 504 730 tons in 1978.

Leading Firms. — Though some of the most important industries have been nationalised, such as the railways (F.S., *Ferrovie dello Stato*), electricity (E.N.E.E., *Enze Nazionale Energia Elettrica*), and certain other sources of power (E.N.I., *Enze Nazionale Idrocarburi*), Italy lives, on the whole, under a regime of private enterprise.

In the motor field, FIAT (Fabbrica Italiana Automobili Torino), Lancia, Ceat and Michelin have their headquarters at Turin, while Alfa-Romeo, Autobianchi, Innocenti and Pirelli are Milanese concerns.

At the head of the chemical industries, the Montedison Company is followed by Anic, the Società Italiana Resine, the Rumianca, the Mira Lanza, the Solvay group, which specialises in the processing of sodium, and by the St-Gobain Company, which has a factory at Pisa and another at Caserta. E.N.I., along with the main foreign firms, are the principal groups in the petroleum industry.

The leader of the steel industry is Finsider, whose production in 1978 amounted to 48 per cent of the national output and about 87 per cent of cast iron. Light engineering firms known far beyond the national frontiers include Olivetti at Ivrea (typewriters and calculating machines).

The largest undertakings in the wool textile industry are Marzotto at Valdagno, Lanerossi at Vicenza and Zegna at Trivero and Valle Mosso. Montefibre and Snia-Viscosa of Milan between them control the synthetics market.

Establishments with a European reputation are Motta and Alemagna (confectionery, pastries and ices) at Milan, Perugina (confectionery) at Perugia, Ferrero (confectionery) at Alba, Buitoni (macaroni) at San Sepolcro, Cirio (preserves) at Naples for foodstuffs. Rizzoli at Milan, Mondadori at Milan and Verona, the De Agostini Geographical Institute at Novara (Piedmont) and Ilte at Turin are known throughout Europe for printing and publishing. The Finmare group is the main shipping line. Alitalia, Alisarda, Ati and Itavia operate airlines.

Merchant Navy. — The Italian Merchant Navy is specially active in the sea routes to the Far East and North and South America. Merchant shipping in 1977 amounted to 11 398 000 gross tons. Modern liners, such as the *Leonardo da Vinci,* the *Eugenio C* and the *Cristoforo Colombo* illustrate the Italian sea-faring tradition.

MODERN BUILDING ON THE GRAND SCALE

Town Planning. — The Italian school of town planning is world famous; it is enough to mention the Città E.U.R., the Stazione Termini and the Olympic stadia and other buildings in Rome, the skyscrapers and new business quarter in Milan. Gio Ponti was the architect of the Montecatini and Pirelli buildings in Milan, Pier-Luigi Nervi, the master of reinforced concrete, the designer of the permanent buildings of the Turin Trade Fair and one of the co-designers of the UNESCO building in Paris.

Civil Engineering. — Italy comes second to Germany in Europe in the construction of motorways. The network (5 431 km - 3 373 miles) depends overall on two main axes, one west to east, the other north to south — the Turin-Milan-Venice Motorway (A4) and the Motorway to the Sun (A1, A2, A3). The latter, in spite of mountain and other barriers, links Milan to Rome, Naples and Reggio di Calabria, and is one of the finest in the world. Great feats of engineering were called for in its construction, particularly in the crossing of the Apennines where in a stretch of only 90 km - 56 miles — there are 25 tunnels and 45 bridges or viaducts.

The Italians in co-operation in one case with the Swiss and in the other with the French have completed the construction of the road tunnels beneath the Great St. Bernard Pass, the San Bernardino Pass, Mont Blanc and the Tenda Pass. Also in co-operation with Austria, Italy has built the only motorway to cross an alpine pass, namely the Brenner Pass, thus linking Northern Italy with Innsbruck.

DEVELOPMENT OF THE SOUTH

Below a line joining the Gulf of Gaeta and the Gargano Massif, lies the famous South which remains economically impoverished. A programme of public works, undertaken under the Vanoni Plan, named after the Finance Minister who worked it out, has noticeably improved conditions.

The first step in redevelopment was in agrarian reform (allotment of fallow land into small holdings in Apulia, Lucania and Sardinia), encouragement of new crops (cotton in Sicily and Calabria), reclamation of poor and marshy lands (Sila, Calabria, the coastal plains round the Bay of Taranto) and afforestation (Sicily). Trade fairs have also been organised at Cagliari, Naples, Bari, Messina and Palermo.

But by far the greatest effort has been made in industrialisation. Oil prospecting has been undertaken (Sicily), dams constructed (Sila and Sicily) and water piped. Large industrial centres have now developed at such places as Gela, Ragusa, Augusta, Syracuse, Catania and Cagliari.

The "triangle" evolved of Taranto, which has become a steel town, Bari and Brindisi is famous throughout Europe.

A finance organisation, the *Cassa del Mezzogiorno,* has invested between 1950 and 1975 the sum of 15 195 000 million lire in this gigantic enterprise.

HISTORICAL FACTS

Roman History

From the Origins to the Empire (753-27 BC)

BC	
753	Foundation of Rome by Romulus according to legend. (In fact it was born of the union of Latin and Sabine villages in the 8C).
7-6C	Royal Dynasty of the Tarquins: Tarquin the Elder and Servius Tullius enlarge Rome and surround it with ramparts. Power is divided between the king, the senate, representing the great families, and the *comitia*, representing the rich families.
509	Establishment of the Republic: the king's powers are conferred on two consuls, elected for one year.
451-449	Law of the XII Tables, instituting equality between patricians and plebeians.
390	The Gauls invade Italy and take Rome.
281-272	War against Pyrrhus, King of Epirus; submission of the south peninsula to Rome.
264-241	First Punic War; Carthage abandons Sicily to the Romans.
219-201	Second Punic War. Hannibal crosses the Alps and defeats the Romans at Lake Trasimeno *(details p 239)*. Hannibal routs the Romans at Cannae and halts at Capua *(p 75)*. In 210, Scipio carries war into Spain and takes Cartagena. In 204, Scipio lands in Africa. Hannibal is recalled to Carthage. Scipio defeats Hannibal at Zama in 202.
146	Macedonia and Greece become Roman provinces. Capture and destruction of Carthage.
133	Occupation of all Spain.
133-121	Failure of the policy of the Gracchi, who promoted popular agrarian laws.
118	The Romans in Gaul.
112-105	War against Jugurtha, King of Numidia (now Algeria).
102-101	Marius, vanquisher of Jugurtha, stops invasions of Cimbri and Teutons.
88-79	Sulla, the rival of Marius, triumphs over Mithridates and establishes his dictatorship in Rome.
70	Pompey and Crassus, appointed Consuls, become masters of Rome.
63	Plot of Catiline against the Senate exposed by Cicero.
60	The first Triumvirate: Pompey, Crassus, Julius Caesar. Rivalry of the three rulers.
59	Julius Caesar as Consul.
58-51	The Gallic war (52: Surrender of Vercingetorix at Alesia).
49	Caesar crosses the Rubicon and drives Pompey out of Rome.
49-45	Caesar defeats Pompey and his partisans in Spain, Greece and Egypt. He writes his history of the Gallic War.
early 44	Caesar is appointed Dictator for life.
March 15	Caesar is assassinated by Brutus, his adopted son, among others.
43	The second Triumvirate: Octavius (nephew and heir of Caesar), Anthony, Lepidus.
40-30	Open struggle between Octavius and Anthony. Defeat (at Actium) and death of Anthony.

The Early Empire (27 BC to AD 284)

27	Octavius, sole master of the Empire, receives the title of Augustus Caesar and plenary powers.
AD	
14	Death of Augustus.
14-37	Reign of Tiberius.
54-68	Reign of Nero, who causes the death of Britannicus, his mother Agrippina and his wife Octavia, and initiates violent persecution of the Christians.
69-79	Reign of Vespasian.
96-192	The Century of the Antonines, marked by the successful reigns of Nerva, Trajan, Hadrian, Antonius and Marcus Aurelius, who consolidated the Empire.
235-268	Military anarchy; a troubled period. The legions make and break emperors.
270-275	Aurelius re-establishes the unity of the Empire.

The Later Empire (AD 284-476)

284-305	Reign of Diocletian. Institution of Tetrarchy or 4-man government.
303	Persecution of the Christians: these called the reign of Diocletian "the age of martyrs".
306-337	Reign of Constantine, who establishes Christianity as the state religion.
313	Edict of Milan: Constantine decrees religious liberty.
379-395	Reign of Theodosius the Great, the Christian Emperor. At his death the Empire is divided between his two sons, Arcadius (Eastern Empire) and Honorius (Western Empire) who settled at Ravenna.
5C	The Roman Empire is repeatedly attacked by the Barbarians.
411	Alaric, King of the Visigoths, captures Rome.
455	Capture and sack of Rome by the Vandals under Genseric.
476	Deposition by Odoacer of the Emperor Romulus Augustus. End of the Western Empire.

From the Roman Empire to the Germanic Holy Roman Empire

493	Odoacer is driven out by the Ostrogoths under Theodoric.
535-553	Reconquest of Italy by the Eastern Roman Emperor Justinian (527-565).
568	Lombard invasion.
752	Threatened by the Lombards, the pope appeals to Pepin the Short, King of the Franks.
774	Pepin's son, Charlemagne (Charles the Great), becomes King of the Lombards.
800	Charlemagne is proclaimed Emperor by Pope Leo III.
9C	The break-up of the Carolingian Empire causes complete anarchy and the formation of many rival states in Italy.
951	Intervention in Italy of Otto I, King of Saxony, who becomes King of the Lombards.
962	Otto I, now crowned Emperor, founds the Holy Roman Empire.

The Quarrel of the Church and the Empire

11C	Progressive establishment of the Normans in Sicily and southern Italy.
1076	Quarrel between Pope Gregory VII and the Emperor Henry IV about Investitures.
1077	Humbling of the Emperor before the Pope at Canossa *(details p 72)*.
1155	Frederick Barbarossa crowned Emperor. Resumption of the struggle between the Empire and the Papacy, with the **Ghibellines** supporting the emperor and the **Guelphs** supporting the pope.
1176	Reconciliation between Frederick Barbarossa and Pope Alexander III.
1216	Triumph of the Papacy on the death of Pope Innocent III.
1227-1250	A new phase in the struggle between the Empire (Frederick II) and the Papacy (Gregory IX). New triumph of the Papacy.

French Influence and Decline of Imperial Power

1265	Charles of Anjou, brother of St. Louis, crowned King of Sicily.
1282	Sicilian Vespers: massacre of French settlers in Sicily *(details p 279)*.
1303	The Anjou Dynasty establishes itself in Naples.
1303	Attack of Anagni, instigated by King Philip of France, on Pope Boniface VIII.
1309-1377	The popes established at Avignon, France.
1328	Failure of the intervention in Italy by the Emperor Ludwig of Bavaria.
1402	Last German intervention in Italy (emperor defeated by Lombard militia).
1442	Alfonso V, King of Aragon, becomes King of the Two Sicilies.
end 15C	Florence, Milan and Venice organise themselves as powerful independent states.
1494	Intervention of King Charles VIII of France, who established himself for three months in Naples.

From the 16C to the Napoleonic era

1515-1526	François I, victor at Marignano but vanquished at Pavia, is forced to give up the Italian heritage.
1527	Capture and sack of Rome by the troops of the Constable of Bourbon, in the service of Charles V.
1559	Treaty of Câteau-Cambrèsis: Spanish domination over Naples and the district of Milan.
17C	Savoy becomes the most powerful state in northern Italy.
1713	Victor-Amadeus II of Savoy acquires Sicily and the title of King.
1720	The Duke of Savoy is compelled to exchange Sicily for Sardinia.
1796	Napoleon's campaign in Lombardy. Creation of the Cispadan Republic.
1797	Battle of Rivoli. Treaty of Campo-Formio. Creation of the Cisalpine and Ligurian Republics.
1798	Proclamation of the Parthenopaean (Naples) and Roman Republics.
1805	Napoleon transforms the Italian Republic into a Kingdom, assumes the iron crown of the Lombard Kings and confers the vice-royalty on his stepson, Eugène de Beauharnais.
1808	Rome is occupied by French troops. Murat becomes King of Naples.
1809	The Papal States are attached to the French Empire. Pius VII is taken to France as a prisoner (1812).
1814	Collapse of the Napoleonic régime. Pius VII returns to Rome.

Towards Italian Unity (1815-1870)

1815	Congress of Vienna. Hegemony of Austria.
1815-1832	The "Carbonari" patriots oppose the Austrian occupation but their revolts are crushed (Piedmont, Lombardy, Naples in 1820, Modena, Sardinia, the Papal States in 1831).
1831	Founding of the Young Italy movement by Mazzini. Growth of national feeling against Austria: the **Risorgimento**.
1834-1837	Revolts at Genoa and in the Kingdom of the Two Sicilies.
1848	General insurrection against Austria, led by the King of Sardinia, ruler of Piedmont. Italian successes followed by a violent Austrian counter-attack.
1849-1850	Accession of Victor Emmanuel II. Cavour's government reorganises the State of Piedmont.
1854	Participation of Piedmont, with Britain and France, in the Crimean War.
1856	Paris Congress. Cavour officially raises the question of Italian unity.
1858	Meeting of Cavour and Napoleon III at Plombières. Alliance between France and Piedmont.
1859	War declared by Austria against Piedmont and France. Franco-Piedmontese victories of Magenta and Solferino and Villafranca Armistice. Piedmont obtains Lombardy and France, Savoy and the County of Nice.
1860	Bologna, Parma, Modena and Tuscany unite with Piedmont. Expedition of Garibaldi and the Thousand to Sicily and Naples. Union of the South.
1861	Proclamation of the Kingdom of Italy with Turin as its capital. Death of Cavour.
1865-1870	Florence becomes the capital of the Kingdom of Italy.
1866	Austria at war with Prussia and Italy. Venetia united to Italy.
1867	Garibaldi, marching on Rome, is defeated at Mentana.
1870	Occupation of Rome by the Piedmontese. Rome becomes the capital of Italy. Italian unity is complete.

From 1870 to the Present Day

1882	Italy, Germany and Austria sign the Triple Alliance.
1885	The Italians gain a footing in Eritrea and on the Somali Coast.
1900	Assassination of King Umberto I by an anarchist. Accession of Victor Emmanuel III.
1904-1906	Rapprochement of Italy with Britain and France.
1912	Tripolitania and Cyrenaica recognised as Italian possessions.
1915	Italy enters the First World War on the side of the Allies.
1919	Treaty of St. Germain: Istria and the Trentino are attached to Italy.
1921	Social disturbances fomented by Mussolini's Fascist Party.
1922-1926	The March on Rome. Mussolini becomes Prime Minister, then *Duce* (Leader).
1929	Lateran Treaties concluded between the Italian Government and the Papacy.
1936	Italian occupation of Ethiopia. Rapprochement with Germany.
1937	Rome-Berlin Axis formed.
1940	Italy enters the Second World War against Britain and France.
1943	Fall and arrest of Mussolini. Italy goes to war with Germany.
1945	Execution of Mussolini by Italian anti-Fascists.
May 1946	Abdication of Victor Emmanuel III and accession of Umberto II.
June 1946	Proclamation of the Republic after a referendum.
1954	Trieste is attached to Italy.

ITALY TODAY

The leading feature of Italian social life is its intense provincialism, a survival of the times when Italy was divided into states whose capitals competed with one another. Rome remains a residential city inhabited by officials, while Milan claims the rôle of economic capital and Florence, Bologna and Padua claim to be the cultural centres. Turin, Naples, Palermo and Genoa have become important industrial centres. Venice keeps its fascinating character.

Political and Administrative Organisation. — The referendum of June 1946 set up the Republic and the Constitution of 1 January 1948, a Parliamentary Republic headed by a President elected for seven years, with two Houses of Parliament the Chamber of Deputies and the Senate, whose members bear the title *Onorevole* (Honourable).

For administrative purposes Italy is divided into 20 regions which have some legislative, administrative and financial powers, and 94 provinces. The various districts are each headed by a *Sindaco* elected by the municipal councillors.

Sicily, Sardinia, the Trentino — Alto Adige and Friuli — Venezia Giulia and the Valle d'Aosta are under a special statute and have a certain amount of administrative autonomy.

The Press. — This is greatly decentralised, at least as far as daily newspapers are concerned. The Turin *Stampa* and the Milan *Corriere della Sera* are the only papers distributed all over Italy. But Venice has its *Gazzettino*, Bologna the *Resto di Carlino*, Genoa *Il Secolo XIX°*, Florence the *Nazione*, Naples the *Mattino* and Palermo the *Giornale di Sicilia*. Even the Roman newspapers, *Messaggero* and *Tempo* though well produced and financially powerful, hardly penetrate the north.

Political journals have rather small circulations: chief among them are the Communist *L'Unità* and *Paese Sera*, the Socialist *Avanti* and the Christian-Democrat *Il Popolo*. Illustrated periodicals like *Oggi*, *Tempo*, *Epoca*, *L'Europeo*, *L'Espresso*. *Panorama* and *Gente* have many readers. The weekly *Fiera Letteraria* in Rome is among the leading publications devoted to art and letters. The Vatican newspaper, *Osservatore Romano*, has a world-wide circulation.

Emigration. — Unemployment is very high. Nevertheless the very large population and long tradition still make emigration an important feature of Italian life. In 1973, 98 970 Italians moved to other countries in Europe, 24 832 went to America and to other continents. On the other hand, 125 968 returned to their native land.

THE PAPACY

Rome, the capital of Roman Catholicism. — The Vatican City forms a Free State of which the pope is the sovereign. The spiritual influence of the Roman Catholic Church radiates throughout the world through the person of the Sovereign Pontiff.

From the Birth of the Church to that of the Papacy. — The Roman Empire, then at its zenith, was being governed from Rome by Tiberius Caesar when Jesus preached. After the Passion of Christ, the Apostles, as witnesses of the various episodes of His earthly life and of His miracles, propagated His Word and described the scenes at which they had been present. Thus Christianity was born in the Levant but reached the west through the agency of the Apostles and their disciples. The Gospels — those of St. Matthew, St. Mark and St. Luke, followed later by that of St. John — helped to lay the foundations of the early Church, which by the end of the 1C was formed of small communities directed by bishops and deacons.

About AD 200 six important centres — Rome, Lyons, Carthage, Alexandria, Ephesus and Antioch — bore witness to the vitality of the Christian religion. By the end of the 2C AD the Bishop of Rome, the capital of the Empire, claimed primacy over the other bishops on the authority of St. Peter, the first Apostle, whom Christ had made the foundation-stone of His Church, and of St. Paul, one of the great teachers of the Church, and took the name of Pope (low Latin Papa: Father).

The Church and the Persecutions. — At first regarded as a harmless cult, Christianity was considered in the reign of Nero to be subversive of public order, and many Christians were tracked down, arrested and suffered martyrdom. Many bishops and priests fell victims to the persecutions instituted by certain emperors such as Domitian (1C), Decius and Valerian (3C), who saw in the expansion of the Church a threat to the stability of imperial rule. At the beginning of the 4C Diocletian, Galerius and Maximinus redoubled the persecution but failed to check the spread of Christianity.

In 313 the Emperor Constantine, who himself converted to Christianity the following year, gave complete religious freedom to Christians by the Edict of Milan.

This alternation of favours and repressions set the seal on Christianity and stimulated its development throughout the Empire. When it was recognised as the state religion it became the surest support of the imperial power, and when Rome crumbled under the repeated assaults of the Barbarians it formed the last bulwark of civilisation.

Influence of the Papacy in the West. — When the Empire broke up, the Church stood out as the only great moral force left in a distracted and divided world.

After the disappearance of the Western Roman Empire, Rome was ruled by the Byzantine Emperor who was represented by a governor established in Ravenna. But the authority of the pope and the ascendancy of the church grew all the stronger due to the strong personality of Gregory the Great, the pope who in AD 752 faced with the occupation of the imperial territories by the Lombards, appealed to Pepin the Short, King of the Franks and initiated an era of alliances with the Carolingian dynasty culminating in the coronation of Charlemagne (Charles the Great) as Emperor of the West in the year AD 800. The King of the Franks gave an undertaking to Gregory the Great to return all the occupied territories by the donation of Quiersy-sur-Oise in AD 756. This donation is the origin of the Papal States and of the pope's temporal power.

The Great Popes of the Middles Ages. — The privileged position of the Church vanished with the fall of the Carolingian Empire at the end of the 9C. The anarchy which then obtained in Europe was for the papacy a period of great laxity (traffic in church property, marriage of ecclesiastics). After the foundation of the Germanic Holy Roman Empire, Gregory VII stands out as a reformer. His decreees led to the Quarrel of the Investitures, a long drawn-out conflict between the pope and the emperor. Urban II, by taking the initiative of the First Crusade, reaffirmed the pre-eminence of the successor of St. Peter.

Religious Crisis and Ecclesiastical Restoration. — The papacy emerged weakened from the Captivity of Avignon (1309-1377) but it had to face a still more serious crisis when the Great Schism of the West occurred in 1378, and again in 1520, when the Reformation started by Martin Luther began to spread. All the energy of Pius IV, Pius V end Sixtus V (second half of the 16C) was needed to restore the shaken authority and influence of the Church. The creation of new religious orders and the promulgation of decrees extending the prerogatives of the bishops helped to do this.

In this way every religious crisis tended to be followed in due course by a reaffirmation of papal authority. In the 18C the Church survived the philosophical movement, and at the fall of Napoleon the temporal powers of the pope were restored within his own domain.

The "Roman Question". — As the spiritual head of the Church but also a temporal sovereign, the pope was involved, in the 19C, in the problem of Italian unity. That unity, brought about by the House of Piedmont-Sardinia, could be complete only if he renounced all temporal power in the peninsula. At the occupation of Rome by the troops of Victor Emmanuel II in 1870 Pope Pius IX was forced to consider himself a prisoner in the Vatican Palace.

This situation continued under Leo XIII, Pius X and Benedict XV. It was Pius XI who obtained the territorial independence of the Holy See by the Lateran Treaties of 1929. From that time on the pope enjoyed complete freedom of action within the Papal State. The authority of the church was also recognised in the fields of education and marriage. It was on this basis that in 1947 the Constitution of the Italian Republic defined the relations between the church and the state.

Pontifical Election and Authority. — The pope is elected by the cardinals, forming the Sacred College and meeting in conclave in the Sistine Chapel. A majority of two-thirds plus one is required to make an election valid. The coronation then takes place, accompagnied by majestic ceremonies in the grandiose setting of St. Peter's.

Though the pope in relation to the priesthood has no powers superior to those of a bishop, he is in the hierarchy the head of the whole Roman Catholic Church. As the successor ot St. Peter and the Vicar of Christ he governs that Church by virtue of powers received from God. In 1870 the Vatican Council declared him infallible in matters of dogma.

Councils. — These are meetings of bishops at which questions of doctrine and ecclesiastical discipline are dealt with. The Oecumenical Councils bring together all the bishops of the Roman Catholic Church. The most famous have been those of Nicea (AD 325) which condemned Arianism, Constance (1414-1418) which condemned John Huss and tried to end the Great Schism of the West, Trent (1545-1563) which decided on a reform of the Church as a means of opposing Protestantism, and the Vatican (1870, 1962).

ANCIENT CIVILISATIONS

Since 2000 BC and throughout Antiquity, Italy, the meeting-place of races, has seen the Etruscan, Greek and Latin civilisations flourish on her soil. Two thousand years later, western civilisation is still impregnated with them.

Greeks, Etruscans and Romans were preceded by two peoples who came from the north: the Ligurians, who also occupied southern Gaul and the Iberian Peninsula, and the Italics or Italiots, who settled in Umbria and Latium and from whom the Latins sprang. The former transmitted their fair hair and blue eyes to some of the present inhabitants of Liguria. The latter built temples of which the gigantic foundations still exist in some places, as for instance at Alatri in Latium.

THE GREEKS

Cities and Men. — The shores of Sicily and southern Italy had a sort of fascination for the ancient Greeks, who regarded them as the limits of the inhabited earth. Many scenes of Greek mythology are set there: the Phlegrean Fields, near Naples, hid the entrance to the Kingdom of Hades; Zeus routed the Titans, with the help of Hercules, on the site of Etna, where the Cyclops lived and Hephaestus, the God of Fire, had his forges; Kore, the daughter of Demeter, was kidnapped by Hades, who had emerged from the Tartara River near Enna.

In the *Odyssey*, Homer (9C BC) relates the adventures of Ulysses (Odysseus) after the siege of Troy, sailing between Scylla and Charybdis in the Straits of Messina and resisting the temptations of the Sirens in the Gulf of Sorrento. Thucydides and Pindar (5C BC) describe these mysterious shores, to which Virgil also refers in the *Aeneid*.

After the Phoenicians had settled at Carthage and their seamen had set up a few trading posts, the Greeks founded, as early the 8C BC, a large number of colonies on the coasts of Sicily and southern Italy. The whole settlement took the name of **Magna Graecia**. In it were Ionian, Achaean and Dorian colonies, named after the Greek peoples who had developed them. The social unit was the "city". One of them, Crotone, was governed by a school of philosophers, the Phytagoreans.

The 6C and 5C BC marked the zenith of Greek civilisation in Italy, corresponding with the period of Pericles in Athens. It was then that the great Doric buildings were erected. The Greek cities drew such profit from their seaborne trade that Syracuse became a rival to Athens.

Philosophers, scientists and writers settled in Sicily. Aeschylus, who lived at Gela, was killed there by a tortoise which an eagle was said to have dropped on his bald pate. At Syracuse, Theocritus laid down the rules of bucolic poetry. The philosopher Plato visited the town three times and the geometrician Archimedes died there, murdered by a Roman soldier.

Unfortunately the number and diversity of these cities led them to fall into rivalry and dissension. Warfare between the "tyrants" of neighbouring towns and Carthaginian raids caused a decline which ended in a Roman conquest at the end of the 3C BC. Syracuse and Taranto, the two main centres of this declining but refined civilisation, were conquered by the Romans in 213-212 and 272 BC respectively.

Today, on the shores of the Ionian and Tyrrhenian Seas, Greek ruins combine with the attractions of the Italian countryside and civilisation to offer beautiful sights rivalling the more evocative charms of Greece.

An ancient temple

Art in Magna Graecia.
— The 7 and 6C BC saw the building of the temples of Paestrum, Selinus and Agrigento, magnificent examples of Doric architecture whose vigorous design contrasts with the delicate grace of the Ionic order. These gigantic buildings give an impression of hard, sober grandeur.

At the end of the 5C BC the Doric style was still used for the beautiful temple at Segesta and that

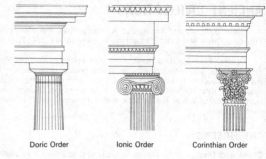

Doric Order   Ionic Order   Corinthian Order

of Athena at Syracuse, while in Greece itself the Ionic style was at its height and the Corinthian style was just making its appearance *(see sketches above).*

Decline began in the 4C BC, after the Peloponnesian War between Sparta and Athens, which impoverished the Greek world. This was the beginning of the so-called Hellenistic period, marked by the neglect of architecture in favour of sculpture.

The museum of Naples, Paestum, Palermo and Syracuse illustrate the development of sculpture from the archaic bas-reliefs of the metopes of Paestum or Selinus and the monumental telamones (male figures used as pillars) of Agrigento to the delightful statuettes of the decadence, resembling Tanagra figures, modelled at Taranto in the 3C BC. Between these extremes, innumerable youths, Apollos and Aphrodites issued from the sculptors' studios. They were all more or less copied from Phidias, Praxiteles, Scopas or Lysippus, but their harmony of form and proportion remained admirable.

THE ETRUSCANS

While the Greeks were impregnating the south of the peninsula and Sicily with their civilisation, the Etruscans were building up in central Italy, from the 8C BC onwards, a powerful empire whose growth was checked only by that of Rome. They are a little known people whose alphabet along with certain tombstone inscriptions, have now been deciphered. Some authorities think they were natives of these parts; others, following the examples of Herodotus, say they came from Lydia in Asia Minor. The Etruscans at first occupied the Apennines, the Arno and the Tiber *(map p 21)* but later spread into Campania and the Plain of the Po. They reached their zenith in the 7-6C BC. **Etruria** then comprised a federation of twelve city-states known as *lucumonies,* among which are named Veii, Bolsena, Tarquinia, Volterra, Perugia, etc.

Having grown rich by working iron (Island of Elba), copper and silver mines and by trading in the western Mediterranean, the Etruscans, who were artisans and technicians, had a civilisation derived from a mixture of savagery and refinement. In religion their gods were the same as those of the Greeks. They believed in survival after death and in divination, and they studied the entrails of animals (for haruspices) and the flight of birds (for auspices), a form of superstition which the Romans adopted and developed.

Their towns, built on elevated sites with walls of huge stones, show an advanced sense of town planning. Near them are vast burial grounds with underground chambers or hypogea filled with utensils and having painted walls. These reveal the customs of the Etruscans, which formed the basis of one branch of Latin civilisation.

The Etruscans were finally defeated by the Romans in the 1C BC.

Etruscan Art. — Etruscan art is primitive in character, though strongly influenced by the Orient and especially by Greece from the 5C BC onwards. It has a marked individuality sustained by realism and expressive movement.

Etruscan art was discovered in the 18C, but was for long regarded only as an offshoot of Greek art. The discovery in the 19C of masterpieces like the Apollo and Hermes of Veii and the systematic study in the 20C of pottery, bronzes, utensils and ornaments unearthed in excavations made it possible to give this vigorous and refined art the place it deserved.

Sculpture. — Since architectural specimens are lacking, sculpture appears to us as the artists' favourite medium. The great period is the 6C BC, when large groups of statuary adorned the frontons of the temples: the famous Apollo and Hermes of Veii (both in the museum of the Villa Giulia in Rome) in which Greek influence is obvious, belongs to this period. Some portrait busts are more original in their striking realism, intensity of expression and stylised features: their large prominent eyes and enigmatic smiles are characteristic of the Etruscan style. The same remarks apply to the famous groups of semi-recumbent figures on the sarcophagi, many of which are portraits.

The sense of movement is shown mainly in sculptures of fantastic animals and in figurines representing warriors fighting, women at their toilet, etc.

Painting. — The only surviving specimens are in the burial chambers of the cemeteries, where they were supposed to remind the dead of the pleasures of life: banquets, games and plays, music and dancing, hunting, etc. The delicate paintings in colours laid on flat show surprising powers of observation. They form an excellent record of Etruscan life.

Pottery and Goldsmiths' work. — Even more than artists, the Etruscans were artisans of genius.

In pottery they used the *bucchero* technique, about which little is known, producing black earthenware with figures in relief. Initially decorated with motifs in *pointillé,* the vases developed into more elaborate shapes. In the 5C BC they modelled beautiful burial urns, *canopae,* in animal or human shape adorned with geometric designs. Inca and Aztec pottery bears a striking resemblance to the Etruscan.

In the domain of goldsmiths' work, both men and women wore heavy gold ornaments of remarkable workmanship: they were mounted with the rather clumsy lavishness characteristic of "barbarian" art. Engraved mirrors, scent-burners and bronze candlesticks of great decorative elegance also show the skill of the artisans.

(After photo in Libreria dello Stato)

Etruscan pitcher

22

THE ROMANS

For about twelve centuries, from the foundation of Rome in 753 BC to the end of the Western Empire in AD 476, a civilisation from which Western Europe emerged reigned in Italy. Royal Rome (753-509 BC) was followed by the Republic (509-27 BC) and then the Empire (27 BC to AD 192). The Roman eagle then spread its wings from Britain to the Persian Gulf and from Africa to Germany. It was only at the time of the Later Empire (AD 284-476), which was harried by barbarian invasions, that the decline set in *(see Historical Facts, p 18)*.

Political and Social Life. — At the time of the kings, the political organisation of Rome comprised two bodies, the Senate and the *Comitia,* composed of patricians. These were a privileged class who kept idle but devoted hangers-on. The plebeians had no access to public affairs. At the bottom of the scale the slaves formed the servile mass of the population, but they could be freed by their masters.

Under the Republic, power was given to two consuls, elected for one year and assisted by quaestors in charge of public finance and the criminal police, together with censors of public morals, aediles in charge of the municipal police and judicial praetors. The Senate had a consultative rôle and sanctioned laws. Ten Tribunes of the People watched over the rights of the masses. Consuls or proconsuls, praetors or propraetors administered the provinces conquered by the legions.

Generally speaking, the Empire kept the administrative structure of the Republic, but the powers of the consuls were taken by an emperor *(Imperator)* who was commander-in-chief of the army; he appointed the Senate, and had the right to make peace or war. Under the Later Empire the power of the emperors became absolute, and the Senate played only an honorary part.

Outside the State, society was divided into clans *(gentes),* or groups of people descended from a common ancestor, and families, each under a *pater familias* who wielded absolute authority.

Religion. — Religion played a part in every event of public or private life.

Domestic Cults. — A small oratory called the *lararium* enshrined the household gods, Lares and Penates, before whom a sacred flame burned always. The souls of the dead were also venerated.

Public worship took place in buildings copied from the Etruscan or Greek temples *(sketch p 21)*. Sometimes, however, they were circular in form, as in the case of temples dedicated to Vesta.

The twelve chief gods were derived from the Greek gods of Olympus:

Greek Gods	Roman Gods	Attributes	Symbols
Zeus	Jupiter	Master of the Gods. All-powerful ..	Eagle, sceptre, lightning.
Hera	Juno	Wife of Jupiter. Marriage	Peacock.
Athena	Minerva	Daughter of Jupiter. Wisdom and the Arts	Owl, olive tree.
Apollo	Apollo (or Phoebus)	Son of Jupiter. Sun and the Arts ..	Lyre.
Artemis	Diana	Daughter of Jupiter. Moon, hunting, chastity	Bow, quiver, stag.
Hermes	Mercury	Messenger of the Gods. Trade, eloquence	Wings, caduceus.
Hephaïstos .	Vulcan	Fire, metal	Anvil, hammer.
Hestia	Vesta	Hearth	Fire.
Aries	Mars	War	Helmet, arms.
Aphrodite ..	Venus	Born of the sea. Love and beauty .	Dove.
Demeter ...	Ceres	Agriculture	Sheaf, sickle.
Poseidon ...	Neptune	The sea	Trident.

A Roman Town (1)

Planning. — Roman towns often have a military origin: when the land placed under their control was shared out, the legionaries and veterans who had stayed in the camps were joined by the civil population. Towns which had been surrounded with walls during troubled periods were divided, whenever possible, into four quarters by two main streets, the *decumanus* and the *cardo,* intersecting at right angles and ending in gateways. Other streets parallel to these two gave the town a chess-board plan of which Pompeii, Herculaneum and Ostia are excellent examples.

Streets. — The streets were edged with footpaths, sometimes 1 ft. 6 in. high, and lined with porches to shelter pedestrians. The roadway, paved with large flagstones laid diagonally, was crossed at intervals by stepping-stones laid at the same level as the pavements but between which horses and cart-wheels could pass.

The Roman House. — Excavations at Herculaneum, Pompeii and especially Ostia have uncovered Roman houses of various types: the small bourgeois house, a dwelling of several storeys, shops open to the street and finally large, luxurious patrician mansions.

The latter had a modest external appearance owing to their bare walls and few windows. But the interiors, adorned with mosaics, statues, paintings and marbles and sometimes including hot baths and a fish pond, revealed the riches of their owners. The entrance was often surmounted by a mosaic or an inscription warning the visitor to beware of the dog: *Cave canem.* A vestibule and a corridor led to the *atrium.*

A Roman house

---

(1) *The personal records of M. Jules Formigé (1879-1960), Inspector-General of Historical Monuments were consulted for this section.*

The **atrium** (1), which opened on the street through a vestibule containing the porter's lodge, was a large rectangular court open, in the middle, to the sky. A basin called the *impluvium*, under the open section, caught rainwater. There were three types of atrium: the **"Tuscan" atrium**, the most ancient, has single-span pillars supporting the roof which at their point of intersection form the frame of the open section; the **"tetrastyle" atrium** with the roof resting in the centre on four columns, each one standing at an angle of the *impluvium;* and the **"Corinthian" atrium** with several columns all round the *impluvium.* The rooms *(cubiculae)* opened off the atrium, which was the only part of the house to which strangers were usually admitted. At the far end was the **tablinum** (2) or study or reception room of the head of the family. Money and books were kept there. All ordinary writings were made with a style on small wooden tablets coated with wax; these were bound together with rings, forming notebooks. Books were in the form of scrolls of papyrus or sheets of parchment bound together. The text was written in red or black ink with split-pointed reeds.

The atrium and the adjoining rooms represent the primitive, simple house of the poorer citizen. High officials, rich colonials and prosperous tradesmen often added a second house, of the more refined Greek type, joining on to the *tablinum.*

The **peristyle** (3) was a court surrounded by a portico (a gallery with a roof supported by columns) in the centre of the part of the house reserved for the family. It was reached from the atrium along a corridor called the *fauces*. Here the peristyle was generally made into a garden with basins lined with mosaics, fountains and statues. The living quarters opened on to it all round : bedrooms, dining-rooms, or the **triclinium** (4) and the main saloon or **œcus** (5).

The bedrooms were simple sleeping chambers. They contained a stone or marble dais built against the wall or a movable bed. There were mattresses, cushions and blankets but no sheets.

In the dining-room, the guests reclined on couches placed on three sides of the table, the fourth being left open for service. Earthenware dishes were used as plates. Meat was served already cup up and was eaten with the fingers. Spoons were used, however. Goblets and drinking-cups were made of clay, metal or glass. Flagons were usually made of clay.

The servants' quarters included the kitchen with a sink and drain, a built-in stove and an oven for roasting and pastry; baths, which were like the public baths on a smaller scale, and the slaves' quarters, attics, stables, etc.

The Forum. — The forum was a large square, often surrounded by a portico. Originally it was a market, usually at the crossing of the two main streets, but it became the centre of the public and commercial life of Roman Towns. Men came there to read public notices, listen to political speakers, stroll and talk. The women did their shopping, either in shops round the square or from hawkers and artisans who set up their stalls under the porticos. Slavemarkets were held on certain days.

Government offices were placed round the forum. These included the *curia* or headquarters of local government; the voting hall for elections; the public tribune from which candidates for office harangued the crowd; the Temple of Money or exchange; the municipal treasury; the public granaries; the Temple of Justice or law courts; the prison, and one or more temples. The largest fora that remain are those of Rome and Pompeii.

The Tombs. — Roman cemeteries were placed along the roads, a little away from the towns. The most famous in Italy is that on the Via Appia Antica, south of Rome. Directly after death the body of the deceased was exposed on a funeral couch surrounded with candlesticks and wreaths of flowers. Then it was buried or burnt by the family. The deceased was provided with funeral furnishings for use in his second life.

Buildings

Great Builders. — The art of building was highly developed by the Romans. The speed with which they erected their buildings was due less to the number of workmen employed than to the special training of workers, the methods of work and the use of lifting devices such as levers, winches and tackle to move heavy material into place. The Roman vault is semicircular in shape. At the end of the Empire, brick was used in preference to stone.

The Orders *(see sketch p 22)*. — The Roman architectural orders were derived from the Greek orders, from which they are distinguished by certain details. Roman Doric, the simplest and strongest, is found in the ground floors of buildings. Ionic, which was elegant but lacking in pomp, was despised by the Roman architects. On the other hand Corinthian was a favourite style for its rich decoration, consisting chiefly of acanthus leaves. The "composite" style is a fusion of the Corinthian and Ionic styles.

Temples. — Rome liberally adopted gods from all the mythologies. The emperors, when raised to divine status, were themselves objects of worship. The Roman temple consists of a closed chamber, the *cella* (sanctuary), containing the image of the god, and an open vestibule *(pronaos)*. The building is surrounded, partly or completely, by a colonnade or peristyle.

Triumphal Arches. — In Rome these commemorated the "triumphs" of generals or conquering emperors. The bas-reliefs on the arches recorded their feats of arms.

In the provinces, such as Aosta, Benevento and Ancona, are municipal arches commemorating the founding of a city or erected in honour of some member of the imperial familiy.

The Baths *(see plan p 189)*. — The Roman baths, which were public and free, were not only baths but centres of physical culture, casinos, clubs, recreation centres, libraries, lecture halls and meeting-places, which explains the amount of time people spent in them. Decoration in these great buildings was lavish: columns and capitals picked out in bright colours, mosaic ornaments, coloured marble facings, richly coffered ceilings, mural paintings and statues. The most luxurious baths were built in Rome by the emperors.

The Roman "Bath". — The bather followed a medically designed circuit. From the changing-room, he entered the gymnasium *(palestra)*; then a luke-warm room *(the tepidarium)* to preprare him for the high temperature of the hot room *(caldarium)* and the steam-room. Then came the hot cleaning-bath, the tepid transition-bath and the cold plunge *(frigidarium)* to tone up the skin. Vigorous massage with oil ended the bath proper. Rest, physical culture, reading, strolling and conversation followed it.

Central Heating. — To heat air and water a number of underground furnaces (hypocausts) like bakers' ovens, in which roaring fires were kept going, were used. The hot gases circulated among the brick pillars supporting the stone floors of rooms and baths and rose through flues in the walls to escape from chimneys. In this way the rooms were heated from below and from the sides as in modern buildings. The warmest room, facing south or west, had large glazed windows for sun-bathing. Water at three different temperatures, cold, lukewarm and hot, circulated automatically by thermo-siphon.

The Amphitheatre. — This is a Roman structure. It had on the outside two tiers of arcades surmounted by a low storey called the attic. On the attic were fixed posts to carry a huge adjustable awning, the *velum*, to shelter the spectators from the sun and rain.

Inside, enclosing the arena, a wall protected the spectators in the front rows from the wild animals, released in the ring. Above this wall were seats reserved for distinguished persons: consuls, senators, ambassadors and magistrates. Another series of seats was reserved for priests, knights and Roman citizens. The rest of the seats were occupied by the crowd whose social status declined in importance the higher the seats, with the women and finally the freedmen and slaves in the highest (and therefore most distant) places.

Numbered gates under the arcades, three circular galleries forming promenades and various staircases and corridors *(vomitoria)*, made it possible for all the spectators to reach their seats quickly without crowding and without any mingling of the classes.

These buildings are often well preserved. Among them the Coliseum in Rome and the amphitheatres of Verona and Pozzuoli may be mentioned.

The Games. — The games included fighting of three kinds (between animals, between gladiators and animals, and between gladiators), Olympic games and chariot races. Performances were announced in advance by painted posters, giving the names of the performers and details of the programmes in sensational terms. Long before opening time the crowd, who loved to see bloodshed and prowess in the arena, waited at the doors. As soon as these were opened they invaded the upper tiers of seats. Distinguished spectators arrived on litters or in sedan-chairs.

To neutralise the smell of animals and stables incense-burners were set up in the arena and slaves armed with scent sprays aimed clouds of perfume *(sparsiones)* at the notables. An orchestra punctuated the games with gay music. Friends met in the promenades during the intervals, and food and drink were sold in the galleries.

The Animals. — Carnivorous and exotic beasts: lions, tigers, panthers, elephants and rhinoceroses, brought over in small numbers from the African provinces, were reserved for Rome or for games in the provinces attended by the emperor. To relax the nerves of the spectators after sensational contests, birds of prey were released against hares, rabbits and pigeons, while dogs got bloody muzzles by attacking porcupines. Performing animals were also on show.

The Gladiators. — Most gladiators were slaves or prisoners but among them, also, were free Barbarians: Germans, Syrians or Berbers who had entered this dangerous profession for sheer love of fighting. These combatants had barracks to themselves; they formed teams carefully trained by impresarios who hired them out, for large fees, to rich citizens, usually candidates for high office. Games offered to the people were a form of electoral propaganda; hence the promise: *Panem et Circenses* (bread and circuses).

The Combats. — In principle, a duel between gladiators had always to end in the death of one of the opponents. A man who could fight no more would raise his finger to ask for quarter. If he had pleased the public, the President of the Games would turn up his thumb, and the man would be reprieved; if he turned down his thumb, the winner would cut the loser's throat. During the games slaves armed with whips with leaden weights on the lashes drove on beasts and men and cruelly rounded up any who tried to escape. In order to make bloodstains less conspicuous the sand of the arena was sometimes sprinkled with red powder.

The victorious gladiator received a sum of money or a ribbon which exempted him from further fighting if he were a freeman or freed him if he were a slave. Apart from gladiatorial combats there were fights between boxers wearing leather gloves and clenching their fists round lumps of iron which could cause serious wounds.

Theatres. — Theatres had rows of seats, usually ending in colonnades, a floor occupied by distinguished spectators or used for acting, and a raised stage.

The actors performed in front of a wall pierced with three doorways, through which they made their entrances. At its two ends the wall formed a right angle with a door in each wing. The actors and the various animals and vehicles used in the play came in and out through these side doors.

The stage wall was the finest part of the building; its decoration included several tiers of columns, niches containing statues, marble facing and mosaics. Behind this were the actors' dressing-rooms and the stores. Beyond these again was a portico open to the garden, through which the actors entered the theatre. In it spectators would stroll during the intervals or take shelter from the rain.

The Sicilian theatres are among the largest and best known. Those of Taormina and Syracuse are most admirable.

Scenery and Machinery. — Some scenes were fixed; some were superimposed and uncovered by sliding others sideways. Scenes between the lower columns were mounted on three-sided, prism-shaped panels. Quick changes of scene, like those dear to our modern producers, could be made by revolving these panels through one-third of a turn.

The curtain was only 3 m - 10 ft high. It dropped into a slit at the beginning of the play and rose at the end. The basement contained the machinery and communicated with the stage through trap-doors on which the actors could rise from or sink into the ground. Other machines, mounted in the flies, lowered gods or heroes from the heavens or raised them into the clouds. The effects men knew how to create smoke, lightning, thunder, ghosts and the accompaniment of apotheoses.

Performances. — The Roman theatre was used as a hall for political meetings, lectures and concerts. Competitions, lottery drawings and distribution of bread or money took place there. Conjurors, bear-leaders, tight-rope dancers, illusionists, sword-swallowers, jugglers, acrobats, mimes and marionettes could be seen, and there were already cock-fights. But the chief function of the theatre was the performance of comedies and tragedies.

Actors. — Until 100 BC all actors wore wigs of different shapes and colours according to the nature of the character they represented; after that date they adopted pasteboard masks. Each kind of character: the father, the mother, the daughter, the young man, the parasite, the slave, had a distinctive mask; as soon as the character entered, one knew what he or she was. Tragic actors, to make themselves more impressive, wore buskins or sandals with thick cork soles. Spectators would express displeasure by throwing things at the actors, as they do today.

Wonderful Acoustics. — All sorts of means were used to obtain perfect acoustics. The mouths of the actors' masks were little megaphones; the large sloping roof over the stage threw the sound downwards, the upward curve of the seats received it smoothly, the colonnades broke up the echo and carefully graduated sounding-boards under the seats acted as loud-speakers. One detail will show how far these refinements were carried: the doors on the stage were hollow and made like violins inside. When an actor wished to amplify his voice he would stand against one of these sound-boxes.

ITALIAN ART

From the earliest days of Christianity to the present time Italian art, as the heir of the Greek, Etruscan and Latin civilisations, has given the world such a profusion of marvels that a journey to Italy becomes a pilgrimage to the sources which every man who cares for culture should make. No album of pictures can take the place of direct contact with these masterpieces.

General Features. — The diversity of the Italian character and, before the formation of a united Italy, the number of small independent states, account for the great number of provincial schools, each with its own characteristics, which will arouse the curiosity of the art lover. Thus Lombardy, Venice, Florence and Siena, Parma, Rome, Naples and Sicily are all distinct art centres.

Unity in diversity : such is the characteristic of Italian art, for while execution varies in different regions certain features inherent in the national mind and soul appear everywhere. Both as an idealist and as a mystic, the Italian worships beauty. Nowhere else, except perhaps in Greece, has the perfection of the pure face of a woman or girl been better expressed thanks to the passionate research of the great minds of the Renaissance into the rendering of forms. Nowhere else has the artist enjoyed such social prestige, due above all to universal talent. From Giotto to Bernini, not to mention Leonardo da Vinci and Michelangelo, many of these creators excelled in several arts: painting, architecture, sculpture and even literature.

The sense of form and taste for harmony of the Italian artists appear in soft outlines and, in painting, in light colours which banish both the bareness and stiffness sometimes found in French art and the detailed realism of the Flemish and Germanic countries. Still in the domain of painting, subjects are bathed in a living, vibrant light and atmosphere: figures stand out against backgrounds of landscape or architecture in which the air circulates freely.

The mingling of the sacred and profane in the Italian outlook is found in Italian art. The pretty mistress of a painter or a sculptor often lends her features to the Virgin Mary; the Madonna with Saints takes part in sacred conversations. From the 15C onwards parish churches take on the appearance of theatres or drawing-rooms decorated with paintings and stucco. Art plays an important part in the lives of all classes of the people, and it is wonderful to see the humblest peasant or labourer deep in contemplation of a fine landscape or a graceful Virgin.

BYZANTIUM

When Constantine transferred the seat of the Empire to Constantinople in the 4C AD, Rome began to decline and ancient Byzantium became the centre of a brilliant civilisation, while part of Italy was overrun by the Barbarians.

After Honorius, who with his sister Galla Placidia fixed the capital of the Empire at Ravenna, this town became the setting of the brilliant reign of Justinian (AD 527-565) and his wife Theodora, successors of King Theodoric of the Ostrogoths, who had been beguiled by Ravennan art.

The Byzantine Emperors held the region of Ravenna and Venezia Giulia only until the 9C, but they kept a footing in Sicily and part of southern Italy until the 11C.

Byzantine art was born of the Christian art of the catacombs and early Christian basilicas and the Greek Oriental style, with its taste for mass, rich decoration and colour. The capital of Byzantine art in Italy was Ravenna, whose tradition was carried on by Venice, Rome, Sicily and even Lombardy to the beginning of the 13C.

The Byzantine artists had a sense of sanctity which appears in their works, with their air of grandeur and mystery.

Architecture and Sculpture. — The palaces have vanished but religious buildings remain. They are built in brick, with domes, on the basilical plan *(see sketch)* inspired by the Roman basilica and by the two basilicas of St. Apollinaris in Ravenna, and on a circular plan for mausolea (Galla Placidia at Ravenna) or baptistries. In the 11C St. Mark's in Venice became the rival of St. Sophia in Constantinople.

On the sides of sarcophagi, chapel walls, pulpits and diptychs, sculpture assumed an essentially decorative character: bas-reliefs represented stylised symbolic animals (lambs, peacocks, doves) and borders were deeply carved with a basic pattern of rosettes which was to inspire Lombard sculpture.

Mural paintings on large surfaces depicted majestic, hieratical figures, the symbols of a religion full of grandeur. The Benedictine fresco (Monte Cassino) was derived from these.

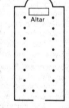

Basilical plan

Mosaics. — Byzantine artists showed their full powers in this sumptuous art form. Mosaics were composed of *tesserae,* or fragments of hard stone, irregularly cut to catch the light. They covered oven-vaults, walls and cupolas, their gold scintillating gently in mysterious semi-darkness. Enigmatic and grandiose figures stood out against midnight blue backgrounds and landscapes enlivened with trees, plants and animals, depicted with surprisingly accurate observation.

The most famous mosaics are those of Ravenna, dating from the 5 and 6C; however, the Byzantine style still prevailed in the 11-12C at St. Mark's in Venice, in Sicily (Cefalù, Palermo, Monreale) and as late as the 13C in Rome.

MEDIAEVAL ROMANESQUE AND GOTHIC (11-14C)

As in every country in Europe, cathedrals were built all over Italy, but here faith remained on the human level and architecture did not reach the sublime heights of the great achievements of religious art in France.

Romanesque Period. — Romanesque architecture in Italy received constant contributions from the Orient and, in the 12C especially, underwent influences from France, notably from Normandy and Provence.

The most flourishing school was that of Lombardy, whose master masons, the *maestri comacini,* created a style which spread all over north and central Italy *(sketch p 27)*. They built great vaulted churches decorated on the outside with bands and arcades, detached bell-towers and elaborately carved façades preceded by porches supported by lions (Como, Milan, Pavia, Verona, etc.).

The Pisan style, which was highly original *(see sketch below)*, included tiers of arcades and geometrical decorations based on lozenge shapes.

The Florentine Romanesque style *(see sketch below))* is characterised by simple lines inspired by antique art and by the decoration of façades with white and green marble used alternately.

In Latium and as far as Campania, in the 12-13C, the **Cosmati**, a Roman guild of mosaic and marble workers, held sway. They specialised in paving, walls, pulpits or ambos, ciboria, etc.

Finally, in southern Italy and Sicily, Lombard, Saracen and Norman influences mingled, the first two exercising their effect chiefly on decoration and the last on the building plan. The combined result was the Sicilian-Norman style *(see sketch below)*.

| Lombard Style | Pisan Style | Florentine Style | Sicilian-Norman Style |

Sculpture, being closely linked with architecture, which was essentially religious and decorative, felt French influence, but as early as the 12C Italian sculptors, unlike the French, began to sign their works. Masters like Wiligelmo and Antelami at Parma seem to have been acquainted with St-Trophime at Arles and with Chartres Cathedral respectively.

Gothic Period. — The Gothic style did not reach maturity until the beginning of the 14C.

Architecture. — The Italians of Piedmont probably invented Gothic vaulting, but they did not immediately realise its importance and they adopted it only when it returned, improved, from France. The Lombards and Pisans kept the Romanesque forms until the 14C.

It was the Cistercians who systematically introduced Gothic formulae into Italy in the 13C, starting at the Abbey of Fossanova; the Franciscans (at Assisi) and the Dominicans (at Florence) followed their example. In the same period the Angevin architects imported by the Anjou Dynasty, which reigned at Naples, spread arched vaulting and façades flanked by turrets in part of southern Italy. In the 14C the Cathedral of Genoa and the huge unfinished *Duomo* at Siena were derived from Burgundian art, but in the 15C the great church of S. Petronio at Bologna and the gigantic and florid Milan Cathedral marked the end of a style for which the Italians never showed much enthusiasm. In the Gothic period, also, many municipal palaces and loggias were built in which citizens met under shelter from rain and sun.

A little apart from these, the **Venetian style**, which had already been the subject of experiment in the Romanesque period and was confined almost wholly to civil buildings (palaces), was characterised by the use of internal courts *(patios)*, loggias and windows in groups of three in the façades. Venetian Gothic was to persist until the end of the 15C and its peculiar designs were still employed in later centuries *(see sketch below)*.

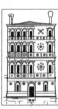

| Romanesque | Gothic | Renaissance | Classical | Baroque |

Venetian Palaces

Sculpture. — Decorative sculpture hardly advanced, but the round boss marked a return to antiquity mainly among the Pisans (Nicolò, Giovanni, Andrea and Nino Pisano); the Sienese, Tino di Camaino, and the Florentines, Andrea Orcagna and Arnolfo di Cambio (also architects), were more nearly followers of the international Gothic style. Stylised Madonnas, pulpits and funeral statues were the favourite subjects of these Gothic masters.

Painting. — The painted Crucifixes in relief which appeared in the 12C were the first specimens of Italian painting. In the 13C a Roman, Pietro Cavallini, executed frescoes and mosaics at S. Maria del Trastevere before leaving for Naples at the bidding of Charles of Anjou. His Florentine contemporary, Cimabue (1240-1302), who was praised by Dante, adorned the Upper Basilica of Assisi with dramatic frescoes.

Giotto (1266-1337) revolutionised painting by introducing naturalism into his works: movement, depth and atmosphere were indicated or suggested, and emotion came to light in the frescoes at Assisi and Padua. Among Giotto's pupils Bernardo Daddi was his most successful imitator.

At Siena at the same time **Duccio** (born about 1255) was still impregnating his painting with Byzantine influence, but he already showed the naïve grace and mannered charm which, together with the gilded backgrounds, lend such attraction to the Sienese school of painting. His disciple Simone Martini gave extraordinary delicacy to his colour; he became the favourite painter of Robert of Anjou at Naples and was invited with Petrarch by the French Popes to Avignon, where he died in 1344. The brothers Pietro and Ambrogio Lorenzetti cultivated minute, delicate detail. A famous school of miniaturists was founded at Rimini.

The leaders of the Florentine Trecento period (14C) were Andrea Orcagna and Andrea da Firenze, the decorator of the Spaniards' Chapel in S. Maria Novella and of the Campo Santo at Pisa. Their mystical and realistic style became known as **International Gothic**. Several artists of the Marches, Umbria and Lombardy, such as Allegretto Nuzi and Gentile da Fabriano, worked in this style, as also did the Veronese, Stefano da Zevio and Pisanello (1394-1450), a portraitist, animal painter and distinguished medallist.

THE QUATTROCENTO (15C)

The Quattrocento, or 15C, is the most important period in the history of the arts in Italy In this period a multitude of artists of genius, mostly working in Florence and encouraged by the Medicis, were to revolutionise forms and technique.

Architecture. — While the Flamboyant style flourished in France, **Brunelleschi** (1377-1446), formerly a talented gold-smith and sculptor and a rival of Ghiberti and Donatello, revealed himself as a great traditionalist in the art of building. Drawing on Antique sources, he advocated simplification of forms and his works (the Pazzi Chapel and the Dome of Santa Maria del Fiorè in Florence) have a purity and elegance reminiscent of Greece. Among his disciples were Michelozzo (1396-1472) and Leone Battista Alberti, a remarkable character, humanist and poet and designer of the Temple of the Malatestas at Rimini. The brothers Antonio and Bernardo Rossellino and Giuliano and Benedetto da Maiano, all four both sculptors and architects, worked in a supple, elegant style derived from Brunelleschi, as were those of Francesco di Giorgio Martini at Siena and of a Dalmatian, Luciano Laurana, at Urbino.

Sculpture. — The doorways of the baptistry at Florence gave sculptors their first opportunity of shaking off the Gothic tradition still followed by the Sienese, Jacopo della Quercia (1374-1438), who took part in the competition for the execution of these doorways and was eliminated, as was Brunelleschi, in favour of **Ghiberti** (1378-1455). The latter introduced into the design of the famous Gate of Paradise a freedom of modelling and sense of perspective which served as models for several generations of sculptors.

(After photo by Hachette)

Florence—The Annunciation,
by Donatello

Equally at ease in the modelling of forms (St. George) and in dramatic expression (St. John the Baptist), **Donatello** (1384-1466), though a Florentine, worked in all parts of Italy and cast in bronze at Padua the first great equestrian statue since the time of the Romans.

A contemporary of Donatello, **Luca della Robbia**, specialised in *putti* (cherubs — choristers of the Cantoria in the Duomo in Florence) and in coloured and glazed terracotta figures which were continued by his nephew Andrea and later by his grand-nephews, Girolamo and Giovanni.

Among Florentine artists who were disciples of Donatello, but less vigorous than their master are Agostino di Duccio, Desiderio da Settignano and Mino da Fiesole.

ITALIAN RENAISSANCE

(Chart)

SIENESE SCHOOL — **SCHOOL OF ROME** — **FLORENTINE SCHOOL**

(13 th c.)

DUCCIO

Pietro Cavallini
Jacopo Turriti

Cimabue

TRECENTO (14 th c.)

Ambrogio Lorenzetti
Simone Martini
Pietro Lorenzetti

GIOTTO

Lippo Memmi

Traini — Andrea Orcagna — Bernard Daddi
Taddeo Gaddi

Mino del Pelliccaio

SCHOOL OF UMBRIA
ASSISI

Giovanni da Milano

Andrea da Firenze — Antonio Veneziano — Giottino

Bartolo di Fredi
Andrea Vanni
Paolo di Giovanni

Allegretto Nuzi
(International Gothic)
Ottaviano Nelli

Spinello Aretino
Agnolo Gaddi

Taddeo di Bartolo

Gentile da Fabriano

Masolino
Lorenzo Monaco

N. di Pietro Gerini

Domenico di Bartolo

Donatello *(Sculptor)*

MASACCIO

QUATTROCENTO (15 th c.)

Sassetta

PERUGIA

FRA ANGELICO
Domenico Veneziano

Neri di Bicci

Lorenzo Vecchietta

Giovanni Boccati
Giovanni di Paolo

Andrea del Castagno

Fra Filippo Lippi
Pesellino

Sano di Pietro

Matteo da Gualdo

Piero della Francesca

Paolo Uccello
Antonio Pollaiuolo
Baldovinetti

Benedetto Bonfigli
Niccolo da Foligno

Benozzo Gozzoli

Piero Pollaiuolo
Cosim Rossel

Matteo di Giovanni

Fiorenzo di Lorenzo

Melozzo da Forli

Verrocchio

D. Ghirlandajo

Francesco di Giorgio

Pinturicchio

Giovanni Santi

Signorelli
Lorenzo di Credi

BOTTICELLI

Piero di Cosim

CINQUECENTO (16 th c.)

Benvenuto di Giovanni

Perugino
Palmezzano

Filippino Lippi

LEONARDO DA VINCI

Fra Bartolomeo

Baldassarre Peruzzi

Lo Spagna

RAPHAEL
Perino del Vaga
Giulio Guanuzzi

Solario

Boltraffio

Andrea del Sarto

MICHELANGELO

Le Rosso

Pontormo

Il Sodoma
(School of Milan)
Beccafumi

Giovanni da Udine
Il Primaticcio

SCHOOL OF MILAN
Bernardino Luini
Il Sodoma Gaudenzio Ferrari

Bronzino

SCHOOL OF FONTAINEBLEAU

28

At the end of the Quattrocento, **Verrocchio** (1435-1488), who was also a painter, showed remarkable power in the famous statue of Colleoni at Venice, while Antonio Pollaiuolo (1432-1498), a painter, medallist and sculptor in bronze, excelled in anatomy.

The most remarkable sculptor outside Florence was Francesco Laurana, a medallist (Louis XI, René d'Anjou) and a carver of the utmost sensibility of female busts in white marble (Eleonora of Aragon).

Painting. — Painting drew profit from the progress made by sculptors like Ghiberti and Donatello in the matter of depth.

Florence. — With **Masaccio** (1401-1428), a new era opened for Italian art. He was the first to insist, in the Carmine frescoes, on the volume of forms and the notions of space and light.

Fra Angelico (1387-1435), a Dominican friar trained by another monk, the charming Lorenzo Monaco, adopted the new style but preserved the Gothic spirit. His frescoes and altarpieces are notable for their freshness and an angelic simplicity of vision combined with purity of drawing and colour. His successors such as Domenico Veneziano and Fra Filippo Lippi (1406-1469) display attractive qualities of composition and drawing combined with sincere piety. Benozzo Gozzoli (1420-1498) also recalls Angelico by the fineness of his brush, but his taste for what is brilliant and descriptive is purely secular.

No one has expressed with more poetry than **Sandro Botticelli** (1444-1510), a pupil of Filippo Lippi, the gentleness and tenderness of the Madonnas or of allegorical scenes; no one has produced better than he that miraculous purity of line, which was to be sought in vain by Filippino Lippi, the son of Filippo. Baldovinetti (1427-1490), with his rather precious grace, adopted the same manner as Botticelli.

On the other hand Andrea del Castagno (1423-1457), emphasised modelling and monumental qualities in his frescoes of Famous Men and of the Last Supper. Paolo Uccello (1397-1474) made clever use of foreshortening in his equestrian portraits and battle scenes.

Piero della Francesca (1416?-1492) was a remarkable portraitist and a powerful fresco painter (Arezzo) with a sculptural style, notable for its majesty and impassivity, using pure, light colours. His subjects are bathed in an atmosphere of mystery. He worked for long at the court of Urbino, where the Montefeltri gathered writers, musicians and artists.

Finally, Siena was the home of several delightful minor masters whose art, still Gothic, shows rare charm and delicacy. Among them Taddeo di Bartolo, Sassetta, Giovanni di Paolo, Sano di Pietro and Matteo di Giovanni exemplified this tendency.

Northern Italy. — At Mantua, the capital of the Gonzaga family, the leading painters were **Mantegna** (1431-1506) and his pupils. The master of the Dead Christ, with his passion for anatomy and his interest in archaeology, composed scenes full of grandeur and discipline. Among the most highly esteemed of contemporary artists were the Lombard, Butinone and Cosimo Tura (1430-1495), the leader of the Ferrara school of painting, whose accentuated and sometimes rather angular realism occasionally recalls the Flemish style.

A painter of Romagna, Melozzo da Forli (1438-1518) was somewhat influenced by Piero della Francesca. He was especially successful in painting angels.

Venice. — The first Venetian painters to emerge from the Byzantine mass were the Vivarini, and the famous Bellini family, with the father, Jacopo, and the two sons, Gentile and especially Giovanni. **Giovanni Bellini** or Giambellini (1430-1516), the brother-in-law of Mantegna, was both sensitive and realistic. He painted his compositions for altarpieces on landscape backgrounds using deep colours. Antonello da Messina (born c. 1430), who resembles Bellini, learned the secrets of oil painting from Van Eyck. Crivelli (1430-1494), a precise and minute painter, and Carapaccio are hardly more than chroniclers.

The art of **marquetry** or inlaying, which derives from painting, is typically Italian. Fra Giovanni da Verona and Cristoforo da Lendinara vied in the composition of perspectives.

CINQUECENTO (16C)

The 16C was marked by a transition from a religious (Christian) atmosphere to one of human sensibility. Artists were attracted more and more by Antiquity, mythology and the discovery of man. Papal influence caused the artistic centre to move from Florence to Rome.

Architecture. — It was in the course of this century that the style of the Florentine palace was formed. Its features were embossing, ringed columns, triangular and curved frontons or pediments and projecting cornices (see sketch p 30).

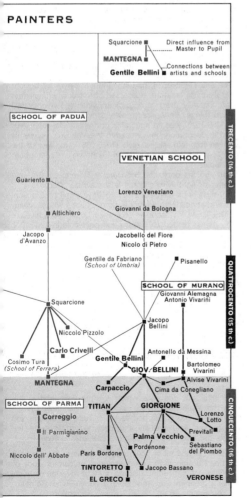

PAINTERS

Squarcione ■   Direct influence from Master to Pupil
MANTEGNA ■
Gentile Bellini ■   Connections between artists and schools

SCHOOL OF PADUA

VENETIAN SCHOOL

TRECENTO (14 th c.)

Guariento ■

Lorenzo Veneziano

Giovanni da Bologna

■ Altichiero

Jacopo d'Avanzo

Jacobello del Fiore
Nicolo di Pietro

Gentile da Fabriano
(School of Umbria)

■ Pisanello

QUATTROCENTO (15 th c.)

SCHOOL OF MURANO
Giovanni Alemagna
Antonio Vivarini

■ Squarcione

Jacopo Bellini

Niccolo Pizzolo

Carlo Crivelli

Antonello da Messina

Cosimo Tura
(School of Ferrara)

Gentile Bellini

Bartolomeo Vivarini

MANTEGNA

GIOV. BELLINI

Alvise Vivarini

Carpaccio

Cima da Conegliano

SCHOOL OF PARMA

TITIAN

GIORGIONE

CINQUECENTO (16 th c.)

Correggio

Lorenzo Lotto

Il Parmigianino

Previtali

Palma Vecchio

Sebastiano del Piombo

Niccolo dell' Abbate

Paris Bordone

Pordenone

TINTORETTO ■   Jacopo Bassano

EL GRECO ■

VERONESE

29

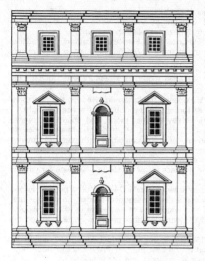

(After photo by T.C.I.)

Bramante's "rhythmic bay'

Florence — Palazzo Medici

Bramante (1444-1514), who was also a painter, was the leading figure of the period. He invented the "rhythmic bay" (a façade composed of alternating windows, pilasters and niches: *see sketch above*). A keen student of antique art, he worked at Milan and at the court of Urbino before conceiving the central plan of St. Peter's, Rome. Raphaël succeeded him as the architect of that church, followed by Giuliano da Sangallo, Baldassarre Peruzzi, Antonio da Sangallo and Michelangelo who designed the dome and at the same time completed the Farnese Palace.

Vignola (1507-1573) and **Palladio** (1508-1580) both wrote treatises on architecture.

Sculpture. — Michelangelo (1475-1564) was the most outstanding character of the 16C. After having served his apprenticeship in Florence he came to Rome to make the tomb of Julius II, whose favourite artist he was. He ended his life in Florence after finishing the tombs of the Medicis in which his appealing mannerisms were given free rein.

His contemporaries paled beside him; yet among them were Benvenuto Cellini (1500-1571), Florentine goldsmith and bronze worker, famous for his Perseus, and Giovanni da Bologna, born at Douai (France) in 1529, who worked at Bologna and at Florence.

Painting. — The 16C is an important period for painting. Interest shifted, however, from Florence to Rome, Venice and a few other centres under the influence of Luca Signorelli, in whom the Biblical greatness of Michelangelo already lay. There had appeared also the Umbrians, Perugino and Pinturicchio who were to be Raphaël's earliest models.

Verrocchio, the teacher of **Leonardo da Vinci** (1452-1519), had little influence over his brilliant pupil. Leonardo was an extraordinary and alarming creature, possessed of universal knowledge. He is famous in painting for his *sfumato* (literally mist), a sort of impalpable, luminous veil which seems to emanate from persons and things. He worked mostly at Milan but died at the court of François I at Amboise. **Raphaël** (1483-1520) was an admirable portraitist. His calm, harmonious genius is incomparably displayed in decoration (the Stanze in the Vatican), where his exceptional mastery of composition is given free rein. **Michelangelo** (1475-1564), the last of the three great men, wanted to be a sculptor, and his sense of relief and his power are triumphant in the gigantic frescoes of the Sistine Chapel.

Let us also mention Andrea del Sarto and the portraitist Bronzino at Florence, Il Sodoma at Siena and Correggio at Parma, a painter of light whose grace is somewhat affected.

The Venetian school began with the mysterious **Giorgione** (1477-1510), a pupil of Giovanni Bellini. His wonderful sense of landscape and atmosphere are felt in compositions whose meaning remains hidden to us (The Storm, The Three Philosophers). Lorenzo Lotto (1480-1556), a portraitist and painter of religious compositions, tended to realism and cold colour.

Titian (1490-1576), a disciple of Bellini, had a proud and varied talent. As much at home in portraiture as in great mythological or religious compositions, he worked with Giorgione in his youth and then for all the European princes, including François I and Charles V.

Tintoretto (1518-1594), a profound and tormented spirit, made play with dramatic light effects in his passionate religious compositions; he appears voluptuous and upsetting in his profane subjects (Suzanna and the Elders). Tintoretto had a notable influence on his amiable pupil, the Cretan, Theotocopoulos, known as El Greco (the Greek).

Veronese (1528-1588) was first and foremost a decorator in love with luxury and sumptuous architecture as can be seen in his Apotheosis of Venice, in the Doges' Palace.

As for Jacopo Bassano (1518-1592), he handled rustic and nocturnal scenes with a freedom of touch which influenced many adepts of dark painting before Caravaggio.

ART OF THE COUNTER-REFORMATION AND MANNERISM (16-17C)

The Counter-Reformation (mid 16-mid 17C) marks the transition between Renaissance and Baroque art.

Architecture. — As regards religious architecture, the style which is often described as the "Jesuit" style in view of the role played by the Jesuit Order in the reaction of the Catholic Church to the Reformation movement headed by Luther and Calvin, led to the building of austere and sublime churches with a single nave, spacious and well-lit, and designed to facilitate the preaching. The Church of Gesù in Rome is the most characteristic example of this style.

Sculpture and Painting. — During the same period many sculptors and painters followed the style of Michelangelo and Raphaël. This trend designated as **mannerism** with its careful study of attitudes and expression, of foreshortening, of light that distorts and of over-ornateness, sometimes leads to artificiality. The main exponents of this style include Giulio Romano, Cavaliere d'Arpino, Daniele da Voltera, Pomarancio, Baroccio and Rosso Fiorentino.

BAROQUE (17-18C)

The Baroque style which developed in the 17C and during part of the 18C, is governed by irregular contours and generous forms; it seeks above all what is picturesque and theatrical.

Painting. — In reaction against mannerism, a group of Bolognese artists under the leadership of the Carracci family and of Caravaggio paved the way for Baroque art.

The **Carracci** (Annibale, the most original, Ludovico and Agostino, academic decorators) tried to codify beauty in large, careful but rather cold compositions. Their Bolognese followers, Guido, Albano and Guercino, continued this manner with rather more vigour.

But the personality of **Caravaggio** (1573-1610), with his stormy life, was pre-eminent in Rome and later in Naples and Sicily. His violent and dramatic work shows scenes and popular figures in a contrasting light which was widely imitated (Orazio and Artemisia Gentileschi, Caracciolo, Giuseppe Ribera, Bernardo Strozzi). In Naples, Porpora, Ruoppolo and Recco painted strange still-lifes.

The characteristics of Baroque art are effects of movement, perspective and *trompe-l'œil* as illustrated by Bernini, sculptor and architect, Pietro da Cortona who was also an architect, Lanfranco and Luca Giordano. In Rome, Father Pozzo excelled in fresco painted in *trompe-l'œil.*

The 18C was not over rich in genius. At Venice, however, the school of painting remained active with Tiepolo, an accomplished decorator, Canaletto, Guardi and Longhi, faithful interpreters of Venetian life and light. At Bergamo we find the portraitist Fra Vittore Ghislandi, in Rome, Piranese, a draughtsman of ruins and architecture, and at Genoa, especially, the curious Magnasco (1667-1747), who depicted fantastic subjects and was far ahead of his time.

Architecture and Sculpture. — The Baroque style was born of "mannerism" and exaggeration of movement and expression, of which Michelangelo and Giulio Romano were the leading exponents. It goes further still, seeking for dramatic and spectacular effect in the exuberant play of curve, counter-curve and scroll-work, the relief making for contrasts of light and shade.

Under the sway of the Jesuits architecture and sculpture acquired a florid and theatrical quality with architects such as Carlo Maderno, Borromini and especially **Bernini** (1598-1680), the architect, sculptor and painter who designed the

(After photo by Nathan)

Syracuse — Baroque façade of the Cathedral

colonnades of St. Peter's, the canopy and tombs inside the basilica and the Fountain of the Four Rivers in Rome. Pietro da Cortona (1596-1669), architect and painter, also worked in Rome.

MODERN ART

In the middle of the 18C Neo-classicism developed and was upheld by the architect Vanvitelli, the sculptor Canova (1757-1822) and the painter Appiani (1754-1817). In the second half of the 19C the **Macchiaioli** (from *macchia:* stain or blot) group was formed in Florence. Their technique was individual touches of paint and colour effects to create a realistic impression. The principal artists among this group were Cecioni, Fattori, Signori and Lega.

The beginning of the 20C saw a certain awakening. Severini and Modigliani of Leghorn belonged to the Paris school, but painters like Boccioni, Giorgio da Chirico and Carlo Carra and the poet Marinetti and sculptors such as Marino Marini and Manzù made their marks in Futurism and Surrealism. Architecture has inspired many talents, among them those of Pier-Luigi Nervi and Gio Ponti, creators of new, pure and sober forms and experts in the use of reinforced concrete and plastic materials.

VILLAS AND GARDENS

Italian achievements in this domain have won great fame abroad, especially in France, where the gardens of Amboise, Blois, St-Germain and Gaillon were inspired by Italy. Terraces and fountains are their principal features.

Roman Villas. — Villas were country houses built by the Roman patricians on the slopes of the Castelli Romani, at Tivoli, Frascati and other places, where they commanded fine views. The most famous example is Hadrian's Villa near Tivoli.

Renaissance Gardens. — In the Quattrocento the best-known villas were at Florence (Careggi, Fiesole and Poggio at Caiano) where the architect planned the gardens, making wide use of the system of terraces. Michelozzo and Sangallo the Elder were the chief designers.

In the 16C Raphaël planned the Villa Madama in Rome. At Castello, near Florence, grottoes, fountains and statues appeared. The Boboli Gardens contains vistas, a grotto, an avenue of cypresses and fountains adorned with statues by Giovanni da Bologna.

With the Villa d'Este at Tivoli cypresses and running water took on added importance; there were cascades, basins, fish-ponds, fountains and cooling sprays of water. Still in central Italy, you can admire the Villa Lante at Bagnaia, near Viterbo, the Villa Giulia and the Villa Farnesina in Rome, the Villa Caprarola, north of Rome, proud of its great loggia.

In northern Italy, Palladio and Scamozzi built villas inspired by Antiquity.

Baroque Gardens. — These were plentiful in the 17-18C. The Aldobrandini villa at Frascati dates from the 17C; the gardens are again terraced. The Villa Doria-Pamphili in Rome has wonderful gardens which have been turned into a public park. The Farnese Gardens extend over part of the Palatine Hill. The Villa Marlia, near Lucca, and the terraces of the Isola Bella in Lake Maggiore are of the same period. The flower-beds of the Villa Carlotta on Lake Como were laid out in the 18C. The gardens of the Palace of Caserta, near Naples, and those of the Palace of Colorno, near Parma, are also noteworthy.

THE MASTERPIECES OF ITALIAN ART

Architecture in bistre. Sculpture in black. *Paintings and mosaics in italics.*

MUSIC — THEATRE — CINEMA

Music and Bel Canto. — As early as the end of the 10C a Benedictine, Guido Monaco, of Arezzo, had invented the scale, naming the notes with the initial syllables of the first lines of John the Baptist's hymn. Palestrina reformed religious music in the 16C. But it was only in the 17-18C that Italy acquired a true musical school, marked by the charm and freshness of inspiration of Corelli (1653-1713), the originator of the *Concerti grossi*, Scarlatti (1659-1725), who was above all a harpsichord player, Boccherini (1743-1805) and the Venetian, **Vivaldi** (1675-1741), whom Bach admired so much. Throughout the 19C Respighi, the author of two symphonic poems, *The Pines of Rome* and *The Fountains of Rome*, was the only composer of instrumental music of any reputation, while in the 20C Dallapiccola is regarded as the head of the dodecaphonic school, and Petrassi remains true to the great tradition. Luigi Bono, Bruno Maderna and Nino Trota represent the new Italian School.

Among esteemed Italian conductors Arturo Toscanini (1867-1957) dominated his colleagues with the verve and originality of his interpretations.

Other famous names are De Sabata and nowadays, Nello Santi, Claudio Abbado, Carlo Maria Giuglini, Ricardo Muti, director of the Florence Music Festival held in May. The Neapolitan school of Bel Canto *(see p 153)* is world famous.

Opera, which displays the register and quality of voices, is more popular than comic opera, mingled with *recitative*, of which Rossini is the leading champion *(the Barber of Seville)*. Opera is considered to have been born with Claudio Monteverdi, the author of *Orfeo* (1607), who was followed in lighter vein by Pergolesi, Cimarosa and Paisiello in the 18C. The Romantic period produced a crop of composers, including Bellini *(Norma)*, Rossini, Donizetti *(Lucia di Lammermoor)*, Puccini *(Tosca, Madame Butterfly, La Bohème)* and Mascagni *(Cavalleria Rusticana)*. The most popular of all is **Verdi** (1813-1901), who composed *Aïda, Rigoletto, La Traviata, Otello* and especially, the admirable *Requiem*. The modern composer Menotti is the promoter of the Spoleto Festival.

The incomparable Scala at Milan, for which Visconti created marvellous sets, the San Carlo theatre at Naples, the theatres of Palermo and Turin and those of Venice (La Fenice) and Rome vie in inviting the famous singers: Graziella Sciutti, Fiorenza Cossotto, Mirella Freni, Katia Riciarelli, Corelli, Capuccini, Raimondi, Pavarotti, Carlo Bini, who have succeeded the great Pagliacci, Lina Cavalieri, Renata Tebaldi, Maria Callas, Caruso, Tito Schipa, Beniamino Gigli, Toti del Monte, Giuseppe Di Stefano, Mario del Monaco and Tito Gobbi. The amphitheatre in Verona and Caracalla's Baths in Rome are the scene of impressive performances.

The Commedia dell'Arte. — This form of theatre implies very considerable powers of imagination. The comedy consists of an improvisation or *imbroglio* based on a theme fixed beforehand and called the *scenario*, with *lazzi* (gags) uttered by masked actors representing stock characters: the braggart, the valet, the lady's maid, the lover, the knave, the old fox, the clown and the musician who are called Pulcinella, Harlequin, Columbine, Pierrot, Scapino, Scaramouch, Pantaloon and Mezzetino. Its element of caricature sometimes springs from triviality.

| Scapino | Pantaloon | Fracasso | Pulcinella | Scaramouch | Mezzetino |

Silence! filming in progress... 1904-1911: the Italian cinema industry was born in Turin with comic strips, documentaries and newsreels. In 1935 the Cinematographic Centre (pupils: Rossellini, Antonioni, De Santis) and the Cinecittà studios were established in Rome.

1942: Visconti made *Ossessione:* neo-realism is born, a doctrine which sets out to give an intimate and spontaneous picture of life, with filming in the street, few or no stars and characters filmed among people going about their daily business. Political and social events in Italy at the end of the war led to the fullest development of this movement.

1945-1950's: Rossellini also inspired by these events created *Rome Open City* and *Paisan*, which shows a distressed Italy. Vittorio De Sica, assisted by C. Zavattini, created *Sciuscia* (Shoeshine) and *Bicycle Thieves* with touching simplicity. Visconti, inspired by one of Vergas novels, realised *The Earth Trembles*, with the aid of the fishermen of Aci Trezza in Sicily. Add to this brilliant list *Bitter Rice* by De Santis and the whole world knows about neo-realism. Antonioni introduced a highly developed psychological element into his descriptions with *Il Grido* (The Cry), then *L'avventura*, *La Notte* (The Night). Fellini showed his mastery with *Vitelloni* (the Loafers/The Young and the Passionate), the unforgettable *La Strada* (The Street) and *The Nights of Cabiria*. With *Senso* (The Wanton Countess) Visconti starts a fresco of decadence.

1960-1970: After creating *Accattone*, the description of a wretched person's life in the Roman suburbs Pasolini disconcerted the critics with *Theorem;* he made a return to Mythology with *Oedipus Rex* and *Medea* — the latter has fantastic scenery. De Seta realised *Banditi a Orgosolo*, painting a moving picture of the life of the Sardinian shepherds. Rosi made the famous bandit relive in *Salvatore Giuliano* and denounces the housing deficiencies of Naples in *Hands over the City*. Fellini made a brilliant picture of life with *La Dolce Vita* and followed this with *Eight and a Half*, an appraisal of the life of a film director, and returned to the theme of decadence with the very controversial *Fellini-Satyricon*. Visconti followed up his description of a decadent nobility in *The Leopard* and *The Damned*.

And since...: Marco Ferreri analysed the alienation of man in modern society in *Blow Out* and *The Last Woman*. After the controversial *Last Tango in Paris*, Bertolucci depicted class struggle in 20C Italy in the historical saga *"1900"*. Antonioni's *The Passenger* deals with identity crisis. In the unforgettable *Death in Venice*, Visconti draws inspiration from the decline of man and the decay of society. After filming stories from classical literature including the *Decameron*, Pasolini delved into decadence and terror with *Salò*. After *Amarcord* and *Roma* which combine autobiography and fantasy, Fellini described brilliantly decadence and superficiality in *Casanova*. Dino Risi, Ettore Scola and Franco Brusati, the masters of Italian comedy, deal with grave sociological problems in a humorous vein.

LETTERS

St. Francis of Assisi (1182-1226), in the *Canticle of the Sun,* was the real originator of poetry in the language of the people, only Latin having been used previously. Italian literature, however, had its true birth with **Dante** (1265-1321), the author of the *Divine Comedy,* an epic of the Christian West. **Petrarch** (1304-1374) of the *Sonnets* and **Boccaccio** (1313-1375) of the *Decameron* form, with Dante, the Florentine trio who set the Italian language on a firm foundation.

Humanism flourished in the Quattrocento (15C) under the patronage of Lorenzo de' Medici (1149-1493), an occasional poet, supported by the writer Politian (1454-1494) and such philosophers as Pico della Mirandola. Artists like Alberti and Leonardo da Vinci also wrote poems and treatises.

The 16C is distinguished by famous poets, story-tellers and philosophers.

Ariosto (1475-1533), a native of Ferrara, wrote *Orlando Furioso,* an epic poem in episodes, which enjoyed an extraordinary vogue. His successor in this genre and at the court of Ferrara, Torquato Tasso (1544-1595), published his *Jerusalem Delivered,* but later went mad and died in prison.

Most of the prose writers were connected with Florence. Among them were **Machiavelli** (1469-1527), a political theorist and the originator of Machiavellism *(The Prince),* and the historians Guicciardini and Vasari.

Aretino (1492-1556) was admired as a story-teller for his elegant style.

The 17C was a period of decadence, but the 18C gives us the Venetians, Goldoni (1707-1793), who has been called the Italian Molière, and Casanova (1725-1798), the author of licentious *Memoirs* written in French. In the 19C writers celebrated national feeling, hitherto suppressed. **Leopardi**, the great lyric poet, Alfieri, Foscolo, Carducci, Pascoli composed songs, while the novelist Manzoni produced his masterpiece, *The Bethrothed.*

Making the transition to the 20C are Panzini and Grazia Deledda. Finally came D'Annunzio (1863-1938), an extraordinary character, a brilliant soldier and conqueror of cities (Fiume), a novelist *(The Child of Lust)* and a poet *(Alcyon).* Among his contemporaries, the Sicilian, Pirandello (1867-1934) created a new stage technique and the Neapolitan, Benedetto Croce (1866-1952) professed an idealistic philosophy. Giovanni Papini concentrated particularly on religious problems.

Contemporary Novelists. — They have given truthful descriptions of the land and people of Italy. Moravia describes the Roman petty bourgeois and working people *(The Indifferents, Roman Tales),* while Malaparte, who was born at Prato, tends rather to study Neapolitans and Tuscans *(Kaputt, The Skin, The Tuscans).*

Vasco Pratolini describes the humbler quarters of Florence in *The Quarter, Chronicles of Poor Lovers* and *Young Girls of San Frediano.*

Sicily has inspired Tomaso di Lampedusa *(The Leopard).* Danilo Dolci *(Report from Palermo),* Vittorini *(Conversation in Sicily, Erica and Her Brothers)* and Brancati *(Bel Antonio),* proving the attraction for Italian writers of that primitive south of which Carlo Levi described the poverty in *Christ Stayed at Eboli.* On the other hand, Ignazio Silone *(Bread and Wine, The Seed under the Snow, The Secret of Luke)* and Giuseppe Marotta *(Naples Gold)* described the splendour as well as the poverty of the south.

Finally, Mario Soldati draws a vivid picture of the Piazza di Spagna quarter in Rome and of the Isle of Capri *(Letters from Capri)* while Giovanni Guareschi is the author of *Don Camillo.*

FOLKLORE, ARTS AND CRAFTS

Survival of Folklore. — The old costumes are still worn daily in the Valle d'Aosta, the Abruzzi, Calabria and especially Sardinia, where great folk festivals take place at Cagliari and Sassari. The traditional fêtes bring together enthusiastic crowds of people both to watch and to take part. As for the religious ceremonies, they arouse great popular fervour and are always occasions for mass demonstrations.

Vitality of Arts and Crafts. — Many tourists like to bring home some souvenir of their journey: an ornament for their rooms or something they can use with pleasure. Italy, as a country where individual skill has held its own against mass production, offers a variety of mementoes, sometimes very simple, which give pleasure without being the sort of bazaar stuff that has nothing to do with local art.

The adjacent map shows the towns and districts where the tourist can obtain the best known specialities.

SPECIALITIES AND SOUVENIRS

A gourmet...?

If you are, look in the current **Michelin Red Guide Italia**
for the establishment with stars.

FOOD AND DRINK

Italy is rich in tasty products and its cooking is among the best known in the world.

Hors d'Œuvre and Soups. — *Antipasti* or hors d'œuvre consist of raw salads, vegetables dressed with oil or vinegar and fine pork-butchers' meats. Minestrone, vegetable or macaroni soups, often thick, are also served at the beginning of a meal.

Entrées: macaroni in its various forms, plain or combined with various sauces and trimmings (in bouillon or with sea-food, minced meat or grated cheese), is the traditional entrée. It has various names, according to its shape: *macaroni* and *spaghetti* (thick and thin), *tagliatelle* (strips), *lasagne* and *tortellini, agnellotti, cannelloni, ravioli,* etc. *Pesto alla genovese, ragù alla bolognese* and Neapolitan *pommarola* are the commonest sauces served with it. In the north, rice, grown in Piedmont and Lombardy, is also consumed. Fish or sea-food soups are to be had all along the Italian coast.

Fish and meat: fried dishes like *fritto misto* (mixed fry or grill) take a prominent place.

Cheeses: the cheeses made from cows', goats', ewes' and buffaloes' milk are delicious.

Dessert: Cakes, pastries and sweets *(dolci)* and ices *(gelati)* are popular in Italy.
Wine is the national drink and is grown in all districts. **Mineral waters** are popular.

After the meal you should try the black *espresso* coffee, which is strong and aromatic.

SOME REGIONAL SPECIALITIES *(see map of districts, p 3)*

Piedmont. — Cooking here resembles French cooking and is done with butter. A popular dish is **fonduta**, melted cheese with milk, eggs and white truffles *(tartufi bianchi). Cardi* (chards) are prepared *alla bagna cauda,* i.e. with a hot sauce containing oil or butter, anchovies, garlic and truffles. Monferrato produces delicious wines: Barolo, Barbaresco, Barbera, Grignolino, red Freisas, white **Asti**, still or sparkling *(spumante),* with a strong flavour of grapes.

Piedmont produces **vermouths** (Martini, Cinzano, Carpano) and *gressini* — bread sticks.

Lombardy. — Milan, where cooking is done with butter, gives its name to several dishes: *minestrone alla milanese,* a soup of green vegetables, rice and bacon; *risotto alla milanese,* rice cooked with saffron; **costoletta alla milanese,** a fillet of veal fried in egg and breadcrumbs with cheese; *osso buco,* a knuckle of veal with the marrow-bone; *panettone,* a large fruit cake containing raisins and candied lemon peel. Here the commonest cheese is the excellent **Gorgonzola.** Few wines are produced, apart from those of Valtellina or the Pavia district, but Piedmont is near. Milan makes ices which are sold all over Italy (Motta, Alemagna).

Venetia. — As in the Po Plain, the people eat *polenta,* a form of semolina made from maize, sometimes accompanied by little birds, *risi e bisi* (rice and peas), and **fegato alla veneziana** (calf's liver fried with onions). The shell-fish, eels and dried cod *(baccalà)* are excellent. The best wines come from the district of Verona; **Valpolicella** and Bardolino, *rosé* or red, perfumed and slightly sparkling, and Soave, which is white and strong.

Liguria. — The chief speciality of Genoa is **lasagne al pesto,** flat leaves of *pasta* backed in the oven and seasoned with *pesto,* a sauce based on olive oil in which basil, pine-kernels, garlic and ewes' cheese have been steeped. Sea-food is famous, including *zuppa di datteri,* a shell-fish soup with which the Ligurians drink Cinqueterre or Corona, strong, liqueur-like white wines.

Emilia Romagna. — This is an eminently gastronomical region, whose pork-butchers' meat is the most famous in Italy: Bologna **salami** and **mortadella,** Modena *zamponi* (pigs' trotters), Parma *prosciutto* (ham). *Pasta* in the form of *lasagne,* egg *tagliatelle, tortellini* and stuffed *cappelleti* are varied and tasty when served *alla bolognese* — that is, with meat-gravy and tomato sauce. **Parmesan cheese** *(parmigiano),* hard and pale yellow, is strong and delicate in flavour. Emilia produces Lambrusco, a fruity, sparkling red wine, and white Albano.

Tuscany. — This is where Italian cooking was born, at the court of the Medici. Florence offers its *alla fiorentina* specialities: died cod *(baccalà)* with oil, garlic and pepper, *costata* grilled fillets of veal with oil, salt and pepper, *fagioli* (beans with oil, onions and herbs); Leghorn produces red mullet *(triglie)* and *cacciucco* (fish soup) and Siena offers the *panforte,* a sugar cake containing almonds, honey and candied melon, orange or lemon. **Chianti** (both red and white) is drunk everywhere.

Umbria, Marches. — The regional dish is the *porchetta,* a whole sucking pig roasted on the spit. The wines are white, including the famous **Orvieto** of Umbria, the Verdicchio of the Marches and the delicious Moscato of San Marino.

Latium. — There are many Roman specialities: **fettucine** or strip macaroni, **gnocchi** alla Romana, **saltimbocca,** a fillet of veal rolled in ham, fried in butter and flavoured with Marsala and flavoured with sage, and *abbacchio al forno* or roast lamb. Vegetables include *carciofi alla Giudia,* or artichokes cooked in oil with garlic and parsley. *Pecorino,* ewes' milk cheese, and the famous white wines of Montefiascone *(see p 150)* and the **Castelli Romani** (Frascati) will satisfy the most discerning gourmet.

Abruzzi, Molise. — Among the *pasta* note *maccheroni alla chitarra,* made by hand and cut into strips, and *pincisgrassi,* cooked in the oven with meat-gravy and cream sauce. *Latticini* (fresh mountain cheeses) are popular.

Campania. — Naples is the home of **spaghetti,** which is often prepared with shell-fish *(alle vongole). Trattorie* and *pizzerie* serve *costata alla pizzaiola,* a fillet steak with tomatoes, garlic and wild marjoram, *mozzarella in carrozza* (cheese savoury) and especially the **pizza,** a cheese *(mozzarella)* tart containing tomato, anchovy and herring and flavoured with capers and wild marjoram. Wines from volcanic soil have a delicate, slightly sulphurous taste: red and white Capri, white Ischia, white Lacryma Christi and red Gragnano (Vesuvius wines).

Apulia, Basilicata, Calabria. — The oysters *(ostriche)* of Taranto are tasty. The most original dish is *capretto ripieno of forno,* a roast kid stuffed with herbs.

Sicily. — The island is rich in fruit (lemons, oranges, mandarines, olives, almonds), pastries and ices. The real Sicilian **cassata** is a partly iced cream cake containing chocolate cream and candied fruits. Other specialities : *cuscusu* (couscous) and fish-tunny, sword-fish, anchovies. The best known wine is **Marsala,** which is dark and strong, but Malvasia and the white wines of Etna and Lipari are also delicious.

Sardinia. — *Porchetta* (see Umbria) and *prosciutto di cinghiale* (smoked wild boar ham) are the most characteristic dishes, together with *succutundu,* a highly concentrated bouillon with balls of semolina. Vernaccia is a well known wine.

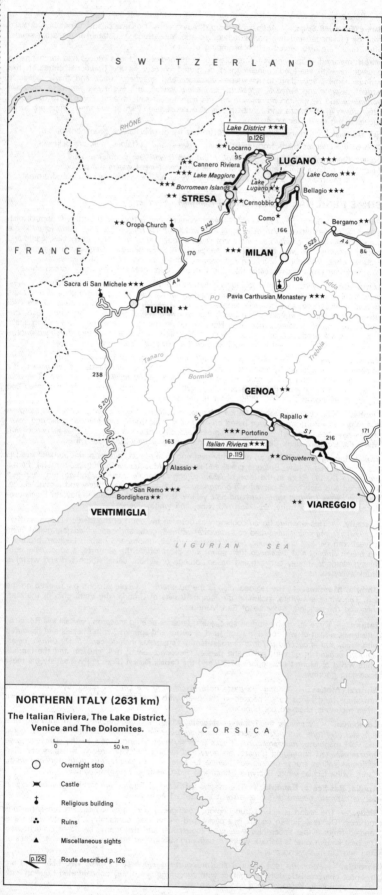

S W I T Z E R L A N D

RHÔNE

Inn

Lake District ★★★
p.126

★★ Locarno
95
★★ Cannero Riviera
★★★ *Lake Maggiore*
★★★ *Borromean Islands*
★★ **STRESA**

LUGANO ★★★

Lake Como ★★★

Lake Lugano ★★
Bellagio ★★★

Cernobbio ★

Como

Bergamo ★★

★★ Oropa Church
Ticino

S 142

166

S 525

★★★ MILAN

A 4
84

170

Sacra di San Michele ★★★
A 4

104
Adda

TURIN ★★

PO
Pavia Carthusian Monastery ★★★

Tanaro

238

Bormida

Trebbia

S 20

GENOA ★★

Rapallo ★

★★★ Portofino
S 1
216

Italian Riviera ★★★
p.119
★★ *Cinqueterre*
171

163

Alassio ★

San Remo ★★★
Bordighera ★★

★★ VIAREGGIO

VENTIMIGLIA

F R A N C E

L I G U R I A N   S E A

C O R S I C A

NORTHERN ITALY (2631 km)

The Italian Riviera, The Lake District,
Venice and The Dolomites.

0 ———— 50 km

○   Overnight stop

⚔   Castle

♀   Religious building

⚉   Ruins

▲   Miscellaneous sights

p.126   Route described p.126

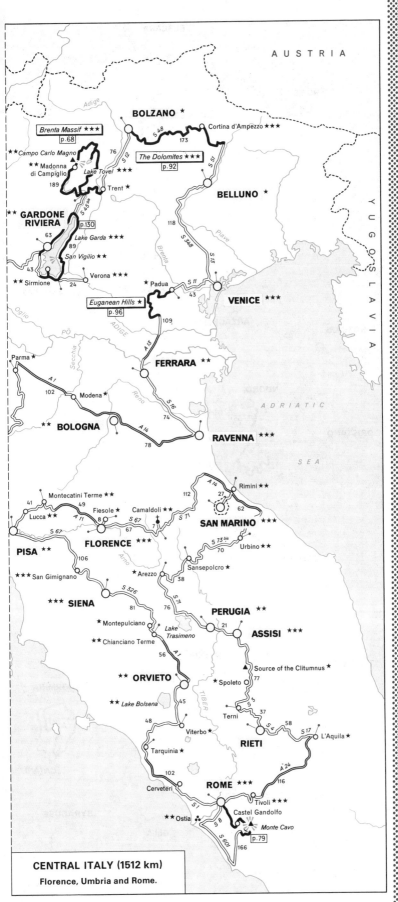

AUSTRIA

BOLZANO ★

S 48   Cortina d'Ampezzo ★★★
173

Brenta Massif ★★★
p.68

★★ _Campo Carlo Magno_   76   _The Dolomites ★★★_
                                 p.92
★★ Madonna
di Campiglio   _Lake Tovel_
189   Trent ★   BELLUNO ★

GARDONE
★★ RIVIERA
p.130   118

63   _Lake Garda ★★★_   S 348
89   _San Vigilio ★★_

43   _Sirmione_   Verona ★★★
          24   ★ Padua   S 11
                           43   VENICE ★★★

          Euganean Hills ★
          p.96
                    109

Parma ★

          A1   FERRARA ★★
102   Modena ★
                    S 16
                    74
★★ BOLOGNA   A 14
          78   RAVENNA ★★★

                                     SEA

          Montecatini Terme ★★   112   Rimini ★★
41   49   27
Lucca ★★ A 11   Fiesole ★   Camaldoli ★★   62
          8   S 67   S 71   SAN MARINO ★★★
          67
PISA ★★   FLORENCE ★★★   S 73 bis   Urbino ★★
          106   70
★★★ San Gimignano   ★ Arezzo   Sansepolcro ★
                    38
★★★ SIENA   S 326
          81   76   PERUGIA ★★
★ Montepulciano   _Lake
               Trasimeno_   21   ASSISI ★★★
★★ Chianciano Terme
               56   A1   ▲ Source of the Clitumnus ★
★★ ORVIETO   77
                    ★ Spoleto ○
★★ _Lake Bolsena_   45   S 3
               48   Terni   37
          Viterbo ★   S 4   58   S 17
                    RIETI ★   L'Aquila ★
Tarquinia ★
               102   A 24
Cerveteri   ROME ★★★   116
               S1   Tivoli ★★★
★★ Ostia   Castel Gandolfo
               Monte Cavo
               p.79
               166

CENTRAL ITALY (1512 km)
Florence, Umbria and Rome.

PESCARA

★★ San Clemente
a Casauria Abbey
Popoli
San Giovanni in Venere

★★★ ROME
A 24   A 25
169
31
72
S 5
Sangro

★★ SCANNO
73
27
298

S 6
158
★★ Casamari Abbey
★★ Barrea
The Abruzzi ★★★
p. 41

Abbey of Monte Cassino ★★
9

Volturno

105   A 2

Caserta ★

SARDINIA (1220 km)
Key p. 36

★★★ NAPLES
48   Vesuvius ★★★
Pompeii ★★★
★★ SORRENTO   69   SALERNO ★
Amalfi ★★
★★ Capri   Paestum ★★★
195
S 18

Amalfi Coast ★★★
p. 44

Máddalena
Archipelago ★★

SASSARI   S 133
135   ARZACHENA
Neptune's   63
Grotto ★★★   S 127bis
S 125
S 151
Alghero ★   153

T Y R R H E N I A N

S E A

125   Tirso
NUORO   32
33   p.270   Dorgali

ORISTANO   ★★★   69   S 125
Gennargentu
Santa Giusta   Mountains ▲
189   Arbatax ★
Barumini
73   9   81
S 151
47   p.269   Muravera
64   S 125
CAGLIARI

0   50 km

SICILY (1285 km)
Key p. 36

TRAPANI   PALERMO ★★★
Erice ★★   S 113   Cefalù ★   S 113
29   Monreale ★★★   S 113   204   ★★★ TAORMINA
118   73   177   S 120
Segesta ★★★   p.276   ▲ *Etna*   14
50   39
Mazara del Vallo   Aci Trezza ★
Selinus ★★   129   ★ Enna   S 127
★ CATANIA

92   Piazza Armerina
S 115   S 610
89
★★★ AGRIGENTO   S 417   ★★★ SYRACUSE
GELA   160   ★ Noto

M E D I T E R R A N E A N   S E A

38

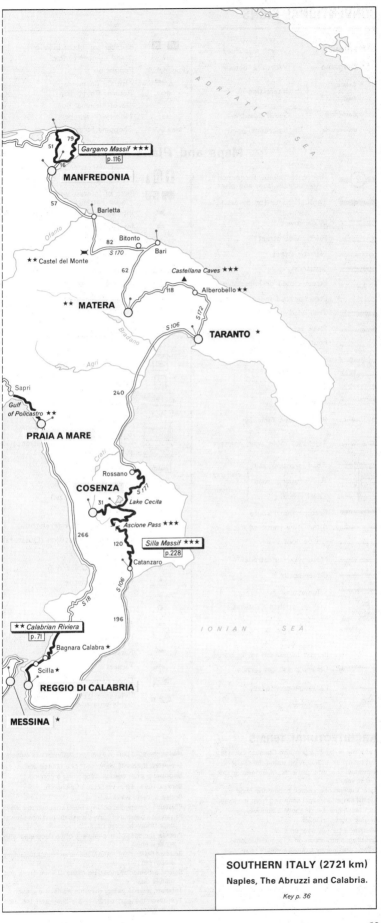

51 79 *Gargano Massif* ★★★
p.116
MANFREDONIA
16

57

Ofanto

Barletta

82 Bitonto
S 170
Bari

★★ Castel del Monte

62

Castellana Caves ★★★

★★ **MATERA**
118 Alberobello ★★

S 106 S 172

S 106 **TARANTO** ★

Bradano

Agri

240

Sapri

*Gulf
of Policastro* ★★

PRAIA A MARE

Crati

Rossano

COSENZA
S 111
31 *Lake Cecita*

Ascione Pass ★★★

266

120 *Silla Massif* ★★★
p.228

Catanzaro

S 106

S 18

196

I O N I A N   S E A

★★ *Calabrian Riviera*
p. 71

Bagnara Calabra ★

Scilla ★

REGGIO DI CALABRIA

MESSINA ★

A D R I A T I C   S E A

SOUTHERN ITALY (2721 km)

Naples, The Abruzzi and Calabria.

Key p. 36

39

CONVENTIONAL SIGNS

*** **FIRENZE**	Worth a journey	988 - 26 / 12	Number of Michelin map and number of fold
** **Bergamo**	Worth a detour	Pop 4,925	Population
★ **Cefalù**		△ 1483	Altitude (in metres)
Bari	Interesting	Rtn	Return; Round trip
Castiglione	See if possible	S7	No of National Road
Domodossola	Reference point	A3	Motorway number
		Roma (Via)	Shopping Street

Maps and Plans

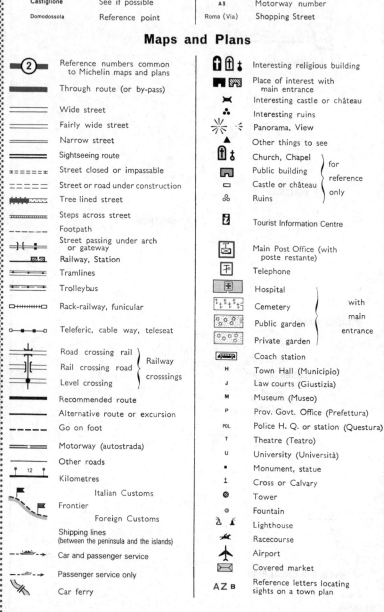

Reference numbers common to Michelin maps and plans	Interesting religious building
Through route (or by-pass)	Place of interest with main entrance
Wide street	Interesting castle or château
Fairly wide street	Interesting ruins
Narrow street	Panorama, View
Sightseeing route	Other things to see
Street closed or impassable	Church, Chapel
Street or road under construction	Public building } for reference only
Tree lined street	Castle or château
Steps across street	Ruins
Footpath	Tourist Information Centre
Street passing under arch or gateway	Main Post Office (with poste restante)
Railway, Station	Telephone
Tramlines	Hospital
Trolleybus	Cemetery } with main entrance
Rack-railway, funicular	Public garden
Teleferic, cable way, teleseat	Private garden
Road crossing rail	Coach station
Rail crossing road } Railway crossings	Town Hall (Municipio)	H
Level crossing	Law courts (Giustizia)	J
Recommended route	Museum (Museo)	M
Alternative route or excursion	Prov. Govt. Office (Prefettura)	P
Go on foot	Police H. Q. or station (Questura)	POL.
Motorway (autostrada)	Theatre (Teatro)	T
Other roads	University (Università)	U
Kilometres	Monument, statue
Italian Customs	Cross or Calvary
Frontier	Tower
Foreign Customs	Fountain
Shipping lines (between the peninsula and the islands)	Lighthouse
Car and passenger service	Racecourse
Passenger service only	Airport
Car ferry	Covered market
	Reference letters locating sights on a town plan	AZ B

ARCHITECTURAL TERMS

Ambo: the pulpit of a primitive Christian basilica.
Ambulatory: an aisle curving round the chancel.
Apparatus: the arrangements of stones or bricks in a structure.
Apse: the end of a church behind the choir.
Apsidal Chapel: a chapel springing from the apse.
Archivolt: highest arch above a doorway.
Bossing: stones in relief.
Ciborium: a canopy over an altar.
Corbelling: a projection on a façade (balcony).
Foliage: ornamental foliated scroll or stem.
Gable: a decorative, acute-angled structure over a window or doorway.
Lintel: the horizontal traverse over an opening.
Machicolations: a corbelled balcony at the top of a wall, supported by consoles or brackets.
Mascaron: carved medallion in form of human mask.

Merlon: the solid part of a parapet between two crenels.
Misericord: the small tilting seat of a church stall.
Modillion: a small console supporting a cornice.
Narthex: the internal vestibule of a church.
Oculus: a round window.
Pilaster: a rectangular column often attached to a wall.
Polyptych: a painted or carved panel divided into several bays (triptych: three bays).
Predella: the base of an altarpiece often decorated with small scenes.
Recessed Orders: concentric receding arches surmounting a doorway.
Stucco: ornamental moulding made of lime, chalk and marble dust.
Triforium: a small gallery over the aisles of a church.
Tympanum: the part between the lintel and the arch of a doorway.

TOWNS, SIGHTS
AND TOURIST REGIONS

ABBIATEGRASSO Lombardy

Michelin map **988** 3 13 — 23 km - 14 miles — southwest of Milan — Pop 27 629

Abbiategrasso is an agricultural market town. It has a church dating from the end of the 14C, with an imposing Renaissance portico attributed to Bramante.

Morimondo Abbey (Abbazia di Morimondo). — *South, 6 km — 3 1/2 miles.* Leave Abbiategrasso by the road to Pavia. The Abbey of Morimondo was founded in the 12C by Cistercians from Morimond in the Haute-Marne Department of France. It is a good example of Romanesque-Gothic architecture. Inside the abbey church, which is beautifully simple, stands a 6C Lombard stoup; the chancel is lined with seventy 16C stalls, carved and inlaid. To the right of the church are the cloisters, into which the chapterhouse opens.

ABETONE★★ Tuscany

Michelin map **988** 14 — 50 km - 31 miles — northwest of Pistoia — Alt 1 388 m - 4 554 ft — Pop 859

Abetone is pleasantly situated near the pass of the same name, from which pretty views may be enjoyed. Two pyramids facing each other, dated 1777, record the opening of the road.

The town is surrounded by 4000 ha - 10 000 acres — of majestic fir forests, known in Italian as *abeti,* of which some of the most gigantic were felled when the road was made.

The ABRUZZI★★★

Michelin map **988** 26 27 — *Local map p 42*

The Abruzzi Massif, the highest of the Apennine range, is a harsh region which remained isolated for a long time and has preserved its beautiful landscapes and noble traditions. There is now a motorway to Rome and winter sports centres are spreading : Gran Sasso, northeast of L'Aquila (Campo Imperatore, Monte Cristo, Prati di Tivo) ; Campo Felice and Monte di Magnola (Ovindoli) to the south ; Campo di Giove and la Maiella to the east of Sulmona ; the Pescocostanzo, Rivisondoli, Roccaraso region ; Colle Rotondo near Scanno and Pescasseroli in the National Park area.

The region of Sulmona, Scanno and the Upper Sangro Valley, in the heart of the Abruzzi Massif, forms a refuge for wild life. Woods of oak and beech at first and then of conifers cover the lower slopes ; above come mountain pastures, swept by strong winds.

(After photo by T.C.I.)

Abruzzi landscape

Green Pastures. — Between Sulmona and Castel di Sangro extend, at an altitude of over 1 000 m - 3 000 ft — the Great Plateaux crossed by the former Roman Consular road. Over these plateaux, which have been described as "long, silent rivers", wander cows guarded by herdsmen skilled in making *latticini* (milk products) and notably *scamorza,* a pressed, egg-shaped white cheese which is sold chiefly at Rivisondoli.

The largest of the five plateaux is the deserted **Piano delle Cinquemiglia,** so-called because it was five Roman miles long (8 km). Coaches used to hurry across it in fear of ambuscades, and travellers were sometimes buried in the snow. In 1529 over 300 German foot-soldiers perished in this way.

★★★TOUR STARTING FROM L'AQUILA
308 km - 191 miles — plus 4 hours sightseeing excluding l'Aquila — allow one day

You can make an interesting tour in the Abruzzi, across the Great Plateaux with their wide horizons, then through the Castel di Sangro Basin and the Upper Sangro Valley. This forms the setting of the National Park, bounded on the west side by the Devil's Pass (Passo del Diavolo).

L'Aquila★. — *Description p 50.* Leave L'Aquila by ②, road S 17.

Popoli. — Popoli is a small trading town on the Pescara River, overlooked by the ruins of a former fortress. Its centre, the Piazza Grande, is adorned with the Church of St. Francis (San Francesco), which has a Gothic façade with a Baroque summit.

The **Ducal Tavern★** (Taverna Ducale), in a narrow street alongside the Piazza Grande, is a graceful and curious little Gothic edifice, formerly used for collecting tithes payable to the prince. Here can be seen the coats of arms of the dynasties that governed the Abruzzi (House of Anjou, Aragon etc) and amusing bas-reliefs of animals, dancers and musicians.

Corfinio. — *7 km - 4 miles from Popoli, take the road to Avezzano on the right.* Away from the town stands the **Basilica di San Pelino o Valvense,** in the Romanesque style, with the adjoining 12C chapel of Sant'Alessandro where Lombard and Byzantine influences are noted. Walk round it to look at the **apse★,** which is remarkably decorated. The church contains a fine pulpit dating from the 12C.

The ABRUZZI★★★

Sulmona★. — *Description p 233.*

Pescocostanzo★. — The peculiar character of this town is due chiefly to its shops and old houses with overhanging roofs, outside staircases and windscreens. Artisanship, particularly wrought iron, copper, gold and silver, wood and lace still flourish.

The **Collegiate Church of St. Mary on the Hill** (Santa Maria del Colle) in the Renaissance style with a few Romanesque survivals, has a Baroque wooden ceiling, and in the north aisle, a remarkable grille, also Baroque.

Roccaraso. — Winter sports centre with immense snowfields.

Castel di Sangro. — The town, which stands at an altitude of 800 m - 2 625 ft — overlooks a basin framed by mountains. A cathedral halfway up the slope, planned in the shape of a Greek cross, is surrounded by Renaissance gateways.

Alfedena★. — Well sited at the mouth of the Upper Sangro Valley, Alfedena gathers its houses round a rock crowned by a ruined castle. Paths lead northwards towards the antique Alfedena, of which only the megalithic walls and a burial ground remain.

Abruzzi National Park★★★ (Parco Nazionale d'Abruzzo). — *Delimited by a dotted line on the plan.* The park, founded privately in 1921 and formally recognised by the state in 1923, was created to protect the fauna, flora and natural beauties of the region. It has an area of approximately 40 000 ha -155 sq miles — mostly forests, with beech and maple dominating. A rare species of birch, dating from the ice age, is to be found near Barrea. The park is delimited to the north by the peak, Montagna Grande, and includes the Upper Valley of the Sangro as far as 'the Barrea Gorges *(gole)* and further to the south the Melfa Valley. Living in peace within the park are the royal eagle, the Apennine wolf, the brown bear, the chamois, the wild cat and more recently the roe deer and red deer. Car worthy roads and well marked rides cut across the park which includes a natural history museum, a zoo and a botanical garden (near Pescasseroli).

Barrea★★. — Built in an unusual setting, it lies within view of a lake of variable level, formed by a dam beyond which deep, narrow gorges can be seen.

Villetta Barrea. — In a curious site at the entrance to a narrow valley, slopes like an amphitheatre down to the Sangro river.

Opi. — Opi crowns a rocky spur barring the valley. Upstream there was once a lake 4 km -2 1/2 miles — long; downstream, the overflowing waters have dug narrow gorges.

Pescasseroli. — The birthplace of the philosopher Benedetto Croce, is the chief centre in the valley, and the park is administered from it. The village lies in a basin with sides covered with beech and fir woods. Wood craft is a popular activity. Beyond Villetta Barrea take road S479 which climbs in hairpin bends through a countryside of pines and mountain pastures to a pass 1 564 m - 5 131 ft — high. It drops steeply after the pass to Scanno.

Scanno★★. — *Description p 224.* After **Lake Scanno★** enter the deep Valley of the Sagittario.

Sagittario Gorges★★. — *Description p 224.*

Anversa degli Abruzzi. — Anversa lies in a pretty setting on a height overlooking the valley.

AEOLIAN Islands See Lipari Islands, p 277.

AGNO, Val d'

Michelin map **988** 4

In this industrialised valley which leads to Recoaro Terme, are to be found at **Trissino** two villas standing side by side in the centre of beautiful terraced gardens.

Valdagno, the wool town, is the domain of the Marzotto textile industry.

Recoaro Terme is a popular spa where disorders of the stomach and liver are treated with the local ferruginous waters which are widely available as a mineral water. It is a ski resort.

ALATRI★ Latium

Michelin map **988** 26 — 11 km - 7 miles — north of Frosinone — Pop 21 855

The **site★** of Alatri is pleasing ; the town stands on a hill overlooking the Frosinone Valley. Its originality is due to its ramps and stairways and alleyways lined with artisans' shops and Gothic houses with pointed arches. Alatri has kept a great part of its Cyclopean walls (4C BC).

Acropolis★. — *1 hour.* The acropolis can be reached by road or, on foot by the stairway at the Porta di Cività, whose architrave is formed of a single block of stone 3 m - 10 ft — long.

The acropolis, which has a trapezoidal plan, is a very fine example of construction on a vast scale. Its summit forms a great esplanade from which superb **views★★** of Alatri and the Frosinone Valley can be enjoyed. The cathedral, the bishop's palace and the presbytery are built on an ancient platform which was once the sacrificial altar.

Church of St. Mary Major★ (Santa Maria Maggiore). — St. Mary's Church stands in a quiet square adorned with a fountain. It is a fine Romanesque-Gothic building with an elegant rose window and a majestic campanile.

ALBA Piedmont

Michelin map **988** 12 — 60 km - 37 miles — southeast of Turin — Pop 31 350

Alba was the ancient Roman city of Alba Pompeia, which gave Rome the Emperor Pertinax (126-193 AD). It is a gourmets' resort made famous by its delicious *tartufi bianchi* (white truffles), which are found by dogs trained at the truffle-hunting dog's school at Roddi, southwest of the town (a truffle fair is held in the autumn at Alba each year). It is also an important grape and wine market (Barolo, Barbaresco) and the headquarters of a school of oenology (the study of wines) in Italy. The town boasts several towers, churches and mediaeval houses. Inside the cathedral will be seen inlaid Renaissance stalls, skilfully carved. South of Alba the **Langhe**, a region of chalk hills covered with clay and planted with vines and oak trees afford wide panoramas. Take the Alba-Ceva road, which frequently follows the crests.

ALBENGA Liguria

Michelin map **988** 12 — 7 km - 4 miles — north of Alassio — *Local map p 199* — Pop 21 491

Albenga lies a little distance from the sea in an alluvial plain with rich market gardens. Tall reddish brick towers give it a distinctive appearance. It was a busy port in the Roman period; amphorae have been recovered from a ship sunk about half a mile from the coast in the 1C BC.

Cathedral Quarter★ (Quartiere della Cattedrale). — The 13C cathedral, with a Baroque doorway, is dominated by a late 14C campanile, pierced with twin windows.

Opposite stands the tower of the Municipio (Town Hall), and at the end of the square, the Peloso-Cepolla Palace contains the Roman naval museum *(open 9 am to noon and 3 to 6 pm; closed Mondays; 500 lire)* : amphorae. Beside the cathedral *(apply to the Municipal Museum)* the tower of the former communal palace (60 m - 197 ft — high : panorama), built in the year 1300, marks the transition from Romanesque to Gothic architecture. At its foot the 14C palace itself, crowned with merlons and containing a fine Gothic communal loggia, houses the Municipal Museum *(open 9 am to noon and 3 to 6 pm; closed Mondays; 500 lire)* : archaeology. The **baptistry** *(tickets at the museum)* is built on an octagonal plan and dates from the 5C. In the centre is a baptismal font. An early Christian mosaic in a niche is adorned with symbolic Christian emblems.

The lover of architecture and carved or painted decoration will linger near the cathedral and baptistry and in the Via Bernardo Ricci and Via Medaglie d'Oro. Here towers, old houses and palaces have been restored during the last few years.

EXCURSION

Neva Valley (Val Neva). — *17 km - 11 miles.* Cross the plain where the Arroscia torrent and the Neva meet to form the Centa. After Leca you enter the Val Neva, enclosed between rocky slopes to which the old village of Zuccarello clings. Farther on, at Erli, a by-road to the right climbs to the mediaeval village of **Castelvecchio** *(restoration work in progress),* whose old stone houses (13-16C) with terraced roofs combine with the castle (11-12C) to make up a curious scene.

ALBEROBELLO ★★ Apulia

Michelin map **988** 29 — 45 km - 28 miles — north of Taranto — Pop 9 966

Alberobello, whose charm is so strange that one feels one has been transported to another planet, is almost entirely composed of *trulli (p 243).* There are nearly 1 000 of these.

"Zona monumentale"★★★. — The monumental zone is the most characteristic part of Alberobello and that in which there are most *trulli.* It lies to the south of the town on the slopes of a dell, beyond a mall. The quarter is all white and seems to have been built for Snow White and the Seven Dwarfs by oriental magicians. In the upper part of the quarter stands the Church of St. Antony (Sant'Antonio), which is in the form of a *trullo.*

Trullo Sovrano★. — This is the largest and most elaborate of the *trulli.* It has two storeys and stands behind the principal church in Alberobello.

AMALFI ★★ Campania

Michelin map **988** 27 — *Local map p 44* — Pop 6 419

Amalfi, which has given its name to the beautiful Amalfi Coast *(description p 44),* is a rather Spanish-looking little town of tall white houses built on rocks facing a blue bay, which makes a wonderful **site★★★**. It is flanked by an old Saracen tower and a Capuchin monastery (12 to 16C — fine cloisters), now converted into an hotel.

Amalfi enjoys a very mild climate and the **Corso Flavio Gioia**, a promenade planted with pine trees is crowded at all seasons. Steamers from Naples, Capri and Salerno call at the port.

The Maritime Republic of Amalfi. — Amalfi is mentioned in the 6C and traded with Constantinople and the Levant in the 9C while taking part in the struggle against the Saracens. The town enjoyed its greatest prosperity in the 11C, at the time when shipping in the Mediterranean was regulated by the *Tavole Amalfitane* (Amalfi Navigation Tables), the oldest maritime code in the world, now preserved in the town hall. It was also in the 11C that Flavio Gioia, presumed to be a citizen of Amalfi, was said to have invented the mariner's compass. The Republic had an arsenal where galleys with as many as 120 oars, the largest of that period, were built. The Amalfi fleet played an important part in carrying Crusaders to the Levant.

■ SIGHTS *time : 2 hours*

St. Andrew's Cathedral★ (Sant'Andrea). — The building dates from the 11C, but many changes have been made. It shows the liking of maritime cities for oriental splendour.

The façade, rebuilt in the 19C on the original model, stands at the top of a stairway and attracts attention by its varied geometrical designs in stone. The Romanesque bell-tower is in the Sicilian-Arab style with a curious summit roofed with green and yellow glazed tiles.

The stairway ends in a spacious atrium whose sharply pointed arches are built in alternate layers of black and white stone. The curious bronze door at the far end bears an inscription stating that it was cast in Constantinople in 1066 by Simeone di Siria and sent to Amalfi by Pantaleone di Mauro Comite, the head of the Amalfi colony in Constantinople.

AMALFI★★

The interior of the cathedral is Baroque. At the entrance to the chancel, however, stand two Antique columns and two candelabra decorated with mosaics; two 12-13C pulpits stand on either side of the high altar. The relics of St. Andrew are kept in the crypt. They are said to exude a miraculous oil locally called "the manna of St. Andrew".

Cloisters of Paradise★★ (Chiostro del Paradiso). — *Open 9.30 am to 1 pm and 2.30 to 7 pm (10 pm 10 October to 31 May); 100 lire.* Built in 1103 by Master Giulio di Stefano and arranged as a churchyard about 1266. The Romanesque austerity of the architecture mingles with the Arabian fantasy of the decoration producing an outstanding effect. Fine sarcophagi are to be seen in the galleries.

"Valle dei Mulini"★★. — An hour's walk will reveal picturesque scenes. Starting from the pretty Piazza del Duomo, adorned with a fountain of St. Andrew (1760), follow the Via Genova, from which many alleys, stairways and roofed passages open into little squares with fountains. Note the variety of façades with re-entrant angles, supporting arches and corbels; also the balconies, niches and terraces brightened by flowers. Finally, pause in front of the Renaissance doorways with vault-bosses or the Baroque doorways decorated with scrolls, consoles and shells. Following the course of the torrent, confined between its rocky shores, you pass mills, cascades and suspended foot-bridges.

Arsenal. — The original 12C ribbed vaulting over the workshops can still be seen near the Piazza Flavio Gioia.

Cape Atrani. — At the eastward exit from Amalfi this rocky promontory, partly occupied by a tower and a Minor Brothers' monastery converted into a hotel, affords a pretty view★ of the Bay of Amalfi.

AMALFI Coast ★★★ (COSTA AMALFITANA)
Michelin map 988 27 28

The *corniche* road which follows the rocky coast between Sorrento and Salerno is the finest in Italy. Its innumerable bends, following the coastline, afford constantly changing views of enchanting landscape, wild, fantastically shaped rocks plunging vertically into an empty, crystal-clear sea, deep gorges spanned by dizzy bridges, and Saracen towers, once the haunts of pirates, perched on peaks or reefs.

The charm and softness of certain scenes contrast with the sublime awe, as it has been described, of the picture as a whole. Orange trees, citron trees, olives, almonds, vines, camellias and oleanders relieve the bareness of naked stone. Fishermen's villages and little towns of white houses nestling in the bays, preserve the charm of a past age.

GEOGRAPHICAL NOTES

The Amalfi Coast forms the fringe of the Lattari Mountains, a limestone range broken and worn by running water which has formed deep gorges, and jumbled masses of rocks fantastically poised. This constant erosion has sometimes caused landslides : one, in 1954, claimed several victims.

Diet here consists chiefly of sea-food : crustaceans, fish (tunny, red mullet, sole, dorado, etc.), cuttle-fish, squid and shell-fish. The local cheese is *mozzarella,* a fresh, white pressed variety. The best wines are red Gragnano and white or rosé Ravello or Positano.

★★★ROAD FROM SORRENTO TO SALERNO
69 km - 43 miles - about 1 day.

Leave Sorrento *(p 229)* by ①.

Peninsula of Sorrento★★★. — The coast road, hewn in the rock, is winding and boldly sited and runs between gardens planted with orange and lemon trees : then, after crossroads where you turn to the right, it begins to climb towards the **Colli di San Pietro** (Hills of St. Peter), revealing extensive views of Sorrento and its Gulf.

You can also reach the Colli di San Pietro by passing through Sant'Agata sui Due Golfi *(p 230).* On the other slope the steep descent is even more spectacular. Far below, you can see the sea, dotted with rocky islands, through a curtain of pines or occasional almond trees.

The balcony road then crosses the **Ponte dei Libri,** spanning a deep cleft in the rock, before reaching the Positano Belvedere.

Positano Belvedere★★★. — Provides a remarkable bird's-eye view of Positano.

Positano★★. — This fishermen's village lies in a delightful **setting★★.** Positano is much frequented by foreigners, both in winter and in summer, and artists find an infinity of subjects there. The houses, white cubes scattered on the slopes among terraced gardens facing the sea, are of the Moorish type with flat roofs and balconies beneath arcades.

Vettica Maggiore. — Its houses, in a pretty setting, are scattered over slopes. From the church esplanade there is a fine view of the coast and the sea.

The road passes through the little resort of **Praiano** sheltered by Cape Sottile, before reaching the Furore Valley.

Furore Valley★★ (Vallone di Furore). — The Furore Valley, between two tunnels, is the most impressive section of the coast owing to the dark depths of its steep, rocky walls and in stormy weather the thunder of wild, rough seas. A fisher-

(After photo by Arthaud)

Positano

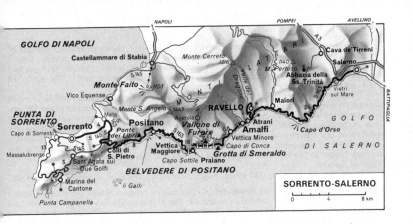

men's village has, nevertheless, been built where a small torrent gushes into the sea. The houses clinging to the slopes and vividly coloured boats drawn up on the shore make a somewhat surprising picture. To discover the full variety of the spot, take the path that goes along one of the side walls of the gorge.

Emerald Grotto★★ (Grotta di Smeraldo). — *Guided tours 1 March to 31 May, 9 am to 5 pm; 1 June to 30 September, 8.30 am to 6.30 pm; 1 October to 28 February, 10 am to 4 pm; 1000 lire (reached from the road by lift); 1000 lire (access by boat) visited only when the sea is calm.* This marine cave at the end of a rocky creek washed by the sea is visited by boat. The exceptionally clear water is illuminated indirectly by rays of light which give it a beautiful emerald colour. The bottom looks quite near, though the water is 10 m - 30 ft — deep. Fine stalactites add to the interest of the trip. The cave became submerged as a result of variations in ground level under the influence of volcanoes, which affect the whole region.
You next pass through Vettica Minore, surrounded by vegetables and olive trees, and suddenly emerge into a marvellous landscape.

Amalfi★★. — *Description p 43.*

Atrani★. — This pleasant fishermen's village at the mouth of the Valle del Dragone has two old churches. The chief one, St. Saviour's (San Salvatore), near the viaduct, was founded in the 10C. It has a fine bronze door cast in Constantinople in the 11C.
An excellent winding road through the vineyards of the Dragon Valley (Valle del Dragone) rejoins Ravello.

Ravello★★★. — *Description p 94.*
Continue down to Minori on the shores of a cove with the road following every curve.

Maiori. — A pretty little village with a beach in the centre of a wide bay. It is surrounded by orange and lemon plantations.
Climb by another spectacular *corniche* to Cape Orso.

Cape Orso★. — The cape, consisting of oddly formed rocks, affords an interesting view of Maiori Bay.
Finally, Salerno *(description p 218)* and its Gulf come into view.

AMATRICE Latium
Michelin map **988** 26 — 65 km - 40 miles — northeast of Rieti — Pop 3376

Amatrice occupies a pleasant site on the slopes of the green Valley of the Tronto. The village is the birthplace of the early 16C painter-architect Cola dell'Amatrice. The town has an elegant Gothic church of yellowish sandstone, with a plain but graceful façade.

Lake Scandarella★. — Pretty views of this small artificial lake at the exit from Amatrice may be had from the road to L'Aquila or the road to Rieti.

ANAGNI★ Latium
Michelin map **988** 26 — 65 km - 40 miles — southeast of Rome — Pop 17 464

Anagni is a picturesque little mediaeval town, built on a rocky spur, where time seems to have stood still. It was the birthplace of four popes, including Boniface VIII. The Via Vittorio Emanuele runs right through the town.

A Slap. — Philip the Fair, King of France, who tried to obtain funds from the clergy, was excommunicated by Pope Boniface VIII. Philip then sent to Anagni, where the pope had his summer residence, men-at-arms led by his Chancellor, Guillaume de Nogaret, and the Roman, Sciarra Colonna, who had been sent to the galleys by Boniface, an enemy of the Colonna family. On 7 September 1303, at dawn, Nogaret and Colonna got into Anagni (where the gates had been opened by the governor) and reached the Papal Palace where the pope was waiting, crowned with his tiara and holding in his hand the keys of St. Peter and a crosier. Colonna so far forgot himself as to strike the old man in the face with his iron gauntlet, at which the pope said : "Here is my head. Here is my neck." The next day the inhabitants of Anagni took up arms and set Boniface free. He died in Rome a month later.

■ **SIGHTS** *time : 1 hour*

Cathedral★★ (Duomo). — The cathedral, in the upper part of the town on the site of a former acropolis, is a Romanesque building erected between 1072 and 1104 and remodelled in the Gothic style in the 13C. The excommunication of Frederick Barbarossa was pronounced here in 1160.
Before entering you should glance at the three Romanesque apses, with Lombard mouldings and arcades, and at the 14C statue of Boniface VIII over the left loggia. A massive Romanesque campanile, from a point near which there is a view of the neighbouring hills, stands away from the façade.

45

The interior contains three aisles of which the 13C **paving★** shows geometrical designs of remarkable variety. The high altar is surmounted by a Romanesque ciborium or canopy; behind it and to the right a twisted paschal candelabrum, adorned with encrustations, rests on two sphinxes and ends in a little statue supporting a socket for the paschal candle. The work, like the nearby episcopal throne is signed Vassaletus (13C).

The **crypt★★★** *(apply to the sacristan)* was consecrated in 1255. The visitor will find himself walking on a beautiful patterned pavement *(p 201)* of the same period. Frescoes of the 13C entirely cover the walls and vaulting. They depict the story of the Old Testament, scenes from the lives of the saints and the scientific doctrines and are curious in the care for detail and the persistence of Greco-Byzantine influence that can be discerned. The most interesting, in a lunette on the right as you come in, is of Galen and Hippocrates facing one another, recalling the famous School of Medecine of Salerno and the fact that this church was founded by Bishop Peter of Salerno.

In the **treasury** are many 13C robes, notably Boniface VIII's cope of embroidered red silk.

Mediaeval Quarter★ (Quartiere Medioevale). — This quarter consists almost entirely of buildings dating from the 13C and is particularly evocative. The Piazza Bonifacio VIII, the Via Tufoli, the Piazza delle Carceri (of the Prisons) are its most characteristic spots. In the Vicolo San Michele (Alley of St. Michael) imposing arches are all that remain of the palace in which Boniface VIII was slapped.

Piazza Cavour. — Here you can enjoy a pretty **view★** of surrounding hills and country : the Sacco Valley and the Lepini Mountains.

Town Hall (Palazzo Comunale). — 12-13C. The palace stands on a huge **arch★** through which you must pass to look at the rear façade, which overlooks the Piazza delle Carceri. Note the Gothic bays in the Cistercian style and the small loggia added in 1404.

ANCONA ★ Marches

Michelin map **988** 16 - Pop 108 466

Town plan in Michelin Red Guide Italia (hotels and restaurants).

Ancona, the chief town, in the Marches, an Adriatic province of Italy, is built in the form of an amphitheatre on the slopes of a rocky promontory forming an acute angle from which the name of the town is derived (Greek *ankon* — elbow). This is the only town in Italy where the sun both rises from and sets in the sea.

Ancona was founded in the 4C BC by the Syracusans under the protection of the Emperor Trajan, and was an independent maritime republic in the Middle Ages and at the Renaissance. It was included in the Church States only in 1532.

Garibaldi (Corso)	ABZ
Stamira (Corso)	ABZ

Giovanni XXIII (Via)	AY 6
Leopardi (Via)	AZ 8
Pizzecolli-Ciriaco (Via)	AYZ 13
Plebiscito (Piazza)	AZ 14
Repubblica (Piazza)	AZ 17
Thaon de Revel (Via)	CZ 21
24 Maggio (Piazzale)	BZ 23

Ancona, the port of embarkation for Yugoslavia and Greece and a busy commercial centre, is among the major ports of the Adriatic. The large Fish Fair, which takes place each year from 11 to 16 May, provides a display of one of the town's basic industries. The most typical, at least gastronomically, among the local sea-foods are the *crocette,* a delicious type of shell-fish served with a piquant sauce including herbs.

The rough, austere seamen's quarter near the port is very picturesque; the horseman who appears in the coat of arms of the town is reproduced in bas-relief on several façades.

The busy Corso Garibaldi joins the old town with the new. The latter extends eastwards in the direction of a rocky coast, pleasantly furnished with gardens.

The accordion, electronic organ and guitar making industries flourish in Ancona; some 150 000 instruments are produced annually.

■ **MAIN SIGHTS** *time 1/2 hour*

Cathedral★ (Duomo San Ciriaco). — The cathedral building stands on Mount Guasco (Colle Guasco) where it occupies the site of a former temple of Venus. It was placed under the invocation of St. Lawrence and then St. Cyriac, 4C martyr and patron of Ancona. From it there is a **view★** of Ancona, its port, its shipyards, the coast and the sea.

The Romanesque building has mingled Byzantine and Lombard architectural features : the Greek cross plan and the dome, and the mouldings and arcades on the outside walls. The façade is preceded by a majestic Gothic porch in pink stone, supported by two lions. The symbols of the Evangelists are carved above the capitals.

The interior, noble and simple, has a nave and two aisles supported by monolithic marble columns topped by Romanesque-Byzantine capitals. Under the dome, note the clever transition from the square base of the transept to the 12-sided drum supporting the cupola. The tomb of Cardinal Giannelli (1509) in the north wall of the chancel is the work of a Dalmatian sculptor, Giovanni da Traù.

Merchants' Loggia★ (Loggia dei Mercanti). — This hall, built in the 15C, was intended for merchants' meetings. The Venetian Gothic façade bearing the heraldic horseman of Ancona and statues of the Virtues (Hope, Strength, Justice and Charity) is the work of a Dalmatian, Giorgio Orsini.

■ **ADDITIONAL SIGHTS**

Church of Santa Maria della Piazza★ (AZ B). — *Restoration work in progress.* This little 10C Romanesque church has a charming façade (1210) attributed to a Lombard master. It is faced with marble and adorned with amusing popular figures, especially on the mouldings round the doorway : fantastic animals, horsemen, men-at-arms, artisans, musicians, etc. In the course of restoration work, traces of two earlier churches dating from the 5 and 6C, together with fragments of mosaic pavements, were discovered beneath the present building.

National Museum of the Marches (Museo Nazionale delle Marche) (AY M1). — *Closed for restoration.* The museum is in the Palazzo Ferretti, built by Tibaldi in the 16C and altered later by Vanvitelli. Among the interesting prehistoric and archaeological collections on view, are Attic urns from the cemetery of Numana, *oreficerie* from the Gallic cemeteries with golden crowns from Montefortino, and an exceptional series of 1C Roman gilt bronzes.

Podesti Public Gallery (Pinacoteca Comunale Francesco Podesti) (AYZ M2). — *Open 10 am to 7 pm weekdays; 10 am to 1 pm Sundays and holidays. Closed Mondays, Sunday afternoons, 1 January, Easter, 15 August, 1 November, 25 and 26 December.* Arranged in the Palazzo Bosdari, you will see a delicate Madonna by the Venetian, Crivelli, a Madonna and two saints by Titian on a fine background of lagoon landscape, and works by Lotto, Andrea del Sarto, Maratti, etc.

The **Gallery of Modern Art** has works by Luigi Bartolini, Massimo Campigli who combines poetic inspiration and figurative style, Bruno Cassinari who was influenced by Cubism but belongs to the Fauvist school through his exuberant use of colour, and Orfeo Tamburini.

Trajan's Arch (Arco di Traiano) (AY C). — The arch was erected in AD 115 in honour of the Emperor Trajan, who built the port.

Piazza Plebiscito (AZ 14). — In this elongated square stands the **Government Palace** (AZ P) finished in the 15C by Francesco di Giorgio, a pupil of Laurana. You enter the courtyard, with its ogive gateway and fine windows, through a handsome Renaissance arcade. At the end of the square is the 18C Church of St. Dominic (San Domenico).

Church of St. Francis on the Steps (San Francesco delle Scale) (AY D). — St Francis on the Steps has a superb Venetian Gothic doorway by Giorgio Orsini. On the tympanum St. Francis is depicted receiving the stigmata.

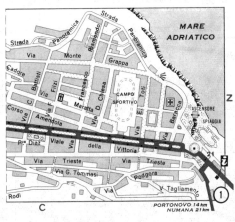

MARE ADRIATICO

EXCURSION

Portonovo★. — *14 km - 9 miles.* Leave Ancona by ①. After about 10 km - 6 miles — bear left into a small road which drops rapidly down to the sea: a track on the right leads through the woods to St. Mary's Church. In the picturesque **setting★** formed by the rocky coastline of the **Conero Massif** lies Portonovo, in a pretty cove. The charming 11C **Church of St. Mary★**, is built on an almost square plan inspired by Norman churches. It once sheltered a Camaldulian monastery. *Ask for the key at the house on the right, at the end of the short alley that leads to the church.*

ANSEDONIA Tuscany _____

Michelin map **988** 25

The ruins of the **ancient city★** of Ansedonia crown a height at the neck of the **Orbetello** Peninsula, linked with the coast by lagoons in which eels are found. *(From the Via Aurelia, 2 km - 1 1/4 miles — plus 1/2 hour on foot Rtn.)*

This former Roman town, originally called Cosa, is girt with walls built of enormous blocks and occupies a beautiful site within view of the lagoon, the old island of Orbetello and Mount Argentario. Crickets chirp among aromatic plants and olive trees.

A tower where Puccini is said to have composed part of *Tosca*, stands by the sea.

ANZIO ★ Latium

Michelin map **988** 26 — Pop 26 806

Anzio stands under a promontory along a beautiful and spacious bay forming, with **Nettuno**, a pleasant modern seaside resort. It has a popular yachting harbour.

Anzio is the Antium of Antiquity, a Volscian city where Coriolanus took refuge in 490 BC after his mother had begged him not to engage in a fratricidal struggle with Rome. Antium was also the birthplace of Nero, in whose villa were found the statues of the Apollo Belvedere, the Fanciulla (young girl) of Anzio and the Borghese Gladiator, now respectively in the Vatican, the National Roman Museum in Rome, and the Louvre in Paris.

The name of Anzio is remembered also for the Anglo-American landing of 22 January 1944. The Germans were at first taken by surprise, but they counter-attacked and the Allied troops were never able to penetrate inland. Under the guns of their fleet, however, they held a bridgehead which threatened the German flank until the general Anglo-Franco-American offensive ended in the taking of Rome on 4 June 1944.

Over 8 000 soldiers are buried in the American cemetery at Nettuno which is dominated by a memorial consisting of a chapel with walls faced with Carrara marble, and a museum which retraces the operations carried out in Sicily and on the mainland between 1943 and 1945. A thousand British soldiers are buried in the cemetery which is situated near Anzio, on the road to Albano.

From Anzio one can reach the volcanic and wild looking **Island of Ponza★**, where small beaches nestle along a rugged coast. At the southeast end of the island, the village of Ponza raises its serried houses in a semicircle round a small harbour favoured by underwater fishermen. *In summer there is a car ferry service (3 days a week in June and September, daily in July and August; time — 3 hours; apply to the CAREMAR Co., Porto Innocenziano, Anzio, ☎ 984 60 73) and a hydrofoil (aliscafi) service (daily from May to October; time — 1 1/4 hours; apply to Helios, 18 Porto Innocenziano, ☎ 984 50 85).*

AOSTA ★ Valle d'Aosta

Michelin maps **988** 2 and **26** 26 — *Local map p 50* — Pop 39 131

The capital of the Valle d'Aosta, overlooked from the south by Monte Emilius, was originally named Augusta Pretoria in honour of the Emperor Augustus. The geometrical plan, like that of a military camp, and some interesting buildings denote its Roman origin. The walls, which are also Roman, have been remodelled several times. Aosta, an active religious centre in the Middle Ages, was the birthplace of the theologian St. Anselm, who became Archbishop of Canterbury where he died in 1109. Today it has steelworks, which are supplied with iron ore from Cogne, in northwest Italy.

A good general **view** of Aosta can be had from a point about 2 km - 1 mile away on the road to the Great St. Bernard.

The St. Orso fair is held on 1 February, the Saint's feast day, and there is a sale of products from local crafts — woodwork, wrought iron and lace.

At the beginning of the 19C, in his novel, *The Leper of Aosta,* a masterpiece of sentimental literature, the Savoyard writer Xavier de Maistre describes the wretched state of a leper shut up for thirty years, from 1773 to 1803, in a tower (Torre del Lebbroso) which is still pointed out in the western section of the ramparts.

Roman buildings★. — The most important buildings, going from west to east, are the Pretoria Gateway (Porta Pretoria) **(A)**, a structure of the 1C BC built of huge blocks of stone, the majestic Arch of Augustus (Arco di Augusto) **(B)** of the same period and the Roman bridge **(G)**. From the Pretoria Gateway you may also reach the remains of the theatre **(D)** beside which a Roman road has recently been discovered. A few arcades of the amphitheatre (anfiteatro) **(E)** remain in the garden of a convent nearby.

Collegiate Church of St. Orso (Collegiata di Sant'Orso). — Placed under the invocation of an archdeacon (5-8C), this church has an 11C crypt and a 12C Roman campanile. The nave is Gothic, as is the chancel beyond the Baroque rood-screen. The chancel has historiated stalls; that of the prior is surmounted by a canopy. A rich treasure is kept in the sacristy *(a canon accompanies visitors).*

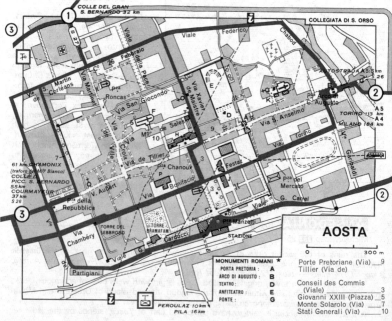

MONUMENTI ROMANI ★	
PORTA PRETORIA :	**A**
ARCO DI AUGUSTO :	**B**
TEATRO :	**D**
ANFITEATRO :	**E**
PONTE :	**G**

Porte Pretoriane (Via) __9
Tillier (Via de)

Conseil des Commis
(Viale) _____3
Giovanni XXIII (Piazza) _5
Monte Solarolo (Via) ___7
Stati Generali (Via) _____10

AOSTA

A stairway, built to the left of the chancel, leads up to the roof, where frescoes dating from the 11C which represent scenes from the life of Jesus and his Apostles, have been restored. Only the upper parts of the original frescoes remain.

A door, opening off the south aisle near the stairway down to the crypt, leads to a delightful, small Romanesque **cloister★** dating from the 12C, shaded and with twin columns running the full length of one side. Splendid historiated **capitals★★** depict the Old and New Testaments, the Prophets, and the life of St. Orso; note also the fable of the fox and the stork.

A lime tree 400 years old grows opposite the church.

Priory of St. Orso (Priorato di Sant'Orso) (K). — This Renaissance style building was erected between 1494 and 1506. The windows are framed in delicate terracotta mouldings.

Cathedral (F). — This has a façade dating from 1848 ornamented with 16C sculptures. The rest of the church dates from various periods from the 12C and 13C to the 15C. The campanile is 12-13C. In the chancel *(apply to the sacristan)* are a 12C mosaic pavement, 15C Gothic choirstalls and the 14C tomb of Thomas II of Savoy. The sacristy contains the rich treasure, an ivory diptych of AD 406 and the 15C reliquary of St. Grato.

Cloisters built in the 15C stand on the north side of the cathedral *(to visit the treasure and the cloisters apply to Canon Edoardo Brunod, 2 Piazza Giovanni XXIII)*. Opposite stand the ruins of the Roman forum.

EXCURSION

Pila (alt 1790 m - 5873 ft). — *South of the plan: 16 km - 10 miles — Bus service available.* From Pila, a winter sports centre, the **view★** includes to the east, the Matterhorn (Cervin) and Monte Rosa, north, the Grand Combin, and, west, Mont Blanc.

AOSTA, Valle d' ★★

Michelin maps **988** 12 and **26** 1 to 4, 12 to 14

A characteristic region formed by the Valley of the Dora Baltea and adjacent valleys, the Valle d'Aosta is surrounded by high mountains: Mont Blanc, the Matterhorn (Cervin) and Monte Rosa to the north and the Gran Paradiso to the south. Marvellous views, secluded valleys, forests of pine, beech and larch, and several castles make it attractive. The Valle d'Aosta communicates with Switzerland by the Great St. Bernard Pass and Tunnel and with France by the Mont Blanc Road Tunnel *(see p 89)* and the Little St. Bernard Pass. Since 1947 it has been, for purposes of administration, an autonomous district governed by a Council.

Life in the Valle d'Aosta. — The mountain peasant remains, especially in the high valleys, attached to the French language and customs.

Living in houses roofed with flat stone slabs called *lauzes,* storing their hay in open-sided barns called *raccards* built of larch logs and standing on piles, the people of the valley raise cattle, prepare a cheese called *fontina* in *tsaudières* or cauldrons with which they make a dish of hot melted cheese in an earthenware pot, and carve wood during the winter evenings.

The Church is still powerful: in the mountains and remote valleys the parish priest enjoys a patriarchal authority in places where ancient rites and religious processions across the pastures are popular. Pretty costumes are worn on feast days. In summer the mountain people play a curious ball game called *tsan.*

(After photo by Arthaud)

Valle d'Aosta — A hamlet in the mountains

FROM COURMAYEUR TO PONT-ST-MARTIN
145 km - 90 miles — Local map p 50

Courmayeur★★. — *Description p 89.*

Gran Paradiso National Park★★ (Parco Nazionale del Gran Paradiso). — The park created in 1922 covering an area previously preserved as a royal hunting ground, extends over 60 000 ha - 1390 sq. miles. It can be reached by the Rhêmes, Savarenche, Cogne or Locana Valleys *(see p 125).* The park is rich in wildlife: chamois, marmots, martens, polecats, royal eagles... Ibex, a threatened species in Europe, and some of the rarest specimens of Alpine flora can be seen in the park and the Paradisia gardens at **Valnontey** respectively. Gran Paradiso extends westwards into France to become the Parc National de la Vanoise.

Rhêmes Valley★★ (Val di Rhêmes). — *From Villeneuve, 20 km - 12 miles.* The countryside, which is still little frequented, green, and sometimes austere, is among the finest in the region. The road ends at Rhêmes-Notre-Dame, at the foot of the Grande Sassière glaciers.

Savarenche Valley★ (Val Savarenche). — *From Villeneuve, 27 km - 17 miles.* Torrents, meadows, escarpments and stone roofed houses make this valley attractive. Pont is the starting-point of many excursions into the mountains, in particular by the Victor Emmanuel II refuge (2732 m -8964 ft). Beyond Pont, the road *(cars are banned)* leads to the **Nivolet Pass** which can also be reached from the south, from Ivrea *(see p 125).*

Cogne Valley★ (Val di Cogne). — *21 km - 13 miles.* The characteristics of this valley, which leads to **Cogne,** itself a resort and winter sports centre, are its wild nature and the many opportunities it affords for excursions into the mountain range of the Gran Paradiso.
Cogne is also famous for its iron mines.

Aosta★. — *Description p 48.*

Fénis. — An imposing 14C **fortress★** with a graceful galleried courtyard adorned with frescoes. The rooms contain fine carved furniture in the style of the Valle d'Aosta. *Open 9.30 to 11.30 am and 2 to 4.30 pm (4 pm 1 December to 28 February); closed Tuesdays; 500 lire.* From Châtillon one can go up the **Valtournenche** as far as Breuil to view the Matterhorn.

AOSTA, Valle d'★★

Breuil-Cervinia★★. — *Description p 70.*

St-Vincent★. — St-Vincent enjoys a mild climate and has become fashionable; its Casino of the Valley, standing in a beautiful garden, is much frequented. There are fine views from the terrace of Ussel Castle.

Montjovet. — The ruins of this castle and the fortress of Bard *(see below)* command the Upper Dora Baltea Valley.

Verrès. — The 14C fortress is built on a square plan. *Open 9.30 to 11.30 am; 2 to 4.30 pm (4 pm 1 December to 28 February); closed Wednesdays; 500 lire.*

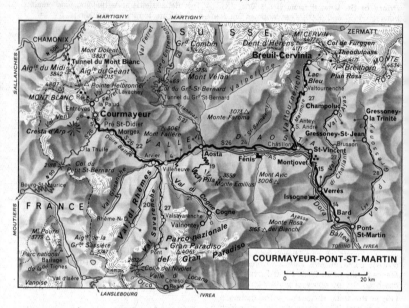

COURMAYEUR-PONT-ST-MARTIN

Champoluc. — *From Verrès, 27 km - 17 miles.* The Val d'Ayas, planted with orchards and chestnut groves, leads to this resort, lying in a beautiful combe. It is an excursion centre for the Breithorn.

Issogne. — The castle was built at the end of the 15C by the Challant family. The courtyard, with its fountains surmounted by a wrought iron grenadier, is remarkable. *Open 9.30 to 11.30 am and 2 to 4.30 pm; 4 pm 1 December to 28 February; closed Mondays; 500 lire.*

Bard. — The colossal fortress, dismantled on the orders of Napoleon in 1800, rebuilt during the 19C, commands along with the remains of Montjovet, the Upper Dora Baltea Valley.

Pont-St-Martin. — Roman bridge guarded by a chapel dedicated to St. John Nepomucene.

Gressoney-St-Jean. — *From Pont-St-Martin, 28 km - 17 miles.* A resort in the Lys Valley. About 6 km - 4 miles — beyond it is **Gressoney-la-Trinité**, the starting point of many mountain climbs.

L'AQUILA ★ Abruzzi

Michelin map **988** 26 — Alt 721 m - 2365 ft — Pop 66215

L'Aquila is a severe looking town, but it matches the majestic circle of mountains that surrounds it and enjoys a cool climate, pleasant in summer.

Legend relates that the town sprang up by a miracle, with 99 *rioni* (quarters) surrounding 99 castles, 99 squares, 99 fountains and 99 churches. The Fontana della 99 Canelle (Fountain of the 99 Conduits) still exists, and in the evening a bell in the old tower in the Law Courts tolls 99 times.

L'Aquila was founded in the 13C on the initiative of the Emperor Frederick II of Hohenstaufen, who gave it an imperial eagle for its emblem and attached it to the Kingdom of Naples. Parts of the ramparts, built by Charles I of Anjou round the town, can still be seen.

The town, built in fine golden tinted stone, has many ancient houses, often marked with coats of arms or with the initials IHS *(Iesus Hominum Salvator* — Jesus Saviour of Mankind), affixed after the preaching of St. Bernardino, whose motto it was.

Traditional crafts in L'Aquila include wrought iron, copper, embroidery and pottery.

St. Bernardino's Basilica★★ (Basilica di San Bernardino). — *1/2 hour.* This superb building was erected between 1454 and 1472. In 1527 Cola dell'Amatrice added a remarkable façade. The arrangement of the three orders of superimposed columns separated by cornices of diminishing size, the placing of the niches between the columns, the oculi and, on the top storey, the emblems of St. Bernardino, all of which are symmetrical, create a fine architectural rhythm.

The interior is spacious and well lit with aisles on either side of a nave which is roofed by a rich wooden ceiling in the Baroque style with the emblem of St. Bernardino at the centre. In the fifth chapel on the right the imposing **mausoleum★** of St. Bernardino of Siena (who died at L'Aquila in 1440) is adorned with figures and bas-reliefs by Silvestro dell'Aquila and his school (1505).

On the south wall of the chancel is a Crucifixion painted by Fiammingo; on the north side is the **sepulchre★** of Maria Pereira (d. 1496), in which Silvestro dell'Aquila has combined Tuscan grace with Roman grandeur. The recumbent figure of Maria's baby daughter, who died at the age of fifteen months, lies beneath the sarcophagus.

Castle★ — *Open 9 am to 2 pm weekdays; 9 am to 1 pm Sundays and holidays. Closed Mondays, 1 January, 25 April, 1 May, 15 August, Easter and Christmas; 500 lire.* On the highest point in the town stands a castle with an elegant gateway, built in 1530 by Luigi Pirro Scrivà. It is a good example of military architecture.

CASTELLO ★
SAN BERNARDINO ★★
Sta M^a DI COLLEMAGGIO ★

L'AQUILA

0 _____ 400 m

Federico II (Corso) _____ Z
Vitt. Emanuele (Corso) ____ YZ

Arco Pizzoli (Via) _____ Y 2
Bafile (Via A.) _____ Y 3
Fonte Secco (Via) _____ Y 4
Guasto (Via del) _____ Y 5
Indipendenza (Via) _____ Z 6
Palazzo (Piazza del) _____ Y 8
Principe Umberto (Corso) Y 9
S. Agostino (Via) _____ Z 10
Tre Marie (Via) _____ Z 12

The **National Museum of the Abruzzi**★★ is remarkably arranged in the great rooms. The ground floor is devoted to Roman archaeology, with an outstanding collection of mediaeval art and modern art on the upper floors. You will notice curious 12C carved wooden door panels (in the Abruzzian style) and a superb coloured wooden statue of St. Sebastian by Silvestro dell'Aquila (1478). The local goldsmiths' art is represented by a rich processional cross by Nicola da Guardiagrele (15C). There is also a collection of Abruzzian pottery and lace.

Also displayed is the nearly intact skeleton of an "Elephas Meridionalis", an elephant bigger than the African elephant, which lived in Europe a million years ago.

Santa Maria di Collemaggio Basilica★. — The church is beautifully sited in a large square at the end of a wide path. The building was begun in 1287 at the instance of Pietro da Morone, a hermit of the Abruzzi and founder of the Celestine Order, who was crowned Pope with the name of Celestine V and canonised in 1313.

The wonderful **façade**★★ of white and pink stone pierced with three rose windows and three rounded doorways with twisted recessed orders was added in the 14C.

Fountain of the 99 Conduits★ (Fontana delle 99 Cannelle). — This huge fountain near the Rivera Gate (Porta Rivera) is said to date from 1272, but it was remodelled in the 15C; 99 masks spout water into its basins. The sides of the fountain are covered with pink and white stone, giving a pleasant effect.

Church of St. Joseph (San Giuseppe). — This church, formerly dedicated to St. Blaise (San Biagio), stands in a beautiful square which also contains the Church of St. Catherine (Santa Caterina), with its pretty 18C façade. Inside St. Joseph's, on the north wall, the Gothic **Camponeschi monument**★ is the work of Gualtiero di Alemania (1432). An arch shelters the equestrian statue of a Camponeschi and the reclining figure of his wife.

EXCURSIONS

Campo Imperatore★★. — *Northeast. Description p 72.*

Pineta di Roio★. — *Southwest, 8 km - 5 miles.* The road begins by climbing in hairpin bends and affording good views of the Aterno Valley, before it plunges into the pinewoods to reach the summit of Mount Luco (from the Latin *lucus*: a sacred wood). There is a good view of L'Aquila.

Lake Campotosto★. — *North, 47 km - 29 miles.* This is an artificial lake in a region of wide mountain pastures. The scene will please lovers of solitude and simplicity.

Velino Gorges★. — *Northwest, 48 km - 30 miles.* Between Antrodoco and Posta, the Via Salaria follows the impressive gorges of the Velino River, hemmed between purple rocks over which cascades tumble. Cultivated terraces and fir woods cover the slopes intermittently.

If you intend combining your tour of Italy
with journeys through Germany, Switzerland or Austria,
remember to take the
Michelin Green Guides
Germany, Switzerland and **Austria.**

Michelin map **988** 6 — 36 km - 22 miles — south of Udine — Pop 3063

While the plan of the town was being outlined with the plough, according to Roman custom, an eagle *(aquila)* hovered overhead: hence its name. Aquileia was a flourishing market under the Roman Empire and was used as general headquarters by Augustus during his war with the Germans. In the Middle Ages it was the capital of a patriarchate ruled by bishops.

Basilica★★. — *3/4 hour.* Alone in its setting of pines, cypresses and lime trees, this was built in the 11C by the patriarch Poppone on the foundations of a 4C building; it was restored in the 14C. An imposing campanile, 73 m - 240 ft — high, stands on the left.

The most striking feature of the interior, which is pleasantly simple, is the splendid 4C **paving★★**, with its curious symbolism. Near the entrance can be seen the portraits of the donors; then a contest between the cock and the tortoise, representing the antagonism between Catholics and heretics; scenes depicting the offering of gifts (nave); the Good Shepherd (south aisle), and a picture of Jonah among little goblins busy fishing (transept).

The timberwork and the arcades are both 14C, the capitals Romanesque and the transept decoration Renaissance (elegant tribunes). In the transept notice the 15C *pietà.*

Under the chancel a 9C Carolingian crypt *(apply to the sacristan to visit; 50 lire)* is entirely covered with Romanesque **frescoes★★** depicting scenes from the lives of Christ (below and from left to right), the Virgin, St. Mark and St. Ermagora.

The **Cripta degli Scavi** is reached from the entrance to the north aisle. Excavations in the crypt have uncovered fine mosaic pavements dating from Roman and early Christian times. *Open 9 am to 2 pm (1 pm Sundays and holidays); closed Mondays, 1 January, 25 April, 1 May, 15 August, 25 December; 500 lire, free on Sundays and holidays; the ticket for the crypt also admits to the archaeological museum.*

Roman Ruins. — *Open 8.30 am to sunset.* Excavations have uncovered the remains of Roman Aquileia. Behind the basilica, the Via Sacra, lined with cypresses, leads to a river port with quays, mooring-rings and the foundations of warehouses.

Archaeological Museum. — *Same times of opening as for the Cripta degli Scavi in the Basilica.* A fine series of portraits including remarkable busts of Tiberius and Augustus as a youth, rich mosaics and collections of precious stones, amber and glass.

AREZZO ★ Tuscany

Michelin map **988** 15 — Pop 92087

The old town of Arezzo is built in terraces on a hill crowned by a citadel, in the centre of a fertile basin where cereals, fruit trees and vines flourish. Hilltop view.

After being first a rich Etruscan city and then a rich Roman one, Arezzo was a free community before it was absorbed by Florence in 1384. It was the birthplace of Maecenas, a Minister of Augustus and a rich patron of arts and letters, of Petrarch, of Guido d'Arezzo (11C), the inventor of the musical scale, of Pietro Aretino, a writer banished for a satirical sonnet against Indulgences, of Giorgio Vasari, the painter, architect and historian, and of Concino Concini, Marshal of Ancre and favourite of Marie de' Medici.

A Well Known Glass-Stainer. — **Guillaume de Marcillat** (1467-1529), born at La Châtre in Berry, France, served his apprenticeship as a glass-stainer at Bourges and then worked at Nevers, where he was a Dominican monk. His skill with stained glass led to his being summoned to Rome by Pope Julius II. He worked at the Vatican with Raphaël and Michelangelo, then settled at Arezzo, where he made many beautiful windows showing consummate skill in perspective and anatomy. Vasari said of his work: "These are not stained glass windows but marvels fallen from Heaven for the consolation of men."

■ **MAIN SIGHTS** *time: 2 hours*

St. Francis' Church (San Francesco). — This church is large, being designed for preaching; it was built for the Franciscans in the 14C, in the Gothic style. These monks, as guardians of the Holy Places, particularly venerated the Holy Cross. They asked Piero della Francesca to decorate the chancel of their church. The Church was remodelled in the 17 and 18C.

Frescoes of Piero della Francesca★★★. — These frescoes depict the **Legend of the Holy Cross.** Executed between 1453 and 1464, they form an admirable whole and a noble masterpiece of well balanced composition, with soft tones and gentle lights.

South Wall: on the tympanum, the death and burial of Adam; his son Seth plants a branch of the Tree of Paradise on his grave. The Queen of Sheba prostrates herself before a beam of the bridge made from this tree; has a vision of Christ crucified on this wood and explains her vision to Solomon, who has the beam buried. Below, the victory of Constantine over Maxentius under the sign of the Cross. Central Wall: the Jews make the Cross with wood from the beam which they have unearthed. Below, the dream of Constantine. North Wall: the Empress Helen finds the three crosses of Calvary; that of Christ is identified by the resurrection of a dead man. Below, the victorious Heraclius kills Chosroes, who had stolen the Cross.

On leaving the church note inside the façade an oculus fitted with a splendid stained glass window bearing the arms of Berry with *fleurs-de-lys.* It is by Guillaume de Marcillat, who depicted in it his native arms and St. Francis offering roses to the pope in mid-January.

Piazza Grande★. — The square is surrounded by mediaeval houses with battlemented towers, the galleried Romanesque apse of Santa Maria della Pieve, the late 18C court house, the palace of the Lay Brotherhood, half-Gothic and half-Renaissance, and the 16C galleries, the *logge* designed by Vasari and formerly closed to the common people. The Saracen's Tournament takes place in this square during the second week in September. The best horsemen of Arezzo attack a dummy figure with lances before a great crowd of extras in 12C costume.

Church of Santa Maria della Pieve★. — A tall campanile, known as that "of the hundred holes" because of its many windows (40 in number), stands over this fine Romanesque church built from the 12 to 14C and altered in the 16C by Vasari among others. The **façade★★**, inspired by the Pisan Romanesque style *(p 27),* has its three tiers of small columns, adorned with various patterns and standing more closely together as the height increases. The lively styled figures adorning the upper arch of the central doorway symbolise the twelve months of the year. On the high altar is a remarkable polyptych (1320) by the Sienese, Pietro Lorenzetti.

The **Via dei Pileati,** with its palaces, Gothic towers and old houses, is curious. The 14-15C Palazzo Pretorio is adorned with the coats of arms of *podestàs* or Florentine governors.

AREZZO

Cavour (Via)	BY
Grande (Piazza)	BY
Italia (Corso)	ABYZ

Giotto (Viale)	BZ 2
Madonna del Prato (V.)	AZ 3
Mecenate (Viale)	AZ 4
Niccolò Aretino (Via)	AZ 5
Pellicceria (Via)	BY 6
Pescioni (Via)	BY 7
S. Clemente (Via)	AY 12
Sasso Verde (Via)	BY 13

— · · — · · —	S. FRANCESCO
— · — · — · —	PIAZZA GRANDE★
— — — — —	S.TA MARIA DELLA PIEVE★

■ ADDITIONAL SIGHTS

Archaeological Museum★ (Museo Archeologico) (AZ M[1]). — *Open 9 am to 2 pm (1 pm Sundays and holidays); closed Mondays.* The collections of Aretian vases made in the Roman period and of Etruscan bronze statuettes, dating from the 6-5C BC, are outstanding.

Cathedral (Duomo) (BY D). — This cathedral was built between 1286 and 1510 but has a modern façade. There is a Romanesque-Gothic doorway in its south front.

Inside are fine **works of art★:** stained glass windows by Marcillat (Expulsion of the Money-Changers from the Temple), a fresco by Piero della Francesca of Mary Magdalen in the north aisle, the 14C tomb *(arca)* of St. Donatus at the high altar and 16C marble pulpits.

St. Dominic's Church (San Domenico) (BY B). — This 13C Gothic church has an asymmetrical façade. Inside, you will notice frescoes by the Giotto school and by Spinello Aretino and his followers and, at the high altar, an admirable **Crucifix★★,** an early work (1260-65) by Cimabue.

Vasari's Mansion (Casa del Vasari) (AY A). — *Open 8 am to 2 pm weekdays; 9 am to 1 pm Sundays and holidays; closed Mondays.* The house was gorgeously decorated in 1540 by Vasari, a painter, sculptor, architect and writer and a symbol of the Renaissance with his versatile talent. Also exhibited are works by Tuscan mannerists.

Church of St. Mary of Grace (Santa Maria delle Grazie). — *1 km - 3/4 mile — southwards along the Viale Mecenate.* In front of the church is a light, graceful **portico★** by the Florentine, Benedetto da Maiano (15C). Inside the church a marble altarpiece by Andrea della Robbia frames a picture by Parri di Spinello, St. Mary of Grace.

Museum of Mediaeval and Modern Art (AY M²). — *Open 9 am to 2 pm (1 pm Sundays and holidays); closed Mondays, 1 January 1 May, 15 August, Easter and Christmas.* The gallery and the museum are both in the 15C Bruni Palace. Works by Margarito d'Arezzo, Guido da Siena, Parri di Spinello, Bartolomeo della Gatta, Luca Signorelli, Cigoli, Vasari, Salvator Rosa and Gaspard Dughet may be seen. The 19C is represented by some of the most famous painters of the Macchiaioli school: Fattori, Signori... There are also coins, bronzes, glass, arms and ceramics (remarkable collection of the Renaissance period and of the 17 and 18C).

ASCOLI PICENO ★★ Marches

Michelin map **988** 16 — Pop 56 420

Ascoli, an austere but picturesque town lies in a narrow valley at the confluence of the Castellano and the Tronto. The town is rich in Roman and mediaeval buildings.

■ MAIN SIGHTS *time: 1 hour*

Piazza del Popolo★★. — The People's Square, elongated and well proportioned and paved with large flagstones, is surrounded by Gothic buildings and Renaissance arcades. The square is the favourite meeting-place of the people and it provides the scene for the Carnival and the parade leading up to the Quintana festival on the first Sunday in August.

People's Palace★ (Palazzo del Popolo). — The People's Palace is an austere 13C building dominated by a tower. An imposing doorway (1549) surmounted by a statue of Pope Paul III was added by Cola dell' Amatrice at the Renaissance. The palace has a Renaissance inner court.

St. Francis' Church★ (San Francesco). — This interesting church was begun in 1262 and consecrated in 1371. The apse is particularly curious with its seven Lombard apsidioles, two hexagonal towers and a dome over the transept crossing. A statue of Pope Julius II surmounts a Romanesque doorway on the right. The cloisters are on the north side of the church.

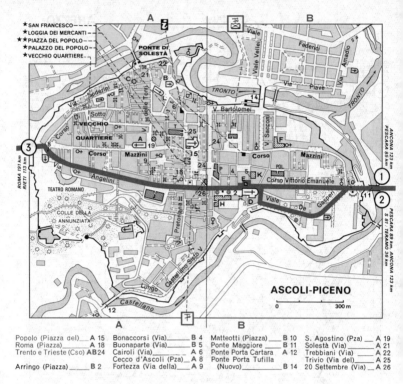

Merchants' Loggia★ (Loggia dei Mercanti). — The Merchant's Loggia abuts on the south front of the Church of St. Francis. It is light and graceful and was built at the beginning of the 16C under Tuscan influence as is revealed by the shape of the capitals.

Old Quarter★ (Vecchio Quartiere). — The quarter lies between the Corso Mazzini and the Tronto River. The main street is the Via delle Torri, prolonged by the Via Solestà — both are lined with old houses. At the entrance to the Via delle Torri is the Renaissance façade of **St. Augustine's** (Sant'Agostino — A A) which has a moving fresco of Christ bearing the Cross by Cola dell' Amatrice (north wall). Twin towers stand in the little square. The Via delle Torri ends at the 14C Church of **St. Peter the Martyr** (San Pietro Martire — A L).

The Romanesque Church of **Sts Vincent and Anastasius★** (Santi Vincenzo e Anastasio - A B), behind San Pietro, has a curious 14C façade formerly painted with frescoes.

The **Ercolani Tower** (Torre Ercolani — A C) in the Via Soderini, to the right, is the tallest (40 m — 131 ft) of the feudal towers of Ascoli. The Palazzetto Longobardo, a 12C Lombard Romanesque mansion, abuts on it.

Through a mediaeval gateway, the single arched Roman bridge, the **Ponte di Solestà★ (A),** spans the Tronto at a height of 25 m - 80 ft. From the end of the bridge on the left bank there is an attractive view of the town gate and the towers with which the old quarter bristles.

■ ADDITIONAL SIGHTS

Corso Mazzini★ (A B). — This street, lined with old mansions, crosses the town from east to west. Note the 16C **Malaspina Palace (B F)** at No. 224.

Cathedral (Duomo) (B D). — In the Chapel of the Holy Sacrament (south aisle) is a superb **polyptych★** (1473) by Crivelli in a finely carved period frame. The Madonna and Saints are painted on the panels and Christ and the Apostles on the predella, on a gilded background and in bright and pleasing colours.

The **baptistry★ (B E),** square at the base and octagonal above, standing on the left of the cathedral, was originally a pagan temple converted in the 5 and 6C. The facing on the outside walls is the work of 12C Lombard masters.

Near the baptistry, in the Via Buonaparte, is the fine 16C **Palazzo Buonaparte (B K).**

Picture Gallery (Pinacoteca) (B H). — *Open 2 May to 30 September, 10 am to 1 pm and 4.30 to 6.30 pm; 1 October to 30 April, 9 am to 1 pm; Sundays and holidays 10 am to noon. Closed 1 January, 1 May, 15 August, 1 November, Easter and Christmas.* The collections are displayed on the first floor of the Communal Palace and include the works of Crivelli and his pupil Pietro Alamanno (15C), portraits by Carlo Maratti (17C) and Van Dyck, a Titian (St.Francis Receiving the Stigmata), canvases by the Venetian painters Bellotto and Guardi and the Genoese Strozzi, Magnasco and Orazio De Ferrari (18C), a painting of the Annunciation by Guido Reni, and two works by Callot. The 19C is well represented by Palizzi, Induno, Morelli and Mancini. However, the pride of the collection is a precious 13C English work "The Cope of Nicholas IV".

EXCURSION

Colle San Marco Road★. — *Southeast, 13 km - 8 miles.* Leave by ② road S 81 to Teramo; at the roundabout about 200 m - 656 ft — after crossing the river, bear right into Viale Marconi which leads to the road to Colle San Marco on the right. This very winding road rises gently through poplars, chestnuts and acacias, affording many views of the town as it climbs.

As you reach the Hotel Miravalle, at an altitude of 700 m - 2 300 ft — you will discover a splendid **panorama★★**: in the foreground lies the Ascoli Piceno Basin dominated to the north by Mount Ascensione with its deeply scored slopes; to the east the Tronto Valley can be seen opening out as it flows towards the Adriatic, while on the west stands the vast chain of the Sibillini Mountains; southwards lie the last foothills of the Laga Mountains.

ASSISI ★★★ Umbria

Michelin map 988 16 — Pop 24 777

Assisi, the city of birds and silence under the protection of St. Francis, is built of pink stone and prettily spread in a fan shape on the slopes of Monte Subasio. Its narrow streets are lined with old façades whose flower decked balconies make delightful pictures. The town, which is still enclosed by ramparts, has hardly changed since the Middle Ages.

Mementoes of St. Francis and St. Clara combined with such a poetic setting and a gentle light, give Assisi a moving beauty all its own.

St. Francis (1182-1226). — Francis was the son of a rich Italian linen-draper and a French woman. He was a brilliant youth with a taste for high society, and he dreamed of military glory. But when made a prisoner during a war with Perugia in 1201, and suffering from fever, he saw the light and was converted. Several apparitions of the Virgin and of Christ appeared to Francis: the most famous is that of La Verna *(p 259)*, during which he received the stigmata. But this mystic also had a deeply poetic soul, and he wrote the first poems in Italian. A lover of the beauties of nature, he preached kindness to animals and praised the gift of Joy in the service of God becoming known as "God's Song-writer".

Francis was followed by many disciples in his life of prayer and penitence. He befriended a young woman of rare beauty, Clara, who founded the Order of Poor Clares. He himself died in 1226 after having founded, in 1210, the Order of Minors, mendicant monks known thereafter as Franciscans.

Art at Assisi. — Leaving aside Roman remains, art at Assisi is essentially religious. It developed under the influence of St. Francis and St. Clara and culminated in the Gothic period.

Franciscan architecture is governed by austerity of style and the importance given to preaching. That is why the churches have single, spacious naves lit by tall windows, and one or several pulpits.

In painting, after Cimabue, Giotto was the great interpreter of Franciscan mysticism, which he illustrated in accordance with the Legend of St. Francis as related by St. Bonaventure. Abandoning Byzantine design and gilded backgrounds he gave great prominence to animals and nature, brought together in a spiritual atmosphere, emphasised by simplicity and concentration of expression, restraint in gesture and harmony in composition and landscape.

■ SIGHTS *time: 5 hours*

St. Francis' Basilica★★★ (San Francesco) (A). — The basilica, supplemented by a monastery whose supporting arches overhang the valley, consists of two superimposed churches and a crypt. The whole building, constructed to the plans of Brother Elias, was consecrated in 1253.

Lower Basilica. — The lower church, dark, low and austere, is adorned with an admirable series of **frescoes★★★** *(some can be lit by request)*.

As you enter the narthex you will see, against the south wall, a Gothic memorial, a gallery and finally the tomb of Philip I of Courtenay, Emperor of Constantinople. At the far end of the narthex is the Chapel of St Catherine, with curious 15C stained glass windows. The chapel is decorated with picturesque frescoes by Andrea da Bologna (14C) depicting the life of St. Catherine.

From the Chapel of St. Catherine you pass through the Chapel of St. Anthony the Abbot into the 15C **Cloisters of the Dead★★★** (Chiostro dei Morti). These cloisters have two storeys and are full of charm, gentleness and peace.

Returning to the church you walk along the nave, whose walls are covered with original (13C) frescoes. They represent, on the right, the Passion, and on the left, the life of St. Francis.

The walls of the first chapel on the left are covered with **frescoes★★** by Simone Martini illustrating the life of St. Martin. These are remarkable for their delicate drawing and colour, graceful composition and beauty of expression. They show St. Martin dividing his cloak (to share it with a beggar) at the gates of Amiens and being dubbed a knight by the Emperor. Finally, they depict his death and his funeral at Tours.

(After photo by T.C.I.)

View of the Basilica of St. Francis

Farther along on the left is the 13C pulpit over which you will see a fresco of the Coronation of the Virgin attributed to Maso, a pupil of Giotto (14C). ·

In the crypt is the saint's tomb, discovered in 1818.

The **vaulting★★** above the Gothic high altar was painted in the 14C with scenes symbolising the Triumph of St. Francis and the Virtues practised by him: towards the nave, the saint's Marriage with Poverty; towards the south transept, Chastity in her tower; towards the north transept, Obedience laying her yoke on a Franciscan; towards the apse, the Triumph of St. Francis.

On the vaulting of the south transept are frescoes devoted to the Childhood of Christ. You will also notice, on the right, a **Madonna with Four Angels and St. Francis★★**. This majestic work by Cimabue is characterised by nobility of form and simplicity of expression.

The north transept is decorated with **frescoes★★** of the Passion. Those on the ceiling, attributed to pupils of Pietro Lorenzetti, are valued for their narrative design and charm of detail; those on the walls, probably by Pietro Lorenzetti himself, are striking for their dramatic expression (Descent from the Cross). Pause before the Virgin and Child between St. Francis and St. John the Evangelist, a composition of poignant sadness.

From the north transept a stairway leads up to the main cloisters built in the Renaissance style. Remarkable view of the apse. The **treasure★★** *(open 9 am to noon and 2 to 6 pm 15 March to 5 November; closed Mondays; 500 lire)* includes many valuable pieces.

Upper Basilica. — This tall and graceful nave, bathed in light, contrasts with that of the lower church. The apse and transept were painted with frescoes, since unfortunately damaged, by Cimabue and his school. In the north transept Cimabue painted a **Crucifixion★★★** of unforgettably tragic intensity. The 13C stained glass windows in the apse and the transept are the work of French craftsmen.

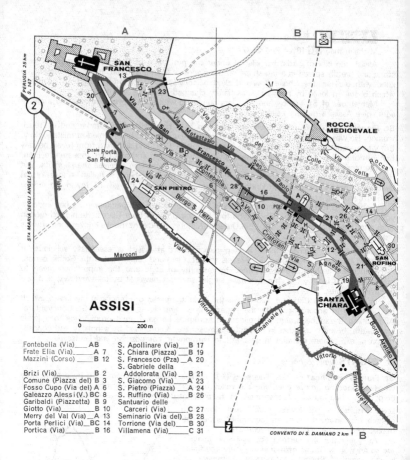

Finally between 1296 and 1304, Giotto depicted the Life of St. Francis in a now famous cycle of **frescoes★★★**. There are twenty-eight scenes, the last four ascribed to a painter called the Master of St. Cecilia. View them from left to right, starting from the transept.

Step out of the basilica on to the esplanade which is overlooked by a harmonious façade with a Gothic doorway and a rose window surrounded by symbols of the Evangelists.

St. Clara's Church★★ (Santa Chiara) (B). — This church is preceded by a terrace from which there is a pretty view of the Umbrian countryside. It was built between 1257 and 1265. To the left of the pink and white façade great supporting arches create patches of light and shade. The interior is plain and austere. Behind the high altar hangs an immense painted Crucifix of the 14C; above, in the vaulting of the transept crossing, are four delicate early 14C frescoes by an Umbrian painter representing St. Clara, her sister St. Agnes, St. Catherine and St. Lucia. The apse and the transept are decorated with 14C frescoes: Death and Funeral of St. Clara and the Nativity.

The Crucifix of St. Damian, which is said to have spoken to St. Francis, can be seen in the small Church of St. George, which adjoins the south aisle, and is now divided into two chapels. It was here that St. Francis lay buried till 1230. In the crypt may be seen a coffin containing the remains of St. Clara.

Mediaeval Castle★★ (Rocca Medioevale) (B). — *Open 8 am to 1 pm and 2 pm to sunset.* This former mediaeval fortress is an example of the military architecture of the 14C. Entering through the castle outpost climb a ramp to the lower court from which you reach the dwelling-house and the court of honour. From the top of the square keep is a **panorama★★** of Assisi and the plain.

Cathedral★ (Duomo San Rufino) (B). — The cathedral was built from 1140 onwards. The **façade★★**, flanked by a square campanile, is one of the finest in Umbria. The doorways and rose windows are decorated with Romanesque sculptures characteristic of Umbrian art.

The interior, on the plan of a basilica, was rebuilt in 1571. On the right is the font in which St. Francis, St. Clara and the Holy Roman Emperor Frederick II (1194-1250) were baptised.

The diocesan museum, the Romanesque capitals that once formed part of the cloisters and a Roman cistern may also be seen. *Open 8 am to noon and 2 to 7 pm (6 pm in winter); closed while services in progress.*

Piazza del Comune★ (B 3). — This square, bordered by two mediaeval castles, occupies the site of the forum.

The **Temple of Minerva★ (B A)** (Tempio di Minerva), converted into a church, is a noble Roman building with a portico comprising six majestic Corinthian columns.

Via San Francesco★ (AB). — A picturesque street lined by mediaeval and Renaissance houses. At No 11 the **Pilgrims' Oratory (A B)** (1431) is decorated inside with frescoes of the 15C, by Matteo da Gualdo.

St. Peter's Church★ (San Pietro) (A). — A Romanesque church, with decorative rose windows in the façade, built by the Benedictines.

The interior is severe and bare, with a pointed central vault and a curious dome which seems to derive from Provençal architecture.

In the chapel on the left of the chancel there is a charming triptych executed by Matteo da Gualdo in the 15C.

EXCURSIONS

Carceri Hermitage★★ (Eremo delle Carceri). — *East, 4 km - 2 miles. One may be accompanied by a Franciscan. Open 7 am (8 am in winter) to sunset.* Leave Assisi eastwards by the Via Santuario delle Carceri. The road climbs through olive groves and among broom and cypresses. It affords excellent **views★★** of the plain.

The hermitage, which originally consisted only of cave cells scattered among the holm oaks, was established by St. Bernardino in the 15C. Beyond an arcade is a delightful small terraced court with a beautiful view. You may visit the cave containing St. Francis' bed and the minute church, hollowed out of the rock, which was already in existence when the *carceri,* or cells, provided a retreat for the saint.

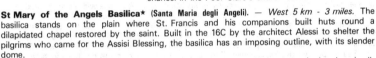

Convent of St. Damian★ (Convento di San Damiano). — *South of Porta Nuova, 2 km - 1 1/4 miles. Follow the road signs. One may be accompanied by a Franciscan. Open 8 am to 12.30 pm and 2 to 7 pm (5 pm 4 October to Easter).*

The convent, standing alone among olive and cypress trees in deep silence, offers a view of the plain.

It was when praying before the Crucifix in this little church that St. Francis heard the order that decided his vocation. St. Clara and her nuns lived in this blessed place. Above the portico, in the façade of the church, is the raised doorway from which St. Clara put to flight the Saracens. The interior is humble and austere; you will see on the right the window from which St. Francis threw a purse of money which the priest of St. Damian had refused, although it was intended to pay for the rebuilding of the church. The frescoes date from the 14C and the fine wooden Christ in the south chapel from the 17C.

After the church you may visit the convent, which is plain but peaceful and graceful in its simplicity. The roof garden is a small terrace looking out on the landscape where St. Francis is believed to have composed the verses of his *Praises of the Creatures.* St. Clara died in the bare dormitory of the convent in 1253. The refectory has not changed since the 13C. In this modest, low-roofed room St. Clara and her companions took their meals, and the Cross appeared on bread broken by the saint. The chancel in the Poor Clare's church contains the old stalls.

St Mary of the Angels Basilica★ (Santa Maria degli Angeli). — *West 5 km - 3 miles.* The basilica stands on the plain where St. Francis and his companions built huts round a dilapidated chapel restored by the saint. Built in the 16C by the architect Alessi to shelter the pilgrims who came for the Assisi Blessing, the basilica has an imposing outline, with its slender dome.

Inside *(to visit, apply to a Franciscan near the sacristy),* under the dome, is the chapel called the **Porziuncola,** or little portion, because of its small size. It was in this chapel that St. Francis consecrated St. Clara as the Bride of Christ and where he had the vision which inspired the Pardon of Assisi.

In the chancel, on the right, the Transito Chapel is the former hospital where St. Francis died on 3 October 1226. The saint's statue in white terracotta is by Andrea della Robbia.

In a little court *(reached through the south transept)* is the rose-bush *(roseto)* into which St. Francis threw himself in order to overcome temptation. The plant lost its thorns from that moment. The former convent and the cave in which the saint retired for prayer may also be visited.

ASTI Piedmont _____
Michelin map **988** 12 — 55 km - 34 miles — east of Turin — *Local map p 148* — Pop 79 644
Town plan in Michelin Red Guide Italia (hotels and restaurants).

Asti, which has given its name to one of the best known of Italian wines, was a powerful communal republic; several seignorial towers still remain from this period.

Asti was also the home town of the tragic poet, Vittorio Alfieri (1749-1803)

A *Palio* or horse race takes place yearly on the third Sunday in September and is preceded by a procession with many of the participants dressed in the costumes of the various quarters of the town, thus bringing alive the past for a day. A wine festival is also held in September.

Cathedral (Duomo). — The cathedral is a large 14C Gothic building with a 13C Romanesque campanile. On the south side is a fine porch adorned with statues and terracottas. The vast nave is covered with Baroque paintings. To the left of the cathedral are the cloisters and baptistry of St. John (San Giovanni) with, below, a 9C crypt.

Church of St. Secundus (San Secondo — 13-15C). — The church, which is dedicated to the patron saint of Asti, has a fine façade and an early Christian crypt.

St. Peter's Church (San Pietro). — The church dates from 1467; adjoining is a 12C baptistry.

ATRI Abruzzi _____
Michelin map **988** 27 — 29 km - 18 miles — northwest of Pescara — Pop 11 502

Atri has a fine situation within sight of the sea.

Cathedral★ (Duomo). — Built in the 13-14C on the foundations of a Romanesque edifice, this structure is in the transitional Romanesque-Gothic style. A fine sightly projecting Romanesque doorway with geometrical decorations adorns the façade. Another Romanesque doorway on the south side of the building is beautifully carved. The square part of the tower is Romanesque, but changes to Gothic in its polygonal upper part.

The interior has large Gothic arcades and elegant 15C frescoes. The cathedral museum contains ecclesiastical plate, sacerdotal ornaments and pottery from the Castelli.

Michelin map **988** 12 — 24 km - 15 miles — west of Turin — Pop 9 333

The town, overlooked by the ruins of a castle dismantled by Louis XIV's Marshal Catinat in 1691, still has some attractive old houses. Two glacial lakes lie to the south.

St. Anthony of Ranverso's Abbey (Abbazia di Sant'Antonio di Ranverso). — *4 km - 2 miles.* Take the Turin road and after 2 km - 11/4 miles — turn right. The abbey was founded in 1186 by the Hospitallers of St. Anthony, who nursed patients suffering from the "burning sickness", also called "St. Anthony's fire". This epidemic disease was caused by bad flour, milled from rusty wheat and rye, and seemed to burn the limbs. The parent abbey was at St. Antoine-en-Viennois in France. The 14-15C **church★** in the French Gothic style is remarkable for its façade with tall gables, its chancel decorated with lifelike and picturesque frescoes (1426) and the altarpiece of its high altar bearing a Nativity, the masterpiece of Defendente Ferrari (16C). The precious fresco by Jaquerio, the Ascent to Calvary, may be seen in the sacristy.

BARI Apulia

Michelin map **988** 29 — Pop 388 336
Town plan in the Michelin Red Guide Italia (hotels and restaurants).

Bari, the capital of Apulia and an agricultural and industrial trading centre, is primarily important as a port. The Levantine Fair *(Fiera del Levante)* is held in September.

Bari has two distinct areas: the old town tightly clustered on its promontory and the modern town with wide airy parallel roads and streets.

According to legend, Bari was built by the Illyrians and later colonised by the Greeks. From the 9 to the 11C it became the centre of Byzantine rule in South Italy. It was prosperous in the Middle Ages but declined under the Sforzas of Milan and Spanish domination in the 16C.

A Saintly Miracle-Worker. — St. Nicholas, Bishop of Myra in Asia Minor, achieved fame by resurrecting three children whom a butcher had cut up and put in brine. In 1807 sailors from Bari stole his relics and brought them home, and the people of Bari decided to build a church to him. The feast of St. Nicholas (8 May) is celebrated at sea, the faithful coming in boats to pray before the saint's statue. A historical procession parades in the town on the eve of the feast.

■ **MAIN SIGHTS** *time: 1 hour*

St Nicholas' Basilica★ (San Nicola). — The basilica in the heart of the old town was begun in 1087 at the behest of the Norman prince, Roger Guiscard, and was finished in 1197. Of the former residence of the Byzantine governors, on whose site the church was built, there remain large sections, mainly of the façade. The building, which is one of the most remarkable examples of Romanesque architecture in Apulia, has been reconstructed several times. The façade, divided into three tiers, is very plain but has considerable style with its sculptured doorway and tall windows. On the north side stands the rich Lions' doorway.

Inside are three aisles. Three transverse arches were added to the central aisle in the 15C. A large 12C ciborium (canopy) surmounts the high altar behind which is an unusual **episcopal throne★** in white marble resting on small figures. In the south apse is a fine altarpiece, Madonna and Saints, painted by the Venetian, Bartolomeo Vivarini. A museum has been installed in the galleries formerly reserved for women. The tomb of St. Nicholas is in the crypt.

Lungomare Nazario Sauro★. — A seaside promenade interrupted at intervals by squares.

■ **ADDITIONAL SIGHTS**

Cathedral★. — Overall the building is 11-12C Romanesque, with parts added in the 13C, although it has been reconstructed and restored. The façade has an elaborate frieze and a large rose window surrounded by monsters and beasts. The side walls include arcades supporting galleries. Fine carvings adorn the great window in the apse and the twin windows on the north side. The interior has three aisles which end in three oven-shaped vaults. Recent restoration work has uncovered the remains of an early Christian church with mosaic pavements dating back to different periods.

Castle★. — *Admission : 100 lire.* The castle, which goes back to the Norman Kings, was reconstructed in 1233 by the Emperor Frederick II of Hohenstaufen. The massive bastions at the corners were added in the 16C. The inner court dates from the same period.

Archaeological Museum. — *Piazza Umberto I. Open 9 am to 2 pm (1 pm on holidays); closed Sundays, 1 January, 25 April, 1 May, first Sunday in June, 15 August and Christmas.* Greco-Roman collections from the excavations made throughout Apulia.

BARLETTA Apulia

Michelin map **988** 29 — Pop 80 489
Town plan in the Michelin Red Guide Italia (hotels and restaurants).

A seaport with two bathing beaches, Barletta has a certain commercial importance due to its production of salt and wine.

The Colossus★★ (Statua di Eraclio). — This gigantic bronze statue (5 m - 16 1/2 ft — tall) of a figure holding a stone ball, apparently the terrestrial globe, in his left hand and a cross in his right, is believed to represent a Byzantine emperor whose identity is uncertain (Valentinian?). Probably 4C, it marks the transition from decadent Roman to early Christian art. The inhuman air of the figure and its rigidity combined with a certain inner strength are typical.

The **Church of the Holy Sepulchre** (San Sepolcro), near the Colossus, dates from the 12C and displays the transitional Romanesque-Gothic style. Inside, on the right, is a 13C font. There is a small museum devoted to Limousin art.

Cathedral★ (Duomo) — 12-14C. The building is dominated by a majestic campanile on arches, and shows Burgundian influence, especially in the walled Gothic chancel.

The great arches of the interior are Romanesque, with ogive vaulting.

Castle★. — This massive and imposing castle, built by the Hohenstaufens on the foundations of a former Norman fortress, was enlarged by Charles of Anjou in the 13C. The bastions were added by the Spaniards in the 16C.

BASSANO DEL GRAPPA ★ Venetia

Michelin map **988** 5 — 42 km - 26 miles — north of Padua — Pop 37 589

Bassano del Grappa, a pottery town which also produces *grappa* or brandy, is built in a smiling setting on the Brenta. It is pleasant to walk in its narrow streets and squares lined with arcades and houses painted in the Venetian fashion. From the Viale dei Martiri on the north side a fine **view★** opens out over the Plateau of the Seven Communes (or of Asiago) on the left and the Monte Grappa on the right, separated by the cleft made by the Brenta River.

Jacopo da Ponte (died 1592). -- Jacopo da Ponte, otherwise called **Bassano** or the Bassan, was the best known member of a family of artists. He was the originator of Bassanism, which was marked by a love of picturesque realism in the depicting of popular scenes. Bassano loved gay colours, fantastic skies and contrasts of light and shade; in this he was the precursor of Caravaggio, but his drawing was weak and he lacked imagination. He was a remarkable animal painter and an expert in *trompe-l'œil* (false perspective created by shadow-painting).

■ **SIGHTS** time: 3/4 hour

Covered Bridge (Ponte Coperto). — This wooden bridge is well known in Italy. It has been rebuilt several times; the present structure dates from 1945 and is a copy of the original.

Municipal Museum (Museo Civico). — Standing on the Piazza Garibaldi is the 12-14C Church of St. Francis. The museum is in the adjoining convent *(open 10 am to 12.30 pm and 3 to 6.30 pm; closed Sunday afternoons, Mondays and on some public holidays; 500 lire)*. The **picture gallery** (first floor) illustrates Bassanism. Jacopo da Ponte's masterpiece is displayed, St. Valentine baptising St. Lucia, about which Tiepolo commented "I saw a miracle at Bassano — black material appeared white" (St. Lucia's robe). Other Venetian painters, such as Guariento and Vivarini, are represented. There is also an amazing canvas by the Genoese painter Magnasco, Monks burying one of their Brethren, and a gallery devoted to the sculptor Canova. The Remondiniana Collection contains nearly 10 000 engravings.

EXCURSIONS

Monte Grappa★★★. — *32 km - 20 miles, plus 1/2 hour sightseeing.* Monte Grappa is reached by the Strada Cadorna, at first lined with acacias and wild roses before it crosses austere mountain pastures. Splendid views of the Brenta Valley and the Venetian Plain open out, especially at Campo Solagna. The mountain (alt 1 775 m - 5823 ft) was one of the strongpoints bravely defended by the Italians during the Austrian offensive (winter of 1917 to June 1918). A huge **ossuary** contains the remains of 25 000 Italian and Austrian soldiers. On a clear day the **panorama★★★** from the summit includes Venice and Trieste.

Asolo. — *14 km - 9 miles.* Asolo situated east of Bassano is overlooked by a castle. The town guards the memory of the poet Robert Browning and Duse, the famous Italian tragic actress who interpreted the works of Gabriele D'Annunzio, who now lies buried in the peaceful cemetery at Sant'Anna. Arcaded streets, Venetian palaces painted with frescoes and the cathedral, which contains interesting old pictures, make Asolo attractive.

BELLAGIO ★★★ Lombardy

Michelin maps **988** 3 and **26** 9 — *Local map p 129* — Pop 3 289

Bellagio, the Pearl of the Lake, occupies a magnificent **site★★★** on a promontory dividing Lake Lecco from the south branch of Lake Como. It is a resort with a world-wide reputation offering the tourist walks, views, villas and gardens. Luxurious hotels, a bathing beach and many amusements help to make a stay there delightful. Bellagio still has narrow streets, picturesque staircases and its Romanesque Church of St. James (San Giacomo).

Villa Serbelloni. — *Guided tours of the park (time: about 2 hours), 10 am to 4 pm. Closed Mondays, Sundays and holidays and 15 October to Easter; 1 000 lire.* This is the jewel of Bellagio. The **gardens★★★**, famous for their luxuriant vegetation, offer lovely glimpses of the lake. The scene from the flower decked terraces, adorned with grottoes, is unforgettable.

Villa Melzi. — *Open mid-March to 10 November 9 am to 6 pm (5 pm October and November); 1 500 lire.* The villa stands on the lake shore near San Giovanni, where you should see the charming landing-stage. The villa was built (1802) in the Empire style by Duke Francesco Melzi, Vice-President of the Italian Republic. From the splendid **gardens★★** there is a magnificent view of Tremezzo. See also the orangery which has been converted into a museum (archaeological collection, souvenirs of Napoleon), and the chapel.

EXCURSION see local map p 129

Tour of the Madonna del Ghisallo★★. — *37 km - 24 miles — about 1 1/2 hours.* The tour should be made in the direction Bellagio-Onno-Asso-Ghisallo-Bellagio. From Bellagio to Onno there are wide views of Lake Lecco. From Onno to Asso the road is panoramic and picturesque. From the **Church of the Madonna del Ghisallo,** the patroness of racing cyclists (ex-voto bicycles), there is a remarkable panorama of Lake Lecco and part of Lake Como, towards Gravedona. The descent to Bellagio, known as the Bellagio Ladders, affords superb views of the lakes; stop at the Grigne belvedere, after Civenna cemetery, to look at the view.

BELLUNO ★ Venetia

Michelin map **988** 5 — *Local map p 93* — Pop 37 053
Town plan in the Michelin Red Guide Italia (hotels and restaurants).

Belluno stands on a rocky spur at the confluence of the Piave and the Ardo. To the North lie the Dolomites with the Schiara Massif (2 563 m - 8 409 ft) and to the South are the Belluno Pre-Alps with Nevegal (1 763 m - 5 784 ft).

Walk along the Via Rialto (through the 13C Dojona gateway — remodelled in the 16C), across the Piazza del Mercato *(see p 60)*, along the Via Mezzaterra and the Via Santa Croce to the Rugo gateway (restored in the 17C). From the Via del Piave, Piazza Castello and Piazza dei Martiri you can enjoy pretty **views★** of the Piave Valley. A chair-lift runs from Nevegal *(southeast, 12 km - 7 miles)* to **Mount Faverghera** (1 610 m - 5 282 ft) near the Botanical Garden.

Piazza del Mercato★. — A square lined with arcaded Renaissance houses and where the fountain (1409) is surmounted by a bishop's statue. The façade of the 15C Monte di Pietà Palace is decorated with coats of arms.

Piazza del Duomo★. — Several notable buildings stand in the square. The **Rectors' Palace** (late 15C), formerly the residence of the Venetian governors, is in the Venetian style (paired windows). On the right stand the Bishops' Palace and the civic tower (12C, rebuilt in the 17C).

The 16C **Cathedral**, restored in the 18C, is flanked by a campanile in the Baroque style by Juvara. It contains good pictures of the Venetian school, notably by Jacopo Bassano. In the crypt are a 14C polyptych attributed to Francesco da Rimini and a 14C marble tomb.

The 17C **Jurists' Palace** houses the **municipal museum**. This consists of an art gallery containing paintings by Bartolomeo Montagna (Virgin and Child), Solario, Longhi (Portrait of a Child), and local painters such as Marco and Sebastiano Ricci, archaeological and numismatic departments and documents on the Risorgimento. *Open 1 April to 30 October, 10 am to noon, 3 to 6 pm; closed Mondays and Sunday and holiday afternoons.*

BENEVENTO Campania _____

Michelin map **988** 27 — Pop 62358

Benevento, the former capital of Samnium, lies in a smiling countryside and was an important agricultural centre in Roman times. Under Lombard rule, in the Middle Ages, it was still the seat of a duchy and later of a powerful principality. Benevento is famous throughout Italy for its Strega liqueur and its nougat.

Trajan's Arch★ (Arco di Traiano). — The arch was constructed in 114 AD at the beginning of the road built by Trajan. It bears bas-reliefs dedicated to the glory of the emperor: low down on either side, the Return of the Emperor to Rome from Germania; on the vaulting, his coronation.

Church and cloisters of St. Sophia (Santa Sofia). — The church has a polygonal plan. To the left of the church stand the cloisters, dating from the 12C; note the slenderness of the columns supporting the Moorish type arcades and the ornament on the Romanesque capitals.

St. Sophia houses the **Samnium Museum** *(open 9 am to 1 pm; closed Mondays)*. The archaeological collections include Egyptian sculptures which adorned the temple of Isis at Benevento, and Greek ceramics decorated with figures; Greek silver coins, Byzantine gold coins and others struck by Lombard masters in Benevento. The mediaeval and modern art department contains paintings of the Neapolitan school (Giordano, Solimena).

The history department (documents on Talleyrand and mementoes of the Risorgimento) is located in the castle (Rocca dei Rettori).

Roman Theatre (Teatro Romano). — This theatre, which is one of the largest still in existence, was built in the 2C BC in the reign of the Emperor Hadrian and was restored by Caracalla.

BERGAMO ★★ Lombardy _____

Michelin map **988** 3 — Pop 126479

The modern lower town, pleasant and airy, has in its centre the Piazza Matteotti. The old upper town is quiet and very picturesque.

Masks and Bergamasques. — The *commedia dell'arte (p 33)* originated at Bergamo in the 16C. It is a comedy of improvisation in which the masked characters, of Venetian origin, mock the rustics *(facchini)* of the region and notably Harlequin, a stupid but cunning peasant of the Brembana Valley. The citizens of Bergamo love music. The composer Donizetti (1797-1848), the prolific author of *Don Pasquale* and *Lucia di Lammermoor*, was born in the town.

The vivacity of the people is displayed in the local folklore such as the *Bergamasque*, a lively dance, and in the groups of public musicians *(pifferi)* who play reed instruments.

■ **UPPER TOWN★★★ (Città Alta)** *time: 2 hours*

The Upper Town is a repository of treasures protected by 16C Venetian walls (pretty views). The funicular ends in the picturesque Piazza del Mercato delle Scarpe (Square of the Shoe Market), which may be used as a starting point for the following tour: Via Gombito, Piazza Vecchia, Piazza del Duomo, Via Donizetti.

Piazza Vecchia★. — This is the historical centre of the town. The Palazzo della Ragione *(restoration work in progress)* — the oldest communal palace in Italy — dates from 1199 but was rebuilt in the 16C; it has graceful arcades and windows and a balcony surmounted by the Lion of St. Mark. A 14C covered stairway gives access to the majestic 12C bell-tower with its 15C clock; the bell still rings for curfew at 10 pm; from the top *(lift)* there is a view of the square and the Colleoni Chapel. The white marble Scamozziano Palace (1610) is Palladian in style *(p 263)*.

The Via Bartolomeo Colleoni is lined with old dwellings, among them, at Nos. 9 and 11, the 16C Colleoni Mansion contains a drawing-room adorned with allegorical frescoes.

Passing beneath the arcades of the Ragione Palace you come to the Piazza del Duomo.

Baptistry (Battistero) (AY B). — This octagonal structure by Giovanni da Campione (14C) has slender pillars and statues of the Virtues in red marble.

Colleoni Chapel★★ (Cappella Colleoni). — *Open 1 March to 30 September, 8.30 am to 12.30 pm and 2 to 7 pm; 1 October to 28 February, 9 am to noon and 2.30 to 4.30 pm. Closed Mondays and Christmas.* The architect of the Carthusian monastery at Pavia, Amadeo, designed this marvellous structure from 1470 to 1476 as a mausoleum for Bartolomeo Colleoni (1400-1475). As at Pavia, the façade is covered with precious multicoloured marble and lavishly decorated with delicate sculptures: medallions, allegories and scenes from the Old Testament and the legend of Hercules (at the base).

The interior *(ask the guide for the plan)* is decorated with bas-reliefs of extraordinary delicacy, frescoes by Tiepolo (1696-1770) and stalls in Renaissance marquetry. The Colleoni monument is surmounted by an equestrian statue of the leader in gilded wood and is delicately carved; there are scenes from the New Testament, statuettes of the Virtues and portraits of the leaders' children. His favourite daughter, Medea, lies near him in a tomb by Amadeo which is a marvel of delicacy and purity. *Ask for the marquetry below to be displayed and lit.*

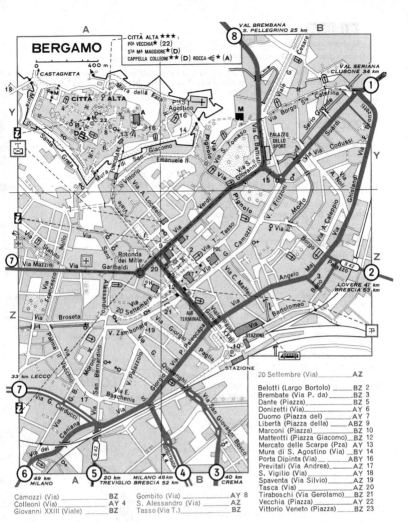

Church of St. Mary Major★ (Santa Maria Maggiore). — This church dates from the Romanesque period (12C). The 14C north and south doorways are by Giovanni da Campione. The interior was remodelled in the Baroque style in the late 16 — early 17C. Inside are splendid **tapestries★★**, some of them Italian and beautifully designed as in the series on the Life of the Virgin from cartoons by A. Allori (Florence, 1583-1586), others Flemish like the Crucifixion from drawings by L. Van Schoor (Antwerp, 1696-1698). Note also the 14C frescoes decorating the transept, a curious 18C Baroque confessional and superb 16C inlaid **panels★★** (scenes from the Old Testament) made from designs by Lorenzo Lotto *(ask for them to be uncovered)*.

Citadel (Rocca). — 14C, remodelled by the Venetians. **View★** of the old town from the tower.

■ LOWER TOWN

Carrara Academy★★ (Accademia Carrara) (BY **M**). — *Open 9.30 am to 12.30 pm and 2.30 to 5.30 pm; closed Tuesdays, 1 January, Easter and Christmas, and afternoons in winter;1000 lire.* In addition to the works of Bergamask portrait painters such as Cariani and Moroni from the 16C and Fra Galgario from the 18C, the Venetian school is also well represented, especially by Lorenzo Lotto who worked at Bergamo for many years.

After the famous portraits of Giuliano de' Medici and Lionello d'Este by Botticelli and Pisanello, come the Madonnas of Giovanni Bellini and his brother-in-law Mantegna, in similar taste. These are followed by works of Cariani and Lotto, the latter showing an admirable picture of the Holy Family with St. Catherine. A room is devoted to portraits by Moroni and also works by Dürer and Clouet. Note the room devoted to Fra Galgario, the still lifes of musical instruments by the Bergamask, Baschenis (1617-1677), the Guardis and the Flemish-Dutch collection dominated by a delightful seascape by Van Goyen.

Via Pignolo★ (BYZ). — A picturesque street winding among old palaces, mostly 16C, and churches containing works of art, notably pictures by Lorenzo Lotto: in Santo Spirito in the second chapel on the right and in San Bernardino in the chancel.

EXCURSIONS

Val Brembana★ – *25 km - 16 miles* — Leave Bergamo by ⑧. The road follows a beautiful, green valley cut through the chalk and occasionally opening out into a basin. You will see caves and curious two coloured chalk strata. The large thermal spa of **San Pellegrino Terme★★**, with pleasant gardens, produces alkaline waters which are good for disorders of the kidneys.

Val Seriana. — *49 km - 30 miles.* Leave Bergamo by ①. The valley is picturesque in its upper part. From Clusone, whose Oratorio dei Disciplini contains a curious Dance of Death (1485), you go up to the **Presolana Pass**, amid fine scenery. From the pass, it is possible *(1/2 hour on foot Rtn)* to climb a rock providing a sheer drop, known as the Married Couples' Leap (Salto degli Sposi), and also a spectacular if vertiginous **view★★** of the deep valley below.

BIELLA Piedmont

Michelin maps 988 2 and 26 15 — Pop 56070

Town plan in the Michelin Red Guide Italia (hotels and restaurants).

Lying at the feet of pleasant hills, Biella is an industrial centre handling wool and cotton. The town is divided into two quarters: **Biella Piano**, which has a curious 10C baptistry and a Renaissance church, and **Biella Piazzo** on the hill *(funicular)*, where you will see 15 and 16C dwelling houses.

EXCURSION

Oropa Church★★ (Santuario d'Oropa). — *Northwest, 13 km - 8 miles.* A popular place of pilgrimage (April to September). The 17-18C buildings shelter a famous Black Virgin which is supposed to have been carved by St. Luke.

From the church cable-cars climb *(8 minutes)* to the Mucrone refuge (view), from which you can reach the pretty **Lake Mucrone★★** at an altitude of 1 900 m - 6 234 ft *(30 minutes on foot Rtn)*.

A cable-car takes one to Monte Camino (2 391 m -7 845 ft) — *time: ascent 12 minutes —:* panorama of the Alps and of the Po plain.

BITONTO Apulia

Michelin map 988 29 — Pop 47 508

This little old town is a busy centre of the grain and fruit trade and produces some of the best olive oil in Italy.

Cathedral★ (Duomo). — The 12-13C cathedral, among the finest of the Romanesque churches in Apulia, is copied from the cathedrals of Trani and of St. Nicholas of Bari.

The façade, flanked on the left by an elegant little loggia, is finely designed: two buttresses divide it into sections corresponding with the nave and aisles. The rose window, paired windows and doorway are richly carved. On the south side arcades support a gallery with delicately turned little columns.

Inside, columns with fine capitals support the galleries reserved for women. A remarkable pulpit (1229) at the entrance to the transept is reached by a staircase on which Frederick II of Hohenstaufen and his family are portrayed.

BOLOGNA ★★ Emilia-Romagna

Michelin map 988 14 15 — Pop 476471

Town plan in the Michelin Red Guide Italia (hotels and restaurants).

The capital of Emilia is a city of many faces: "Bologna the Turreted", bristling with towers and campaniles; "Bologna the Fat", a sanctuary of good fare; "Bologna the Learned", famous for its wise men and its University, the oldest in Europe. Finally, Bologna is a city of art and an important industrial and commercial centre producing steel, electrical equipment, shoes, macaroni and sausages. Various events are held there: the International Fair and Food Fair *(late May - early June)*, the Shoe Fair *(5-8 September)*, the Fashion Show *(18-21 September)*... One of the features of the town is the great number of arcades lining the principal streets.

Fortunes and Misfortunes. — Etruscan Felsina was invaded in the 1C BC by the Boïan Gauls, who, on being driven out in their turn by the Romans, settled in Bohemia. Roman Bononia fell under the sway of the Barbarians and did not revive until the 12C.

From the 13 to the 16C the city enjoyed independent communal government. In the 13C the Guelphs and Ghibellines *(p 18)* fought one another; the Guelphs prevailed and, in 1249, defeated the Imperial Army of Frederick II at Fossalta and took prisoner his son Enzo, who remained at Bologna until his death in 1272. Bologna reached its zenith: the University flourished and city walls, towers, palaces and churches were built. Certain families, such as the Visconti, the Pepoli and especially, after 1400, the Bentivoglio, distinguished themselves. Giovanni II Bentivoglio threw Bologna open to the Tuscan Renaissance.

Bologna was under the control of the popes from 1506 to 1797.

"Long Live the Students". — The University, founded in 425, had 10 000 students in the 13C. At that time the professors were often women and a solemn chronicler reports that one of them, Novella d'Andrea, was so beautiful in face and body that she had to give her lectures from behind a curtain to avoid distracting her pupils.

Teaching concentrated on Roman law and theology.

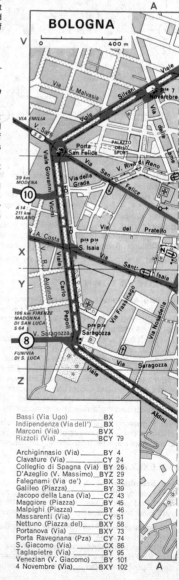

BOLOGNA

Bassi (Via Ugo)	BX
Indipendenza (Via dell')	BX
Marconi (Via)	BVX
Rizzoli (Via)	BCY 79
Archiginnasio (Via)	BY 4
Clavature (Via)	CY 24
Colleglio di Spagna (Via)	BY 26
D'Azeglio (V. Massimo)	BYZ 29
Falegnami (Via de')	BX 32
Galileo (Piazza)	BY 39
Jacopo della Lana (Via)	CZ 43
Maggiore (Piazza)	BY 45
Malpighi (Piazza)	BY 46
Massarenti (Via)	CY 51
Nettuno (Piazza del)	BXY 58
Portanova (Via)	BXY 73
Porta Ravegnana (Pza)	CY 74
S. Giacomo (Via)	CX 86
Taglapietre (Via)	BY 95
Venezian (V. Giacomo)	BY 101
4 Novembre (Via)	BXY 102

At the Forefront of Scientific Progress. — Science has always been honoured at Bologna. As early as the 14C anatomy lessons were given with limewood dummies, or better still with fresh corpses. More recently Guglielmo Marconi (1847-1937) studied Hertzian waves (wireless telegraphy) there.

At the present time the University has first class medical and surgical laboratories, also institutes of traumatology, radiology and preventive medicine for the treatment of tuberculosis and the Rizzoli Institute, which specialises in orthopaedics. An atomic research centre is now engaged in nuclear physics.

■ **MAIN SIGHTS** *time: 3 hours*

Two adjoining squares, the **Piazza Maggiore** and the **Piazza del Nettuno★★★**, form, with the Piazza di Porta Ravegnana, the heart of Bologna. This is an ensemble of rare beauty.

Communal Palace★ (Palazzo Comunale). — The façade is made up of structures of various periods. The building on the left, resting on arcades, is 13C. To the right, there is a façade which dates from the beginning of the 15C but is still Gothic. In the centre, the great 16C doorway by Alessi is surmounted by a statue of Pope Gregory XIII, who was born at Bologna and in 1582 established our present Gregorian calendar. Above and to the left of the doorway is a statue of the Virgin and Child in terracotta by Nicolo dell'Arca (1478).

Cross the courtyard diagonally; at the opening of a corridor, on the left, a superb gently sloping **staircase**, once mounted by horses, leads to the first floor and, from the far end of a gallery, continues up to the second storey. Opening off the vast Farnese chamber at its far end (note the 17C frescoes) are the sumptuous 17-18C saloons containing the art collections, pictures and furniture *(open 9 am to 2 pm and 9 am to 12.30 pm Sundays; closed Tuesdays and holidays)*.

Left of the Communal Palace stands the 14-15C Gothic Palace of Notaries.

Governor's Palace★ (Palazzo del Podestà). — The Renaissance façade facing the Piazza Maggiore, has arcades separated by Corinthian columns on the ground floor and is surmounted by a balustrade. The upper storey has pilasters and an attic pierced by oculi (round windows).

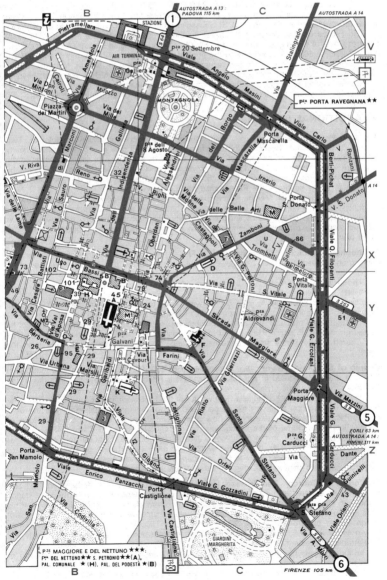

King Enzo's Palace (Re Enzo) stands next to the Governor's Palace, looking out over the Piazza del Nettuno. It has a fine inner courtyard and a magnificent staircase which leads out to a gallery on whose left is a minute court overlooked by the Arengo Tower.

Neptune's Fountain★★ (Fontana del Nettuno — 1566). — This is the work of a Frenchman, Jean Bologne known as Giovanni da Bologna, born at Douai in 1529. The muscular bronze Neptune, nicknamed the Giant, is armed with a trident; four sirens riding dolphins spout water from their breasts. The whole group suggests a rather rough vigour characteristic of Bologna.

St. Petronius' Basilica★★ (San Petronio). — This huge building, dedicated to the patron saint of Bologna, was begun in the Gothic style in 1390 and remained unfinished; only the nave was built. Charles V was crowned Emperor there by the pope in 1530.

The façade, the upper part of which lacks its marble facing, is remarkable chiefly for a main **doorway★★** on which a Sienese, Jacopo della Quercia, worked from 1425 to 1438. On the tympanum the Virgin and Child are enthroned between St. Petronius and St. Ambrose. The lintel, uprights and embrasures are adorned with small, expressive bas-reliefs, rather pagan in spirit. Note especially the story of Adam and Eve.

(After photo by T.C.I.)

Bologna—The central doorway of
St. Petronius

The interior is gigantic: 132 m long in six bays only, 44 m high and 58 m wide (433 ft, 144 ft, 190 ft). The total length was to be 217 m - 712 ft - and the height of the dome nearly 152 m - 500 ft — (St. Paul's, London: 463 ft long, 93 ft high, 125 ft wide.)

There are many **works of art** in the north aisle. Note a fine fresco by Giovanni da Modena in the fourth chapel, a Martyrdom of St Sebastian (Ferrara school, late 15C) and a 15C pavement in Faenza ceramics in the fifth chapel. In the seventh chapel are a Madonna (1492) by Lorenzo Costa of Ferrara, and the tomb of Elisa Bacciochi, Napoleon's sister. A sundial designed by Cassini in 1656 is marked out on the floor of the north aisle. An aperture in the roof admits a beam of light to shine on it and record local time according to the sun. Note the canopy by Vignola over the high altar, and the organ (15C) on the right which is the oldest in Italy.

Before leaving walk round, outside, through the **Pavaglione Portico**, along the Via dell'Archiginnasio. On your right are single columns of the transept of the unfinished basilica.

■ ADDITIONAL SIGHTS

Piazza di Porta Ravegnana★★. — This is the most characteristic square in Bologna. Two strange, leaning towers, belonging to noble families, stand in it *(see p 220)*. The taller is nearly 100 m - 330 ft — high and has a tilt of over 2 m - 7 1/2 ft; a staircase of 486 steps leads to the top, from which there is a fine view. This tower was built by the Asinelli family in 1109; the other, known as the Garisenda, is 50 m - 165 ft — high and leans 3 m - 10 ft — out of the vertical. No. 1 in the square is the Renaissance Linen Drapers' Palace.

The 14C **Mercanzia** or Merchant's House in the next square on the south side, was the headquarters of the corporations whose arms can be seen in the frieze on the façade. It bears statues of saints in lateral niches and that of Justice beneath the balcony from which court judgments and bankruptcies were announced. Nearby are curious houses supported on brick or wood piles.

St. Stephen's Church★★ (Santo Stefano) (CY F). — This building contains several sanctuaries opening on a square lined with old houses and remarkable 15-16C palaces. They are, from right to left:

The **Church of the Crucifix**, 11C but remodelled.
Church of the Holy Sepulchre, 12C.
Church of Sts. Vitalis and Agricola, 8-11C, with plain, massive lines. In the north apse is a curious 14C Adoration of the Magi composed of roughly carved wooden statues.

Through the Church of the Holy Sepulchre you reach the **Court of Pilate**, which gets its name from a basin in which Pilate is said to have washed his hands before the Crucifixion. The 13C Church of the Trinity stands opposite. Entrance to the Romanesque cloisters is on the right.

Church of St. James Major★ (San Giacomo Maggiore) (CX D). — The church was founded in 1267 and drastically altered in the 15C. A Renaissance doorway on the north side has a fine 15C frieze in the antique style.

The **Bentivoglio Chapel★** (Cappella Bentivoglio) is the funeral chapel of the Bentivoglio family. In the Renaissance style, it used to be linked by an underground passage with the Bentivoglio Palace, on whose site a theatre now stands. The altarpiece is one of the best works of Francia (late 15C). Some of the frescoes are by the Ferraran, Lorenzo Costa (1489).

Opposite the chapel, in the ambulatory, Jacopo della Quercia made the tomb of the jurist Antonio Bentivoglio in 1435: the teacher with his students is portrayed on the base.

In the **St. Cecilia Oratory** *(apply to the sacristan)* are remarkable **frescoes★** (1506) by Francia, Lorenzo Costa and their school, depicting the life of the saint.

St. Dominic's Church★ (San Domenico) (BZ K). — The church was built between 1221 and 1233 and was restored in the 18C. The famous and beautiful **tomb★★** *(arca)* of the saint stands in the sixth chapel on the right. His life is depicted in bas-reliefs (1267) by Nicola Pisano and his pupil Fra Guglielmo. The monument is crowned with a Flamboyant arch of original and graceful design carried out from 1469 to 1473 by the sculptor Niccolò da Bari, who was afterwards known as Niccolò dell'Arca. The Kneeling Angel (in front and to the right), St. Proculus and St. Petronius Protecting Bologna are believed to be early works by Michelangelo.

In the chancel, the richly inlaid stalls (1541-1551) are the work of Brother Damiano of Bergamo.

North of the church is the **tomb★** of the lawyer Rolandino dei Passeggeri (14C).

St. Francis' Church (San Francesco) (AX N). — 13C but extensively remodelled. At the high altar is a magnificent **altarpiece★** (1392), the work of Venetian sculptors. In the centre can be seen the Crucifixion, the Virgin and Child, the Eternal Father and the Coronation of the Virgin. In the niches are St. Petronius holding a model of Bologna, and the plague-stricken St. Roch and his dog. The life of St. Francis is depicted on the predella.

Bevilacqua Palace★ (Palazzo Bevilacqua) (BY E). — This, the finest palace in Bologna, is late 14C, Florentine Renaissance in style with arch bosses. The Council of Trent sat here in 1547. The court, in two storeys, with a sculptured frieze, is pleasant.

Stada Maggiore★ (CY). — The street is lined with crenellated Gothic mansions (No. 19) and Classical palaces (Nos. 22, 24, 34...). A palace dating from 1658 (No. 44) houses the Davia Bargellini Gallery (open 9 am to 2 pm; 9 am to 12.30 pm Sundays; closed Tuesdays, weekday holidays, 25 and 26 December) which contains furniture and pictures including a splendid Madonna painted in 1345 by Vitale da Bologna.

Municipal Archaeological Museum★ (Museo Civico Archeologico) (BY M[1]). — Open 9 am to 2 pm (12.30 pm Sundays and holidays); closed Mondays.

Egyptian antiquities; head of the Pharaoh Amenophis IV and bas-reliefs from the tomb of Harembab; Greco-Roman antiquities: good Roman copy of the head from the Acropolis of Athena Lemnia by Phidias; Etruscan antiquities: stelae and vases among which is a famous water pitcher (situla).

Near the museum, at No. 1, is the 16C **Palazzo dell' Archiginnasio** with a graceful court adorned with the coats of arms of priors and professors. It housed the University until 1803 and today contains the library (10 000 manuscripts).

Picture Gallery★ (Pinacoteca) (CX M). — Open 9 am to 2 pm (1 pm on Sundays and holidays). Closed Mondays; 500 lire. The Bologna school of painting in the 14C and the Renaissance and Baroque periods can be studied here.

Its characteristics are: in the Middle Ages, Byzantine survivals; under the Renaissance, mannerism, idealism, science and composition; with the Carracci, realism, vigour and colour; with the pupils of the Carracci (Domenichino, Guido Reni, Albani and Guercino), an academic style.

The school of Bologna influenced French painters of the 17 and 18C of whom several, including Fragonard and Vigée-Lebrun, were members of the Bologna Academy. The first rooms are devoted to 14C Bolognese painters: Vitale da Bologna, Jacopo and Simone de' Crocefissi. One room displays the frescoes, by Vitale da Bologna and his pupils, which originally came from the former church of St. Apollonia di Mezzaratta (now private property).

Those which follow contain works of the pronouncedly realistic Ferrara school, Ercole de' Roberti, Francesco del Cossa and Lorenzo Costa. After a canvas by Francia, The Adoration of the Child, comes a famous picture of truly classical beauty by Raphaël: St. Cecilia with St. Paul, St. John, St. Augustine and Mary Magdalen.

The Bolognese school of the 17C follows with the Carracci brothers and their disciples: St. William of Aquitaine, a masterpiece by Guercino (clever light effects) and works by Albani, Domenichino, and Guido Reni. Paintings of the Bolognese school of the 18C.

Tapestry Museum (Museo Nazionale Storico della Tappezzeria) (BY M[2]). — Open 10 am to noon, 4 to 7 pm; closed Saturdays and in August. The museum is installed in the Salina Palace.

EXCURSIONS

Madonna di San Luca. — 5 km - 3 miles. Leave Bologna by ⑧. On a hill ascended by a portico of 666 arches, stands the 18C church containing, in the chancel, the Madonna of St. Luke, a 13C Byzantine painting.

From the church there is a fine **view★** of the town and the Apennines.

Hills (Colli). — Town plan in Michelin Red Guide Italia. The hill roads south of the town offer pleasant excursions and sights; superb **panorama★** from the slopes of **Monte Donato.**

BOLSENA Latium

Michelin map 𝟵𝟴𝟴 25 — Pop 3997

Bolsena, the ancient Etruscan city Volsinii, built on a slope facing a lake, whose shady shores welcome many visitors attracted by a soft and limpid light that gives the landscape an ethereal air.

The old part of the town rises in terraces up a small hill, its squat houses built of sombre stone; there is a good view from road S 2.

The Miracle of Bolsena. — A Bohemian priest had doubts about the Transubstantiation, that is, the incarnation of Christ in the Host. But, it is related, at the moment of Consecration when he was celebrating mass at St. Christina, the Host began to bleed profusely. The priest no longer doubted the mystery and the Feast of Corpus Christi was instituted.

The Lake★★. — This is the largest lake of volcanic origin in Italy. Earth tremors constantly agitate it and change its level. At one time malaria was prevalent along its shores, so that most of the nearby towns were built on the pumice-stone hills.

The lake swarms with eels which are so delicious that in the 13C they made Pope Martin IV fall into the sin of gluttony: it is true that he was from Touraine where stewed eels with onions has many devotees. For a fault so benign Dante, who had opposed the French ever since they had exiled him from Florence, placed the cleric in Purgatory in his Divine Comedy.

Drive round the lake (68 km - 42 miles). The road runs close to the eastern shore; it turns away from the western bank and climbs into the hills, affording superb views.

The most interesting places are **Montefiascone** (p 50) and **San Lorenzo Nuovo**, which enjoys a fine view of the lake.

St. Christina's Church★ (Santa Cristina). — The Renaissance façade is adorned with a Madonna between St. George and St. Christina, in terracotta, of the school of della Robbia. The interior is supported by Roman columns. In the central apse is a polyptych by Sano di Pietro (15C Siena school). From the north aisle you enter the **Chapel of the Miracle**, where the paved floor stained by the blood of the Host is revered (see above), and then the Grotto of St. Christina, where the Altar of the Miracle, surmounted by a 9C canopy, will be found. A reclining terracotta statue of the saint at the far end is attributed to Giovanni della Robbia.

Michelin maps **988** 4 and **24** 20 — *Local map p 92* — Pop 106 464

Bolzano, the capital of the Alto Adige and formerly a possession of the Bishops of Trent, is an industrial town (electrical, paper and steelworks) and a tourist centre thanks to its proximity to the Dolomites. The town is bilingual and, in the older part, rather German in character.

■ SIGHTS *time: 1 hour*

Via dei Portici★ (Laubengasse). — This is the most characteristic and the most commercial street in the old town. It starts from the picturesque Piazza delle Erbe, where a lively fruit market is held and is lined with porticoes and 15, 16 and 17C houses with oriel windows (small loggias) and curious doorways.

Cathedral (Duomo). — Built in the Romanesque Gothic style in pinkish stone and roofed with multicoloured tiles, the cathedral is remarkable for its open belfry (14 and 16C), 65 m - 213 ft — high. The interior is plain, in the style of a German hall church, and is characterised by three aisles of equal height. The **pulpit★** is carved with Germanic realism.

Dominican Monastery (Convento dei Domenicani). — The Chapel of St. John on the south side of the chancel in the church contains a fine series of **frescoes★** dating from the 14C. Other, equally remarkable, frescoes adorn the nave and the Gothic cloisters.

Church of the Franciscans (Chiesa dei Francescani) (B A). — 14C, restored. In a chapel to the left of the chancel you will see a Flamboyant altar (1500). There are delightful little 14C cloisters, peaceful and flower decked, with graceful subdivided vaulting.

Gries Parish Church (Chiesa Parrocchiale di Gries). — *Access by Corso Libertà.* The beautiful Gothic Church of Gries, a parish pleasantly situated on the west side of the town at the foot of Mount Guncinà, contains a carved **altarpiece★** (1471) by Michael Pacher of Brunico.

Erbe (Piazza)	B	Dodiciville (Via)	B 7
Mostra (Via della)	B 15	Domenicani (Piazza)	B 8
Museo (Via)	AB	Garibaldi (Via)	B 10
Portici (Via dei)	B	Marconi (Via G.)	A 14
Walther (Piazza)	B 21	Ospedale (Via)	A 16
		Parrocchia (Piazza)	B17
Alto Adige (Via)	B 2	Stazione (Viale)	B 19
Brennero (Via)	B 3	Streiter (Via Dottor)	B 20

EXCURSIONS *see map p 92*

San Genesio Atesino★ (Jenesien) (1 087 m - 3 566 ft). — *North, 1 km - 3/4 mile — plus 1/4 hour Rtn by cable-car; departures about every hour from the Sarentino road, after the bridge over the Talvera; 2 300 lire Rtn.* A village surrounded by pinewoods. View★ of the Dolomites.

Roncolo Castle★ (Castel Roncolo or Runkelstein). — *North, 2 km - 1 1/4 miles.* An eagle's eyrie perched on a rock, the castle dates from the 13C. It was decorated with interesting frescoes in the 15C. *Open 10 am to noon, 3 to 6 pm; closed Sundays, Mondays and holidays, and from 1 November to end of February.*

The High Plateau of the Renon★ (alt about 1 200 m - 4 000 ft). — There is a splendid panorama to be seen from this green plateau which overlooks the town from the northeast. A cable-car takes one to **Soprabolzano** *(time: ascent 1/4 hour; 1 800 lire Rtn); view★* of the Dolomites; the curious "crowned girls" or limestone pinnacles *(3/4 hour on foot Rtn).* A cog railway leads from Soprabolzano to **Collalbo** *(1/4 hour),* from which there is another fine view★ of the Dolomites. A road links Bolzano to Soprabolzano.

Guncinà. — *Northwest, 2 km - 1 1/4 miles.* View★ overlooking Bolzano, the Adige basin and the Dolomites.

BORMIO Lombardy

Michelin maps **988** 4 and **24** 17 — Alt 1 225 m - 4 019 ft — Pop 4 150

Bormio is a climatic and winter sports resort with a few old buildings (painted houses, towers, churches). Bagni di Bormio, known for its hot springs (warm water swimming pool – 37°C.: 98.6°F.), adjoins the resort. A funicular and teleseat take you to Rocca *(50 minutes Rtn)* from which there is a **view★** of Bormio, lying in its basin surrounded by mountains.

To the south of Bormio both a road *(8 km - 5 miles long and narrow in certain sections)* and cable-car *(10 minutes)* lead to **Bormio 2000.** From there a second cable-car *(8 minutes)* climbs to **Cima Bianca** (3 020 m - 9 908 ft): **panorama★★★** of the surrounding valleys and the Ortlès group of glaciers.

EXCURSIONS

Road to Lakes Cancano and San Giacomo★★. — *46 km - 29 miles — about 1 1/2 hours.* At Bagni di Bormio take the Livigno road from which, soon branching off to the right, a splendid, winding road through wild landscape leads to the dams built below the sources of the Adda, at an altitude of 1 902 m and 1 950 m - 6 239 ft and 6 398 ft. These have formed the two reservoir lakes of Cancano and San Giacomo.

Valfurva★ — *13 km - 8 miles.* The picturesque road runs alongside fields before plunging between two fir clad mountains. From **Santa Caterina,** which has charming old houses, there is a **view★** of the Forno Glacier.

The road to the **Gavia Pass★★★** *(description p 116)* starts from Santa Caterina.

The BORROMEAN Islands ★★★ Piedmont

Michelin map **26** 67 — *Local map p 128*

The islands are usually approached from Stresa, Baveno or Pallanza. Day tickets are available between March and October which enable the visitor to journey from island to island, stopping at each; time: 3 hours; 4 200 lire.

The Borromean Islands are world famous; no tourist travelling in these parts should pass them by without breathing their intoxicating perfume. Since the 12C the islands have belonged to the Borromeos, a princely family who gave a saint to Italy and who, since the 17C, have created the present appearance of this marvellous archipelago.

The **Isola Bella** (Beautiful Island), which is the most famous, is also the most frequented *(guided tours, 1 April to 31 October, 8.30 am to noon and 2 to 5.30 pm; 2 500 lire; fare from Stresa or Baveno: 1 000 lire; from Pallanza: 1 000 lire).* The palace, built in the 17C, is richly furnished and decorated. Note the Medals' Room, the Great Saloon, the Conference room (where MacDonald, Mussolini and Laval met in 1935), the room in which Napoleon slept, the tapestry galleries, the Zuccarelli room and the underground rooms laid out as grottoes. The gardens, laid out in superimposed terraces, form an extraordinary museum of statuary and botanical specimens. Aromatic shrubs scent the air. From the topmost terrace, on which stands a unicorn (the Borromeo crest), there is a matchless view.

The tiny **Isola dei Pescatori** (Fishermen's Island) or Isola Superiore (Upper Island) *(fare from Stresa and Baveno: 1 000 lire; from Pallanza: 1 000 lire),* is the one on which the original atmosphere is best preserved, with the narrow alleys of the fishing village, the port and esplanade, and many viewpoints.

The **Isola Madre** (Mother Island — *same times of admission as Isola Bella; 2 500 lire; fare from Stresa and Baveno: 1 000 lire; from Pallanza: 1 000 lire)* has an 18C palace and splendid gardens, even more luxuriant than those of the Isola Bella. It contains a cypress 140 years old, the tallest palm trees in Italy and a wistaria over 80 yds long. Peacocks and golden pheasants strut slowly in the flower and botanical gardens. There is a splendid panorama of the lake shores.

BRACCIANO Latium

Michelin map **988** 25 — Pop 10 579

The smiling little town of Bracciano overlooks the lake of the same name.

Castle★. — The castle was built in the middle of the 15C by Napoleone Orsini and now belongs to the Odescalchi family. Its outside aspect, overlooking the town and the lake, is imposing. The long battlemented walls are interrupted by massive towers, rounded at the corners and semicircular on the faces. The apartments *(guided tours Thursdays, Saturdays and Sundays: 1 April to 30 September, 9 am to noon and 3 to 6 pm; 1 October to 31 March, 10 am to noon and 3 to 5 pm; 1 000 lire)* are richly furnished and decorated with stucco and frescoes. Charles VIII, King of France, lived here during the Italian wars (1495). A magnificent panorama can be seen from the parapet walk.

. **The Lake★.** — A road affording varied views leads down from Bracciano to the lake. This is of volcanic origin and symmetrical in shape. It is surrounded by hills which are cultivated or planted with olive groves and umbrella pines, and its banks are fringed with rushes.

The Paolo Aqueduct (43 km - 27 miles), built by the Emperor Trajan and rebuilt by Pope Paul V in the 17C, brings the lake water to the Paolina Fountain on the Janiculum, and so supplies the Vatican City.

In 1804 the people living near the lake saw a huge fire-balloon, launched from the parvis of Notre-Dame in Paris at the coronation of Napoleon, descend into the lake.

You may have difficulty

in finding a room for the night

during the summer season—

book well in advance.

Michelin map **988** 4

The wild limestone Brenta Massif prolongs the Dolomites beyond the Adige Valley. Its features are deep valleys, lonely lakes and sheer, multicoloured rocks, worn by erosion.

★★★TOUR STARTING FROM TRENT — *233 km - 146 miles — allow 2 days — local map below*

Tourists who can spare only half a day may be content to skirt the massif from Tione di Trento to Malè, with an excursion into the Genova Valley.

Lake Toblino★ (Lago di Toblino). — This lake is the most charming in the Sarca Valley. It appears pale green and fringed with tall rushes, against a background of rocky walls. An attractive little castle, once the summer residence of the Bishops of Trent, stands on a small peninsula.

Rendena Valley★ (Valle Rendena). — Green, sunny valley containing churches covered with 15-16C outdoor frescoes, protected by widely overhanging roofs. The church of St. Anthony the Abbot, near **Pelugo**, is small, charming, and has frescoes dating from 1493. That of St. Vigilius (San Vigilio) near **Pinzolo** has a Dance of Death (1539) by Simone Baschenis on its south wall.

Genova Valley★★★ (Val di Genova). — This valley, carved out of the granite of the Adamello Massif, is one of the best known in the Trentino for its wild grandeur. The road, which branches off north of Pinzolo, runs through chestnut groves and then climbs slopes planted with pine trees. Threading its way among jumbled rocks and skirting a torrent in which scattered boulders lie, it reaches the impressive **Nardis Waterfall** (Cascata di Nardis — 100 m - 300 ft).

Madonna di Campiglio★★. — This famous resort and winter sports centre at the head of the Rendena Valley, between the Brenta Massif to the east and the Adamello and Presanella Massifs to the west, consists of hotels and villas scattered among fir trees. Its position at the foot of the Brenta and the local walks (several small lakes) attract many tourists. There is a **view★★** of the surrounding massifs from **Monte Spinale** *(cable-car: 5 minutes)*.

Campo Carlo Magno★★. — A supposed visit by Charlemagne gave its name to this place, which in recent times has become a winter sports centre. From the pass there is a typical view of the Pietra Grande (Great Rock) and its Dolomite precipices. A cable-car climbs from Campo Carlo Magno to the Grostè Pass (Passo del Grostè), which lies at an altitude of 2 437 m - 7 996 ft — at the foot of the Pietra Grande.

Lake Tovel★★★ (Lago di Tovel). — On leaving Tuenno the road, after passing through wild gorges, reaches the clear, lonely lake, lying in the hollow of a valley whose slopes are covered with woods that shelter the last brown bears left in the Alps. Lake Tovel, which is also known as the Lago Rosso (Red Lake), sometimes takes on in summer, in certain parts, a reddish colour due to the presence of unique minute water creatures.

Andalo★. — Andalo, surrounded by great pine forests, is set in majestic scenery typical of the upper Alpine valleys.

Paganella Mountain★★ (Monte Paganella). — *From Andalo, 1/2 hour by telecabin; from Lavis, 10 minutes by cable-car.* **Panorama★★** of the Alps, the Dolomites and Lake Garda from the summit.

Molveno. — This choice resort is situated among gently sloping meadows at the north end of a great **lake★★** which lies on the floor of an amphitheatre overlooked by slopes covered with fir trees and surmounted by Dolomite precipices. The lake supplies the Santa Massenza power station to the southeast, linked to it by high-pressure mains.

The BRENTA Riviera ★★ Venetia

Michelin map **988** 5

Between Fusina and Stra, along the Brenta Canal, stand the **villas★** to which the Venetian patricians used to retire in summer, giving night fêtes by lantern light while orchestras hidden in bowers softly played the music of Vivaldi, Pergolese or Cimarosa.

Boat Trip. — During the summer *(early May to early October)*, a boat makes a tour several times a week of the Venetian Villas, recalling the well known **Burchiello**, a luxurious boat, which, in the 17 and 18C, plied along the Brenta Canal, linking Venice and Padua.

The excursion (which takes a full day) can be made from Venice or Padua; the return journey is by bus; fare: 16 000 lire (including visits, lunch and return bus journey). Apply: in Venice to C.I.T., Piazza San Marco (☎ 85480); in Padua to C.I.T., Via Matteotti 12 (☎ 25349) or to SIAMIC EXPRESS, Via Trieste 42 (☎ 664755).

As the boat glides slowly along the calm green waters of the canal, one can admire the splendid patrician villas built in the Classical style by either Palladio (p 263) or Sansovino.

Palladio built the **Villa Foscari** at **Malcontenta** in 1574. A member of the Foscari family banished his wife to it, which made her "malcontent", whence the local name for the town.

At **Stra**, the Villa Pisani or **Villa Nazionale★** *(visit on the excursion from Padua to Venice only)* is virtually a palace adorned with remarkable gardens *(description p 232)*.

Palazzo Foscarini. — A palace situated in **Mira** where Byron and Sir Thomas More stayed.

Brescia lies at the feet of the Lombard Pre-Alps, not far from Lakes Garda and Iseo. It is well known as an industrial centre for iron and steel, mechanical engineering and the manufacture of arms, which is traditional. For the tourist, however, its chief points of interest are its fine Renaissance buildings: palaces, churches, etc.

The town has been nicknamed the City of Beautiful Fountains; a 16C traveller wrote: "in this town there are so many beautiful fountains that it is a real paradise". Brescia forms a quadrilateral enclosed in fortifications. Life centres on the Corso Zanardelli, the Via delle 10 Giornate and the modern Piazza Vittoria.

Brescia was the starting and finishing point of the famous Mille Miglia (1 650 km - 1 025 miles) motor race, which was forbidden after a series of fatal accidents in 1957.

Brescia, called Brixia by the Romans, became later a Lombard duchy and then, in the 11C, a free commune. In the Middle Ages it was one of the most prosperous towns in Italy, thanks to its famous manufactures of arms and armour, which supplied all Europe until the 18C. From 1496 to 1797 Brescia was part of the Venetian domains. In 1849 it rebelled against the Austrians and resisted them for ten days, earning the nickname of Leonessa (the Lioness).

The Siege of Brescia (February 1512). — When Louis XII occupied the district of Milan, the Venetians, at the instigation of Pope Julius II, seized the town, to the cry of "Long live St. Mark!" Gaston de Foix, returning from Bologna by forced marches in abominable weather, attacked in unfavourable circumstances. During the attack Bayard, a famous French soldier (1473-1524), who was said to have "the assault of a ram and the defence of a wild boar", was severely wounded in the thigh by a pike-thrust. Thinking him dead, the French poured into the town, killing, looting, raping and drinking according to the custom of the time. The loot was worth 3 000 000 gold crowns.

Venus changed to Minerva. — In the middle of the 16C Tullia of Aragon charmed all Brescia. She was one of the most famous of the *cortigiane oneste* (well-born courtesans) who abounded in the free-thinking society of the Renaissance, taking the place reserved formerly to the Greek *haeteras* and today by the Japanese geishas. Tullia was a cultivated woman, familiar with the Greek and Latin writers, an artist and a musician, and she attracted the most distinguished company. Moretto da Brescia painted her portrait as Salome, and a diplomat described her in these terms: "She is fascinating, wise and discreet; she sings and composes melodies and motets; she is so well educated that she has no rival in conversation on any subject. Whoever meets her is instantly captivated by the charm of her person, the sound of her voice and the graciousness of her talk."

■ **MAIN SIGHTS** time: 2 1/2 hours

Piazza della Loggia★. — The citizens of Brescia are proud of their Loggia, with its graceful outline and fine decoration, which is now the town hall. The ground floor, sober and harmonious with busts in medallions in the corners, is said to have been built in 1489 to designs by Bramante. The upper storey is the work of Sansovino and Palladio. The roof, in the characteristic Palladian form, was restored in 1914.

The Palace of the Clock (Palazzo dell'Orologio), opposite the Loggia, is surmounted by Venetian *Mori* (Moorish figures — jaquemarts).

On the south side of the square are the graceful palaces of the Monte Vecchio (1484) in the Venetian Renaissance style, and of the Monte Nuovo (1497), in the Classical style, which were used as pawnbroking establishments. To the north of the square is a picturesque popular quarter with arcades and old houses.

Picture Gallery★ (Pinacoteca). — *Open 9 am to noon and 2 to 5 pm; closed Mondays and public holidays.* Here you will see works of the Brescian school, characterised by richness, refined and well balanced composition. The leader of the school was Moretto (1498-1555) a mystical and serene author of religious scenes and a remarkable portraitist, like his pupil Moroni (1520-1578) and like Romanino (1485-1566), another lavish interpreter of religious scenes in the Venetian manner.

Pictures by Moretto can be seen on the grand staircase and in three other rooms, where they are coupled with those of Romanino. The rooms containing a portrait of Henri III by Clouet, a Nun by the Master of Utrecht (early 16C), a Christ giving His Blessing and an Angel by Raphaël and three early 16C Nativities by Savoldo, Moretto and Lorenzo Lotto are remarkable. Finally, you will notice the curious Seasons, composed in the manner of Arcimboldi, and a painting attributed to Jan ("Velvet") Breughel.

Piazza del Duomo (BCY 5). — The 17C Duomo Nuovo (New Cathedral) seems to crush, with its mass of white marble, the Duomo Vecchio (Old Cathedral), a Romanesque rotunda-shaped building which succeeded a 7C basilica. A magnificent sarcophagus in rose marble surmounted by the recumbent figure of a bishop faces the doorway. In the Gothic chancel are pictures by the Brescian painters Moretto and Romanino, and, in the 11C crypt, sarcophagi.

In the square, opposite the Duomo Vecchio, is an 18C fountain.

To the left of the Duomo Nuovo the **Broletto**, a communal palace of the Middle Ages, is an austere Romanesque building dominated by the massive tower, the Torre del Popolo. On the façade is a balcony for the reading of proclamations. The court is unusual, being mediaeval on three sides and Baroque on the fourth, where strange masks grimace and grin.

■ **ADDITIONAL SIGHTS**

Via dei Musei★ (CY). — *The museums are open from 9 am to noon and 2 to 5 pm; closed Mondays and public holidays.* The **Roman Museum (M)** in this picturesque street is built into the ruins of the **Capitoline Temple** (AD 73). It contains a magnificent Winged Victory, one of the most famous pieces of Roman sculpture and fine bronze busts. To the right of the temple and the museum are the remains of the theatre and to the left of the forum, the last traces of the east gate. The **Museum of Christian Art (CY M¹)** *(being restored)* is in the Classical church of the Monastery of Santa Giulia. It contains excellent specimens of pre-Romanesque and Renaissance art, cameos, gems and *intaglio* (engraved designs) of rare purity adorning the famous 8C Cross of Desiderio, a 4C ivory casket, medals by Pisanello (15C) and the 16C Martinengo tomb. From the museum you pass into the Basilica of St. Saviour (San Salvatore), founded in the 8C (crypt). It has columns of Roman origin, Romanesque capitals and frescoes. Continuing along the Via dei Musei, note, on the left, the 12C Oratory of Santa Maria in Solario, where Ermengarda, repudiated wife of Charlemagne and daughter of the Lombard King Didier, died.

BRESCIA★

Castle (CY). — The imposing mass of a much-restored mediaeval castle stands in a park; it affords a panorama of Brescia and the plain.

It houses a small museum devoted to the Risorgimento *(open 9 am to noon and 2 to 5 pm; closed Mondays and public holidays).* An arms museum is being set up. There is also a zoological garden in the grounds.

Churches. — Nearly all contain paintings of the Brescian pictorial school, mostly by Moretto and Romanino. Note the Churches of St. Francis (San Francesco — **BY A**), Lombard Romanesque in style with Gothic cloisters; St. John (San Giovanni) **(BY E)**, built in the 15C and rebuilt in the 17C, Sts. Nazarius and Celsus (San Nazaro e San Celso) **(AZ N)** with Moretto's masterpiece, the Coronation of the Virgin, in the second chapel on the left, and a fine polyptych by Titian in the apse and, finally, St. Alexander (Sant'Alessandro) **(CZ G)** in which hangs an Annunciation by Jacopo Bellini.

EXCURSION

Monte Maddalena★ (alt 875 m - 2 871 ft). — *East, 10 km - 6 miles.* Leave Brescia by the Via Panoramica which leads to the summit of Mount Maddalena, from which there is a good panorama of the Pre-Alps, Lake Garda and the Po Plain.

BRESSANONE ★ (BRIXEN) Trentino - Alto Adige

Michelin map **988** 4 5 — *Local map p 92* — Pop 16170

Town plan in Michelin Red Guide Italia (hotels and restaurants)

Bressanone lies at the confluence of the Rienza and the Isarco. It enjoys a dry, bracing climate, with an average of 200 fine days in the year. The streets and squares have kept their old Tyrolean style of architecture, with oriel windows; the Via di Ponte Aquila is picturesque.

Cathedral (Duomo). — This is a 13C building remodelled in the 18C, with a Baroque interior. Beside the cathedral, fine 12C Romanesque **cloisters★**, whose vaulting was reconstructed with ogive arches in the 14C, are covered with curious 14 to 16C frescoes.

St. John the Baptist's Chapel (San Giovanni Battista). — 11C. The chapel opens on the cloisters. Early 13C Romanesque and 14C Gothic frescoes (Beheading of John the Baptist).

Palace of the Prince-Bishops (Palazzo Vescovile). — Enter the late Renaissance (17C) building by a bridge over a moat. Within is a three-storey court with arcades.

Novacella Monastery★ (Convento di Novacella). — *North 3 km - 2 miles; guided tours every hour: 9 to 11 am and 2 to 4 pm. Closed Sundays; 500 lire.* Leave Bressanone by ①. The monastery was founded in 1142 and remodelled in the 15 and 18C. Note the Church of Our Lady in the Bavarian Baroque style, the library, containing priceless manuscripts, the restored cloisters (frescoes by Pacher, 1480) and the remarkable fortified Chapel of St. Michael in the form of a late 12C rotunda, remodelled in the 16 and 19C.

BREUIL-CERVINIA ★★ Valle d'Aosta

Michelin maps **988** 2 and **26** 3 4 — *Local map p 50*

Breuil-Cervinia (alt 2 050 m - 6 726 ft), which stands on an impressive **site★★**, at the head of the Valtournenche, is a fashionable winter sports resort and mountaineering centre. The resort is dominated by the Jumeaux precipices (alt 3 875 m - 12 713 ft) to the west, and to the north by the huge but slender shape of the Matterhorn (alt 4 477 m - 14 689 ft).

From the resort, two teleferics *(leaving every 1/4 hour from 8 am to 5 pm — except in October and May)* will take you to many magnificent viewpoints. East is the **Rosa Plateau** (Plan Rosa) from which there are **views★★★** (alt 3 480 m - 11 418 ft; *time: 1/2 hour; 12 000 lire)*; in *3/4 hour on foot Rtn* you gain the **Theodulpass** and a **panorama★★★**. Northeast lies the **Furggen Pass** (alt 3 491 m - 11 454 ft) with another **view★★** — take the same teleferic but branch off at the Maison Plateau (Plan Maison — *time: 1/2 hour; 12000 lire)*.

From Breuil the classic excursion is to the **Blue Lake** (Lac Bleu — *south, 2 km — 1 1/4 miles)*.

The BRIANZA

Michelin map **26** 9 19 — *Local map p 129*

The Brianza lies between Milan and Lake Como and is a region of hills and calm lakes, smiling villages and villas surrounded by pretty gardens. Mulberries and vines grow there, and orchards prosper.

The fast Milan to Lecco road *(leave Milan by ② of plan)* which you leave after 30 km -19 miles — (take road to Erba), and the Bellagio road cross the Brianza, giving glimpses of **Inverigo,** whose Rotunda (1833) dominates the landscape, and **Erba,** near the pretty Lakes Pusiano and Alserio. The panoramic road to the Madonna del Ghisallo *(p 59)* begins after Asso. Total distance: 72 km - 45 miles.

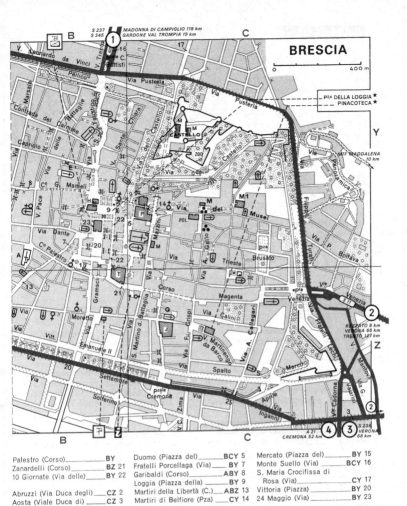

BRESCIA

S 237 MADONNA DI CAMPIGLIO 118 km
S 345 GARDONE VAL TROMPIA 19 km

PZA DELLA LOGGIA ★
PINACOTECA ★

MTE MADDALENA 10 km

RIZZATO 8 km
VERONA 66 km
TRENTO 127 km

S 236 VERONA 68 km
CREMONA 52 km
A 21

Palestro (Corso)	**BY**		Duomo (Piazza del)	**BCY** 5		Mercato (Piazza del)	**BY** 15
Zanardelli (Corso)	**BZ** 21		Fratelli Porcellaga (Via)	**BY** 7		Monte Suello (Via)	**BCY** 16
10 Giornate (Via delle)	**BY** 22		Garibaldi (Corso)	**ABY** 8		S. Maria Crocifissa di	
			Loggia (Piazza della)	**BY** 9		Rosa (Via)	**CY** 17
Abruzzi (Via Duca degli)	**CZ** 2		Martiri della Libertà (C.)	**ABZ** 13		Vittoria (Piazza)	**BY** 20
Aosta (Viale Duca di)	**CZ** 3		Martiri di Belfiore (Pza)	**CY** 14		24 Maggio (Via)	**BY** 23

If you are puzzled by an **abbreviation** or a **symbol** in the text or on the maps, look at the key on p. 40.

BRINDISI Apulia

Michelin map 988 30 — Pop 88 795
Town plans in Michelin Red Guide Italia (hotels and restaurants)

Brindisi has a modern look and is an important naval and trading port on the Adriatic. It is from here that the famous *India Mail,* used by Phileas Fogg in his journey *Round the World in 80 Days* (Jules Verne's romance), sailed after the opening of the Suez Canal in 1869.

Virgil died suddenly at Brindisi on his way home from a visit to Greece.

Roman Column★. — This column near the harbour, one of a pair that marked the end of the Appian Way, is 20 m - 66 ft — high, made of marble and ends in a capital carved with figures of the gods.

CALABRIAN Riviera ★★ (RIVIERA CALABRESE) Calabria

Michelin map 988 38 39.

Between Gioia Tauro and Reggio the *corniche* road affords fine views of the coast, the sea, Sicily and the Lipari (Æolian) Islands, with Stromboli crowned with a plume of smoke.

Gioia Tauro. — A seaside place near olive groves, in the shade of which farmhouses nestle.

Bagnara Calabra★. — A small town in a picturesque setting facing the sea, with villas scattered among gardens. From the road to the north of the town there is a fine **view★★** of the town, the Peloritani Mountains in Sicily and the Lipari Islands.

From April to July the people of Bagnara hunt swordfish, which are sometimes over 15 ft long and come from the Arctic Ocean to spawn in the Mediterranean. Until 1956 fishermen harpooned them like the ancient Greeks.

Scilla★. — The town is built at the base of the Scylla rock on which a castle stands. On this rock, according to Homer's *Odyssey,* ships which had successfully avoided the violent currents in the Gulf of Charybdis often came to grief.

A high-tension cable spans the straits to carry electric current from the Sila Massif *(p 228).*

Villa San Giovanni. — Linked with Sicily by a ferry-boat and a car-ferry service *(every 1/2 hour).*

Reggio di Calabria. — *Description p 197.*

CAMALDOLI

Tuscany

Michelin map **988** 15 — 46 km - 29 miles — north of Arezzo — Alt 816 m - 2 677 ft *18 km - 11 miles from Poppi via Moggiona.*

Camaldoli, in the heart of the mountains and the great forest, was the cradle of the Camaldulian Order, founded in the 11C by St. Romuald, who imposed strict rules.

The narrow **road**★★ affords views of Poppi and the Arno Valley, climbs the slopes of a small valley, then runs through rugged country.

(After photo by T.C.I.)

Camaldoli — View of the Monastery

The 16C church and **monastery** will be found at an altitude of 816 m - 2 677 ft at the end of a dark valley with pine clad slopes. Climbing steeply along the torrent in the midst of the forest you reach the **hermitage**★ *(open 8 to 11.30 am and 3.30 to 6.30 pm)* in a severe, secluded setting. You will see the Baroque church and St. Romuald's cell.

Behind the monastery, from the Apennine crest, there are splendid **views**★ over the Tuscan and Romagnan countryside.

CAMONICA, Val

Michelin map **988** 4.

The Val Camonica, between Lovere and Edolo, incorporates the Valley of the River Oglio; it is particularly picturesque in its upper reaches, where castle ruins stand out against the valley slopes. Engravings discovered on the rock walls of the Val Camonica and the adjacent valleys prove that the area was inhabited in the earliest times. A national park has been created in the valley.

Darfo-Boario Terme is a spa from which you can make an excursion to the spectacular **Dezzo Gorges**★, which extend for 10 km - 6 miles and through which runs the Via della Val di Scalve.

Breno, dominated by the ruins of its 10C castle and with two fine churches, St. Anthony's (Sant'Antonio) and St. Saviour's (San Salvatore), is the major centre in the valley.

CAMPO IMPERATORE ★★ Abruzzi

Michelin map **988** 26 — 20 km - 12 miles — northeast of L'Aquila — Alt 2 130 m - 6 987 ft

From L'Aquila, 22 km - 14 miles, plus 1 hour Rtn, including 1/2 hour by cable-car. The Sasso road provides glimpses of the Aterno Basin and, far away, of the Gran Sasso (2 914 m - 9 560 ft). After Paganica, the road runs through gorges before climbing and affording superb views of Monte Portella with its steep and deeply scored sides and, later, of the Val di San Franco to the west. A road and cable-car climb from Fonte Cerreto (1 100 m - 3 609 ft), 1 000 m - 3 000 ft — up to Campo Imperatore, a winter sports centre between November and May. It was from this spot that Mussolini escaped on 12 September 1943, thanks to a daring raid by German airmen whose plane landed and took off near the hotel in which the Duce had been interned after Badoglio's *coup d'Etat.*

The road continues, highly scenic, beyond Fonte Cerreto, to end at an altitude of 2 000 m - 6 560 ft — at the base of the Gran Sasso peaks.

CANOSA DI PUGLIA Apulia

Michelin map **988** 28 29 — Pop 30 854

Canosa is a town of Roman origin which still has an 11C Romanesque cathedral; this, however, has been restored and undergone Byzantine influence, as the domes show. The **tomb**★ of Bohemund, the son of Robert Guiscard (1015-1085), a Norman adventurer who campaigned in southern Italy, is a domed cube in the Moslem style, recalling that this Norman, who died in 1111, had reigned over the principality of Antioch, in Syria.

CANOSSA Emilia-Romagna

Michelin map **988** 14 — 34 km - 21 miles — southeast of Parma.

Canossa was a stronghold belonging to the Great Countess of Tuscany, Matilda (1046-1115), who supported the pope against the emperor for thirty years during the quarrel over the investiture of bishops and abbots. Only the romantic ruins, perched on a rock, remain of the imposing castle to which the Emperor Heinrich IV of Germany came through the snow, barefooted and in his shirt, to make amends to Pope Gregory VII (1077). He had to wait three days for his absolution. This is the origin of the expression "to go to Canossa", that is, to humble oneself after a quarrel.

From the top of the rock there is a **view**★ of a desolate landscape.

CAPRAROLA Latium

Michelin map **988** 25 — 19 km - 12 miles — southeast of Viterbo — Pop 4 636

This little town, built of black volcanic stone, is strung out along a rather steep slope.

Villa Farnese★. — *Guided tours from 9 am to one hour before sunset; closed Mondays, 1 January, 25 April, 1 May, first Sunday in June, 15 August, Christmas; time: 1/2 hour.* This curious villa was built in the 16C for Cardinal Alessandro Farnese. Its architect was Vignola (1507-1573), the author of a *Treatise on Architecture* (1562), who was much esteemed, worked in his youth at Fontainebleau with Il Primaticcio, and oddly mingled Classical proportions and Baroque decoration in his work.

To appreciate the theatrical appearance of the building you should stand at the end of the astonishing perspective formed by the terraces linked by great horseshoe staircases.

The **palace** has five storeys: first basements and then separate floors for prelates, nobles, knights and servants. The structure is built on a pentagonal plan round a circular court, and includes a Doric portico, an Ionic loggia and an attic.

To the left of the entrance hall a graceful and originally designed spiral **staircase**★★ can be admired. A hollow column serves to draw off rainwater.

The apartments are decorated with a series of frescoes by the Zuccaro brothers and Tempesta (16C).

Pretty views may be enjoyed in the **gardens,** ornamented with terraces, fountains and a charming *palazzina* (villa) designed by Vignola. *(To visit, ask for a written authorisation from the Soprintendenza per i Beni ambientali e architettonici del Lazio, Via Cavaletti 2, 00186 Rome.)*

(After photo by T.C.I.)

Caprarola — View of the Villa Farnese

EXCURSION

Lake Vico★ (Lago di Vico). — *West, 7 km - 4 miles.* Make for San Rocco. Bear left into the Viterbo-Ronciglione road (Via Cimina), from which there is a superb view of the lonely lake lying in a crater of the Cimini Mountains. The conical, isolated Monte Venere (834 m -2 736 ft) to the north is covered by fine beech woods; to the east you can see as far as the Valley of the Tiber and the Sabine Mountains. Branching off to the right of the Via Cimina, a small road leads to Punta del Lago, on the lake shore.

CAPRI, Isle of ★★★ Campania

Michelin map 988 27 — Pop 12512

Capri, the Island of Dreams, is one of the high spots of international tourism. Its incomparable beauty, exceptional climate and superb hotel facilities have attracted many celebrities. An almost inaccessible coast, honeycombed with fairy grottoes, and blissful scenes under sub-tropical vegetation dotted with a myriad of small white houses, form a heavenly picture framed between a sky which is always clear and a deep blue, crystal clear sea. Capri has been praised by many writers including Norman Douglas, *Footnote on Capri* and Axel Munthe, *The Story of San Michele.*

Capri captivated two Roman emperors: Augustus exchanged it for Ischia and paid several visits, and Tiberius spent the latter part of his life there in voluntary exile.

Capri appears in the form of two rocky massifs separated by a depression at the ends of which lie the two beach-harbours of Marina Grande and Marina Piccola. It is 6 km - 4 miles — long and 3 km - 2 miles — wide, its limestone mass prolonging the Sorrento promontory.

The climate is warm (average temperature, 10°C = 50°F in winter, 25°C = 77°F in summer), but is cooled by the sea-breeze in summer and favours the growth of a varied flora: pine, juniper, lentisk, arbutus, asphodel, myrtle, acanthus, etc.

Access. — There are boat services from **Naples,** Mole Beverello (some take cars): *apply to CAREMAR Company, ☎ 332860; or to the Libera Navigazione del Golfo Company, ☎ 320763 in Naples.* From **Sorrento** (some take cars): *apply to CAREMAR Company, ☎ 8781282 in Sorrento.* From **Amalfi** (in season only): *apply to Scarano Agency, Via G. Vicinanza 16, ☎ 225322 in Salerno.* From **Salerno** and **Ischia** (in season only): *apply to Scarano Agency (address above).*

There are hydrofoil services from **Naples:** *apply to CAREMAR Company (Mole Beverello), ☎ 322860 in Naples; or to ALILAURO (Port Sannazzaro at Mergellina), Via Caracciolo 13, ☎ 681041; or to the Aliscafi SNAV Company (Port Sannazzaro), Via Caracciolo 10, ☎ 660444.* From **Sorrento** (in season only): *apply to ALILAURO, ☎ 8783476 in Sorrento.* From **Amalfi** (in season): *apply to ALILAURO in Naples (address above).* From **Positano** (in season): *apply to ALILAURO in Naples (address above).*

Transport. — *Visitors are not allowed to bring cars to the island between 1 June and 30 September.*

There is a bus service *(every 1/4 hour)* linking Marina Grande and Marina Piccola with Capri and Anacapri. A funicular railway links Marina Grande with Capri *(service every 1/4 hour).*

TOUR *allow one day*

One of the charms of Capri is that wild and lonely spots can still be found near crowded and lively scenes. Walkers can wander in a constantly changing landscape; painters will find a picture at every step and archaeologists will be rewarded in their search for ancient relics. As for gourmets, they will enjoy seafood washed down with the local white wine, which is clear and appetizing.

Visitors disembark at **Marina Grande★ (Y)** with its white and colourful houses nestling round the bay framed by the spectacular cliffs of the Anacapri plateau to the right and of Mount Tiberius to the left.

Blue Grotto★★ (Grotta Azzurra) (Y) and Tour of the Island★★★. — Motor-boats take visitors from Marina Grande to the entrance of the grotto where they are transferred to small craft. It is also possible to make a tour of the island by boat with a visit to the grotto included.

Blue Grotto★★. — *Guided tour 9 am (10 am 1 October to 30 April) to sunset. Boat fare and admission: 2200 lire. Time — about 1 hour. No visits are made if there is a sea swell.*

The grotto may also be reached from Anacapri by a road *(4 km - 2 miles)* affording beautiful views.

The Blue Grotto is the most famous among the many sea caves on the island. It is 54 m long, 30 m high, 15 m wide, and the depth of the water in it is 16 m (177 ft, 98 ft, 49 ft, 52 ft). The light enters, not directly but by refraction through the water, giving it a beautiful blue colour, while submerged objects take on a fine silvery hue.

Tour of the Island★★★. — *Boat fare: 1600 lire per person. Minimum number: 15. Time — about 2 hours.*

Visitors will discover a rugged coastline with sheer cliffs dipping vertically into the sea, pierced with caves and fringed with creeks and fantastically shaped rocks.

The east and south coasts are the steepest. Starting from the east you will come first to the Bove Marino Cave (Sea Ox Cave) which derives its name from the roar of the sea gushing into the cave in stormy weather. Then round the Cape (Punta del Capo) dominated by Mount Tiberius (334 m - 1083 ft) where the Roman emperor spent the latter part of his life at Villa Iovis *(see below).* According to legend, he had his victims thrown from the impressive cliff called Salto di Tiberio.

At Punta di Tragara stand the famous **Faraglioni**, rocky islets carved into fantastic shapes by the waves. The Arsenal Grotto (Grotta dell'Arsenale) was decorated as a nymphaeum during the reign of Tiberius. Continue past the small port of **Marina Piccola** *(see below)* to reach the west coast which is less craggy with deeper coves.

The **Blue Grotto** *(see p 73)* lies on the north face of the island.

Capri★★. — Capri is like a scene in an operetta: it has little squares, little white houses, rustic alleys forming passageways with a Moorish look.

Piazza Umberto I★. — This famous piazzetta onto which all streets converge, is surrounded by the clock tower, the town hall and cafe terraces where fashionable crowds foregather. Smart shops line the busy side streets (Via Le Botteghe, Via Vittorio-Emanuele...)

Via Vittorio-Emanuele leads to Viale Matteotti. Take Via Certosa on the left.

Carthusian Monastery of St James★ (Certosa di San Giacomo). — *Restoration work in progress.* This 14C building was extensively restored in the 16C. In a cell opening on to small cloisters there are Roman statues recovered from the Blue Grotto.

Return by the Viale Matteotti, a pleasant promenade through the gardens.

Augustus Gardens (Giardini Augusto). — From the gardens which overlook Via Krupp with its hairpin bends, there is a beautiful **view★★** of Marina Piccola, the Faraglioni and Punta di Tragara.

Via Krupp★. — This narrow track clinging to the rock face leads to Marina Piccola *(about 1/2 hour)* and affords remarkable views.

Marina Piccola (Y). — Well **sited★★** at the foot of the rock wall of Monte Solaro, Marina Piccola also possesses beautiful small beaches frequented by fishing boats.

Return to Capri by bus (10 minutes).

Cannone Belvedere. — *1/2 hour on foot, Rtn.* From Piazza Umberto I go up the steps leading to the church. Past a house decorated with arches take Via Certosa on the right which is almost entirely covered. Bear left at a junction.

The visitor will discover another aspect of Capri, quiet and mysterious with its covered and winding alleys interrupted by steps. Past the old quarter the road is lined with villas and gardens, with fine views of Capri.

The Belvedere commands an outstanding **view★★** of the bay of Marina Piccola with Punta di Tragara and the Faraglioni to the left and further down the Carthusian Monastery of St. James and the Augustus Gardens.

Villa Iovis★★ (Y). — *1 1/2 hours on foot, Rtn. Open 9 am (10 am 1 October to 31 March) to one hour before sunset. Closed on Mondays. 500 lire.* Approach from Via Tiberio. Villa Iovis or Jupiter's Villa was once the Emperor Tiberius' palace. Tiberius was nearly 70 years old when he came to live here about the year 27 AD. He spent the last ten years of his life in seclusion and died at Misena.

He ruled the empire from this palace, one of the twelve built on the island during his reign and that of Augustus. News of Christ's crucifixion reached him there. Mysterious and cruel legends supported by the writings of Tacitus and Suetonius, are attached to this place and to the life led by the emperor.

Steps lead from the entrance to the excavations to the top of the headland, passing, on the way up, the impressive remains of the palace. From the palace a passage descends to a loggia surrounded by luxuriant vegetation and affording a splendid **panorama★★★** of the island.

Anacapri★★★ (Y). — *Town plan in the Michelin Red Guide Italia (hotels and restaurants).* The visitor approaches Anacapri up a most beautiful **corniche road★★★** providing breathtaking views of the sea.

Less crowded and less fashionable than Capri, Anacapri is a delightful village where life centres round the Piazza della Vittoria. Cool, shady streets thread their way between gardens, villas, little squares and white houses forming terraces, oriental looking with their flat roofs.

The via San Michele leads from the Piazza della Vittoria (bus terminus) to the **Villa San Michele** (Y A) *(open: 1 April to 30 September, 9 am to sunset; 1 October to 31 March, 10 am to 4 pm; 500 lire).* The villa was built nearly a hundred years ago for the Swedish doctor-writer Axel Munthe (died 1940) who lived there up to 1910 and described the atmosphere of the island in *his Story of San Michele* (J. Murray, London).

The house contains 17 and 18C furniture, copies of ancient works and some original pieces from the Roman era (heads of Medusa and Aphrodite), but the chief interest of a visit lies in the garden and the magnificent **panorama★★★** of Capri, Marina Grande and at the far end, Mount Tiberius.

The **Scala Fenicia**, a stairway which numbers nearly 900 steps, leads up to just below the villa. The legend is that it was built by the Phoenicians and was for a long time the only access from Anacapri to the port. This is where Axel Munthe met the old Maria "Porta-Lettere" who delivered the mail although she could not read and who is depicted in his novel.

Monte Solaro★★★ (Y). — *Reached by chair-lift from Anacapri, 9 am to 7 pm — time: 12 minutes; change of altitude 290 m - 951 ft; 1000 lire Rtn.* The chair-lift swings pleasantly above gardens and terraces planted with vines and tropical plants. From the summit there is an unforgettable **panorama★★★** of the whole island and the Bay of Naples as far as the Island of Ponza to the northwest, the Apennines to the east and the mountains of Calabria to the south.

CAPUA Campania

Michelin map 🲹🲹🲹 27 — 38 km - 24 miles — north of Naples — Pop 18417

Capua, a town which exhales the atmosphere of Old Campania, stands on the Volturno River. Ancient Capua, where Hannibal grew soft in luxury, was on the present site of Santa Maria Capua Vetere *(p 223).*

In 1501 Cesare Borgia besieged the town in the name of the pope. On 24 July he entered by treachery and massacred 5000 inhabitants. The cathedral bells ring a knell every year on the anniversary of this bloody affair.

Castle (Castello delle Pietre). — This palace of the Norman princes was built in the 11C with stones from the amphitheatre of Santa Maria Capua Vetere.

Campano Museum. — *Guided tours: 9 am to 2 pm (1 pm on Sundays); closed on Mondays and holidays.* The museum has an archaeological department (Greek vases, Roman statues and mosaics) and a mediaeval section (sculpture).

CARRARA Tuscany

Michelin map 🲹🲹🲹 14 — *Local map p 200* — Pop 70213

Carrara lies in a smiling basin on the edge of the limestone massif of the Apennines, which is rugged and spectacular and so white that it appears to be snow-clad. It is known the world over for its white marble, of unequalled texture and purity (except perhaps for that of Paros in the Cyclades Archipelago). It has been quarried since the time of the Romans and Michelangelo used to come in person to choose the blocks from which he carved his masterpieces. Among modern sculptors who visit the quarries to choose blocks on which to work is Henry Moore.

The Romanesque-Gothic cathedral (11-14C) has a façade in the Pisan style adorned with a delicately carved marble rose-window.

Colonnata and Fantiscritti Quarries★★ (Cave). — *3/4 hour by car Rtn a morning visit is preferable; take care.* The wild and broken countryside, the flow of white marble fragments and the gigantic nature of the work afford a spectacular sight. Water and sand which has an abrasive action, are flushed through the grooves of steel cables used for quarrying. The blocks are then carried down to the plain where they are cut and treated in factories.

Marina di Carrara, 7 km - 4 1/2 miles — to the southwest, is the port for shipping marble, which may be seen piled in huge stacks.

CASAMARI Abbey ★★ Latium

Michelin map 🲹🲹🲹 26 — 14 km - 9 miles — east of Frosinone.

Casamari Abbey (Abbazia), built on a lonely site surrounded by barren mountains, as the rules required, but near a watercourse, was consecrated in 1217 by Pope Honorius III. It is a typical specimen of the first Gothic buildings erected in Italy by monks from Cîteaux, in Burgundy, on the plans *(details p 115)* and according to the principles laid down by St. Bernard, the founder of the Cistercian Order. These principles were: austerity and insistence that the community must be self-supporting.

Tour. — *1/2 hour.* The gateway is interesting. Two gates, one for vehicles, the other for pedestrians, both with pointed arches, are preceded by a great semicircular arch supporting a covered gallery with paired windows. From the Renaissance onward this was the lodging of the commendatory abbot, who enjoyed the revenues of the abbey but was not compelled to reside in it.

Note on the left of the courtyard, the façade of the **abbey church,** a typically Burgundian structure with its porch in front of a fine round arched doorway, its transept tower and its rose window. The interior *(if closed, ring at the monastery door)* is spacious, austere and solemn and still displays Cistercian features: massive cruciform pillars and hanging columns supporting tall ogive vaulting; a Latin cruciform plan; a flat, shallow chancel, and a transept with square apsidal chapels. The huge 18C canopy seems out of place in such a setting.

From the church you pass into the cloisters with their twin columns. On the east side, in its traditional position, is the chapterhouse with its massive fasciculated columns.

The **monastery buildings** may be visited under the guidance of a monk, *9 am to noon and 3 to 7 pm; March to September, 9 am to noon and 3.30 to 7 pm.* One goes through the refectory, the picture-gallery and a museum.

CASERTA  ★ Campania

Michelin map **988** 27 — Pop 66898

Thirty kilometres - 19 miles — from Naples, in the middle of fertile Campania, Caserta is the Versailles of the Kingdom of Naples. It is reached by a straight, majestic avenue, flanked by side-avenues, and planted with plane trees.

■ LA REGGIA★★ *time: 2 hours*

The name designates the truly royal ensemble formed by the palace and the park.

Closed 1 January, Easter Monday to Wednesday (royal apartments only), 25 April, 1 May, first Sunday in June, 15 August, Christmas, and Mondays (if Monday is a holiday, closed the following day). Tickets (on the left as you go in) are issued up to 1/2 hour before closing time for the palace and 1 hour for the park. Royal apartments: 500 lire; park: 500 lire, plus 750 lire per vehicle. You may leave your car in the palace courtyard.

The Palace. — *Open 9 am to 2 pm (1 pm Sundays and noon holidays).* The building was begun in 1752 by Vanvitelli for the Bourbon King, Charles III, who dreamed of another Versailles, and was completed in 1774. The brick and stone palace is built on a great rectangular plan about 253 m long and 202 m wide (275 × 220 yds). The façades with outside colonnades are grand but rather monotonous: each is pierced with some 250 windows. Altogether the building contains 1 200 rooms, and 34 staircases. The inner plan includes four courts surrounded by buildings arranged round the rotunda.

From the centre of this rotunda there is a good view of the courtyards, the long vestibule, the monumental entrance, and farther off on one side, of the approach to the palace, and on the other, of the park and the grand waterfall. On the right, the monumental staircase with 116 marble steps leads to the grand vestibule which is also in the form of a rotunda: the overall architectural effect (turn when halfway up the staircase) is admirable.

The Royal Apartments, which lead out of one another, are richly decorated with gold, stucco and marble and contain Empire style furnishings and fine pavements.

The apartments of the Bourbon King Ferdinand IV (1780) include a library of 10 000 volumes and an 18C Neapolitan crib *(p 159)* with more than 1 200 figures carved upon it. In the other wing, the bedroom of Joachim Murat, King of Naples (1767-1815), contains a superb Empire bed decorated with pikes and warlike emblems.

The Park★. — *Open 9 am to one hour before sunset; 100 lire. You can use your car except on Sundays and holidays when a bus service is available.* The park was designed by Vanvitelli. With an area of some 100 ha - 250 acres — and partly on a hillside, it is planned round a 3 km - 2 mile — long vista enclosed between thickets, dotted with basins, fishponds and fountains which ends in a monumental cascade. An alley opposite the first fountain leads off on the left to the Peschiera Grande, a huge pond with in the centre, a minute island bearing a small temple. In the central alley are the Dolphin's Cascade, the Aeolus Fountain with small winged figures representing the winds, the Ceres Fountain and, finally, that of Venus and Adonis.

The great **cascade★★**, whose waters fall over massive blocks of stone from a height of 78 m - 256 ft — is fed from an aqueduct. The overflow basin is adorned with groups surrounding Diana and Acteon: Diana, bathing among the nymphs, is surprised by the hunter Acteon; he is turned into a stag by Diana and devoured by his own hounds. At the top of the cascade steps is a grotto and a good view of the park.

To the right of the cascade is the **English Garden** *(closed 1 hour before the park)*, created in 1782 for Maria-Carolina of Austria. Winding and picturesque, rich in cypresses, cedars, palms, tropical plants and artificial ruins, it is further embellished with a small lake.

EXCURSION

Caserta Vecchia★. — *9 km - 5 miles.* This little mediaeval looking town retains the imposing ruins of its 11C castle. The 12-13C Romanesque **cathedral** stands in a lonely square. It shows certain features of Moslem art as seen in Sicily, notably in the bell-turrets on the campanile and the arches of the gable on the façade. The interior, with monolithic pillars surmounted by fine capitals, contains a 12C pulpit.

CASSINO Latium

Michelin map **988** 27 — Pop 31 241

Cassino stands on the Rapido River in a wide valley surrounded by mountains. It is of Roman origin and has been rebuilt since its complete destruction in the 1939-1945 War.

The Battle of Cassino (October 1943 - May 1944). — After the capture of Naples by the Allies, the Germans made Cassino the key point in the centre of the Gustav Line, a system of fortified positions guarding the approaches to Rome.

The assaults against this bastion failed, despite the great heroism and heavy losses of the Polish Corps under General Anders, who were given the task of storming Monte Cassino in difficult terrain, strewn with land mines. Following this assault the monastery was destroyed by bombardment from the air, led by the Americans. Then the 5th U.S. Army proceeded to attack, but without success.

Following a crucial action by the French troops under General Juin, who were advancing in the Aurunci and Ausoni mountains, and the attempt by the British army to surround the German position, the final assault, with the Polish Corps as the spearhead, was launched on 17 May. After a raging battle, the Germans abandoned Cassino on the following day allowing the Allies to join forces and leaving open the road to Rome.

■ ABBEY OF MONTE CASSINO★★ (Abbazia di Montecassino)

This is one of the holy places of Roman Catholicism.

The Cradle of the Benedictine Order. — The monastery of Monte Casino, the mother house of the Benedictines, was founded by St. Benedict in 529. It was here that the saint was said to have worked many miracles and drew up a remarkably complete and precise set of rules. Intellectual study and manual labour were combined with the virtues of chastity, obedience and poverty. This was where Benedict died in AD 543, forty days after his sister, Scolastica, who had come to join him.

In the 11C under Abbot Didier the abbey was considered the richest in the world, and during the Middle Ages its influence was considerable. The library still contains numerous volumes in spite of repeated pillage and destruction. The monks were skilful artists. Miniatures in manuscripts, frescoes and mosaics attained such perfection that their technique was imitated all over Europe, notably in France, and especially at Cluny, where the miniature and the Romanesque fresco were inspired by the models of Monte Cassino, themselves based on Byzantine art.

(After photo by T.C.I.)

The Abbey of Monte Cassino

The Abbey. — *Open 7 am to 12.30 pm and 3 to 7 pm (sunset in winter).* The abbey's majestic outline can be seen from afar.

The access road branches off from the Via Casilina and climbs in hairpin bends, affording remarkable bird's-eye views of the valley. Before you reach the abbey you will see, on the right, the obelisk that commemorates the battle, and then the military cemetery, in which lie 1 100 Polish soldiers.

The abbey has been completely destroyed four times since its foundation. It was reconstructed after the bombings of 1944 to the old plans and in the Classical and Baroque styles. A balcony in one of the cloisters before the church affords a bird's-eye view of the Liri Valley.

The basilica is richly decorated with marble, stucco, mosaic and gilding. An urn containing the remains of St. Benedict and St. Scolastica has been placed under the high altar.

CASTEL DEL MONTE ★★ Apulia

Michelin map **988** 28 29 — 55 km - 34 miles — west of Bari

This massive, proud and solitary castle, standing on the top of a bluff, dominates the surrounding plain. It was built in about 1240 by the Emperor Frederick II of Swabia. In the 14C members of the House of Anjou used it first as a prison and later as a country residence and hunting lodge. The building has been considerably restored in recent years.

The Castle★★. — *Open 9 am to 1 pm and 3 to 6 pm (9 am to 2 pm 1 October to 30 April). Closed Mondays and Sunday and holiday afternoons. Time: about 3/4 hour.*

The castle is built in pale stone on an octagonal plan and furnished at the corners with eight towers, themselves octagonal and almost 24 m - 80 ft — high. It combines balance, logic and strict planning with delicate decoration.

The superb gateway, shaped like a triumphal arch, though belonging to the Gothic period, is of ancient inspiration, but the magnificent marble which used to adorn it has disappeared. After passing through the guard-house the tourist enters the great court, on to which three doorways open. The internal plan includes eight large trapezoidal rooms with ogive vaulting on the ground floor and as many on the floor above, where the decoration is elaborate, including huge, finely carved capitals, delicate window-frames and small marble columns. The arrangement of water-conduits is highly skilful.

From the summit there is a panorama of Apulia, Trani, Barletta and Andria.

There are resemblances between this dwelling, of great luxury for the period, and the castles built in Syria by the Crusaders which Frederick II had seen during a visit to the Levant.

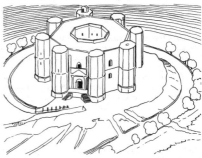

(After photo by S.M. Aeronautica)

The Castel del Monte

CASTELFRANCO VENETO ★ Venetia

Michelin map **988** 5 — Pop 28 354

Castelfranco is a picturesque stronghold surrounded by moats. It has a few pretty houses painted with frescoes on the outside walls in the Venetian manner.

The painter **Giorgione** was born here in 1478. He died at the age of 32, and little is known of his life. He exercised a peculiar influence over his contemporaries by reason of his knowledge of colour, his delicate draughtsmanship and the airy and poetical atmosphere that pervades his works. These have sometimes been confused with those of Titian, who was his pupil. The house where he was born is to be turned into a museum for his work.

The **Cathedral of St. Liberalis** (Duomo San Liberale) contains (in a chapel to the right of the chancel) a masterpiece by Giorgione, the **Madonna and Child★★** between St. Francis and St. Liberalis. From this traditional theme Giorgione has drawn a composition full of grace and nobility, balance and restraint *(the picture can be lit; 9 am to noon and 3 to 7 pm).*

EXCURSION

Cittadella. — *Southwest 12 km - 7 1/2 miles.*

This stronghold was built by the Paduans in 1220 in reply to the fortifications of Castiglione built by the Trevisans. The high brick **walls★** are 1 350 m - 1 476 yds long, with thirty-two square towers, parapet walks and four gates facing the cardinal points of the compass.

This was the former Roman town of **Stabiae**. In the 18C, the Bourbons undertook excavations, repaired the port, built shipyards which are still in use. Castellammare is an industrial centre and a thermal spa.

The **Villa Comunale**, a pleasant promenade by the sea, and the **"Strada panoramica"** (Road S 145) which overlooks the town, afford pleasant views over the Bay of Naples.

Stabiae. — Stabiae was occupied successively by the Oscans, the Etruscans and the Samnites before the Romans established their rule by the middle of the 4C. Two hundred and fifty years later, the town rebelled against the Romans and was crushed by Scylla.

It was reconstructed in small sections spread out over the area and luxury villas were built on the high ground. A friend of Cicero, the sage Marcus Marius, and Pomponius, a friend of Pliny the Elder, lived there.

The new Stabiae was recovering from an earthquake which occurred in 62 AD when it was hit in 79 AD by the eruption of Vesuvius and was wiped out along with Herculaneum and Pompeii. The naturalist Pliny the Elder, admiral of the Misena fleet, sailed to Stabiae to help those in danger and to observe the phenomenon at close range and met his death.

■ SIGHTS *time: 3/4 hour*

Antiquarium. — *2 Via Marco Mario. Open 9 am to 1.30 pm; closed Mondays, 1 January, 25 April, 1 May, first Sunday in June, 15 August and Christmas.* Objects and paintings discovered when excavation work was carried out for the ancient city of Stabiae which uncovered villas *(see below)* and a burial ground from pre-Roman times. You will notice in Room 1, a funerary stela dating from prehistoric times; in Room 4, a fresco depicting the abduction of Amymônê by Poseidon; in Room 7, a tomb dating back to the iron age; in Room 8, a milliary column (from Hadrian's reign) and a fine 3C sarcophagus; in Room 11, a statue of a shepherd carrying a kid on his shoulders. It is from the portrayal of sheperds by the Romans, itself based on the depiction of Hermes bearing the ram with the golden fleece by the Greeks, that is derived the image of the Good Shepherd adopted by the early Christians.

Roman Villa of San Marco★. — *East, 2 km - 1 miles. Open 9 am to 6.30 pm (4 pm in winter). Closed Mondays, 1 January, 25 April, 1 May, first Sunday in June, 15 August and Christmas.* Take the road to Gragnano and after 300 m - 984 ft — turn sharp left into a steep road. Past Hotel Torre Varano, the road to the left of the signpost "Scavi archeologici" leads to the villa (after 100 m - 328 ft — the road passes between two houses).

This is one of the elegant villas built in terraces facing the sea with an incomparable view of the bay and of Vesuvius. Its dimensions, extensive gardens, large swimming pool and refined architecture indicate that it was a magnificent villa built on two levels.

A large *lararium* opens on to the *atrium*. The villa had large baths. On this side of the building, there is a garden with a swimming pool. There remain only 17 columns with alternating spiral fluting from the peristyle situated on the upper level.

EXCURSIONS *local map p 162*

Monte Faito★★. — *Tour 48 km - 30 miles — about 2 hours.* Access by a steep toll road *(500 lire)*. Monte Faito is part of the Lattari range, a headland which separates the Bay of Naples and the Gulf of Salerno and forms the Sorrento Peninsula. Its name is derived from *faggeto* (beech grove). The air is pleasantly cool in summer.

The narrow, steeply winding road overlooking the coast, offers remarkable views of the Bay of Naples through openings in the vegetation, and leads to a roundabout. From the **Capi Belvedere** *(behind a bar)*, there is a wide and splendid **view★★★** of the Bay of Naples. The coast spreads out in an immense arc dominated by Vesuvius in the centre and flanked by Cape Miseno and the islands of Ischia and Procida on the right and by the Sorrento Peninsula and Capri on the left.

Follow the road uphill (signpost "Hotel Monte Faito") and after 1 km - 1/2 mile — take the turning on the right to the **San Michele Chapel** from where there is a superb and immense **panorama★★★**: the wild landscape of the Lattari mountains contrasts strongly with the smiling scenery of the Bay of Naples and the Sarno plain.

Return to the roundabout and go down to **Vico Equense**, a small health resort. The terrace road is well laid out and affords attractive **views★★** of the Bay of Naples and the Sorrento Peninsula.

Cable-car. — You can also go up to the summit of Monte Faito by cable-car *(1 April to 31 October; 800 lire)*: remarkable views unfold as you climb. From the upper station, walk to the Capi Belvedere *(see above)* — about 45 minutes Rtn.

Torre Annunziata. — *Northwest, 9 km - 5 miles.* Buried under the lava of Vesuvius seven times, the centre of the famous Neapolitan spaghetti and macaroni industry and the start of Naples' crowded industrial suburbs, this town is known for the luxurious **Roman Villa** which has been excavated near the Sarno canal bearing out the theory that on the site of Torre Annunziata formerly stood several villas lining a road along the seashore, and which early writers referred to as **Oplontis**.

The villa that has been unearthed is of exceptionally vast dimensions and the painted decoration is in the 2nd Pompeiian style *(p 187)*. It was an imperial villa, which probably belonged to Poppea, wife of Nero. You may visit the villa *(open 9 am to 1 hour before dusk)* except for the part where excavation work is in progress.

CASTELL'ARQUATO Emilia-Romagna
Michelin map **988** 13 — 41 km - 25 miles — west of Parma — Pop 4 452

This mediaeval town is built in terraces on a hill. The chief buildings will be found on the summit, in the delightful little **Piazza del Municipio★**. They include the 14C Rocca or castle, and the 13-15C fortified Palazzo Pretorio with an outside stairway, a loggia and a bell-tower.

The 12C Romanesque **collegiate church** shows remarkable unity of design and has four apses. The plain, harmonious interior contains interesting capitals. A charming little Renaissance cloister *(apply to the sacristan)* leads to the parish museum, which contains precious Byzantine embroidery and 15 and 16C gold plate.

From the Piazza della Rocca there is pleasant view of the Arda Valley.

Castelli Romani or Roman Castles is the name given in the Middle Ages to the region southeast of Rome. Thirteen villages were converted into fortified places by the Patricians fleeing from the anarchy prevailing in Rome. Their sites were Frascati, Grottaferrata, Marino, Castel Gandolfo, Albano Laziale, Ariccia, Genzano, Nemi, Rocca di Papa, Rocca Priora, Monte Compatri, Monte Porzio Catone and Colonna.

Nowadays, it is a favourite recreation spot for the Romans who are attracted by its cool climate, the distant views and the bright golden light.

Geographical and Historical Notes. — The Castelli are in the region of the **Alban Hills** (Colli Albani) which are of volcanic origin. They form a great circle whose crest encloses a vast crater, itself pitted with small secondary craters in which lie lakes.

Vegetation includes pastures and chestnut groves on the upper levels and, lower down, olives and vines. The latter produce the famous Castelli wine. The black volcanic earth in the valleys grows excellent early vegetables.

The history of the Alban Hills is closely linked to that of Rome. Cicero and the Emperors Tiberius, Nero and Galba had summer villas in the area and Cato the Censor was born in 234 BC near Camaldoli.

★★TOUR STARTING FROM ROME

122 km - 76 miles — allow one day — Local map below

Leave Rome by Via Appia Nuova.

From Via Appia Nuova, you will enjoy fine views of the Roman Campagna: remains of aqueducts and Villa dei Quintili on the Via Appia Antica.

Castel Gandolfo. — Castel Gandolfo stands on the edge of a crater overlooking Lake Albano. It is the summer residence of the Pope.

Alba Longa. — The site of ancient Alba Longa has been identified as that of Castel Gondolfo. It was the most ancient town in Latium founded, according to legend, about 1150 BC. Its rivalry with Rome found expression in the famous combat of the Horatios and the Curiaces. The two cities, weary of a costly war, decided to settle their quarrel by confiding their fortunes to three champions each: the three Horatios for Rome and the three Curiaces for Alba. At the first clash two of the Horatios were killed and all three Curiaces were wounded. At this the last Horatio pretended to flee in order to separate his adversaries and then faced about and felled them one by one. On his return to Rome, Horatio found at the Capena gate, his sister Camilla mourning for her fiancé, Curiace, and cursing Rome as "the one object of her hatred". He killed her and was arrested but later acquitted.

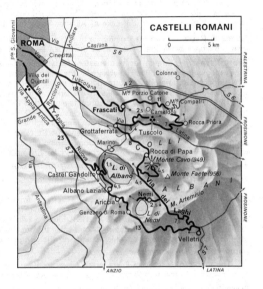

CASTELLI ROMANI

Papal Villa (Villa Papale). — *Not open to visitors.* The entrance to the villa is in the main square. The Holy See acquired "Castello" Gandolfo at the end of the 16C. In 1628, Urban VIII had a villa built by Maderno on the site of Domitian's Villa (81-96 AD) which extended as far as the present town of Albano Laziale. The villa houses the astronomical observatory (Specola Vaticana) since the time of Pope Pius IX.

Lake Albano★ (Lago di Albano). — From a terrace at the entrance to the village there is a fine **view★** of the lake. A road leads from Castel Gandolfo to Lake Albano which lies in the crater of an extinct volcano.

Albano Laziale. — Its name is derived from that of Domitian's villa, Villa Albana.

Church of Santa Maria della Rotonda★. — *At the far end of an alleyway at right angles to Via Aurelio Saffi.* The church was built in a nymphaeum in Domitian's villa. Its ancient brickwork has been restored. Impressive 13C Romanesque campanile.

Porta Pretoria. — *At the bottom of Via A. Saffi in Via A. De Gasperi.* Ruins of the gateway to a fortress built by Septimus Severus (193-211 AD).

Villa Comunale★. — *Piazza Mazzini.* In this large public garden are scattered ruins of a villa which once belonged to Pompey (106-48 BC).

Tomb of the Horatios and the Curiaces★. — *On the road to Ariccia, on the right and below the road.* This tomb is made up of large tufa blocks bounded by truncated cones. In fact it dates only from the latter part of the Roman Republic.

Ariccia. — The main square adorned by two fountains is the achievement of Bernini (1664). On the left is the mansion of the Chigi, a banking family, who became the owners in the 17C; on the right, the **Church of the Assumption** with two elegant porticos (the domed interior on a circular plan is worth a visit).

Velletri. — Velletri witnessed all the events of Italian history. It made a stand against Joachim Murat, was conquered by Fra Diavolo, leader of the Calabrese bandits, it was the scene of fights between supporters of Garibaldi and Neapolitan troops and was damaged by the bombings during the second World War. It is now a prosperous town situated on the southern slope of the crater in the midst of the Alban Hills, and is the centre of a good wine-growing district.

In Piazza Cairoli stands the impressive 14C **Trivio Tower**.

CASTELLI ROMANI★★

Chapter Museum. — *Open Saturdays 3 to 6 pm and holidays 9 am to 12.30 pm; 500 lire.* The museum contains fine paintings (Madonna and Child by Gentile da Fabriano, 15C) and precious objects (remarkable 11C reliquary cross, 14C vestment belonging to Benedict XI etc...).

From Velletri turn back and take the Via dei Laghi on the right.

Via dei Laghi★. — The road winds through groves of chestnut and oak trees.

Nemi. — Nemi occupies a pleasant **site★★**. It is built in the shape of an amphitheatre on the steep slopes of a crater in which Lake Nemi lies. A tower of the Castle of Ruspoli subsists from the "Castello" of the Middle Ages. In June you can taste delicious wild strawberries.

Lake Nemi (Lago di Nemi). — The road winds down through fields of daisies, poppies and strawberries. The lake is called the Mirror of Diana because the sacred grove near the goddess's temple used to be reflected in it. In 1929 the level of the lake was lowered by 9 m - 30 ft — to uncover two galleys dating from the time of Caligula (37-41 AD). They were destroyed by fire during the war and the remains are kept in the nearby museum *(closed).*

Return to the Via dei Laghi then bear left and take the road on the right to Monte Cavo.

Monte Cavo. — Alt 949 m - 3 124 ft. *By the toll road: 300 lire.* Alongside the steep road are the large flagstones of the Roman Via Sacra leading to the Temple of Jupiter which crowned Monte Cavo. There in the 5C BC met the representatives of cities belonging to the Latin League. Rome was a member until the 4C BC when it triumphed over the other cities. This marked the beginning of its expansion in the peninsula and the birth of Latium.

The place of the Temple of Jupiter has been taken by a monastery, which in turn has been converted into an hotel-restaurant. From the nearby promenade there is a **view★** of the Apennines, the Castelli Romani, the Lake of Albano, Rome and the Roman Campagna.

Rocca di Papa. — The **site★** of Rocca di Papa is picturesque: the country spreads like a fan over the slopes of Monte Cavo, facing the Alban lakes and mountains, and is rich in game.

Grottaferrata. — Known for its monastery founded in 1004, on the site of a Roman villa, by Greek monks from Calabria. The **abbey★**, at the end of a street at right angles to the street that runs through Grottaferrata, is surrounded by ramparts and ditches added in the 15C, giving it the appearance of a fortress. Monks of the Greek Orthodox Church keep it today.

The church is fronted by a portico containing a fine 10C marble font *(on the left).* It has a fine Byzantine doorway decorated with carvings, 11C carved wooden doors, and an 11C mosaic. Inside (restored in the 18C), the triumphal arch is decorated with a great 12C mosaic of the Pentecost. On the right side, the Chapel of St. Nilus has a 17C coffered ceiling and is adorned with frescoes (1608-1610) by Domenichino. In the south aisle is the *crypta-ferrata*, a room of the Roman villa which was converted for Christian worship in the 5C.

Take Via Latina, and then the road on the left to Tuscolo.

Tuscolo. — It was in a villa at ancient Tusculum that Cicero gave a series of lectures which were published under the title *Tusculanae Disputationes.*

The city was the fief of the Counts of Tusculum; from the 10 to 12C this powerful family governed most of the Castelli and extended their rule to Rome to which they gave several popes. It was completely destroyed in 1191 during a battle with the Romans and was never rebuilt. Some vestiges remain; the ruins of a small theatre and beyond those of a cistern can be seen on the way to the cross which stands on the site of the fortress.

Return to Via Latina and bear left.

The road climbs to **Rocca Priora** which clings to the north ledge of the great crater formed by the Alban hills and from which there are fine views of **Monte Compatri** and **Monte Porzio Catone.**

Frascati★. — All the gilded youth of Rome came here for recreation. From the main square there is a wide view as far as Rome and of the Villa Aldobrandini.

The fame of Frascati is based on its white wine and its 16 and 17C villas. A fine example is **Villa Aldobrandini★** which is adorned with terraces, paths with clipped trees, fountains and rockeries. *The gardens only are open, mornings only. Apply to Azienda di Soggiorno e Turismo, 1 Piazza Marconi; ☎ 940-331 — closed Sundays.*

Via Tuscolana leads back to Rome and goes past **Cinecittà**, the Italian "Hollywood".

CASTIGLIONE OLONA — Lombardy

Michelin maps ▨ 3 and ▨ 18 — 12 km - 7 miles — southeast of Varese — *Local map p 129* — Pop 7 075

Castiglione is an old village of which Cardinal Branda Castiglioni (1350-1443) was the benefactor. The early Renaissance Castiglioni mansion stands in the main square, together with a small 15C church built on a square plan. Surmounted by a dome this edifice is in the style of the Florentine architect Brunelleschi. On the façade are colossal 15C terracotta statues of St. Anthony the Abbot and St. Christopher.

Higher up, in the village, is the Gothic **collegiate church.** A Tuscan painter, Masolino da Panicale, who worked with Masaccio in the same style as he between 1418 and 1430, painted, in 1428, delicate **frescoes★** depicting the Life of the Virgin. In the nearby baptistry the same painter executed, in 1435, other admirable frescoes depicting the Story of St. John the Baptist, the Baptism of Jesus, etc.

Castelseprio. — *6 km - 4 miles to the south.* The simple church (7-8C) in this village contains remarkable **frescoes★** (7-8 or 9C) in the Byzantine tradition.

CATANZARO — Calabria

Michelin map ▨ 39 — *Local map p 228* — Pop 93 538
Town plan in Michelin Red Guide Italia (hotels and restaurants).

Catanzaro is a busy town built on a hill within sight of the sea. Founded in the 10C by the Byzantines it was named the Magnificent and Very Faithful by Charles V, on whose behalf it had resisted the French troops of Marshal de Lautrec (1528). Also famous for its silk industry, introduced from the East in the 11C, it specialised in making velvet. In 1470 artisans from Catanzaro taught the weavers of Tours to weave the cloth known as *gros de Tours.*

In the nearby villages, notably at **Tiriolo** *(18 km - 11 miles)* women still wear the delightful, vividly coloured, local costume.

Villa Trieste. — From the Piazza M. le Pera go down towards the villa's **public garden★** covering the eastern edge of the ridge on which the town stands. There is a beautiful view of the valley sloping down towards the sea.

St. Dominic's Church (San Domenico). — At the altar (early 17C) in coloured marble in the north transept, stands the altarpiece of the **Madonna of the Rosary★.** The central panel depicts the Virgin and Child giving a rosary to St. Dominic. Fifteen small panels relate scenes from the life of the Virgin and of Jesus. The polyptych attributed first to Palma the Elder and then to Titian, is probably the work of a late 16C painter of the Neapolitan school (Fabrizio Santafede?) who was influenced by Venetian painters working in southern Italy. The painting is remarkable for its draughtsmanship (two angels at the top) and the harmony, softness and delicacy of its colours.

CAVA DE' TIRRENI Campania

Michelin map **988** 27 — 7 km - 4 miles — northwest of Salerno — *Local map p 45* — Pop 51 007

Cava de' Tirreni is a summer resort on a green and airy site, surrounded by plantations of tobacco and fruit trees.

Abbey of the Most Holy Trinity★ (Abbazia della Santissima Trinità). — *West, 4 km — 2 1/2 miles. Guided tours, 9 am to 12.30 pm. Closed 1 January, from Wednesday before Easter to Tuesday after Easter, Whit Sunday and the following Monday and Tuesday, and Christmas; to see the monastery, apply to the custodian.* The church, with its elegant 18C façade, contains a fine pulpit and a paschal candelabrum, both 12C. In the monastery are Romanesque cloisters with a few 14 and 15C frescoes (St. Louis of Toulouse and St. Stephen of Hungary), the "Lombard cemetery", the 11C crypt on Roman columns used again, and a museum arranged in the 13C Hall of Honour.

CERTALDO Tuscany

Michelin map **988** 14 — 47 km - 29 miles — southwest of Florence — Pop 15 899

The village of Certaldo is built of pink brick in the attractive Elsa Valley. Here, Giovanni Boccaccio, the writer and incomparable narrator, the friend of Petrach, grew old and died in 1375. He was born in Paris in 1313, the son of a merchant, Boccaccio di Chellino da Certaldo and a high born Frenchwoman.

When a young man at the court of Naples, **Boccaccio** fell in love, in a church, with the natural daughter of the Good King Robert of Anjou, the blonde Maria d'Aquino, whose praises he sings under the pretty name of Fiammetta (Little Flame). Though tender at heart, Boccaccio was a mocker of all things; he represented the Italian *bourgeois* of the 14C, in love with pleasure and with letters. He became a canon but remained both gracious and cynical. At Florence, in a rhythmic, limpid style, he composed his *Decameron,* ten days, in which ten youths and ten women describe, sometimes with a touch of irony, the charm of the countryside and its cultured life under the Renaissance.

In the **upper town,** which is girt with ramparts, the **house and museum of Boccaccio,** largely destroyed during the war, has been rebuilt *(open 9 am to noon and 3 to 7 pm — 6 pm 1 October to 31 May).* Still higher up is the 13C Church of St. James (San Jacopo), where the storyteller now lies: a stone, laid in 1954, marks the spot where he was buried; the memorial against the south wall was erected in 1503.

Nearby is the Palazzo Pretorio *(open 9 am to noon and 3 to 7 pm; closed Mondays; 300 lire),* with a façade adorned with terracotta or marble coats of arms, a small arcaded court and Italian style staircases. Inside are 15C frescoes by Pier Francesco Fiorentino. From the top of the tower there is a fine view of the town and the Elsa Valley.

CERVETERI Latium

Michelin map **988** 25 — southeast of Civitavecchia — Pop 10 532

The Etruscan town stood to the east of the present Cerveteri. Southeast and northwest of ancient Caere were the two vast necropolises of Monte Abetone and Banditaccia separated from the town by two gorges (Fosso della Mola and Fosso del Manganello).

Historical Notes. — Ancient Caere was one of the great maritime centres of the Etruscans. It was founded in the 8C BC and attained great prosperity in the two following centuries, a period of Etruscan expansion overseas and of victorious warfare, with the support of the Carthaginians, against the Greek colonies. Caere was then the centre of a refined culture: many sanctuaries were built.

The 4C saw Caere decline. In 384 BC the tyrant Denys of Syracuse captured the port of Pyrgi (now Santa Severa) and ravaged the sanctuary which stood there. The city was subjugated by Rome in the early 3C and continued to decline under the Empire and in the Middle Ages. The population was decimated by malaria, and fearing Saracen invasions, abandoned ancient Caere for the present site.

Excavations were undertaken in the 19C and work has been carried out since 1911. Objects found during excavations at Caere are to be seen in the British Museum and the Louvre in Paris, and, in greater number, in the Vatican Museums and the Etruscan Museum at the Villa Giulia in Rome. A **museum** installed in Palazzo Ruspoli at Cerveteri displays recent finds.

■ **BANDITACCIA NECROPOLIS★★ (Necropoli della Banditaccia)** *time: 1 1/2 hours*

2 km - 1 1/4 miles — north of Cerveteri. Open 1 May to 30 September, 9 am to 1 pm and 4 to 7 pm; the rest of the year, 10 am to 4 pm (11 am to 4 pm Sundays and holidays). Closed Mondays, 1 January, 25 April, 1 May, first Sunday in June, 15 August, and Christmas; 500 lire.

The access road is lined with *tumuli* (earth mounds) marking graves. The extent and splendour of the remains of this cemetery show the importance of the town and the mastery of the Etruscans as regards funerary architecture. The Etruscans believed in the afterlife and often built their tombs on the same pattern as their houses. Consequently, the discovery of the burial chambers provided useful information on the life of the Etruscans.

CERVETERI

In a pleasant setting of cypresses, broom and pine trees, the necropolis is like a city with its main thoroughfare lined with tombs. There are underground burial chambers reached through a door simply decorated with fine mouldings. A vestibule leads into the burial chambers which often contain two funeral beds placed side by side: one is adorned with a small column if the deceased is a man (the breadwinner) and the other with a small canopy in the case of a woman (the guardian of the home).

Other tombs are characterised by *tumuli* and usually date back to the 7C BC. They are conical earth mounds *(tumuli)* resting on a circular base which is sometimes decorated with mouldings, with the burial chambers underneath.

Tomba dei Rilievi★★. — *On an esplanade shaded by a big oak tree. Apply to the keeper.* It is one of the most recent (4-2C BC) tombs without tumulus. According to an inscription inside, it belonged to the Matuna family. Its main interest lies in the painted stucco bas-reliefs decorating the walls of the underground chamber and giving a realistic picture of everyday Etruscan life. It is possible to identify dogs, various weapons, tongs, knives, cooking utensils, etc.

CERVINIA - BREUIL *See Breuil-Cervinia p 70.*

CESENA Emilia-Romagna
Michelin map 988 15 — Pop 90046

The town nestles at the foot of a hill on which stands the great 15C Castle of the Malatestas. It contains the Renaissance **Malatestiana Library★** (Biblioteca Malatestiana). The interior comprises three long aisles with vaulting supported on fluted columns with fine capitals. On display are valuable manuscripts, including some from the famous school of miniaturists at Ferrara, as well as the Missorium, a great silver-gilt dish possibly made in the 4C. *Open weekdays: 15 June to 15 September, 8.30 am to 12.30 pm and 5 to 7 pm (4 to 6 pm from 1 September); the rest of the year, 9.30 am to 12.30 pm and 4 to 6 pm. Sundays and holidays, 10 am to noon 15 June to 15 September only. Closed Monday mornings, 14 and 15 August and holidays between 16 September to 14 June.*

EXCURSION

Bertinoro. — *West, 11 km - 7 miles. Take the Forlì road and after 8 km - 5 miles — turn left.* Bertinoro is famous for its panorama and its yellow wine (Albana). In the middle of the village is a "hospitality column" fitted with rings, each corresponding with a local hearth. The ring to which the traveller tethered his horse used to decide which family should be his hosts. From the nearby terrace there is a wide **view★** of the Romagna.

CESENATICO Emilia-Romagna
Michelin map 988 15 — 15 km - 9 miles — northeast of Cesena — Pop 20183

Cesenatico is a large seaside resort on the Adriatic. Its **canal-port★**, with many boats with brightly coloured sails and trawlers is picturesque. The port built in 1302 was an outlet for Cesena. Nearby is an old fishermen's quarter with low houses and a fine arcaded square.

CHIANCIANO TERME★★ Tuscany
Michelin map 988 15 — Pop 7294

Chianciano is an important and fashionable thermal spa, pleasantly situated within view of a pretty, hilly landscape. The sulphur and calcium springs were known to the Etruscans and Romans and are now used against disorders of the liver. It has up-to-date equipment, both residential and medical, and fine, shady parks.

CHIAVENNA Lombardy
Michelin maps 988 3 and 24 14 — north of Lake Como — Pop 7587

Chiavenna is the capital of the Valchiavenna, a region of wild valleys, and the key *(chiave)* to the roads over the Splügen and Maloja Passes.

The **Collegiate Church of St. Lawrence** (San Lorenzo) is dominated by a tall slim campanile. A 17C four-sided doorway opens on to the baptistry which contains a curious Romanesque baptismal basin (1156) on which the ceremony of baptism is depicted as it was practised 800 years ago. In the treasury is a valuable lectern-cover of 12C Rhenish (or French) workmanship. *(To visit the baptistry and treasury, apply to the sacristan.)*

Close by, on the rock known as Il Paradiso is a botanical and archaeological garden *(open 2 to 5 pm; closed Mondays; 200 lire).* At the foot of the rock stands the 15C Palazzo Balbiani which has been rebuilt.

EXCURSION

Road from Chiavenna to the Splügen Pass. — *30 km - 19 miles.* This road is one of the boldest and most spectacular in the Alps. The **Campodolcino-Pianazzo section★★★** is the most amazing, with tunnels and hairpin bends superimposed on the flank of a precipice.

CHIETI Abruzzi
Michelin map 988 27 — Pop 56459
Town plan in Michelin Red Guide Italia (hotels and restaurants).

Chieti, the ancient Roman Theate Marrucinorum, is built on the summit of a hill planted with olive trees and offers varied panoramas. Corso Marrucino is the town's busiest street.

Villa Comunale. — At the west end of the town these pleasant **gardens★** are planted with acacias, cedars and Judas trees. In the evening the people of Chieti come here to take the air and the young people play the tambourine. From the esplanade behind the villa there is a fine **view★** southwards of the Maiella Massif.

Abruzzi Archaeological Museum. — A museum has been installed in Villa Comunale *(open 2 May to 30 September, 9 am to 1 pm and 4 to 7 pm (9 am to noon only Sundays and holidays); the rest of the year, 9 am to 12.30 pm only (noon Sundays and holidays). Closed Mondays, 1 January, 1 May, first Sunday in June, 15 August and 25 December).* On the ground floor are exhibited Roman statues and objects dating from the Republic and the Empire. Note in particular a marble statue of Hercules (in the vestibule), discovered in Alba Fucens near Avezzano, dating from the late Grecian period; in Room 3, a portrait of Sylla; in Room 5, a fine bronze of Hercules leaning on his club, probably executed by a Taranto workshop in the 1C BC; in Room 9, a funeral couch from Amiternum, near L'Aquila, a rare example of bronze work, probably from Taranto workshops. On the first floor which is devoted to pre-Roman Italic civilisation, is the **Warrior of Capestrano** (a necropolis southeast of L'Aquila) dating from the 6C BC, which is remarkably well preserved.

Roman Remains. — Chieti has preserved much from its heritage as a Roman city. Three adjoining and minute temples were discovered in 1935 near the post office and the Corso Marrucino. The temples' small rubble walls rest on massive foundations. A little farther to the east, beside the national road S 81, water tanks cut out of the hillside and intended to supply water for the baths remain fairly well preserved.

CHIUSI Tuscany

Michelin map 📖 15 — 54 km - 34 miles — southwest of Perugia — Pop 9 108

Standing on an easily defensible height, Chiusi is today a quiet and hospitable little town. It was once one of the twelve sovereign cities of Etruria.

Etruscan Museum★ (Museo Etrusco). — *Open 9 am to 2 pm; Sundays and holidays, 9 am to 1 pm. Closed Mondays.* The museum is at the entrance to the town, near the cathedral, and contains many sarcophagi and other objects from the burial grounds in the neighbourhood. Very fine and of great interest are the *canopae* or cremation urns in human form, designed to hold ashes and adorned with griffins to frighten away evil spirits. There are also a bronze vase for offerings to Charon, the ghostly ferryman of the Styx, jewels and *cippi*, rounded tombstones, which were placed on the graves.

If you have a car you can be accompanied by the museum keeper to the remaining and most interesting tombs. One of them, the **Tomba della Scimmia**, the Monkey Tomb, dates from the 5C BC, and is adorned with paintings.

CINGOLI Marches

Michelin map 📖 16 — Pop 10 528

The former Roman town of Cingulum is famous for the **panorama★★** stretching away to the sea, which has earned it the nickname Balcony of the Marches.

Note the 13C Church of Sant'Esuperanzio and that of St. Nicholas (San Nicolò), which contains the Madonna of the Rosary (1539) painted by the Venetian, Lorenzo Lotto.

CINQUETERRE ★★ Liguria

Michelin map 📖 13 — *Local map p 200*

Lying northwest of the Gulf of La Spezia, the **Cinque Terre** (Five Lands), which up till now have been linked only by a mule track and accessible by rail or water, form one of the most astonishing districts in Italy. The old customs of the Ligurian fishermen survive in the setting of a steep, rugged coast, wild but hospitable, where famous vines yield a strong, sweet wine known to the natives as *sciacchetrà*.

A *corniche* road *(work now suspended)* will eventually connect La Spezia and Sestri Levante; the Spezia-Manarola section is finished. Monterosso has recently become accessible by way of Levanto or the Via Aurelia (fork at Pian di Barca).

■ TOWNS AND SIGHTS

Corniglia. — A small church adorned with a rose window.

Manarola. — Its houses cling to the slope which goes down to the dock. The small church dates from the 14C. The Via dell'Amore (Road of Love), a curious road hewn out of the rock and overhanging the sea, links Manarola and Riomaggiore.

Monterosso al Mare. — This is the only place with an equipped beach.

Riomaggiore. — This mediaeval village lies in the narrow valley of a torrent.

Vernazza★. — This, with Riomaggiore, is the most typical and full of character of the Cinqueterre. Narrow streets, arcades, little squares, old houses, forts and bell-towers in a marvellous setting form a picture of unforgettable shapes and colour.

CITTÀ DI CASTELLO Umbria

Michelin map 📖 15 — Pop 37 335

Città di Castello, on the left bank of the Tiber, is a notable art centre. The former Roman Tifernum has given its name to the present inhabitants, who call themselves Tifernati.

Communal Palace (Palazzo Comunale). — This elegant Gothic building with paired windows dates from the 14C.

Cathedral (Duomo). — The cylindrical campanile only subsists of the original 12C Romanesque church. The present church dates from late 15C to early 16C. The Baroque façade was added between 1632 and 1646. The dome is late 18C. A small museum in the sacristy displays a collection of silver church utensils (5-6C) and a remarkable 12C **altarfront★** *(paliotto)* in silver-gilt.

Vitelli alla Cannoniera Palace (Palazzo Vitelli alla Cannoniera). — The palace (1521-1532) includes a picture gallery. Vasari designed the façade. The first gallery contains pictures by painters of the 14C and 15C; in the next hangs a Saint Sebastian by Luca Signorelli and in Gallery III are two standards painted by Raphaël in his youth, a Coronation of the Virgin by Ghirlandaio, and a Head of Christ by Just de Gand. There are also several délla Robbia terracottas on display.

CIVIDALE DEL FRIULI ★ Friuli-Venezia Giulia

Michelin map 988 6 — 17 km - 11 miles — northeast of Udine — Pop 11 279

The ancient Forum Julii in time became the chief town of the Friuli district and gave the town its modern name. Its setting and monuments add to its attraction. It was for long independent and became the residence of the Patriarchs of Aquileia (p 52). From the 15C onwards it belonged to Venice. It was hit by the earthquakes that ravaged the district in 1976.

Cathedral (Duomo). — The Cathedral which dates from the middle of the 15C, was extensively rebuilt in the 16C. The sober, tasteful façade, marking the transition from Gothic to Renaissance, is pierced with an elegant central doorway. The interior is Renaissance with Gothic survivals and the campanile is Classical.

The nave, of a noble simplicity, has gigantic columns and wide arcades. The 12C Veneto-Byzantine silver-gilt altarpiece of the high altar was presented by the Patriarch, Pellegrino II. The **chapter museum** (open 9 am to noon and 2.30 pm to sunset) opens off the south aisle. It contains the valuable baptismal font of the Patriarch Callisto, redesigned in the 15C with some 8C features (delicate symbolic reliefs: peacocks, griffins, etc.) and the 8C "altar" of Duke Ratchis in marble with carved slabs depicting Christ Triumphant, the Epiphany and the Visitation.

The **Communal Palace**, Palazzo Comunale, facing the cathedral has pointed arcades and is decorated with coats of arms.

Archaeological Museum★. — Open 9 am to 1.45 pm (12.45 pm Sundays and holidays). Closed Mondays, 1 January, 25 April, first Sunday in June, 15 August and 25 December. The museum which was damaged by an earthquake has been restored and reorganised.

Tempietto★★. — Temporarily closed. At the end of the square, to the left of the cathedral, pass under an arch, go down some steps and turn to the left into a street spanned by two monumental gateways. The Oratory of Santa Maria in Valle, known as the Tempietto or Little Temple, stands on a pretty site near the Piazza San Biagio. This is a charming building in which the Byzantine or Romanesque styles are mingled (8C). Inside note the decoration of the end wall in stylised stucco of surprising dignity, depicting vine leaves and six enigmatic women. Some of the frescoes date from the 8C; the stalls are Gothic.

CIVITA CASTELLANA Latium

Michelin map 988 26 — 36 km - 22 miles — southeast of Viterbo — Pop 15 911

Civita Castellana occupies the site of the ancient Falerii Veteres which was destroyed by the Romans after a rebellion in AD 241. The town was not rebuilt until the 8 or 9C.

Cathedral (Duomo). — This 11C Romanesque building is fronted by an elegant **portico★** built in 1210 by the Cosmati (see p 201). It is supported by Ionic columns, and the whole structure foreshadows the Renaissance style. The right doorway has a tympanum decorated with a mosaic by Jacopo Cosma, depicting Jesus giving His Blessing. The interior, remodelled in the 18C, contains two 13C superb marble and mosaic pulpits made by the Cosmati.

Castle (Rocca). — Pope Alexander VI had this massive fortress built by Sangallo the Elder between 1494 and 1500. Cesare Borgia lived in it, and the political prisoners of the Papal State were held there in the 19C.

EXCURSIONS

Falerii Novi★. — Northwest, 6 km - 4 miles. Leave Civita Castellana by the Vignanello road. This city was built by the Romans after the destruction of Falerii Veteres. Its **ruins★** stand on the left of the road among fields, surrounded by a wall more than 2 100 m - 1 1/4 miles — long, with fifty towers and nine gates. Near the West Gate stand the romantic ruins of the Romanesque Church of Santa Maria di Falleri.

Castel Sant'Elia. — Southwest, 17 km - 11 miles. Leave Civita Castellana by the road to Nepi and at the entrance to the town turn left. The 11C Romanesque Basilica of Sant'Elia stands on a pretty site. The interior is divided into three aisles by antique columns. You will notice the 12C pulpit and ciborium (canopy) and the 11-12C frescoes showing Byzantine influence, in the transept and apse.

CIVITAVECCHIA Latium

Michelin map 988 25 — Pop 47 988

Civitavecchia — formerly Centumcellae in the Roman era —, which has been the port of Rome since the reign of Trajan (AD 98-117), also handles maritime traffic with Sardinia. The port is guarded by the Fort of Michelangelo, which was realised by Bernini and Sangallo the Younger and completed by Michelangelo.

Succeeding the son of David, the painter, Henri Beyle, alias **Stendhal** (1783-1842), a lover of Italy, was appointed Consul at Civitavecchia in 1821, thanks to his friends in the Liberal party. He still held the position at the time of his death. The post left its occupant plenty of leisure and Stendhal took advantage of it to write his Memoirs of a Tourist (1838), The Charterhouse of Parma (1839) and innumerable articles and essays.

Trajan's Baths (Terme Taurine). — Northeast, 3 km - 2 miles — Restoration work in progress: temporarily closed to the public. There are two groups: the first (to the west) dates from the end of the Republican era (1C BC); the other which has brick walls, is better preserved and was built by Trajan's successor, the Emperor Hadrian (2C AD). The largest section is the caldarium.

CLITUMNUS River Source ★ (FONTI DEL CLITUNNO) Umbria

Michelin map 988 16 26 — 13 km - 8 miles — north of Spoleto.

The **Source of the River Clitumnus★** near the Via Flaminia, appears as a spring within a pool of marvellously clear water with blue-green depths. The waters rise among aquatic vegetation to form a peaceful little lake shaded by weeping willows and tall poplars. The source was sacred to the Romans who plunged animals into its waters before sacrifice: by virtue of the Clitumnus' magic powers the animals emerged a dazzling white. Virgil, Propertius, the Younger Pliny and, in the 19C Byron and the poet Giosué Carducci have all described this sacred spot.

One kilometre - 1/2 mile — to the north, below the Via Flaminia, stands the **Temple★** of Clitumnus, a pretty early Christian building dating from the 5C (To visit apply to the next house, uphill from the main road).

COLLE DI VAL D'ELSA ★ Tuscany ─────────────

Michelin map **988** 14 15 — 27 km - 17 miles — northwest of Siena — Pop 15618

Colle Alto is more interesting than Colle Basso. You should enter it, preferably, through the massive Volterra fortified gateway and follow the central street, Via del Castello, lined with mediaeval towers, palaces and old houses, among which No. 53, with the tall tower, was the birthplace of the gloomy Florentine architect-sculptor-poet Arnolfo di Cambio (about 1250-1302).

The **cathedral** contains a lectern designed by Pietro Tacca and, in the baptistry, a Quattrocento (15C) font. The frescoes of Pietro and Ambrogio Lorenzetti, in the **Episcopal Palace**, have been restored. One corner of the Piazza del Duomo is the starting point of a curious roofed street.

COMACCHIO Emilia-Romagna ─────────────

Michelin map **988** 15 — 53 km - 33 miles — southeast of Ferrara — Pop 21197

Comacchio is built on sand and water; it resembles Chioggia and, with the help of a little imagination, Venice. Its fishermen's houses, canals crossed by little operetta type bridges, its barges and canoes give it an odd and not unattractive look.

Built in 1634, at an intersection, the Trepponti (Three Bridges) flanked by towers, are a picturesque sight.

For a long time, the main activity in Comacchio was eel fishing. The region in the Po Delta, once poor and unhealthy, has been turned into rich agricultural land reclaimed by pumping and drainage as in the polders of Holland.

EXCURSION

Valli. — South of the Po Delta lie the Valli di Comacchio, lagoons of melancholy beauty. The region abounds in wildlife and is a hunting and fishing area (the eels are famous).

In the districts of the Valli Pega and Trebba *(west, 5 km - 3 miles)* near the Ferrara road, excavations on the site of the ancient Etruscan town of **Spina** have uncovered two burial grounds and precious objects which are now on view at the Ferrara archaeological museum *(p 101)*.

COMO ★ Lombardy ─────────────

Michelin maps **988** 3 and **26** 8 9 — *Local map p 129* — Pop 96733

Como lies at the south end of the lake of the same name. It is the centre of an active silk industry and an important town whose business life is concentrated in the Piazza Cavour, opening on the lake and the landing stages. Many visitors make a tour of the **lake★★★** by boat *(p 127)*.

The city was already prosperous under the Romans, thanks to its favourable position at the outlet of the lakes and the Alpine Passes, Bernina, Splügen and St. Gothard. It reached its zenith in the 11C; was destroyed by the Milanese in 1127 but was rebuilt by the Emperor Frederick Barbarossa (1123-1190). From 1355 onwards Como followed the fortunes of Milan.

The town is built on the regular plan of the former Roman camp and part of its wall is still standing, notably the 12C 40 m - 130 ft — high tower, the Torre di Porta Vittoria.

Maestri Comacini. — The *maestri comacini* (master builders), known as early as AD 643, were masons, architects, sculptors and decorators who spread the Lombard style throughout Italy and over Europe as far as the Lower Rhine. It has been suggested that their name is derived from Como, but it seems more likely to mean simply associated masons *(co-macini)*.

Their rivals and imitators were the *maestri campionesi (p 127)*, who came from Campione on Lake Lugano.

Cathedral★★ (Duomo). — *Time: 1/2 hour.* The cathedral is built entirely of marble. It was begun in the Gothic style at the end of the 14C, completed under the Renaissance and crowned in the 18C with the dome, 75 m - 246 ft. — high, by Juvara, an architect from Turin.

To the left of the façade, the Broletto (1215), a municipal palace on arcades, has a balcony for the reading of proclamations. It is dominated by the austere municipal belltower.

Façade — This is the most remarkable part of the cathedral and was built in 1487. It was abundantly and delicately decorated by the Rodari brothers: four pilasters are adorned from top to bottom with statues; the central doorway is surmounted by statues of saints or

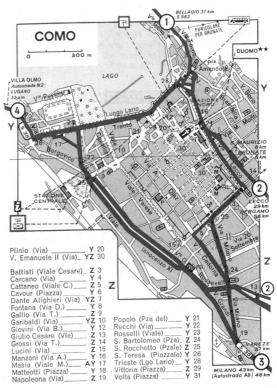

COMO

Plinio (Via)	Y 20
V. Emanuele II (Via)	YZ 30
Battisti (Viale Cesare)	Z 3
Carcano (Via)	Y 4
Cattaneo (Viale C.)	Z 5
Cavour (Piazza)	Y 6
Dante Alighieri (Via)	YZ 7
Fontana (Via D.)	Y 8
Gallio (Via T.)	Z 9
Garibaldi (Via)	YZ 10
Giovini (Via B.)	Y 12
Giulio Cesare (Vle)	Z 13
Grossi (Via T.)	Z 14
Lucini (Via)	Z 15
Manzoni (Via A.)	Y 16
Masia (Viale M.)	AY 17
Matteotti (Piazza)	Y 18
Napoleona (Via)	Z 19
Popolo (Pza del)	Y 21
Recchi (Via)	Y 22
Rosselli (Via)	Y 23
S. Bartolomeo (Pza)	Z 24
S. Rocchetto (Pzale)	Z 25
S. Teresa (Piazzale)	Y 26
Trieste (Lgo Lario)	Y 28
Vittoria (Piazza)	Z 29
Volta (Piazza)	Y 31

heroes and framed by niches containing the seated statues of the Latin writers Pliny the Elder and Pliny the Younger, both of whom came from Como. The Rodari brothers showed their skill in the north door, known as the Porta della Rana because a frog *(rana)* is carved on one of the pillars. They also were responsible for the south door whose decoration is exquisitely delicate; the tympanum bears a Flight into Egypt surrounded by the Seven Virtues.

Interior. — The interior, full of solemn splendour, displays Gothic architecture and Renaissance decoration. Curious banners and magnificent 17C **tapestries★** illustrating the Old Testament and the Life of the Virgin are hung between the pillars. Near the entrance is an elegant 16C *tempietto* or shrine, which is used as a baptistry.

In the south aisle are a bishop's sarcophagus (1347), a late 15C altarpiece of wood, richly carved and gilded and pictures of the Lombard school (beginning of 16C): an Epiphany by Bernardino Luini and a Flight into Egypt by Gaudenzio Ferrari.

An interesting **old quarter** lies round the cathedral. Note the Romanesque Church and Square of San Fedele. The curious apse doorway of the church is adorned with sculptures in bas-relief.

Villa Olmo. — *3 km - 2 miles — about 1/2 hour sightseeing.* Leave Como by ④, and turn right immediately into the road S 340 which runs beside the lake. The villa, a large Neo-Classical building of the late 18C containing a small 18C theatre still in use, is surrounded by a park from which there are pretty **views★** of the lake and its frame of hills.

Brunate. — *6 km - 4 miles.* Leave Como by the Via Tomaso Grossi, a narrow, winding road. The funicular station is the lower one at the north end of the Lungo Lario Trieste; *departure every 1/4 hour; time for trip: 7 minutes; 1250 lire Rtn.* There is a fine **view★** from Brunate, a pleasant country resort, of Como and its hill encircled lake and, in the distance, of the Apennine Alps.

The road continues up to San Maurizio *(2 km - 1 mile),* where there is an impressive **view★** of the lake at your feet.

CONEGLIANO Venetia

Michelin map **988** 5 — 28 km - 17 miles — north of Treviso — Pop 35 685

Conegliano is surrounded by pleasant hills planted with orchards and vineyards whose tall vines produce excellent white wine. A castle overlooks the town and a **museum** is housed in one of the towers still standing. Note the frescoes by Pordenone, a painting by Palma the Younger and an early 20C bronze sculpture by Arturo Marini.

The fine **Via 20 Settembre,** interrupted halfway along its length by the Piazza Cima, is lined with Renaissance palaces in the Venetian style, some of them painted with frescoes. The **Cathedral (Duomo),** preceded by a 14-15C portico with pointed arches, adorned with frescoes by Pozzoserrato on its façade, possesses a Madonna between Saints and angels playing musical instruments, by Cima di Conegliano (1459-1517), a successor of Giovanni Bellini, and superb colourist, who introduced the landscape of the Venetian hills into his pictures.

Beyond the Cathedral, in Calle S. Maria dei Battuti, is situated a hall, known as ''dei Battuti'', whose walls are decorated with 15-16C frescoes in the style of the Lombard and Venetian schools.

CORI Latium

Michelin map **988** 26 — 17 km - 11 miles — southeast of Velletri — Pop 9 972

Cori is of Roman origin and still has visible portions of its girdle of Cyclopean walls (i.e. wall built of huge, irregular stones), dating from the 4C BC.

Temple of Hercules★ (Tempio d'Ercole). — The temple dates from 90 BC and resembles the temple of Fortuna Virilis in Rome. It includes a graceful atrium with columns up to 9 m - 30 ft — high. A small Romanesque church has been incorporated in the temple.

From the belvedere near the temple, is a view of the Latium countryside.

CORTINA D'AMPEZZO ★★★ Venetia

Michelin map **988** 5 — *Local map p 93* — Alt 1 204 m - 3 950 ft — Pop 8 426

Town plan in Michelin Red Guide Italia (hotels and restaurants).

Cortina, the capital of the Dolomites *(p 92),* overlooked from the west by the huge twin masses of the Tofane, is a mountain resort of worldwide fame at the end of the Dolomite road. Lying in the middle of the well known Combe of Ampezzo, sunny and sheltered, the resort is excellently equipped. The Olympic winter sports were held there in 1956. Cortina offers a wide variety of entertainment, sporting and artistic events.

The mountain people have preserved their customs, skills and their local Ladin-Romansh dialect deriving from Latin. Local costumes are worn on *fête* days.

(After photo by Arthaud)

Cortina d'Ampezzo—General view

Tondi di Faloria★★★ (alt 2 343 m - 7 667 ft). — *Access by cable-car. Departures every hour from the lower terminus near the bus station, starting at 8.15 am ending 6.45 pm in summer; 9 am to 4.45 pm in winter; fare: 6000 lire Rtn.* From the summit there is a grand **panorama★★★.**

Pocol Belvedere★★ (Belvedere Pocol). — *Bus service. Departures from the main square in the village: every hour from 7.30 am to 8 pm; fare: 1000 lire Rtn.*

The **panorama★★** of the combe is best seen at sunset. Nearby, an **ossuary**, the **Sacrario Pocol**, contains the remains of 10 000 soldiers killed in the War of 1914-1918.

Tofana di Mezzo★★★ (alt 3244 m - 10673 ft). — *Access by cable-car. Departures from the lower terminus near Stadio del Ghiaccio every 1/2 hour (every 20 minutes in winter) from 9 am to 6.15 pm (5.15 pm in winter); 7500 lire Rtn.* A cable-car climbs to the summit: imposing **panorama★★★** of the Dolomites, Central Alps and Po plain.

CORTONA ★ Tuscany

Michelin map 988 15 — 33 km - 21 miles — southeast of Arezzo — Pop 22561

Cortona in a remarkable **site★**, clings to the steep slopes of a hill planted with olive trees overlooking a valley near Lake Trasimeno. The town is grim and silent; it has not changed since the Renaissance and still has steep, narrow streets paved with flagstones, opening on to irregularly shaped squares bordered with arcades and buildings. A girdle of mediaeval ramparts dominated by a massive citadel *(fortezza)* has taken the place of the Etruscan walls.

Art and Religion. — Cortona attracted artists as early as the 14C. After the Sienese, Fra Angelico came there to paint, but its claim to fame is that it was the birthplace of distinguished masters. In painting, **Luca Signorelli** (1450-1523), by his dramatic temperament and sculptural modelling, showed himself the precursor of Michelangelo; he died as a result of a fall from the scaffolding he was using to paint the frescoes in the Villa Passerini, a little to the east of Cortona. In the 16C Cortona gave France an architect, Domenico Bernabei, known as **Boccadoro** (Mouth of Gold) or Becalor.

Pietro da Cortona (1596-1669), painter and architect and one of the masters of Roman Baroque, has a lively imagination and was highly skilled as a decorator. When in Rome he liked to go with his friends Poussin and Claude Lorrain and the sculptor Duquesnoy to admire the Bacchanalia of Titian at the Casa Aldobrandini. His major works are the Church of St. Mary of Peace (Santa Maria della Pace) in Rome and the decorations in the Pitti Palace in Florence and the Barberini Palace in Rome.

The people of Cortona revere especially St. Francis, who founded a hermitage not far away, St. Margaret, the 13C Magdalen, and finally Brother Elias, friend and disciple of St. Francis, who directed the building of the Basilica of St. Francis in Assisi.

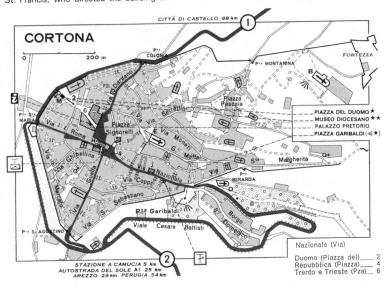

■ MAIN SIGHTS *time: 2 hours*

Piazza Garibaldi. — The **view★** extends to Lake Trasimeno and Montepulciano.

Piazza del Duomo★. — The square enjoys an ecclesiastical seclusion. Its position on the edge of the ramparts gives it a bird's-eye view over the valley. The **Cathedral (Duomo)**, of Romanesque origin, was entirely remodelled at the Renaissance.

Diocesan Museum★★ (Museo Diocesano). — *Open 9 am to 1 pm and 3 to 6.30 pm (5 pm 1 October to 31 March). Closed Mondays; 500 lire; ring.* The Gesù Church, opposite the cathedral, has a fine sculptured ceiling (1536) and contains rich collections. The "divine Angelico" is represented by two of his best works: a beautiful **Annunciation**, remarkable for the drawing of the Virgin's hands and face and for the placing of the head of the Angel, standing out against a large halo which is accentuated by red drapery; and a picture of the Madonna surrounded by saints. This should be noted more for the tenderness of Mary's face than for the interpretation of the scenes from the life of Christ, which are handled as though for an altarpiece.

Remarkable paintings of the Sienese school are also shown: they include a Madonna by Duccio, a Madonna with Angels and a large Christ on the Cross, with livid flesh tints, by Pietro Lorenzetti (late 14C), and a triptych (restored) of the Madonna and Child by Sassetta (1434).

The museum contains a choice collection of pictures by Signorelli: the best are a Communion of the Apostles and a Descent from the Cross whose intensity is enhanced by the softness of the landscape background. Note also, among the paintings, a realistic and clear-cut Ecstasy of St. Margaret by the Bolognese artist, Crespi (1665-1747).

Distinguished pieces of gold plate adorn a small room. The Vagnucci reliquary is the work of Justus of Florence (15C).

CORTONA*

Praetorian Palace (Palazzo Pretorio). — This is also called the Palazzo Casali after its former owners, who were local lords. It was built in the 13C and remodelled later: the façade on the right, covered with the coats of arms of governors, is Gothic, but that which faces the Piazza Signorelli dates from the beginning of the 17C.

A stairway leads from the courtyard to the **museum★**. *Open 10 am to 1 pm and 4 to 6 pm (1 October - 30 May, 9 am to 1 pm and 3 to 5 pm). Closed Mondays; 500 lire, free on Sundays.* The most important exhibits are in the great central hall. Among the Etruscan specimens, note an astonishing 5C BC bronze oil lamp with a gorgon's head for its base, surrounded by 16 figures of Sileni and female divinities supporting 16 burners. Etruscan and Roman bronze statuettes. Ceramics. Among the pictures hung on the walls note a superb Miracle of St. Benedict of the 17C Spanish school.

■ **ADDITIONAL SIGHTS**

St. Margaret's Church (Santa Margherita) (B). — The modern Church of St. Margaret, in the upper part of the town, contains the Gothic **tomb★** of the saint, surmounted by gables. It dates from 1362 and is of unusual design. 17C campanile.

From the esplanade there are **views★** of the town, the valley below and Lake Trasimeno.

St. Francis' Church (San Francesco) (E). — This church was begun to the design of Brother Elias in 1245. It is a Gothic building with a graceful doorway and an open belfry. In the interior (remodelled in the 17C) you will see a late 16C picture depicting St. Anthony of Padua and the Presentation of the Host to the Mule (on the fourth altar on the right), the 10C Byzantine style reliquary of the Holy Cross on the high altar, an Annunciation by Pietro da Cortona (on the third altar on the left) and a Martyrdom of St. Lucy by Sagrestani (on the second altar on the left). Brother Elias was buried in the chancel. Luca Signorelli is believed to have been buried there, too.

St. Dominic's Church (San Domenico) (D). — St. Dominic's is early 15C Gothic. The interior contains a few good pictures: a Madonna with angels and saints by Luca Signorelli in the south apse, a triptych of the Coronation of the Virgin (1402) by Lorenzo di Niccolò at the high altar, an Assumption by Bartolomeo della Gatta (1480-1485) near the north apse, and a fresco representing a Madonna between two Dominicans, attributed to Fra Angelico.

A pleasant promenade beyond St. Dominic's offers bird's-eye views of Lake Trasimeno.

EXCURSION

Church of Santa Maria del Calcinaio★. — *3 km - 2 miles.* Leave Cortana by ②, going towards road S 71. Santa Maria, built between 1485 and 1513, is the work of the excellent Sienese painter-sculptor-architect Francesco di Giorgio Martini. It is built in dark coloured stone which emphasises its outlines, and is remarkable for the grace and harmony of its design and its well balanced proportions. A dome surmounts the interior, which is well lit, graceful and built on the plan of a Latin cross. In the oculus of the façade is a remarkable stained glass window (1516) depicting the Madonna of Pity, designed by a native of the Berry district in France, Guillaume de Marcillat.

A short distance westward is the so-called **Tomb of Pythagoras**, really an Etruscan sepulchre of the 4C BC.

COSENZA Calabria

Michelin map **988** 39 — *Local map p 228* — Pop 102629
Town plan in Michelin Red Guide Italia (hotels and restaurants).

Cosenza is at the confluence of the Busento and Crati Rivers, between the plain and the mountains.

King Alaric of the Visigoths, after the capture and looting of Rome by his army in 410, made for Sicily, which he intended to conquer, but died on the way at Cosenza. His warriors are believed to have buried him secretly, with all his treasures, under the bed of the Busento River.

The town is dominated by a Norman castle in which Louis III of Anjou, brother of Good King René, was married to Margaret of Savoy in 1431.

The lower quarters of Cosenza are modern and crossed by broad avenues. The picturesque old town climbs up the hill with the Corso Mazzini as its principal axis.

Cathedral (Duomo). — This was begun in the Romanesque style after 1185 and finished, with a Gothic façade, in 1222. It was rebuilt in 1750 but a recent restoration has revived its original form.

The façade is pierced with three tierce-point doorways and with rose windows.

The three aisles rest on overlapping arches which are themselves supported by Romanesque pillars. In the north transept is the **tomb** of Isabella of Aragon, the wife of Philip III (the Bold), King of France and son of St. Louis. Accompanied by her husband, Isabella was returning from Tunis, where the sainted King had died, when she fell from her horse at Cosenza and, being pregnant, died as she gave birth to her child (1271). The mausoleum, the work of a French artist (1275), shows the royal couple saluting a graceful Virgin and Child. The queen's face, which is striking, was modelled from a cast taken after her death.

Villa Comunale. — This shady, flower decked garden is laid out in terraces at the top of the old town above the Crati River and facing the foothills of the Sila Mountains.

When visiting London use the Green Guide "London"

- *Detailed descriptions of places of interest*
- *Useful local information*
- *A section on the historic square mile of the City of London with a detailed fold out plan*
- *The lesser known London boroughs — their people, places and sights*
- *Plan of selected areas and important buildings.*

COURMAYEUR ★★ Valle d'Aosta

Michelin maps 988 1 2 and 26 1 — *Local map p 50* — Alt 1228 m - 4029 ft — Pop 2685
Town plan in Michelin Red Guide Italia (hotels and restaurants).

Courmayeur is a well-known summer resort, mountaineering and winter sports centre at the foot of the Mont Blanc massif.

The construction of the Mont Blanc Tunnel has put this resort, formerly isolated at the far end of the Valle d'Aosta, firmly on one of the main international tourist routes.

The Mont Blanc Tunnel. — The tunnel, which was opened in July 1965, links **Entrèves** with the hamlet of Les Pèlerins in France. It is 11,6 km - 7 miles 366 yds — long, which makes it one of the longest road tunnels in the world.

For all information concerning passage through the tunnel, see the current Michelin Guide France (hotels and restaurants).

EXCURSIONS

Crossing the Mont Blanc Massif★★★. — *4 km - 2 miles* — to La Palud, then by cable-car to the Pointe Helbronner followed by a telecabin to the Aiguille du Midi.

The Aiguille du Midi cable-car goes down to the Plan de l'Aiguille and Chamonix.

For a detailed description see the Michelin Green Guide "Alpes".

Cresta d'Arp★. — *Access by cable-car from Courmayeur to Plan Chécrouit, and by telecabin to the Altiporto; and then by cable-car to Cresta di Youla from where another cable-car climbs to the Cresta d'Arp. Time for the trip: about 3/4 hour; Rtn fare: 8500 lire.* From the belvedere at the upper cable-car station, which is at an altitude of 2763 m - 9065 ft there is a splendid **panorama★★** of the high Alpine peaks: to the north and quite close are Mont Blanc, the Aiguille du Géant and the Grandes Jorasses; farther away, to the northeast are the Grand Combin and the Matterhorn and beyond the Monte Rosa. Southeast lies the Gran Paradiso.

Val Ferret. — *10 km - 6 miles* — to Lavachey. This densely wooded valley is bordered on the north by the vertiginous slopes of the Mont Blanc mountain range.

CREMONA ★ Lombardy

Michelin map 988 13 14 — Pop 82 169

Cremona is a fine town at the south end of Lombardy. It became famous for its stringed instruments and is today also an agricultural centre.

Town life in Cremona centres on the Piazza Roma, where there is a public garden, and where the Corso Mazzini and also the commercial Via Solferino both end.

Song of a Marshal. — In 1702 the French Marshal Villeroy held the town. The historian Saint-Simon relates that he allowed himself to be captured while his troops were repelling a surprise attack by those of Prince Eugen. Hence the ditty:

"Français, rendons grace à Bellone,   *("Frenchmen, give thanks to Bellona,*
Notre bonheur est sans égal!   *Our joy is quite phenomenal,*
Nous avons conservé Crémone   *For we have held on to Cremona*
Et perdu notre général!"   *And we have lost our General!")*

The Violin Makers of Cremona. — In the 17 and 18C Cremona's violin makers were a source of local pride. Amati, **Stradivarius** and Guarnerius remain famous: their knowledge and incomparable skill in the choice and fashioning of pine wood and the mixing of varnish gave an almost supernatural resonance to the "souls" of their instruments.

Stradivarius Cremonensis (1644-1737), the genial pupil of Amati, was the greatest violin maker in the world. He himself said to one of his pupils: "You will never make a violin better than mine." Wearing a white cap and a white leather apron, he worked hard and became so prosperous that there was a saying at Cremona: "As rich as Stradivarius."

The International School of Violin Making in the Piazza Marconi carries on the tradition.

Another Cremonese, the composer Monteverdi (1567-1643), created modern opera with his *Orfeo.*

■ **PIAZZA DEL COMUNE★★** *time: 3/4 hour*

This is one of the finest squares in Italy.

Cathedral★★ (Duomo). — This magnificent Lombard building was begun in the Romanesque style and later completed in the Gothic and Renaissance styles.

On its left, linked to the façade by a Renaissance gallery, is the **Torrazzo★★★**, a beautiful campanile and the tallest in Italy (112 m - 387 ft). Built at the end of the 13C, it has a 16C clock and bears the coat of arms of Cremona.

The façade, faced with marble, has belonging to all periods.

The columns of the Gothic porch rest on two lions; their capitals represent Roland sounding his horn and Charlemagne. The upper loggia contains a statue of the Madonna between two saints attributed to Gano da Siena; a small frieze depicts the Work of the Months in the Middle Ages. The 13C rose window is surmounted by a pediment designed 300 years later.

In the centre of the early 13C doorway stand statues of four of the prophets.

To the right of the façade is a 12C baptistry, remodelled during the Renaissance.

Before entering the cathedral, walk round the building to admire the magnificent proportions of the transept, the tower and the apse.

The central nave and the chancel are decorated with an astonishing series of **frescoes★** depicting from left to right the New Testament by Boccaccino (Life of the Virgin), the Campi, Bembo and Romanino da Brescia (Jesus before Pilate, the Flagellation, the Crowning with Thorns, *Ecce Homo),* Pordenone painted on the reverse of the façade, two compositions (the Crucifixion, the Descent from the Cross) already Baroque in style but full of power, and finally Gatti, completing the cycle with a Resurrection.

Splendid tapestries woven in Brussels in the 17C, relating the story of Samson, hang between the pillars. In the chancel are fine inlaid stalls dating from 1490.

At the entrance to the chancel, on the face of the right-hand pillar of the triumphal arch, is a graceful high-relief by the Pavian sculptor, Amadeo (late 15C). It shows St. Imerio giving alms.

A staircase behind this pillar leads to the crypt *(open 6 am to noon and 3 to 7 pm)* containing a tomb by Briosco, a pupil of Amadeo.

CREMONA

0 _____ 500 m

Municipal Palace (Palazzo Comunale) (BZ H). — *Open 15 June to 1 September, 8.30 am to 12.30 pm (9 am to noon Saturdays); the rest of the year 8.30 am to 12.30 pm and 2.30 to 5 pm; closed at Easter and Christmas.* The palace was built in the 13C then remodelled and decorated with terracottas at the Renaissance. The rostrum for speech-making is placed, unusually, on the ground floor.

Inside, on display, are the Cremona 1715 violin by Stradivarius and also an instrument by Amati.

To the left of the palace is the 13C **Loggia dei Militi** (Soldiers' Loggia).

■ ADDITIONAL SIGHTS

Fodri Palace★ (Palazzo Fodri) (BZ D). — This early 16C building in the Renaissance style stands among other palaces at No. 17 Corso Matteotti. The façade bears a remarkable terracotta frieze composed of mythological scenes and lifelike busts in relief. The delightful court is surrounded by galleries with columns and pilasters adorned at the base with fleurs-de-lys, the French royal badge, because Louis XII occupied the district of Milan at the time. A terracotta frieze and frescoes in monochrome depict camp and battle scenes.

Municipal Museum (Museo Civico) (ABY M). — *Open 10 am to noon and 3 to 6 pm (2 to 5 pm 1 October to 31 March); Sundays and holidays 9 am to noon throughout the year; closed Sunday afternoons, Mondays and 1 January, 25 April, 1 May, Easter, 15 August, 1 and 13 November, 8, 25 and 26 December; 100 lire.* The museum, which includes a **picture gallery**, is in the Palazzo Affaitati (1561), with its monumental staircase. The gallery is rich in works by the artists of Cremona, graceful and serene, especially those of Bembo (15C) in Room II, those of the Campi family (16C) in Room VI and those of Boccaccino (died 1525) in Room VIII. Note also a Diogenes by Salvator Rosa and a curious Bacchanalia by Elsheimer (Room IX); a still-life by Nuvolone and a strange composition of the school of Arcimboldi (Room XI). Room XII is devoted to foreign schools: Provost and ''Velvet'' Breughel, while in Room XIII are fantastic landscapes by the 18C Magnasco.

On the second floor is exhibited the Cathedral's treasure which includes 25 illuminated missals (15-16C) and a large inlaid cabinet by the Cremonese artist Platina (1477).

On the ground floor are located the archaeological section and collections of local ceramics (8-15C) and of wrought iron (15-19C).

The **Stradivarius Museum**, which is housed in the palace, has an interesting collection of souvenirs of the violin makers of Cremona.

Palaces. — Not far from the Affaitati Palace, in the Via Palestro, opposite San Vincenzo, the Palazzo Stanga (AY E), whose court is decorated with splendid 16C terracottas and the Palazzo Raimondi (AY F), in the Corso Garibaldi, which has a slightly embossed stone façade with pink marble pilasters and a cornice painted with Renaissance figures, are among the several palaces worth looking at.

St. Augustine's Church (Sant' Agostino) (AZ B). — The church is in the Lombard style, with a façade pierced with five oculi. It was built by Augustinians in 1339.

In the third chapel in the south aisle there are portraits of Francesco Sforza and Bianca Visconti by Bembo and on the left in the same aisle, a stoup surmounted by a pretty 14C bas-relief. Farther on at the end in the centre of an altarpiece is a Madonna between Sts. James and Augustine (1494) by Perugino.

St. Sigismund's Church (San Sigismondo). — *2 km - 1 1/2 miles — east, on the road to Casalmaggiore. Leave by ③.* The church was built in 1463 by Francesco Sforza, Duke of Milan, and his wife, Bianca Visconti, on the site of a chapel in which their marriage had taken place. Inside are frescoes by the Campi family (16C).

CROTONE Calabria

Michelin map **988** 40 — Pop 56427

Crotone stands on a promontory. It is an ancient town and was an Achaean colony of Magna Graecia, founded in 710 BC and celebrated in Antiquity for its riches, the beauty of its women and the strength of its athletes.

Crotone is today a prosperous maritime town with an active commercial and tourist port, and important chemical and metallurgical industries. It is also a holiday resort with fine rugged beaches.

A Greek Samson. — **Milo of Crotone,** who lived in the 6C BC, was tremendously strong and greedy and won the championship six times at the Olympic Games. Sometimes he would tie a cord round his head and hold his breath; the blood, rising to his head, then swelled his veins to such an extent that the cord snapped. One day, according to popular report, after running round the stadium with a bull on his shoulders, he killed the bull with a blow of his fist and ate it.

His death served as Puget's subject for the marble group now in the Louvre: in his old age, Milo tried to tear apart a split tree-trunk with his bare hands, but the wood caught and held his hands. He was then devoured by wild beasts.

At the same period, Crotone boasted another famous resident, Pythagoras, who settled in the town around 530 BC.

CUMAE * (CUMA) Campania

Michelin map **988** 27 — 7 km - 4 miles — northwest of Pozzuoli — *Local map p 164*

Cumae, one of the oldest Greek colonies, is believed to have been founded in the 8C BC. The city dominated the whole Phlegrean area *(see p 163),* including Naples, between the 7th and 6th centuries BC. Its splendour was at its height under the tyrant Aristodemus. Cumae defeated the Etruscans in a naval battle in 474 BC but was captured by the Romans in 334 BC. It became a naval base which the Romans linked with Lake Avernus *(p 163).* Its decline then set in and continued until AD 915, when it was looted by the Saracens.

The dead town of Cumae stands in a serene and solemn setting near the sea. You can visit the ruins of the upper town — the Acropolis — where several temples stood. But, in the area of the lower town, excavations have revealed the remains of an amphitheatre near the road to Baia, the vestiges of a temple (Tempio Capitolino) dedicated to the Capitoline Triad (Jupiter, Juno, Minerva) near the forum, and a short distance away, baths *(terme).* To the north of the town was a large burial ground.

Acropolis★★. — *Open 9 am to one hour before sunset. Closed Mondays (Tuesday when Monday is a holiday), 1 January, 25 April, 1 May, first Sunday in June, 15 August, and 25 December; 500 lire. Tour: about 1/2 hour.* The acropolis is on a lava hill a short distance from the sea, in lonely surroundings, overlooking the plateau on which the lower town was built. Go down an alley bordered with laurels to reach the ruins.

After a large cavern on the left, appears the gallery which leads to the **Sibyl's cave★** (Antro della Sibilla). One of the most venerated spots of Antiquity, it was hollowed out of the rock by the Greeks in the 6 or 5C BC. At the end of the gallery is a cave on which open three small niches. Here the Sibyl rendered her oracles. Her cult was officially abandoned in the early days of the Empire, in the 1C AD. At a later stage, the Romans converted this part of the cavern and built three cisterns half way along the gallery.

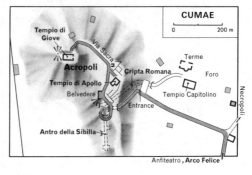

Facing the entrance to the gallery, lower down is the entrance to the **Roman crypt** (Cripta Romana), an underground gallery almost 200 m - 656 ft — long, which was probably an extension of Cocceio's cave *(p 163).*

At the top of the gallery leading to the Sibyl's Cave, go down a stairway on the left and along a paved road, the ancient Via Sacra of the Romans, to the **lower esplanade** of the Acropolis: from a platform which has been turned into a belvedere (objects recovered from the excavations are on show), there is a view of the islands of Procida and Ischia. Further up to the right, are vestiges of the **Temple of Apollo** (Tempio di Apollo). You can also see the remains of a Greek cistern and of a Christian octagonal font.

Keep to the ancient Via Sacra which turns into a narrow path (on the left), go up some steps and after about 200 m - 656 ft — you reach the **upper esplanade** which is crowned by the remains of the **Temple of Jupiter** (Tempio di Giove). It was rebuilt during the reign of Augustus and transformed by the early Christians into an important basilica with five aisles (note in the centre a large circular font with marble facing). Christian tombs have been discovered beneath the pavement. From the edge of the hill which rises steeply above the sea, you will enjoy a magnificent **panorama★★** from Cape Miseno (on the left) to the Gulf of Gaeta.

Arco Felice★. — *On the small road linking Cumae to Road S 7 Quater.* This triumphal arch, 20 m - 65 ft — high, was erected under the Emperor Domitian (AD 81-96), on a beautiful site. The road linking Cumae with Pozzuoli and Naples passed at the summit.

Join us in our never ending task of keeping up to date. Send us your comments and suggestions, please.
**Michelin Tyre Co Ltd
Tourism Department
81 Fulham Road, LONDON SW3 6RD**

Michelin map 🔢 4 5.

This rugged and grandiose limestone massif displays many colours, some harsh, some soft, which change with the light. It makes a splendid haunt for snowshoe runners and skiers as well as for ordinary tourists. Excellent roads, well made paths, immense panoramas and well equipped hotels combine to please the traveller.

GEOGRAPHICAL NOTES

The Dolomites are bounded roughly by the Adige River and its tributary, the Isarco, in the west, the Brenta in the south, the Piave in the east and the Rienza in the north. The Brenta Massif *(description p 68),* rising beyond the Adige, has the same geological formation as the Dolomites.

Most of the range is formed of limestone rocks called "dolomites" after a French geologist, Gratet de Dolomieu, who was the first to study their formation at the end of the 18C. A few nuclei of volcanic rock are to be found in the centre and west and schist (slate or shale) in the southwest: Cima d'Asta. The nature of the soil and the effect of erosion have created a distinctive landscape: steep, rugged rocks take the forms of towers, belfries, or domes, with gentler slopes at their feet covered with alpine pastures, conifers or crops. The steepness of the upper slopes has prevented the formation of glaciers.

The various massifs. — To the south, near the Cima della Vezzana, the Pale di San Martino, which are deeply fissured, are divided into three chains separated by a high plateau. The Massifs of the Latemar and the Catinaccio, on which the well known Towers of the Vaioletto (Torri del Vaiolet) stand, enclose the Costalunga Pass (Passo di Costalunga). To the north are the Sasso Lungo and the Sella Massif (Grupo di Sella), a colossal and spectacular mass which can be admired from all sides, for a road runs round it. To the east, the chief summits in the Cortina Dolomites are the Tofane and the Sorapis.

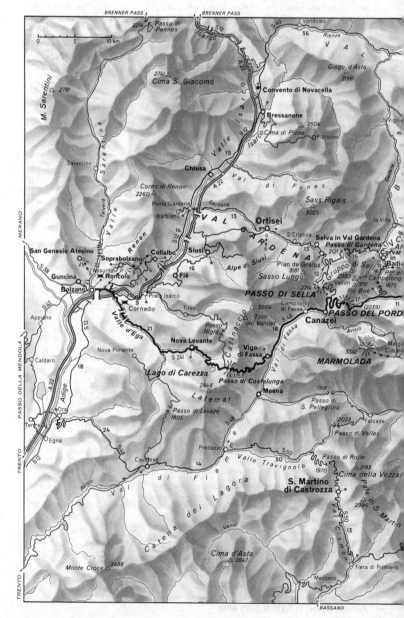

Finally, to the south in the heart of the range stands the formidable Marmolada Massif (Gruppo della Marmolada), which rises to the highest point in the Dolomites *(see p 94)*.

The Cadore district prolongs the Dolomites to the east and southeast of Cortina; its axis is the Piave Valley and its capital is Pieve di Cadore. Here the highest summits are the Antelao (3 263 m - 10 705 ft) and the three Cime di Lavaredo (2 998 m - 9 836 ft).

Fauna and Flora. — Birds and animals are those of the Alps: royal eagle, chamois, deer, hawks and woodcock in the coniferous forests.

In spring the fields are covered with brightly coloured flowers: edelweiss, deep blue gentian, white, or mauve crocus, blue campanula, six-petalled anemones, starry white saxifrage or five-petalled rock flowers, fringed mauve soldanellas and purplish-pink Turk's Cap lilies. Market gardens and vineyards flourish in valleys dotted with large farmhouses with wooden balconies.

***DOLOMITE ROAD from Bolzano to Cortina
109 km - 68 miles — about 1 day

The main touring route in the Dolomites is the great Dolomite Road, which is shown in black on the map below. Several secondary tours, also superb, can be combined. We show them in black, but thinner, on the same map. The sites and localities along the routes, are described in alphabetical order on p 94 under the title of "Other towns and sights in the Massif".
The Dolomite Road, a wonderful and world famous example of road engineering, links Bolzano and Cortina, following the central depression of the massif. It runs through a landscape which is always majestic and varied.

The road was already used at the Renaissance by merchants going from Venice to Germany. It began to be modernised in 1895, was used for military purposes in 1915-1918 and was improved after 1918.

Leave Bolzano *(p 66)* to the east to take the S 241.

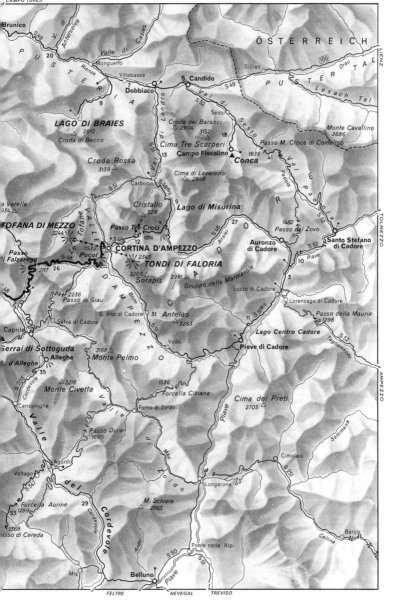

The DOLOMITES★★★

Ega Valley Gorge. — A narrow gorge guarded by **Cornedo Castle.**

Nova Levante★. — A smiling little village on the Dolomite Road, with pretty houses bordering a torrent.

Lake Carezza★★ (Lago di Carezza or Karer See). — This tiny lake is set in a dark expanse of fir woods with the sharp, jagged peaks of the Latemar and the Catinaccio Massifs for background.

Costalunga Pass★ (Passo di Costalunga). — From this pass on the Dolomite Road, also called the Passo di Carezza, there is a **view★** over the Catinaccio on one side and the Latemar on the other. The soil on the mountainsides is contained by brushwood faggots.

Vigo di Fassa. — This resort, very well placed in the famous Val di Fassa, is a mountaineering and excursion centre in the Catinaccio Massif.

Canazei★★. — Canazei lies deep in the heart of the massif, framed between the Catinaccio, the Towers of Vaioletto (Torri del Vaiolet), the Sella Massif and the Marmolada, on the Dolomite Road. This is the usual base for most of the excursions and difficult climbs in the Marmolada range.

Pordoi Pass★★★ (Passo del Pordoi). — This, the highest and most impressive pass on the Dolomite Road, goes through Dantesque **scenery★★★**, between huge blocks of rock with vertical sides and shorn-off tops.
From the road on the west slope the **view★★** includes the Sasso Lungo, the precipices of the Boè Peak, the Fassa Valley and Canazei.

Falzarego Pass (Passo di Falzarego). — The wild, desolate Falzarego is an important pass on the Dolomite Road. View to the west of the Marmolada and a big glacier. 9 km - 6 miles — to the south and below it you can turn off to Caprile (Romanesque campanile) and Alleghe along a **panoramic road★★★** which dizzily overlooks the valley.

Monte Crepa Tunnel. — View of Cortina *(p 86).*

OTHER TOWNS AND SIGHTS IN THE MASSIF

Alleghe. — Pleasantly situated on the shore of a pale green **lake★** formed in 1771 by a landslide which dammed the river. Alleghe offers an impressive view of the rocky wall of Monte Civetta. It is a good centre for excursions in the **Cordevole Valley★★** (Valle del Cordevole).

Siusi Alp (Alpe di Siusi). — The Alpine pastures overlooking the Isarco Valley from the southeast form splendid snow-slopes in winter and idyllic fields of flowers in early summer. A panoramic road turns off road S 12 at Prato Isarco, and enables one to reach Fiè and, later, Siusi. Farther on a fine road leads to the Siusi Alp.

Auronzo di Cadore★. — White houses scattered among greenery form the pretty country resort of Auronzo, on the edge of its lake, overlooking a picturesque valley.

Lake Braies★★★ (Lago di Braies). — Alt 1495 m - 4905 ft. The lake appears, encircled by grim mountains dominated by the bare mass of the Croda di Becco. Its winding banks enclose crystal clear, emerald-green water swarming with trout *(boats for hire).*

Bressanone★. — *Description p 70.*

Brunico. — Mountain town and centre for excursions into the Anterselva Valley.

Campo Fiscalino. — A narrow, winding road skirting the torrent up the Val Fiscalino ends in an impressive **amphitheatre★★** enclosed by a wall of jagged mountains.

Chiusa. — This little town deep in the Isarco Valley has kept some of its old Tyrolean character, having corbelled houses painted with frescoes and wrought iron signs in the main street. The Sabiona Monastery, above Chiusa, was once the residence of the Bishops of Bressanone.

Corvara in Badia. — Corvara, a resort and winter sports centre, is the starting point for three excursions to the Alto Pass (by chair lift), to the Vallon refuge (by cable-car and then by chair lift) and to Pralongià (by chair lift) from where lovely **views★★** of the neighbouring valleys may be enjoyed.

Dobbiaco (or **Toblach**). — Lying at the junction of several valleys and commanding the approach road to the north of the Dolomites, Dobbiaco is a pleasant country resort.

Gardena Pass (Passo di Gardena). — The **road to the Gardena Pass★★** is lonely and impressive. It offers remarkable views of the Sella Massif (Gruppo di Sella).

Gardena Valley★★★ (Val Gardena). — This valley, which opens into the Isarco Valley, is attractively beautiful, green and winding, widening and narrowing by turns. Its slopes are covered with coniferous forests, cascades and typical mountain dwellings. The inhabitants still speak the Ladin dialect *(p 86)* and stick to their ancestral habits and customs. They are clever woodworkers. Main centres: Ortisei, Santa Cristina and Selva.

Ortisei★★. — Ortisei is strung out among fir woods. A teleferic links Ortisei with the ski slopes on the Siusi Alp.

Selva in Val Gardena★. — A resort at the bottom of the Gardena Valley and at the foot of the impressive, precipitous Sella Massif. The hamlet of Plan de Gralba, in an excellent skiing area, adjoins it. The inhabitants are clever woodworkers.

Marmolada Massif (Gruppo della Marmolada). — This is the highest point in the Dolomites (3342 m - 10964 ft) with its own great glacier complex offering the fastest ski-run. A teleferic starting from Malga Ciapela goes up to 3270 m - 10728 ft — from where there is an admirable **panorama★★★** of the main massifs and summits around Cortina.

Lake Misurina★★ (Lago di Misurina). — A popular lake set in rolling parkland overlooked by the three Lavaredo Peaks *(Cime).* To the south, the horizon is bounded by the Sorapis. The lake was used as a racing ice-rink in the 1956 Olympic Games.

Moena★. — A rather popular winter sports resort with a remarkable view of the Catinaccio and Sasso Lungo mountain groups.

Pieve di Cadore★. — *Description p 182.*

San Candido★ or **Innichen.** — Situated amid larch and fir woods within view of the Croda dei Baranci and the Three Cobblers Peak (Cima Tre Scarperi).

San Martino di Castrozza★★. — At the feet of the famous Pale di San Martino mountain peaks, in a splendid **setting★★★**, lies San Martino (1467 m - 5575 ft), an ideal centre for winter sports, mountaineering and excursions to the Rolle Pass (Passo di Rolle), the road to Predazzo (splendid **viewpoints★★**) or the Cismon Valley. There is a strong folk tradition in the region (costumes).

Santo Stefano di Cadore. — A village built at a junction of valleys. Northwards are fine pinewoods with slim, straight trees. Chalets with open attics, balconies under which wood is stored and overhanging roofs, can be seen here and there.

Sella Pass★★★ (Passo di Sella). — One of the most extensive and most characteristic **panoramas★★★** in the Dolomites, including the Sella, Sasso Lungo and Marmolada Massifs.

Serrai di Sottoguda★★. — Impressive gorges formed by the Pettorina River in the Marmolada Massif.

Tre Croci Pass (Passo Tre Croci). — Glimpses through the larch trees of the Sorapis and the Marmarole. Nearby is the lower station of the cableway leading to Monte Cristallo.

ELBA, Isle of ★ Tuscany

Michelin map 988 24 — Pop 28 429

Elba, the island of sea-horses, is the largest in the Tuscan Archipelago. Tourists have, these last few years, been attracted to it by its lonely scenes, its quiet and its dry warm climate. The two chief towns are Portoferraio and Porto Azzurro.

Access. — *Car ferries ply between Piombino and Portoferraio (apply to the TOREMAR ☎ 92022 at Portoferraio or the NAVARMA, ☎ 92133 at Portoferraio); between Piombino and Porto Azzuro (apply to the TOREMAR, ☎ 95004 at Porto Azzurro). There is also a hydrofoil (aliscafi) service operating between Piombino and Portoferraio (apply to the TOREMAR, ☎ 92022).*

By air, there are flights from Milan to Marina di Campo (apply to S.O.R.E.M., ☎ 97011 at Marina di Campo).

GEOGRAPHICAL NOTES

In the Primary Era Elba was part of a vanished continent, Tyrrhenia, which sank into the sea in the Quaternary Era, leaving as vestiges the Islands of Corsica, Sardinia, the Balearics, Elba, and the Maures and Estérel Massifs on the French Riviera coast.

Elba is mountainous and culminates at Monte Capanne (1 019 m - 3 343 ft), overlooking a granite massif on which quarries are worked. The coastline is much indented and forms natural sheltered creeks containing small beaches. Under-water fishing is practised among the steep rocks of the west coast, which are pierced with sea-caves. Professional fishermen capture tunny and anchovies. Vegetation is of the Mediterranean type, comprising palms, eucalyptus, cedars, magnolias and, in great quantity, olives and vines. Two strains of vines yield strong, perfumed wines: white Moscato and red Aleatico. The island is particularly beautiful in June when the broom is in flower.

Iron Mines. — These were prospected and worked by the Etruscans as early as the 6th century BC. The open-cast mines are in the eastern part of the island, at Cape Calamita, and between Rio nell'Elba and Cavo. Lighters towed by tugs carry the ore to the blast furnaces at Piombino.

NAPOLEON ON ELBA (3 May 1814 - 26 February 1815)

After the abdication of Napoleon I the Isle of Elba and its neighbour Pianosa were formed into a principality for the fallen sovereign. Napoleon was surrounded by a small court under the control of Bertrand, the Grand Marshal of the Palace, and about 1 000 soldiers. To the 100 grenadiers and light infantrymen of his Guard and 300 others who had accompanied him from the first, there came a further 600, including Polish lancers under the command of Drouot and Cambronne; he also had a naval force consisting of the brig *Inconstant*.

During his short stay he wandered about the island, brooded over the sight of his native Corsica, lying on the horizon, and sailed round his kingdom in the brig. He constructed roads, using the Cambronne veterans and Polish lancers, improved farming, developed the iron mines and modernised the street planning of Portoferraio.

★TOUR STARTING FROM PORTOFERRAIO

81 km - 50 miles — about 5 hours

The Island of Elba is a place for a stay rather than for an excursion. But you can see it in a day, either in your own car or in one hired at Portoferraio.

Portoferraio. — Lying on the shore of a beautiful bay, guarded by ruined walls and two forts, Portoferraio is the island's capital. In the upper part of the town the **Villa dei Mulini** (Mill Villa) is a simple house which Napoleon sometimes occupied during his brief local reign. His personal library and various mementoes are kept there. *Open weekdays, 9 am to 1.30 pm; Sundays and holidays, 9 am to 12.30 pm. Closed Mondays, 1 January, 25 April, 1 May, first Sunday in June, 15 August and Christmas; 500 lire, valid on the same day for Napoleon's Villa.*

The **road★** to Marciana Marina is recommended for the bird's-eye views it offers of **Procchio** and its bay.

Biodola. — A large beach of fine sand.

Marina di Campo. — *A journey of 5 km - 3 miles — from Procchio.* Lying on the edge of a plain dotted with olive groves and vineyards, Marina di Campo is sought after for its fine beach. The busy fishermen lend plenty of life to the charming little port.

Marciana Marina. — The pleasant sea promenade is lined with palm trees, oleanders and magnolias.

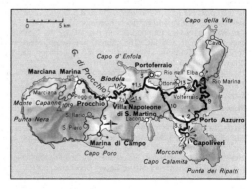

ELBA, Isle of*

Returning, on the right is a by-road leading to Napoleon's villa at San Martino.

Napoleon's Villa at San Martino★ (Villa Napoleone). — *Same times of opening as the Villa dei Mulini.* The setting of silent hills, planted with groves of evergreen oaks and terraced vineyards, has not changed; nor has the view. Unfortunately Prince Demidoff, the son-in-law of King Jerome, had a Neo-Classical palace built to house a museum just below the modest house which was the ex-Emperor's summer residence, with its garden shaded by fine trees. The internal decoration has been restored.

From the terrace there is a good view of Portoferraio Bay.

Capoliveri. — From the western boundary of this village there is a **panorama★★** known as the Three Seas because it shows the three Bays of Portoferraio, Marina di Campo and Porto Azzurro. One also overlooks, to the south, the road and beach of **Morcone.** The view extends beyond to the Islands of Pianosa and Monte-Cristo in the east.

Porto Azzurro. — Formerly called Porto Longone, Porto Azzurro is a pretty port overlooked by a fortress, which is now used as a prison. Cacti and agaves are typical vegetation.

Return to Portoferraio by a high altitude **road★★** *(not surfaced for most of the way and rough,* which affords remarkable views of the ruins of Volterraio, Portoferraio Bay and the sea.

TUSCAN ARCHIPELAGO★ (Arcipelago Toscano)

The archipelago includes, with the Isle of Elba, those of Gorgona, Pianosa, Capraia, Giglio and Giannutri, and finally the famous **Monte-Cristo** *(no boat service operating, landing prohibited)* which has been turned into a national park.

Several of these islands contain prison colonies. A steamer service *(from and to Leghorn)* makes it possible to see Gorgona and Pianosa, and visit Capraia and Elba.

ESTE Venetia

Michelin map **988** 5 — southwest of Padua — *Local map p 97* — Pop 18 300

The ancient Ateste, dating from before the Roman era, was also the cradle of the Este family, who reigned over Ferrara. North of it stand the ramparts of a castle built in the 14C by a member of the Carrara family who ruled over Padua; there is a public garden within its walls. From the keep a panorama of the Euganean Plain and Hills can be seen *(see below).*

Atestino National Museum★ (Museo Nazionale Atestino). — *Closed for restoration work; opening due early 1981.* This museum, in the late 16C Palazzo Mocenigo, whose façade is the wall of the old castle, contains interesting archaeological collections, including Venetian antiques (ceremonial pitchers shaped like animals, richly engraved bronze vases and amusing statuettes), and Roman antiques (mosaics and coins).

Northwest of the museum, in the hills, among the pines, are the Palazzo dei Principi (Palace of the Princes) and also the charming Benvenuti and Kunkler Villas, where Byron and Shelley lived.

Cathedral (Duomo — 17C). — The church contains a fine picture by Tiepolo (18C) of St. Tecla delivering Este from the plague.

EUGANEAN Hills ★ (COLLI EUGANEI) Venetia

Michelin map **988** 5.

These hills, whose highest point, Monte Venda, reaches an altitude of 602 m - 1 975 ft — are of volcanic origin, which explains the characteristic sugar-loaf shape of their summits and the numerous hot springs. Owing to their isolation they are used for television and radar relay stations.

The country is unusually rich and was already inhabited in the Palaeolithic era. Orchards of apple, pear and peach trees alternate with vineyards. The latter produce excellent red and white wines.

TOUR STARTING FROM PADUA — *105 km - 65 miles — 1 day*

Leave Padua *(p 169)* by ⑤.

Abano Terme★ and Montegrotto Terme. — These resorts have been famous since the time of the Romans for their mud baths, which are excellent for rheumatism. The waters have a temperature of 87°C (188·6°F) and contain radio-active algae.

Rua Hermitage (Eremo di Rua). — The hermitage is occupied by Camaldulian monks. *Only men may enter the monastery: open Tuesdays, Thursdays and Saturdays, 9.30 am to 12.30 pm and 3.30 to 5.30 pm in summer; 8.30 to 11.30 am and 2.30 to 7.30 pm in winter. Sundays and holidays the church only may be visited. Closed Saturday before Easter.* There is a good view from the monastery of the hills, Padua and the plain as far as Venice.

Praglia Monastery (Monastero di Praglia). — *Guided tours, Easter Monday to 30 September, 3.30 to 5.30 pm; the rest of the year, 2.30 to 4.30 pm; closed Mondays, Maundy Thursday to Saturday before Easter, and religious holidays.*

The monastery was founded late in the 11C by the Benedictines but the present buildings date only from the 16 and 17C. The church, fine raised cloisters with uncluttered lines and the refectory with its Baroque stalls and late 15C Crucifixion painted by Montagna above the abbot's chair, are the most remarkable features.

Having crossed the little **Teolo Pass,** planted with acacias and chestnut trees, the route then skirts the western boundary of the hills, allowing a visit to Este.

Este. — *Description above.*

Monselice★. — A large section of the walls is intact on the north side of this charming place which is dominated by the romantic ruins of a castle. In the centre of the town is the graceful **Piazza Mazzini** in which stands the *Torre Civica* (Municipal tower — 13-16C). From this square the picturesque Via del Duomo runs uphill, and on its left is the entrance to the 13-14C **castle** of the Paduan, Ezzelini da Romano.

Higher up is the **cathedral,** a Romanesque building, and higher still rise two adjoining buildings the early 17C Sanctuary of the Seven Churches and the Villa Balbi from which there is a good view.

Arquà Petrarca. — Petrarch, the leading humanist of the Renaissance, died in this mediaeval looking town. The great Italian lyric poet was born at Arezzo in 1304, but he spent nearly all his
youth at Avignon, at the Papal Court, and it was in a church there that he met Laure de Sade,
the "ideal" mistress, whom he was to immortalise in his melancholy *Sonnets.* Petrach was a
diplomat and a great traveller, employed in turn by Robert of Anjou at Naples, by the Pope, by
the Visconti at Milan, by the Doges of Venice and by the Carrara of Padua; he was crowned
Prince of Poets in the Capitol in Rome with a laurel wreath sent by the University of Paris. In
1370 he retired to Arqua and four years later, on the morning of his 70th birthday, he was
found dead in his library with his
head resting on a page of the Latin
author he had been reading.

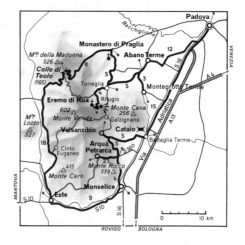

In this attractive house on the top
of the hill are moving souvenirs
such as the chair in which the poet
died and a visitors' book containing the signatures of Mozart and
Byron amongst others *(open
17 March to 15 October: 9 am to
12.30 pm and 2 to 7 pm; the rest
of the year: 9.30 am to 12.30 pm
and 1.30 to 4.30 pm. Closed Mondays, 1 January, Easter and
Christmas; 300 lire).* Petrarch's
tomb, a plain pink marble sarcophagus, was set up in the
church square in 1830.

Valsanzibio di Galzignano. — The 17C
Villa Pizzoni-Ardemani, formerly
called the **Villa Barbarigo★,** is surrounded by a pretty Italian garden:
ponds, grottoes, statues and a
maze. *Open 1 May to 15 October,
10 am to noon and 3 to 7 pm; the
rest of the year, 10 am to noon
and 2 to 5 pm. Closed Monday mornings and 30 November to 15 March; 1 000 lire.*

Cataio Castle (Castello di Cataio). — A fine 16C castle.
Rejoin the Via Adriatica to return to Padua.

In addition to Faenza other centres of Italian ceramic production included:
Urbino: *Under the patronage of the Montefeltros factories produced 16C majolica.*
Gubbio: *Again patronised by the Montefeltros the
artisans produced the famous iridescent red or metallic lustre.*
Castel Durante: *This 16C group of majolica factories
were known for the art of Istoriato painting.*

FABRIANO Marches ─────────────────────────────

Michelin map **988** 16 — 55 km · 34 miles — northeast of Assisi — Pop 28 951

Industrious Fabriano, lying in its basin, has manufactured paper since the 13C, but it has
also given birth to delightful artists like Allegretto Nuzi (14C) and Gentile da Fabriano
(1370-1427), both exponents of the international Gothic style *(p 27).*

Piazza del Comune★. — This square in the centre of Fabriano has preserved the rather severe
charm of the mediaeval city. The grim grey stone Governor's Palace (1225), in the
Romanesque-Gothic style, crowned with Ghibelline merlons, is lit by windows of three adjacent
bays beneath a single supporting arch. To the left is the municipal loggia.
    Three basins, one fitted with small columns, make up the elegant Gothic fountain (1351).
The Piazza del Duomo is reached by a stairway starting under the arcades.

Piazza del Duomo★. — The square is pink-walled, quiet and charming; only the sound of
water from the simple Classical fountain breaks the silence. The brick buildings surrounding the
square are, from left to right, the bishop's palace (1545) and the façades of the cathedral and
the hospital.
    The **Hospital of St. Mary, Mother of Jesus** (Ospedale di Santa Maria del Buon Gesù) dates
from 1456. The graceful Gothic façade, pierced with paired trilobar windows, rests on a portico
under which two 15C frescoes are visible. The cloisters and well are of the same period.
    The early 17C **cathedral** has kept a polygonal 14C apse and a 13C sacristy. In the interior the
Chapel of St. Lawrence (San Lorenzo) near the chancel is covered with frescoes by Allegretto
Nuzi depicting the life of St. Lawrence.

FAENZA Emilia-Romagna ─────────────────────────

Michelin map **988** 15 — Pop 55 630

Town plan in the Michelin Red Guide Italia (hotels and restaurants).

Formerly the Roman Faventia and still girt with 15C ramparts, Faenza has given its name to
the ceramics known as faïence.

Ceramics. — In Italy *faïence* is also known as *majolica* because it originated in Majorca. The
15C Faenza potters were inspired by ceramics imported from the Balearic Isles. Production
began in Faenza in the 12C and reached its zenith in the 15-16C, after the "hot-fire" process
had been adopted. The earthenware is coated with a glaze containing tin salts; the decoration
is painted on the glaze and melted into it by baking at high temperature (950°C = 1 742°F.).
This technique has drawbacks: correction is impossible and only pure colours can be used.
    Subjects placed dead centre, sometimes poorly drawn, brilliant colours and floral decora-
tion are the characteristics of Faenza ceramics.

■ **SIGHTS** *time: 2 1/2 hours*

International Ceramics Museum★★ (Museo Internazionale della Ceramica). — *9.30 am to 1 pm and 3.30 to 6.30 pm (2.30 to 5.30 pm 1 October to 31 May). Closed Mondays, 1 January, 25 April, 1 May, 15 August, Easter and Christmas, Sunday and holiday afternoons; 500 lire, Sundays and holidays 200 lire.*

Ceramic development in all parts of the world can be studied from the vast collections.

A history of the art of ceramics is displayed on the first floor. The most interesting works are in gallery IX: popular Italian art in all its provincial variety (there is some amusing Sardinian pottery). Galleries II, VII and VIII contain a large collection of majolica of the Italian Renaissance from Urbino, Castel Durante and especially Liguria, whose style was copied in the blue patterns of Nevers (France). In galleries IV, V and VI there is a display of local work, 14-19C. Also worth a visit are an oriental collection, an archaeological collection of the classical era *(temporarily not on view)*, and works from pre-Columbian America and Africa.

On the ground floor, the contemporary collection comprises Italian works and an international collection, which is a remarkable exhibition of modern pottery by Matisse, Picasso, Chagall, Léger, Lurçat and members of the Vallauris school.

Rooms containing records, a library and photographs complete the museum.

Municipal Picture Gallery and Museum★ (Pinacoteca e Museo Civico). — *Open 9.30 am to 12.30 pm and 2.30 to 4.30 pm. Closed Mondays, Sunday and holiday afternoons, I January, Easter Monday, 25 April, 1 May, 15 August, 1 November, 8, 25 and 26 December.*

In the entrance gallery, on the right hand wall is a Byzantine Madonna (gilded background) by Giovanni da Rimini. The next room contains pleasantly coloured works by Palmezzano da Forli, and especially a masterly and dramatic statue in wood of St. Jerome the Hermit, attributed to Donatello. Room III contains a Madonna between four cherubs and two saints, a charming picture of the Ferrara school (1484). In Room IV an attractive bust of St. John the Baptist as a child is the work of Antonio Rossellino.

Among the works shown in the remaining rooms note The Lovers, painted by Simon Vouet, a superb portrait of a Magistrate (Lombard or Flemish school, 17C) and a portrait of King Charles I of England by Franz Pourbus the Younger.

The Modern Art department *(closed afternoons)* is housed in a nearby building at 2 Corso Matteotti.

Cathedral (Duomo). — The cathedral was built in the Quattrocento (15C) by the Florentine architect Giuliano da Maiano, but the façade was left unfinished.

In the chapel to the left of the chancel Benedetto da Maiano, the nephew of Giuliano, carved the tomb of Bishop St. Savinus, whose life is depicted in six bas-reliefs. On the cathedral esplanade is a 17C fountain.

Piazza del Popolo. — The square is elongated and unusual, with arcades surmounted by galleries. The 12C Governor's Palace and the 13-15C town hall stand face to face.

EXCURSION

Brisighella★. — *Southwest, 13 km - 8 miles. Leave Faenza by   on the plan, road S 302.*

Brisighella is a picturesque town, dominated by a 13C castle and a tower dating from 1503. It lies in a pretty, verdant setting. The Piazza Marconi, in the centre of the town, is overlooked by the **Via Borgo**, a curious covered alley with arcades.

FANO ★ Marches ──────────────────────────

Michelin map **988** 16 — Pop 53 027

Town plan in the Michelin Red Guide Italia (hotels and restaurants).

Fano is a small town and a favourite seaside resort, with sand and pebble beaches bordered by a pleasant marine promenade.

Whom should we believe?. — Montaigne passed through Fano in April 1581. "This town", he wrote, "is famous above all others in Italy for its beautiful women. We saw only very ugly ones, and when I questioned a good man of the place he said the time of the beauties was past." One hundred years later Huguetan, a lawyer from Lyons, declared: "The place is reputed to have the most beautiful women in Italy. I saw two dead women lying in a church with their faces exposed. Both were of surpassing beauty and seemed only asleep. If the dead are so beautiful, what must the living be?"

■ **SIGHTS** *time: 1/2 hour*

Santa Maria Nuova Church. — 16-18C. This contains **works★** by Perugino which are admired for their fine draughtsmanship and soft colour as well as for this painter's fondness for ideal beauty. An exquisite Madonna and Child (1497) may be seen at the third altar on the right. The Virgin is surrounded by saints, among them St. Peter and, in the foreground, St. John the Baptist and Mary Magdalen. A *pietà* is painted above them and scenes from the life of the Virgin are depicted with much charm on the predella. The second altar on the left is adorned with a graceful Annunciation (1498), also by Perugino.

Fountain of Good Fortune (Fontana della Fortuna). — In the Piazza 20 Settembre stands the Fountain of Good Fortune which is the symbol of the city. The protecting goddess, perched on a pivoting globe, forms a weather-vane, catching the veering wind in her cloak.

Arch of Augustus (Arco d'Augusto). — The arch dates from the 1C AD and spans a driveway and two footpaths. It was formerly surmounted by arcades, which were destroyed in 1463 by the artillery of Federico da Montefeltro.

A 15C bas-relief on the graceful façade of the little Church of St. Michael (San Michele), nearby, reproduces the arch in its original form.

EXCURSION

Corinaldo. — *Southeast, 35 km - 22 miles.* This small town is surrounded by an interesting system of **fortifications★**, walls and gateways of the 15C.

FARA IN SABINA ★ Latium _____

Michelin map 🔢 26 — 38 km - 24 miles — southwest of Rieti — Pop 7725

Fara is a typical mediaeval city which has not changed since ancient times, and in which life goes on in rarely broken silence. The district produces an excellent white wine, generous and amber-tinted, also a fuller flavoured cheese, the *pecorino*.

The little town, with its narrow streets hemmed between market stalls and flower decked balconies, is perched on a knoll. From this there is an extensive and beautiful **view★** of the Sabine Mountains and the Roman Campagna, covered with vineyards and olive groves.

Farfa Abbey (Abbazzia di Farfa). — *6 km - 4 miles — plus 1/4 hour sightseeing.* In the village built round the monastery you will see hemp-weavers and houses still decorated with wrought iron signs. Farfa Abbey was founded in the 5C, rebuilt in 680, and became an important cultural centre in the Middle Ages. A Románesque-Gothic doorway adorned with a 15-16C fresco leads to the court in front of the church. The latter was rebuilt in the 16-17C but still has its 12C columns and its Romanesque mosaic paving.

FELTRE ★ Venetia _____

Michelin map 🔢 5 — 57 km - 35 miles — northwest of Treviso — Pop 22335

Feltre is grouped round its castle, which dates from the time of the Lombard King Alboin. Napoleon I presented the duchy to his War Minister, General Clarke. The town has kept part of its ramparts (Porta Oria, 1502) and its old houses, mostly Renaissance, adorned with frescoes in the Venetian manner (Via Mezzaterra).

Piazza Maggiore★. — This square in the centre of the town, overlooked by the Classical façade of St. Roch (San Rocco) and by the ancient castle, is beautiful with its irregular plan, its Gothic architecture with painted frescoes, and especially its noble Renaissance buildings, its arcades, stairways, terraces edged with balustrades and its narrow vistas.

Museum. — *Via Lorenzo Luzzo, near the Porta Oria. Open Tuesday to Friday, 9 am (10 am Friday) to noon; Saturday, 9 am to noon and 3 to 5 pm; Sunday 10 am to noon and 4 to 6 pm; closed Mondays; 300 lire.* On view are local works, notably by Pietro Marescalchi and Lorenzo Luzzo (1474-1527) who was called the "deadman of Feltre", because of the pallor of his complexion. It was said he was Giorgione's rival in love. The paintings include a remarkable portrait by Gentile Bellini, a Virgin between St. Denis and St. Victor, by Cima da Conegliano and four landscapes of which one is a seascape by Marco Ricci. Note also the Crown of Thorns a naïve and realistic work (German school of first half of 16C) a St. Bernardino of Siena attributed to Jan Metzys. (There are two copies of this: one in the Louvre, attributed to Memling, the other, in a Portuguese collection of paintings, to Quentin Metzys, Jan's father.)

The museum includes an historical section (Risorgimento) and an archaeological collection.

FERENTINO ★ Latium _____

Michelin map 🔢 26 — 12 km - 7 miles — northwest of Frosinone — Pop 17430

Like many other towns in Latium, Ferentino, which stands in a magnificent position overlooking the Sacco Valley, has kept its mediaeval air. It still has part of its Cyclopean walls and its acropolis, from which an extensive view can be enjoyed.

Church of St. Mary Major (Santa Maria Maggiore). — In the lower part of the town, at the end of the Via Cavour, stands the 13C Cistercian church with Gothic features: a façade pierced with rose windows, a flat chevet, a tower at the transept crossing and crotcheted capitals. The central rose window is surmounted by a statue of St. Bernard.

FERMO ★ Marches _____

Michelin map 🔢 16 — Pop 35192

Fermo is one of the artistic and cultural centres of the Marches. In an exceptional **site★** on the slopes of a hill overlooking the countryside and the sea, it displays the exclusive spirit of a little town still surrounded by ramparts and much attached to its old customs.

Piazza del Duomo★. — Right on top of the hill, where the feudal castle stood, is a wide esplanade, shady and flower decked, whose horizon is bounded by the façade of the cathedral. From this open space, which is also known as the Girifalco, splendid **views★★** can be enjoyed of the Sibillini Mountains and the Ascoli district to the west, of Gran Sasso to the south and of the sea and the Monte Conero Peninsula, near Ancona, to the north.

Cathedral (Duomo). — A majestic Romanesque-Gothic building, the Cathedral of Fermo was rebuilt in 1227 by Maestro Giorgio da Como to take the place of the earlier building, burnt down by Frederick Barbarossa in 1176. The stately **façade★** in white Istrian stone, remarkable though asymmetrical, is pierced with an elegant 14C rose window. A delicately carved doorway shows Christ with the Apostles on the lintel and symbolic scenes or figures on the uprights; among them are doves drinking from the Spring of Life, a pelican symbolising the Church, and again the Church in the form of a mother offering the fruit of the vine (the Eucharist) to a child representing the Faithful; also the Signs of the Zodiac, etc.

In the late 18C interior note: in the narthex, to the right, the 14C sarcophagus of Giovanni Visconti, overlord of the town; in front of the chancel, a 5C mosaic paving; in the crypt, a Christian sarcophagus of the 4C with high reliefs depicting the life of St. Peter; and finally at the 4th altar in the south aisle, a precious 13-14C Byzantine icon of the Virgin.

The chasuble of St. Thomas à Becket, made in Almeria in 1116, is kept in the sacristy. *Open weekdays, 8 am to noon and 3 to 6 pm (4 to 8 pm I July to 15 September). Closed in June and 16 September to 30 April.*

Piazza del Popolo★. — The Piazza del Popolo lies in the centre of the town and is surrounded with 16C arcades and the elegant portico of the church of San Rocco. At the far end, to the right, the sober town hall (1446) has a double flighted staircase leading to a loggia finished with the statue (1590) of Pope Sixtus V, who bestowed the bishopric on Fermo.

At the far end, to the left, the 16C Palazzo degli Studi (Palace of Learning) which now houses an important library, was the seat of the university, until it was abolished in 1826. The busts surmounting the windows are of papal benefactors.

A 16C archway between the two palaces leads to a steep, picturesque street lined with towers of nobility *(see p 220)*, palaces and ancient churches.

Many Sleeping Beauties' Palaces, with memories of the Princes of Este and their brilliant, artistic and lettered court, give Ferrara a rather melancholy charm which is apparent near the castle and in the avenue, Corso Ercole d'Este. Except for a nucleus round the cathedral the plan of the town, modern in conception with its gardens and wide, airy streets, dates from the Renaissance. With 100 000 inhabitants Ferrara was in the 15C the equal of Milan, Venice and Florence.

HISTORICAL NOTES

At first an independent community, Ferrara belonged to the House of Este from 1208 to 1598. It then became papal territory and was, under Napoleon, the departmental capital of the Lower Po.

The Estes. — The members of this famous family were often cruel, but they were also discriminating patrons of arts. Niccolò III (1393-1441) murdered his wife Parisina and her lover, Ugo. But he begat Lionello and Borso, generous administrators and enlightened patrons.

Ercole I (1471-1505) was highly intelligent and able. He tried to poison his nephew Niccolò, who claimed the duchy, married Eleonora of Aragon, a capable woman who later succeeded, in the absence of her spouse, in defeating an attempted *coup* by Niccolò, who was captured and beheaded. He was then buried in a solemn ceremony at which Eleonora burst hypocritically into tears, followed by the whole court. Ercole encouraged artists, as did his two famous daughters, Beatrice and Isabella d'Este. **Alfonso I,** the son of Ercole, became the third husband of Lucrezia Borgia, an angel or devil whose charm and supple, blonde beauty were irresistible, as her serving knight, the handsome Pietro Bembo, insists in one of his books, *The Asolani.* Another famous couple was **Ercole II** (1534-1558) and Renée of France, the daughter of Louis XII, who took Marot and the Calvinists under her protection.

Several of the Estes including Lucrezia, are buried in the 15C **Church of Corpus Domini** (BZ C).

Two Best Sellers. — *Orlando Furioso (Roland the Mad)* was the *Gone with the Wind* of the Renaissance: it was similar in length, in popular appeal and in theme. In it **Ariosto** (1474-1533) related the adventures of a coquette, Angelica, and of two suitors bewitched by her beauty, Rinaldo and Orlando, the knight whom the lady succeeded in driving mad.

The success of *Orlando Furioso* was tremendous. Ariosto was compared to Virgil and Homer, and portrayed by Titian. It was said that one day he was attacked by educated highwaymen who recognised him, treated him with respect and escorted him to the end of his journey, for the roads, they said, were not safe.

Torquato Tasso (1544-1595) was the author of the epic poem *Gerusalemme Liberata (Jerusalem Delivered),* the subject of which, the capture of Jerusalem by Godefroy de Bouillon, is enlivened by episodes in the love-story of Rinaldo and Armida. The poem enchanted Mme de Sévigné, Napoleon Bonaparte and the Romantics such as Chateaubriand, Lamartine. Shelley took as a souvenir a piece of brick from the cell in the mental hospital of St. Anne, where Alfonso d'Este had the poet, who was subject to fits of insanity, confined.

The Ferrara School of Painting. — Together Van der Weyden, who arrived at Ferrara in 1450, and the Veronese, Pisanello, who painted Niccolò III and Lionello d'Este, introduced painting to Ferrara. The leader of the local school, the peculiar **Cosimo Tura** (1425-1495), was soon followed by **Francesco Cossa** (1435-1477), Ercole dei Roberti, Lorenzo Costa (1465-1530), the colourist Dosso Dossi, a friend of Ariosto, and Garofalo (died 1559), an imitator of Raphaël. The characteristics of the Ferrara school, which was both powerful and original, are a taste for picturesque and fantastic detail, firm drawing, realistic observation balanced by absence of idealisation and imagination, and lack of beauty in facial expression.

■ **MAIN SIGHTS** *time: 3 1/2 hours*

Este Castle★ (Castello Estense). — *Open 9.30 am to noon and 3 to 6 pm (2 to 5 pm 1 October to 31 May). Closed Mondays, 1 January, Easter, 1 May and Christmas.* This 14C castle was the seat of the court under the Renaissance. It is guarded by moats and four fortified gateways with drawbridges. The marble balustrades and crowns of the towers, added in the 16C, give it an unusual appearance.

Visitors are shown the great and the small Games' Rooms and the Aurora Room, in the last of which are four frescoes representing the four times of day, and the small Bacchanalia Room. All these rooms are painted with mythological and allegorical frescoes dating from the 16C attributed to Filippo and Filippino Lippi. The Chapel of Princess Renée of France, who was a Protestant, is decorated with porphyry and marble. Also to be seen are the duchess' hanging garden and the cell in which Parisina and Ugo were murdered in 1425.

Cathedral★. — Begun in 1135 the cathedral is in the Romanesque-Gothic Lombard style *(pp 26-27).* The triple **façade★★,** which is very wide and all in marble, is remarkable for its sculptures and the arrangement and variety of the openings. The upper part is Gothic and the central doorway Romanesque. You should walk round the building to the right to judge its great size and see the Renaissance campanile.

There are inlaid stalls in the chancel and a 16C Last Judgement on the ceiling.

Above the narthex is the cathedral **museum★** *(open 10 am to noon and 3 to 5 pm; closed Sundays and holidays)* in which are kept amusing and expressive late 12C bas-reliefs representing the months taken from the south door, which was destroyed in the 18C; two early 15C statues by the Sienese, Jacopo della Quercia, one representing the Virgin with a Pomegranate; 16C tapestries portraying St. George and St. Maurillo, the patron saints of Ferrara; and above all, two outstanding **masterpieces★★** by Cosimo Tura: an Annunciation and a St. George slaying the Dragon and so saving the Princess of Trebizond.

The 13C **town hall,** facing the cathedral, is a former ducal palace joined by a gallery with the Este Castle. The façade was rebuilt in 1924; at the back is a grand staircase (1481).

Schifanoia Palace★ (Palazzo Schifanoia). — 14-15C. *Schifanoia* means carefree, and the Estes called this palace the House of Joy. The doorway has noble lines.

Inside is the **Municipal Museum** *(open weekdays, 9 am to 12.30 pm and 3 to 6 pm (2.30 to 5.30 pm in winter); Sundays and holidays, 9.30 am to 12.30 pm and 3.30 to 6.30 pm. Closed 1 January, 25 April, 1 May, 25 and 26 December)* with its displays of medals and a rich collection of missals and antiphonaries illuminated with beautiful miniatures, archaeological exhibits,

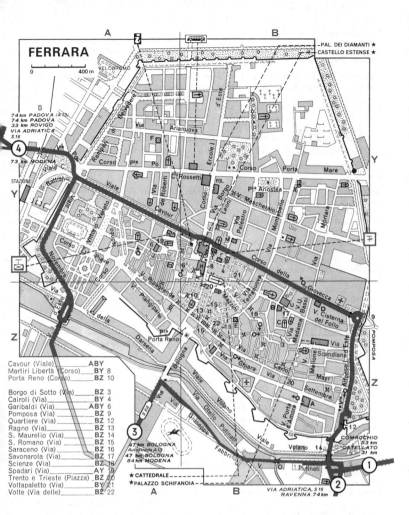

- PAL. DEI DIAMANTI ★
CASTELLO ESTENSE ★

FERRARA	
Cavour (Viale)	ABY
Martiri Libertà (Corso)	BY 8
Porta Reno (Corso)	BZ 10
Borgo di Sotto (Via)	BZ 3
Cairoli (Via)	BY 4
Garibaldi (Via)	ABY 6
Pomposa (Via)	BZ 9
Quartiere (Via)	BZ 12
Ragno (Via)	BZ 13
S. Maurelio (Via)	BZ 14
S. Romano (Via)	BZ 15
Saraceno (Via)	BZ 16
Savonarola (Via)	BZ 17
Scienze (Via)	BZ 18
Spadari (Via)	AY 19
Trento e Trieste (Piazza)	BZ 20
Voltapaletto (Via)	BY 21
Volte (Via delle)	BZ 22

★ CATTEDRALE
★ PALAZZO SCHIFANOIA

Renaissance ceramics and small bronzes, and 14-17C paintings and sculptures. The Room of the Months is adorned with admirable **frescoes★★** full of life and charm (1467-1470). Francesco Cossa, Ercole dei Roberti and some unknown masters have painted, from left to right, allegories of the months and scenes from the life of Borso d'Este in three superimposed orders.

The **Basilica Santa Maria in Vado**, near the palace, has in its south transept a 16C shrine *(tempietto)* in which the stains made by drops of blood said to have sprung from the Host at Easter, 1171, are worshipped *(ask the sacristan to light the shrine)*.

Palace of Diamonds★ (Palazzo dei Diamanti). — 15-16C. — This owes its name to the 12 500 blocks of marble of its façade, cut in facets like diamonds. The sumptuous building has delicate Renaissance patterns on the corner pilasters and a projecting balcony. The Palazzo Prosperi, at the opposite corner of the square, has a graceful Renaissance doorway.

Picture Gallery★★. — *Restoration work in progress; only some of the rooms being reorganised are open: 9 am to 2 pm except Mondays; 9 am to 1 pm Sundays and holidays*. The gallery has a valuable collection of paintings of the Emilian school and in particular of the Ferrara school of the 15 and 16C including such artists as Cosimo Tura, Ercole dei Roberti, Garofalo (the Raphaël of Ferrara) and Dosso Dossi. There are interesting 13-14C frescoes in the Great Hall.

■ ADDITIONAL SIGHTS

Palace of Ludovico the Moor★ (Palazzo di Ludovico il Moro) (BZ A). — *Open 1 June to 15 September, 9 am to 12.30 pm and 3.30 to 6 pm; the rest of the year, 9 am to 1.30 pm (12.30 pm Sundays and holidays). Closed Mondays, Sunday and holiday afternoons, 1 January, 25 April, 1 May, first Sunday in June, 15 August and 25 December; 500 lire.* This palace, built at the end of the 15C, for Ludovico Sforza, the Moor, husband of Beatrice d'Este, has a great courtyard with arcades which was completed only on two sides. On either side of the portico leading to the garden are two rooms, one of which has a painted ceiling, probably by Garofalo, while the other contains two curious boats, each carved out of a gigantic tree-trunk and recently found in the Spina marshes *(p 85)*, near Comacchio.

The other rooms of the palace contain an **archaeological museum**: finds from the excavations of the Etruscan city of Spina, and an outstanding collection of ceramics brought over from Greece, dating from 5 and 4C BC, and found in the tombs at Spina.

Romei House★ (Casa Romei) (BZ B). — *Guided tours with the caretaker.* A delightful 15C house with decorated courts. Opposite the entrance is a palace in which Renée of France, daughter of Louis XII, lived.

Palazzina di Marfisa d'Este★ (BZ D). — *Open 1 April to 30 September, 9 am to noon and 5 to 6 pm (9 am to noon Sundays and holidays); the rest of the year, 10 am to 12.30 pm and 2 to 5 pm (9 am to 12.30 pm Sundays and holidays); closed Mondays.* This elegant single storey residence (1559) was frequented by many friends of that charming Marfisa d'Este of whom Tasso sang. The house is interesting for its painted ceilings, rare 16C furniture, garden and outdoor theatre with frescoes of a trellis perched on by flocks of birds.

FERRARA★★

Old Streets. — In the southern part of the town, in the Via delle Volte, there are many covered alleys and corbelled houses.

House of Ariosto (AY F). — *Open 9 am to noon and 3 to 6 pm; closed Sundays and holidays.* The house was built for Ariosto, with a garden in which he grew roses and jasmine. On the first floor is the room with 16C furniture in which he died. His tomb lies in the library of the Paradise Palace (palazzo del Paradiso — **BZ E**).

FIDENZA Emilia-Romagna _____

Michelin map **988** 14 — 23 km - 14 miles — west of Parma — Pop 24 117

Fidenza has resumed its Roman name after having been known as Borgo San Donnino for a long time.

Cathedral★. — San Donnino (late 12C) is a remarkable building in the Lombard Romanesque style *(p 26)*. The arcades along the sides of the cathedral and the interior decoration are of the same period. The facings and the decoration of the façade, twin towers, apse and chancel in a similar style date from a later period (13C) and mark the transition between the Romanesque and Gothic style.

The doorways in the façade are admirable; they recall those of Provence.

The sculptured decoration of the **central porch★★**, full of nobility and expression, seems to be of the school of the Parmesan sculptor Antelami. This porch is supported by two Lombard lions which appear ready to spring. The vaulting is adorned with the figures of two angels, Old Testament prophets and apostles surrounding Christ the King. A frieze on the lintel and sides of the doorway relates the life and martyrdom of St. Donnino, who was beheaded but carried his head away in his hands like St. Denis.

FIESOLE ★ Tuscany _____

Michelin map **988** 14 15 — 8 km - 5 miles — north of Florence — *See town plan of Florence p 103* — Pop 14 788

The ancient Etruscan and Roman city of Fiesole, the mother of Florence, standing on its hill, is a delightful place. The slopes going down towards Florence are covered with rows of cypresses and sumptuous villas.

It was at the foot of the hill, in the garden of the Villa Palmieri, that Boccaccio set the action of his *Decameron;* it was on the terrace of the Villa Medici that Lorenzo de' Medici entertained his literary friends, Politian and Pico della Mirandola. This quiet landscape and subtle atmosphere attracted writers like Shelley, Dickens, Lamartine, Anatole France and the art-historian Berenson.

View of Florence★★. — This outstanding memory of a visit to Italy can be seen from the terrace near the peaceful **Monastery of St. Francis** (San Francesco). The latter has charming small 14C cloisters (which you can see through a grille) and tiny cells, one of which was occupied by St. Bernardino of Siena. At the foot of the stairway in front of the monastery, you will see the **Church of St. Alexander** (Sant'Alessandro) with its ancient columns and capitals. It was built on the site of a Roman temple, dedicated to Bacchus, and then transformed into a church, probably by Theodoric the Great (King of the Ostrogoths from 474 to 526) at the beginning of the 6C.

Cathedral (Duomo). — Founded in the 11C and enlarged in the 13 and 14C, the building was extensively restored between 1878 and 1883 when the façade was completely rebuilt. It is surmounted by a battlemented campanile built in 1213; the upper section has been renovated. The austere interior is on a basilical plan with a raised chancel. The columns support antique capitals. The Salutati Chapel, on the right in the chancel, has frescoes by Cosimo Rosselli (15C) and two handsome **works★** by Mino da Fiesole: the bust of Bishop Salutati (1464) adorning his tomb, and a carved altarpiece full of grace and delicacy depicting the Virgin at Prayer with St. John and other saints. At the high altar there is a Virgin in Majesty with saints by Bicci di Lorenzo (1440).

FIESOLE

FIRENZE 8 km

Archaeological Site. — *Open 1 May to 30 September, 10 am to noon and 3 to 7 pm; March, April and October, 10 am to 12.30 pm and 2.30 pm to 6 pm; 1 November to end of February, 9.30 am to 12.30 pm and 2 to 5 pm. Closed Mondays and Christmas; 500 lire.* In a pretty hill setting stands a **Roman theatre★** (about 80 BC) which is remarkably well-preserved. Plays are now performed there. There are ruins of a temple (on the left) and of baths (on the right) near the entrance stands a small archaeological museum **(M)**.

Bandini Museum (M¹). — *Open 9 am to 12.30 pm and 3 to 6 pm (2 to 5 pm November to end of March); Sundays and holidays 9 am to noon. Closed for 5 days for 15 August celebrations; 500 lire.* On view on the ground floor are terracottas by della Robbia, and on the first floor, works by 14 and 15C Florentine masters: note in Room 1, Bernardo Daddi (an Evangelist), Bicci di Lorenzo (St. Catherine of Alexandria and the Emperor), Taddeo Gaddi (the Annunciation), Niccolò di Tommaso...; in Room 2, Jacopo del Sellaio ("Triumphs" after Petrarch's masterpiece).

San Domenico di Fiesole. — *South, 2.5 km - 1 1/2 miles.* The church dates from the 15C and was remodelled in the 17C when the porches and campanile were added. Fra Angelico made his vows here. A **picture★** of the Madonna and Saints by the artist is exhibited in the first chapel on the left (in 1501 Lorenzo di Credi collected together the elements of this work originally designed as a triptych). Note an Annunciation (third chapel on the left) by Jacopo da Empoli (1615) and a Baptism of Christ (second chapel on the right) by Lorenzo di Credi.

Badia Fiesolana. — *South, 3 km - 2 miles.* The church and the cloisters of this abbey *(badia)* were rebuilt in the 15C in the graceful style of Brunelleschi. The marble façade of the small Romanesque church that previously stood on the site, was included in the new façade.

FLORENCE ★★★ (FIRENZE) Tuscany

Michelin map 988 14 15 — Pop 463 826

Florence the Divine gathers within its boundaries every form of beauty. Lying between the hills of the Arno Valley, idealised by a diaphanous, amber light, it mingles art and life gracefully under the town's heraldic sign of the red Turk's Cap lily.

Tour of Florence. — The tourist may linger in front of the jewellers' shops on the Ponte Vecchio. He may stroll along the area — between the Ponte Vecchio and Piazza San Giovanni — bounded by Via Por Santa Maria, Calimala and Roma and by Via Calzaiuoli, the other street linking Piazza San Giovanni and Piazza del Duomo, where abound luxury shops specialising in fashion, footwear and fine leather goods. He may pause among the booksellers near the Annunziata and Via Cavour, he may explore the Flea Market in Via Pietrapiana or the antiquaries' shops in Borgo Ognissanti and Via Maggio and Serragli or he may stroll under the loggia in the New Market, along the arcades of Piazzale degli Uffizi and round San Lorenzo which is lively with open-air souvenir stalls. When tired by the bustle of the traffic he may sit on the terraces of one of the cafés of the Piazza della Signoria or Piazza della Repubblica, and enjoy an ice or a cup of coffee (a *gelato* or an *espresso*). At meal-times he will seek out a *trattoria* or *buca* (cellar) where he can sample the delicious Tuscan cuisine *(p 35)*. As he walks he will see palaces adorned with embossing and façades decorated with paintings and sculptures and he will identify the six-balled shield of the Medicis. He will also discover the characteristics of the Florentine: courtesy, discretion, quick wits, artistic sense and sophistication.

Traditional Events. — Easter Sunday is celebrated in the Piazza del Duomo by the *scoppio del carro* or blowing up of a float, sparked by a dove sliding along a wire from the high altar in the cathedral to the vehicle. May in Florence is a time of concerts, opera and ballet. On Ascension Day the people of other times hunted for crickets in the Cascine Park. Today, they are content to buy them on the Sunday following Ascension Day.

The famous *Calcio Fiorentino* is a ball game, preceded by a magnificent procession in 16C costume. This is held on the Feast of St. John (mid-summer) and 28 June (fireworks display in Piazzale Michelangiolo). September 7 marks the Rificolona festival: floats, coloured paper lanterns. There is dancing and music in the streets and local folk-songs are sung.

Florence hosts an Antique Fair every two years *(odd years, mid-September to mid-October),* which is held in the Strozzi Palace *(p 112)* and a biennial exhibition of gold and silver plate *(end of September to beginning of October, even years).*

Craftsmanship flourishes in Florence: there are fashion-houses, leather, gold and silversmiths' workshops and strawmakers, and hard stone workers' shops.

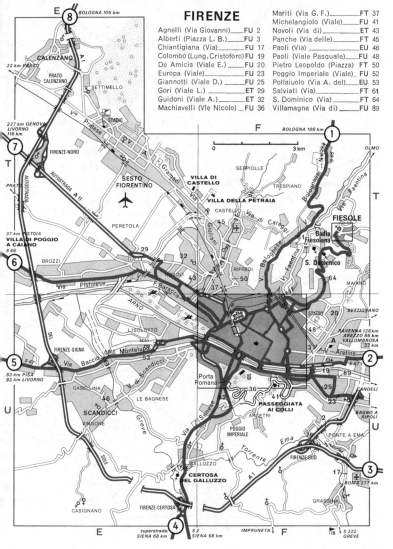

FIRENZE

Agnelli (Via Giovanni)	FU	2
Alberti (Piazza L. B.)	FU	3
Chiantigiana (Via)	FU	17
Colombo (Lung. Cristoforo)	FU	19
De Amicis (Viale E.)	FU	20
Europa (Viale)	FU	23
Giannotti (Viale D.)	FU	25
Gori (Viale L.)	ET	29
Guidoni (Viale A.)	ET	32
Machiavelli (Vle Nicolo)	FU	36
Mariti (Via G. F.)	FT	37
Michelangiolo (Viale)	FU	41
Novoli (Via di)	ET	43
Panche (Via delle)	FT	45
Paoli (Via)	EU	46
Paoli (Viale Pasquale)	FU	48
Pietro Leopoldo (Piazza)	FT	50
Poggio Imperiale (Viale)	FU	52
Pollaiuolo (Via A. del)	EU	53
Salviati (Via)	FT	61
S. Dominico (Via)	FT	64
Villamagna (Via di)	FU	89

FLORENCE★★★

HISTORICAL NOTES

Florence grew up from 200 BC onward round the Via Flaminia, which crossed the Arno at the site of the present Ponte Vecchio (Old Bridge). But its power dated only from the 11-12C. This period saw the rise of trades organised in powerful guilds, the appearance of a currency based on the florin and the growth of exports of Florentine cloth.

Internal Strife. — The Guelphs, who supported the Pope, and the Ghibellines, who were partisans of the Holy Roman Emperor, appeared in the 13C *(see p 18)*. The Guelphs at first had the advantage; but the Ghibellines, after being driven out of Florence, allied themselves with its enemies, notably Siena, and defeated the Guelphs at Montaperti. The Guelphs counterattacked and defeated the Ghibelline nobles in 1266. They established government by the *Signoria,* in which the *Priori* sat. There then occured a split between White Guelphs and Black Guelphs which lasted until 1348, when the Black Death decimated the townspeople.

Money Power. — Succeeding the Lombard and Jewish money-lenders, the Florentine bankers became famous all over Europe. As early as 1199 they kept up relations with England and in 1262 they issued the first bills of exchange, which gave an incredible stimulus to Florentine and European trade. The leading bankers were the Bardi-Peruzzis, who advanced huge sums to Edward III of England at the beginning of the Hundred Years War (1338-1453). The Pitti, the Strozzi, the Pazzi and the Medicis were the other outstanding families of Florence.

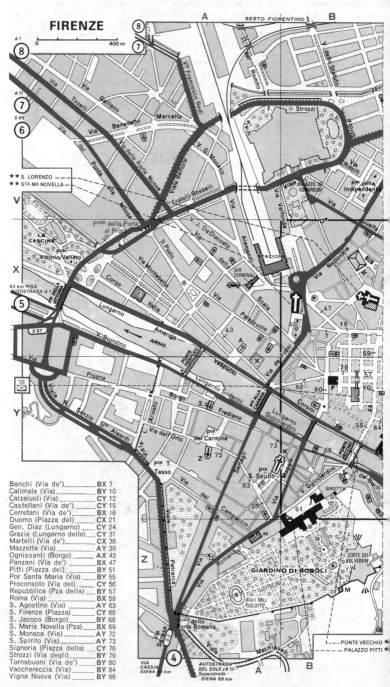

FIRENZE

The Medicis. — Giovanni di Bicci (1360-1429), a banker, was the founder of this illustrious dynasty of patrons of the arts. Cosimo the Elder (1389-1464), the Grand Merchant of Florence, the Father of the Land, who was both rich and generous, gathered artists round him. Lorenzo the Magnificent (1449-1492), a prodigy of intelligent ugliness, nicknamed *Lauro* (Laurel) by his friends, was a talented poet. He founded the Platonic Academy, the Laurentian Library and his death marked the end of the Medici Century.

The sceptre descended to the junior branch, who were also descended from Giovanni di Bicci. Cosimo I (1519-1574), the son of the leader, Giovanni delle Bande Nere, annexed Siena and became the first Grand Duke of Tuscany; Francesco (1541-1587), whose daughter Maria was to marry Henri IV King of France, named as his second wife the beautiful Venetian Bianca Cappello. The last prominent Medici was Ferdinand I (1549-1609).

Savonarola. — The Dominican from Ferrara, Savonarola (1452-1498), the fanatical and ascetic Prior of the monastery of St. Mark, was the antithesis of the Florentines, who were artists and high livers, but submitted to his influence. In 1493 he thundered from the pulpit of Santa Maria del Fiore against the pleasures of the senses and of the arts so vehemently that he terrified his audience. He had Pietro II de' Medici, the son of Lorenzo, banished for his cowardice before the French, but in 1494 he himself welcomed Charles VIII. In 1497 he organised, in the Piazza della Signoria, a bonfire of vanities on which wigs, musical instruments, books of poetry and works of art were burnt. A year later he was burnt at the stake on the same spot.

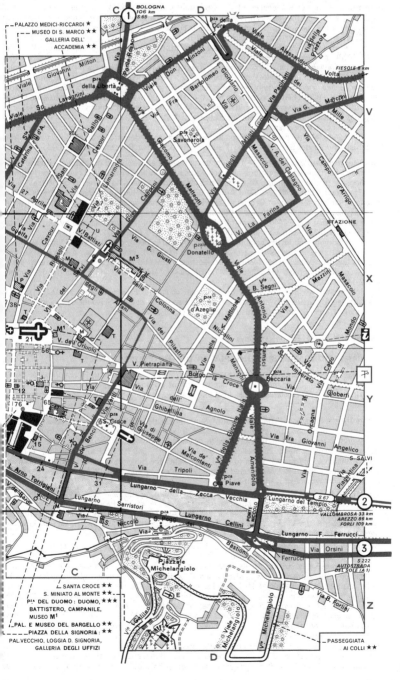

FLORENCE★★★

LETTERS

The Italian language developed with Dante on the banks of the Arno, and it is in the Florence region that the purest Italian is spoken today.

Dante Alighieri (1265-1321) was a prior at Florence in 1300 and was banished two years later; he then travelled all over Italy before dying at Ravenna. Beatrice Portinari, whom he met when she was ten and who died at twenty-four, inspired all his work, especially the *Vita Nova* (New Life). But his masterpiece remains the *Divina Commedia* (Divine Comedy), the highest achievement of spiritual knowledge of the age, in which Dante, led by Virgil and then by Beatrice, visits the Inferno, Purgatory and Paradise. The 14C was dominated by the names of Petrarch *(p 97)* and Boccaccio *(p 81)*.

Machiavelli (1467-1527), born in Florence and the statesman on whose account Machiavellism became a synonym for cunning, was both the pioneer of Italian unity and the author of *Il Principe* (The Prince — 1513), an essay on political science and government dedicated to Lorenzo II de' Medici.

THE ARTS

From the 12 to the 16C — from Byzantine traditionalism to decadent mannerism — Florence saw an extraordinary blossoming of the visual arts, which reached their zenith in the century of the Medicis.

Painting. — The characteristics of the Florentine school *(see table p 28)* are the search for beauty of form and the desire to present an idealised picture of nature, together with balanced composition and perspective. Giorgio Vasari (1511-1574) is the historian of this movement.

Cimabue (1240-1302) was still close to the mosaicists, but **Giotto** (1266-1337) freed himself from the Byzantine tradition in his search for truth, movement and expression. **Masaccio** (1401-1428), a pioneer in the matter of foreshortening, studied the depth of space, while the "blessed" Fra Angelico (1387-1455) expressed a suave mysticism in a still Gothic technique. Paolo Uccello (1397-1475) and Andrea del Castagno (1423-1457) worked especially at the rendering of volume, unlike such sharp and delicate draughtsmen as Filippo Lippi (1406-1469) and Gozzoli the historian (1420-1498). The summit and the decline of the first Florentine Renaissance are marked by the Pollaiuolo brothers, **Botticelli** (1444-1510), Domenico Ghirlandaio (1449-1494) and Filippino Lippi (1459-1504), the son of Filippo.

The second Renaissance, in the 16C, was dominated by the great names of Leonardo da Vinci, *(p 264)*, Michelangelo and Raphaël, who made their début at Florence, by the brilliant colourist Andrea del Sarto (1486-1531) and by the portraitist Bronzino (1503-1572).

Architecture and Sculpture. — The architects created a style based on restraint coupled with grandeur: harmonious proportions and geometrical decoration in coloured marble for religious buildings, a massive structure of embossed stone and overhanging cornices for palaces.

The great Gothic masters were Arnolfo di Cambio (died 1302) and Giotto, pioneers of the Renaissance and teachers of Orcagna (1308-1368), a painter, sculptor and architect. The typical Renaissance architects fell back on the Classical tradition: among them was the refined and sober **Brunelleschi** (1377-1446), a rival of Ghiberti in sculpture. He was followed by Leon Battista Alberti (1404-1472), who was also a poet, and Michelozzo (died 1472).

Outstanding among the sculptors are Ghiberti (1378-1445), **Donatello** (1386-1466), with his realistic and stylised genius, Luca della Robbia (1400-1482), who was also a specialist in terracotta and Verrocchio (1436-1488). Donatello had many and charming imitators, among them Desiderio da Settignano (1428-1464), Mino da Fiesole (1430-1484) and Benedetto da Maiano (1442-1497).

In the 16C we find the names of two great sculptors, **Benvenuto Cellini** (1500-1571), who was above all a goldsmith and also, at times, a memorialist and Giovanni da Bologna (Jean Bologne), a Frenchman who settled at Bologna (1529-1608).

■ MAIN SIGHTS *time: 4 days*

DAY 1: **MONUMENTS OF THE PIAZZA DEL DUOMO★★★** *morning*

The cathedral stands in the Piazza del Duomo and in the adjoining Piazza San Giovanni, and together with the campanile and baptistry forms an admirable group.

Under the 14C **Loggia del Bigallo (CXE)**, which is in the Gothic style, lost or abandoned children were exhibited.

Cathedral★★ (Duomo). — The Cathedral of Santa Maria del Fiore was built and paid for by the Florentine Republic and the cloth-makers' guild. It is one of the largest cathedrals in the Christian world. It was begun in 1296 by Arnolfo di Cambio and was consecrated in 1436; the huge and magnificent dome by Brunelleschi (height, 106 m - 348 ft; St. Paul's London, 111 m - 365 ft), which took fourteen years to build, completed the building in 1434. Multicoloured marble forms the geometrically decorated facing. A modern façade (late 19C) has taken the place of one which was destroyed in 1588.

Exterior. — Note the late 14C Canons' Door in the south façade, and then make for the Mandorla Door, walking round the building (from the corner of Via Proconsolo, there is an impressive view★★ of the apse and the dome). An Assumption between the archivolt and the gable represents the Virgin in a *mandorla* (almond), supported by angels. The Annunciation is depicted in mosaic on the tympanum (1490).

Interior. — This is impressive for its size and bareness. High Gothic vaulting rests on sturdy arches: there are only four in the nave.

The **dome★★★** is striking for its great height. It is painted with a huge fresco of the Last Judgement, the work of Vasari and Federico Zuccari, and lit by stained glass windows from cartoons by Donatello, Paolo Uccello, Andrea del Castagno and Lorenzo Ghiberti. You can go up to the inner gallery and on to the top *(464 steps)* of the dome *(open 8.30 am to noon and 2. 30 to 6 pm — 5 pm, 1 October to 31 March — tickets on sale up to 1/2 hour before closing-time; closed for the main religious festivals; 500 lire; entrance on the north side of the nave)*. From the gallery there is a bird's-eye view of the cathedral nave, and from the top a magnificent **panorama★★** of Florence.

The great octagonal chancel under the dome, surrounded by a delicate marble balustrade made in 1555, is dominated by a large 15C Crucifix by Benedetto da Maiano. The sacristy doors on each side of the high altar have tympana adorned with pale blue terracottas by Luca della

Robbia, representing the Resurrection and the Ascension. A dramatic episode of the **Pazzi conspiracy** took place in the chancel. The Pazzis, who were rivals of the Medicis, tried to assassinate Lorenzo the Magnificent on 26 April 1478, during the Elevation of the Host. Lorenzo, though wounded by two monks, managed to take refuge in a sacristy, but his brother Giuliano fell to their daggers.

The axial chapel contains a masterpiece by Ghiberti, the sarcophagus of St. Zanobi, the first Bishop of Florence. One of the bas-reliefs shows the saint resurrecting a child.

Go down the north aisle: at the first bay on the right a fresco of 1465 shows Dante explaining the *Divine Comedy* (Inferno, Purgatory and Paradise) to Florence. Farther along on the right two frescoes by Uccello (1436) and Andrea del Castagno (1456) depict portraits of local leaders.

A little further on, at the far end of the north aisle and of the nave, stands *(provisionally)* the famous **Pietà★★** which Michelangelo, at the age of eighty, left unfinished.

A stairway on the other side of the nave, between the first and second pillars, leads to the **Santa Reparata crypt** *(open 9.30 am to noon and 2.30 to 6 pm — 5 pm 1 October to 31 March; closed Sunday afternoons, 1 January, Easter, 1 May, Corpus Christi, 15 August, 1 November, 25 and 26 December; 300 lire, free Sundays).* You will see the vestiges of a Romanesque basilica demolished when the present cathedral was built, which have been excavated recently. The basilica itself was formerly an early Christian church (5-6C). Now visible are traces of mosaic paving belonging to the original building and Brunelleschi's tomb (behind a grille at the bottom of the stairs, on the left).

Campanile★★. — *Open 8.30 am to 12.30 pm and 2.30 to 6 pm (5 pm 1 October to 31 March); tickets on sale up to 1/2 hour before closing time. Closed 1 January, Easter, Corpus Christi, 25 and 26 December; 1 000 lire.* The tower is slim and tall (82 m - 269 ft) and goes well with Brunelleschi's dome, the straight lines of the former balancing the curves of the latter. Giotto drew the plans for it and began building in 1334, but died in 1336. The campanile was completed at the end of the 14C; it belongs to the Gothic period but is Classical in spirit in its regular lines, emphasised by multicoloured marble.

The admirable bas-reliefs at the base of the campanile have been replaced by copies. Those on the lower band were executed by Andrea Pisano and Luca della Robbia and those on the upper band by pupils of Andrea Pisano, but the general design was due to Giotto. The original bas-reliefs are in the Cathedral Museum.

From the top of the campanile there is a fine **panorama★★** of the cathedral and the town.

Baptistry★★ (Battistero). — *Open 9 am to 12.30 pm and 2.30 to 6 pm (5 pm 1 October to 31 March).* The building is decorated with white and green marble in a quiet and well balanced Romanesque style. The **doors★★★** are world famous.

The South Door (main door), by Andrea Pisano (1330), is Gothic; above are scenes from the life of St. John the Baptist and below, the Virtues, three theological (Faith, Hope and Charity) and five cardinal. The door-frames, which show extreme skill are by Vittorio Ghiberti, son of the designer of the other doors.

The North Door (1403-1424) was the first done by Lorenzo Ghiberti. This was the winner in a competition in which Brunelleschi, Donatello and Jacopo della Quercia also took part. Scenes from the Life and Passion of Christ are evoked with extraordinary nobility and harmony of composition.

The East Door (1425-1452), facing the cathedral, is the one that Michelangelo declared worthy to be the Gate to Paradise. In it Ghiberti recalled the Old Testament *(see sketch);* prophets and sibyls adorn the niches. The artist portrayed himself, bald and malicious, in one of the medallions.

Interior★★. — With its 25 m - 82 ft — diameter, its black and white marble and its paving decorated with oriental motifs, the interior is grand and majestic.

The dome is covered with magnificent **mosaics★★★** of the 13C. The Last Judgement is depicted on either side of a large picture of Christ the King; on the five concentric bands that cover the other five panels of the dome, starting from the top towards the base, note the Heavenly Hierarchies, Genesis, the Life of Joseph, scenes from the Life of the Virgin and of Christ, and the Life of St. John the Baptist.

On the right of the apse is the tomb of the Antipope John XXIII, friend of Cosimo the Elder, a remarkable work executed in 1427 by Donatello assisted by Michelozzo.

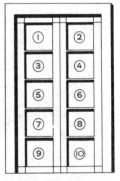

Baptistry: Gate to Paradise.

1 Adam and Eve.
  The Temptation.
2 Cain and Abel.
3 The Deluge. Noah's Drunkenness.
4 Abraham. The Sacrifice of Isaac.
5 Esau. Isaac blesses Jacob.
6 Joseph sold by his Brethren.
7 Moses receives the Law.
8 Joshua. The Taking of Jericho.
9 David and Goliath.
10 Solomon and the Queen of Sheba.

Museum of the Cathedral Building and its Possessions★
(Museo dell' Opera di Santa Maria del Fiore). — *Open 9.30 am to 1 pm and 3 to 6 pm (2 to 5 pm 1 October to 31 March). Closed Sunday afternoons, 1 January, Easter, 1 May, 15 August, 25 December; 500 lire, free Sundays.* Statues from the former façade of the Cathedral (Pope Boniface VIII by Arnolfo di Cambio, the four Evangelists), equipment used by Brunelleschi to build the dome, and gold plate are collected on the ground floor.

On the mezzanine is exhibited an impressive repentant **Magdalen★** carved in wood by Donatello.

In the large room on the first floor are two famous statues by Donatello of the prophets Jeremiah and Habakkuk, the latter being nicknamed *Zuccone* (vegetable marrow) because of the shape of his head. In the same room are the famous **Cantorie★★**, choristers' tribunes, from the cathedral; on the left, that of Luca della Robbia is the best known (the independent panels on the base are original, the upper section has been remodelled with copies); it bears figures of choir boys, dancers and musicians of exquisite charm. Donatello's tribune, opposite, is more elaborate and less natural but its decorative carvings are effective.

The room to the right contains the famous silver **altarpiece★** depicting the life of St. John the Baptist, a masterpiece of 14-15C Florentine craft. In a room on the left are exhibited the admirable **bas-reliefs★★** from the campanile: those by Andrea Pisano and Luca della Robbia which are hexagonal in shape and very picturesque, depict the creation of Adam and Eve and various human activities; the rest are diamond-shaped and represent the planets, the virtues, the liberal arts and the Sacraments.

FIRENZE

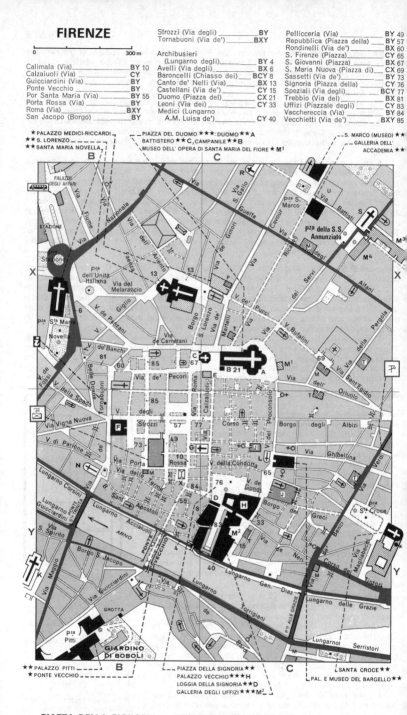

★PALAZZO MEDICI-RICCARDI — PIAZZA DEL DUOMO ★★★ :DUOMO ★★A — S. MARCO (MUSEO) ★★
★★S. LORENZO — BATTISTERO ★★C,CAMPANILE ★★B — GALLERIA DELL' ACCADEMIA ★★
★★SANTA MARIA NOVELLA — MUSEO DELL'OPERA DI SANTA MARIA DEL FIORE ★M¹

★★PALAZZO PITTI — PIAZZA DELLA SIGNORIA ★★ — SANTA CROCE ★★
★PONTE VECCHIO — PALAZZO VECCHIO ★★★H — PAL. E MUSEO DEL BARGELLO ★★
LOGGIA DELLA SIGNORIA ★D
GALLERIA DEGLI UFFIZI ★★★M²

PIAZZA DELLA SIGNORIA★★ AND PONTE VECCHIO★ afternoon

Piazza della Signoria★★. — This was, and still is, the political stage of Florence, with a wonderful backcloth formed by the Palazzo Vecchio and the Loggia della Signoria. The many statues make it virtually an open-air museum of sculpture: near the centre of the square, the equestrian statue of Cosimo the Younger, after Giovanni da Bologna, and at the corner of the Palazzo Vecchio, the Fountain of Neptune (1576) near which a bronze plaque marks the spot where Savonarola was burnt. In front of the Palazzo Vecchio are the proud *Marzocco,* or Lion of Florence, the famous bronze of **Judith and Holofernes★** by Donatello and a copy of Michelangelo's David.

Palazzo Vecchio★★★. — *Open 9 am to 7 pm (8 am to 1 pm Sundays and holidays; closed Saturdays, 1 January, Easter, 1 May, 24 June, 15 August and Christmas; 500 lire, free on Sundays and holidays.* The Old Palace's powerful yet graceful mass is dominated by a lofty belltower, 94 m - 308 ft — high. Built between 1299 and 1314 in a severe Gothic style complete with battlements, parapet walks and crenellations the edifice is thought to have been designed originally by Arnolfo di Cambio. The elegant interior is a complete contrast. The **court★** was restored by Michelozzo in 1453 and delicately decorated a century later. The 16C fountain is surmounted by a delightful winged goblin holding a dolphin, a copy of a work by Verrocchio (the original is in the palace).

The apartments are lavishly decorated with paintings by Vasari and Bronzino (16C), and sculptures by Benedetto and Giuliano da Maiano to the glory of Florence and the Medicis. On the first floor the great Sala dei Cinquecento, painted with frescoes by several artists, including

Vasari, contains a group carved by Michelangelo, The Genius of Victory. The walls of the magnificent **studiolo★★**, or study of Francesco de' Medici, which was designed by Vasari were painted by several Florentine mannerist painters including Bronzino who was responsible for the medallion portraits of Cosimo I and Eleonora of Toledo. On the second floor, the former apartments are open: in the Priors' Apartments, note the Sala dei Gigli which is adorned with a splendid coffered **ceiling★** by Giuliano da Maiano, the Guardaroba lined with 16C maps and in the adjoining small room the winged goblin by Verrocchio; the Apartments of Eleonora of Toledo were designed and decorated by Vasari with the exception of the chapel which was adorned with frescoes by Bronzino. The visit ends with the Apartments of Cosimo I, known as Quartieri degli Elementi because of the allegorical scenes painted by Vasari and his assistants to decorate the first room.

Loggia della Signoria★★. — Built at the end of the 14C, the loggia was the assembly hall and later the guard-room of the *Lanzi* (foot-soldiers) of Cosimo the Younger, Duke of Tuscany. It contains antique and Renaissance statues: the Rape of a Sabine (1583), Hercules and the centaur Nessus by Giovanni da Bologna and the wonderful **Perseus★★★** showing the head of Medusa, a masterpiece of Renaissance sculpture executed by Benvenuto Cellini between 1545 and 1553.

Ponte Vecchio★. — The bridge is unique in appearance and dates from the 14C. On each side of the road across the bridge are jewellers' shops *(closed Sundays)* which have been there since the 16C. Above the shops the **Corridoio Vasariano,** a corridor built by Vasari, links the Uffizi with the Pitti Palace.

DAY 2: BARGELLO★★ AND SANTA MARIA NOVELLA★★ *morning*

The Bargello Palace and Museum★★. — *Open 9 am to 2 pm (1 pm Sundays and holidays). Closed Mondays, 1 January, 1 May, 15 August, Easter and Christmas; 750 lire.*
  The Palazzo del Bargello was formerly that of the Governor and then that of the Constable *(Bargello).* It is a fine example of 13-14C mediaeval architecture planned round a majestic **courtyard★★.** A museum of sculpture and decorative art is now housed in it.

Ground Floor. — One room is devoted to Michelangelo and to 16C Florentine sculpture. Note a Bacchus drunk, a Brutus, a marble medallion (the Tondo Pitti) depicting the Virgin and Child and St. John, and an Apollo (or David) by Michelangelo. There are also works by Cellini, Giovanni da Bologna etc.

First Floor. — The Great Saloon (to the right) contains many **works by Donatello★★★,** including St. George, St. John the Baptist as a Youth, the famous **David,** etc. In the other rooms is displayed the large Carrand collection: enamels, jewels, remarkable ivories.

Second Floor. — Room I contains excellent terracottas by the della Robbias. In the other rooms you will see many Renaissance sculptures, the famous bronze statue of **David** by Verocchio as well as delicate little bronzes and a remarkable collection of arms and armour.

Santa Maria Novella★★. — The church of Santa Maria Novella and the adjoining monastery were founded in the 13C by the Dominicans.

Church★. — Begun in 1246, the church was completed only in 1360, except for the **façade★** with harmonious lines and geometric patterns in white and green marble, designed by Alberti (upper section) in the 15C. It is a large church (100 m - 330 ft) designed for preaching. On the wall of the third bay in the north aisle is a famous **fresco★★** of the Trinity with the Virgin, St. John and the donors in which Masaccio, adopting the new Renaissance theories, shows great mastery of perspective. In the north transept, the Strozzi Chapel (raised) is decorated with **frescoes★★** (1357) by Ørcagna depicting the Last Judgement with great scope and originality. The sacristy contains a fine **Crucifix★** by Giotto. In the Gondi Chapel (1st on the left of the chancel) is displayed the famous **Crucifix★★** by Brunelleschi which so struck Donatello that he is said, on first seeing it, to have dropped the basket of eggs he was carrying. The chancel *(illumination: 100 lire)* is ornamented with admirable **frescoes★★** by Domenico Ghirlandaio who, on the theme of the Lives of the Virgin and of St. John the Baptist, painted a dazzling picture of Florentine life in the Renaissance era.

Cloisters. — *Open 9 am to 2 pm; closed Fridays, 1 January, 1 May, 24 June, 15 August, Easter and Christmas; 500 lire; free Sundays and holidays. Entrance north of the church.* The finest are the **Green Cloisters★,** so-called because of the predominant colour of the frescoes *(presently removed for restoration)* painted by Paolo Uccello and his school. Into them opens the famous **Spaniards' Chapel,** covered with **frescoes★★** of intricate symbolism by Andrea di Buonaiuto (late 14C). Facing the entrance the Ascent to Calvary, the Crucifixion, the Descent into Limbo; on the vault, the Resurrection; on the wall to the left, the Triumph of Divine Wisdom and Glorification of St. Thomas Aquinas; on the vault, Pentecost; below, a Dominican theologian enthroned and surrounded by the Wise Men of the Old and New Testament, represents Catholic Doctrine thanks to which the Liberal Arts (below right) and the Sacred Arts (left) symbolised by 14 female figures are animated by the Holy Spirit. On the right wall, the Church Militant and Triumphant and the glorification of the action of the Dominicans: on the vault, St. Peter's fishing boat symbolises the Church; on the wall, below, standing in front of a church are the Pope and the Emperor (the two foremost dignitaries in the human hierarchy); the flock of the faithful is watched over by the Dominicans *(Domini Canes* — the Hounds of the Lord) symbolised by dogs attacking heretical wolves; above, after the sacrament of Confession, the souls purified of the deadly sins (seated on the right) gain admission to Heaven.

UFFIZI MUSEUM★★★ (Galleria degli Uffizi) *afternoon*

  Open on weekdays, 9 am to 7 pm (1 pm Sundays and holidays); closed Mondays, 1 January, 25 April, 1 May, first Sunday in June, 15 August and 25 December; 1 250 lire. The **Uffizi Museum** is housed in the Renaissance palace, designed by Vasari (1560), which contained the offices *(uffizi)* of the Medicis' administration. Today this is one of the finest museums in the world. The rich collections of drawings and prints are on the first floor; the museum proper (paintings and sculpture), in three galleries, is on the second floor, overlooking the Uffizi court with its adjacent rooms.

The Galleries. — The walls are hung with an admirable series of 16C **tapestries:** the Months and the Fêtes given at the courts of Catherine de' Medici and of Henri II, of the Flemish school — in these the Tuileries and the Châteaux of Anet and Fontainebleau can be recognised. Other subjects are the Passion of Christ from the Florentine looms, etc. Classical statues, mostly Roman copies, and a fine series of busts of the Imperial era are also on view.

FLORENCE★★★

Rooms of the first Gallery of Painting. — The first room *(closed for restoration)* is devoted to Classical sculpture; the ten which follow contain Florentine and Tuscan paintings from the late 13 to 16C and the remaining rooms are reserved for the Italian and foreign schools of the 15 and 16C and miniatures.

Tuscan late 13-14C. — Note especially the works of Cimabue, Giotto and Duccio (Madonnas: Room 2) and the famous **Annunciation** of Simone Martini (Room 3).

Florentine 15C. — Here you can admire: in Room 7 Masaccio (St. Anne, the Virgin and Child); Paolo Uccello **(Battle of San Romano:** the two other panels are in the Louvre and in London); Fra Angelico (Coronation of the Virgin), Piero della Francesca (Portrait of the Duke of Urbino); in Room 8 Filippo Lippi (Nativities, **Virgin and Child,** Coronation of the Virgin); in Room 9, the Pollaiuolos. The **Botticelli Room★★★** (10-14), which is the most remarkable in the museum, contains the **Birth of Venus, Spring** and Madonnas as well as beautiful Flemish primitives: Van der Goes **(Portinari Altarpiece),** Van der Weyden (Entombment), Memling (portraits).

The next rooms (15-16) contain two masterpieces by Leonardo da Vinci: the unfinished **Adoration of the Magi** and the famous **Annunciation.**

The Tribune (Room 18). — This is octagonal in shape with red hangings and was designed by Buontalenti (1588). It contains the famous **Medici Venus** carved by a Greek sculptor in the 3C BC, and several portraits of the Medicis by Pontormo, Bronzino, Vasari...

Italian and Foreign Schools of the 15-16C. — Note in Room 19, Perugino and Signorelli; in Room 20, Cranach **(Adam and Eve,** Luther) and Durer **(Adoration of the Magi);** in Room 21, Giovanni Bellini **(Sacred Allegory)** and Giorgione; Correggio etc...

Miniatures Room. – *(Temporarily closed).* Miniatures from the 15 to the 19C.

Second gallery of Painting *(coming back).* — The first eleven rooms are devoted to the Italian Cinquecento (16C): Michelangelo (Room 25: **Holy Family**); Raphaël (Room 26: **Leo X, Madonna with a Thistle);** the "mannered" schools: Florentine (Rooms 26-27: Andrea del Sarto — the famous Virgin with Harpies, Pontormo, Rosso, etc.), Emilian (Rooms 29-31: Parmigianino, Dosso Dossi), and Venetian.

There are some splendid Titians (Room 28: Flora, **Venus,** portraits), Veroneses (Room 34: the Holy Family and St. Barbara) and Tintorettos (Rooms 35: **Leda and the Swan,** portraits).

Next is Italian and foreign painting of the 17 and 18C. The 17C Flemish school is represented in Room 30 by Rubens **(Isabella Brandt)** and Van Dyck (portraits). The Niobe Room (42) contains views of Venice by Guardi and Canaletto, a Tiepolo and works of the French school: Chardin (Boy playing Cards), Nattier (Three portraits of Louis XV's daughters). The landscape painters (Room 43) include Ruysdael and Claude Lorrain. Finally in Room 44 are several Caravaggios **(Bacchus as a Youth)** and remarkable portraits by Rembrandt.

Corridoio Vasariano. — *Guided tours (1 hour); apply in writing well in advance to the Uffizi Administration; same times and ticket as the museum. Access by the door near Room 25.* Remarkable collection of self-portraits by Italian and foreign artists.

DAY 3: THE PITTI PALACE★★ (Palazzo Pitti) *morning*

Open 9 am to 2 pm (1 pm Sundays and holidays); closed Mondays, 1 January, 1 May, 15 August and Christmas; 1 000 lire. This 15C Renaissance building, of rugged but imposing appearance, with huge embossing, was built to the plans of Brunelleschi. The two wings were added in the 18C. Maria de' Medici lived here, in the Palazzo Pitti.

Palatine Gallery★★ (1st floor). — This contains a wonderful **collection★★★** of Titians and Raphaëls, among them: by Titian, **La Bella,** the Aretino, a copy of a portrait of Julius II by Raphaël, **the Concert** (Hall of Venus) and the Portrait of the **Grey-eyed Nobleman** (Hall of Apollo); by Raphaël, **Woman with a Veil** (Hall of Jupiter), remarkable portraits and the famous **Madonna del Granduca** and the **Madonna della Seggiola** (Hall of Saturn). Among other masterpieces are two admirable seascapes by Salvator Rosa (Hall of Venus), Charles I, King of England, and his wife Henrietta of France by Van Dyck (Hall of Apollo), the **Four Philosophers** by Rubens and **Cardinal Bentivoglio** by Van Dyck (Hall of Mars), a Descent from the Cross by Fra Bartolomeo (Hall of Jupiter), a gloomy Mary Magdalen by Perugino (Hall of Saturn), fine portraits by Sustermans, and Eleonora of Mantua as a Child by Pourbus (Iliad Room), and an amazing Sleeping Cupid by Caravaggio (Hall of the Education of Jupiter), and a Virgin and Child by Filippo Lippi (Hall of Prometheus).

Royal Apartments. — *First floor.* These are lavishly adorned with pictures, works of art and admirable tapestries.

Silver Museum★ (Museo degli Argenti). — *Ground floor. Open Wednesdays, Fridays and Sundays.* This contains an exceptional collection of hard stone carvings, ivories, glassware and silver plate largely from the Medici treasury.

Modern Art Gallery. – *2nd floor. 1 000 lire.* Works, mostly Tuscan, illustrating the trends that influenced Italian painting and sculpture in the last century. In the section devoted to Neo-Classical and Romantic Art, note works by the Benvenuti, Canova, Bezzuoli, Hayez and Bartolini. The *"Macchiaioli"* school *(p 31)* is represented by its most famous masters: Fattori, Lega, Signorini, Cecioni...

SANTA CROCE★★ AND A TRIP TO THE HILLS★★ *afternoon*

Santa Croce★★. — The church and cloisters of Santa Croce give onto one of the town's oldest squares, which is lined by several palaces which are typically Florentine in style.

Church★. — This is the church of the Franciscans. It was started in 1294 and completed in the second half of the 14C. The façade and the campanile date from the 19C. The **interior★★** is vast (140 m by 40 m - 460 × 130 ft) as the church was designed for preaching and consists of a simple spacious nave and a slender apse with fine stained glass windows (15C). The church is paved with 276 tombstones, and along the walls are sumptuous tombs.

SOUTH AISLE: By the first pillar, a Virgin and Child by A. Rossellino (15C); opposite, the tomb of Michelangelo (died 1564) by Vasari; opposite the second pillar, the funerary monument to Dante (died 1321, buried at Ravenna); by the third pillar, a fine pulpit by Benedetto da Maiano (1476) and facing it the monument to V. Alfieri (died 1803) by Canova; opposite the fourth pillar, the 18C monument to Machiavelli (died 1527); facing the fifth pillar, an elegant bas-relief of the **Annunciation★** carved in stone and embellished with gold by Donatello; opposite the sixth pillar, the **tomb of Leonardo Bruni★** (a humanist and chancellor of the Republic, died 1444) by B. Rossellino, and next to it the tomb of Rossini (died 1868).

SOUTH TRANSEPT: At the far end, the Baroncelli chapel with frescoes (1338) depicting the Life of the Virgin by Taddeo Gaddi; at the altar, the Coronation of the Virgin from Giotto's workshop.

SACRISTY *(access by the corridor on the right of the chancel):* This dates from the 14C and is adorned with frescoes★ including a Crucifixion by Taddeo Gaddi and, in the fine Rinuccini Chapel, with scenes from the Life of the Virgin and of Mary Magdalen by Giovanni da Milano (14C).

At the far end of the corridor is the harmonious Medici Chapel built by Michelozzo (1434) with a fine altarpiece in glazed terracotta by Andrea della Robbia.

CHANCEL: The first chapel to the right of the altar contains moving frescoes★★ (c 1320) by Giotto depicting the life of St. Francis; in the third chapel is the tomb of Julie Clary, the wife of Joseph Bonaparte.

The chancel proper is covered with frescoes★ (1380) by Agnolo Gaddi relating the legend of the Holy Cross.

NORTH TRANSEPT: At the far end is a famous Crucifix★ by Donatello, which Brunelleschi tried to surpass at Santa Maria Novella.

NORTH AISLE *(coming back):* Next to the second pillar, a fine monument to Carlo Marsuppini by Desiderio da Settignano (15C); facing the fourth pillar, the tombstone of L. Ghiberti (died 1455); the last tomb (18C) is that of Galileo (died 1642).

This church is one of the Florentine monuments that suffered most in the 1966 floods as water rose to a height of 3 m within the building and 5 m in the cloisters.

Cloisters. — *Open 9 am to noon and 3 to 6 pm (5 pm 1 October to 31 March). Closed Wednesdays, Sunday afternoons and holidays; 500 lire. Entrance to the right of the church.*

The museum of Santa Croce *(entrance in the first cloister on the right)* installed in the former refectory contains a famous Crucifix★ by Cimabue which was seriously damaged by the 1966 floods.

The Pazzi Chapel★★ *(at the far end of the first cloister)* is the work of Brunelleschi. Entered through a domed portico, it is a masterpiece of the Florentine Renaissance remarkable for its originality, noble proportions and harmonious decoration (glazed terracotta from the della Robbia workshop).

The Great Cloister★ *(entrance at the far end of the first cloister, on the right)* is very elegant and was designed by Brunelleschi shortly prior to his death (1446) and was completed in 1453.

A Trip to the Hills★★ (Passeggiata ai Colli). — *By car (1 hour). See plans pp 105 and 103. Leave by the Piazza F. Ferrucci (DZ).* The Viale Michelangiolo climbs the flank of the hill, affording pretty views. From the Piazzale Michelangiolo can be seen a panorama★★ of the town. A stairway nearby leads to the pretty early 16C Church of San Salvatore al Monte (DZ E) which Michelangelo referred to as *"la bella villanella"* "the pretty little country church".

Overlooking the town, the church of San Miniato al Monte★★ built from the 11C to early 13C is one of the most remarkable examples of Florentine Romanesque architecture with its façade decorated with geometric designs in white and green marble. The harmonious interior also ornamented with white and green marble contains a 13C pavement with a very fine marble mosaic in the centre. The Chapel of Cardinal James of Portugal opens out of the north aisle; it is a fine Renaissance structure with a ceiling adorned with medallions by Luca della Robbia. The cardinal's tomb (1459-1461) is by Rosellino and there is an Annunciation by Alessio Baldovinetti. In the centre of the nave is a chapel by Michelozzo (1447) containing a Crucifix; the coffered ceiling in glazed terracotta is by Luca della Robbia. The raised chancel is closed by an admirable balustrade★ on which rests the pulpit, beautifully inlaid with marble and dating from the early 13C. The apse has elegant blind arches and is adorned by a mosaic (late 13C) depicting Christ giving his blessing. The Gothic sacristy to the right of the chancel is covered with frescoes (1387) by Spinello Aretino relating the life of St. Benedict. The 11C crypt has fine columns with antique capitals.

From the esplanade in front of the church, there is a fine view★ of Florence.

DAY 4: MUSEUM OF ST. MARK★★ AND THE ACADEMY★★ *morning*

Museum of St. Mark★★ (Museo di San Marco). — *Open 9 am to 2 pm (1 pm Sundays and holidays); closed Mondays, 1 January, 25 April, 1 May, first Sunday in June, 15 August, 25 December; 750 lire.* The museum in a former Dominican monastery rebuilt in 1437 by Michelozzo, is virtually the Fra Angelico Museum★★★. Purity, delicacy, gentleness and humility are the qualities of the Blessed Angelico.

The cloisters, which are shaded by a famous cedar, have tympana adorned with frescoes (late 16-early17C).

On the ground floor, on the right, the former guest quarters contain many works of this Dominican, including the Linaioli Madonna surrounded by twelve Angel Musicians which are among the best known figures painted by Fra Angelico, the great triptych depicting the Descent from the Cross, three small paintings in the style of miniature painters (Coronation of the Virgin, Madonna with a Star, Annunciation), the admirable series of large wall paintings depicting the life of the Virgin and the Life of Christ, and the famous Last Judgement. The vast and famous fresco of the Crucifixion adorns the chapterhouse. In the small refectory is an admirable Last Supper★ by Ghirlandaio.

The monks' cells on the first floor were decorated by Fra Angelico and his assistants with edifying scenes designed to encourage meditation. His own masterpiece, the Annunciation, faces the staircase.

Following the corridor to the left of the stairs, note the Apparition of Christ to the Penitent Magdalen (1st cell on the left), the Annunciation (3rd cell on the left), the Transfiguration (6th cell on the left), and the Coronation of the Virgin (9th cell on the left). Savonarola's cell contains mementoes and his portrait, a fierce, passionate and obstinate man, as seen by Fra Bartolomeo, whom he had converted. The library, an elegant room with three aisles that gives onto the corridor on the right, is by Michelozzo.

Academy Gallery★★ (Galleria dell'Accademia). — *Open 9 am to 2 pm (1 pm Sundays and holidays). Closed Mondays; 150 lire. Entrance in Via Ricasoli, No. 60.* The main gallery contains works by Michelangelo★★★, among them Four Slaves (unfinished) destined for the tomb of Julius II (the remaining two are in the Louvre Museum) and the famous David.

The picture gallery *(partially closed for reorganisation)* has on display in the three rooms to the left of the gallery Florentine primitives (13-14C). In the first room as you enter, you will see the delightful Madonna of the Sea by Botticelli.

SAN LORENZO★★ AND MEDICI PALACE★ *afternoon*

San Lorenzo★★. — Situated a short distance from the Medici Palace, this was the parish church of the Medicis.

Church★. — This Renaissance building was designed by Brunelleschi and his pupils.

The **former sacristy★** *(door at the end of the north transept)* is the work of Brunelleschi and is a very successful harmony of geometrical lines: note the effective use of the bluish grey stone *(pietra serena)* to highlight the architectural features. Much of the decoration is by Donatello (coloured medallions in the pendentives and lunettes, bronze doors and the surmounting bas-reliefs, heads of the cherubs on the frieze of the entablature). The funerary monument of Pietro and Giovanni de' Medici is by Verrocchio (1472).

Laurentian Library★. — Access is through the charming cloisters built in the 15C in the style of Brunelleschi *(entrance to the left of the church).* A majestic staircase executed by Ammannati on a design by Michelangelo leads to the great room also designed by Michelangelo. Some of the library's 10000 manuscripts are on display in rotation *(open 9 am to 5 pm; closed Sundays, holidays and 1 to 15 September).*

Medici Chapels★★ *(entrance on the Piazza Madonna degli Aldobrandini).* — Open 9 am to 7 pm *(1 pm Sundays and holidays); closed Mondays, 1 January, 1 May, 15 August and Christmas; 800 lire.* These include the Princes' Chapel and New Sacristy.

The **Princes' Chapel** (17-18C) is faced inside with hard stone and precious marble and contains the funerary monuments of Cosimo I and his descendants, the Grand-Dukes of Tuscany, in the crypt below.

The **New Sacristy★** is the work of Michelangelo as regards its architecture and sculpture. He started work in 1520 but he departed from Florence in 1534 leaving the building unfinished (it was completed in 1555 by Vasari and Ammannati).

The famous **tombs★★★** were designed by the great artist so that Giuliano de' Medici (died 1516) appears as Action, Lorenzo II de' Medici (died 1519) as a Thinker. The power, originality and skill in design and execution are incomparable.

Drawings (nudes, face studies and architectural designs) attributed to Michelangelo, have been discovered recently in the basement *(group tours every 1/2 hour).*

Medici Palace★ (Palazzo Medici-Riccardi). — *Open 9 am to 1 pm and 2 to 5 pm; Sundays and holidays 9 am to noon; closed 1 January, Easter and Christmas.*

This noble building, with its huge bosses, is typical of the Renaissance style. It was begun by Michelozzo on the order of his friend, Cosimo the Elder, in 1444. The Medicis lived in it from 1460 to 1540.

Chapel *(1st floor, entrance by the first stairway on the right — closed also on Wednesdays).* — A tiny chapel decorated with admirable **frescoes★★** (1459) by Benozzo Gozzoli. The Procession of the Kings is a vivid picture of Florentine life; included are portraits of the Medicis and of famous dignitaries from the East who had assembled for the council meeting in Florence in 1439: the Magi appear with the features of the Patriarch of Constantinople in the front (north wall), and of the Byzantine Emperor (wall opposite the altar), with Lorenzo the Magnificent as a child (south wall). In the middle of the group following is Benozzo himself wearing the hat inscribed Opus Benotii.

Luca Giordano Gallery *(lst floor, entrance by the second stairway on the right).* The Apotheosis of the Second Dynasty of the Medicis, a Baroque fresco painted in 1683 by Luca Giordano, covers the entire roof.

■ ADDITIONAL SIGHTS

Strozzi Palace★★ (BY F). — *Open Monday, Wednesday and Friday 4 to 7 pm; apply to Gabinetto Vieusseux, 4 Piazza Strozzi; closed 10-20 August.* Dating from the end of the 15C, this is the finest privately owned palace in Florence with its rusticated stonework, cornice and arcaded court. There is a small museum in the basement where are displayed a wooden model of the palace by Giuliano da Sangallo, documents on the Strozzi family and documents on Florence since the beginning of the century.

Boboli Garden★ (Giardino di Boboli) (ABZ). — *Open 9 am to 7 pm (6 pm 1 March to 30 April and 1 September to 31 October, or 5 pm 1 November to end of February).* This Italian-style terraced garden designed in 1549 by Tribolo, to which Ammannati (1550) and Buontalenti (1583) also contributed, is ornamented with antique and Renaissance statues. At the end of an avenue, left of the Pitti Palace, you will see the façade of the Buontalenti **grotto.** Crossing the amphitheatre you reach the highest point of the garden from which, on the right, the **Viottolone,** an avenue of pines and cypresses, runs down to the **Piazzale dell' Isolotto,** a circular pool with a small island, bearing citrus trees and a fountain by Giovanni da Bologna.

A pavilion *(access by a path to the right at the top of the avenue on the same line as the palace)* houses a **Porcelain Museum** (BZ M): porcelains from Sevres, Austria, England and Italy (Doccia, Naples). *Open Tuesdays, Thursdays, Saturdays, 9 am to 2 pm.*

The **Citadel Belvedere,** at the top of the hill, affords a splendid **panorama★★** of Florence and of the celebrated Florentine countryside which has inspired many painters.

Church of Santa Maria del Carmine (AYZ). — Built between the 13 and 15C, the church was extensively remodelled in the late 18C. The Brancacci Chapel in the south transept contains an exceptionally fine series of **frescoes★★** of the life of St. Peter painted (1427) at the age of twenty-six shortly before his death by Masaccio, a pioneer of the Renaissance in his use of relief and expression. The themes are original sin and the life of St. Peter (upper part: on the left **Adam and Eve being banished from the Garden of Eden** and the Payment of the Tribute, at the far end to the right of the altar St. Peter Baptising, and next to it on the right wall, St. Peter healing a cripple; lower part: at the far end to the right of the altar, St. Peter giving alms, and to the left St. Peter healing the sick; next to it on the left wall, St. Peter preaching). The remaining frescoes on the same themes are by Masolino (1424) and Filippino Lippi (1481).

Orsanmichele★ (BCY G). — Originally a wheat granary, Orsanmichele was rebuilt in 1337 in a transitional Gothic-Renaissance style, delicate and ornate. Between 1380 and 1404 the arches were walled up and the building raised to serve as an oratory for the craftsmen and guilds of Florence.

Outside, the niches between the pillars contain statues of the patrons of the corporations; these statues alone are a museum of 14 to 16C Florentine sculpture. Note by the Via Calzaiuoli: St. John the Baptist by Ghiberti, the Doubting St. Thomas by Verrocchio, St. Luke by

Giovanni da Bologna; by Via Orsanmichele: St. Peter by Donatello, St. Philip and four crowned Saints by Nanni di Banco, and a copy of St. George (the original is in the Bargello Museum) by Donatello; by Via dell'Arte della Lana: St. Matthew (1) and St. Stephen (2) by Ghiberti; by Via dei Lamberti: St. John the Evangelist (4) by Baccio da Montelupo. Inside, in the south aisle, is a splendid 14C Gothic **tabernacle★★** by Orcagna. It is decorated with coloured marble, mosaics, gold and charming bas-reliefs of the Life of the Virgin *(illumination: 100 lire).*

Refectory of St. Apollonia (Cenacolo di Sant'Apollonia) (CX R). *1 Via 27 Aprile. Open weekdays 8 am to 2 pm; apply for permission to the Soprintendenza ai Beni Artistici e Storici, 5 Via Ninna.* In the refectory of this former Camaldulian monastery, there hangs a remarkable **Last Supper★★** (1430) by Andrea del Castagno.

Refectory of San Salvi (Cenacolo di San Salvi) (FU A). — *Access by the quays on the right bank of the Arno, the Via Piagentina (DY), the Piazza L.B. Alberti, the Via Aretina and the Via San Salvi (No. 16; 500 lire).* The former refectory of the abbey contains an admirable **Last Supper★★** (1526-1527) by Andrea del Sarto.

Piazza della Santissima Annunziata★ (CX). — This fine square is adorned with an equestrian statue of Ferdinand I de' Medici by G. da Bologna and two charming 17C Baroque fountains. Round it stand the late 16C Classical palace of the Brotherhood of the Servants of Mary (on the left facing the church), the Church of the Annunciation and the Foundlings' Hospital (on the right).

The **Church of the Santissima Annunziata (CX S)**, or Holy Annunciation, is Renaissance. It is much loved by the Florentines and was built for the Servants of Mary, whose Order was founded by St. Philip Benozzi, in the 13C and was reconstructed by Michelozzo in the 15C. It is preceded by an atrium decorated with **frescoes★** *(some have been removed for restoration)* by several artists, including Baldovinetti, Andrea del Sarto, Il Rosso and Pontormo.

The Baroque interior is richly decorated. At the end of the north transept, through a little door above which (outer side) is a delightful Madonna with a Bag by Andrea del Sarto, you reach the Cloisters of the Dead onto which opens on the right the Chapel of St. Luke, where Cellini, Il Pontormo and others were buried *(apply at the sacristy).*

The **Foundlings' Hospital** (Ospedale degli Innocenti) **(CX M⁴)** *(open 9 am to 6.30 pm 1 April to 30 September; 9 am to 1 pm the rest of the year; Sundays and holidays 9 am to 1 pm throughout the year; closed Mondays; 500 lire)* is entered through a pretty 15C portico by Brunelleschi, with corners decorated with touching **medallions★** of children (1463) by Andrea della Robbia. The art gallery *(second floor)* contains: in the great hall, by the wall to the right of the entrance, a **Coronation of the Virgin★** — a fine painting by Neri di Bicci (15C) — and a Virgin and Child with an Angel, an early work of Filippo Lippi; in a small adjoining room, the great **Adoration of the Magi★** (1488) by Domenico Ghirlandaio, a fine Virgin and Saints by Piero di Cosimo (c 1462 to c 1520) and a Virgin and Child in glazed terracotta by Luca della Robbia.

Archaeological Museum★ (Museo Archeologico) **(CX M³).** — *Open 9 am to 2 pm (1 pm Sundays and holidays); closed Mondays; 750 lire.* Interesting collections of Etruscan, Egyptian and Greco-Roman art.

New Market Loggia★ (Loggia di Mercato Nuovo) **(BY X).** — Renaissance. It houses a market for Florentine craft: straw-work, leather-work, embroidery, articles in gilded and painted wood. On one side stands the small fountain of the Porcellino (so called after the boar that surmounts it) sculpted by Tacca (16C).

Cascine★ (AX). — Park laid out in the 18C round the Grand Ducal dairy farms *(cascine).*

Casa Guidi (AY). — *8 Piazza S. Felice. Open 4 to 7 pm; closed Mondays, weekends, holidays and 22 December to 5 January.*

Florentine home of the Victorian poets Robert and Elizabeth Barrett Browning.

Church of the Holy Spirit (Santo Spirito) (BY K). — This Renaissance church, built between 1444 and 1487 to the plans of Brunelleschi (two years prior to his death) with a simple, graceful interior, contains many **works of art★**, notably a fine Madonna by Filippino Lippi *(fifth chapel in the south transept).* The sacristy *(on the left)* is by Giuliano da Sangallo.

La Badia (CY L). — This is the church of a former Benedictine abbey *(badia).* It contains several fine Renaissance **works★**: on the left as you enter is a picture by Filippino Lippi of the Virgin appearing to St. Bernard; opposite is a charming relief sculpture by Mino da Fiesole (Virgin and Child with Saints) who also carved the tombs of Bernardo Giugni (south transept) and of Count Ugo (north transept) — he worked on the latter for more than ten years. From the upper gallery of the cloister *(door to the right of the altar)* executed between 1435-1440 by Bernardo Rossellino, there is a view of the Romanesque-Gothic bell-tower.

Holy Trinity Church (Santa Trinità) (BY N). — The Sassetti Chapel *(second on the right of the chancel)* was decorated by Ghirlandaio with **frescoes★** of the life of St. Francis (1486). The **Adoration of the Shepherds★** by the artist is on the altar. In the north transept *(second chapel on the left of the chancel)* stands the fine marble tomb of Bishop Federighi, by Luca della Robbia.

All Saints (Ognissanti) (AX A). — The church dates from the 16-17C, but the campanile is 13-14C. The Coronation of the Virgin over the main door is attributed to Giovanni della Robbia. In the monastery refectory, *(ring at No. 42, on the right on leaving the church; open 9 am to noon and 4 to 6 pm; closed Sunday afternoons and holidays)* are a **Last Supper★** *(end wall)* and St. Jerome *(north wall)* by Ghirlandaio, and St. Augustine *(south wall)* by Botticelli.

EXCURSIONS See plan p 103

Fiesole★ (FT). — *8 km - 5 miles. Description p 102.*

Villas★★. — Three Renaissance villas, former residences of the Medicis.

Villa della Petraia (FT). — *North, 3 km - 2 miles. Closed for restoration.* This was formerly a castle. In 1576 Cardinal Ferdinando de' Medici commissioned the architect Buontalenti to convert it into a villa. In the **garden★** (16C), there is a remarkable fountain *(near the house)* by N. Tribolo and a bronze statue of Venus by Giovanni da Bologna.

Villa di Castello (EFT). — *North, 5 km - 3 miles (garden only open to the public).* The villa, bought by the Medicis in 1477, was embellished by Lorenzo the Magnificent and restored in the 18C. It is surrounded by a 16C terraced garden, exquisitely proportioned, to set off a beautiful central fountain by Tribolo adorned with a group by Ammannati of Hercules and Cacus.

Villa di Poggio a Caiano★. — *Northwest, 17 km - 11 miles. Leave by ⑥ of plan. Near the road to Pistoia (S 66). Restoration work in progress. The drawing-room only is open (except Mondays) to visitors. Apply to the Soprintendenza ai Beni Ambientali e Architettonici 1 Piazza Pitti, Florence.* The villa was built in 1485 by Sangallo for Lorenzo the Magnificent.

Francesco I de' Medici and Bianca Capello, it is said, were poisoned there in 1587. The magnificent drawing-room has a coffered ceiling and frescoes started in 1521 by Andrea del Sarto, Pontormo and Franciabigio, which were completed in 1579 by Alessandro Allori; the fresco by Pontormo representing Pomona and her spouse Vertumnus (God of Spring) is particularly remarkable.

Galluzzo Carthusian Monastery (Certosa del Galluzzo) (EFU). — *South, 6 km - 4 miles. Guided tours: 9 am to 11 am and 3 pm (2.30 pm in winter) to 4.30 pm; time: about 1 hour; donation.*

The monastery was founded in the 14C and remodelled many times. The adjoining palace contains frescoes (1522) by Pontormo depicting scenes from the Passion of Christ *(first room)*. From the church (14C with 16C façade and stalls) go through to the early 15C Gothic Chapel of Santa Maria. The monks' cells *(one may be visited)* give onto the great Renaissance **cloister★**, which is adorned with medallions by the della Robbias.

Vallombrosa. — *East, 33 km - 21 miles. Leave by ② of plan.* Vallombrosa, sung by Milton in *Paradise Lost* and by Lamartine, is much appreciated for its **setting★**, its **views★★**, its magnificent forest and its excursions in the Pratomagno Massif. The Monastery of Vallombrosa, founded in the 11C, remodelled and enlarged in the 16 and 17C, is once more occupied by monks, who have made it a cultural centre.

FOLIGNO Umbria

Michelin map ▓▓▓ 16 — 18 km - 11 miles — southeast of Assisi — Pop 52 393

Foligno, a modern looking town on the plain, is an active commercial centre.

The game of the Quintana takes place on the second Sunday in September, when horsemen in 17C costumes, representing the different quarters of the town, must carry away, with the points of their spears, a ring which is hung from the outstretched arms of the Quintana, an early 17C wooden statue.

Piazza della Repubblica. — The chief buildings in Foligno, the town hall (13-17C), the cathedral and the Palazzo Trinci, are here.

The **Cathedral**, which is joined by an arch to the Palazzo Trinci, is of Romanesque origin. Its main façade gives on the Piazza del Duomo, that on the Piazza della Repubblica is the right façade and dates from 1201. It has a fine Lombard doorway with geometrical decoration and a wooden door (1620) vigorously carved with saints and angels.

The **Palazzo Trinci**, built of brick, had a Neo-Classical façade added in the 19C. The greater part of the building, however, dates from the 15C. It contains a **picture gallery** in large rooms adorned with interesting 15C frescoes *(open 8 am to 8 pm (9 am to noon and 3 to 6 pm October to May); 9 am to noon Sundays and holidays).*

EXCURSIONS

Bevagna. — *West, 9 km - 6 miles.* Leave Foligno by the road to Perugia and take the first road to the left. Fine mediaeval buildings form a homogeneous framework for the **Piazza della Libertà★** (or Silvestri): they are the Palazzo dei Consoli (the Consuls' Palace — 1270), with an outdoor staircase, paired windows and Gothic vaulting and the Romanesque Churches of St. Silvester (San Silvestro) and St. Michael (San Michele), built by Maestro Binello at the end of the 12C and restored in 1952-1957.

Trevi★. — *South, 12.5 km - 8 miles.* This small town is perched on a hill in a pleasant **setting★** amidst olive groves. From the boulevard A. Ciuffelli which runs along the access road into the town between the Piazza Garibaldi and the church of San Martino, there is a splendid **view★** over the valley.

Sassovivo Abbey (Abbazia di Sassovivo). *East, 4.5 km - 2 1/2 miles.* Come out by the Tolentino road. After half a mile take a little road on the right *(signpost)* and bear left. In a lonely setting overlooking a small valley, the Benedictines, in the 11C, founded their abbey. A beautiful Romanesque cloister remains, its semicircular arches supported on slender twin columns. Coloured marbles and mosaic form the decoration.

FONDI Latium

Michelin map ▓▓▓ 26 — 17 km - 11 miles — northeast of Terracina — Pop 27 136

Fondi belonged to the Volsci; it is built on a picturesque site at the foot of the Ausoni Mountains. It is an important agricultural centre, famous for its early glasshouse production.

Fondi has preserved remains of its **Cyclopean walls**, rebuilt by the Romans and again in the Middle Ages. Its most interesting buildings are the 13C Church of St. Peter (San Pietro), containing a fine pulpit of the same period, a 15C Prince's Palace where the influences of Anjou and Aragon are mingled, and the 14C castle in which the French Antipope Clement VII was elected in 1378, marking the beginning of the Great Schism of the West *(see p 20).*

FORLÌ Emilia-Romagna

Michelin map ▓▓▓ 15 — Pop 110 275

Town plan in the Michelin Red Guide Italia (hotels and restaurants).

Forlì was an independent domain in the 13 and 14C. Its citadel, or *Rocca* was heroically defended in 1500 by Caterina Sforza. She answered the cruel Cesare Borgia, who threatened to sacrifice her children, with the words: "I am still young enough to have others". Forlì is the birthplace of the painter Melozzo da Forlì (1438-1494).

Basilica di San Mercuriale. — The Basilica in the great Piazza Saffi is dominated by an imposing Romanesque campanile 75 m - 246 ft — high. Although rebuilt several times, it still has a Romanesque doorway with a lunette adorned with a 13C bas-relief of the Adoration of the Magi. In the south aisle is the shapely tomb of Barbara Manfredi (died 1466), a member of the powerful Manfredi family of Faenza and wife of Pino Ordelaffi, ruler of Forlì.

FOSSANOVA Abbey ** Latium

Michelin map **988** 26 — 4 km — 2 miles — south of Priverno.

Standing, as the rules prescribe, on a lonely site, the Cistercian Abbey of Fossanova is the oldest of the Order in Italy. Monks from Cîteaux (France) settled there in 1133. In 1163 they began to build their abbey church, which was to serve as a model for many Italian churches (Casamari, for instance). Its name is derived from a great ditch dug by the monks to drain the waterlogged soil of the Pontine Marshes.

A typical Cistercian Abbey. — Although rather heavily restored, Fossanova is one of the few Cistercian houses in Europe which have kept their original architecture and arrangements intact. It was designed in accordance with the rules of austerity laid down by St. Bernard.

The well lit church, with its flat chevet, had to include in its transept several altars for the monks to serve mass. The monastery buildings were divided into two parts: one, in the east, for the monks, was a continuation of the transept and chancel of the church; the other, in the west, was for lay brothers, who were allowed only in the nave. The outhouses, needed by any self-sufficient community, stand nearby.

TOUR

If the abbey is closed, ring at the third door on the right; guided tours, 9 am to noon and 3 to 7 pm (3 to 5 pm in winter).

The **church (1)**, which was consecrated in 1208, is in the Burgundian Gothic style with a number of Romanesque survivals; such decoration as there is recalls the Lombard technique with traces of the Moorish style.

As regards the exterior, the Latin Cross plan with a flat chevet, the transept crossing tower, the rose windows and the triple bayed window in the chevet are typically Cistercian.

The interior, which is impressively plain, also has Cistercian features: a central nave balanced by aisles with ribbed vaulting, large double moulded pointed arches, binding-joists supported by pilasters resting on stems, and bracketed capitals.

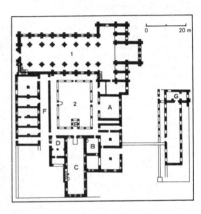

The **cloisters (2)** are picturesque with three Romanesque sides and the fourth or south side in the transitional late 13C Romanesque Gothic style. The small columns are Lombard in form and decoration.

Beyond the transept of the abbey church you will see in succession *(see sketch)* the fine Gothic chapterhouse (1250-**A**), opening into the cloisters through wide twin bays (through which the lay brothers, who were not allowed in the chapter, could watch proceedings); the passage to the garden and the boiler-room (the only room in which a fire was lit — **B**); the refectory (**C**) with lectern, and the kitchen (**D**), which communicated with the refectory through a service hatch. Opposite the refectory is an elegant lavabo (**E**) at which the monks washed their hands before and after meals. Next come the rooms reserved for the lay brothers and the "alley" (**F**), a corridor used by them. On the upper floor are the dormitories and libraries.

The guest house (**G**) stands alone. In it St. Thomas Aquinas died on 7 March 1274.

The beach of fine sand is fashionable and well equipped. The beautiful **pinewood★**, 4 km long and 1 km wide — 3 × 3/4 miles — consists of sea pines, growing close together. Villas and bungalows are scattered under the trees (restaurants, dance halls).

This former fortress, still partly walled, is admirably sited at the end of a promontory bounding a beautiful **bay★** beside which runs the road, affording magnificent views. Gaeta has a pleasant beach of fine sand, facing south, at the neck of the promontory — the Serapo Beach.

Cathedral (Duomo). — The cathedral is interesting especially for its 12-13C Romanesque-Moorish campanile adorned with porcelain and resembling the Sicilian or Amalfi towers. Inside, the late 13C **paschal candelabrum★** is remarkable for its size and for its forty-eight bas-reliefs depicting scenes from the lives of Christ and of St. Erasmus, the patron saint of sailors.

A picturesque mediaeval quarter lies near the cathedral.

Castle. — The castle, dating from the 8C, has been altered many times. The lower castle derives from Anjou, the upper from Aragon. In the fortress was buried the High Constable of Bourbon, a traitor to his king, killed when Rome was captured by Charles V.

Roland's Tower (Torre d'Orlando). — This tower on the summit of Monte Orlando is the tomb of the Roman Consul Munatius Plancus, a friend of Caesar's, who founded the colonies of Lugdunum (Lyons) and Augusta Raurica (Augst near Basle).

RATING OF THE SIGHTS AND POINTS OF INTEREST

★★★　Worth a journey

　★★　Worth a detour

　　★　Interesting

GARGANO Massif ★★★ Apulia

Michelin map **988** 28.

The Gargano Massif, shining white under a blue sky, projects like a spur from the "boot" of Italy. It is one of the most attractive natural features of Italy with its wide horizons, its deep and mysterious forests and its lonely, rugged coastline.

Physically, Gargano is quite independent from the Apennine Mountains; it is a limestone plateau fissured with crevasses into which water runs. The present peninsula was once an island, since connected with the mainland by deposits from the rivers flowing down from the Apennines.

Today the promontory wears the appearance of a chalky massif riven by high valleys in which arable soil, which can be cultivated, has accumulated. Its eastern end is covered with forest. The scanty pastures and moors on the plateaux support flocks of sheep and goats and herds of black pigs.

The picturesque Tremiti Islands belong to the same geological formation. They can be reached by boat from Manfredonia *(see p 136)*, Pugnochiuso, Vieste, Peschici, Rodi, Garganico and Termoli.

★★★TOUR STARTING FROM MONTE SANT'ANGELO

146 km - 91 miles — 1/2 day

From Monte Sant'Angelo *(p 152)*, in the heart of the Gargano Massif, a tour, shown in black on the map below, through varied country will enable you to see the main features of the massif. It is equally possible to follow the coast road linking Peschici and Mattinata, which affords splendid views of the coast.

Starting along the inland road, you descend into the valley dominated by the rock on which Monte Sant'Angelo is perched. The road then climbs in hairpin bends along the slopes opposite Monte Sant'Angelo, affording pretty **views** of the town. The route next crosses a deserted plateau of moors and woods before reaching **Bosco d'Umbra**, a huge clump of venerable beeches in the middle of which is the Cantina d'Umbra, a forest lodge.

GARGANO

You now start descending towards Vico del Gargano and **Peschici**, well sited on its rock. As you go you will catch glimpses of the sea through the sea pines which embellish the entire coastal area from Peschici to Mattinata. Though it does not closely follow the sea, the road is often a high *corniche* overlooking creeks and inlets.

The bird's-eye views are most beautiful before you reach **Mattinata**, which is perched above a coastal plain planted with olives. The light all along the coast is of rare quality.

You can return to Monte Sant'Angelo by the coast road overlooking Manfredonia and its bay. Road S 89^D, which is 3 km - 2 miles — shorter, affords much the same views and is also picturesque.

GAVIA Pass ★★★ Lombardy

Michelin map **988** 4 — Alt 2 621 m - 8 599 ft

The Gavia Pass (Passo di Gavia) links the Valtellina *(p 249)* and the superb Valfurva *(p 67)* with the Val Camonica *(p 72)*. It is impressive in its wildness and the marvellous views it affords of the Ortlès Alps. The narrow, difficult and dangerous road, with its gradients of 1 in 6, should please lovers of mountain driving.

Enquire at Santa Caterina Valfurva or at Ponte di Legno whether the road is passable (generally snowbound between October and June).

Michelin Red Guides

Benelux, Deutschland, España/Portugal, France, Great Britain and Ireland, Italia (hotels, restaurants, lists of sights).

Michelin Green Guides

Austria, Germany, Italy, Portugal, Spain, Switzerland
(sights and touring programmes described)

Michelin Main Road Maps

Great Britain/Ireland 986, Germany 987, Italy/Switzerland 988, France 989, Spain/Portugal 990, Yugoslavia 991.

GENOA ★★ (GENOVA) Liguria _____

Michelin map **988** 13 — *Local map pp 199-200* — Pop 789 057
Town plan in the Michelin Red Guide Italia (hotels and restaurants)

Genoa the Superb, the greatest seaport in Italy, spreads its hundreds of palaces, its streets and quarters over a mountain amphitheatre. It is a city of surprises and contrasts, where the most luxurious palaces stand side by side with the humblest alleys. The busy centre of the town is the Piazza De Ferrari.

HISTORICAL NOTES

Genoese Expansion (12-15C). — This was based on a strong fleet already comprising seventy ships in 1104, all built in the famous local dockyards: they were rowing and sailing craft (galleys, caravels, carracks, cutters, galleasses, galleons and sloops). Seasoned sailors led by clever admirals (Grimaldi, the Dorias) made this fleet a weapon which French Kings Philip the Fair and Philip of Valois, used against the Barbary pirates and the English.

The Crusaders offered the Genoese an opportunity of planting their flag, charged with St. George's cross, on the shores of the Eastern Mediterranean. Their trading posts, which rivalled those of Pisa and later of Venice, were run by the famous Bank of St. George.

Andrea Doria (1466-1560). — He was the most glorious representative of a line of adventurous fighting seamen. A bold but prudent leader and legislator, Doria entered the service of France after having distinguished himself against Consalvo de Cordoba and the Turks. During the French war with Italy he served François I, and after Pavia he covered the French retreat into Provence, supplying Marseilles and cutting the sea communications of Charles V with Spain. In 1528, indignant at François I's unjust treatment of him, he entered the service of Charles V. Loaded with honours and favours by the Emperor, he received him in 1533 in a way which remained famous in history. For twelve days Doria fêted the Emperor with incredible lavishness; he gave a great banquet on board his flagship, anchored in the middle of the harbour: when the silver-gilt tableware was soiled it was thrown into the sea.

Genoa declined under Spanish rule. Louis XIV had it bombarded by Duquesne in 1684 and the Doge had to humble himself at Versailles. In 1775 the town ceded its rights in Corsica to France. Genoa was French under the First Empire and under the French marshal Masséna withstood siege by the Austrians. Later, after indulging the republican spirit of its own citizen, Giuseppe Mazzini, it became one of the cradles of the Risorgimento.

FINE ARTS

As in many countries, the decline of commercial prosperity in the 16 and 17C coincided with intense artistic activity, evidenced in the building of innumerable palaces and the arrrival at Genoa of well known artists, especially Flemings.

In 1607 Rubens, who later produced a work on the *Palazzi di Genova,* and from 1621 to 1627 Van Dyck, came to portray Genoese nobility, the *grandezza.* Van Dyck painted more than fifty pictures, many of which are still in Genoese galleries. Puget lived at Genoa from 1661 to 1667, working for patricians like the Dorias and the Spinolas.

Among local painters were the decorator Luca Cambiaso (16C), the realist Strozzi (17C) and above all **Magnasco** (18C), a precursor of modern art with the dramatic lyricism expressed by his brush in quick, sharp, colourful touches. In the domain of architecture, Alessi (17C), when at his best, was the equal of Sansovino and Palladio in the nobility and ingenuity of his designs.

■ MAIN SIGHTS *time: 4 hours*

The Port★★. — *Tour by boat; landing-stage to the right of the main marine station; about 1 hour; 1 000 lire per person.*

You can also get a good general view of the port by going from west to east along the raised roads (Strada Sopraelevata) which runs round it.

The harbour, protected by a breakwater 5 km - 3 miles — long, has five major basins: on the east the *Avamporto,* a harbour reserved for pleasure boats; in the centre the *Bacino delle Grazie* where naval equipment and repairs are undertaken, and the *Bacino Porto Vecchio* which now has two railway stations.

To the west the modern port consists of the *Lanterna* and *Sampierdarena* basins with, rising between them, the oldest Genoese lighthouse, the *Lanterna* (1544).

West of the town and protected by the Christopher Columbus Airport (Aeroporto Cristoforo Colombo), which has been built entirely on land reclaimed from the sea, an oil tanker port has been constructed. An oil pipeline network links the port to the refineries in the Po Valley, to Aigle in Switzerland and to Ingolstadt in Bavaria.

Genoa is the largest Italian port: in 1978 nearly 8 000 ships docked there carrying about 1 265 000 passengers and 51 149 000 metric tons of merchandise. The 25 km - 15 1/2 miles — of quays are laced by 135 km - 84 miles — of railway tracks; freight consists chiefly of imported raw materials (imports make up 87 % of the traffic handled): oil and petrol, coal, minerals, cereals, metal, wood, oleaginous products, cotton, and exported manufactures — chemical products, machines, cars, textiles, etc.

The sailors' quarter extends from the main railway station to the **Palazzo San Giorgio (BY G),** a 13C building which was formerly the headquarters of the bank of the same name. Behind the palace are the Loggia dei Banchi (of the Banks) and the picturesque Via degli Orefici (Goldsmiths' Street).

Via Garibaldi★. — This street of palaces, once known as the Via Aurea, was built according to the plans of Alessi. The **Palazzo Cataldi** (No. 4) designed by Alessi in 1558 has a lovely vestibule decorated with frescoes and a dazzling gilded **gallery★** *(open 8.30 am to noon and 2.30 to 6.30 pm — 8.30 am to 6.30 pm July and August; apply to the keepers; closed Saturday afternoons, Sundays and holidays).*

No. 9, the 16C **Palazzo Doria Tursi** *(apply to the Direzione Pubbliche Relazioni; open, 9 am to noon and 2 to 5 pm; closed Saturdays, Sundays and holidays)* is now the town hall; within are a bronze table dating from 117 BC, a violin of Paganini, who was a Genoese and manuscripts by Christopher Columbus. No. 11, the 16C **Palazzo Bianco,** contains an **art gallery★★** in an especially luxurious setting; there is a particularly good collection of Flemish (Provost, Van der Goes, Gerard David, Van Dyck and Rubens) and Dutch paintings as well as the best of the local school *(same opening times as the Palazzo Rosso, p 118).*

GENOA★★

The 17C **Palazzo Rosso** at No.18 also contains works of art. The fine **pinacoteca★** or picture gallery *(open weekdays 9 am to 8 pm (Mondays 2 to 7 pm); Sundays 9 am to 12.30 pm; closed holidays)* has local artists' work, also examples of Veronese, Tintoretto, Caravaggio and Il Guercino; finally there are some Dürer canvases and an especially fine collection of Van Dyck portraits as well as sculpture, ceramics and medals, etc.

Via Balbi★. — This street is joined to the Via Garibaldi by the Via Cairoli and is also lined with palaces.

The **Royal Palace** (Palazzo Reale) formerly the Balbi Durazzo, at No. 10 *(open Tuesdays, Thursdays and Sundays 9 am to 1 pm; closed holidays),* contains a Van Dyck room and antique furniture.

The **University Palace★** (Palazzo dell'Università — 17C) at No. 5 has a majestic court and staircase. The 17C **Palazzo Durazzo Pallavicini** is at No. 1.

St. Lawrence's Cathedral★ (San Lorenzo). — The cathedral façade is Gothic; French influence appears in the placing of the doorways and the large rose window. The carving of the pedestals on the central doorway represents a Tree of Jesse on the right and scenes from the Life of Christ on the left. The tympanum bears a Christ between Evangelical Symbols and a Martyrdom of St. Lawrence. Above the side doorways are statues of the Virgin and Child and of St. John the

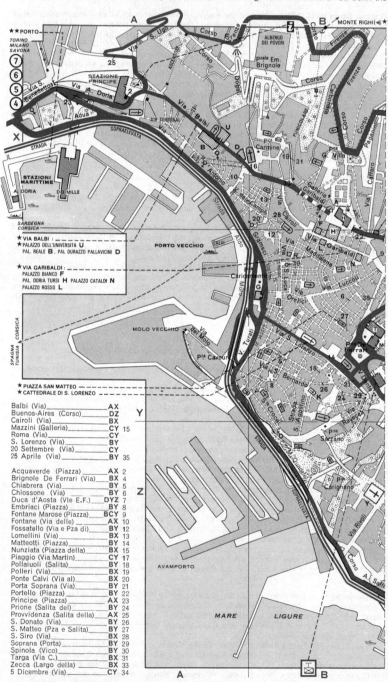

The names of the main shopping streets are in brown.

Baptist. In the right corner of the façade the early 13C knifegrinder resembles the angel at Chartres, performing the same function. Two fine lions, 19C, flank the steps. The side door-ways of St. John and St. Gothard are in the Romanesque style.

The transept crossing is crowned with a Renaissance dome by Alessi.

Inside, the Gothic nave rests on marble columns. The Renaissance Chapel of St. John the Baptist in the north aisle contains the bones of St. John.

The **treasure★** *(open 9.30 to 11.45 am and 3 to 5.45 pm; closed Sundays, Mondays and holidays; 100 lire)* is housed in the archiepiscopal palace which possesses the famous *Sacro Catino*, a cup given to Solomon by the Queen of Sheba, from which Christ is said to have drunk at the Last Supper.

Piazza San Matteo★. — The square is small but harmonious and lined with palaces that belonged to the Doria family. No. 17 is a Renaissance building presented by the community to Andrea Doria.

The 13C Church of St. Matthew (San Matteo) has a façade adorned with inscriptions com-memorating the Dorias.

The interior decoration is Renaissance. The tomb and sword of Andrea Doria are in the crypt. To the left of the church are small 14C cloisters.

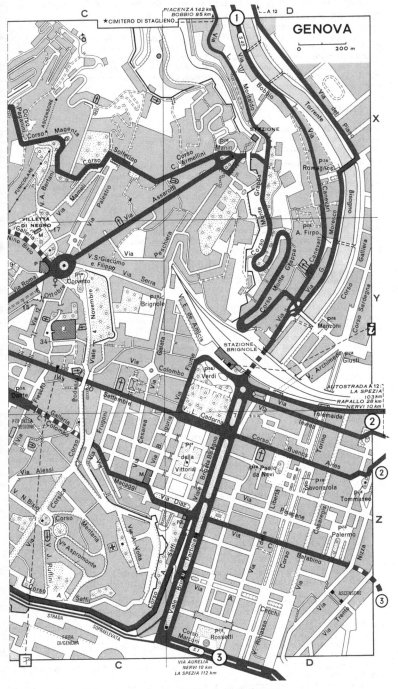

The maps and plans are orientated with north at the top.

■ ADDITIONAL SIGHTS

Piazza De Ferrari (BY). — This square, the heart of modern Genoa, is bordered by the remains of the Opera, built in 1828 and partly destroyed in 1944, the palaces of the Academy, the Exchange, the Italia Navigation Company, and the 18C Ducal Palace, former residence of the Doges.

The nearby Piazza Matteotti is overlooked by the façade of the Ducal Palace, rebuilt in the 19C, and by the church of St. Ambrose (Sant'Ambrogio) which contains an Assumption by Guido Reni (at the altar in the third chapel on the right), and a Circumcision (behind the high altar) and a St. Ignatius Exorcising (third chapel on the left) by Rubens.

Church of St. Donatus (San Donato) (BY K). — A splendid **Adoration of the Magi★★**, attributed to Joos Van Cleve (16C), may be seen in the north aisle of this church in the old town.

Villetta Di Negro (CXY). — This is a sort of belvedere-labyrinth with cascades and artificial grottoes. From a terrace there is a **view★** of the town and the sea.

Church of Santa Maria di Carignano (BZ Y). — The church was built in the 16C to the plans of Alessi. Under the dome are four large Baroque statues and opposite and to the right, the **St. Sebastian★** of Puget, a theatrical work, but one displaying great skill.

Castelletto (BX A). — From the terrace (reached by lift) there is a fine **view★** of the town.

Palazzo Spinola Gallery (BY R). — Open 9 am to 4 pm (1 pm Sundays and holidays). Closed Mondays, 1 January, Easter, 25 April, 1 May, 15 August, 1 November, 8, 25 and 26 December.

The decoration of the apartments, the items displayed and the furnishings form a pleasing whole. There are fine ceilings by Tavarone (large rooms on the first and second floor), by Lorenzo de Ferrari (Hall of Mirrors) and by Sebastiano Galeotti (small rooms); and a collection of pictures by painters of the Italian and Flemish Renaissance (Antonello da Messina: *Ecce Homo*, Joos Van Cleve: *Madonna*), of the Flemish 17C (Van Dyck: Portrait of a Child, the Four Evangelists) and the Italian 17C (principally Genoese). The furniture is contemporary.

EXCURSIONS

Monte Righi★★. — Reached by cable-car from the Largo della Zecca; 10 or 20 minute intervals; 200 lire. From this point 302 m - 991 ft — above sea-level there is a remarkable **view★★** of the town and the Italian Riviera.

Cemetery of Staglieno★ (Campo Santo). — 1.5 km - 1 mile. Leave Genoa by ①, road S 45. To the left of the road is one of the most curious Italian cemeteries, with galleries holding the sumptuous tombs of the great families of Genoa and popular clay *tumuli* formed into sepulchres. Mazzini's tomb lies approximately in the centre, on the side of the hill.

Nervi. — East, 9 km - 5 1/2 miles. Leave Genoa by ③, road S 1. This pleasant town near the sea, surrounded by luxuriant vegetation, is the oldest residential resort on the Eastern Riviera (Riviera di Levante). There is a fine **view★** of the sea from the Serra and Groppallo parks, which are planted with exotic trees, sea pines and orange trees, and also from the **Passeggiata Anita Garibaldi★** which runs along the seashore.

GORIZIA Friuli-Venezia Giulia
Michelin map 988 6 — Pop 42 748

The town, almost entirely destroyed in the 1915-1918 War, has a modern appearance with the exception of the Church of St. Ignatius (Sant'Ignazio), built by the Jesuits in the Austrian Baroque style with its onion domes, and the mediaeval castle enlarged and fortified by the Venetians in 1508. From the castle there are views of the town and the Isonzo Valley.

North of Gorizia you can go up to the Monastery of Castagnevizza in Yugoslav territory. Charles X of France, when in exile, took refuge and died there of cholera in 1836; he was buried in Gorizia church as are the Duke and Duchess of Angoulême, daughter of Louis XVI, and the Comte de Chambord, unsuccesful contender for the French throne in 1871.

GRADARA Marches
Michelin map 988 16 — 15 km - 9 miles — northwest of Pesaro — Pop 2 181

Gradara is a mediaeval town, almost intact, surrounded by walls and battlemented gateways. The **Rocca★** (open 1 June to 30 September, 2.30 to 7 pm; the rest of the year, 9 am to 1.30 pm and 9 am to 12.30 pm Sundays and holidays. Closed Mondays, 1 January, 25 April, 1 May, 1 June, 15 August and 25 December; 1 000 lire), a fortress at the summit, built on a square plan with corner towers, is a well preserved example of military architecture in the 13 and 14C. The interior contains old furniture, frescoes, etc.

It was built by the Grifis and afterwards belonged to the Malatestas and Sforzas. It is here that Gianni Malatesta is said to have murdered his wife Francesca da Rimini and her lover Paolo Malatesta at the end of a tragic love-story mentioned by Dante in his *Divine Comedy*.

GRADO ★ Friuli-Venezia Giulia
Michelin map 988 6 — Pop 10 200

At the time of the Barbarian invasions the inhabitants of Aquileia took refuge in the marshy solitudes of the lagoon and founded Grado, now a busy little port with a popular bathing beach.

The arrival at Grado along the dyke which crosses the lagoon is now without grandeur: you will see great stretches of water, many sea birds, thatched houses and the town skyline.

Old Quarter. — This is made picturesque by narrow *calli* or alleys forming a network between the canal-port and the cathedral.

The **cathedral** (duomo), built on the basilical plan, dates from the 6C. It has marble columns and Byzantine capitals, a curious 6C mosaic pavement, a 10C ambo (pulpit) with 6C panels bearing the symbols of the Evangelists, and finally, at the high altar, a valuable silver-gilt **altarpiece★**, Venetian work of the 14C.

Beside the cathedral stands the **baptistry** dating from the 6C and adorned with mosaics. Beside it, again, is the little 6C Basilica of St. Mary of Grace (Santa Maria delle Grazie).

GUBBIO ★★ Umbria

Michelin map **988** 16 — Pop 32 507

Gubbio stands at the mouth of a gorge hollowed out by a torrent on the steep slopes of Monte Ingino, which overlooks an inner valley enclosed by hills. The town is girt with ramparts and seems to have been forgotten in the passage of time, whence its nickname: The City of Silence. The yellow ochre of its stone buildings, the toast-like tint of its Romanesque tiled roofs, and the austere grandeur of its treeless site make it one of the Italian towns in which the harsh atmosphere of the Middle Ages is most easily imagined. Since mediaeval times the artisans of Gubbio have specialised in ceramics. One of them, Mastro Giorgio, produced the famous iridescent red lustre — the secret of which was never discovered by nearby towns.

HISTORICAL NOTES

In the 11 and 12C the free community of Gubbio, fiercely Ghibelline, enjoyed a period of expansion marked by a surprising victory over a league of eleven other towns. After being governed by the Montefeltro *(see p 248)* family from 1384 to 1508, and then by the Della Roveres, the town became a papal possession from 1624 to 1860.

The Wolf of Gubbio. — At the time of St. Francis (13C), legend has it that a gigantic wolf devasted the countryside. The *Poverello* (St. Francis) heard of it and, when passing through Gubbio, sought out the ferocious quadruped to reproach him for his misdeeds. The wolf then burst into tears, swore never to hurt anyone again and, to prove his submission, offered his paw to the saint. After this he was adopted and fed by the people.

The Race of the Ceri. — On 15 May this traditional fête recalls the help given by the Bishop of Gubbio, St. Ubald, in the miraculous victory of 1151 over the eleven other towns. The *ceraioli*, members of the Guilds, the merchants, masons, peasants and students, wearing ancient costumes and carrying the *Ceri,* curious wooden poles surmounted by statues of Sts. Ubald, George and Anthony 5 m - 16 ft high, race along a course between the town centre and the Monastery of St. Ubald (Sant'Ubaldo — *see p 122).* This exhausting uphill race is run in the late afternoon and is the highlight of a day rich in folk events.

■ MAIN SIGHTS time: 2 hours

Old Town★★★ (Città Vecchia). — *See the route marked in black on the plan.* This quiet quarter round the Piazza della Signoria is pleasant. The most picturesque streets are the Via Piccardi, Galeotti, dei Consoli, 20 Settembre and Baldassini, and the banks of the Camignano torrent. There are houses flanked by towers of nobility *(see p 220),* palaces like the 15C Bargello and the Consuls' Palace *(p 122),* squares with fountains, and hermitages clinging to sheer rocks.

Along streets either cobbled or paved with bricks or roughly spaced stones, the houses are often occupied by the shops of artisans (potters) lit by the entrance door alone, like those in pictures by the followers of Caravaggio. Some houses have two doors, one for everyday use, the other narrower and known as the Door of Death, through which coffins were brought out. Other characteristics of the façades are: a structure of squared stone alternating with rubble and brick; supporting arches; convex moulding and brackets; embossed coach-doors; small Gothic windows irregularly placed; larger Renaissance bays, niches, lamps, etc.

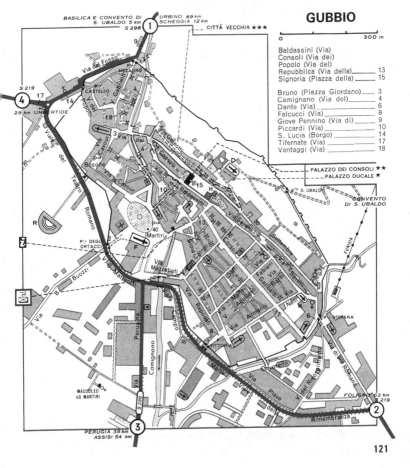

GUBBIO

CITTÀ VECCHIA ★★★

0 _____ 300 m

Baldassini (Via)
Consoli (Via dei)
Popolo (Via del)
Repubblica (Via della) _____ 13
Signoria (Piazza della) _____ 15

Bruno (Piazza Giordano) _____ 3
Camignano (Via del) _____ 4
Dante (Via) _____ 6
Falcucci (Via) _____ 8
Giove Pennino (Via di) _____ 9
Piccardi (Via) _____ 10
S. Lucia (Borgo) _____ 14
Tifernate (Via) _____ 17
Vantaggi (Via) _____ 18

PALAZZO DEI CONSOLI ★★
PALAZZO DUCALE ★

GUBBIO★★

Consuls' Palace★★ (Palazzo dei Consoli). — *Open 1 May to 30 September, 9.30 am to 12.30 pm and 3.30 to 7 pm; the rest of the year, 9 am to noon and 3 to 5 pm; 500 lire.* This imposing Gothic building, supported by great arches rising above the Via Baldassini, has a severe façade accentuated by strong buttresses resting on the balcony foundations. The first floor windows are late 15C. A loggia on the left overlooks the lower quarters. On the palace walls are rings for tethering horses.

You can visit the municipal council chamber *(Salone)*, the picture gallery and especially the museum containing the bronze *Tavole eugubine*, a series of tablets recording the ancient Umbrian language, as well as old coins and pottery by Mastro Giorgio. A splendid panorama can be seen from the top of the tower. A cross-bow contest takes place in the Piazza della Signoria on the last Sunday of May.

Ducal Palace★ (Palazzo Ducale). — *Restoration work in progress. Courtyard only open 9 am to 2 pm (1 pm Sundays and holidays); closed Mondays.* The palace was built from 1476 onwards for Federigo da Montefeltro, Duke of Urbino, to the plans of Francesco di Giorgio Martini, who was inspired by the ducal palace at Urbino.

Pass through the elegant courtyard, where faded red bricks blend with grey stone. Note the delicate ornament on the capitals. The inside of the palace, whose rooms have massive doors, is adorned with frescoes and finely carved chimney pieces. The *Salone* is very interesting.

■ ADDITIONAL SIGHTS

Roman Theatre★ (Teatro Romano) (R). — The theatre is well preserved from the time of Augustus. From the top there is a fine view of Gubbio.

Cathedral (Duomo) (D). — The cathedral presents a plain façade adorned with bas-reliefs showing the symbols of the Evangelists. The interior consists of a single nave. The bishop's chapel opens to the right. It is a luxurious sitting room, adorned with marbles and gilding (1670), from which the bishop could follow the services.

Church of St. Francis (San Francesco) (F). — The Gothic church has three polygonal apses and a slim campanile. The inside walls of the north apse are covered with remarkable early 15C frescoes★ by the local painter Ottaviano Nelli depicting scenes from the Life of the Virgin.

Church of Santa Maria Nuova (K). — This church contains the Madonna of the Belvedere between St. Emiliano, St. Anthony the Hermit and angel musicians, a charming fresco★ by Ottaviano Nelli.

EXCURSION

Basilica and Monastery of St. Ubald (Basilica e Convento di Sant' Ubaldo). — *5 km -3 miles.* Go out by ① and about 2 km - 1 mile — away, after two bridges over the torrent, take the turning to the right which goes up to the monastery situated above Gubbio at 820 m - 2 690 ft. One can also get there by cable-car *(operating from 8 am to 1 pm and 2 to 8 pm; 8 minutes by cable-car plus 5 minutes Rtn on foot; 1 000 lire Rtn):* panorama of the Umbrian countryside and the encircling hills. The basilica contains the remains of St. Ubald and the three *Ceri,* which are carried by the *ceraioli* in the race of 15 May *(see p 121).*

From the recently restored Rocca (castle) there is an extensive **view★★** of the Apennines and the plain.

HERCULANEUM ★★ (ERCOLANO) Campania

Michelin map **988** 27 — *Local map p 162* — Pop 56 468

Founded, according to tradition, by Hercules, this Roman town on the seashore was overwhelmed during the eruption of Vesuvius in AD 79.

In 1709 Emmanuel de Lorraine, Prince of Elbeuf, discovered the theatre when having a well dug. He immediately exploited his find, taking possession of the statues which were laid bare. In 1738 systematic excavation by means of underground tunnels was undertaken at the instigation of the Bourbons of Naples. The numerous and remarkable works of art which were then found are now in the Naples national museum. The town has been gradually uncovered since 1828, but it is only since 1927 that excavations have been carried out on a regular basis.

A Peaceful City. — In the 1C AD, Herculaneum with a population of barely 5 000 inhabitants was a less important but more peaceful town than Pompeii. The commercial and political life was also less active and the town knew less prosperity. Its port was frequented by fishing boats and coastal vessels and it attracted many craftsmen. It was also a resort. Excavations have revealed many elegant dwellings built by rich and cultured patricians who were probably drawn to Herculaneum because of its beautiful setting and of the Hellenic culture that still prevailed under the influence of neighbouring Naples.

The site has since greatly changed. The eruptions of Vesuvius raised the ground level and the sea receded as the two creeks that formed the bay were filled in.

The Dead City. — Herculaneum had five quarters and three main streets *(decumani).* One can see various types of dwellings which illustrate the development of the traditional Italic and Greek house into a more airy structure divided into units or its conversion into shops and apartments, sometimes on different levels. The villas of the propertied classes were on the outskirts with views of the sea. They are similar in plan to the villas of Pompeii *(for Roman town planning, see p 23).* As at Pompeii, different building methods *(p 187)* as regards building material and construction were used.

The lower part of the town has been unearthed, but the upper part is still buried under the modern settlement. Digging is going on near the palestra and the Forum which was crossed by the main street — Decumanus Maximus — has been partially excavated.

The interest of a visit to Herculaneum lies in the good state of preservation of private houses and in the feeling of intimacy and life that strikes the visitor. Unlike Pompeii which was buried under gravel and ashes, the town was overwhelmed by a sea of mud which afterwards solidified and in some places is over 20 m - 65 ft — deep. This hard crust has made excavation work harder than at Pompeii but the parts built in wood which there were burned down, were preserved in this hard shell. It is particularly moving to see the houses with frames, beams, staircases, doors, window frames, walls and complete with furniture. The houses were empty as the inhabitants had time to flee from the catastrophe.

TOUR *about 3 hours*

If you are coming from Naples, take the motorway rather than the coast road. Open 9 am to 1 hour before sunset; closed Mondays, 1 January, 1 May, 15 August, Easter and Christmas; 150 lire. The chief houses are closed; apply to the keepers.

From the access road *(go on foot)* just before reaching the excavations, there is a fine view of the luxurious villas with terraces facing the sea.

Casa dell'Albergo (A). — This vast house, the House of the Inn, was originally a patrician villa; a part was later turned into an apartment house. It was badly damaged by the eruption.

House with the Mosaic Atrium★★ (Casa dell'Atrio a mosaico). — The house is so-called because the atrium beyond the entrance is paved with mosaic. Although not far from the Casa dell' Albergo, it suffered relatively little damage. The ripples in the ground were caused as the ground caved in under the weight of the lava flow.

The garden on the right is surrounded by a peristyle with windows connecting the columns (the wooden frames are still standing). On the left are the bedrooms and at the far end, the nicest part of the house with a large *triclinium* (dining-room) opening on to a gallery; the terrace overlooking the sea is flanked by two small rest-rooms where one could enjoy the view and the sunshine.

The Wooden Trellis House★★ (Casa a Graticcio). — The house gets its name from the wooden trellis *(graticcio)* forming the walls. It is the sole example of this type of house that has survived from antiquity. This building technique, inexpensive but not very sound, was used for shops, secondary rooms and parts jutting over the street. The house

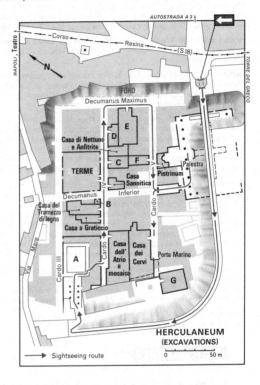

HERCULANEUM
(EXCAVATIONS)

→ Sightseeing route   0   50 m

has an original plan: it has two separate flats, one at ground level which also includes a shop, and the other on the first floor with a loggia supported by a portico giving on to the street.

House with the Wooden Partition★ (Casa del Tramezzo di legno). — The façade is remarkably well preserved. This is an example of a patrician dwelling with floors added to house several families. The *atrium* is separated from the *tablinum* (living room) by a **wooden partition★** *(tramezzo di legno)* to make the latter more comfortable; only the sides of the partition remain standing. One can also see the charred remains of a bed and of foodstuffs. Alongside, in the Decumanus Inferior, is a **dyer's shop (B)** containing a well preserved wooden clothes-press.

Casa Sannitica★★. — Although the house has been modified, it retains the very simple plan of dwellings built by the Samnites, the Italic race that ruled over Campania before they were absorbed by the Romans. The **atrium★** in the Tuscan style *(p 24)* is splendid: it is surrounded by a gallery with Ionic columns inspired from Greek architecture. The decoration at the entrance is in the first Pompeian style *(p 187)* and the outer rooms are adorned with frescoes.

Baths★★★ (Terme). — The baths of Herculaneum were built at the time of Augustus. They are not sumptuous but they show a remarkable degree of practical planning.

The **men's baths** are entered through a corridor (No. 7) ending at the *palestra,* a gymnasium communicating at the far end, on the right, with the *apodyterium* **(a)**, a cloakroom with partitioned shelves for clothes. The skeletons of the bath attendants, who took cover there during the eruption of Vesuvius, lie in a corner. The *apodyterium* communicates on one side with the *frigidarium* **(b)**, with its circular cold bath with the dome ornamented with marine animals reflected in the blue-green water creating an aquatic setting, and on the other with the *tepidarium* **(c** — steam and tepid water) followed by the *caldarium* **(d** — steam and hot water).

The entrance to the **women's baths** is at No. 8. The waiting-room and cloakroom (*apodyterium* — **e**), adorned with a mosaic pavement representing Neptune, come before the *tepidarium* **(f)**,and the *caldarium* **(g)**.

Men's Baths
Women's Baths

House with the Charred Furniture★ (Casa del Mobilio carbonizzato) (C). — This small but rather elegant house was decorated with paintings in false relief prior to the destruction of the town. The small court with its *lararium* in painted stucco is charming and intimate. But the main interest lies in the charred furniture that has been recovered.

House with the Neptune and Amphitrite Mosaic★★ (Casa del Mosaico di Nettuno e Anfitrite). — This house at No. 7, almost opposite the baths, is equipped with a **shop★** (No. 6) in an admirable state of preservation. The counter which included containers for the foodstuffs on sale opened on to the street and inside are the original wooden shelves on which stood the amphorae.

Mosaics depicting Neptune and Amphitrite adorn the nymphea in the inner court.

Casa del Bel Cortile★ (D). — The house with a fine court at No. 8 is one of the most original in Herculaneum. It has no *atrium* but a raised court, and with its stone staircase and balcony brings to mind a mediaeval castle of Central Italy. On display are foodstuffs, crockery, coins, buttons, dice, jewellery and bronze statuettes unearthed during the excavations.

Casa del Bicentenario★ (E). — This house was laid bare in 1938, two hundred years after digging officially started. The austere *atrium* is in the Tuscan style. One of the smaller rooms *(alae)* opening off it is closed by a charred folding door. The *tablinum* (living room) is adorned with a marble pavement and frescoes in the 4th Pompeiian style: painted panels (Venus and Mars) with medallions (Sileni, Bacchae...) framed by bands with plant motifs, and above a cornice adorned with cupids, scenes and vistas. In a small room on the upper floor, in which, no doubt, a Christian lived, you will see a small cross incorporated in a stucco panel above a small wooden altar. This is the oldest evidence of the Christian religion in the Roman Empire.

House with the Wooden Cupboard (Casa del Sacello di legno) (F). — No.31. In a room to the right, after entering the house, you will see a wooden cupboard *(sacello di legno)* probably also used as a shrine.

Pistrinum★★ (Bakery). — No. 8. An inscription reveals that the bakery belonged to Sextus Patulcus Felix. In the shop are two flour mills and in the back room, a large oven and bronze bread moulds. Opposite the Decumanus Inferior (there is a fountain at the corner) is the entrance to the *palestra*.

Palestra★. — *Partly excavated.* This huge building (over 100 m by 80 m - 328 × 262 ft) was used for athletic sports. It is lined with shops and tenement houses along Cardo V, with porticoes on the inside. A swimming pool in the shape of a cross has been uncovered (in the centre is a fountain around which is curled a snake with water spouting from its five heads); there is also a large room with a niche which held a statue of the Emperor or of an important personage. Trophies for the champions were displayed on the marble table.

House of the Stags★★ (Casa dei Cervi). — This rich patrician mansion at No. 21 probably the most beautiful among those overlooking the bay, is adorned with numerous works of art and frescoes of the time of Nero in the red and black style of Pompeii. From the *atrium* you enter the *triclinium*, where there are two admirable sculptured groups of stags, hence the house's name, being attacked by dogs. In the next room is the statue of a satyr carrying a leather bottle. The garden, complete with peristyle, is surrounded by a portico into which the rooms open. In one of them is a statue of Hercules, drunk; facing the sea is a *solarium* (sun porch).

A steep, sunken road leads to **Porta Marina** which opened on to the port.

Small Baths★ (Terme Suburbane) (G). — *Closed for restoration work.* The baths lie below the House of the Stags, to the left of the road going down towards the former Lido of Herculaneum. Recent excavations have revealed a magnificent group. The building which was erected shortly before the town was buried, is well preserved.

Theatre★ (Teatro). — At No. 119, Corso Resina *(closed for restoration work)*. At the time of Augustus the theatre could accommodate 2 000 spectators.

ISCHIA, Isle of ★★★ Campania

Michelin map 988 27 — Pop 43 628

The Emerald Isle, near the edge of a transparent sea and clothed in vines, tropical vegetation, olives and pinewoods, is one of the major attractions of the Bay of Naples. A clear, sparkling light plays over varied landscape, a coast indented with bays and creeks, and small wine growing villages scattered over the slopes.

The island has many hot springs with various properties. Monte Epomeo, an extinct volcano, rises to a height of 788 m - 2 585 ft.

Access. — Boats (some take cars) leave for the island from **Naples** *(apply to the CAREMAR Company, Mole Beverello, Naples ☎ 313 882; or to the Libera Navigazione LAURO Society, Mole Beverello, ☎ 323 013); from* **Pozzuoli** *(apply to the CAREMAR Company, Pozzuoli, ☎ 867 13 35); or to the LAURO or TRAGHETTI Societies, at the harbour, Pozzuoli ☎ 867 37 36); from* **Procida** *(apply to the CAREMAR Company, Pro-*

(After photo by T.C.I.)

View of the Castello d'Ischia

cida ☎ 89 67 280); from **Capri** (in season and passengers only) *(apply to the LAURO Company, Marina Grande, Capri ☎ 837 75 77); from* **Sorrento** *(apply to the LAURO Company, Piazza Marinai d'Italia, Sorrento ☎ 877 1506).*

A hydrofoil *(aliscafi)* service also operates from **Naples** *(apply to the ALILAURO Company, Via Caracciolo Mergellina, Naples ☎ 68 10 41 or to the CAREMAR Company, Mole Beverello, Naples ☎ 313 882); from* **Pozzuoli** *(apply to the CAREMAR Company, Pozzuoli ☎ 867 13 35).*

Life on Ischia. — For the most part, the island villages have kept their ancient appearance and most of them remain very small. The white cottages, sometimes roofed with a dome and with outside staircases, often have walls covered with vines. The vines grown on the slopes of Mount Epomeo produce a delicious white wine which has a slightly iodised flavour.

The tourist is driven in a Vespa sidecar shaded by a parasol, or in an open cab covered by an awning and drawn by horses wearing straw hats.

Ischia★★. — *Town plan in Michelin Red Guide Italia (hotels and restaurants).* The capital is divided into two settlements, Ischia Porto and Ischia Ponte, joined by the Corso Vittoria Colonna, an avenue lined with cafés, restaurants and smart shops.

The harbour of **Ischia Porto** lies in the crater of an extinct volcano, which was joined to the sea by a canal in 1854. A tiny island rises in the middle of the basin.

Ischia Ponte owes its name to the bridge built by the Aragonese to link the coast with the rocky islet on the summit of which stands the **Castello d'Ischia★★** *(open 9 am to sunset; 1 300 lire on foot; 2 000 lire by lift).* This is a group of buildings comprising an Aragonese castle of the 15C and several churches. From the esplanade in front of the castle there is a splendid panorama of the Bay of Naples. Castello d'Ischia is the oldest settlement in the island.

Tour of the Island★★★. *34 km - 21 miles — about 2 hours.* There is something enchanting about this tour. The lonely road winds among the vines, past caves hewn in the rock. From time to time a white village of Moorish appearance comes into sight. There are many views of the coast. The most remarkable are those from Barano d'Ischia, Fontana and Serrara Fontana.

A road to the left on the Serrara Fontana-Panza road enables you to make a detour *(3 km - 2 miles)* to **Sant'Angelo**, a minute fishing village lying at the foot of a rocky promontory. From Panza a path goes *(1/2 hour on foot Rtn)* to La Guardiola (mark 194): good views.

From the Punta del Soccorso Church in the village of **Forio** the view extends as far as the Island of Ponza. **Lacco Ameno** is pleasantly sited. From halfway between Lacco Ameno and **Casamicciola Terme** can be seen a curious mushroom-shaped rock, Il Fungo.

ITRI Latium
Michelin map 988 26 27 — 16 km - 10 miles — north of Gaeta — Pop 6 867

Itri was an important strategic point because of its position on a pass used by the Appian Way (Via Appia). The town occupies a **site★** hemmed in between impressive walls of rock.

Fra Diavolo. — Michele Pezza, who was nicknamed Fra Diavolo because, like the Devil, he eluded all pursuers, was born at Itri in 1771. Half bandit and half soldier, he waged ceaseless guerrilla warfare against the French troops under the Revolution and the Empire. He was arrested at last and hanged in the market-place at Naples on 11 November 1806.

IVREA Piedmont
Michelin maps 988 2 and 26 14 — 50 km - 31 miles — north of Turin — Pop 29 103

Ivrea, at the mouth of the Valle d'Aosta, was the capital of the Dora Department under the French Empire; today it is a busy commercial town with mechanical and textile industries. (The Olivetti typewriter and calculating machine factory is one of the largest in the world.)

The town, known as Beautiful Ivrea, has a cathedral with pre-Romanesque features and a castle built in the 14C by Amadeo VI of Savoy.

East of Ivrea, is the **Serra d'Ivrea**, the greatest moraine wall in Europe, formed by the glaciers which, in the Quaternary Era, gave birth to the Dora Baltea River.

EXCURSION

Nivolet Pass★★. — *West, 80 km - 50 miles.* Take road S 565 to Castellamonte then road S 460 leading to Pont Canavese. Follow the picturesque **Locana Valley** at the bottom of which runs the River Orco. The valley which marks the boundary of the Gran Paradiso National Park *(p 49)*, narrows past Locana and is dominated by the Gran Paradiso Massif. The rugged scenery is impressive. There is a scenic road through gorges, leading to Ceresole Reale, a small tourist resort by a lake.

The spectacular climb to the **Nivolet Pass** (2 612 m - 8 570 ft) cuts through the national park. From the top of the pass, there are superb **views★★** of the massif dotted with high-altitude lakes. One can descend to the small Lake Nivolet. Beyond the lake, the road *(cars are banned)* rejoins the Savarenche Valley *(p 49)*.

JESI Marches
Michelin map 988 16 — 31 km - 19 miles — southwest of Ancona — Pop 42 090

Jesi, like several towns in central Italy, has kept the characteristic appearance of a mediaeval city, enclosed in curious fortified walls with 14C battlements. Under the Renaissance, Jesi was a domain of the Malatesta family and then of the Sforzas. The German Emperor Frederick II of Hohenstaufen was born in Jesi in 1194, and the musician Pergolese in 1710.

Government House★ (Palazzo della Signoria). — Francesco di Giorgio Martini, the pupil of Brunelleschi, was the architect of this sober and elegant Renaissance building in the heart of the old quarter, built between 1486 and 1490. The doorway, which was of later date, 16C, is surmounted by the lion which appears in the coat of arms of the town. Andrea Sansovino designed the court with its superimposed loggias so full of grace and lightness.

Picture Gallery (Pinacoteca). — *Open 9.30 am to 12.30 pm and 4 to 6 pm 1 June to 30 September; 9 am to noon and 3 to 6 pm the rest of the year; 1st and 3rd Sundays in the month: 10 am to noon all the year round. Closed on 2nd and 4th Sundays in the month and in the afternoon on Saturdays and 1st and 3rd Sundays in the month.* The gallery is in the Palazzo Pianetti, via XX Settembre, and contains an important collection of **works★** by **Lorenzo Lotto** (1480-1556). This Venetian painter of religious compositions and portraits lived in the Marches from 1535 until his death at Loreto as an Oblate of the Santa Casa. He came under the influence of German art, was a colourist and a realist and a merciless observer of his models, but he had a sense of light and of crowd movements. This gallery owns one of his best known works, a Santa Lucia whose yellow robe and red scarf make an astonishing colour harmony.

Michelin maps **988** 2 3 4 and **26** 6 to 10 — *Local maps pp 128-130*

The words Italian Lakes conjure up an idyllic fairyland of blue waters at the foot of shapely mountains, sailing-boats, villas, terraced gardens and flowers, bathed in brilliant light.

The Lake District extends from Piedmont to Venetia and Switzerland. It includes Lakes Orta and Varese, Lake Maggiore or Verbano, Lake Como or Lario, Lake Lugano or Ceresio, Lake Iseo or Sabino and Lake Garda or Benaco, all of which are of glacial origin.

The charm and originality of the Pre-Alpine lakes, which are sometimes called the Lombard Lakes, are due to the juxtaposition of Alpine and southern scenery under a clear sky and a mild climate.

Tour. — The route shown in black on the maps on pp 128-130 corresponds to the most picturesque sections.

■ LAKE MAGGIORE★★★ (Lago Maggiore)

Maggiore is the most famous of the Italian lakes, and its beauty is legendary. Luxuriant vegetation and shores, sometimes rugged, sometimes wonderfully smiling give it its particular charm. The central part of the lake, in which the Borromean Islands lie, is world famous.

The lake is 65 km long and 5 km across at its widest part — 40 × 3 miles; its maximum depth, between Laveno-Mombello and Intra, is 372 m - 1 220 ft. Its northern end is in Switzerland; the Ticino and Toce Rivers run through the lake and feed it. In fine weather the lake waters are green in the north and a flawless blue in the south.

The tropical vegetation displays an extraordinary variety of species: magnolias, camellias, azaleas, orange and lemon trees, citrons, pomegranates, palms, rhododendrons, cannas, oleanders, lotus, water-lilies, coffee bushes, tulip trees, coconut palms, cedars, myrtles, etc.

Tour. — A boat tour of the lake is pleasant, for the views from the lakeside road, on which traffic is heavy, are sometimes masked by villas. There is a regular service *(April to October)* on the route Arona-Stresa-Baveno-Intra-Luino-Locarno, taking about 3 1/2 hours *(you may have a meal on board)*. The return trip is by hydrofoil *(aliscafi)* taking 1 1/2 hours. *1 day return ticket, Arona-Locarno, 7 000 lire.*

There are also many sailings from Stresa, Baveno and Pallanza to the Borromean Islands *(description p 67)*. A car ferry links Intra and Laveno *(departures every 20 minutes; time for crossing: 20 minutes; 2 600-4 800 lire)*. *1 to 7 day sailing tickets are available; price: 6 400 lire for 1 day; 16 700 lire for 7 days; half fare for children.*

FROM ARONA TO LOCARNO along the west shore
73 km - 45 miles — about 2 hours — visit to the Borromean Islands not included

Arona. — An old town at the foot of a cliff. When leaving Arona and going towards Stresa a road branches off to the left which leads to the **Colosso di San Carlone**, a gigantic bronze and copper effigy of **St. Charles Borromeo**, 23 m - 75 ft — high, standing on a granite pedestal 12 m -40 ft — high. This statue was erected to commemorate a man who was born at Arona in 1538, was an abbot at twelve and Cardinal Archbishop of Milan at twenty-two. He distinguished himself by the authority he showed in re-establishing discipline and morals in the Church and by his heroic conduct during the plague of 1576. From the terrace *(500 lire)* or from the top of the statue *(somewhat difficult climb-open 8.30 am to 12.30 pm and 2 to 7 pm 1 April to 30 September; 9 am to noon and 2 to 6 pm the rest of the year; closed Tuesday afternoons, Wednesdays from 1 October to 31 March, and holidays in November; 1 000 lire)* there is an extensive view.

Stresa★★. — *Description p 232.*

Borromean Islands★★★. — *Description p 67.*

Baveno★. — A quiet and pleasant holiday resort at which Queen Victoria stayed. The granite quarries, which can be seen alongside the road, are well known.

Pallanza★★. — *Description p 172.*

Premeno. — *11 km - 7 miles — from Intra.* Its villas are scattered in a fine setting overlooking the lake.

Cannero Riviera★★. — Cannero occupies a delightful site among its olive trees, vines and groves of orange and lemon trees. Opposite on two small islands, are the ruins of two curious looking **castles★** which were brigands' lairs in the 15C.

Cannobio. — Cannobio is a small resort near the Swiss border. The Church of the Madonna della Pietà, near the lake, is a fine Renaissance building and the Palazzo della Ragione (Law Courts) dates from the 13C. There are fine old houses. The Sunday market is a colourful event. From Cannobio you can take the road along the Valle Cannobina and, just over 3 km - 2 miles — farther on, you can see the **Orrido di Sant'Anna**, a precipice formed by the torrent. The Valle Cannobina with its typical houses, retains its wild scenery.

Ascona★ (Switzerland). — *See Michelin Green Guide of Switzerland.*

Locarno★★ (Switzerland). — *See Michelin Green Guide of Switzerland.*

SITES AND TOWNS on the east shore

Luino. — An attractive resort, but also an industrial centre, Luino has a cool promenade shaded by plane trees.

Laveno-Mombello. — A large industrial centre where fine porcelain is manufactured. A cableway enables one to reach the **Poggio Sant'Elsa** (alt 972 m - 3 255 ft) about 100 m - 950 ft — below the summit of the Sasso del Ferro *(several departures daily between May and September; Sundays only the rest of the year; time: 15 minutes; Rtn fare: 1 000 lire)*; vast **panorama★★** of Lake Maggiore and the Borromean Islands, and of the other Lombard Lakes; to the west stands the Monte Rosa.

Santa Caterina del Sasso★. — A path branching off to the right from the Laveno-Angera road leads to this church. The building clings to a rock overlooking the lake in a picturesque setting. It was founded at the end of the 14C by an anchorite, Alberto Besozzo.

Angera. — To the north of this place a steep little uphill road leads to the **Rocca**, a 14C Gothic castle *(open 15 March to 30 October, 9 am to noon and 1.30 to 5.30 pm — 6 pm July; 1 500 lire)* which belonged to the Torriani family, then the Viscontis and finally the Borromeos. The view is pretty and the apartments are fairly typical of the life of the aristocracy in the Middle Ages. Note a large Gothic hall decorated, in the 14C, with the Signs of the Zodiac and frescoes depicting the struggle of the Viscontis against Napo Torriani, whom they dispossessed.

■ LAKE ORTA★★ (Lago d'Orta)

Orta one of the smallest Italian lakes, with a very mild climate, is perhaps the most smiling and the most gracious in its setting of wooded hills. It is 13 km long and at the most 2 km wide — 8 × 1 1/2 miles — and is dominated from the northeast by the Monte Mottarone. The outflow is into Lake Maggiore in the north. The tour of the lake *(using the route shown in black on the map, p 128 — 39 km - 24 miles — about 1 hour)* affords good views.

Orta San Giulio★★. — A springtime country resort and delightful site★★★ at the tip of a peninsula. Orta has old houses adorned with wrought iron ornaments of the 17 and 18C and a small, shady square with a 16C town hall above an arcade. From Orta you can go up on foot, by the Via Corinna Cairo Albertoletti and the Via Gemelli *(3/4 hour Rtn)*, to the Sacro Monte (401 m -1 316 ft). Here twenty chapels were built between 1591 and 1770 in a sort of park from which marvellous glimpses of Orta and its lake can be seen.
On leaving Orta you can join the road to Mottarone at Armeno. *Description p 232.*

San Giulio Island★★. — *Reached from Orta by motor-boat (Rtn fare: 4 000 lire for up to 5 people and 750 lire for each additional passenger) or by small motor-boat (2 500 lire per hour without the boatman or 4 000 lire Rtn with the boatman and for up to 5 people).* The island is a jewel 300 m long and 160 m across — 330 × 175 yds. The terraces, clumps of trees and flower gardens, which make it up, are circled by a pleasant road.
The Romanesque **Basilica** of San Giulio is said to date from the 4C, when St. Julius arrived and rid the island of a dragon and the snakes which infested it. The basilica was rebuilt in the 9 and 10C (bas-reliefs, columns) and in the 12C (campanile). Inside, between walls covered with interesting frescoes, you will see the curious 12C pulpit in black Oira marble, adorned with relief sculptures and motifs, and in the crypt a sarcophagus containing the relics of St. Julius. The seminary alongside the basilica dates from 1624.

Boleto. — *Excursion 5.5 km - 3 1/2 miles.* The town is reached by a steep road, which branches off to the right not far from Alzo. From the sanctuary of the **Madonna del Sasso** Church, built at an altitude of nearly 700 m - 2 300 ft — there is a **view★** of almost all of the lake.

■ LAKE LUGANO★★ (Lago di Lugano)

Most of Lugano is in Swiss territory. The Italians, who call it Lake Ceresio, own only the northeast end (Porlezza), part of the southwest shore (Porto Ceresio) and an enclave (Campione d'Italia).
Lake Lugano looks wilder than Lakes Maggiore and Como, being enclosed between the steep but shapely slopes of the Alps (many cableways) on which the olive groves form pale patches. Oddly shaped, it is 35 km - 22 miles — from one end to the other and has a maximum depth of 288 m - 950 ft.
An ugly causeway, carrying the St. Gothard railway and a motorway divides the lake into two bays between which boats can nevertheless pass.

Tour. — The steamship company runs a daily tour of the lake starting from Lugano *(start about 2.25 pm, return about 5.30 pm; fare 15 Swiss francs)* and regular and frequent services to Porlezza, Gandria, Campione, Capolago, Morcote and Ponte Tresa.

TOUR by Morcote
26 km - 16 miles — about 2 hours
See Michelin Green Guide of Switzerland.

FROM LUGANO TO PORLEZZA
16 km - 10 miles — about 3/4 hour

Lugano★★★ (Switzerland). — *See the Michelin Green Guide of Switzerland.*
Gandria★ (Switzerland). — *See the Michelin Green Guide of Switzerland.*
Oria★. — A pretty village at the water's edge.

OTHER TOWNS AND SITES

Campione d'Italia★. — An Italian enclave in Switzerland, Campione is a colourful, smiling village which is highly popular on account of its casino. At Campione the art lover will find the memory of the famous **maestri campionesi**, a guild of masons, architects, decorators and sculptors who, in the 14C, vied with the *maestri comacini (p 85)* in spreading the Lombard style throughout Italy and all over Europe. The St. Peter's Oratory (San Pietro) dates from 1326.
Lanzo d'Intelvi. — *Service temporarily suspended.* A funicular railway starting from Santa Margherita leads to this resort (alt 907 m - 2 975 ft), which can also be reached from Argegno and the picturesque Valle di Intelvi *(see p 128)*. From the upper funicular station there is a fine **panorama★** of Lake Lugano and the Alps.
Monte Generoso★★★ (Switzerland). — *See the Michelin Green Guide of Switzerland.*
Riva San Vitale (Switzerland). — *See the Michelin Green Guide of Switzerland.*

■ LAKE COMO★★★ (Lago di Como)

Of all the Italian lakes, Como has the most variety. Olives, mulberries, chestnuts, walnut and fig trees and oleanders alternate on its shores. Smiling, flower decked villages, little ports, villas, Eden-like gardens, haughty castles and *crotti* (country inns) succeed one another.
The lake is hemmed between mountains (600 m - 2 000 ft high on the south side, 2 600 m - 8 500 ft high on the north side). Halfway along its length it divides into two branches, the eastern branch, which is the wilder, taking the name of Lake Lecco.
Lake Como is 50 km - 30 miles long; its width varies between 4.5 km and about 650 m, - 2 3/4 miles × 700 yds; its depth, the greatest in any European lake, reaches 410 m - 1 345 ft — opposite Argegno. Square-rigged cargo boats glide on its clear waters teeming with fish.
Under the name of Larius the praises of the lake were sung by both Pliny the Younger and the Elder, who had houses on its shores, Virgil, Cassiodorus and Shelley.
Tour. — Lake tours can be made on the Como-Argegno-Bellagio-Menaggio-Colico route in steamers with bar-restaurants *(2 return trips daily including public holidays; time for single trip: about 3 hours; 5 400 lire Rtn).*

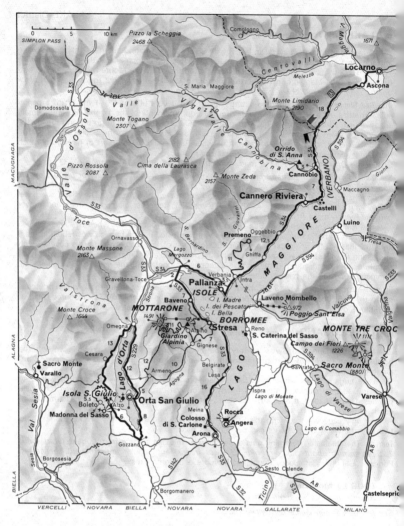

A hydrofoil *(aliscafi)* service operates; from Como to Tremezzo, Bellagio and Menaggio: *3 000 lire;* from Tremezzo, Bellagio and Menaggio to Dongo, Gravedona, Domaso and Colico, and also to Lecco: *2 300 - 3 000 lire;* tickets for Como to Lecco or Colico: *4 400 lire.*

There are car ferries between Cadenabbia and Bellagio, Bellagio and Varenna *(charge: 2 700 - 4 700 lire according to size of car),* and Cadenabbia and Varenna or Menaggio-Bellagio and Menaggio-Varenna. *Tickets available for one to ten days, can be obtained for the tour of the lake; price: 5 500 lire for one day and 16 500 lire for ten days.*

There are also day and night cruises on Saturdays during the summer holidays *(7 000 lire with dancing on board).*

The tourist in a hurry can confine himself to a tour of the western arm of the lake, using the ferry between Cadenabbia and Bellagio.

FROM COMO TO MENAGGIO

35 km - 21 miles — about 1 1/2 hours

Leave Como (p 85) to the northwest by road S 340 which follows the west shore of the lake.

Cernobbio★★. — This modern resort is well equipped. The monumental 16C Villa d'Este, now an hotel, is surrounded by a lovely garden.

Valle di Intelvi★. — A wide smiling valley winds its way between Argegno and Lanzo d'Intelvi. From the road there are views of Lake Como and, later, of Lake Lugano.

Ospedaletto. — A charming village near Ossucio, opposite the Island of Comacina. A curious **campanile★** stands below the road.

The most remarkable sections are the **Tremezzina,** between Ospedaletto and Menaggio which the French writer Maurice Barrès called "the garden of Lombardy".

Comacina Island★. — This is the only island in Lake Como. On it stood a mediaeval fortress in which the King of the Lombards, Berenger, took refuge. Ruins of a church and fortifications.

Balbianello Point. — A verdant point on which the Baroque Arconati-Visconti villa stands.

Lenno. — Well situated town north of the Punta del Balbianello.

Tremezzo★★. — A mild climate, a beautiful **site★** and lovely vegetation combine to make this capital of the Tremezzina a favourite place for a stay.

Between Tremezzo and Cadenabbia the **Villa Carlotta★★★** *(open 1 April to 30 September 9 am to 6 pm; the rest of the year 9 to 11 am and 2 to 4.30 pm; closed 10 November to 28 February; 2 500 lire)* in a beautiful setting forming a belvedere overlooking the lake, is one of the most famous sights of the region. It has terraced gardens with tropical vegetation, enclosed by a splendid grille. May is the time for a visit when the azaleas and rhododendrons are in full flower. The 18C villa contains an interesting collection of early 19C marble statues, including a famous group of **Love and Psyche** by Canova and figures by the Danish Thorvaldsen.

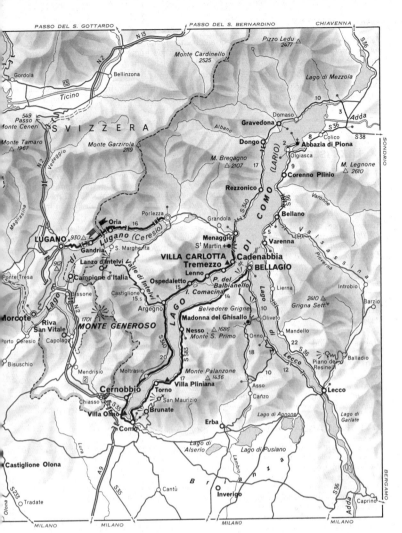

Cadenabbia★★. — On an admirable **site★** opposite Bellagio, Cadenabbia is a delightful holiday resort linked with the Villa Carlotta and with Tremezzo by a splendid avenue of plane trees known as the Via del Paradiso. There is a very good **view★★** of Bellagio and Lakes Como and Lecco from the path *(1 1/2 hours Rtn on foot)* up to the Chapel of St. Martin.

Menaggio. — Favoured by a cool summer breeze, this is one of the lake's smart resorts.

FROM COMO TO BELLAGIO
31 km - 19 miles — about 1 1/2 hours

Leave Como (p 85) to the north by road S 583 which follows the lake's eastern shore.

Torno. — A little port with steep alleys. The Church of Santa Thecla has a fine Lombard doorway. Eastwards is the famous **Villa Pliniana★** *(open 6 September to 20 October 3 to 6 pm)*, so-called because Pliny owned a country house there. It is remarkable for its splendid site and an intermittent spring.

Nesso. — A picturesque village with houses scattered among greenery, Nesso boasts a waterfall, the Orrido di Nesso.

The next stop is at Bellagio (p 59) on a promontory dividing Lake Lecco from the south branch of Lake Como.

OTHER TOWNS AND SITES
From Bellagio to Varenna (Lake Lecco)

Leave Bellagio (p 59) to the south in the direction of Lecco.

Lecco. — An industrial town between Lake Lecco and Lake Garlate.

Varenna★. — This is a delightful town with many gardens and cypresses and pretty little streets running down to the lake. The 16C Villa Monastero has beautiful **gardens★** *(Villa and gardens open 9 am to noon and 2 to 5 pm; 7 pm May to end of August; closed 1 November to 31 March; 500 lire)*. The gardens afford good views of the lake.

From Varenna to Menaggio (the northern arm of Lake Como)

Leave Varenna (see description above) to the north by the road S 36.

Bellano. — A small industrial town (cotton) at the mouth of the Valsassina. The 14C church has a fine façade in the Lombard Gothic style. You can visit the impressive **Orrido di Bellano**, a gorge and cascade formed by the Pioverna torrent.

Corenno Plinio. — The name of this place, prettily built in terraces rising from the lake, is said to be derived from one of Pliny's villas.

Piona Abbey (Abbazia di Piona). — A poor and narrow road *(2 km - 1 1/4 miles — from Olgiasca)* which affords, however, fine glimpses of the lake, leads from road S 36 to this graceful little Romanesque Cluniac monastery: 11C church and remarkable Romanesque **cloisters★** (1252).

Gravedona. — This fishing port is a good excursion centre.

Dongo. — It was near this village, which has busy paper-mills, that Italian anti-Fascist partisans captured Mussolini and his mistress, Clara Petacci, on 27 April 1945. They were shot next day near Mezzegra, south of Tremezzo.

Rezzonico. — The village is prettily situated. It has a 14C castle among cypresses.

Continue along the lakeside road to Menaggio (p 129).

■ LAKE ISEO★ (Lago d'Iseo) *local map below*

Though Lake Iseo is not very well known and luxury villas do not abound on its shores, it has an attractively varied setting of olive trees, wild scenery and high mountain backgrounds with secluded villages and a few industrial centres. The lake is 25 km - 15 1/2 miles — long, with a maximum depth of 250 m - 820 ft — and contains the largest lake island in Italy, Monte Isola *(see below)*. The wines grown on its shores are popular.

Tour. — There are boat services on the Sarnico-Iseo-Marone-Pisogne-Lovere line *(about 3 hours for the single trip)* which make it possible to fit the tour into a day *(for information apply to the Azienda Autonoma Soggiorno, Lungolago at Iseo, ☎ 980209, or the Stazione Autolinee at Bergamo, ☎ 243680).* However, it is better to take the road running round the lake.

Iseo. — The *Pieve* (Romanesque church), facing a charming little square, has a 13C campanile.

Monte Isola★. — This island, reached from Sulzano, covered with chestnuts and olives, rises to a height of 599 m - 1 965 ft and is 9 km - 6 miles — round. From the Church of the Madonna della Seriola, which crowns the summit, there is a panorama of the lake and the Bergamaschian Alps. The run from Peschiera Maraglio to Sensole through olive groves is delightful.

The *corniche* section, between Marone and Pisogne, is particularly picturesque.

Pisogne. — Its industries (iron mines, foundries, spinning mills) give it a certain importance. The 15C Church of St. Mary of the Snows (Santa Maria della Neve) contains 16C **frescoes★** by Romanino da Brescia depicting the Life of Christ.

Lovere. — A prosperous little industrial town. The Tadini Museum *(open 15 April to 30 September, 10 am to noon and 3 to 6 pm; closed in the morning on weekdays; 500 lire)*, near the lake, contains weapons, pictures by Giovanni Bellini and Parmigianino, porcelain, and sculptures by Canova. The route between Castro and Riva di Solto is also picturesque.

■ LAKE GARDA★★★ (Lago di Garda) *local map below*

Garda is the largest lake in Italy. It is 52 km long, with maximum width of just over 18 km — 32 × 11 miles. A depth of 346 m - 1 135 ft — has been plumbed. The lake is a deep blue; the northern extremity is hemmed between mountains like a fjord and the southern section looks like a small inland sea. It is sometimes considered the most beautiful of the Italian Lakes and it enjoys a warm climate, being sheltered from the cold north winds. Its enchanting shores are covered with splendid vegetation: the famous vines of Bardolino, citron, palm, lemon, orange and olive trees, oleanders and venerable cypresses. Stout two-masted sailing boats carry wood and are also used for fishing. This is the "beneficient" lake, the *Benacus* sung by the Latin poets Catullus, Virgil and Pliny, and later by Goethe, and Gabriele D'Annunzio.

Tour. — Tour along the western side of the lake: Desenzano-Sirmione-Salò-Gardone-Riva; *2 Rtn trips daily; time for single trip, about 4 1/2 hours; 3 000 lire; 4 Rtn trips daily by hydrofoil (aliscafi).*

From April to October, swift hydrofoils, leaving Desenzano and Riva, enable one to do the trip in about 2 hours.

A car ferry links Maderno with Torri del Benaco *(8 Rtn trips daily in summer).*

FROM SALÒ TO RIVA
44 km - 27 miles

This most spectacular road follows the *corniche* from Salò to Riva (56 bridges and 70 tunnels in 44 km - 27 miles) and is best in the late afternoon when the sun strikes the east shore.

Salò. — This town, powerful during the domination of Venice, was the birthplace of the supposed inventor of the violin, Bertolotti da Salò. The 15C Cathedral (Duomo) contains works by two painters of Brescia, Moretto and Romanino. The Island of Garda, opposite Salò Bay, contains a magnificent estate belonging to the Borghese family.

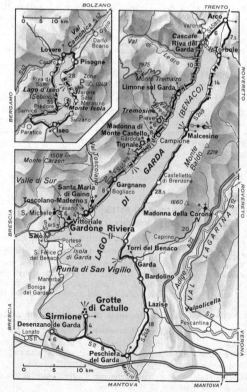

Gardone Riviera★★. — This is a favourite resort for tourists because of its excellent hotel accommodation, bathing-beach, luxuriant vegetation and quiet atmosphere and good walks in the surrounding hills. At 1 km - 3/4 mile — to the northeast, on a hill-top is the **Vittoriale★** estate *(open 8.30 am to noon and 2 to 6 pm or 5 pm 1 October to 31 March and 5.30 pm April-May; 1 000 lire; 2 000 lire including villa; closed Monday mornings)*, comprising a villa and a park which belonged to **Gabriele D'Annunzio** (1863-1938), who is buried there. Mementoes of the extraordinary personality of this poet, novelist, military leader, aesthete and Don Juan, who was famous during and just after the First World War, are collected in the villa. His plays are performed in a theatre in the park in summer. There is a good view from the church chevet of Gardone di Sopra, of the Gardone Riviera, the lake and, on a clear day, of Monte Baldo.

From Gardone di Sopra there is a panoramic road to San Michele *(6 km - 4 miles)* from which there is a magnificent view of the lake and the Sur Valley.

Toscolano-Maderno. — Maderno, built deep in the centre of a bay, possesses most of the tourist attractions of this pretty health resort that extends along both sides of a promontory. Maderno contains a small 12C Romanesque church. From the Church of **Santa Maria di Gaino** which lies to the north *(3 km - 2 miles)* and which is encircled by cypress trees, there is a wonderful **view★★** of the lake.

Gargnano. — This pleasant little place, with greenhouses full of citron and lemon trees, has a 13C church, St. Francis (San Francesco), with 15C cloisters.
The Villa Feltrinelli on the lake shore was a residence of Mussolini during the Fascist Republic (end of 1943 to April 1945).

Tignale. — A spectacular road leading to Tignale branches left off the *corniche* road S 45 *bis* as you come out of the third tunnel.
Follow the branch road for 7 km - 4 miles — then 500 m - 500 yds —, beyond the hamlet of Gardola, take the road to the right. Almost immediately you come on the **Madonna di Monte Castello,** a church perched 600 m - 1 969 ft — above the lake and affording a magnificent **panorama★★★.**

Tremosine. — Near Campione a **road★★** *(6 km - 4 miles)*, impressively beautiful, branches off and climbs through the wild Val Brasa to the Plateau of Tremosine, forming a terrace with splendid views over the lake. *Turn back at Pieve di Tremosine.*

Limone sul Garda. — An attractive fishing port nestling between rocks grooved by glaciers. The figs and honey of Limone are well known.
Once within sight of Riva *(p 198)* the road is nearing the northern tip of Lake Garda.

FROM RIVA TO DESENZANO along the east shore
96 km - 60 miles

The road along the east shore is hardly less beautiful than that along the west shore.

Arco. — A charming little town near the north shore of the lake.

Torbole. — The town is admirably placed at the northeast end of Lake Garda. A health resort, it was formerly famous for its quarries of green marble.

Malcesine★. — A picturesque country holiday resort built on a promontory at the foot of Monte Baldo. On the edge of the lake stands the **Captains' Palace** — the captains were the representatives of the Venetian Republic. It is the 13 and 14C castle of the Scaligers of Verona, however, which dominates the town. Goethe was surprised, arrested and finally imprisoned in Malcesine in September 1786 for drawing the castle from which there is a splendid **panorama★★★** of the lake.
A cable-car climbs from Malcesine to an altitude of 1 765 m - 5 791 ft — on the slopes of **Monte Baldo** *(time: 15 minutes; change cars at San Michele; departures every 1/2 hour for the first stage, every hour for the second; Rtn fare: 4 000 lire; 2 500 lire in winter)*. From the top there is a very good **panorama★★** of the lake; to the north lies the Brenta Massif.

Torri del Benaco. — A pleasant and frequented spot with a port and a 14C castle.

San Vigilio Point★★ (Punta di San Vigilio). — The point makes a romantically beautiful picture, framed in dark masses of ancient cypresses. The lovely gardens of the Villa Guarienti di Brenzone *(visited by permission of the proprietor)* surround a palace built by Sanmicheli in the 16C. From the road there is a superb **view★★** of the lake.

Garda. — A little port at the head of a bay, among cypresses and olives, Garda, an ancient Roman village, has given its name to the lake.
From Garda a road leads *(20 km - 12 miles — about 3/4 hour)* to the Church of the **Madonna della Corona** on a remarkable **site★★** overlooking the Adige Valley.

Bardolino. — The village, famous for its red wine, has a few Renaissance houses. The Church of St. Severinus (San Severo) dates from the 11C.

Lazise. — A tiny fishing port near which, on the water's edge, stand the walls of a castle that belonged to the Scaligers, overlords of Verona.

Peschiera del Garda. — This town of Roman origin at the mouth of the Mincio, an overflow of the lake, is in a remarkable strategic position commanding the northern part of the Po Valley. It is protected on the north side by the lake and the Alps.

Sirmione★★. — *Description p 229.*

Desenzano del Garda★. — This charming little port, dominated by its castle, is sought after as a holiday resort. In the Via Scavi Romani (Street of Roman Excavations) in the north part of the town, the Villa Romana contains remarkable Roman mosaics. There is a Last Supper by Tiepolo in the parish church.

LARDERELLO Tuscany _____
Michelin map **989** 14 — 33 km - 21 miles — south of Volterra.

Larderello is among the metal-bearing hills that were mined formerly. It is known for its volcanic steam jets, which can be seen from afar — from Volterra in the north and Massa Marittima in the south.

Larderello is one of the oddest places in Tuscany for its desolate soil, the roaring of the steam jets and the rumble of machinery. From the steam jets, which blow at a temperature of 100 to 200°C. (212 to 280°F.), chemical substances, particularly boric acid, are extracted. The springs are also used in the production of electrical energy.

LECCE * Apulia

Michelin map **988** 30 — Pop 89 661
Town plans in Michelin Red Guide Italia (hotels and restaurants).

Lecce is an art centre which has been nicknamed the Baroque Florence because of the many buildings in this style. The walls are of fine grained yellow limestone which is easy to work.

Lecce was first a Norman and then an Angevin town. It became part of the Kingdom of Naples from 1463 onward.

Basilica of the Holy Cross★★ **(Santa Croce).** — The basilica, which is sumptuously but not grossly decorated, makes, with the Palazzo del Governo (a museum), a graceful ensemble resembling in ornament the Spanish *plateresque*. The group was completed between 1549 and 1695. The interior of the basilica, which is graceful and well lit, displays pure, simple architecture based on the theories of Brunelleschi with the addition of abundant but delicate Baroque decoration.

Piazza del Duomo★. — This is one of the most remarkable squares in southern Italy for the unity of the Baroque structures standing round it. These are, from left to right: the cathedral campanile, 70 m - 230 ft — high; the cathedral itself; the bishop's palace and the seminary building, with an elegant façade and a court in the centre of which is an elaborate well.

LEGHORN (LIVORNO) Tuscany

Michelin map **988** 14 — Pop 177 101
Town plan in the Michelin Red Guide Italia (hotels and restaurants).

Leghorn is a busy town whose activities are concentrated in the Via Grande, lined with fine modern arcaded buildings, the Via Cairoli and the Via Ricasoli. The fashionable quarter lies near the park of the Villa Fabbricotti. The trading port, which deals chiefly in wood, products from Florentine crafts, marble, rough and finished alabaster, and cars, is one of the most important in Italy; it is further supported by heavy industries. The fishing industry has created two tasty specialities: *cacciucco* or fish soup, and *triglie*, red mullet cooked in the local fashion.

Cosimo I de' Medici built a jetty in 1571 and a canal to link Leghorn with Pisa in 1573. At the beginning of the 17C the town was given the protection of a wall with bastions which can still be seen and in 1620 the work on the "Porto Mediceo" (Medici port) was completed under Cosimo II.

In the Piazza Micheli, from which the 16C Fortezza Vecchia (Old Fortress) can be seen, stands the **monument**★ (Monumento dei Quattro Mori — 1624) to Ferdinand de' Medici. This commemorates a victory won over the Moors by the Knights of St. Stephen *(p 184)*.

Between Leghorn and Ardenza a road called the **Viale Italia** offers views of the Mediterranean. It passes near the Aquarium (Mediterranean fish) and the Naval Academy of Italy.

EXCURSION

Montenero★. — *9 km - 6 miles.* Leave Leghorn by ②, road S 1. After Ardenza, beyond the railway, a winding by-road branches off on the left towards Montenero, from which there is an extensive panorama of the coast and Leghorn. Round the square are the chapels forming the *Famedio* (Temple of Fame) reserved for the burial of distinguished citizens of Leghorn. The Church itself (1721), a point of pilgrimage, is dedicated to Our Lady of Grace, the patroness of Tuscany. Some of the rooms are lined with curious *ex-votos.*

LERICI * Liguria

Michelin map **988** 14 — 10 km - 6 miles — east of La Spezia — *Local map p 200* — Pop 14 070

Lerici lies at the head of a calm, sheltered cove, and is as much frequented in winter as in summer. It belonged to Pisa until 1256, when the Genoese took possession of it.

The imposing mass of a **castle** built in the 13C, demolished, and then rebuilt by the Genoese in the 16C, stands at the tip of a little cape. You can visit the guard room, the fortifications and the 13C Chapel of Sant'Anastasia. There are **views**★★ of Lerici and the Gulf of La Spezia.

EXCURSIONS

Ameglia Panoramic Road★★. — *24 km - 15 miles — about 1 hour.* Go preferably from Ameglia to Lerici. Make for Ameglia by way of Romito and the right bank of the Magra which you follow for a little under 4 km - 3 miles until you come to a crossroads when you take the first on the right. About 1 km - 1/2 mile from Ameglia, as you come out of a bend, you get magnificent **views**★★ of the old village curiously built at the top of a rock spike surrounded by hills. East lies the Magra Estuary, on the horizon, the Apuan Alps.

At Montemarcello the road changes. The last part of the run is along a *corniche.* As you drop down towards Lerici there is a splendid **view**★★★ of the Gulf and port of La Spezia, the Portovenere Point with the Islands of Palmaria and Tino and, just below the road, the little fishermen's villages pressed close into the backs of minute bays.

San Terenzo. — *2 km - 1 1/4 miles.* Byron and Shelley stayed in this pretty village and it was from here that Shelley set out in a sailing boat for Leghorn in July 1822, when a violent storm blew up and he was drowned off Viareggio. The sea threw up the body, and the Ariel of modern times lay for several days upon the beach, the local health regulations preventing his removal. Byron afterwards preserved the heart and had the remains burnt on a pyre in accordance with the rites of ancient Greece.

LIVIGNO Lombardy

Michelin maps **988** 3 4 and **24** 16 — Pop 3 527

The houses of Livigno stand separately along both sides of the road in the charming **setting**★ of a wide valley with green meadows. This arrangement is due to the fear of fire, which might ravage a small town of wooden houses. The construction of a barrage has necessitated the drowning of part of the Livigno valley downstream from the town.

The LOMELLINA Lombardy

Michelin map 988 13 — west of Pavia

The Lomellina, which lies between the Ticino and the Po, is the great rice growing area of Italy. In the spring the landscape is typical of any European rice region: vast stretches of flooded land divided by long lines of willows and poplars.

The chief towns are **Vigevano** where the ouststanding **Piazza Ducale★** was designed by Bramante and whose castle was the residence of the Sforza family; **Mortara** with its 14C cathedral and 16 and 17C Lombard paintings; and **Lomello** after which the region is named, which has several mediaeval monuments (8C baptistry, 10 or 12C Church of St. Mary, 13C Church of St. Michael, and 14C castle).

LORETO ★ Marches

Michelin map 988 16 — 31 km - 19 miles — southeast of Ancona — Pop 10 806
Town plan in Michelin Red Guide Italia (hotels and restaurants).

Loreto is perched on a spur and surrounded by massive brick ramparts with large round towers at intervals. It is the scene of famous pilgrimages to the House of Mary. This building, also known as the Santa Casa (Holy House) was carried, we are told, from Nazareth to a hill near Rijeka, in Slavonia (Dalmatia), by angels in 1291, and then, in 1294, from Slavonia across the Adriatic to the Marches. The angels set the house down in a wood of laurels (in Latin, *lauretum*) which gave its name to Loreto. The most popular pilgrimages take place on the feasts of the Virgin: the Nativity (8 September) and the Translation of the Santa Casa (10 December).

Piazza della Madonna★. — The square is in front of the Basilica. The porticoes of the Apostolic Palace, begun by Bramante and Sansovino in 1510 but left unfinished, give it a noble setting. In the centre is a fine 17C fountain.

Sanctuary of the Holy House★★ (Santuario della Santa Casa). — *Time: 1 hour.* The building, by several Florentine architects including Giuliano da Maiano, was begun in 1468. It possesses an impressive fortified **apse★★**. Guiliano da Sangallo built the dome in 1500 and Bramante the side chapels eleven years later. Vanvitelli designed the bulbous campanile, 76 m - 250 ft — high, in the 18C.

The plain white façade (1587) marks the end of the Renaissance period; the buttresses that frame it are surmounted by an Italian clock with only six hours marked on the left side and an astronomical clock-face indicating twelve hours on the right. In front of the façade, to the left, stands the majestic statue of Sixtus V surrounded by statues symbolising Faith, Charity, Justice and Peace.

The three bronze **doors★★** (late 16 and early 17C) are adorned with statues of Prophets, of Sibyls and bas-reliefs illustrating the Old Testament. Note especially Adam and Eve being expelled from the earthly Paradise, in the central section.

At the end of the south aisle the **Sacristy of St. Mark★** (San Marco) has a dome painted with frescoes by Melozzo da Forli (1477) with an exceptional sense of relief and foreshortening: seraphim and young angels with sweet faces carry the Instruments of the Passion.

Equally fine is the **Sacristy of St. John★** (San Giovanni), opening into the south transept. It is octagonal and paved with mosaic and contains a quaint lavabo designed by Benedetto da Maiano under a vault painted with frescoes by Luca Signorelli and his assistants (1477). Remarkable for their vigour and originality, these represent angel musicians and, at the base of the octagonal dome, the four Doctors of the Church and the four Evangelists alternately.

Standing at the transept crossing, under the dome, the brick-built **Santa Casa** was sumptuously faced with marble carved, in the 16C, by Andrea Sansovino and other sculptors. Prophets and Sibyls are seated in the niches. The panels depict scenes from the Life of the Virgin (an Annunciation by Sansovino facing the nave) and the Translation of the Santa Casa (facing the chancel).

From the north transept you enter a room decorated by Pomarancio (1605-1610) with scenes from the Life of the Virgin, Prophets, Sibyls and other symbols.

Museum-Picture Gallery. — *Open 1 April to 30 September, 9 am to 1 pm and 3 to 6 pm except Friday; the rest of the year, Saturdays and Sundays 9 am to 1 pm. Closed 1 January, Easter, 1 May, 15 August and 25 December; 500 lire.*

The museum housed in the Apostolic Palace, contains a remarkable series of **works★** by Lorenzo Lotto, a 16C Venetian painter who was an oblate of the Santa Casa and died at Loreto; paintings by Simon Vouet (17C), Pellegrino Tibaldi (16C), and Pomarancio; ten Flemish tapestries executed between 1620 and 1624 from designs by Raphaël; a superb collection of Urbino faience vessels (about 500 pieces); furniture and objets d'art ranging from the 16 to the 19C, and mementoes of the popes who visited Loreto.

View★. — From a point behind the basilica, beyond the gate in the ramparts, there is a fine view of the countryside and the sea.

EXCURSION

Recanati. — *Southwest, 7 km - 4 miles.* This little town was the birthplace of the poet Leopardi (1798-1837), whose works are perfect in form and reflect deep melancholy. The **Palazzo Leopardi**, where mementoes of the writer are collected, is open to visitors.

When visiting the continent

use **Michelin Red Guides**

Benelux — Deutschland — España/Portugal — France — Italia
(hotels and restaurants)

and the **Michelin Green Guides**

Austria — Germany — Italy — Portugal — Spain — Switzerland
(sights and tourist routes)

A superb **promenade★** laid out on the 16 and 17C **ramparts★**, shaded by ancient trees, offers a view of this peaceful, artistic little town, full of palaces and churches.

HISTORICAL NOTES

In the Roman era Lucca was an important city and the old town is built on the plan of a Roman military camp. The town became a Commune at the beginning of the 11C; it then passed under the control of the mercenary leader Castruccio, and afterwards, for two periods, under that of Pisa. It bought its independence for 100 000 florins in 1369 and enjoyed peace and prosperity.

The Legend of the Holy Cross. — The Volto Santo (Holy Visage) is a miraculous Crucifix kept in the cathedral. It is said that Nicodemus, after Calvary, depicted the features of Christ on it. The Italian Bishop Gualfredo, when a pilgrim in the Holy Land, obtained possession of the Volto Santo and embarked in a boat without a crew or sails which drifted ashore on the beach at Luni, near La Spezia. As the worshippers at Luni and Lucca disputed possession of the Holy Image, the Bishop of Lucca had it placed on a cart drawn by two oxen; they immediately set off towards Lucca. The fame of the Volto Santo, spread by merchants from Lucca, became very great. A most unusual commemorative procession passes through the illuminated town after dark each year on 13 September.

A Strong Woman. — **Elisa Bonaparte** (1777-1820), Napoleon's sister and the wife of Felice Bacciochi, became Princess of Lucca and Piombino in 1805. She showed remarkable aptitude for public affairs, had roads repaired, laid out the Piazza Napoleone, protected arts and letters, supported agriculture and cleared the district of the brigands who infested it. In this way she gained the nickname of the "Semiramis of Lucca".

Her sister Pauline, Princess Borghese, ended her life in exile at the Villa Paolina *(not open to visitors)* on Monte San Quirico, 1 km - 3/4 mile — north of Lucca, and at the Villa of Compignano, 10 km - 6 miles — to the west.

■ MAIN SIGHTS *time: 2 hours*

From the great Piazza Napoleone you will reach the Piazza San Giovanni, faced by the church of the same name, and then the Piazza San Martino, lined along the left side by the 16C Palazzo Micheletti, designed by Ammannati, and its pretty terraced gardens.

Cathedral★★ (Duomo). — The cathedral is dedicated to St. Martin. It was founded in the 6C but its most important parts are Romanesque outside, Gothic inside.

The Romanesque façade resembles that of Pisa with its superimposed galleries, its columns carved with fantastic animals and its frieze decorated with geometric encrustations or animal forms. The upper part was built by Guidetto da Como in 1210. The slim and powerful campanile crowned with merlons dates from the 13C.

Note in detail the sculptural decoration of the porch; a labyrinth, barking dogs, Roland sounding his horn, a man wrestling with a bear and another stroking his beard.

In the left doorway, known as that of the Santa Croce (Holy Cross) because it leads to the nave where the Volto Santo is displayed, the tympanum is carved with a Descent from the Cross and the lintel with an Adoration of the Magi.

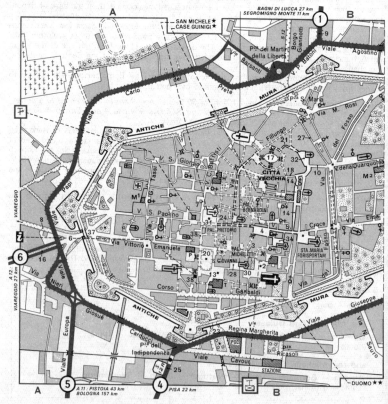

The central doorway evokes the Ascension and that on the right the martyrdom of St. Regulus. Between the doorways are bas-reliefs depicting the Work of the Months and the Life of St. Martin.

Inside the cathedral, behind the façade, is a freely carved 13C statue of St. Martin dividing his cloak; this statue comes from the façade, where a copy has been set in its place. On the left as you enter is the lovely Renaissance *tempietto* (shrine) built by Civitali to shelter the Volto Santo. The Gothic nave is graceful.

A row of columns divides the transept. In the north arm, the white marble **tomb★★** of Ilaria del Carretto is a masterpiece (1406) by the Sienese, Jacopo della Quercia, who also made the statue of an apostle near the first chapel on the left of the chancel. Another chapel in the north transept contains a Madonna between St. John the Baptist and St. Stephen (1509) by the Florentine sculptor Fra Bartolomeo.

In the south transept may be seen works by Civitali: a tomb and angels on the altar of the Chapel of the Holy Sacrament.

St. Michael's Church★ (San Michele). — This 12C Romanesque church is one of the best examples of the Lucca-Pisa style. The Archangel Michael surmounts the remarkable façade, unfortunately restored in the 19C and disfigured by the addition of portrait busts of Garibaldi, Napoleon III, Cavour, etc. Note the four superimposed galleries with light, slim arcades decorated with geometrical designs and animals which are amusing to examine in detail. At the right-hand corner is a graceful Madonna by Civitali.

In the north transept a brightly coloured work by Filippino Lippi represents Sts. Roch, Sebastian, Jerome and Helen. In the south transept is an immense Christ painted on wood at the end of the 12C.

On the far side of the square are the Palazzo Pretorio which dates from the Renaissance and huge *loggia comunale*.

Walk in the Old Town★ (Città Vecchia). — *Follow the route outlined in black on the plan — about 1 hour on foot.*

The streets and squares of old Lucca are full of atmosphere with their cool courted palaces, their lordly towers, old shops and sculptured niches and doorways.

Starting from the Piazza San Michele, follow the Via Roma and the Via Fillungo to the Piazza del Mercato situated inside the Roman amphitheatre. From this go towards the Piazza San Pietro (12-13C church) and then take the Via Guinigi where you will see the **Case Guinigi★**. These mansions belonged to the family of the same name. One, No. 20 has a Gothic façade with triple windows and a tall tower of nobility with trees on its summit. The other palace is at No. 29.

Continue to the Romanesque Church of Santa Maria Forisportam, so-called because it stood outside the Roman walls.

The Via Sante Croce, the delightful Piazza dei Servi and the Piazza dei Bernardini, where the 16C palace of the same name stands, lead you back to the Piazza San Michele.

■ ADDITIONAL SIGHTS

St. Frigidian's Church (San Frediano) (AB A). — This Romanesque church is dedicated to the Irish, St. Frigidian who founded it in the 6C and is buried under the high altar. The mosaic on its façade is restored. White stone contrasts with brown brick, and arches, becoming more numerous at successively higher levels, give the imposing **campanile★** a decorative touch. It is most attractive seen from the ramparts.

Inside, bas-reliefs on a Romanesque **font★** depict the story of Moses (end of 12C), the Good Shepherd and the Months.

In the fourth chapel on the left are a marble altarpiece (1422) and two tombs by Jacopo della Quercia. In the fifth chapel on the right is an Assumption by Masseo Civitali.

Picture Gallery (Pinacoteca) (A M1). — *Open 9 am to 2 pm; closed Mondays, 1 January, 25 April, 1 May, 15 August, 25 December; 500 lire.*

Recently installed in the Mansi Palace. Note the portrait of Princess Elisa by Marie Benoist. The collection is encircled by works by Tintoretto, Lanfranco, Luca Giordano as well as Dutch and Florentine masters.

Villa Guinigi (BC M²). — *Open 9 am to 2 pm (1 pm Sundays and holidays); closed Mondays, 1 January, 25 April, 1 May, 15 August, 25 December.*

The villa was built in the 15C and now contains a museum: sculpture of the Pisan school, lovely bas-relief of the Annunciation attributed to Civitali (15C); among the paintings are a triptych (The Mystic Marriage of St. Catherine) by the local 14C painter, Puccinelli, and works by local 15C masters. Two balanced compositions by the Florentine, Fra Bartolomeo (early 16C) and a colourful and well drawn Ecstasy of St. Catherine by Pompeo Batoni are outstanding.

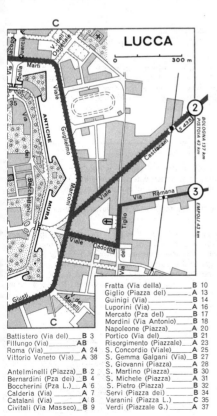

LUCCA

0   300 m

EXCURSIONS

Villa Reale, Marlia. — *8 km - 5 miles. Guided tours every hour of gardens only: July to October, only Tuesdays, Thursdays and Sundays, 9 am to noon and 4 to 7 pm; 1 500 lire; the rest of the year open every day except Mondays: 9 am to noon and 3 to 6 pm; 1 000 lire.* Leave Lucca by ①, road S 12. After 6 km - 4 miles — turn to the right towards Marlia *(signpost)* and cross the railway. The Villa Reale is surrounded by magnificent 17C **gardens★★**, modified by Elisa, a lemon orchard, a 17C nymphea and an open air theatre with statues, clipped yews and bays.

Villa Torrigiani★. — *Northeast, 12 km — 8 miles. Guided tours 1 May to 15 November: 10 am to 1 pm and 3 to 7 pm; 2 000 lire.* Leave Lucca by ② and at Borgonuovo, take the road on the left. This 16C villa situated in Camigliano, was converted in the 17C into an elegant summer residence by Marquess Nicolao Santini, ambassador of the Lucca republic to the Papal Court and to the Court of Louis XIV. The gardens designed by Le Nôtre, are adorned with fountains, grottoes and nymphea. The villa which has a delightful rococo façade, contains rooms ornamented with frescoes and a picture gallery where are exhibited works of 17 and 18C Italian and Flemish artists. Many illustrious guests have stayed at the villa in the 19 and 20C.

LUCERA Apulia

Michelin map **988** 28 — 18 km - 11 miles — west of Foggia — Pop 33 090

Already important in Roman times, Lucera in Capitanate, a dependency of the Kingdom of Naples, was allotted by Frederick II of Hohenstaufen to the Saracens of Sicily, who numbered 20 000. Tired of their excesses, the grandson of St. Louis, Charles II of Anjou (died 1309), expelled them and built a cathedral in place of the mosque.

Castle★. — The long high walls, furnished with towers, of the fortress built between 1263 and 1283, enclose the ruins of Frederick II's castle and a Franciscan church founded by Charles I of Anjou in the 13C.

An excellent view of the castle can be had from the public garden, which overlooks the plain.

Cathedral (Duomo). — Pierre d'Agincourt, the favourite architect of Charles II of Anjou, built this great cathedral in the Angevin style. It is of brick and stone with a projecting transept, lancet windows, a wide façade flanked by a polygonal tower, and doorways with lofty tympana. The central doorway bears the coat of arms of Anjou.

The interior consists of three plain aisles. In the chapel on the right of the high altar lies a recumbent figure said to be that of Charles II of Anjou.

LUMIEI Valley ★★ Friuli-Venezia Giulia

Michelin map **988** 5.

A road from Ampezzo to Lake Sauris reveals one of the strangest landscapes in Europe, consisting of deep gorges, gigantic fissures, rugged, broken rocks and foaming cascades. Stop on the bridge over the torrent to look at a wild scene.

The jade green **Lake Sauris**, a jewel of the Carnic Alps, was formed by a dam.

MACUGNAGA ★ Piedmont

Michelin maps **988** 2 and **26** 5 — Alt 1 327 - 4 354 ft — Pop 758

The picturesque Val Anzasca leads to Macugnaga, a well known climbers' and winter sports resort with typical old wooden houses in a remarkable **setting★★** at the foot of the imposing rocky walls of the Monte Rosa (4 634 m - 15 204 ft). A plaque in the church recalls the ascent of Monte Rosa by Pope Pius XI in 1889. The resort has several cableways and chairlifts enabling the visitor to enjoy remarkable panoramas. Those from the **Monte Moro Pass** and Pedriola, facing the eastern slope of the Monte Rosa, are among the best.

MANFREDONIA Apulia

Michelin map **988** 28 — *Local map p 116* — Pop 52 333

This little port, dominated by its castle of the Angevin period, is now almost deserted. In the Middle Ages, at the time of the Crusades, it swarmed with pilgrims and knights embarking in Genoese or Venetian ships for the Levant. Many Gothic miniatures depict the animation of the harbour basins at this period.

In the hinterland, 23 km - 14 miles — from Manfredonia, is **San Giovanni Rotondo** where lived Padre Pio. It is now a pilgrimage centre.

St. Mary's of Siponte★ (Santa Maria di Siponto). — *3 km - 2 miles — on the road to Foggia.* This church, standing alone among the pines, and the ruins of an early-Christian church are the only vestiges of the ancient city of Siponte. The Romanesque style shows strong Pisan and Moslem influence (blind arcades and lozenges and square plan and flat roof, respectively). The church was dedicated to the Virgin by Pope Paschal II in 1117 and elevated to the rank of a minor basilica by Pope Paul VI in 1977. It was remodelled several times. It has a richly decorated doorway and in the interior, a fine crypt.

Michelin main road maps (scale 1:1 000 000)

986 *Great Britain, Ireland*
987 *Germany, Austria, Benelux*
988 *Italy, Switzerland*
989 *France*
990 *Spain, Portugal*
991 *Yugoslavia*

MANTUA ★ (MANTOVA) Lombardy

Michelin map 988 14 — Pop 64 329

Mantua is a severe but attractive town, partly encircled on the north side by three lakes formed by the course of the Mincio. It is rich in buildings and historical memories which have earned it the adjective *gloriosa*. There is an interesting view of the town from the Verona road.

HISTORICAL NOTES

Although according to a legend quoted by Virgil, Mantua was founded by Manto, daughter of the divine Tiresias, its origin seems to have been Etruscan. It developed in the Roman era.

Publius Vergilius Maro. — Virgil, that gentle poet, a lover of nature and of solitude, was born in 70 BC at Andes, a village near Mantua, which was destroyed by order of Bonaparte. The fields of the Mantuan countryside, lying in a soft, misty light and often under a cloudy sky, explain the melancholy of the author of the *Bucolics*, the *Georgics* and the *AEneid*.

The Gonzagas. — The members of this family, having succeeded the Captains of the People, proved to be enlightened rulers and patrons of the arts and letters. Thus Gianfrancesco Gonzaga (1407-1444) confided his children to the famous **Vittorino da Feltre** (1379-1446), the father of teaching, who was Rabelais' model for his Ponocratus, the tutor of Gargantua.

Ludovico (1448-1478), Vittorino's pupil and an army officer by profession, was a typical Renaissance patron, distributing land to the poor peasants, having a new port dug and the streets of Mantua paved. He protected the humanist Politian, the Florentine architect Leon-Battista Alberti and the fanciful Paduan painter Mantegna, who often quarrelled with his neighbours and tried to drive out the priests, whom he disliked.

Francesco II (1484-1519) married Isabella d'Este, a lettered and artistic woman, as beautiful as she was wise, and according to her motto moved by "neither hope nor fear" *(nec spe, nec metu)*.

The collateral branches of the family owned the duchies of Sabbioneta and Guastalla; at the end of the 16C a Gonzaga became Duke of Nevers and Overlord of Charleville, both in France. He introduced faïence to Nevers and his son Charles had the famous Place Ducale at Charleville built.

■ MAIN SIGHTS

time: 2 hours

Piazza Sordello★. — This great square is surrounded by fine buildings. It is divided by the Arch of St. Peter (Arco San Pietro) from the Piazza Broletto. The Cathedral has a Baroque façade and a tower in the Romanesque style; in the north aisle is the Chapel of the Incoronata (Crowned Virgin) attributed to Alberti. To the left of the cathedral, telamones adorn the Baroque façade of the 18C **bishop's palace.**

Next to the bishop's palace is the 13C **Palazzo Bonacolsi**, now known as the Palazzo Castiglioni, divided into two buildings.

Ducal Palace★★ (Palazzo Ducale). — *Guided tours 9 am to 2 pm (1 pm Sundays and holidays); closed Mondays, 1 January, 25 April, 1 May, first Sunday in June, 15 August and Christmas; 750 lire.*

This comprises the palace proper (largely 16C) facing the Piazza Sordello, the Castello San Giorgio, a 14C fortress, and the Renaissance ducal Chapel of Santa Barbara. The whole group includes fifteen courts, squares, gardens and more than 450 rooms.

The **apartments★★★** *(entrance in the Piazza Sordello)* are luxurious and were sumptuously decorated in the 16 and 18C (outstanding ceilings). They contain many works of art. In the Guastalla apartments on the 1st floor is an interesting collection of mediaeval and Renaissance statues. The Greco-Roman sculptures, consisting principally of statues collected by Isabella d'Este, have been distributed throughout the rooms of the Corte Nuova, decorated by Giulio Romano and his school. The gallery contains fine pictures by Rubens, Morone, Tintoretto, Feti, etc. The tapestry rooms, formerly known as the Green Apartment, in the 18C Neo-Classical style, are hung with splendid Brussels tapestries after Raphaël. You can also see the Zodiac Room, the 18C Room of the Rivers, the roof gardens (1581), and especially the famous 16 and 18C Hall of Mirrors. The Paradise Apartment (del Paradiso) is so-called because of its marvellous view of the lakes. It was decorated at the end of the 16C by Antonio Viani. On the way down from the Paradiso is the tiny and unusual Dwarfs' Apartment also of the late 16C.

On the ground floor are the Isabella Rooms, with delicately carved ceilings.

In the **Castello** may be seen the famous Spouses' Room (Camera degli Sposi) with frescoes (1465-1474) by Mantegna. Mantegna creates an impression of space by his knowledge of foreshortening and perspective.

The tall Torre della Gabbia, nearby, still bears, on the façade overlooking the Via Cavour, the cage in which wrongdoers were exhibited.

Piazza Broletto. — In this square stands the **Palazzo Broletto**, a municipal building of the 13-15C; it has on its façade a statue of Virgil, seated (1225). Four large rings under the arch were used as pulleys for hoisting condemned criminals.

Piazza delle Erbe★. — The Square of Herbs has kept its old setting among public buildings. Awnings and parasols, shading the market stalls, are erected there every morning.

On one side, the 13C **Palazzo della Ragione** (Law Courts) is flanked on the right by the 15C Clock Tower. The rotunda (Church of San Lorenzo) is Romanesque. A 15C house to the right of the rotunda has pretty Gothic terracotta decorations.

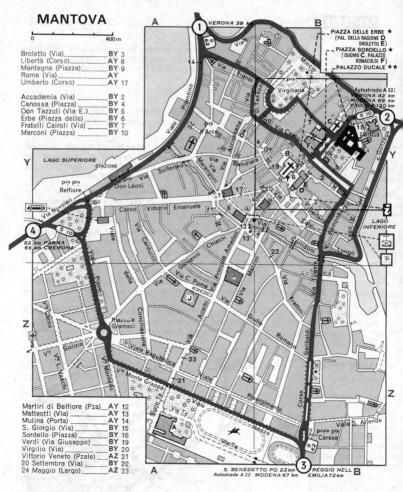

MANTOVA

0   400 m

Broletto (Via) _____ BY 3
Libertà (Corso) _____ AY 8
Mantegna (Piazza) ____ BY 9
Roma (Via) _____ AY
Umberto (Corso) _____ AY 17

Accademia (Via) _____ BY 2
Canossa (Piazza) _____ BY 4
Don Tazzoli (Via E.) __ BY 5
Erbe (Piazza delle) ___ BY 6
Fratelli Cairoli (Via) _ BY 7
Marconi (Piazza) _____ BY 10

PIAZZA DELLE ERBE ★
(PAL. DELLA RAGIONE D)
BROLETTO E
PIAZZA SORDELLO ★
(DUOMO C, PALAZZO
BONACOLSI F)
PALAZZO DUCALE ★★

Martiri di Belfiore (Pza) __ AY 12
Matteotti (Via) _____ AY 13
Mulina (Porta) _____ AY 14
S. Giorgio (Via) _____ BY 15
Sordello (Piazza) _____ BY 16
Verdi (Via Giuseppe) ____ BY 19
Virgilio (Via) _____ BY 20
Vittorio Veneto (Pzale) __ AZ 21
20 Settembre (Via) _____ BY 22
24 Maggio (Largo) _____ AZ 23

■ ADDITIONAL SIGHTS

St. Andrew's Church★ (Sant'Andrea) (BY B). — The Renaissance church was built to the plans of Alberti, but the Gothic belfry is older (1414). The dome was added between 1732 and 1782 by an architect from Turin, Juvara. The porch has exquisite Renaissance decorations.

The nave is very wide; its vaulting, also that in the chancel and the transept are painted in *trompe-l'œil*. In the first chapel on the left *(ring for the sacristan)* are the tomb of Mantegna and a Holy Family painted by that master, who is himself portrayed in a vigorous bronze medallion. In the crypt is kept the blood of Christ preserved, according to tradition, by Longinus, the Roman Legionary who pierced the Saviour's side with a spear.

A door at the far end of the north transept leads to the Piazza Alberti, from which the best view of the building can be seen.

Te Palace★ (Palazzo Te) (AZ A). — *Open 9.30 am to 12.30 pm and 2.30 to 5 pm; 9 am to 1 pm Sundays. Closed Mondays and holidays; 750 lire.*

This summer palace was built between 1525 and 1535 by Giulio Romano for Federigo II in a forceful style with embossing and monumental columns. The interior is decorated with huge frescoes by Giulio Romano and his pupils, who displayed astonishing skill and imagination. The duke's favourite Mantuan horses are depicted in one room and the story of Psyche in another. Yet another room is decorated with stucco mouldings by Il Primaticcio. The Giants' Room is the best known; in it, with a remarkable sense of the colossal, Giulio Romano depicted the giants trying to reach Olympus and being crushed by rocks and falling buildings.

The west wing of the palace houses a gallery of modern art *(installation in progress)*.

Law Courts (Palazzo di Giustizia) (AZ J). — The Courts were built in the 16C to the drawings of Giulio Romano who also designed the monumental façade with caryatids. At No. 18 in the same street is Romano's house, built to his own plans.

EXCURSION

San Benedetto Po. — *22 km - 14 miles.* Go out by ③, road S 62. After 4.5 km - 3 miles - turn left. The church, rebuilt by Giulio Romano in 1542, was part of a Benedictine abbey. Inside is the tomb of Countess Matilda of Tuscany. The cloisters are Gothic.

MAROSTICA Venetia

Michelin map **988** 5 — 28 km - 17 miles — north of Vicenza — Pop 12 480

Marostica is a little town, of ancient appearance, enclosed in fortifications. It has two castles; from the top of the second, the Rocca, there is a pretty **view★**. The Church of St. Anthony (Sant'Antonio), reconstructed in the 18C, still conserves some 13C elements.

A curious game of chess, with people in costumes for pieces, is played in front of the Castello da Basso (Lower Castle) every second year, on the first Sunday in September and the preceding Saturday. The square is transformed for the occasion into a giant chess-board.

MASER Venetia

Michelin map **988** 5 — 29 km - 18 miles — northwest of Treviso — Pop 4 571

The famous **Villa Barbaro★★** at Maser *(open Tuesdays, Saturdays, Sundays and holidays: 3 to 6 pm 1 June to 30 September; 2 to 5 pm the rest of the year; closed Easter and Christmas Eve to Epiphany inclusive; 1 500 lire)* is now called the Villa di Maser. It was built by Palladio *(p 263)* for the brothers Marcantonio and Daniele Barbaro. Inside the villa, Veronese painted one of his best decorative schemes, in which he used all his amazing knowledge of perspective, trompe-l'œil (false relief) and foreshortening and his sense of movement and colour. The frescoes include the famous group of Venus and Apollo, Bacchus, the gods on Mount Olympus on the ceiling of the saloon, and the Seasons.

A car museum has been opened near the villa. *Open 3 to 6 pm (2 to 5 pm 1 October to 31 May); closed Easter Sunday, Good Friday to Epiphany and religious holidays falling on weekdays; 800 lire.*

MASSA MARITTIMA ★ Tuscany

Michelin map **988** 14 — 65 km - 40 miles — southwest of Siena — Pop 10 297

Massa Marittima stands on the last foothills of the metal-bearing mountains, with iron, copper and pyrite mines buried in a wild landscape. Massa Marittima is so-called because it was once near the sea, which covered the whole Maremma district. Far from main roads, it is a town of ancient appearance and had an intense communal life.

Piazza Garibaldi★. — The square, paved with broad flagstones, has an impressive unity, lined as it is by the Palazzo Pretorio (Law Courts) with paired windows crowned with merlons, the town hall and the cathedral, three Romanesque buildings erected in the 13C.

Cathedral★ (Duomo). — This majestic building in the Pisan Romanesque style, is adorned with blind arcades and dominated by a fine Tuscan **campanile★** pierced with windows which increase in number towards the top. On the façade are roaring lions, delicately carved capitals and the central doorway depicting the life of St. Cerbonius, patron saint of the city. The slim, graceful apse is by Giovanni Pisano (1287).

Inside, a strange baptismal font with a Romanesque basin ornamented with bas-reliefs depicts the life of St John the Baptist. At the back of the façade are the naïvely carved fragments of IIC bas-reliefs. In a room beneath the chancel *(door to the left of the high altar)* is the *arca,* or marble sarcophagus made in 1324, for St. Cerbonius.

Candeliere Tower, Sienese Fortress and Arch★ (Torre Candeliere, Fortezza e Arco Senesi). — The Via Moncini leads from the Piazza Garibaldi through the upper part of the town to the massive Candeliere Tower, built early in the 13C. An arch, with pure lines and a wide span, reaches from the tower to the ramparts, all that remain of a 14C Sienese fortress.

EXCURSION

San Galgano Abbey★. — *Northeast, 32 km - 20 miles.* A short distance from the Massa Marittima-Siena road stand the noble ruins of a Gothic Cistercian abbey built by monks between 1224 and 1288.

This church, on which is modelled the Siena Cathedral, is a good example of traditional Cistercian architecture *(p 115)*. The chapterhouse and refectory can also be seen.

MATERA ★★ Basilicata

Michelin map **988** 29 — Pop 49 954

Matera overlooks a ravine separating it from the Murge Mountains in the heart of a region cut by erosion into deep gorges and forming a desolate landscape with wide horizons.

The lower town, today almost deserted, is one of the most curious in existence with its ancient appearance and houses indistinguishable at times from the rocks.

The upper part of Matera, the modern part, is the centre of all activity, provincial capital, and the part occupied by the majority of the buildings to be seen.

Old Town★★★ (Città vecchia). — *Time: 1/2 hour.* The old town, with all the appearance of a mountain village of former times, lies on either side of and below the rock on which the cathedral stands. Many streets run close to the roofs of houses whose lower storeys are built into the rock. Little whitewashed cottages and stairways overlap and overhang one another in a labyrinth which it is difficult to unravel.

Strada dei Sassi★★. — *Time: 1/2 hour.* This panoramic street, which lies below the cathedral rock in the old town, skirts the wild gorge, flown over by crows. It is partly hewn out of the rock, like the cave-dwellings that line it. At one end, in a quiet oblong square, the Baroque Church of San Pietro Caveoso stands at the foot of the rock, the Sasso Caveoso, while above and built into the living rock stands the Church of Santa Maria in Idris.

Cathedral (Duomo). — The **exterior★** of this church in the 13C Apulian Romanesque style is particularly interesting. It has a fine square campanile in two storeys and a façade in three sections with a rose window and a single doorway. The south side of the building is adorned with blind arches, trilobar windows and two richly carved doorways.

Piazza Pascoli. — From the Piazza Vittorio Veneto, follow the main streets which form the axis of the upper town (Via Umberto I and Via Ridola) and are lined with charming Baroque churches. You reach the Piazza Pascoli, a terrace in front of a small Baroque monastery now used as an art gallery.

From the terrace there is a characteristic **view★★** of the old town with its tiled roofs, staircases, rocks and gorges honeycombed with caves in the background. The chaotic appearance makes a curious scene.

Ridola National Museum. — *Open 9 am to 2 pm (1 pm Sundays and holidays); closed Mondays, 1 January, 25 April, 1 May, first Sunday in June, 15 August and Christmas.* The museum at No. 24 Via Ridola has a rich prehistoric collection.

St. Francis' Church (San Francesco). — Inside this Baroque church a Madonna between Saints on a remarkable polyptych, the work of the Venetian, Bartolomeo Vivarini (15C), adorns the organ loft.

MENDOLA Pass ★★ Trentino-Alto Adige

Michelin maps 988 4 and 24 20 — 25 km - 16 miles — southwest of Bolzano

This broad, wooded pass, which begins at an altitude of 1 363 m - 4 427 ft — connects the Adige Valley with that of the Noce River. The surroundings are attractive to the tourist who likes varied and easy drives and walks, shady trees and frequent views.

From the pass itself he will see an immense **panorama★★** of the Adige Valley, the Dolomites and the Brenta.

MERANO ★★ Trentino-Alto Adige

Michelin maps 988 4 and 24 10 20 — Pop 34 560

Merano, lying at the end of the Val Venosta in the Adige Valley, is an important tourist centre and spa. There are numerous quick ways of reaching **"Merano 2 000"**: chair lifts, cable-cars and telecabins. All are appreciated by winter sports enthusiasts and for excursions into the mountains.

It is also at the centre of a prosperous fruit growing area, particularly dessert grapes of which it produces 3 000 tons a year.

The **Via Portici (Laubengasse)**, a street lined with porticoes sheltering curious shops with sculptured façades (Nos 203 and 213), is both busy and picturesque.

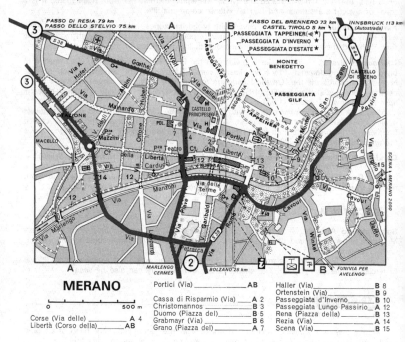

MERANO

0 _____ 500 m

Portici (Via)	AB		Haller (Via)	B	8
			Ortenstein (Via)	B	9
Cassa di Risparmio (Via)	A	2	Passeggiata d'Inverno	B	10
Christomannos	B	3	Passeggiata Lungo Passirio	A	12
Corse (Via delle)	A 4		Duomo (Piazza del)	B	5	Rena (Piazza della)	B	13
Libertà (Corso della)	AB		Grabmayr (Via)	B	6	Rezia (Via)	A	14
			Grano (Piazza del)	A	7	Scena (Via)	B	15

Winter and Summer Promenades★ (Passeggiate d'Inverno e d'Estate). — These promenades follow the Passirio River. The first, facing south, is continued by the **Passeggiata Gilf** which ends near a powerful waterfall at the foot of the 12-13C St. Zeno Castle (Castello di San Zeno). The summer promenade, on the opposite bank, is shady and flower decked.

Passeggiata Tappeiner★. — This magnificent promenade, — 4 km - 2 1/2 miles — long, winds 150 m - 500 ft — above Merano affording remarkable views of the town and the valley.

Cathedral (Duomo) (B A). — This Gothic building, dedicated to St. Nicholas, is dominated by a massive bell-tower fronted by a façade with a crenellated gable. It is adorned on the outside with frescoes; note the 15C frescoes beneath the belfry arch and the large statue of St. Christopher on the façade.

EXCURSIONS

Val Passiria★. — *To the Rombo Pass, 50 km - 31 miles.* Leave by ①. Road S 44 follows the line of the winding and smiling Passirio Valley as far as San Leonardo where you turn off left. Beyond San Leonardo the road *(usually blocked by snow from October to July beyond Moso)* rises above the ground, crossing the always steep hillsides. Impressive views of the mountains on the frontier appear (the Granati to the south). The road, often cut out of the living rock reaches the **Passo del Rombo**, and an altitude of 2 509 m - 8 232 ft. The pass connects the Upper Valley Passiria with the Ötztal in Austria.

Beyond San Leonardo, road S 44 leads to the **Monte Giovo Pass** (Passo di Monte Giovo) at an altitude of 2 094 m - 6 870 ft — from which there is a splendid panorama and from which one reaches the Brenner road.

Tirolo Castle (Castel Tirolo). — *5 km - 3 miles.* Leave Merano by the Via Monte San Zeno. *Open in summer 10 to 11 am and 5 to 6.30 pm; the rest of the year 11 am to noon and 3 to 4 pm; closed Mondays and from 15 November to 15 March; apply in advance to Sir Plaseller Walter, director of Albergo Castel; 500 lire.* The castle, which was built in the 12C, was the seat of the Counts of Tyrol who, until the 14C, ruled the Upper Adige and the Upper Inn region.

In addition to fine carved doorways, the visitor sees the Romanesque chapel which is built on two levels and adorned with 14C frescoes, the knights' hall and the throne room. There is a good view.

MILAN ★★★ (MILANO) Lombardy

Michelin maps 988 3 and 26 19 — Pop 1 693 361

Town plan in Michelin Red Guide Italia (hotels and restaurants).

Milan is the second city in Italy in population and first in economic importance. It has a continental climate and its people are enterprising and show a keen taste for productive work.

The town is bounded by two concentric boulevards: the shorter has taken the place of the 14C ramparts, of which traces remain, among them the Porta Ticinese in the south and the Porta Nuova in the north. The castle was part of this defence system.

Besides the artistic evidences of its past, Milan, the home town of the famous architect, Gio Ponti, is proud of its modern town planning. Modern buildings are to be seen in the Piazza Cavour (Swiss Bank: 22 storeys), the Via Turati (Montecatini Company), the Piazza della Repubblica (more than 30 storeys) and finally the Piazza Duca d'Aosta (Pirelli skyscraper of 36 storeys) around which a large business centre is springing up.

An extensive programme of road improvements has been undertaken both within the city and on the outskirts.

HISTORICAL NOTES

Milan is probably of Celtic origin, but it was the Romans who subdued the city in 222 BC. The Emperors of the West resided there from AD 305 to 402, and in 312 one of them, Constantine, published in Milan the Edict making Christianity the official religion of the Empire. In 375 St. Ambrose, a Doctor of the Church and the initiator of the Ambrosian liturgy, which is still used at Milan, became bishop of the town. His gift of persuasive speech worked wonders, and the name *ambrosia* was given to honey liqueur as a symbol of religious eloquence. The Barbarian invasions of Attila, the Franks and the Burgundians took place in the 5 and 6C. Then the Longobards kingdom was invaded in 756 by Pepin, King of the Franks, whose son, Charlemagne, was to wear the Iron Crown of the Kings of Lombardy.

The Viscontis. — In 1277 the Viscontis seized power. Bernabò (1319-1385) left memories of extreme cruelty. Having received a Bull of Excommunication from two Benedictine monks and escorted them to a bridge spanning a torrent, he suddenly asked them whether they wished to eat or drink. The two monks feared drowning and said they would prefer to eat. Thereupon Bernabò forced them to swallow the parchment bull.

Gian Galeazzo (1347-1402) was a conspirator, an assassin and a war leader. He was also a pious and lettered artist: he ordered the building of the Carthusian Monastery and Cathedral of Pavia. His wife, Isabelle de Valois, gave him a daughter, Valentine, who married Louis, Duke of Orleans, the father of the poet Charles d'Orléans and grandfather of Louis XII. This family connection explains the origin of the later French expeditions into Italy.

The Sforzas. — After the death of the last Visconti, Filippo-Maria (1447), and three years of the Ambrosian Republic, the Sforzas took over the rule of Milan, thanks to Francesco, the son of a simple peasant but also a military leader and son-in-law of Filippo-Maria Visconti. The most famous figure in the Sforza family, Ludovico il Moro (1451-1508), married Beatrice d'Este and made Milan a new Athens by bringing to it the geniuses of the time, Leonardo da Vinci, Bramante, etc. Ludovous was captured by Louis XII in 1500 and died in the castle at Loches, on the Loire.

Milan under Napoleon. — In 1797 the troops of the French Army of Italy entered Milan under a rain of flowers. Milan then became the capital of the Cisalpine Republic and later of the Kingdom of Italy. In 1805 Napoleon placed the Iron Crown on his own head with the words: "God gave it to me. Woe to him who touches it." Eugène de Beauharnais, the viceroy, adopted as his favourite architect the Milanese, Antolini.

ECONOMY

Milan is by tradition a European trading centre, and every year businessmen attend its famous International Fair. As a silk market, Milan rivals Lyons.

The town has 432 banks and branches (812 in the district as a whole) which have taken the place of the Lombard money-changers and moneylenders who were famous in Europe in the Middle Ages.

Industry is concentrated on the outskirts of the town and in particular to the northeast along the Milan to Monza road.

LIFE IN MILAN

Life in Milan is most pleasant. The French writer Stendhal (Henry Beyle) was captivated by its liveliness and gaiety. He wished his tomb to be inscribed with the words: "Henri Beyle, Milanais" (Henri Beyle, man of Milan).

The most frequented parts of Milan are in the heart of the city. At the **Galleria★**, the centre of political and local life, near the cathedral, the Milanese come to talk or read their *Corriere della Sera* (the famous Milanese evening newspaper) on the terraces of the big cafés. Fashionable shops are to be found in the Corso Vittorio Emanuele and the Corso Venezia and also along the Via Monte Napoleone, where the antiquaries' shops are. The cabarets are round the Piazza San Babila. The cafés and tea-shops *(Motta, Alemagna)* in this quarter are thronged with Milanese sipping coffee made in *espresso* machines.

The most remarkable gardens are the **Parco Sempione** *(see p 145)* and the **Giardini Pubblici**.

The **Scala Theatre** *(p 144)* is also a centre of attraction. There Toscanini and his pupil Guido Cantelli directed the operas of Donizetti, Puccini and Verdi, with the help of *divas* like Maria Callas, Renata Tebaldi, Graziella Sciutti, Suzanna Danco, etc. The *Piccolo Teatro* (Little Theatre) is valued as an advanced playhouse.

Sport has its enthusiasts and many competitions take place in the Ice Palace (skating), at the Lido, at the Idroscalo (water sports), at the famous Vigorelli velodrome, where the start and finish of the *Giro* (cycle race round Italy) take place and in the vast St. Siro stadium, and racecourse of the same name and the grandiose new sports centre.

Milanese cooking is done with butter. It is a pleasure to taste Milanese *minestrone* (vegetable and pork soup), grilled fillets of veal in breadcrumbs *alla milanese*, saffron-tinted *risotto*, *osso buco*, a marrow bone (shin of veal) with its meat, and *panettone*, a very light currant cake. Favourite cheeses are *Gorgonzola* (green and strong), *Taleggio* and *Grana*. There are few Lombard wines except those of the Valtellina, but the Piedmontese vintages are near at hand.

MILANO

0 _____ 500 m

142

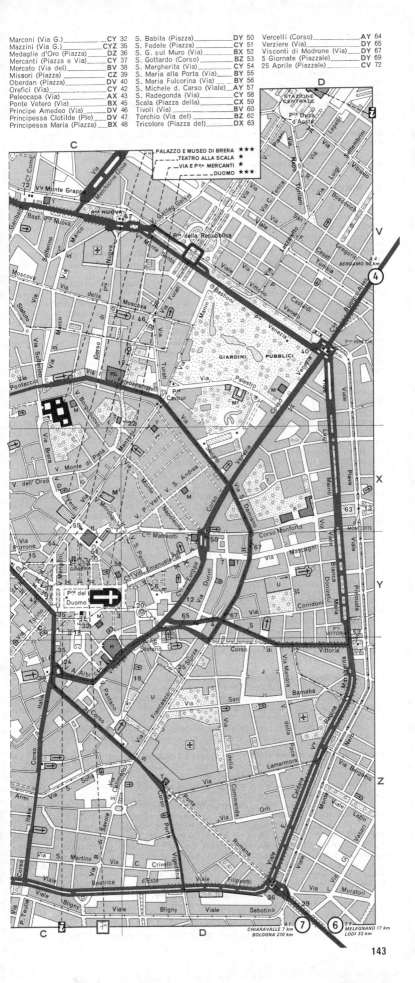

143

SCHOOLS OF ART

In architecture, the *duomo* (cathedral) marks the climax of the Flamboyant Gothic period. Prominent architects under the Renaissance were the Florentine, Michelozzo (1391-1472) and especially **Bramante** (1444-1514), the favourite master mason of Ludovico il Moro and a man of universal knowledge with a talent distinguished by lofty inspiration.

In painting, the Lombard school sought beauty and grace above all else. Vincenzo Foppa (1427-1515), Bergognone (1450-1523) and Bramantino, loved strong colours, beauty of line and intensity of expression. The Lombard school then came under the influence of Leonardo with Andrea Solario (1460-1520), a conscientious painter who specialised in portraiture, Boltraffio (1467-1516), sensual and refined, and last but not least **Bernardino Luini** (1475-1532), who search- ed for sweetness of expression in feminine beauty.

■ MAIN SIGHTS *time: 1 day*

Parking is difficult in the centre of the town; there are, however, paid carparks and under- ground garages such as those below the Piazza Diaz **(CYZ 18)** and the Via San Marco **(CV)** or multi-storey carparks as at the Via Santa Radegonda **(CY 58)**. Cars may also be left in the outer boulevards, or in the carparks built beside certain peripheral underground stations.

Cathedral★★★ (Duomo). — This marvel of white marble, both colossal and ethereal, bristling with belfries, gables, pinnacles and statues, stands at one end of a great paved esplanade. It should be seen late in the afternoon in the light of the setting sun.

The cathedral was begun at the chevet in 1386 on the orders of Gian Galeazzo Visconti, and building continued in the 15 and 16C under the direction of Italian, French and German master masons. The façade was finished only between 1805 and 1809, by order of Napoleon.

You should walk round the cathedral to see its apse with three huge bays of curved and counter-curved tracery, magnificent stained glass and wonderful rose windows. The overall design is the work of a French architect, Nicolas de Bonaventure, and of a Modenese architect, Filippino degli Organi. The interior is bare, severe and imposing. The nave and four aisles are separated by more than fifty pillars of tremendous height; the transepts have three aisles. The length of the building is 148 m and the width across the transepts 91 m — 485 1/2 × 298 1/2 ft — St. Paul's London, 463 × 228 ft.

The mausoleum of Gian Giacomo de' Medici in the south wall of the south transept is a fine work by Leoni (16C), inspired by Michelangelo. On the left is the curious statue of St. Bar- tholomew, who was martyred by being flayed alive. The sculptor, Marco d'Agrate, modestly compared himself with Praxiteles in the inscription in Latin on the base. Passing under the dome, you enter the north transept, where you will notice a magnificent bronze candelabrum, French work of the 13C. In the crypt, the tomb of St. Charles Borromeo, Archbishop of Milan who died in 1584, was the gift of Philip II of Spain.

In the Treasury *(near the crypt, closed Mondays; 100 lire)* is a fine collection of gold plate and ivories dating from the 4C to the present day.

Walk on the Roofs★★★. — The building is adorned with 135 pinnacles and numerous white mar- ble statues, full of grace and elegance. They can be admired in detail by going up on to the roof *(9 am to 6 pm 1 March to 30 October and 9 am to 4 pm the rest of the year; go up either by the stairs — entry outside the north transept, 500 lire; or by lift — by two doors to the right or left of the apse, 1 000 lire)* and thence to the top of the Tiburio or central tower (108 m - 354 ft), surmounted by a small gilded statue, the Madonnina (1774).

Under the square in front of the Cathedral are ruins of a 4C baptistry *(access through the cathedral; closed Mondays)*.

The Royal Palace, built in the 18C by Piermarini, contains the rich Museum of Cathedral Works *(open 10 30 am to 12.30 pm and 3 to 6 pm; closed Mondays, 15 August and Easter and Christmas; 1 000 lire, free on Sundays)*: sculptures, stained glass, tapestries and religious vestments from the 14 to the 20C.

Via e Piazza Mercanti★. — In the Via Mercanti stands the Palace of Jurisconsults, built in 1564 with a façade adorned with a statue of Ambrose teaching. The Piazza Mercanti is quiet and picturesque. The charming Loggia degli Osii was built near the dwelling of the Osii family. It is of white and black marble and is adorned with statues of the saints in addition to possess- ing a balcony from which penal sentences were proclaimed. To the right of the loggia is the Baroque palace of the Palatine schools; the statues in the niches are of the poet Ausonius and St. Augustine.

La Scala, Milan★ (Teatro alla Scala). — *For permission to visit, apply to the theatre museum 805 95 35; closed during August.* This, the most famous opera house in the world, was built from 1776 to 1778 on the site of the Church of Santa Maria della Scala. The auditorium can ac- commodate more than 3 000 spectators; the acoustics are perfect. In the foyer are four statues; Rossini, Bellini, Donizetti and Verdi. The Scala Museum is rich in theatrical mementoes.

The 16C Marino Palace opposite, by the Genoese architect Alessi, has a remarkable court. Its rear façade, which is the more interesting, gives on the Piazza San Fedele.

Brera Palace and Picture Gallery★★★ (Palazzo e Pinacoteca di Brera). — *Open 9 am to 2 pm (1 pm Sundays and holidays). Closed Mondays, 1 January, 25 April, 1 May, first Sunday in June, 15 August, and 25 December; 750 lire.*

The palace is 17C. You are greeted in the court by a statue of Napoleon I, whom Canova depicted in 1809 as a victorious Caesar.

This picture gallery is rich in the works of Lombard and north Italian artists. Among the masterpieces, note the famous painting by Mantegna, the **Dead Christ**, admirable in its realism and knowledge of foreshortening. Until his death, Mantegna would not part with this picture. There are also the exquisite Madonna of the Rose Tree by Bernardino Luini; frescoes of the 15-16C Lombard school by Bergognone and the Piedmontese artist Gaudenzio Ferrari; the famous **Pietà** and some pathetically expressive Madonnas including a "Greek" Madonna by Giovanni Bellini; St. Mark Preaching (1507) by Gentile and Giovanni Bellini; works of admirable delicacy by Crivelli such as the Madonna with a Candle; St. Stephen Preaching by Carpaccio; a Miracle of St. Mark and a St. Helena by Tintoretto; a Last Supper and a Baptism of Christ by Veronese; and paintings by Tiepolo, Canaletto and Guardi.

Among the paintings by artists from other parts of Italy, note works by Bramante; the Marriage of the Virgin by Raphaël, full of grace and harmony, a Flagellation by Luca Signorelli and the Last Supper at Emmaus by Caravaggio.

The gallery also contains works by El Greco, Rembrandt, Rubens and Van Dyck.

Castle of the Sforzas★★ (Castello Sforzesco). — This building, a huge brick quadrilateral of rather crushing majesty, stands on the site of a former castle built in 1368 during the rule of Galeazzo Visconti. Partly destroyed, it was rebuilt by Francesco Sforza and later remodelled many times over the centuries. Several rooms bear the stamp of the various occupants at the time when the castle was the residence of the Dukes of Milan.

The **Municipal Museum of Art★★** (open 9.30 am to noon and 2.30 to 5.30 pm; closed Mondays, 1 January, 1 May, 15 August, Easter and Christmas) housed in the castle since 1900, contains admirable sculptures, among them a head of the Empress Theodora — the work of a 6C Byzantine artist —, the tomb of Bernabò Visconti surmounted by his equestrian statue (14C), the reclining figure of Gaston de Foix, who was killed at Ravenna in 1512, and the unfinished Rondanini Pietà, Michelangelo's last work. Among the pictures are works by Fillipo Lippi, Mantegna, Bellini, Foppa, Boltraffio, Correggio, Tintoretto, Magnasco, Guardi and Tiepolo. There are also precious ivories, gold and silver plate, and tapestries depicting the Months.

Beyond the castle lies the **Sempione Park★** (47 ha - 116 acres) in which are a stadium, the Arena (1805), the Neo-Classical Arch of Peace (1807-1838) and a tower built of steel tubing, 109 m - 360 ft — high.

Church of St. Mary of Grace (Santa Maria delle Grazie). — A Renaissance building erected by the Dominicans from 1465 to 1490. In the interior, restored, you will see in the fourth chapel on the right lifelike frescoes by Gaudenzio Ferrari, the impressive gallery and **dome★** by Bramante, the Baroque Chapel of the Madonna delle Grazie (at the end of the north aisle) and charming cloisters by Bramante (entered from the north transept).

To the left of the church, in what used to be the monastery refectory, is the world famous **Last Supper★★★** (Cena), painted by Leonardo da Vinci from 1495 to 1497 at the request of Ludovico il Moro. The fresco (not on view as restoration is in progress following damage incurred in June 1980) has already been restored several times. It depicts with dramatic expressiveness the moment when Jesus says: "One of you will betray me".

St. Ambrose's Basilica★ (Sant'Ambrogio). — The basilica was founded at the end of the 4C by St. Ambrose, Bishop of Milan, who baptised St. Augustine in it. The present building is in the 11-12C Lombard Romanesque style with a fine **atrium★★** (interesting capitals). The campanile on the right dates from the 9C, that on the left from the 12C. The doorway carries bas-reliefs from the time of St. Ambrose and two 9C bronze doors. In the crypt lie the remains of St Ambrose, St. Gervase and St. Protais.

The 5C Basilica of San Vittore is entered through the seventh chapel on the right. At the end of the north aisle is the entrance to the Bramante portico and court of the Oratory of St. Sigismund. A fine golden Carolingian altar frontal of the 9C forms the high altar. It is protected by a glass screen.

Church of St. Eustorgius★ (Sant'Eustorgio). — This Romanesque basilica was founded in the 9C and belonged to the Dominicans. The side chapels were added in the 15C. The church has been considerably restored recently.

Behind the choir is the **Portinari Chapel★★**, a jewel of the Renaissance of really Classical purity by the Florentine, Michelozzo. Foppa decorated it with frescoes depicting the life and death of St. Peter the Martyr. A Dance of Angels is carved round the base of the dome. In the centre of the chapel is a richly carved marble tomb, the work of Giovanni di Balduccio (1339).

■ ADDITIONAL SIGHTS

Ambrosian Library★ (Biblioteca Ambrosiana) (BY A). — Open 9 am to noon and 2.30 to 4.30 pm. Closed Saturday afternoons, Sundays and on some holidays including Easter Sunday and Monday, 15 and 16 August, 25 and 26 December. In the library, which is in a palace built in 1609 for Cardinal Frederico Borromeo, are shown Virgil's manuscript with notes by Petrarch and miniatures by Simone Martini (14C).

The **picture gallery★★**, 1st floor (open 9.30 am to 5 pm; closed Saturdays, Easter Sunday and Monday, 15 and 16 August, 25 and 26 December; 500 lire). After passing through several rooms , you come to a series of paintings by "Velvet" Breughel including Earth and Air and the delightful **Mouse with a Rose★**. In the room devoted to Leonardo da Vinci, note two remarkable **portraits★★★**, one of the musician Gaffurio, the other presumed to be of Beatrice d'Este, attributed sometimes to Ambrogio da Predis. Raphaël's **cartoons★★★** for the frescoes of the Athenean School for the Vatican are admirable. Note in the centre Plato depicted with Leonardo's features; another interesting detail, the portrait of Michelangelo, a late addition to the fresco, does not appear on the drawing. There are also drawings by Polidoro da Caravaggio (16C), famous for the decoration of façades in chiaroscuro. Another room contains the Basket of Fruit by Caravaggio and an exquisite **Nativity★★** by the mannerist painter Barocci. In a large room are collected reproductions from the 1 750 drawings in the great Codex Atlanticus, where the universal genius of Leonardo is powerfully displayed, and Arabic manuscripts.

Poldi Pezzoli Museum★★ (Museo Poldi Pezzoli) (CX M1). — Open, 9.30 am to 12.30 pm and 2.30 to 5.30 pm (6 pm Tuesdays and Wednesdays); 1 500 lire. The museum is also open on Thursdays from 9 to 11 pm except in August; closed Sunday afternoons from 1 April to 30 September, afternoons on 25 April, 7 and 8 December; closed Mondays and holidays. The valuable exhibits are well presented in a mansion furnished and decorated with taste.

Ground floor. — Arms and armour of the 14 to the 18C; 15-16C collection of materials.

1st floor. — Three galleries are devoted to the Renaissance Lombard school: there are works by Luini (Marriage of St. Catherine), Boltraffio, Foppa, Solario... Farther on are the portraits of Luther and his wife by Cranach. It is in the Gold Saloon, where there is also a splendid **Persian carpet★** dated 1522, that the most beautiful paintings hang: the **portrait of a woman★★★** (in profile) in which the artist Antonio Pollaiuolo has caught perfectly the trembling expression of the face, St. Nicholas of Tolentino by Piero della Francesca, a gently melancholic Virgin and Child by Botticelli, a dramatic **Ecce Homo★★** by Bellini and a Madonna by Mantegna. In other galleries are a Venetian Lagoon scene by Guardi, and works by Palma the Elder, Pietro Lorenzetti, Tiepolo, Filippo Lippi, Crivelli and Lotto. There are also collections of antique watches and clocks, and especially of small bronzes (15-18C).

Leonardo da Vinci Museum of Science and Technology★ (Museo della Scienza e della Tecnica Leonardo da Vinci) (AY M1). — Open 9 am to 12.30 pm and 2 to 5 pm; closed Mondays unless a holiday, 1 January, 1 May, 15 August and 25 December; 1 000 lire.

Documents on the development of science and technology. A 16C monastery houses the sections devoted to Modern Physics and Measures; the gallery displaying copies of Leonardo da Vinci's drawings and models; and the sections devoted to Electrology, Optics, Horology, Astronomy, Graphic Arts, Telecommunications, Radio, Transport, Petroleum and Metallurgy... In a building reserved for railways, 21 locomotives and engines of different periods are lined up along five platforms. The air and sea section is located in a separate building.

Church of San Satiro★ (CY C). — The square campanile dates from the 9C, the façade from 1871. The rest of the church and the baptistry are by Bramante. The interior, particularly the sacristy and the chancel, has been decorated with antique motifs.

General Hospital★ (Ospedale Maggiore) (DZ U). — This hospital, founded by Francesco Sforza in 1456, was completed in the 17C and is at present occupied by the Faculty of Medicine. The oldest part forms the right wing of the façade; on it you will notice a little loggia. The central portion, with its terracotta window-frames and medallions, is 17C, as is the great court with superimposed galleries.

St. Maurice's Church (San Maurizio) (BY E). — This is a monastery church in the Renaissance style, adorned with frescoes★ by Luini and, in the gallery, with figures of saints by Boltraffio.

An **archaeological museum** *(to visit, apply to the Department of Culture and Entertainments in Milan, 7 Via Marino,* ☏ *(02) 620 83856)* with interesting sarcophagi has been installed inside the former conventual buildings.

The Palazzo Litta, facing the church, has an 18C façade.

Gallery of Modern Art (DV M²). — *Open 9.30 am to noon and 2.30 to 5.30 pm; closed Tuesdays, 1 January, 1 May, 15 August, Easter and Christmas.*

This, the former Villa Belgioioso built in 1790 by the Austrian architect Leopold Pollak, and once the residence of Napoleon and Eugene de Beauharnais, contains the municipal collections of Modern Art ranging from the Neo-Classical period to early 20C. The building also houses the Grassi Collection (Impressionists, 19 and 20C Italian artists), and the Marino Marini Museum which has over 200 works by the famous contemporary Italian sculptor.

St. Lawrence's Church (San Lorenzo) (BZ F). — The basilica was founded in the second half of the 4C and rebuilt in the 12C (campanile) and 16C. It has kept its original octagonal plan.

In front of the façade stands a majestic **portico** of sixteen columns, all that remains of the Roman Mediolanum (2 and 3C). Farther on, the ancient **Porta Ticinese (BZ),** a vestige of the *Naviglio* (canal) ramparts, dates from the 14C.

EXCURSIONS

Chiaravalle Abbey★ (Abbazia di Chiaravalle). — *Southeast, 7 km - 4 miles. Open 9 am to noon and 2.30 to 5.30 pm weekdays; 2.30 to 6 pm only Sundays and holidays, except during services.* Leave Milan by the Via San Dionigi. *See town plan of Milan in Michelin Red Guide Italia (hotels and restaurants).*

The abbey, founded by St. Bernard of Chiaravalle in 1135, is dominated by an elegant polygonal tower. The porch was added in the 17C. Inside there are three aisles and 14C frescoes on the roof of the dome. Another fresco in the south transept represents the Tree of the Benedictine Saints. The small cloisters are delightful.

Melegnano. — *Southeast, 17 km - 11 miles.* Leave by ⑥, road S 9. Scene of the battle of Marignano won by the French, led by François I, against the Swiss in 1515. A monument commemorates the king's dubbing as a knight.

MILANO MARITTIMA ★★ Emilia-Romagna _____
Michelin map **988** 15 — 22 km - 14 miles — southeast of Ravenna

This seaside resort, established by the Milanese, is now one of the largest and most elegant in Italy. An immense pinewood runs the full length of the fine sand beach and protects the luxurious villas and modern hotels.

A canal port separates Milano Marittima from **Cervia** another seaside resort and the administrative centre for both towns. Southwest of Cervia, saltpans cover an area of 700 ha -1 730 acres — and produce some 30 000 tons of salt a year.

MODENA ★ Emilia-Romagna _____
Michelin map **988** 14 — Pop 180 557

The local domination of the Este family, who then lived at Ferrara, began in 1289; in 1452 they raised the marquisate of Modena to the status of a duchy. In 1598 they were expelled from Ferrara by the pope, and they then took refuge at Modena, which reached the peak of its prosperity in the reigns of Francesco I and Francesco II. After 1814, when it was subjected to Austrian exactions, Modena rebelled twice, in 1830 and in 1848. It recovered its freedom in 1859 and following a plebiscite in 1860, became again a part of Italy.

Modena, situated between the Secchia and Panaro Rivers, at a major cross-roads (Via Emilia, Autostrada del Sole and Brenner Autostrada), is an active commercial and industrial centre and one of the most important towns in the Emilia-Romagna district. Maserati, Ferrari and De Tomaso, the racing car firms, all have factories in the town.

However, Modena remains a quiet town; the old quarter encircled by great avenues, is adorned by several spacious squares lined with arcades.

Modena has a gastronomic reputation for its excellent *zamponi* (stuffed pigs' trotters) and Lambrusco, a sparkling red wine; its vinegar, walnut liqueur *(nocino)*, and cherries *(ciliegie)* from Vignola (about 20 km away).

■ **MAIN SIGHTS** *time: 2 hours*

Cathedral★★ (Duomo). — The cathedral is dedicated to St. Germinian and is one of the best examples of Romanesque architecture in Italy. In it the Lombard architect Lanfranco gave vent to his sense of rhythm and proportion. The *maestri campionesi (p 127)* put the finishing touches to his work. Most of the sculptured decoration is due to Wiligelmo, a 12C Lombard sculptor.

The central porch is supported by marble lions and surmounted by a loggia and a large marble rose window. The doorways are framed in bas-reliefs by Wiligelmo: from left to right, they represent the Creation, the Life of Adam and Eve, and Cain and Abel.

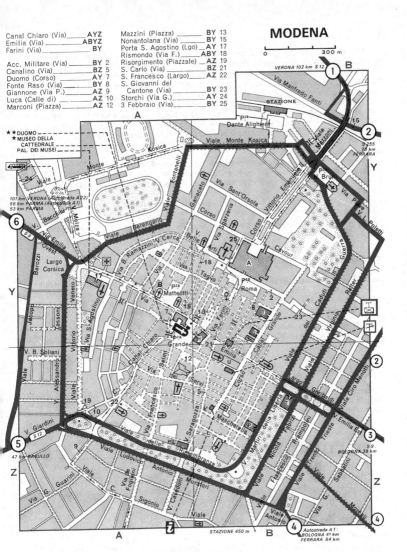

MODENA

The south side of the cathedral is remarkable for its architectural rhythm. From left to right may be seen: the Princes' Doorway, crowned by bas-reliefs carved by pupils of Wiligelmo; the 13C main doorway, known as the Royal Door, and an outside pulpit (1501) ornamented with the symbols of the Evangelists.

The Fish Market Doorway on the north side was also carved by the pupils of Wiligelmo, showing fantastic animals and people, the Work of the Months on the inner faces of the pilasters, and an attack on a town on the extrados (the exterior curve of the arches).

The massive Romanesque campanile built of white marble, 88 m - 289 ft — high, is nicknamed Ghirlandina because of the bronze garland on its weather-vane: it was completed in 1310.

The interior of the cathedral is all of brick, sober and solemn and roofed with ogive vaulting. The great arches rest on massive brick and lighter marble piers, placed alternately. The graceful **rood-screen★★** supported by Lombard lions was carved from 1170 to 1220 by the *maestri campionesi*. Scenes from the Passion are depicted on it.

The crypt, supported on many slender columns, contains a terracotta Holy Family made by the Modena artist, Guido Mazzoni in 1480, and the tomb of St. Geminian, patron saint of the town. In the presbytery *(access by stairs in the south nave)* the chancel is encircled by 15C carved stalls ornamented with realistic marquetry. In the north transept there are a 15C statue of St. Geminian and a 1384 polyptych of the Coronation of the Virgin.

The **Cathedral Museum★** (Museo della Cattedrale) contains the famous 12C **metopes★★**, bas-reliefs which used to surmount the buttresses of the cathedral. They represent buffoons or symbols incomprehensible today, but whose modelling, balance and style have an almost Classical air. *Apply to the sacristan; closed during services.*

Museums' Palace (Palazzo dei Musei). — This 18C palace contains interesting collections.

Este Library★ (Biblioteca Estense). — *1st floor, staircase on the right. The manuscripts only are on display. Open 9 am to 2 pm; closed Sundays, holidays, Holy Week and a fortnight from the last week in August.*

This is one of the richest libraries in Italy, containing 600 000 books and 15 000 manuscripts, the most interesting of which are on view. The prize piece is the Bible of Borso d'Este, Duke of Ferrara and Modena. It has 1 200 pages illuminated during the Renaissance by a team of artists including Taddeo Crivelli.

Este Gallery★★ (Galleria Estense). — *Open 9 am to 2 pm (1 pm Sundays and holidays); closed Mondays, 1 January, 25 April, 1 May, first Sunday in June, 15 August and Christmas; 750 lire.*

The museum which has been recently reorganised according to the latest museum design, is of particular interest.

The exhibits have been carefully selected, especially the Italian works, among which Emilia is well represented.

The Emilian and Tuscan Primitives' Room contains works by Barnaba da Modena (14C) which recall Sienese gentleness, Tomaso da Modena, Giovanni di Paolo, etc.

The Quattrocento is evoked by paintings of the Emilian and Venetian schools (Cima da Conegliano, Bartolomeo Montagna). Note especially a St. Anthony by the Ferrarese, Cosimo Tura, impressive in its ugliness, with bony hands and sallow colouring.

The 16C is represented by painters from Venice such as Veronese, Bassano, Tintoretto (scenes from the *Metamorphoses*), El Greco and painters of the Emilian school such as Correggio, Il Parmigianino, Dossi and Niccolò dell'Abbate (pretty frescoes depicting scenes from the *Æneid*). The 17C is illustrated by the Emilian painters from Carracio to Guercino and by a series of Italian and foreign "Caravaggists", while the 18C includes such Venetian landscape painters as Carlevaris, Guardi, etc.

Two rooms are reserved for foreign schools: French (Corneille de Lyon), German (Baldung Grien) and especially Flemish (Joos van Cleve, author of a delightfully coloured Virgin and Child with St. Anne). There is a portrait of Francesco I d'Este by Velazquez, to represent the Spanish school.

Among the Mediaeval, Classical and Renaissance sculptures in the museum, note a terracotta bust by Niccolò dell'Arca and a bust of Francesco I by Bernini.

Cabinet of Medals★. — *Reorganisation in progress.* The collection includes about 35 000 pieces of rare quality by Pisanello, Sperandio, etc.

■ **ADDITIONAL SIGHTS**

Ducal Palace★ (Palazzo Ducale) (BY A). — This noble and majestic building was begun in 1634 under Francesco I d'Este. It is huge and carefully designed, with windows differing at every storey of the façade. Today it is occupied by the Italian Infantry and Cavalry Schools. The ducal park has been converted into public and botanical gardens.

Church of St. John the Baptist (San Giovanni Battista) (AY B). — The church contains a pietà★ (1476) by Guido Mazzoni comprising eight figures in terracotta of dramatic and extravagant realism.

EXCURSION

Nonantola. — *11 km - 7 miles. Apply to the abbey for a guide.* Go out by ②. The Abbey Church of St. Silvester (San Silvestro) is a vast, sober Romanesque building. The fine sculptures of the doorway are 12C. In the south aisle there is a fresco in the Modena style and on the high altar, a 15C polyptych. The treasury contains precious miniatures and gold plate.

MONFERRATO ★ Piedmont
Michelin map 988 12 13

The Monferrato is a limestone massif situated east of Turin, whose crests rise under a clear but rather hard light. Guarded by many castles and planted with orchards and vineyards, it produces most of the famous Piedmontese wines, the best known of which is Asti.

Towns and Sights in Upper Monferrato

Vezzolano Abbey★. — *From Albugnano, 1 km - 3/4 mile.* The Romanesque church has a graceful façade with a sculptured doorway and three tiers of columns. The building has a nave and one aisle, the position of the second aisle being occupied by one of the cloistral galleries; a curious rood-screen is adorned with Burgundian sculptures devoted to the Virgin. The cloisters are decorated with a fresco of three Dead Men and three Living Men symbolising the vanity of human life.

Asti. — *Description p 57.*

Casale Monferrato. — The town was an important stronghold under the Gonzagas of Mantua, and later under the House of Savoy. Its chief modern products are cement and electrical household appliances.

The 12C but much restored Cathedral of Sant'Evasio has a monumental sized atrium; inside is a Romanesque Crucifix made of silver.

The Church of St. Dominic (San Domenico) has a fine Renaissance doorway attributed to the Venetian, Sanmicheli.

The Synagogue (late 16C, extensively remodelled in the 19C) contains a small museum *(open 10 am to noon and 3 to 6 pm; apply to the keeper ☏ 014271807)* in the section reserved for women, devoted to Sacred Art and religious and historical documents relating to the Jewish community.

Castelnuovo Don Bosco. — St. John Bosco *(see p 245)* was born in this village in 1815.

Chieri. — This is an ancient town known for its *cardi con bagna cauda,* a dish of cardoons with a hot sauce made of olive oil, anchovies and garlic, with which you should drink Freisa, a fruity red wine. Note the Triumphal Arch (1580), the cathedral (11-15C) and the Church of St. Dominic (San Domenico — 13-15C).

Chivasso. — Chivasso is situated on the Po, on the edge of the Monferrato, and has a church with an elegant façade adorned with terracottas. Inside, at the second altar on the right, is a Descent from the Cross painted by Defendente Ferrari (16C), who was born at Chivasso.

Moncalieri. — A rather picturesque little town dominated by a huge 15C castle.

MONTAGNANA ★ Venetia

Michelin map **988** 4 5 — 47 km - 29 miles — southwest of Padua — Pop 10 069

As you drive round this fortified town girt with impressive brick **ramparts★★** of a burnt sienna hue you will notice, at intervals, twenty-four polygonal towers, one of which, higher than the rest, on the northeast face, contains the chapel. The walls are pierced with four gates, including the Porta Legnano in the northwest, 32 m - 105 ft — high, with a gatehouse and a keep, of remarkable, austere beauty.

In the main square, stands the Gothic **cathedral**, with a 16C doorway by Sansovino. To the left as you enter is a 17C picture of the naval battle of Lepanto, at which the Christians defeated the Turks in 1571. The altarpiece of the high altar bears a Transfiguration, painted by Veronese. The oven vaulting is decorated with frescoes dating from the beginning of the 16C.

From the square can be seen the fine Gothic brick belfry of the Church of San Francesco.

MONTALCINO Tuscany

Michelin map **988** 15 — 46 km - 29 miles — southeast of Siena — Pop 5 702

Part of the 13C town walls still surround and the fortress built in 1361 still guards the town of Montalcino built on a hillside. The town was under the domination of Siena for several centuries, only to become the refuge of the Sienese when the Republic of Siena itself fell before Charles V in 1555.

The 13C town hall on the Piazza del Popolo is flanked by a 14-15C arcaded gallery. The **municipal museum**, in the Piazza Cavour, contains 14 and 15C paintings, 14C Majolicas (Italian pottery) and a 12C illuminated Bible.

The **museum of sacred art** (near the Church of St. Augustine) contains a collection of wooden polychrome statues of the 14 and 15C by the Sienese school.

EXCURSION

St. Anthimus Abbey★ (Abbazia di Sant'Antimo). — *South, 10 km - 6 miles. Open 9 am to noon and 3 to 6 pm.* This abbey to St. Anthimus, founded in the 9C, stands alone at the foot of the hill on which was later built the village of Castelnuovo dell'Abate. The church, which was erected in the 12C, is a good example of Cistercian architecture in Tuscany. The bare, spacious interior consists of three aisles divided by columns surmounted by fine alabaster capitals. Note the ambulatory which is of graceful proportions.

MONTECATINI TERME ★★ Tuscany

Michelin map **988** 14 — Pop 21 764
Town plan in Michelin Red Guide Italia (hotels and restaurants).

Montecatini, the most frequented and most fashionable thermal spa (for liver and stomach ailments) in Italy, has ample hotel accommodation and offers a pleasant stay. It has parks, various amusements, a racecourse, etc. The season lasts from 1 April to 30 November.

The Accademia d'Arte *(Viale Diaz, open 1 May to 31 October 4 to 7 pm; 16 March to 30 April 3 to 6 pm; closed Sundays 16 March to 30 April and all Mondays)* contains a small modern art museum. Among the exhibits are paintings by Giovanni Fattori, Guttuso, Primo Conti, Domergue and Fernand Léger, and sculptures by Mascherini and Agenore Fabbri. There are also mementoes of Puccini.

Northeast of the town a cable-way *(departures every half-hour; time: 10 minutes; 600 lire Rtn)* goes up to **Montecatini Alto** (altitude 290 m - 951 ft), a **site★** with a fine panorama.

EXCURSION

Villa Garzoni★ at **Collodi.** — *15 km - 9 miles.* Take the Pescia-Lucca road and turn right 3 km - 2 miles — after Pescia. The villa built in the 18C by the Marchese Garzoni has fine terraced **gardens★**, dating from the 17C *(open 9 am to sunset 1 April to 6 November, 8 am to sunset; 200 lire).* It is usually possible to visit the villa *(3 000 lire)* which contains 18C and Empire furniture. It was in its kitchen that Carlo Lorenzini, alias Collodi, began to relate the adventures of the famous puppet Pinocchio (monument).

MONTEFALCO ★ Umbria

Michelin map **988** 16 — 12 km - 7 miles — southwest of Foligno — Pop 5 500

14C ramparts still encircle this charming little town, which lies among vineyards and olive groves. It is perched — at its name and crest suggest — like a falcon on its nest and has been called the Balcony of Umbria. Owing to its strategic position commanding the Clitumnus Valley, Montefalco has often been a bone of contention. Frederick II destroyed it in 1249, and it was coveted for two centuries by the popes.

Montefalco, won over to Christianity in 390 by St. Fortunatus, has its own saint, Chiara, born in 1268 and not to be confused with the companion of St. Francis of Assisi. It also has a minor master, Melanzio (late 15C and early 16C), who painted in a naïve style.

Before visiting the town, drive round the *Circonvallazione,* a circular road from which you will see remarkable views of the Clitumnus Basin.

Communal Tower (Torre Comunale). — *Open 8 am to 1 pm and 3 to 8 pm (or 2 to 5 pm, 1 November to 30 April); apply to the caretaker, 15 Piazza del Comune.* From the top you can enjoy a beautiful **panorama★★★** of the Clitumnus Basin and nearly all Umbria, embracing, to the north, Perugia, Assisi, Spello and Foligno, Trevi in the east and Spoleto in the south.

St. Francis' Church (San Francesco). — Standing a little below the Piazza Garibaldi, in the Via Ringhiera Umbra, this Gothic Franciscan church with a Renaissance doorway has been converted into a museum. *Guided tours 9 am to 12.30 pm and 3.30 to 6.30 pm; 9 am to noon only Sundays and holidays. Closed 1 January, Easter and Christmas; apply to the caretaker (Signora Servili Clarice), 16 Via Severini,* ☎ *79 146.*

The mid-15C **frescoes★★** by the Florentine painter Benozzo Gozzoli are full of freshness, gentleness and an accomplished picturesqueness of anecdotal detail. In the central nave is the life of St. Francis, in the south aisle are episodes from the life of St. Jerome and, nearby, a Madonna between Saints made delightful by delicate draughtsmanship. Other frescoes of the Umbrian school by Melanzio and Perugino are in the south aisle and nave.

Santa Illuminata Church. — Late 16C. On the tympanum of the main doorway is a Madonna of Pity (Madonna della Misericordia) painted by Melanzio (1500). The interior consists of a single nave with six niches entirely painted, three by Melanzio. These are the second and third niches on the right (Coronation of the Virgin and Resurrection) and the second niche on the left (Holy Spirit).

St. Augustine's Church (Sant'Agostino). — The church is Gothic with frescoes by Umbrian painters of the 14, 15 and 16C.

Church of St. Fortunatus (San Fortunato). — *South, 1 km - 3/4 mile.* Go out by the road to Spoleto, then turn left on to a by-road which leads down to the monastery, half-hidden in a wood of evergreen oaks. The church is fronted by a 14C portico with four antique columns. On the tympanum of the doorway Benozzo Gozzoli painted a **fresco★** remarkable for its pure design and colouring, showing the Madonna between St. Francis and St. Bernard. Inside, the right altar is adorned with a fresco of St. Fortunatus by Gozzoli.

MONTEFIASCONE Latium

Michelin map 988 25 — 17 km - 11 miles — northwest of Viterbo — Pop 12 302

Montefiascone stands on the edge of a crater, facing Lake Bolsena. The countryside is covered with vineyards which produce the delicious *Est, Est, Est wine.*

"Prosit". — A German prelate belonging to the well known Fugger Family of Augsburg, had to go to Rome. As he was fond of good food and especially of generous wine, he sent one of his servants ahead of him with orders to mark the inns where the wine was the best with the word *est* ("is" in Latin) — *Vinum est bonum:* the wine is good. The man did this. When he arrived at Montefiascone the faithful servant found the wine so good that he wrote, in his enthusiasm, *"Est, est, est".* And his master, becoming enthusiastic in his turn, drank so much, much, much of it that he died.

■ SIGHTS

St. Flavian's Church★ (San Flaviano). — The church, consisting of two superimposed buildings, stands on the road to Orvieto, in the lower part of the town. The architecture is in the Lombard Romanesque style, with Umbrian influence in the decoration. The simple but unfinished façade of 1110, is remarkable for the pointed arch of its central doorway. The lower church (1032) is a fine example of plain architecture with superb Romanesque capitals, carved with rare vigour, supporting Gothic vaulting. Three Romanesque oven-shaped apses are adorned with a pretty sculptured frieze. On the right as you come in is the **tombstone** of Johann Fugger, the greedy prelate, with this curious epitaph: *Est, est, est pr(opter) nim(ium) est hic Jo(annès) de Fougg do(minus) meus mortuus est* which may be translated: It is because of too much *est, est, est* that my master Johann Fugger is dead.

On the left, again at the entrance, is a fresco illustrating the Story of the Three Dead and the Three Living Men, symbolising the brevity and vanity of human life. You go up into the upper church, consisting of three asymmetrical aisles which are really large galleries built over the main arches of the lower church.

Castle (Rocca). — From the esplanade, about 350 m - 1 050ft — above the lake, there is a fine **view★** of Lake Bolsena, Monte Amiata and, in clear weather, the Tyrrhenian Sea.

Cathedral (Duomo). — The majestic dome was designed by Sanmicheli in 1519.

MONTEFIORE DELL'ASO Marches

Michelin map 988 16 — 26 km - 16 miles — south of Porto San Giorgio — Pop 2 464

Carlo Crivelli (1430-1495), a painter of courtesans and fair virgins, on being sentenced at Venice in 1457, took refuge in the Marches, Montefiore so gaining a masterpiece.

The Church of St. Lucy (Santa Lucia) contains, in the first chapel on the right, a splendid **polyptych★★**, finely chiselled and picked out in gold, representing six saints. The most successful panel shows the sinner Mary Magdalen richly apparelled in gold and silk brocade, holding the symbolic box of ointment.

MONTELEONE SABINO Latium

28 km - 17 miles — south of Rieti — Pop 1 280

The **Romanesque Basilica of Santa Vittoria★**, founded in the 3C and remodelled in the 13C, stands in a pretty setting on an esplanade lined with cypresses 2 km - 1 1/4 miles — from the village. The façade is decorated with Byzantine symbols. In the interior, which is divided into three aisles by 3C fluted Greco-Roman columns, you will see a miraculous well, a sunken "confessional" dug to enable the faithful to worship the relics, and catacombs containing the sarcophagus of St. Vittoria.

MONTE OLIVETO MAGGIORE Abbey ★ Tuscany

36 km - 22 miles — southeast of Siena

Open 9 am to 12.30 pm and 3 to 7 pm (6 pm in winter); ring; time: 1 hour.

The huge pink brick buildings of this famous abbey lie hidden among cypresses. A fortified gateway adorned with terracottas by Luca della Robbia gives access to the monks' domain.

Monte Oliveto is the Mother House of the Olivetans, a congregation of the Benedictine Order which was founded in 1319 by Blessed Bernard Tolomei of Siena.

Great Cloisters (Chiostro Grande). — The cloisters are decorated with a superb series of thirty-six **frescoes★★** depicting the life of St. Benedict by Luca Signorelli (1498) and Il Sodoma (1505-1508).

The frescoes begin near the entrance to the church, at the great arch where the Christ of the Column and the Christ bearing His Cross, masterpieces of Il Sodoma, are painted. The first fresco represents St. Benedict leaving his family home. Follow on from left to right.

The first nineteen frescoes are by Il Sodoma; then comes one by Riccio; then nine by Signorelli; the remainder (on the last wall) are by Il Sodoma.

Note especially the 3rd fresco in which Il Sodoma has painted himself, turning towards the spectator, with his hair falling to his shoulders; the 12th (first on the south side) in which St. Benedict is receiving two young Romans, Maurus and Placidus; the 19th (last on the south side), in which the courtesans are sent to seduce the monks; the 27th, by Signorelli, which shows St. Benedict discovering the ruse of the Barbarian Totila, who has changed clothes with his standard-bearer; and the 30th by Il Sodoma, in which the saint predicts the destruction of Monte Cassino. Note also the differences of style between Signorelli, who is powerful, sculptural and dramatic, and Il Sodoma, who shows little religious feeling and concentrates on attractive human types, landscape and picturesque detail.

Abbey Church (Chiesa Abbaziale). — The interior was remodelled in the Baroque style in the 18C, but the chancel has kept its **stalls★★** (1505) by Fra Giovanni da Verona, inlaid with birds, architectural perspectives, tabernacles, musical instruments and Sienese buildings (the town hall).

The 15C refectory (access through the great cloisters), the library and the pharmacy are also open to the public (a monk takes visitors round).

MONTEPULCIANO ★ Tuscany
Michelin map **988** 15 — Pop 14 297

Montepulciano, a little town characteristic of the Renaissance period, perched as it is on the crest of a hill of volcanic rock between two valleys, occupies a remarkable **site★★** and is generally most attractive.

Inhabitants of Chiusi, fleeing from the Barbarian invasion, founded the town in the 6C and called it Mons Politianus, which explains why its inhabitants are known as *Poliziani* (Politians).

Poets have sung of its *vino nobile*, a ruby coloured wine.

Politian (1454-1494). — Il Poliziano, one of the most exquisite Renaissance poets, became the friend of Lorenzo de' Medici, whom he called *Lauro* (Laurel). They used to meet at Fiesole, where Lorenzo had given a villa to Politian after he saved him from the assassins of Giuliano de' Medici during the attack in the cathedral in 1478 (p 107). The *Stanzas,* Politian's masterpiece, describe a sort of Garden of Delight haunted by attractive women. Politian's verse matches the painting of his friend Botticelli.

■ OLD CITY (Città Antica) time: 1 1/2 hours

After passing through a fortified gateway bearing the Tuscan shield and alongside the Marzocco or Lion of Florence, one enters the long street that crosses Montepulciano from end to end, although its name changes several times. It is lined with many interesting **palaces★** and churches.

The fine Palazzo Avignonesi in the Via Roma, dating from the end of the Renaissance (16C) and attributed to Vignola, is numbered 37. The Palazzo Cocconi, at No. 72, is believed to have been designed by Sangallo the Elder (early 16C). Farther on, on the right, the Church of St. Augustine (Sant'Agostino) has an elegant Renaissance façade designed by Michelozzo (15C). Opposite stands a tower with a figure of Pulcinella (the Clown) as the Jack-o'-the-clock.

In the Via Cavour the Palazzo Cervini at No. 9, designed by Sangallo the Elder, is a good example of the Florentine Renaissance style with its embossing, and its curvilinear and triangular pediments.

Following the Via Garibaldi and the Via Poliziano (the poet's birthplace is No. 1 in the latter), turn to the right in front of the Church of Santa Maria dei Servi to reach the Piazza Grande.

■ PIAZZA GRANDE★★ (Main Square)

The Piazza Grande is the monumental centre of the town. Its irregular plan and varying styles avoid architectural monotony while blending into a harmonious whole.

Town Hall★ (Palazzo comunale). — The building is Gothic and severe in style, with machicolations, battlements and fine square tower reminiscent of the Florentine Palazzo Vecchio. It was remodelled by Michelozzo in the 15C.

From the top of the tower (for ascent apply to the keeper; the stairs are steep and narrow) you will see an immense **panorama★★★** of the town and its environs (Church of the Madonna di San Biagio), the graceful, hilly Tuscan landscape, Lake Trasimeno and Cortona to the east, Siena to the north, Pienza to the west and Monte Amiata to the south.

The Palazzo Contucci on the other side of the square was begun in 1519 by Sangallo the Elder and completed in the 18C.

Palazzo Nobili-Tarugi★. — This majestic Renaissance palace, facing the cathedral, is attributed to Sangallo the Elder. It has a portico and a great doorway with semicircular arches; six Ionic columns, standing on a lofty base, support the pilasters of the upper storey, where there is, on the left, a blind loggia.

The windows, with curvilinear pediments, rest on small consoles. Note, above and to the left of the central doorway, openings used for observing arrivals.

Standing next to the Nobili-Tarugi Palace is another palace, Palazzo del Capitano.

Well★ (Pozzo). — This well is picturesque, especially its hood, which is formed of two lions supporting the coat of arms of the Medicis.

Cathedral (Duomo). — 16-17C. The cathedral's unfinished façade lacks the customary marble facing.

The interior, which has pure, simple lines, forms three aisles. To the left of the central doorway as you come in is the recumbent figure of Bartolomeo Aragazzi, secretary to Pope Martin V; this effigy was part of a monument designed by the 15C Florentine architect Michelozzo. Two graceful statues flanking the high altar, and the bas-reliefs on the first two pillars, were taken from it.

Over the high altar is a monumental **altarpiece★** (1401) by Taddeo di Bartolo, a Sienese painter who has depicted the Assumption, the Annunciation and the Coronation of the Virgin.

EXCURSION

Madonna di San Biagio★★. – *1 km – 3/4 mile.* Go through the Al Prato gate by which you arrived, take the road to Chianciano, then turn to the right. This pale tinted church in a setting of cypresses stands on an attractive site in the centre of a large meadow. The church, which was consecrated in 1529 by Pope Clement VII de' Medici, is the masterpiece of Sangallo the Elder. The variety and harmony of its architectural lines and the reliefs which create a play of light and shade will please the tourist in search of beauty.

The building is planned in the shape of a Greek cross and is surmounted by a dome; the south transept is prolonged by a semicircular sacristy. Two campaniles flank the main façade. One is unfinished; the other includes the three orders: Doric, Ionic and Corinthian.

The interior gives an impression of majesty and nobility. The high altar dates from 1584. Opposite the church stands the Canonica, or canon's mansion, an elegant porticoed building.

MONTE SANT'ANGELO ★ Apulia

Michelin map **988** 28 — *Local map p 116* — Alt 843 m - 2 755 ft — Pop 17 548

Monte Sant'Angelo stands on a curious **site★★**. The town is built on a spur dominated by the Norman ruins of the Giants' Castle and overlooks the Gargano Massif *(p 116)* and the sea.

This little town has kept up its ancestral customs and its ancient appearance, with steep alleys, stairways and whitewashed houses.

The Legend of St. Michael. — St. Michael, chief of the Heavenly Host, who overthrew the Devil, appeared to some shepherds in a grotto in the year AD 491. When he withdrew he left them his great red cloak. A Christian pilgrimage then took possession of this pagan holy place, where Podalireus, the son of AEsculapius, and the divine Calchas had been worshipped.

In the 8C a French monk, St. Aubert, brought back to his country a piece of the cloak, to shelter which he built the Abbey of Mont St-Michel, in Brittany. During the Middle Ages all the Crusaders, before embarking at Manfredonia, came to pray to the Archangel Michael, the saintly warrior who always appeared in high places. This explains why his statues and churches are always placed on high.

■ **SIGHTS** *time: 3/4 hour*

St. Michael's Church★ (Santuario di San Michele). — The building is designed in the transitional Romanesque-Gothic style. The octagonal bell-tower has four storeys and dates from the end of the 13C. Facing the square is a porch with two arches and two doorways bearing bas-reliefs. The doorway to the right is early 14C. By going down a stairway close by you will come out in front of the façade of the church, which dates from the reign of Charles I of Anjou.

The beautiful bronze door was made in Constantinople. It gives access to the ogive-vaulted nave and the grotto in which St. Michael is said to have appeared; note the 16C statue of the saint and a magnificent episcopal pulpit of the 12C.

From a balcony behind the stalls of the building there is a fine view of the Gargano Massif.

Tomb of Rotharis (Tomba di Rotari). — Go down the stairs opposite the campanile. The tomb, which is on the left in the apse of the ruined Romanesque Church of St. Peter's, is supposed to contain the remains of Rotharis, King of the Lombards, but is really a 12-13C baptistry.

MONZA Lombardy

Michelin maps **988** 3 and **26** 19 — Pop 123 184

Monza is an industrial town (hats, textiles, carpets) on the boundary of the Brianza which is also of real interest to tourists.

Royal Villa (Villa Reale). — The villa is a majestic building in the Neo-Classical style. It was the residence of Eugène de Beauharnais and Umberto I of Italy, who was assassinated at Monza by an anarchist in 1900. In 1806 Eugène de Beauharnais, the French Viceroy of Italy, had the **park★★** landscaped in the English manner (first gate to the left of the main entrance).

The northern part of the former royal estate now includes a racecourse, two golf courses, a swimming pool and the Monza motor **race track** *(see plan in Michelin Red Guide Italia (hotels and restaurants). Open 8 am to noon and 1.30 to 6 pm (1 pm to one hour before sunset 1 October to 31 March); 1 000 lire to visit the installations and 3 000 lire per car on the track).* This comprises a 5.80 km - 4 mile track as well as a 4.25 km - 2 1/4 mile fast circuit, which was reconstructed in 1955, allowing cars to attain a speed of 300 km p.h. - 186 m. p.h. The Italian Grand Prix Formula One is run on this track (September) as well as the 4-hour race (March), the 1 000 km - 620 miles — (April), the Lottery Grand Prix (June) and the motor-cycle Grand Prix for Nations (May-September).

Cathedral (Duomo). — The cathedral was constructed in the 13-14C on the site of a church founded in 595 by the Queen of the Longobards, Theodolinda. The campanile is late 16C.

The Lombard **façade★** in alternating white, green and black marble is remarkable for its harmonious proportions and decorations. It was built by Matteo di Campione in 1390-1396.

The interior was remodelled in the 17C. To the left of the chancel is the chapel of Queen Theodolinda, adorned with 15C **frescoes★** depicting in forty-four scenes the life of this pious sovereign, who is buried behind the altar. Over the altar is a facsimile of the famous Iron Crown of the Kings of Lombardy, so-called because it contained an iron band said to have been forged from a nail of the Holy Cross *(to see the original, apply to the sacristan).*

The treasury, where there are fine pieces of gold plate, is open *(9 am to noon and 3 to 6 pm; 10 am to noon and 3 to 6 pm the museum; 11.30 am to noon and 3 to 5 pm for the Iron Crown; closed Mondays; 1 000 lire for the museum and Iron Crown).*

MORTOLA INFERIORE Liguria

Michelin map **988** 20 — 5 km - 3 miles — west of Ventimiglia — *Local map p 199*

The **Hanbury Gardens★** (Giardini Hanbury), the entrance to which *(open 9 am to 5 pm)* is near the Via Aurelia main road, are laid out in terraces along the seashore. Innumerable colourful and picturesque vistas will be found. The vegetation is extremely varied, and includes some 6 000 species: olive, eucalyptus and palm trees, agaves, cedars, mimosa, cineraria...

NAPLES ★★★ (NAPOLI) Campania

Michelin map **988** 27 — Pop 1 225 377

Town plan in Michelin Red Guide Italia (hotels and restaurants).

The beauties of Naples have been praised by innumerable travellers. A lovely bay, filled by a sea of dark blue, a horizon bounded by Posillipo, the Islands, the Sorrento Peninsula and lofty Vesuvius, all these contribute to the fame of this favoured spot. As for Naples itself, the mingling of gaiety and sadness and the noisiness and vivacity of the people make this town "the permanent playhouse of Italy".

However, the industrial quarter to the east, the busy traffic which throttles the city at certain times of the day, and the light mist that clouds the horizon may at first disappoint tourists who dream of picturesque Naples basking under an ever blue sky in a harmonious setting. Visitors need to have a very flexible outlook but the discovery of the city although not easy, is a rewarding experience.

HISTORICAL NOTES

According to legend, the siren Parthenope gave her name to a town which had sprung up round her tomb; that is why Naples is called the Parthenopaen City and its inhabitants Parthenopaeans. In fact, Naples originated as a Greek colony named Neapolis, which was conquered by the Romans in the 4C BC. Rich inhabitants of Rome like Virgil, Augustus, Tiberius, Nero, etc., used to spend the winter there, but the Neapolitans themselves retained the Greek language and customs until the decline of the Empire.

Since the 12C seven princely families have reigned over Naples. The French Revolution of 1789 brought in French troops, and a Parthenopaean Republic was set up, followed by a French kingdom (1806-1815), under Joseph Bonaparte (Napoleon's brother) and afterwards Joachim Murat (Napoleon's brother-in-law), who promoted excellent reforms. From 1815 to 1860 the restored Bourbons remained in spite of revolts from 1820 to 1848.

"Good King Robert" of Anjou (1309-1343). — The brother of St. Louis, Charles I of Anjou, had been called by the French Pope Clement VI to the throne of Naples. His son, Charles II, and his grandson, Robert I, succeeded him. Robert the Wise, whose brother Louis became Bishop of Toulouse and was canonised, attracted poets, scholars and artists to his court. Giotto and Simone Martini painted masterpieces, but Giotto's, unfortunately, have disappeared. Boccaccio spent twenty years at this court where Petrarch was also well known.

The successor of King Robert, the notorious Queen Jeanne from Provence, romantic and beautiful, clever but cruel, died in the city in 1382, smothered by one of her cousins.

ART IN NAPLES

Mediaeval Sculpture and Architecture. — Under the princes of the House of Anjou, architecture borrowed from France its Gothic style and some of its architects, such as Pierre de Chaulnes and Pierre d'Agincourt. Sculpture was influenced chiefly by Tuscans, such as the Sienese, Tino da Camaino, who held a school in Naples from 1311 to 1324. At the same time Master Goldsmiths Godefroid and Milet of Auxerre specialised in religious work.

As painters of mural frescoes the Florentine, Giotto and Pietro Cavallini, a Roman artist still under Byzantine influence, who lived in Naples in the 14C, were outstanding.

The Neapolitan School of Painting (17-18C). — Though it originated with Spanish and Bolognese masters influenced by Caravaggio, this school had a style of its own in the form of realism in warm colours on a basis of chiaroscuro.

Giuseppe Ribera, *alias* Spagnoletto (1588-1652), a painter of Spanish origin, excelled in gruesome subjects and chiaroscuro. Monsu Desiderio, a Lorrainer by origin, painted strange and fantastic scenes. Mattia Preti and Luca Giordano were more decorative. Salvator Rosa, a passionate and romantic artist, painted landscapes and battle scenes. Ruoppolo (1620-1683) and Recco painted strange still-lifes of shells and fish with scales glimmering in a dim, mysterious light.

THE NEAPOLITANS

The Neapolitans are small and dark, with almost Grecian profiles. They speak either a rather sing-song Italian or the dialect of Naples. They have lively imaginations; they fear the *jettatura* (the Evil Eye), from which they protect themselves by touching a little bone or coral horn they carry in their pockets.

The modern writers, Malaparte, in *Kaputt* and *La Pelle* (The Skin) and Marotta, in *L'Oro di Napoli,* have graphically described these unusual people.

Popular Festivals. — Religious festivals are sumptuous; those of the Madonna di Piedigrotta (first week in September) and Santa Maria del Carmine (16 July) are the best known. Twice a year, on the first Saturday in May and on 19 September, at the cathedral, the Feast of the Miracle of St. Januarius (San Gennaro) is held. The saints' blood, kept dry in a flask, is supposed to liquefy, failing which disaster will come upon the town.

Neapolitan Song. — Naples is the capital of the *Bel Canto,* sometimes joyful, sometimes melancholy, practised to the accompaniment of a guitar or a mandolin. A Neapolitan song festival takes place in September. *Santa Lucia, Marechiare, Funiculi-Funiculà, O Sole Mio!* are among the great successes of the Neapolitan repertory.

Neapolitan Cooking. — The restaurants of Santa Lucia and the *trattorie* and *pizzerie* (restaurants and *pizza*-shops) of the old town serve Neapolitan dishes. Try the *zuppa di pesce* (fish stew), the various forms of spaghetti seasoned with fresh tomatoes and served *al dente* (i.e. lightly cooked); the *vermicelli alla Vongole,* long, thread-like *pasta* mixed with shell-fish, all accompanied by the white wine of Capri or Ischia, the wine of Vesuvius or *Lacryma Christi* (Tear of Christ) or the red wine, Gragnano.

But the local speciality is the famous *pizza,* a sort of tart made with olive oil, *mozzarella* (melted cheese), tomatoes and fillets of herring or anchovy, the whole seasoned with wild marjoram and baked in the oven.

In the Street. — Popular scenes which used to charm the tourists are now a thing of the past. Vendors of glow worms and tortoises have disappeared, the noise of motor vehicles and horns has replaced the music of hurdy-gurdies and of mules bedecked with bells; shoeblacks still operate but few display the elaborate gilded stools which were a feature of Naples.

NAPOLI

However Naples is a world apart: lively but mysterious, disturbing but familiar, fascinating and full of noise and activity.

Traffic is hectic. The town with its narrow streets and layout — it is squeezed between the sea and hills — is unsuited to heavy traffic but cars weave in and out frenetically and only the genius for improvisation, the daring and virtuosity of Neapolitan drivers compensate for their lack of discipline. Tourists need courage and determination to venture across the road, traffic lights are rare and one has to dart across but one needs to be on the alert.

The Quarters. — The port handles more passengers than any other in Italy but is second to Genoa in goods traffic. Tourists embark for Capri, Ischia and Sorrento at the Beverello jetty; hydrofoils operate from the small Sannazzaro port at Mergellina and from the Beverello jetty.

The centre of public life is the Piazza del Plebiscito, close by the Piazza Trento e Trieste, near which is the Galleria with its four arcades which house shops and cafes. Via Roma and Via Chiaia are lined with shops but the luxury shops are near Piazza dei Martiri (CZ). Certain quarters specialize in different trades: antiquaries near Piazza dei Martiri; second-hand book-shops at Via Port'Alba near Piazza Dante **(DY)**; wedding and communion outfitters at Via del Duomo **(EY)**... The working-class quarters, their streets drawn close together and dressed overall with lines of washing, are to be found in the Spacca-Napoli *(see p 160)* and in the area to the left of Via Roma towards Piazza Salvo d'Acquisto. The Posillipo hillside facing the sea is a residential area.

■ **MAIN SIGHTS**
tour: about 2 1/2 days as museums are closed in the afternoon

FROM NEW CASTLE TO MERGELLINA
see local map pp 155-156

The dense traffic and the lack of shady areas along the

Amedeo di Savoia	
Duca d'Aosta (Corso)	BV 2
Angelini (Via Tito)	BV 3
Arena della Sanità (Via)	BV 6
Arenaccia (Via)	BV 7
Bernini (Via G. L.)	BV 12
Buonarroti	
(Viale Michelangelo)	BV 13
Camaldoli (Via nuova)	BV 14
Capodimonte (Via)	BV 16
Caracciolo (Via B.)	BV 20
Caracciolo (Via F.)	BX 21
Cavallino (Via Bernardo)	BV 23
Casanova (Via)	BV 24
D'Annunzio (Piazza G.)	AX 35
Da Caravaggio	
(Via Michelangelo)	AX 39
De Vito Piscicelli	
(Via Maurizio)	BV 44
Di Giacomo (Piazza S.)	AX 45
Di Giacomo	
(Via Salvatore)	AX 46
Domitiana (Via)	AX 47
Don Bosco (Via)	BV 48
Europa (Corso)	BX 52

Fiore (Via Mario)	BV 58
Fontana	
(Via Domenico)	BV 59
Garibaldi (Corso G.)	BV 61
Gigante (Via Giacinto)	BV 65
Giulio Cesare (Via)	AX 67
Leopardi (Via Giacomo)	AX 68
Martini (Via Simone)	BV 74
Mergellina (Via)	BX 78
Mille (Via dei)	BX 80
Morghen (Via Raffaele)	BX 86
Nazionale (Piazza)	BV 93
Nicolini (Via Nicola)	BU 95
Parco Margherita (Via)	BX 107
Partenope (Via)	BX 107
Piedigrotta (Via)	BX 113
Russo (Via Ferdinando)	AX 134
S. Pasquale (Via)	BX 146
S. Raffaele (Salita)	BV 147
S. Teresa degli	
Scalzi (Via)	BV 149
Sanità (Via della)	BV 150
Santacroce (Via G.)	BV 152
Sauro (Via Nazaro)	BX 153
Semmola (Via Mariano)	BV 156
Tecchio (Piazzale V.)	AX 160
Vanvitelli (Piazza)	BX 166
Vergini (Via)	BV 168
Vittorio Emanuele	
(Corso)	BX 170

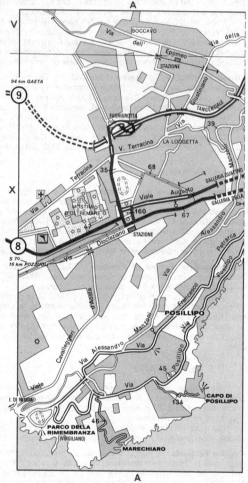

coast lessen the attraction of this itinerary which however takes in some of the most famous spots of Naples and affords lovely views of the town and of the bay.

New Castle★★ (Castel Nuovo). — The castle is imposing and surrounded by deep moats. Built in 1282 by Pierre d'Agincourt, the architect of Charles I of Anjou, it is also called the Castel Angioino (Angevin Castle) since it was modelled on the Castle at Angers. The Aragon dynasty made important alterations.

A remarkable **triumphal arch★★** adorns the entrance. This masterpiece bearing the arms of Aragon was built from designs by Francesco Laurana in 1467. It is ornamented with sculptures: the Triumph of Alfonso of Aragon, Alfonso among his court, four statues of the Virtues in the upper niches and a statue of St. Michael on the summit. The whole shows the Classical spirit in the perfect adaptation of the sculptures to the architectural design, the light reliefs and the influence of ancient bas-reliefs in the central feature.

At the end of the square court stands an elegant Renaissance doorway surmounted by a Virgin by Laurana (1471).

St. Charles' Theatre★ (Teatro San Carlo). — *Open 10 am to noon; closed Mondays and August; 100 lire, free on Sundays.* This grey and white theatre is the most famous in Italy after the Scala of Milan. It was built under Charles of Bourbon in 1737 and rebuilt in 1816 in the Neo-Classical style: the loggia along the façade is ornamented with Ionic columns.

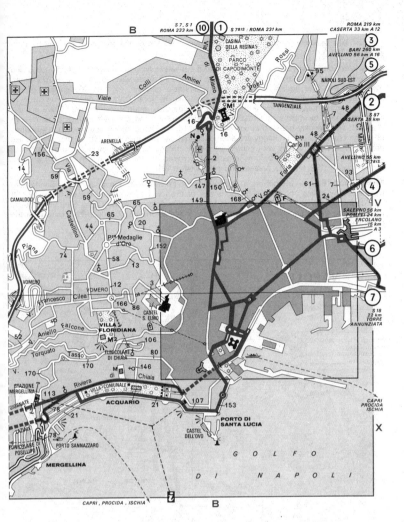

The lavish auditorium is a good example of a classic 18C Italian theatre with boxes on six levels and the magnificent royal box in the centre. To achieve perfect acoustics, the entire decoration is in wood and stucco (with imitation marble facing made of wood). The ceiling is painted with a fresco of Apollo and the Muses.

Piazza del Plebiscito★. — This noble semicircular "square" was laid out in the centre of Naples in the reign of Murat. It is enclosed on one side by the royal palace, on the other by the Neo-Classical façade of the Church of **St. Francis of Paola** (San Francesco di Paola), built on the model of the Pantheon in Rome and prolonged by a curving colonnade. The equestrian statues by Canova in the centre are of Ferdinand and Charles III of Bourbon.

Royal Palace★ (Palazzo Reale). — *Open 9 am to 2 pm (1 pm Sundays); closed Mondays; 750 lire.*

The palace was built at the beginning of the 17C by the architect Domenico Fontana and was remodelled several times. The façade retains more or less its original appearance. Since the late 19C the niches on the façade contain eight statues of the most famous Kings of Naples.

A huge staircase with twin ramps and crowned by a coffered dome, leads to a 17C chapel and to the apartments.

The kings lived in the palace only after 1734. At the foot of the staircase is a bronze door designed by Guglielmo, a Parisian monk, in 1468. Six bas-reliefs depict the struggle of Ferdinand of Aragon against René d'Anjou. The door was taken away by Charles VIII at the time of the campaigns of Italy but was subsequently returned. A canon-ball is still embedded in it.

The theatre is to the right as you enter the apartments. In a series of richly decorated rooms you will see Gobelins tapestries from designs by Lebrun, and others by Pietro Durante, the work of 18C Neapolitan weavers. Among the paintings note in Room V, the Flute Player by Grimou (18C), and in Room VI a Virgin and Child by Francesco Ruviale (16C). In the queen's apartments note a delightful work-table (Room VII), cased in Sevres porcelain, the masterpiece of the Parisian cabinet-maker Carlin and given by Marie Antoinette to her sister Marie Caroline; and an original round table (Room VIII), gift of Tsar Nicholas I to Ferdinand II, which is surmounted by a gilded bronze bird-cage adorned with Sevres porcelain. Room X was the study of Joachim Murat. Room XIV contains portraits by Doyen and E. Vigée-Lebrun.

From the Via Cesario Console which leads to the sea front, there is a partial view of the port.

Port of Santa Lucia★★ (BX). — Santa Lucia is the name of the small suburb that juts out towards the sea. It is best known as the name of a tiny port, immortalized by a famous Neapolitan song, nestling between a rocky islet and the jetty linking it to the shore. People go there to watch splendid sunsets. The quays lined with restaurants built on piles, the *borgo marinaro* and the austere **Egg Castle** (Castel dell'Ovo) make a picturesque scene.

Along the coast from the Via Partenope, there is a splendid **view★★★** of the western part of the bay, especially in the evenings when the buildings on the Vomero and Posillipo hillsides are brilliantly lit up.

The **Villa Comunale** gardens which extend over 1 1/2 km by the sea, were planned by Vanvitelli in 1780.

Aquarium★ (Acquario) (BX). — *Open 9 am to 5 pm weekdays and 10 am to 7 pm Sundays and holidays. Closed Mondays, 1 January, Easter, 1 May, 19 September, 8, 24, 25 and 26 December; 1 000 lire.* The aquarium in the Villa Comunale gardens, exhibits 200 species of sea creatures from the Bay of Naples together with marine flora. They are never all on show at once as some survive only for a short while outside their natural environment. There are sea lilies that move by means of tentacles covered in yellow, red or violet plumes of some sort (Tank 1); small prickly murex that secrete a liquid from which purple was extracted in Antiquity (3); large crustaceans (7); shaggy sea anemones that paralyse their prey (8); asteriae shaped like orange flowers (9); morays with impressive long teeth and as long as snakes — their flesh was considered a great delicacy by the Romans, (11); round flat torpedoes which give out an electric discharge (13); tiny sea horses (20); and jellyfish (21).

Mergellina★ (BX). — Mergellina, at the foot of the Posillipo with the small port of Sannazzaro frequented by sailing and fishing boats, is one of the few places around Naples for a stroll. It affords a splendid **view★★** of the bay: the Vomero hillside crowned by Castel Sant'Elmo slopes gently to the Santa Lucia headland which is extended by the Egg Castle, with Vesuvius in the distance.

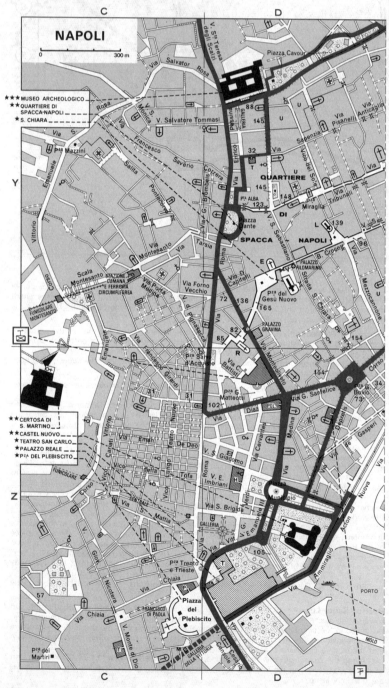

■ NATIONAL ARCHAEOLOGICAL MUSEUM*** (Museo Archeologico Nazionale)

Open 9 am to 2 pm; closed Mondays, 1 January, 25 April, 1 May, first Sunday in June, 15 August, 25 December; 750 lire. The museum is in a 16C palace which was the seat of the university until 1777. It is one of the richest museums in the world devoted to Greco-Roman Antiquity. It contains works of art belonging to the Farnese family and treasures discovered at Pompeii and Herculaneum were installed there.

Greco-Roman Sculptures***. — *On the ground floor.*

Tyrant-Slayers' Gallery. — *Turn to the left at the entrance.* The gallery is devoted to archaic art. The **Aphrodite Sosandra,** with a fine, proud face and elegantly draped robe, which was recovered at Baia, is a splendid copy of a Greek bronze (5C BC). In the middle of the room stands the powerful marble group of the **Tyrant-Slayers,** a copy (1-2C) of a Greek bronze representing Armodio and Aristogeiton who delivered Athens from the tyrant, Hipparchus, in the 6C BC.

Great Masters' Gallery. — *Parallel to the above-mentioned gallery.* This gallery contains the statue of the **Farnese Pallas** (Athena), majestic and serene according to Phidias' ideal; **Orpheus and Eurydice** bidding each other farewell in the presence of Hermes, a bas-relief of touching simplicity copied from the Phidias original (5C BC) and the calm **Doryphorus,** the lance-bearer, a copy of the famous bronze by Polycletus (5C BC).

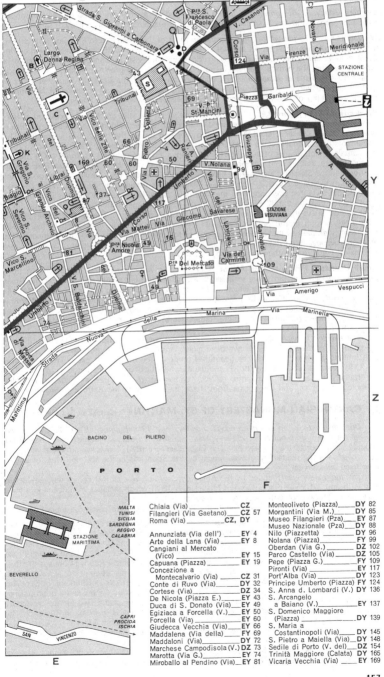

Farnese Gallery. — *At right angles to the two previous galleries.* The **Callipygian Venus**, a Roman copy of the Greek original, stands in Room X. Room XII contains wonderful works: the Aphrodite of Sinuessa, a Greek original of admirable purity and delicacy, is flanked by two male torsos; two other splendid torsos of Aries and Aphrodite near the window are replicas of 4C Greek originals; the famous **Farnese Hercules**, with exaggerated muscles, is a Greek copy of an original by Lysippus, sculptor to Alexander the Great. Almost equally famous is the Farnese Eros, in Room XIII, which Phidias is believed to have given to the courtesan Phryne. A pretty bas-relief on the opposite wall represents Paris, Helen and Aphrodite. In Room XIV is the **Psyche of Capua**, with a beautifully spiritual face. The Capuan Aphrodite recalls the Milos Aphrodite attributed to Scopas. The colossal group, the **Farnese Bull** (Room XV), depicting the death of Dirce, was carved from a single block of marble, and was restored by Michelangelo.

Works in Coloured Marble. — *If the wing of the Farnese Gallery is closed, enter from the great hall (on the right at the far end).* The most famous work is the statue of **Artemis of Ephesus** (2C) in alabaster and bronze, representing the deity venerated at the famous temple by the Aegean sea. She is sometimes considered as a nature goddess in the oriental tradition and is represented with numerous breasts symbolising her motherly nature.

Great Hall. — In the middle row (on the right), the statue of Eumachia discovered at Pompeii *(p 186)* is inspired from Greek art. The expressive face in particular shows Praxiteles' influence.

Greek Portraits. — *On the left at the far end of the hall.* At the entrance on the left is a portrait of Socrates depicted as a silenus. On the second stand is exhibited a fine portrait of Euripides. The famous portrait of the blind Homer (in the centre) is a forceful representation of the misery of blindness.

Emperors' Gallery. — *At right angles to the former gallery; temporarily closed for reorganisation.* Excellent Roman portraits (Caracalla, Agrippina...) are exhibited in this gallery.

Mosaics★★. — *(To the left on the mezzanine).* Most of them come from Pompeii. Note on the left in **Room LIX**, two small works by Dioscurides of Samos (late1C BC) remarkable for their delicate colours and satirical realism: Roving Musicians and Visit to a magician. A portrait of a woman denotes the artist's mastery in portraying facial expression. In **Room LXI**, the famous mosaic of the **Battle of Alexander** which adorned the floor of the Casa del Fauno at Pompeii *(p 190)* depicts with a remarkable sense of movement, the victory of the King of Macedonia over Darius, King of Persia. Note the bronze **Dancing Faun** also from Pompeii.

Works from Villa Pison★★★. — *1st floor, on the right.* The villa which was discovered at Herculaneum in the 18C but was later reburied, is thought to have belonged to L. Calpurnius Pison who was Julius Ceasar's father-in-law. The owner had turned the house into a museum. The documents and splendid works of art from his collections are priceless. The Papyri Room (CXIV) contains photographs of some of the 800 papyri from the library. In Room CXVI are exhibited bronze statues that adorned the peristyle of the villa. Note the **Drunken Faun** lost in euphoria and a **Sleeping Satyr** with a beautiful face in repose. Two lifelike **"Wrestlers"** are inspired from Lysippus (4C BC). The famous **"Dancers from Herculaneum"** probably water carriers, illustrate the style that was popular in the early days of the Empire and which was inspired from the "severe" style (in the 5C BC, this style marks the first stage in the transition from the rigidity of archaic art to the flexibility of classical art in Greek sculpture). The famous **Hermes at Rest**, with a tall, strong figure, reflects Lysippus' ideal. In Room CXVII, in addition to the **portrait** mistakenly identified as that of **Seneca** and one of the most remarkable works from Antiquity for its expressiveness, are exhibited an Ideal Head formerly identified as a portrait of Berenice, and the majestic statue of Athena Promachos (1C BC).

Small Bronzes, Paintings and Minor Arts★★. — *1st floor, on the left.* Works of art from Pompeii and Herculaneum. Note in **Room XC**, a small equestrian statue of Alexander the Great and statues of Apollo and Diana which adorned the Temple of Apollo at Pompeii. **Room XCI** contains a rich collection of small bronzes: graceful shrine statuette (Case II) representing Fortune Enthroned. The objects (vases, plates, lamps, furniture ornaments) on show in **Rooms XCII to XCIV** reveal a keen penchant for ornamentation. Note in Room XCIV, a brazier stand (centre) and heating equipment (by the window).

The exhibits in **Room XCV** (musical, measuring and surgical instruments) conjure up a moving picture of everyday life in the two dead cities. Among the murals in **Room XCVI** is a still life of a fruit bowl where the artist has beautifully rendered the transparent glass. The **Silver Room** (LXXXII) contains sets of vases, bowls and plates which belonged to the patrician families. The set found at Casa del Menandro *(p 189)*, consisting of 115 pieces is decorated with mythological scenes, and the bucket from Herculaneum depicts the Bath of Aphrodite.

■ CARTHUSIAN MONASTERY OF ST. MARTIN★★ (Certosa di San Martino)

Open 9 am to 2 pm (1 pm Sundays, holidays and 19 September, 8 and 26 December). Closed Mondays and holidays; 750 lire. This immense Carthusian monastery is beautifully situated on a spur of the Vomero hill. The **Castel Sant'Elmo (BX)**, a massive structure with bastions overlooks the monastery; it was rebuilt by the Spaniards in the 16C and was for a long time used as a prison.

The monastery was founded by the Anjou dynasty and was almost completely remodelled in the 16 and 17C. There is a museum (installed in 1866) which includes historical and artistic collections. The monumental section can also be visited.

Cross the courtyard and go through the Procurators' Court to reach the museum.

Historical Collections. — The **naval section** is housed in two rooms to the right at the entrance. The rooms devoted to **"Souvenirs of the Kingdom of Naples"** relate the history of the town from the reign of the Bourbons (1734-1860) with two interruptions (the Parthenopean Republic and the reigns of Joseph Bonaparte and Murat). Room 13 deals with the revolution that broke out in 1799 after the French General Championnet had taken Naples. Room 14 houses the Ruffo donation — the Ruffo family supported Ferdinand IV in his attempt to reconquer the kingdom — which includes the portraits of D.L. Ruffo by Vicenzo and of Princess of Sant'Antimo by Hayez. In Room 15 you will see a superb bust of Murat by Castex and a good portrait of him by the French painter François Gérard, Collar of the Order of the Two Sicilies created by Murat. The reform initiated in 1848 by the liberal intellectual elite is reviewed in Room 22. The Risorgimento and Garibaldi's arrival in Naples are dealt with in Room 23.

Room 25 is arranged as a **belvedere** famous for its outstanding **view★★★** over the Bay of Naples.

The **map section** *(parallel to the preceding rooms)* is in Rooms 27 to 30. It includes views of Naples by A. Joli (18C) and Monsu Desiderio (17C) and maps by Antonio Lafrery (1566).

The **section devoted to festivals and costumes** (Rooms 32 to 38) contains an exceptional collection of figurines and **cribs★★**, the famous *presepi* which were a speciality of Naples and Sicily in the 17 and 18C. The exuberance of the Baroque style manifests itself vividly in these scenes with innumerable figures which gave rise to a craft involving wood carvers, potters, costumiers and goldsmiths. The most famous is a large crib by Cuciniello. A Sicilian crib in coral and gilded copper, and another set in an egg shell are also noteworthy.

Art Collections. — Rooms 42 to 77. Paintings and sculptures.

Monumental Section. — This section is a curious example of the Neapolitan Baroque style. The **great cloisters**, all white, and their cemetery show the genius of the architect and decorator, Fanzago. The **church★**, lavishly Baroque, is adorned with a profusion of multicoloured marbles, stuccos, statues and paintings. Note a fine Deposition by Stanzione above the doorway. The **monks' chancel★★** is most remarkable with its superb marble communion table decorated with hard stone, its fine paving, a painting of the Nativity by G. Reni and another of Christ washing the Disciples' Feet by G. Battista Caracciolo. The **sacristy** on the left is adorned with inlaying. The treasury contains a Deposition (at the high altar), a fine triangular composition by Ribera, and a Triumph of Judith (ceiling), the last work of Luca Giordano.

Return to the monks' chancel. The novices' chancel, on the right, contains remarkable 15C stalls. A passage (to the right and then left) leads to elegant small cloisters on to which opens the refectory which has kept its elaborately carved 18C furniture.

■ CAPODIMONTE PALACE AND NATIONAL GALLERIES★★ (BV M¹)

Open 9 am to 2 pm (1 pm Sundays and holidays, 19 September, 8 and 26 December). Closed Mondays, 1 January, 25 April, 1 May, first Sunday in June, 15 August, 25 December; 750 lire. This former **royal estate★**, includes a palace, a landscape garden, a hamlet, Casino della Regina, and the remains of a porcelain factory which was famous in the 18C. The palace, built between 1738 and 1838, is a massive and severe structure.

Picture Gallery★★. — *2nd floor.* The works are displayed in groups illustrating the various artistic movements and influences. At the entrance are Brussels tapestries (1531) after Van Orley, depicting the Battle of Pavia, where the troops of Charles V defeated those of Francois I.

Among the Primitives, the masterpiece (1317) of Simone Martini, **St. Louis of Toulouse**, depicted in the Byzantine style in a hieratic pose against a gilded background, illustrates the Sienese School (Room 4). In Room 5, Florence is represented by a Madonna by Bernardo Daddi (14C), a pupil of Giotto, and by a Miracle of the Snow and a Madonna from the delicate brush of Masolino, the teacher of Masaccio, whose admirable **Crucifixion** remarkable for its deep colours, hangs in Room 6.

In Room 8, devoted to 15C Neapolitan painters, note a picture of a lion being cared for by St. Jerome, executed in the detailed Flemish style by Colantonio. Room 10 contains works of the 16C and of the Mannerist movement *(p 30)*. Giulio Romano, one of the early exponents of this trend is represented by a Holy Family with fine light effects to emphasise perspective.

The elegant Portrait of a Youth by Rosso Fiorentino (Room 12) illustrates the fashion for elongated figures, a feature of mannerism. The 16C Lombard school (Room 14) includes a gentle Madonna by Bernardino Luini whose inner joy is reminiscent of the style of Leonardo da Vinci. Correggio holds a preeminent position among the 16C Emilian Mannerists with his clear colours, the expressive highlighting of his characters and the fluid movement that heralds Baroque art. His Marriage of St. Catherine and delightful **Zingarella** (Gipsy Woman) — Room 14 — are tender and delicate works. The rather stange portraits of his pupil, Il Parmigianino, which include that of **Antea** (Room 15) in sumptuous dress, are more sophisticated and cold.

The 15 and 16C Venetian school (Room 17) is exemplified by the works of the Vivarinis and portraits by Mantegna and L. Lotto, and a **Transfiguration** by Giovanni Bellini whose subtle combination of balanced landscape, harmony of colours and vivid light enhances the religious theme. Christ is depicted with light radiating from his robe against a wonderful landscape which is a masterpiece of colouring in brown, golden brown and greenish blue. There are fine paintings by El Greco on Room 18. The **Titian** room (19) is dominated by the admirable family portrait of Pope Paul III (Alessandro Farnese) with his nephews which is wonderfully expressive. The portrait of Danae shows superb colour effects.

Among the foreign Primitives (Room 20), note the Saxon, Cranach (1472-1553), who painted Jesus and the Woman taken in Adultery, a realistic but pessimistic composition verging on caricature; Breughel the Elder, painter of a Misanthropist and the celebrated **Parable of the Blind** (1568); Joos Van Cleve, Konrad Witz and Van Oostzaanen of Amsterdam (1470-1553).

In reaction against Mannerism, the Carracci (Room 25) with their Bologna Academy (late 16C), opened the way to Baroque art. Their successors include Guido Reni, whose elegant composition in oblique style of Atalanta and Hippomenus hangs in Room 27.

Caravaggio was a decisive influence in the development of painting in the 17C. There is a dramatic Ascent to Calvary in Room 11 and a remarkable **Flagellation** in Room 29. He inspired a southern school through his pupil Caracciolo and later, by his presence in Naples. His sombre realism, violence and use of strong, contrasting light are opposed to Mannerism and have influenced artists from other regions of Italy and foreign painters (Rooms 30-36) besides those of the Neapolitan school (Andrea Vaccaro, Ribera, Artemisia Gentileschi, Stanzione...). The Neapolitan Bernardo Cavallino (Room 35) inspired by his use of light (Judith), achieves original colour effects and an intimate atmosphere in his paintings (St. Cecilia, the Primadonna). The influence of Caravaggio's naturalism is also evident in the sumptuous 17C still lifes (Room 39) of the Neapolitan school (Porpora, Ruoppolo, Recco). The famous banquet scenes (Convito d'Assalonne and Convito di Baldassarre) by Mattia Preti (Room 40) show besides the dramatic treatment favoured by Caravaggio, a Venetian influence in the composition.

Luca Giordano (Room 41) illustrates brilliantly the Neapolitan Baroque movement. In Room 42bis are displayed Battle Scenes by Salvator Rosa and delightful genre paintings by Traversi (18C) marking the last stage of Neapolitan Baroque art.

Royal Apartments. — *1st floor.* The royal apartments contain fine furniture. Beyond the ballroom are displayed the De Ciccio collection of fine porcelain and portraits by E. Vigée-Lebrun and Gérard (Room 80). The **porcelain museum** is housed in Rooms 67 to 71. Retrace your steps and past the ballroom you will see small Renaissance bronzes (Room 87) including Pollaiolo's David. The Chinese style **porcelain room★** executed in the 18C at Capodimonte for the Porticri Palace, has been reassembled in Room 94. Note in Room 92 a polyptych of the Passion in alabaster (15C English art) and a 16C French enamelled Crucifixion. You can also visit the **Arms Rooms** (Bourbon and Farnese collections) and the **gallery devoted to the 19C** (Ottocento).

■ SPACCA-NAPOLI QUARTER★★ (Quartiere di Spacca-Napoli) *time : 2 1/2 hours*

To avoid possible incidents, tourists are advised to dress simply and not to draw attention to themselves in any way. The visit should be made by day; follow on foot the itinerary outlined in black on the map (p 156-157).

This is the heart of old Naples. With its numerous churches, small crafts and businesses, its ancient streets where swarms a lively but secretive populace, it is undoubtedly the most engaging part of the town. Its main axis, formed by the Via Benedetto Croce, San Biagio ai Librai and Vicaria Vecchia beyond the Via del Duomo, follows the course of the Roman Decumanus Maximus.

Church of St. Anne of the Lombards (Sant'Anna dei Lombardi — DYZ R). — A Renaissance building rich in contemporary Florentine **sculptures★**. In the first chapel on the left, the altar surmounted by a crib adorned with carvings, and the tomb of Marie of Aragon are works by Antonio Rossellino (1427-1470); in the first chapel on the right, a delicate Annunciation carved by Benedetto da Maiano adorns the altar; in the chapel to the right of the chancel (at the far end), there is a late 15C terracotta *Pietà*, work of rather dramatic realism, by Guido Mazzoni who introduced this style of sculpture in Naples which became very popular in the 16C. The former sacristy (passage behind the chancel, on the right) contains fine marquetry by Fra Giovanni da Verona (1457-1525) and his assistants.

The 16C **Gravina Palace** (DY) has an embossed façade and is extensively restored.

Church of Gesù Nuovo (DY E). — Its curious façade with nail-headed embossing (late 15C) overlooks a square with a quaint Baroque *guglia* (fountain) in the middle (1751). The church (1601), on the plan of a Greek Cross, with a dome, and a spacious interior decorated with frescoes and marbles, has features in the Jesuit style *(p 30)*.

St. Clara's Church★ (Santa Chiara). — Sancia of Majorca, the wife of Robert of Anjou, had this Church of the Poor Clares built in the Provençal Gothic style, that is, with a flat chevet and a single nave supported by massive buttresses. The detached campanile was finished in the 16C.

The interior is sober and slenderly built. In the chancel are several memorials to the Anjou dynasty. In 1345 Florentine sculptors created the **tomb★★** of King Robert the Wise (behind the high altar). The prince is represented recumbent, watched over by the Sciences and the Arts, and enthroned, with a background of lilies. Pillars bearing six statues of the Virtues support the sarcophagus with sculptures depicting the king, surrounded by his intimates. The tomb of Marie de Valois (near the wall on the right) is the work of Tino di Camaino and his pupils.

Pass along the church to reach the **cloisters★** *(open 8 am to 1 pm and 4 to 7 pm)* where, in the 18C, the close was transformed by Vaccaro into a strange garden: the pillars supporting arbor roofs that shade the walks and benches are faced with coloured Capodimonte faïence depicting landscapes, fruit and rustic scenes, etc. An amusing 17C crib with innumerable figurines occupies a whole wall of a room which opens off the convent entrance hall.

At No. 12 Via B. Croce stands the Filomarino Palace where the philosopher Benedetto Croce lived.

Church of St. Dominic Major (San Domenico Maggiore) (DY L). — Its apse gives on to a square ornamented with a Baroque *guglia* (fountain). The church dates from the 14C and has been remodelled. The interior is of imposing dimensions with Gothic and Baroque features, and it possesses an extremely Baroque high altar. At the entrance to the first chapel on the north side of the chancel, a huge paschal candelabrum (1585) is supported on early 14C **caryatids★** representing the Virtues by Tino di Camaino. Pass through the south aisle to the sacristy to see the panelling; in the gallery above are forty-five coffins containing the remains of members of the dynasty and court of Aragon.

The famous Piazzetta Nilo is adorned with a statue of the river Nile from which it derives its name. Follow the Via Biagio ai Librai which is lined with palaces; the monumental doorways lead to courts which sometimes retain traces of their past splendour.

Take the picturesque Via San Gregorio on the left.

Church of St. Lawrence Major (San Lorenzo Maggiore) (EY K). — The spacious and bright church, on the plan of a Latin cross, has a fine Gothic nave (early 14C) lined with chapels. After renovation, the interior has regained its original bare appearance except for the reverse of the façade which has kept its Baroque additions. An elegant **arch★** spans the transept crossing. The late 13C **polygonal apse★** by Thibaud de Saumur is an interesting specimen of French architecture in Southern Italy; its ambulatory (a rare feature in the region) leads to the chancel through elegant arches crowned by twin bays.

The Via Tribunali on the left leads to the Alba Gate (17C) which opens on to Piazza Dante. The semicircle of buildings was designed by Vanvitelli (1765).

■ ADDITIONAL SIGHTS

Villa Floridiana★ (BX). — *Same visiting times as the Carthusian Monastery of St. Martin; 750 lire.* The villa stands on the bank of the Vomero in a pleasant setting. A graceful white *palazzina* (small palace) in the Neo-Classical style houses the **Duca di Martina Museum★** (M²), which contains enamels, ivories and especially china and porcelain (1st floor). Its fine gardens afford a splendid **panorama★★** of the Bay of Naples from the terrace.

Catacombs of St. Januarius★ (San Gennaro) (BV N). — *Guided tours on Saturdays, Sundays and holidays: 9.30, 10.15, 11, 11.45 am; closed 1 May; 500 lire: apply in advance to Prof. Nicolo Ciavolino, Parish of Santa Maria del Principio, Torre del Greco, ☎ 8812132.* St. Agrippin was buried here in the 13C. The catacombs have been associated with the name of St. Januarius since the 5C when Bishop John I had the remains of the martyred saint transferred there. They extend over two floors and they consist of vast galleries bordered by *loculi* (niches hewn out of the rock, serving as tombs) and with *arcosoli* (arches surmounting the *loculi,* often covered with paintings). They contain interesting 2-9C frescoes and admirable mosaics.

On the upper floor, notice the 5C portrait of St. Januarius, the mosaic portraiture of bishops of Naples and the early 3C paintings, in which one can distinguish Adam and Eve, David and Goliath, and the Allegory of the Tower; three maidens (the Virtues) building a tower (the Church). On the lower floor, the paintings are mainly decorative and symbolic. Notice the delicacy of the motifs (2C) of the arches of the large vestibule. In the middle of the room is the 8C baptismal basin. The visit is completed by a small basilica, where there is an altar, with an opening through which the faithful could touch the relics and bishop's seat hewn out of the bedrock.

Church of Santa Maria di Donnaregina★ (EY B). — *Closed provisionally.* A Baroque church precedes the 14C Gothic building. Inside the Gothic church is the **tomb**★ of Mary of Hungary, widow of Charles II of Anjou. This remarkable work is by a Sienese, Tino di Camaino, who showed the queen both recumbent and kneeling before the Madonna. The sons of Queen Mary, King Robert and St. Louis, are represented standing round the sarcophagus.

The Gothic church: open 9 am to 2 pm; closed Sundays and holidays. The walls of the nuns' chancel are covered with **frescoes**★★ by Pietro Cavallini (14C). Those which represent the Passion, the Apostles and the Prophets are particularly successful.

St. John's Church★ (San Giovanni a Carbonara) (BV F). — *Open Sundays: 11 am to 1 pm.* The church was founded in the 14C and remodelled in the 15C. An 18C stairway leads to an elegant Gothic doorway flanked by statues of saints. Inside, note the imposing monument to Ladislas of Anjou, King of Naples from 1386 to 1414. The circular Caracciolo del Sole Chapel has fine 15C faïence paving and frescoes. The Caracciolo di Vico Chapel is adorned with 16C statues of the Spanish school.

Cathedral (EY C). — Built in 14C Gothic, the cathedral was much altered later. The 19C façade still has its 15C doorways.

The interior has three aisles, remodelled in the 17 and 18C. A new tomb of Charles I of Anjou was erected over the central doorway in 1559 to take the place of the original tomb, which had been destroyed.

In the south aisle the **Chapel of St. Januarius**★ *(open 8 am to noon),* in a rich 17C Baroque style, is preceded by a remarkable 17C bronze grille designed by Fanzago. On the end wall, a reliquary placed below the statue of St. Januarius holds a flask containing the Saint's blood *(p. 153).* Note the altarfront in chased silver which depicts the Translation of the Relics of St. Januarius. The dome is decorated with the host of the blessed painted by Lanfranco with an admirable sense of movement.

The Minutolo Chapel (to the right of the chancel) has kept its original Gothic architecture and its 14C frescoes. Under the chancel is the "confessional" of St. Januarius (Sepolcro di San Gennaro), an elegant Renaissance structure (1508). The Chapel of St. Lawrence (San Lorenzo), to the left of the chancel *(apply to the caretaker)* is adorned with a 14C fresco representing the Tree of Jesse. In the north transept is the tomb of Pope Innocent IV (16C). The tomb of Andrew of Hungary (1345), who was strangled on the orders of his wife, Jeanne I, stands near the entrance to the Basilica of St. Restituta.

A door in the middle of the north aisle gives access to the 4C **Basilica of St. Restituta**, which was altered in the Gothic period and again in the 17C. It contains a 14C mosaic showing the Madonna between St. Januarius and St. Restituta (6th chapel on the left). The 5C baptistry at the end of the south aisle contains mosaics.

Cuomo Palace★ (Palazzo Cuomo) (EY Q). — *Open 9.30 am to 2 pm (Sundays and holidays 1 June to 30 September 9.30 am to 1 pm); closed Mondays; 750 lire.* This majestic late 15C palace, with its embossed stonework, is a reminder of the Florentine Renaissance. It contains the **Filangieri Museum**. There are collections of arms and armour from Europe in the Middle Ages, and from the Orient (samurai armours); ceramics and porcelain (Abruzzi, Naples, Meissen, Vienna, Zurich, Sevres, China, Japan); coins and antique furniture. The first floor is of special interest with paintings by Ribera (St. Mary the Egyptian, Head of St. John the Baptist), by Battistello Caracciolo *(Ecce Homo),* Mattia Preti, Lanino, and the Head of a Youth in glazed terracotta by Giovanni della Robbia.

Capuan Gate★ (Porta Capuana) (EFY D). — This is one of the fortified gateways in the Aragonese walls built in 1484 to the plans of Benedetto da Maiano. It is flanked by two massive towers which contrast with the fine Renaissance decoration of the arch made of white marble.

The **Capuan Castle** (Castel Capuano) (EY S) nearby *(entrance opposite Via Tribunali),* the seat of the courts, is the former residence of the Norman princes and the Hohenstaufens. It was converted into a court-house by the Spanish Viceroy, Don Pedro of Toledo, in 1540.

EXCURSIONS

Follow the itinerary indicated on the map on p 154-155

Posillipo★★ (AX). — *Southwest, 15 km - 9 miles.* The name of this famous hill which forms a promontory and separates the Bay of Naples from Pozzuoli Bay, is derived from a Greek word meaning "that soothes pain". Posillipo, dotted with villas set in lovely gardens and splendid buildings, and offering superb views of the bay, is Naples' main residential area. It is reached by the road along the seashore and the *corniche* passing through Mergellina before it climbs to become Via Posillipo, begun by order of Murat, King of Naples, and completed in 1830. About 300 m — 328 yds past Piazza Salvatore di Giacomo, a square planted with trees, bear sharp left into the winding Via Ferdinando Russo which drops steeply to **Cape Posillipo**; there is a good **view**★ of the bay from the fishermen's hamlet.

Climb back to the Via Posillipo and follow it for 1 km - 3/4 mile; at a road fork beside a petrol station next to a small tree planted square, turn left into the winding Via Salvatore di Giacomo then right at a junction. The road ends at **Marechiaro**★, a small fishermen's village built high above the sea. The wall of an old house facing the sea has inscribed upon it the first line of the Neapolitan song *Marechiare*, marking the window made famous by Salvatore di Giacomo.

Return to the Via Posillipo and turn left into a wide avenue lined with pine trees which ends at the **Garden of Remembrance** (Parco della Rimembranza or Parco Virgiliano) at the top of the hill *(leave the car at the entrance beyond the columns, and go round the promontory by the right on foot).* The **views**★★ are splendid: on one side across Pozzuoli Bay (the view is marred by the Bagnoli factories in the foreground) to Miseno; down below the isle of Nisida, once a volcanic crater and now linked to the coast by a dyke; the islands of Procida and Ischia; and on the other side over the Bay of Naples, the Sorrento Peninsula and Capri. Leave the park by the wide, straight path leading to the gate and turn left into the main road (Via A. Manzoni). At a road fork bear right into Via F. Petrarca, a long and elegant avenue built on the hillside and lined with fine buildings on the left hand side. It slopes down gently towards Naples and affords **views**★ of the bay to the right.

If in doubt where to find a place name or historic reference
look in the index at the end of the guide.

The idyllic Bay of Naples has a well deserved reputation. Its beauty is marred by industrial areas but its islands, capes, creeks and mountains offer unforgettable excursions.

■ THE ISLANDS★★★

These are Capri *(p 73)*, Ischia *(p 124)* and Procida *(p 193)*, to which may be added the Ponza Archipelago *(p 48)*, off Gaeta.

■ VESUVIUS★★★ (Il Vesuvio)

Vesuvius is one of the few still active volcanoes in Europe. Its outline, inseparable from the Neapolitan landscape, has, in fact, twin summits: on the left, Mount Somma (alt 1 132 m - 3 713 ft); on the right Mount Vesuvius proper (alt. 1 277 m - 4 189 ft).

With the slow disintegration brought about by time, the volcanic matter has turned into fertile soil. On the lower slopes and at the foot of the crater, to the east in particular, grow orchards and vines that produce the famous *Lacryma Christi* wine.

The Phases of an Eruption. — A volcano is a chimney communicating with rock in a state of fusion in the depths of the earth's crust. When it is not in eruption, the volcano emits only gases, which form a plume of smoke. When it is quiescent only light vapours escape from the crater.

A volcanic eruption begins with underground rumblings and tremblings of the earth. These are followed by explosions and projections of solid, liquid and gaseous matter. Sometimes half-molten lava blocks the vent of the volcano. The gases then force their way through it in a series of explosions, throwing up "bombs" and clouds of steam or ashes. The solid matter accumulates round the crater, forming a cone of debris.

The Eruptions of Vesuvius. — Until the earthquake of AD 62 and the eruption of AD 79 which buried Herculaneum and Pompeii, Vesuvius seemed extinct; its slopes were clothed with famous vines and woods. By 1139, seven eruptions had been recorded. Then came a period of calm during which the slopes of the mountain were cultivated. On 16 December 1631 Vesuvius had a terrible awakening, destroying all the settlements at its foot. The eruption of 1794 devastated Torre del Greco. The volcano had minor eruptions in 1871, 1900, 1903 and 1904, and a major eruption in 1906. An eruption in 1929 and another in 1944 altered the shape of the crater. Since then Vesuvius has emitted only a plume of smoke but scientists expect a revival of activity.

ASCENT★★★ *see adjoining plan*

From Naples, take Motorway A3 to the foot of Vesuvius (Exit ⑥ on the plan p 156).

This excursion can be combined with a tour of the east slope (see p 164).

You can make the ascent of the volcano either by the west slope *(motorway exit: Ercolano)* or by the south slope *(exit: Torre Annunziata)*. The tour is interesting both for the desolate landscape and for the remarkable views which unfold as you climb.

West Slope. — *46 km - 29 miles — Rtn, 20 minutes by chair lift Rtn or 3/4 hour on foot Rtn. Round tour: 2-2 1/2 hours. This is the easiest route.* On this slope, where was sited a former Camaldulian monastery, famous in the times when the ascent was made on foot or by donkey, the winding road is good. The lava has made enormous blisters in several places along the road and further up, the slope is sparsely covered with

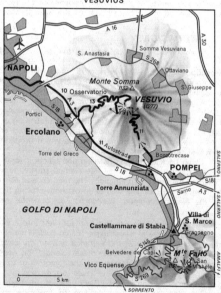

VESUVIUS

scrub and broom. Beyond the **Vesuvius Observatory** (Osservatorio) perched high up on the right, the scenery has been dramatically transformed by the 1944 eruption .

Farther on, at a junction, there are two options open for the last stage of the ascent:

By chair lift. — The road to the right leads to the lower station of a chair lift *(parking: 300 lire)* which climbs to the edge of the crater *(service: 10 am to 5.30 pm 1 April to 30 September; 10 am to 4 pm October; 10.30 am to 3 pm 1 December to 31 March; service not in operation in November; 1 500 lire, guide included for visit of the crater).*

The **panorama**★★★ is immense — Naples, the Bays of Naples and Gaeta, the Islands and the Sorrento Peninsula. The **crater**★★★ *(tour: 20 minutes)* affords an unforgettable sight with its vast size and the desolate spectacle of its walls and the spouting steam jets.

On foot. — The road on the left leads to a car park *(300 lire)*. A narrow path, easy but impressive, climbs the bare slope of the volcano through a leaden scenery of ash and lapilli *(3/4 hour Rtn; wear walking shoes; toll: 450 to 850 lire)*. The path ends near the upper station of the chair lift *(see above, guide compulsory: payment)*.

South Slope. — *64 km - 40 miles — Rtn, 3/4 hour on foot Rtn. Round tour: about 3 hours.*
From Torre Annunziata, make for Boscotrecase. A toll road *(to be taken only in dry weather; 500 lire per person; a guide can be engaged at the tollgate, price to be fixed)* leads to Vesuvius. The road which is only partly surfaced, leads through a fine pinewood and after 3 km - 2 miles — affords a **view**★ of the Sarno plain and of the coast. The last section which is simply a track in the ash and lapilli from the latest eruption (1944), is rough and narrow, very steep and winding. The final part of the car trip is through apocalyptic scenery. The last part of the ascent is made on foot *(40 minutes Rtn, wear walking shoes)*, by a narrow path up the bare slope to the edge of the crater *(see above; at the summit a guide is compulsory: 400 - 600 lire per person)*.
On the way down, you can stop at the tollgate where objects made from the lava from Vesuvius are on show.

■ **POMPEII**★★★ — *Description p 186.*

■ **HERCULANEUM**★★ (Ercolano) — *Description p 122.*

■ **PHLEGREAN FIELDS** ★★ (Campi Flegrei)
75 km - 46 miles — about 1/2 day — see plan p 155, then local map p 164.

This volcanic area, which received its name from the Ancients ("phlegrean" is derived from a Greek word meaning "to blaze"), extends in an arc along the Gulf of Pozzuoli, from Cape Posillipo to Cape Miseno. Hot springs, steam-jets and sulphurous gases rise from the ground and from the sea; lakes have formed in the craters of extinct volcanoes and changes in the ground level are frequent due to its volcanic nature. Generally, the raising of the ground level occurs when the volcano is most active.
With the four centres represented by Cumae, the seat of Greek culture in Italy, the great trading port of Pozzuoli, the naval base of Miseno, and the luxurious thermal spa of Baia (the Romans used the natural hot springs and vapours of the region to establish cleverly designed thermal spas), the coastline to the west of Naples has a rich history.
This landscape inspired Homer and Virgil, who based on it the myths of the Oracle (the Sibyl of Cumae) and the Kingdom of the Infernal Regions *(Odyssey, AEneid)*.
Leave Naples by the Quattro Giornate Tunnel. Continue to Piazzale Tecchio and pass on the left along the Mostra d'Oltremare buildings, the venue for trade events. Then taking Exit ⑧ on the plan, follow Road S 7 Quater, "Via Domiziana" (Direction Pozzuoli). About 300 m - 328 yds — past the Church of San Gennaro, a short passage leads to Solfatara.

Solfatara★★. — *Open 9 am to sunset; 500 lire. Free parking inside. It is advisable to hire a guide (fee to be fixed beforehand).*
This crater is still active, and all the phenomena produced by a volcano which may erupt at any time can be observed; jets of steam charged with sulphurous fumes, miniature volcanoes spitting hot mud, and bubbling jets of sand caused in effect by the escaping gases and fumes. The soil resounds hollowly and is hot to touch. At a depth of 10 m - 33 ft — temperatures of about 110 °C - 230 °F — have been recorded, and of 162 °C - 324 °F — at Bocca Grande (behind a small kiosk).

Pozzuoli★. — *Description p 192.*

Lake Avernus★ (Lago d'Averno). — *Best seen at sunset*. This lake within a crater is sad, still and silent and wrapped in an atmosphere of mystery which was all the more intense in Antiquity as birds flying overhead were hit by the fumes and dropped into the lake to be swallowed up. The Ancients regarded it as the entrance to the Underworld.
Under the Roman Empire, Agrippa, a captain in the service of the Emperor Augustus, developed it as a naval base. The port linked by a canal with Lake Lucrino *(see below)* which in turn opened on to the sea, was practically unassailable. An underground gallery *(not open)* 1 km - 1/2 mile — long, known as **Cocceio's cave** (Grotta di Cocceio) (it derives its name from that of the architect Coceius who built it), connected Avernus with Cumae, thus providing further access to the sea. This tunnel was used to store munitions during the last war and was seriously damaged. The opening on the port was through a grandiose colonnaded vestibule which can be seen from the end of the road that follows the left bank of the Avernus.

Lake Lucrino (Lago Lucrino). — In Antiquity, oyster farming was practised there. It was also a resort famous for its elegant villas and gracious living. One of the villas was owned by Cicero and another was the scene of Agrippina's murder on the orders of her son Nero.

Baia★. — The port of Baia, a rich Greek colony, took its name from Baios, the companion of Ulysses, who died and was buried here. At the time of the Roman Empire this was a fashionable bathing-beach as well as a thermal spa with the most complete equipment in the world for hydrotherapy. The Roman emperors and patricians had immense villas, all of which disappeared under the sea after a change in ground level.
The famous **baths**★★ can be visited. *Open 9 am to 1 hour before sunset; closed Mondays (Tuesday when Monday is a holiday), and holidays; 500 lire; entrance off the Cumae road.*
Standing on the hill, facing the sea, you will distinguish, from south to north, the Springs of Mercury, the Baths of Sosandra and the Springs of Venus.
Outside Baia, the road is overlooked by an imposing castle built by a Spanish Viceroy in the middle of the 16C and later extensively remodelled.

Bacoli. — On the high ground in the old town, you can visit the **Cento Camerelle**★ (d) *(leave your car near the church, keeper at No. 161 Via Cento Camerelle, fee)*. This huge reservoir, which belonged to a private villa, is built on two levels: the grandiose upper level built in the 1C has four galleries and immense arches. The lower part, built much earlier, has a network of low and narrow galleries that emerge high up above sea level.

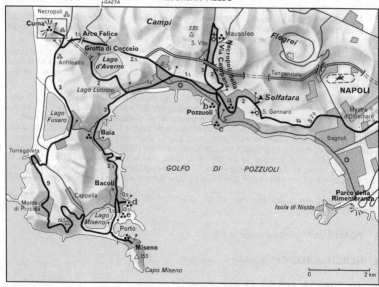

East of the road to Miseno is the famous **Piscina mirabile★ (e)** (magic pool — *keeper at No 9, Via Carannante)*, a cistern designed to supply water to the Roman fleet in the port of Miseno. It is 70 m long, 25 m wide and nearly 15 m high — 75 × 28 × 50 ft — and is divided into five sections whose roofs are supported by forty-eight pillars: remarkable light effects.

Miseno. — The name is that of a lake, a port, a promontory, a cape and a village.

Lake Miseno, a former volcanic crater, was believed by the Ancients to be the Styx, across which Charon ferried the souls of the dead. Under the Emperor Augustus it was linked by a canal with the port of Miseno, which was used as a base by the Roman fleet. The village of Miseno (remains of a Roman theatre) is dominated by Monte Miseno, on which Misenus, the companion of AEneas, is said to have been buried. The slopes of the promontory were studded with luxurious villas, including the one where the Emperor Tiberius choked to death.

The winding road which leads to Lake Fusaro via Monte di Procida, affords fine **views★**, looking back over Cape Miseno, Pozzuoli Bay and the Phlegrean Fields, and as the road descends towards Torregaveta, over Procida and Ischia and finally Lake Fusaro.

Lake Fusaro (Lago Fusaro). — A lagoon containing a small island on which Vanvitelli, in 1782, built a hunting lodge for king Ferdinand IV of Bourbon.

Cumae★. — *Description p 91.*

After passing under the Arco Felice *(description p 91)* the road returns to Naples.

NARNI Umbria

Michelin map 📖 26 — 15 km - 9 miles — southwest of Terni — Pop 20 736

The little mediaeval town of Narni, dominated by its castle, occupies a lofty **site★** on a ridge overlooking the Valley of the Nera River. Enter through a 15C fortified gateway.

Piazza dei Priori★. — The Via Garibaldi opens into this narrow, elongated square. The 14C Priors' Loggia dominated by a tall tower, has a majestic portico and a doorway flanked by a small outdoor pulpit. The 13-16C Governor's Palace is ornamented with Romanesque bas-reliefs. The 14C fountain was inspired by the Great Fountain at Perugia.

Cathedral (Duomo). — The cathedral façade is preceded by a Renaissance portico. The interior, of the basilical type, has Romanesque columns and interesting furnishings (south aisle).

Ponte Augusto. — Below Narni, on the road to Todi, a Roman bridge named after Augustus, used to span the foaming waters of the Nera. The picturesque and massive arches, which are still standing, were painted by Corot in one of his best compositions.

NOVARA Piedmont

Michelin maps 📖 2 3 and 📖 17 — Pop 102 132
Town plan in the Michelin Red Guide Italia (hotels and restaurants).

Novara, lying in a rice and cattle region, is a grim town. It is also an industrial centre. Of Roman origin, it was an important strategic point during the Italian campaigns. The most interesting buildings are the 16-17C church of St. Gaudentius (San Gaudenzio), surmounted by a tall 19C dome, the restored 15C Broletto and the governor's palace, now a Modern Art Gallery.

ORVIETO ★★ Umbria

Michelin map 📖 25 — Pop 23 529

Orvieto was of Etruscan origin and later became a papal stronghold. It makes an interesting halt with its buildings, its old town atmosphere, its narrow and winding streets and finally its remarkable **site★★★** on the top of a pedestal of volcanic rock.

The tourist will enjoy its cool, fragrant white wine, the amateur of ceramics can linger in the pottery market held every Saturday in the Piazza del Popolo. In the Corso Cavour the square Moor's Tower (Torre del Moro) (D) stands 42 m - 140 ft — high.

Religious Festivals. — On Whit Sunday the Feast of the Dove is celebrated on the cathedral parvis to commemorate the descent of the Holy Spirit on the Apostles. The procession to the reliquary of the Holy Corporal takes place at the feast of Corpus Christi.

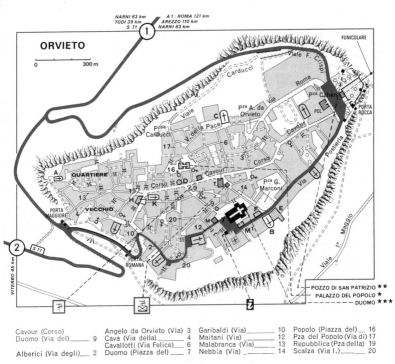

ORVIETO

NARNI 63 km
TODI 39 km
S 71
A 1 : ROMA 121 km
AREZZO 110 km
NARNI 63 km

0   300 m

FUNICOLARE

Viale F. C. Crispi

Carducci
Viale
Roma
Via
Pza Cahen

PORTA ROCCA

P.le
Carducci
Pza A. da
Orvieto
V. della Pace
POL

PORTA MAGGIORE
QUARTIERE
VECCHIO
Corso
Corso Cavour
Corso
Pza G. Marconi
Via
Postierla

PORTA ROMANA

VITERBO 45 km

S 71

Viale 1º Maggio

POZZO DI SAN PATRIZIO ★★
PALAZZO DEL POPOLO ★
DUOMO ★★★

Cavour (Corso)		Angelo da Orvieto (Via) 3	Garibaldi (Via) 10	Popolo (Piazza del) 16	
Duomo (Via del) 9	Cava (Via della) 4		Maitani (Via) 12	Pza del Popolo (Via di) 17	
	Cavallotti (Via Felice) 6		Malabranca (Via) 13	Repubblica (Pza della) 19	
Alberici (Via degli) 2	Duomo (Piazza del) 7		Nebbia (Via) 14	Scalza (Via l.) 20	

■ MAIN SIGHTS *time : 3 hours*

In the heart of the town the quiet Piazza del Duomo, of majestic proportions, contains several interesting buildings. Apart from the cathedral, you will notice on the left a small tower surmounted by a 14C jaquemart (bell-ringing figure) overlooking little houses with flower decked balconies and, on the right, the Palace of the Popes.

Cathedral★★★ (Duomo). — This perfect example of the transitional Romanesque-Gothic style was begun in 1290 to shelter the relics of the Miracle of Bolsena *(p 65)*. It was modified and completed in the 14C. Thirty-three architects, 152 sculptors, 68 painters and 90 mosaicists took part in the building of this imposing masterpiece.

Exterior. — The wonderful **façade★★★** is the boldest and richest in colour among Italian Gothic buildings. The vertical lines are accentuated by the slimness of the gables and especially by the soaring buttresses, which are made up of small panels of coloured marble, elongated in shape and further prolonged by pinnacles. The sumptuous decorative effect is obtained by the use of multicoloured mosaics and marbles and delicate sculpture, inspired by French ivories. This façade, which may be seen in all its glory at sunset, was designed by the Sienese, Lorenzo Maitani (1310-1330) and continued to his plans by Andrea Pisano, Orcagna and Sanmicheli. It was completed only in 1600.

Maitani and his assistants were the authors of the famous **bas-reliefs★★** adorning the pillars. Viewed from left to right and from bottom to top, they depict scenes from the Old Testament (to the left of the central doorway) and the New Testament (to the right). On the second pillar to the right of the doorway is a Last Judgment. Above the pillars are the Symbols of the Evangelists in bronze, also by Maitani. A statue of the Virgin and Child adorns the tympanum of the central doorway. Orcagna was the designer of the rose window fitted into a square frame further adorned with niches containing the Apostles (above) and the Prophets (left and right). Nearly all the mosaics were remade in the 17 and 18C.

The side walls of the building have black and white stone bases (basalt and travertin). On the left are the Porta Canonica with a fresco of 1412 and the Porta Corporale, through which the relics of the Miracle of Bolsena, as recorded on the lintel, used to pass. The bronze doors were made for the cathedral in 1964 by the sculptor Emilio Greco.

Interior. — A nave and two aisles built in alternating courses of black and white stone rest on semicircular arches supported by bracketed capitals. A moulding projects above the arches.

The aisles are roofed with timber, while Gothic vaulting covers the transepts and the chancel. The paving slopes up towards the chancel, reducing the perspective. Alabaster window-panes let in plenty of light. At the entrance you will see a 15C stoup and Gothic font. A fresco of the Virgin and Child in the north aisle is by Gentile da Fabriano (1425).

In the north transept, under the 16C organ is the entrance to the Corporal Chapel, in which the relics of the Miracle of Bolsena, and notably the cloth in which the bleeding Host was wrapped, are kept. A tabernacle encloses the Reliquary of the Corporal, a masterpiece of mediaeval goldsmiths' work (1338) enriched with enamel and precious stones. In the chapel on the right is a Madonna of Pity by the Sienese painter, Lippo Memmi (1320).

A fine Gothic stained glass **window★** in the chancel illustrates the Gospel with recognisable figures of theologians and prophets.

From the south transept, beyond a wrought iron grille (1516), you reach the famous Chapel of San Brizio, painted with admirable **frescoes★★** of the Apocalypse. These were begun in 1447 by Fra Angelico with the help of Benozzo Gozzoli and were entrusted, from 1499 to 1504, to Luca Signorelli, whose masterpieces they are. With his care for truth in anatomy, his dramatic method of composition, his appealing faces and the modelling of his vivid draughtsmanship, Signorelli, though lacking in religious feeling, was a precursor of Michelangelo. On the ceiling, Fra Angelico painted Christ among angels and prophets; the apostles, Christ, virgins, martyrs and patriarchs are by Signorelli. The latter executed wall frescoes of extraordinary power; the Preaching of the Antichrist (first lunette on the left) containing portraits of Signorelli and Fra Angelico; the End of the World (on the reverse side of the entrance) and the Resurrection of the Body (first lunette on the right). The end wall of the chapel is devoted to the Last Judgment. There is a *pietà* of astonishing power in a niche in the right hand wall.

165

St. Patrick's Well★★ (Pozzo di San Patrizio). — The well was dug in the volcanic rock by order of Pope Clement VII de' Medici to supply the town with water in case of siege. Sangallo the Younger was entrusted with the work, which was completed in 1537.

You can go down to the well by two spiral staircases, with 248 steps, lit by seventy-two windows and so arranged that two people, one coming up, the other going down, cannot meet. The well is over 62 m - 200 ft — deep; its water is cold and pure. In Italy they say a spendthrift has pockets "like the well of St. Patrick" — that is to say, bottomless.

From the well terrace a fine view of the Paglia Valley can be seen.

People's Palace★ (Palazzo del Popolo). — The palace is built of weather worn volcanic rock in the Romanesque-Gothic style. The façade has a majestic balcony on corbels, with graceful windows and curious fluted merlons.

■ ADDITIONAL SIGHTS

Old Quarter★ (Quartiere vecchio). — This quiet, unfrequented quarter, west of the Piazza della Repubblica and the town hall, has kept its old houses, Gothic churches and mediaeval towers. From the ramparts there is a good **view★** of a small valley and the Volscian Mountains.

At the western extremity of the quarter, at the end of the Via Malabranca, the **Church of St. Juvenal (A)** (San Giovenale) was formerly the cathedral. The Gothic apse is decorated inside with 13-15C frescoes. View from the terrace of the valley and Abbey of San Severo.

Papal Palace★ (Palazzo dei Papi). **(M1).** — This austere and massive palace, built of volcanic rock in the Piazza del Duomo, dates from the 13C. The great hall on the first floor houses the Cathedral Museum *(open 6 April to 25 September, 9 am to 1 pm and 3 to 6.30 pm; the rest of the year, 9 am to 1 pm and 2.30 to 5 pm; closed Mondays; 400 lire),* containing a Madonna by Simone Martini and sculptures by Arnolfo di Cambio, Maitani and the Pisanos.

St. Bernard's Church (San Bernardino) **(B).** — A charming Baroque monastery church with the refined decoration of a theatre. 17C scroll work façade.

The interior, oval in plan *(apply to the monastery, on the right),* is delightfully decorated in white, gold and pale blue, with loggias with gilded grilles on either side of the altar. The organ, mounted on corbels behind the façade, is carved with female figures.

In the square, note the **Palazzo Marciano (E)**, built to the plans of Sangallo the Younger (16C) and the 13C **Bishop's Palace (F)**, lit by graceful Gothic windows.

Piazza della Repubblica. — The square is on the site of the ancient Forum. The Church of **St. Andrew** (Sant'Andrea) **(K)** has a remarkable 12C Romanesque tower with twelve sides. The **Town Hall (H)** dates from the end of the 16C.

St. Dominic's Church (San Domenico) **(C).** — The church contains the tomb of Cardinal Guillaume de Braye (13C), by Arnolfo di Cambio. Guillaume, a Cardinal from Touraine, belonged to the court of Pope Martin IV, who also originated from Touraine and crowned Charles of Anjou, King of Sicily at Orvieto.

EXCURSION

View of Orvieto★★★. — *West, 4 km - 2 miles.* Go out by ②, take road S 71 towards Montefiascone, cross the valley and stop on a hairpin bend on the slope facing the town. You will have a striking view of Orvieto planted on its rock, dominated by its towers and its cathedral. You will also see an example of tabular formation: the foundations of hard volcanic rock show the former soil level, the softer parts having been washed away.

OSTIA ★★ (OSTIA ANTICA) Latium _____

Michelin map **988** 25 26 — 24 km - 15 miles — southwest of Rome

The **Lido di Ostia** is the nearest seaside resort to Rome and in summer time, the Romans flock to the vast beaches of grey sand.

The only remnant of the old village of Ostia is a 15C **fortress** built by Cardinal Giuliano della Rovere (later Pope Julius II) to defend Rome against invaders from the sea.

The main interest of a visit to Ostia lies in the ruins of the ancient town.

The Roman town was situated near the mouth (Latin: *Ostium)* of the Tiber.

According to legend, Ostia originated at the landing of Æneas, but in fact it was founded in the 4C BC. It became the great trading port of Rome, being used mainly to bring food supplies to the town. From 3C onwards it was also a naval base. At the time of its glory, when the Roman Empire was at its zenith, Ostia had over 100 000 inhabitants.

It began to decline under Constantine, and from the 4C onwards it was depopulated by malaria and the silting up of the harbour. St. Monica, the mother of St. Augustine, died in a house in the city.

Systematic excavation has been undertaken only since 1909. The western quarters were uncovered between 1938 and 1942.

■ VISIT TO THE EXCAVATIONS OF THE ANCIENT TOWN★★

Open from 1 May to 30 September: 9 am to 7 pm (5 pm the rest of the year). Closed Mondays, 1 January, 25 April, 1 May, 15 June, Christmas; 450 lire. Time: about 4 hours.

A visit to these excavations is interesting because the ruins, being only recently uncovered have not crumbled very much. The archaeological excursion is combined with a moving walk; the depth of the sky increases the melancholy of the atmosphere, the silence is accentuated by the whispering of the wind in the pines and cypresses.

Excavations reveal Roman building methods (storeyed houses — *Insula* — and private houses with *atrium* and garden — *Domus)* and their use on a large scale of the arts of mosaic and mural painting. By studying them we can reconstruct the family, religious, business and artistic life of the ancient Romans *(see also p 23).*

On the left past the entrance, **Via delle Tombe** outside the city walls was reserved as a burial place and various types of graves have been found: sarcophagi, columbarium or chapel.

Porta Romana. — This was the town's main gateway which gives onto the **Decumanus Maximus**, the East-West axis in all Roman towns. The Decumanus Maximus, the town's main road, is paved with broad flagstones and was lined with houses with porticoes and warehouses *(horrea).* From the gate started the Via Ostiense, the main thoroughfare to Rome.

Piazzale della Vittoria. — The Square of Victory, to the left as you enter the city, is so-called after a 1C statue of **Minerva the Victorious (1)**, copied from a Greek original and intended to decorate the main gate.

Baths (Terme di Nettuno). — A 2C building. From the terrace *(access by a stairway from the Decumanus Maximus)* there is a view of a superb **mosaic★★** depicting the wedding of Neptune and Amphitrite (2).

Via dei Vigili. — The construction of this street in the 2C required the demolition of earlier buildings to which belonged a **mosaic★** (3) with heads of men and women representing the Four Winds and four great Roman Provinces: Sicily, Egypt, Africa and Spain.

The street passes above the mosaic. The **Caserma dei Vigili**, the firemen's barracks include a courtyard at the end of which stands the Augusteum (4), a temple used for the worship of the Emperors. There are mosaics on the pavement depicting the sacrifice of a bull.

Take Via della Palestra.

Via della Fontana. — This well preserved street contains a public fountain (5) and shops. At the corner of the Decumanus Maximus was the Fortunatus tavern whose paved floor still bears the inscription: *Dicit Fortunatus: vinum cratera quot sitis Bibe* (Fortunatus says: drink your fill of the crater wine) (6).

Horrea di Hortensius★. — This imposing 1C warehouse with a colonnaded court lined with shops, is a remarkable example of *opus reticulatum* (walling of squared stones arranged diagonally). To the right of the entrance is a small sanctuary dedicated by Hortensius. Note the mosaic on the pavement.

Theatre. — The theatre was probably built during the reign of Augustus. Although much restored, it is one of the places most evocative of the life of the city. Note the three fine masks (7) taken from the *proscenium.*

Piazzale delle Corporazioni★★★. — The Corporations' Square was surrounded by a portico below which were seventy commercial offices engaged in world trade whose mottoes and emblems, set forth in mosaic, remain. In this way you can distinguish the trades and native regions of the merchants: grain factors *(mensores frumentarii),* caulkers, ropemakers and shipowners from Alexandria, Arles, Narbonne, Carthage, etc.

In the centre of the square stands a **temple** (8) of which only the podium and two columns remain, sometimes attributed to Ceres, sometimes to the Annona Augusta, or the sacred imperial supply system (Ostia was a centre of the Annona, responsible for the organisation of supplies to Rome).

House of Apuleius (Casa di Apuleio). — The house has a colonnaded *atrium* and rooms with mosaic pavement.

Mitreum of the Seven Spheres. — This is one of the better preserved among the many temples dedicated to the Sun God, Mithras, discovered at Ostia. The two side benches reserved for the initiated and at the far end, a relief depicting the sacrifice of a bull can still be seen.

Return to the Decumanus Maximus.

Via dei Molini. — On the right are the remains of the great warehouses *(horrea)* in which goods were stored. In one of these buildings are the mills *(molini)* (9) which have given their name to the street.

Walk back and take Via di Diana on the right.

Piazza dei Lari (10). — In this square stands an altar dedicated to the household gods. Note also the ruins of the original fortress *(castrum)* in large blocks of volcanic stone.

House of Diana★ (Casa di Diana). — This is a superb example of an *Insula* with rooms and corridors planned round a central court, and with a fine corbelled façade overlooking the Via dei Balconi.

Thermopolium★. — The Thermopolium is a bar with a marble counter, shelves and painted decorations representing fruit and vegetables on sale in the shop.

Insula dei Dipinti. — This group of buildings comprised several houses surrounding an interior garden.

At the far end of Via dei Dipinti, on the right, oil stores (11) with huge jars half sunk in the ground, have been found.

Museum★ (Museo). — *Open 9 am to 1 pm; same ticket and closing days as for the excavations.* Attractive presentation of works from Ostia including a fine series of 2-3C **portraits★**.

Take Via del Capitolium which leads to **Cardo Maximus**, a large street at right angles to the Decumanus.

Capitol and Forum★★. — The **Capitol** was the largest temple in Ostia, built in the 2C and dedicated to the "Capitoline Triad", the three major deities: Jupiter, Juno and Minerva. Although the walls of the temple have lost their marble facing, there are still imposing brick remains and the staircase leading to the *pronaos* (vestibule): the altar has been partly reconstructed in front of the staircase.

The **Forum**, extended in the 2C, still shows several columns of the porticoes that once lined it. At the far end of the Forum, the grandiose 1C **Temple of Rome and Augustus** (Tempio di Roma e Augusto) formerly adorned with marble decorations, bears witness to the loyalty of Ostia to the rule of Rome.

As in all Roman cities, the Forum had its **Basilica**, a covered structure to provide shelter for the citizens and its **Curia**, the seat of the municipal authorities.

Tempio Rotondo. — This circular temple was probably dedicated to the cult of the deified emperors in the 3C.

House of the Lararium★ (Casa del Larario). — This house was occupied by shops that lined the inner court. The pretty niche in ochre and pink brick contained the statuettes of the Lares (Household Gods).

Continue along the Decumanus and take Via Epagathiana on the right.

Horrea Epagathiana★. — These great 2C warehouses *(horrea)* by the Tiber have a fine gateway with columns and a pediment. They were owned by two rich freed slaves, Epagathus and Epaphroditus.

OSTIA (EXCAVATIONS)

0   100 m

~~~~~~~~~ Parts destroyed
——▸—— Sightseeing route

NECROPOLI DEL PORTO DI TRAIANO

House of Cupid and Psyche★★ (Domus di Amore e Psiche — 4C). — The House of Cupid and Psyche is a dwelling which was built like most houses, facing the sea.

There are fine remains of mosaic and marble pavements and of a nymphea adorned with niches, arcades and pillars.

Take Via del Tempio di Ercole on the left then Via della Foce on the right.

Baths of Mithras (Terme del Mitra). — The baths built in the 2C had an arcaded façade. Inside, one can still see the staircase leading to the underground hypocausts (heating system) and vestiges of the *frigidarium* (pool and pillars with Corinthian capitals). There are also remains of mosaic pavements.

Return to Via della Foce.

Insula del Serapide★. — 2C structure comprising two buildings and a court with a portico. They were separated by baths. There are stucco remains of a doorway.

Baths of the Seven Wise Men★ (Terme dei Sette Sapienti). — The baths are part of a group of buildings. The large circular hall retains its fine mosaic pavement. In one of the adjacent rooms, there is a dome adorned with mosaics on a white background.

Insula degli Aurighi. — In the middle of this group of flats there is a pretty court with a portico; some rooms contain remains of paintings.

Take Cardo degli Aurighi then Via delle Volte Dipinte.

Casa delle Volte Dipinte; Casa delle Muse; Casa delle Pareti Gialle. — *To visit, apply to the Museum Office.* 2C dwellings with vestiges of mosaics and paintings.

Garden City (Case Giardino). — This is an example of a 2C residential complex. The apartment buildings were set in a large garden ornamented with fountains (the sites of these remain with a mosaic in one of them).

House of the Dioscuri (Domus dei Dioscuri). — The house was located in a building of the garden city in the 4C. The rooms have fine pavements with coloured mosaics, one of which represents the Dioscuri.

House with a Nympheaum (Domus del Ninfeo). — This house was sited in the 4C in a 2C structure. The hall is reached through three graceful arches supported by small columns decorated with fine capitals.

Porta Marina. — The gate in the Sylla wall (Cinta di Silla) opened towards the sea. Large blocks of pumice stone remain. Note a taverna (12) on the left, and the remains of a tomb (13) on the right outside the wall.

Beyond the gate, the Decumanus led to a large colonnaded square.

Return by the Decumanus.

Schola del Traiano★★. — This imposing 2-3C building was the seat of a traders' guild. On the left of the entrance, there is a plaster copy of a statue of Trajan found in the building. Then you pass into a court lined with brick columns and with a rectangular pool in the centre. The court was remodelled when the rooms at the far end were built in the 3C. In the central hall there is a fine mosaic pavement. To the east of the pool, excavations have revealed a 1C house complete with nymphea (paintings and mosaics) and peristyle.

Christian Basilica. — In this 4C Christian building, note the pillars that divide the aisles, the apse and an inscription on the architrave of a colonnade closing off a room that has been identified as the baptistry.

Market (Mercato). — The market included two fishmongers' shops (14). An alley between the two shops leads to the market place which has a colonnaded podium on the west side. The third pillar from the left bears a Latin inscription "Read this and know that gossip is rife in the market place".

Take Via del Pomerio then Via del Tempio Rotondo on the left.

Forum Baths★ (Terme del Foro). — These were the largest baths in Ostia; the heating pipes running along the walls still remain. Nearby were the public conveniences (15).

Mill (Molino). — On the left of Cardo Maximus, millstones for grinding corn stand under a bower.

Campo della Magna Mater. — In this triangular enclosure are the ruins of the Temple of Cybeles (or Magna Mater) (16). The small shrine of Attis (17) to the east retains its apse with a statue of the goddess, and its doorway flanked by statues of two fauns.

At the far end of Cardo Maximus, the **Porta Laurentina** marked an opening in the Sylla wall.
Take Via Semita dei Cippi on the left.

Go past the **Domus del Protiro.** The doorway with a marble pediment is an unusual feature in Ostia.

Domus della Fortuna Annonaria. — 3-4C house with garden adorned with a well; the rooms have mosaic pavements; one room has three arches opening on to the garden.
Return to the Decumanus Maximus through Via del Mitreo dei Serpenti.

■ NECROPOLIS OF TRAJAN'S PORT★ (Necropoli del Porto di Traiano)

5 km - 3 miles — from the site of the excavations. Access by car: take road S 296 (direction Leonardo da Vinci Airport at Fiumicino) then turn right into the Via Cima Cristallo. Entrance to the necropolis on the left of the access road.
By bus: take No. 02 outside the Ostia Antica station and alight at the Necropoli stop. Open from 1 May to 30 September, 9 am to noon and 3 to 6 pm (2 to 5 pm from 1 October to 30 April). Closed Mondays.

Trajan (98-117) built a port on the right bank of the Tiber roughly on the site of the present Leonardo da Vinci airport.

It was in the shape of a hexagon and was linked to the Tiber by the Fossa Trajana (which would correspond to the present Fiumicino).

The impressive necropolis where the inhabitants of the port area buried their dead in the 2 to 4C, now stands isolated and silent.

There are graves of all sorts. Those of the poor are simply marked by an amphora fixed in the ground or by a group of amphorae laid out in an oval or by tiles forming a small roof. Others built in brick included one or more burial chambers where the sarcophagi were placed. Sometimes a court preceded the chamber reserved for the *colombarium* (with wall cavities to hold the funeral urns) which the owner provided for his staff. Most of the tombs had a low door with the lintel placed directly on the uprights; above an inscription gave the name of the dead and sometimes a bas-relief provided some information about his activity.

PADUA★ (PADOVA) Venetia

Michelin map **988** 5 — *Local map p 97* — Pop 242 816

Even by the time of the Holy Roman Empire, Padua had become an important religious, cultural, artistic and commercial centre. In the heart of the town gay, arcaded squares contrast with the dark narrow streets. The Paduans like to meet in cafés such as the Pedrocchi in the Piazza Cavour, a meeting-place of the liberal *élite* in the Romantic period.

HISTORICAL NOTES

St. Anthony. — This saint, not to be confused with St. Anthony the Hermit, was a Franciscan, born in Lisbon in 1195. He preached in Africa and died in the environs of Padua in 1231. His eloquence was remarkable and he was said to have performed several miracles, as well as preaching to the fishes. His name is invoked in the search for mislaid objects; he is represented holding a book and a lily.

The University. — The university was founded in 1222. Galileo was a professor there and Pic de la Mirandole, Copernicus and Tasso, students. Students came from all over Europe. It became famous at the beginning of the 15C and reached its zenith in the 16 and 17C. The university is a palace known as the "Bo" from the name of an inn with an ox as its sign which stood on the site at an earlier date.

Through a modern court in the Via San Francesco you reach the 16C court, which is adorned with the emblems of students and professors. The anatomy theatre dating from 1594 is perfectly preserved.

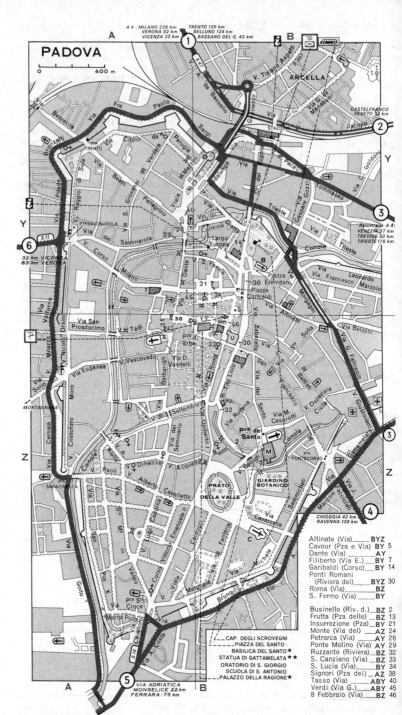

PADOVA

Mantegna (1431-1506). — Mantegna was a painter of powerful originality and a technical innovator in the representation of depth, perspective and anatomy, as is proved by the famous Dead Christ at the Brera in Milan. He was also a humanist and a lover of the antique and of architecture, which he liked to include in his pictures. A student of the Paduan, Squarcione and then of Donatello, he later became brother-in-law to Giovanni Bellini. His colours are rather cold and his drawing a little stiff, but his religious feeling is genuine.

■ MAIN SIGHTS *time: 2 1/2 hours*

Scrovegni Chapel (Cappella degli Scrovegni). — *Open 16 March to 15 October, 9 am to 12.30 pm and 2.30 to 5.30 pm; the rest of the year, 9.30 am to 12.30 pm and 1.30 to 4.30 pm (closed Sunday and holiday afternoons). Closed 1 January, Easter and Christmas; 500 lire weekdays, 300 lire Sundays and holidays.* The chapel, also known as that of the Madonna dell'Arena, was built in 1303 as part of a palace which was demolished in 1820.

Frescoes by Giotto★★★. — The decoration was entrusted to Giotto, who between 1304 and 1306 painted a series of thirty-eight frescoes illustrating the lives of the Virgin and of Christ *(ask the keeper for the plan giving the sequence of scenes)*; the work is concluded by the Last Judgment (on the entrance wall). The Vices and Virtues are depicted on the lower parts of the walls. The most famous scenes are the Kiss of Judas and the Entombment. In dramatic power, harmonious composition, poetry and religious feeling these frescoes reach the summit of the artist's achievement. The Virgin on the altar is by the Pisan Giovanni Pisano (14C).

The Saint's Basilica★ (Basilica del Santo). — The basilica overlooks the square in which, in 1447, Donatello erected an **equestrian statue★★** in bronze of the Venetian commander Erasmo da Narni, who was nicknamed **Gattamelata**. It is a perfectly balanced work, full of power and life, the first of this size to be cast in Italy. Note the contrast between the massiveness of the horse and the slimness of the rider.

The Basilica "Il Santo", dedicated to St. Anthony, was built from 1232 to 1307, in the transitional Romanesque-Gothic style. Its eight tiered domes bring to mind St. Mark's Basilica, Venice.

The imposing interior, 115 m — 377 ft — long, is adorned with works of art and many tombs.

Off the north aisle is the chapel containing the tomb of St. Anthony (Arca di Sant'Antonio) with bas-reliefs (16C) depicting the life of the saint.

In the chancel (to see it, apply to the sacristan) the **high altar★★** is adorned with bronzes, admirably executed by Donatello (1450). They are bas-reliefs of the Life of the Saint, a Crucifix, the Virgin Crowned and Angels. The same sculptor carved the splendid marble bas-relief of the Entombment. To the left of the high altar is a monumental early 16C candelabrum. The walls of the chancel are decorated with bronze bas-reliefs by Bellano (15C). There is also a portrait of St. Anthony.

The treasury chapel (axial) contains the relics of St. Anthony and fine gold plate.

The first chapel in the south aisle contains the recumbent figures of Gattamelata and his son. The third chapel, dedicated to St. Felix, has frescoes by Altichieri (14C).

The basilica's 13-16C cloisters (apply to the sacristan) are open, as are the novices' cloisters from which there is a fine general view of the basilica.

In the square to the right of the basilica the **St. George Oratory** or Oratorio di San Giorgio (apply to the caretaker at the Scuola di Sant'Antonio) was built in the 14C for a noble family of Padua. Altichieri and his pupils painted there, in 1377, twenty-one **frescoes★** representing members of the family of benefactors being presented by their patron saints (left hand wall), the Boyhood of Christ (reverse of the façade), the Coronation of the Virgin, the Crucifixion (at the far end), the legends of St. George (north façade), St. Catherine and St. Lucia (south façade). The **Scuola di Sant'Antonio** alongside the St. George Oratory has walls painted with remarkable 16C **frescoes★**, four from the hand of Titian (fine skies).

Law Courts★ (Palazzo della Ragione). — Open 9 am to 12.30 pm and 2.30 to 5.30 pm (9.30 am to 12.30 pm only Sundays and holidays). Closed Mondays, 1 January, 15 August, Easter and Christmas; 500 lire.

This building, standing between the picturesque Piazza delle Frutta and Piazza delle Erbe, is remarkable for its loggias and its sloping roof. Inside, a room over 80 m - 260 ft — long known as the salone, is decorated with 15C frescoes replacing Giotto's. The subjects (Signs of the Zodiac, Liberal Arts, Trades, Work of the Months) are similar to those chosen by Giotto for the campanile at Florence. The salone contains the Stone of Dishonour on which undischarged bankrupts were exposed, as well as a curious wooden horse used in a tournament in 1446 and said to have been designed by Donatello.

The Palazzo della Ragione is joined by an arch to the 13C Palazzo degli Anziani, which is surmounted by a leaning tower of nobility (see p 220).

Piazza dei Signori (AZ 38). — The Palazzo del Capitanio, one-time residence of the Venetian Governors, is in this square. It dates from the 14C but was almost entirely remodelled late in the 16C. The great early 15C clock was the first of its kind in Italy.

To the left of the Palazzo, the Loggia del Consiglio, or Great Guardroom, is a Renaissance structure, both sober and graceful. Behind the palace is a delightful triangular court planted with acacias.

■ ADDITIONAL SIGHTS

Municipal Museum★ (Museo Civico) (BZ M). — Open 9 am to 1.30 pm (9.30 am to 1 pm Sundays and holidays); closed Mondays, 1 January, 1 May, 15 August, Easter and Christmas; 400 lire.

This museum is in the Monastery of St. Anthony. In addition to a lively 15C Arras tapestry illustrating the Chanson de Geste of Jourdain de Blaye, note, among the paintings, a Crucifix by Giotto, a Madonna and Angels and Celestial Host by the Paduan, Guariento, a remarkable Crucifixion by Tintoretto, a charming Adoration of the Shepherds by Piazzetta, and a good portrait and genre pictures by Longhi.

Church of the Hermits (Chiesa degli Eremitani) (BY B). — The church was badly damaged in 1944 but has been restored to its original early Romanesque style, with a sculptured doorway depicting the Work of the Months and the Annunciation.

In the Ovetari Chapel on the right of the chancel are fragments of **frescoes★** by Mantegna: among them note the Martyrdom of St. James and particularly that of St. Christopher as well as an Assumption.

Botanical Garden (Giardino Botanico) (BZ). — Open weekdays: May to September 9 am to 5 pm, the rest of the year 9 am to 1 pm; Sundays and holidays: May to October and March-April 10 am to 1 pm. Closed 1 January, 1 May, 15 August, 25 December and holidays in November and February; 400 lire. This garden is one of the oldest of its kind in Europe; it was laid out in 1545. In it you can see many exotic species, and, towards the left side of the garden, under glass, the palm tree which inspired Goethe in his reflections on the metamorphosis of plants.

Cathedral (Duomo) (AZ A). — An impressive Classical building with interesting annexes including a canon's sacristy with 14 and 17C paintings. The Romanesque baptistry (restoration work in progress) contains frescoes and a polyptych by Giusto de' Menabuoi (14C).

Prate della Valle (BZ). — This oval garden planted with plane trees dates from the 17C. It is surrounded by statues of famous men and by a canal of still water.

Santa Giustina (BZ C), southeast of the square, is a majestic 16C church surmounted by eight domes. An altarpiece in many colours at the end of the chancel by Veronese, depicts the Martyrdom of St. Justinia — the Church of St. Justinia can be distinguished in the background.

EXCURSION

Brenta Riviera★★. — Description p 68.

PAESTUM ★★★ Campania

Michelin map 988 28 — 50 km - 31 miles — southeast of Salerno

Paestum was an ancient Greek colony founded in the 6C by Achaeans from Sybaris who gave it the name of Poseidonia. The Lucanians, a local tribe, succeeded the Greeks and conquered Poseidonia around the year 400 BC.

It became Roman in the year 243 BC but began to decline towards the end of the Empire because of the malaria which finally drove out its inhabitants.

The Ancient City★★★ (Città Antica). — *Open 9 am to 1 hour before sunset; closed 1 January, 25 April, 15 August, 25 December; 150 lire. Enter by the Porta della Giustizia, in the south, rather than through the temples of Neptune or Ceres on the main road.*

The temples and ruins, built of a fine yellow limestone, stand in a bower of aromatic herbs, asphodel, cypress and oleander. Excavations, have established that the temples belonged to two religious centres: one, in the south, included the Basilica and the Temple of Neptune; the other, in the north, the Temple of Ceres and other shrines.

After passing through the wall built of huge blocks, walk along the Via Sacra. The Decumanus Maximus, formerly the main street, followed the course of the present main road.

"Basilica"★★. — The rear of the "Basilica", so-called by 18C archaeologists, stands on the right of the Via Sacra. This, the oldest temple in Paestum (middle of the 6C BC) was dedicated to Hera (Juno). Facing east, as did all Greek temples, it now consists of 50 archaic Doric columns, barrel-shaped and fluted, without plinths.

The temple stands on a platform, the stylobate, 54 m long and 25 m wide. — 177 × 82 ft. The central part was divided into two aisles. There are remains of the altar of sacrifice at the entrance.

Temple of Neptune★★★ (Tempio di Nettuno). — When Paestum was discovered in the 18C this was thought, because of its size, to be the temple of the god of the town, Neptune (Poseidon in Greek), but it has since been proved that it was dedicated, like the "Basilica", to Hera. Together with the Temple of Theseus in Athens and that of Concord at Agrigento it is the best preserved in Europe. Massive but harmonious, it was designed in an admirably pure Doric style in the 5C BC. It measures nearly 60 m long by nearly 24 m wide — 200 × 80 ft — and comprises a vestibule *(pronaos),* an outer gallery (peristyle) and a sanctuary *(cella).* The entablature and the two triangular frontons are almost intact.

Continuing along the Via Sacra you reach the Forum, where the Greek *agora* stands.

Small Underground Temple. — This was discovered in 1954, beyond the Forum, 130 m - 140 yds — south of the Temple of Ceres. It was dedicated to Hera and contained superb bronze vases. The honey in some of them has remained almost unblemished.

Temple of Ceres★★ (Tempio di Cerere). — Originally erected in honour of Athena (Minerva), the green-eyed goddess, the temple is surrounded by 34 columns. Parts of its frontons remain. A little over 34 m long by 13 m wide — 100 × 42 1/2 ft — it dates from the end of the 6C BC. The deep vestibule had Ionic columns, now in the museum. There is a sacrificial altar.

Museum★★. — *Open 9 am to 2 pm; 1 pm Sundays; closed Mondays and certain holidays.* The museum is not far from the Temple of Ceres but on the other side of the road. The central room contains the products of the most important and characteristic discoveries: round the outer walls are the 34 famous **metopes★★** (bas-reliefs in the Doric style of the 6C BC), which adorned the base of the Temple of Hera near the mouth of the Sele River; also exhibited are the superb bronze vases from the small Underground Temple. In one room can be seen the tomb of the diver *(tomba del tuffatore),* which was discovered in 1968. The paintings which adorn the walls are a unique example of 5C BC painting. The museum also exhibits a number of decorated stone slabs from a Lucanian cemetery situated northeast of the city where about 800 tombs have been discovered. The walls of about a hundred of these were decorated like the "tomb of the diver". This collection is of great interest for the details they reveal of Lucanian life and customs, and they show the evolution of Lucanian painting in the 4C BC. In the upper gallery is a prehistoric department (exhibits from the Sele Plain excavations).

PALESTRINA Latium

Michelin map 988 26 — 38 km - 24 miles — east of Rome — Pop 13 091

The mediaeval city, which stands on the site of a great temple dedicated by the Romans to fortune, forms an amphitheatre on a steep slope in a fine panoramic setting. The musician Palestrina (1524-1594), composer of religious polyphonic music, was born here.

Temple of Fortune★ (Tempio della Fortuna). — The temple, of mythical origin (8C BC), was pulled down by Sulla in 82 BC and rebuilt by him in an enlarged form. The museum contains, among other curiosities, a mosaic from the Nile.

The **Lower Sanctuary** *(to visit apply to the museum)* was behind the cathedral, which was once a Roman temple. Go up the stairs to the left at the end of the square and enter the court known as the *Area Sacra* of the sanctuary through a door and an inside staircase. The court has Roman walls and capitals. Beyond is the Antro delle Sorti (Cave of the Fates).

Return to the car and follow the Via Anicia. Then, turning off to the left, climb by a winding road to the **Upper Sanctuary** which was the centre of the cult of the goddess. The esplanade was surrounded with porticoes, and at the top of the fan-shaped staircase stood the small temple, which was replaced by the Barberini Palace in the 17C. From the terrace there is a splendid **view★★** of the valley.

PALLANZA ★★ Piedmont

Michelin maps 988 2 and 26 7 — *Local map p 128*

Lying not far from the Castagnola Point, whose slopes are covered by an age-old chestnut grove, Pallanza, which belongs to the community of **Verbania,** is a wonderful country resort with fine gardens and magnificent villas. Flowers everywhere deck and scent the town. It is unusually sunny and has quays planted with magnolias from which one embarks for the Borromean Islands.

Villa Taranto. — *Gardens open 8.30 am to one hour before sunset; closed 1 November to 31 March; 2 500 lire.* This is surrounded with splendid experimental **gardens★★** in which more than 20 000 species, including rare tropical plants, not yet acclimatised in Italy, are grown. Particularly worthwhile are the specialised gardens: the rose garden, the valley of rhododendrons and the heather valley.

Parma is built on the banks of a tributary of the Po; its attractions are its streets near the cathedral, its clear light and the refined and gentle manners of its people. Stendhal, who lived here, made it the setting of his well known novel, *The Charterhouse of Parma*.

The Parmesans. — In the fine season the people of Parma are best seen in the great Piazza Garibaldi, which is adorned by the 17-18C town hall and the government palace with its clock tower (1760). On the terrace of the cafés, customers sip cold drinks and watch the wheeling pigeons and shrill martins, while the women of Parma, who are noted for their dignified beauty, do their shopping in the Strada della Repubblica.

Parma violets (rare), hams and Parmesan cheese are the local specialities.

HISTORICAL NOTES

Parma was a Roman colony on the Via Emilia. It declined but revived in the 6C under a Barbarian king, Theodoric. The traditional local autonomy of the Middle Ages ended with papal annexation of the city in 1513. In 1545 Pope Paul III Farnese gave Parma to his son, Pier Luigi Farnese, who was assassinated in 1547. The Farnese dynasty reigned until 1727 and were patrons of the arts and letters.

The Bourbons (1731-1801). — Don Philip, who reigned from 1749 to 1765, married Elizabeth, the favourite daughter of Louis XV, whom the king called Babette. The influence of French customs at Parma began then and lasted for a century: the prime minister, Tillot, an excellent administrator, came from Lyons; many French artists worked at Parma, among them the architect Petitot, the painter Laurent Pécheux and the sculptor Boudard.

Ferdinand of Parma, the son of Don Philip, had a Breton as his tutor and the philosopher Condillac as one of his teachers. He founded the Academy of Fine Arts and was the patron of the famous typographer Bodoni, designer of the type fount which still bears his name.

The Bourbons had their Versailles, now in ruins, at Colorno, northeast of Parma.

The Empress Marie-Louise became sovereign of Parma after the fall of the Empire, and governed the duchy with wisdom.

The Parma School. — This is marked by certain mannerisms and shows a secular spirit even in religious scenes.

Antonio Allegri (1489-1534), known as **Correggio** because he was born at Correggio, east of Parma, was a master of light, chiaroscuro, transparent colour and perspective; his vision was gracefully optimistic and he was influenced by Leonardo da Vinci. Though little known in his lifetime, he became famous in the 17C: Louis XIV bought four of his pictures.

Il Parmigianino or **The Parmesan**, as he was commonly known (1503-1540), liked stylised, elongated forms. His geometrical masses and rather cold colour illustrate an aesthetic canon which influenced the Fontainebleau school through the intermediary of Niccolò dell'Abbate and Il Primaticcio. His masterpiece, the Madonna of the Rose, is in the Dresden Museum.

■ **MAIN SIGHTS** time : 2 3/4 hours

Episcopal Centre★★★ (Centro Episcopale). — This group of buildings, in faded rose brick, is the most harmonious in Italy. It includes the Cathedral, the Baptistry, the Church of St. John and the surrounding palaces.

Cathedral★ (Duomo). — This is in the Lombard Romanesque style *(p 26)* with early Gothic adjuncts such as the late 13C campanile. The façade includes a Lombard porch supported by lions and surmounted by a loggia and three tiers of galeries with little columns. The chevet and apsidal chapels prolonging the transepts are decorated with fantastic animals.

Inside, the nave is painted with 16C frescoes depicting the Life of Jesus. The dome is decorated with the famous **frescoes**★★ of Correggio, very light in colour, masterpieces of life and skill, painted between 1522 and 1530. The Virgin draped in a white cloak is borne heavenwards by a large group of cherubim *(illumination of the dome, 100 lire)*.

On the west wall of the south transept look at the **Descent from the Cross**★, a Romanesque bas-relief of 1178. It is an early work of the Parmesan sculptor Antelami, whose hieratic art recalls Byzantine ivories with the addition of sober yet dramatic expression.

Baptistry★★★ (Battistero). — This baptistry is one of the most remarkable in Italy for the harmony of its architecture and decoration, both carved and painted. It is a majestic Romanesque building in Veronese rose coloured marble, on an octagonal plan, with graceful superimposed galleries and is almost certainly the work of the great local sculptor Antelami.

The tympanum of the west door bears a Last Judgement, while Works of Pity — giving food and drink, clothing and teaching — are depicted on the pilasters. Those of the north door show, on the left, the Twelve Tribes of Israel descended from Jacob, and on the right, the Tree of Jesse. In the rectangular niches on either side are admirable groups inspired by Burgundian sculpture: King David and Jacob, Solomon and the Queen of Sheba.

Interior. — This forms a polygon of sixteen sides containing sixteen niches and graceful galleries similar in design to those on the exterior. The roof of the dome has fan vaulting. The niches and dome are painted with admirable frescoes of the 13C depicting scenes from the Life of Christ, the Golden Legend (St. George and the Dragon, St. Martin), the Prophets and Apostles (in the centre of the dome) and the Life of St. John the Baptist (at the base of the dome). The niches were adorned by Antelami with noble and realistic sculptures of angels, months and seasons, David playing the harp, musicians, Christ the King, etc. *(illumination: 100 lire)*.

St. John's Church (San Giovanni). — The façade is Baroque. The Renaissance interior has a dome with fine **frescoes**★ by Correggio (The Vision of St. John), remarkable for their magical colouring and powerful drawing *(illumination: 200 lire)*. The same artist painted a St. John Writing on the tympanum of a doorway in the north transept. The entrance arches of the first, second, fourth and sixth chapels in the north aisle are covered with frescoes by Il Parmigianino.

By applying to the keeper's lodge (left of the façade) you can visit the Benedictine monastery with Renaissance cloisters *(open 8 am to noon and 3 to 6 pm except Sunday afternoons)*, a library and a 13C dispensary *(the latter has the same times of opening as for the National Gallery; admission free)* with its original shelving and a fine collection of vases and mortars.

Palazzo "della Pilotta". — The palace was so-called because *pilotta* (fives) was played in its courts. This, a huge, sombre building, erected by order of the Farnese between 1583 and 1622, was damaged during the 1939-1945 War. It contains the Museum of Antiquities, the National

Gallery and the Palatine Library. The famous **Farnese Theatre** was built inside the palace in 1619 from plans by Giovanni Battista Aleotti, on the model of Palladio's Olympic Theatre at Vicenza. *Same times of opening as for the National Gallery, admission free.*

National Museum of Antiquities★ (Museo Nazionale d'Antichità). — *Open 9 am to 2 pm; Sundays and holidays 9 am to 1 pm; closed Mondays, 1 January, 25 April, 1 May, first Sunday in June, 15 August and 25 December; 500 lire.* The exhibits include the finds made in the excavation of Velleia (west of Parma). There are pottery, fine statues and a famous Food Table as a reminder of a foundation started in the reign of Trajan for the benefit of 300 poor children. Roman and pre-Roman archaeological items discovered in the Parma region; Greek, Italic and Etruscan pottery; Egyptian funerary objects; medals and coins.

National Gallery★★ (Galleria Nazionale). — *Open 9 am to 2 pm; Sundays and holidays 9 am to 1 pm; closed Mondays, 1 January, 25 April, 1 May, 15 August, 25 December; 150 lire weekdays, 75 lire weekday holidays, free on Sundays.* The first few rooms are devoted to Emilian, Tuscan and Venetian painters of the 14, 15 and 16C. Among them are Dosso Dossi and Francia (remarkable Madonna), Fra Angelico (Madonna), Cima da Conegliano, Bassano and El Greco (Cure of the Blind Man) of the Venetian period, and Il Parmigianino with a Nativity, a Marriage of St. Catherine and a masterpiece, The Turkish Slave, of considerable elegance.

The **Virgin with St. Jerome** (1527-1528), is one of Correggio's greatest works. It has life, charm, gentleness and exceptionally harmonious colour and light effects. Other wonderfully coloured works by Correggio include a Madonna with a Bowl, a Madonna of the Staircase, a Coronation of the Virgin and an Annunciation. A little farther on is an exquisite monochrome painted Head of an Adolescent, by Leonardo.

The following rooms contain specimens of the schools of Parma and Emilia of the 16 to 18C and works by Lombards, Neapolitans, Genoese and Venetians of the 17 and 18C, as well as foreign paintings, mostly Flemish. The last rooms are devoted to French painters of the 18C, who had a connection with Parma. They include Nattier (who painted the Infant Duke of Burgundy in a "Nattier" blue robe), Pécheux (the Infante Don Felipe), Largillière, Doyen (Death of Virginie), Hubert Robert, Vigée-Lebrun (portrait of her daughter) and Roslin.

St. Paul's Room★ (Camera di San Paolo). — *Same times of opening as for the National Gallery; admission free.* This is the former dining-room of the Abbess of the Convent of St. Paul. In 1519 Correggio drew on the ceiling a charming decoration in a secular vein: it includes the Triumphs of Diana, Adonis, *putti* (cherubs), the Three Graces and the Three Fates.

■ ADDITIONAL SIGHTS

Lombardi Museum★ (Museo Glauco Lombardi) (BY M1). — *Open 9.30 am to 12.30 pm and 4 to 6 pm (3 to 5 pm October to April); Sundays and holidays 9.30 am to 1 pm; closed Mondays, 1 and 13 January, Easter, 25 April, 1 May, 15 August, 1 November and Christmas.* The museum is chiefly devoted to life in the Duchy of Parma in the 18 and 19C. It contains paitings and mementoes of the former Empress Marie-Louise who became Duchess of Parma, of Napoleon and of the King of Rome. Their portraits were painted respectively by Lefèvre, Gérard and Prud'hon. Also on view are Napoleon's sumptuous wedding present and a cup by Dagoty, gift of Napoleon to Marie-Louise at the birth of the King of Rome, the Empress' piano, small travelling medicine chest, sewing box, painting set and jewels. There are also letters and watercolours signed by Marie-Louise as well as letters from the King of Rome and the Emperor. A watercolour by Isabey showing Marie-Louise at the Tuileries after the birth of the King of Rome is of documentary interest.

Two rooms are devoted to French painters of the 18 and 19C. There are works by Chardin, Watteau, Fragonard, Boucher, Greuze, La Tour, Hubert Robert, Daubigny, J. Vernet, E. Vigée-Lebrun, David, Millet... and a series of drawings and watercolours by Petitot.

Garden Palace (Palazzo del Giardino) (AY B). — The palace was built in 1560 and remodelled two centuries later by Petitot who also laid out the **ducal garden★** (Parco Ducale) which is adorned with statues by the French sculptor Boudard.

Madonna della Steccata (BY E). — This 16C church, designed by the architects Bernardino and Giovanni Francesco Zaccagni, is a typical example of the Classical style with its dome and its plan in the shape of a Greek cross. The interior contains fine **frescoes★** by Il Parmigianino *(illumination)*. The painter was imprisoned for taking too long to paint them. The mausoleum of Neipperg, whom Marie-Louise married, is on the left, and the tombs of the Farnese family and the Bourbon-Parma are in the crypt.

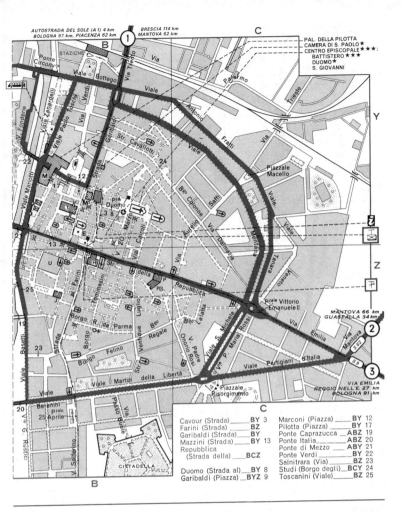

AUTOSTRADA DEL SOLE (A 1) 4 km
BOLOGNA 97 km, PIACENZA 62 km

Cavour (Strada)	BY	3	Marconi (Piazza)	BY	12
Farini (Strada)	BZ		Pilotta (Piazza)	BY	17
Garibaldi (Strada)	BY		Ponte Caprazucca	ABZ	19
Mazzini (Strada)	BY	13	Ponte Italia	ABZ	20
Repubblica			Ponte di Mezzo	ABY	21
(Strada della)	BCZ		Ponte Verdi	BY	22
			Salnitrara (Via)	BZ	23
Duomo (Strada al)	BY	8	Studi (Borgo degli)	BCY	24
Garibaldi (Piazza)	BYZ	9	Toscanini (Viale)	BZ	25

PAVIA ★ Lombardy

Michelin map 988 13 — Pop 87 222

The life of this proud city on the Ticino River, rich in historic buildings, is concentrated along the Strada Nuova. It is, today, the home town of the Necchi sewing machine.

Pavia was originally the Roman Ticinum and later the rival of Milan as the capital of the Lombard kings. In the Middle Ages it was known as *Pappia, civitas centum turrium* — Pappia, the city of a hundred towers. Several of these towers, which symbolised the power of the patricians, still exist, notably the three overlooking the Piazza Leonardo da Vinci, behind the University. This, one of the oldest and most famous in Europe, was founded in the 14C and received Petrarch and Christopher Columbus.

"All but Honour lost..." — Fortune was fickle for King François I in February 1525 at a place called Mirabello, three miles north of Pavia. After having fought with reckless bravery the king had to yield his sword, some say to a Spanish nobleman, others to Lannoy, the Viceroy of Naples. "Sir", said he, "here is the sword of a king who feels he is still entitled to respect because he becomes a prisoner not through cowardice, but through ill-fortune." At this Lannoy knelt on one knee, received François' sword and handed him his own in exchange. Before being taken to Madrid François was imprisoned in a tower near Cremona. He wrote to his mother, Louise of Savoy: "I have nothing left but honour and my life, which has been spared."

■ SIGHTS *time: 2 1/2 hours*

St. Michael's Church★ (San Michele). — This is a magnificent 12C Romanesque church. Charlemagne, Henri II and Frederick Barbarossa were crowned Kings of the Lombards in an earlier building on this site. The façade★★ is outstanding for its balance and the variety of its sculptured ornaments, which make up a curious collection of animals.

A remarkable Romanesque doorway on the right has a lintel on which Christ is seen giving a papyrus volume to St. Paul and the Keys of the Church to St. Peter. Romanesque bas-reliefs (the Annunciation and a Madonna) adorn the wall of the south transept.

Inside, note the great galleries in the nave, the dome resting on squinches and the superb carvings on capitals, friezes and 14C high altar. In the chancel are large fragments of a 12C mosaic pavement, and in the oven-vaulting of the apse, 15C frescoes.

Cathedral★ (Duomo). — This vast building, surmounted by a huge dome (the third largest in Italy), was begun in 1488: both Bramante and da Vinci contributed to the plan. The façade is late 19C. To the left of the façade stands an 11C municipal tower with Lombard bands surmounted by a 16C crown; opposite is the 16C bishop's palace.

Following the Via Amadeo, to the left of the cathedral, you will reach the oblong Piazza Vittoria, surrounded with porticoes. On the south side is the 16C façade of the Broletto or town hall, with a pretty inner court and an interesting view of the cathedral apse. Between the cathedral and the river lies the picturesque old quarter.

175

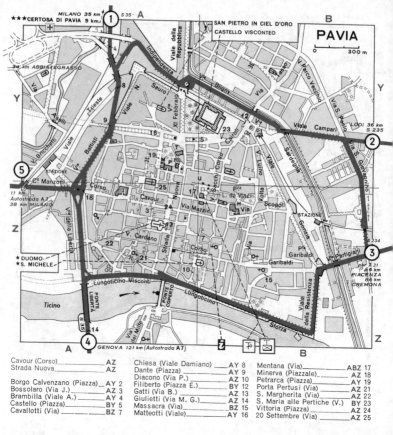

Cavour (Corso)	AZ	Chiesa (Viale Damiano)	AY 8	Mentana (Via)	ABZ 17
Strada Nuova	AZ	Dante (Piazza)	AY 9	Minerva (Piazzale)	AZ 18
		Diacono (Via P.)	AZ 10	Petrarca (Piazza)	AY 19
Borgo Calvenzano (Piazza)	AY 2	Filiberto (Piazza E.)	BY 12	Porta Pertusi (Via)	AZ 21
Bossolaro (Via J.)	AZ 3	Gatti (Via B.)	AZ 13	S. Margherita (Via)	AZ 21
Brambilla (Viale A.)	AY 4	Giulietti (Via M. G.)	AZ 14	S. Maria alle Pertiche (V.)	BY 23
Castello (Piazza)	BY 5	Massacra (Via)	BZ 15	Vittoria (Piazza)	AZ 24
Cavallotti (Via)	BZ 7	Matteotti (Viale)	AY 16	20 Settembre (Via)	AZ 25

St. Peter's Church (San Pietro in Ciel d'Oro). — This Lombard-Romanesque church was consecrated in 1132. You enter through a rich doorway. In the chancel is the white marble **tomb★**
of St. Augustine (Arca di Sant'Agostino), the work of the *maestri campionesi (p 127)*, pupils of
Giovanni Balduccio of Pisa (14C). On the base are Apostles, Virtues and Saints; above,
episodes in the life of St. Augustine who was converted by St. Ambrose, Bishop of Milan.

Castle of the Viscontis (Castello Visconteo). — This impressive building was designed at the end
of the 14C by Galeazzo II Visconti, of Milan, and its building was continued by his son, Gian
Galeazzo. The walls are nearly 30 m - 100 ft high; two of the corner towers were destroyed in
1527 by the French Marshal de Lautrec. An arcade surrounds three sides of the court, with
above, a gallery crowned with Ghibelline merlons. The remarkable library formed by Galeazzo II
is now in the Bibliothèque Nationale in Paris.

The castle houses the **Municipal Museum** (Museo Civici). An interesting **Museum of Archaeology
and Sculpture★** *(open 10 am to 12.15 pm and 2.30 to 5.15 pm — 2 to 4 pm 1 October to
31 March; closed Mondays and holidays)* on the ground floor, contains a fine collection of
glass, mosaics, capitals and bas-reliefs, and a curious 10C seat. There are also 14C and
Renaissance sculpture sections: works by the brothers Mantegazza *(pietà)* and bas-reliefs by
Amadeo and his pupils (the Creation of Eve).

The castle also has a Risorgimento Museum. The art gallery on the first floor, presents
12-17C paintings, wood sculpture and models of Pavia cathedral *(other sections are planned)*.

Church of St Lanfranc (San Lanfranco). — *2 km — 1 1/4 miles — west by the Corso Manzoni.*
A graceful **tomb★** by Amadeo in the 15C, holds the remains of Lanfranc, who died when Bishop
of Pavia in 1198.

PAVIA Carthusian Monastery ★★★ (CERTOSA DI PAVIA) Lombardy

Michelin map **988** 13

The "Gra Car", *Gratiarum Cartusia,* is one of the most remarkable buildings produced not
only by Lombard but also by Italian art. It was founded in 1396 by Gian Galeazzo Visconti of
Milan, and a great part of it was built in the 15 and 16C to the plans of two successive architects, Amadeo and Lombardo. The monastery buildings are 15C. The Viscontis rest in the
building they caused to be constructed so lavishly. *Guided tours 9.30 to 11.30 am and 2.30 to
6 pm (4.30 pm November to end of February); March, April, September, October 9 to 11.30 am
and 2.30 to 5 pm. Time : 1 hour. Closed Mondays unless a holiday.*

The museum, former palace of the Dukes of Milan (1625) , is on the right of the courtyard,
and on the left are the studios of the sculptors in charge of the decoration.

Façade — Even unfinished the façade is, nevertheless, famous for the care and richness of its
decoration. The work of two sculptors can be distinguished. They are Amadeo (end of 15 and
beginning of 16C), who did the lower half, and Lombardo, who completed the building in 1560.
A portrait of Amadeo holding a pair of compasses can be seen low down on the left.

The façade is adorned with multicoloured sculptures in marble, with medallions copied
from antiques at the base, statues of saints in the niches and an endless variety of foliage,
garlands and ornaments. Round Amadeo's famous windows are scenes from the Bible, the Life
of Christ and the life of Gian Galeazzo Visconti. The bas-reliefs round the central doorway by
Briosco depict events in the history of the Carthusians.

Before entering the church walk round it to the left for a general view of the late Lombard
Gothic style, with its galleries of superimposed arcades.

Interior. — This is Gothic although the beginnings of the Renaissance can be detected in the transept and the chancel. Note the late 16C finely wrought bronze grilles. The decoration of the vaultings is by Bergognone (late 15C).

At the upper end of the nave a *trompe-l'œil* painting makes it appear that visitors are being watched by Carthusian monks.

Works of Art. —. *To see these, apply to the guide.* In the second chapel are an Eternal Father by Perugino and Four Doctors by Bergognone.

North Transept. — Over a small door is an *Ecce Homo,* and, higher up, angels by Bergognone, fine bronze candelabra by Fontana (1580), and the famous reclining figures of Ludovico il Moro and Beatrice d'Este by Cristoforo Solari (1499).

Former Sacristy. — This contains a door with seven portraits of the Dukes of Milan by Amadeo and Briosco and a triptych made from hippopotamus teeth (1409) which includes sixty-six small bas-reliefs and ninety-four statuettes.

Chancel. — A 16C marble balustrade and splendid 15C inlaid stalls.

Lavabo. — This contains a Renaissance fountain with curious taps and a well; a door by Amadeo bears seven portraits of Duchesses of Milan; a fresco by Luini represents a Madonna.

South Transept. — The magnificent tomb of Gian Galeazzo Visconti is the work of Cristoforo Romano, assisted by Briosco (1497); it was completed only in 1562. There are also a charming Madonna and bas-reliefs relating the life of Gian Galeazzo.

New Sacristy. — Built in the 15C and decorated in the 16C, with an Assumption by Solario. The ceiling and finely carved wardrobes date from the early 17C.

Chapels in the South Aisle. — These contain several works by Bergognone, including a Crucifixion and altarpiece dedicated to St. Benedict (the predella is in France in the Nantes Museum).

Cloisters. — The small cloisters. into which the lavabo and the refectory open, are decorated with charming terracottas. A good view of the church may be had from these cloisters in which a Baroque fountain plays.

The size of the larger cloisters is striking: there are 122 arches each with terracotta mouldings. Round the cloisters the twenty-four cells each include three rooms and a garden.

PENNE ★ Abruzzi

Michelin map ▨▨▨ 27 — 32 km - 20 miles — west of Pescara — Pop 11 766

Built at an altitude of 498 m - 1 660 ft — within sight of the Gran Sasso, Penne forms an attractive **mediaeval scene**★. Walk along the street which crosses Penne from end to end.

The town, still surrounded by walls pierced with monumental gateways, has steep streets lined with Gothic churches and Renaissance or Baroque palaces, shady promenades and fine viewpoints.

PERTOSA Caves ★★ Campania

Michelin map ▨▨▨ 28 — 75 km - 47 miles — east of Salerno

The approach road branches off road S 19 at Pertosa and crosses the Tanagro.

Open 1 June to 30 September, 8 am to 7 pm; the rest of the year, 9 am to 4 pm. Time ; 1 hour. Closed 1 January, 25 April, 1 May, 2 June, Easter and Christmas; 2 000 Lire.

The great cave, over 35 m - 100 ft — high and reached by boat, has complicated galleries. You visit only part of it (about 2 km - 1 mile): a great gallery, cleverly lit to show off magnificent concretions, a narrow gallery bristling with stalactites, and a belvedere from which an invisible cascade can be heard pouring into a small basin.

PERUGIA ★★ Umbria

Michelin map ▨▨▨ 15 — Pop 138 766

Perugia the Gentle, the mystic and pious capital of Umbria, guarded by its ramparts, overlooks the Valley of the Tiber. Its *rioni* (quarters) have kept their mediaeval character.

HISTORICAL NOTES

Thanks to its strong defences, Perugia was one of the twelve Etruscan strongholds *(see p 22).* None the less it was occupied by the Romans as early as 310 BC.

A Soldier of Fortune. — A curious figure is that of Malatesta Baglioni, who played the terrorist at Perugia and the double agent at Florence when he was defending that town against the Imperial troops. He handled his cannon oddly and sounded the retreat when on the point of victory. Having asked for leave in the hope that it would be refused, he found it granted, a messenger even confirming the news, when he was lying ill. He promptly jumped out of bed, stabbed the messenger and bombarded the town.

Umbrian Painting. — Like their peaceful countryside, the Umbrian painters had gentle, mystic souls. They loved landscapes with pure lines, punctuated with pines and cypresses, and stylised their compositions, giving them a calm but rather mannered grace, noticeable especially in the fair haired women and ethereal angels who were their favourite subjects. Extremely delicate drawing and soft colours distinguish their technique.

The masters of Florence, Fra Angelico, Gozzoli and Piero della Francesca, taught the Umbrian painters of the 15C: Giovanni Boccati (1410-1485), Benedetto Bonfigli (died 1496) Bartolomeo Caporali (1420-1499) and Fiorenzo di Lorenzo (died 1520).

But the local celebrity is the tender Pietro Vannucci, *alias* **Perugino** (1445-1523), the teacher of Raphaël. His favourite subjects were religious (Madonnas, Life of the Virgin); in them he showed his sense of space, atmosphere and landscape, marred only by a touch of mannerism. The charming historical artist Pinturicchio (1454-1518) was influenced by Perugino but painted more naïvely than his predecessor.

Tuscan sculptors liked to work at Perugia; among them, in the Middle Ages, were Nicolò and Giovanni Pisano of Pisa, and under the Renaissance, Agostino di Duccio (1418-1481), a Florentine in love with antiquity.

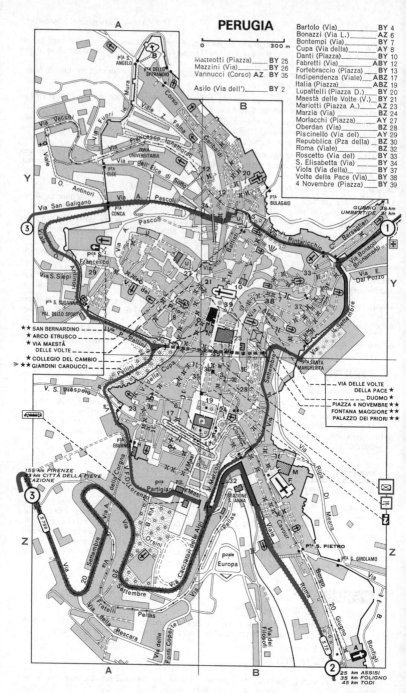

PERUGIA

★★ SAN BERNARDINO
★ ARCO ETRUSCO
★ VIA MAESTÀ DELLE VOLTE
★ COLLEGIO DEL CAMBIO
★★ GIARDINI CARDUCCI

VIA DELLE VOLTE DELLA PACE ★
DUOMO ★
PIAZZA 4 NOVEMBRE ★★
FONTANA MAGGIORE ★★
PALAZZO DEI PRIORI ★★

■ MAIN SIGHTS *time : 4 hours*

Piazza 4 Novembre★★. — This square is the heart of the old town, where the chief buildings of the glorious "communal" period are to be found: the Priors' Palace, the Great Fountain and the Cathedral. One of the most picturesque in Italy, it was the scene of bloody fighting during the struggles between the great families of Perugia, but it was also the spot where St. Bernardino of Siena preached to the assembled people. Leading off from the far end of the square is the picturesque **Via Maestà delle Volte★**.

Great Fountain★★ (Fontana Maggiore). — The fountain was built to the designs of Fra Bevignate and, from 1278 onwards, was decorated with sculptures by Nicolò Pisano and his son Giovanni. It is admirably and majestically proportioned: a bronze cup crowns two polygonal marble basins. The panels of the lower basin are carved with bas-reliefs by Nicolò Pisano; these represent the griffin and the lion, emblems of Perugia, the Work of the Months (two scenes for each month) with the Signs of the Zodiac, the Liberal Arts, episodes from Genesis, the story of the origin of Rome, and AEsop's Fables.

The upper basin carried twenty-four panels bounded by statues attributed to Giovanni Pisano. On a cornice is an inscription in twenty-eight verses relating the history of the fountain.

Priors' Palace★★ (Palazzo dei Priori). — The place was begun in the 13C and enlarged in the 14 and 15C. It forms an ensemble of impressive grandeur.

The façade to the square is the oldest. A majestic outside staircase leads up to a little pink and white marble pulpit from which the priors harangued the people. A 13C griffin and a lion, respectively the symbols of the city and of the Guelph (papist) party *(see p 18)*, surmount the doorway. They are proudly poised and hold the chains which used to close the streets of Siena and were taken from that town after a Perugian victory in 1358.

In the façade to the Corso Vannucci is a fine 14C doorway with a tympanum adorned with the statues of the protectors of Perugia: St. Louis of Toulouse, St. Lawrence and St. Herculanus.

Handsome rooms in the palace include the Notaries' Room (dei Notari) with 14C frescoes and the Collegio della Mercanzia (Trading College) with beautifully carved early 15C panelling.

National Gallery of Umbria★★ (Galleria Nazionale dell'Umbria). — *Open 9 am to 2 pm (1 pm Sundays and holidays); closed Mondays, 1 January, 25 April, 1 May, 2 June, 15 August and 25 December; 750 lire.* The gallery on the top floor of the palace contains many masterpieces of the Umbrian and Tuscan schools.

The great entrance hall is adorned with 14C frescoes from the churches of Perugia and with a Dead Christ, a remarkable wood carving of the 13C. The Umbrian and Sienese Primitives are exemplified by an immense Crucifix by the Master of San Francesco and a Madonna by Duccio, made still more hieratic by its golden background.

The second room contains marble statuettes by Nicolò and Giovanni Pisano and by Arnolfo di Cambio (14C), with lines cleverly emphasised by the veins in the marble. A panel by Francesco da Rimini (14C) of a Magdalen and Four Saints shows the influence of the miniature.

A room is devoted to the Tuscan masters. It contains a polyptych of the Dominicans (1437) by Fra Angelico with "angelic blue" and rose tints and a polyptych of St. Anthony by Piero della Francesca (15C) and his assistants. Only the Annunciation appears to be by the master. A Flagellation (c. 1480) a bronze bas-relief is by the Sienese Francesco di Giorgio.

In the next room are several works, including the famous Virgin with Angels, by the charming Boccati (15C), a notable Umbrian master, anecdotal and full of gentleness and pure draughtsmanship. Next come the Umbrian masters: Bonfigli, whose delightful angels are his speciality, Caporali and Fiorenzo di Lorenzo, a narrative painter who loved the picturesque.

But the most attractive room in the gallery is that containing the masterpieces of Pinturicchio, with their deep colours and harmonious landscapes, and those of Perugino, including on one hand a Dead Christ whose livid flesh stands out against a black background, and on the other an admirable Madonna of Consolation.

The 15C Priors' Chapel is dedicated to St. Herculanus and St. Louis of Toulouse, whose story is told by Bonfigli in a remarkable series of frescoes.

Note also 13-14C French enamels and ivories and sculptures of Agostino di Duccio.

Exchange Building★ (Collegio del Cambio). — *Open 9 am to 12.30 pm and 2.30 to 6 pm (5 pm 1 November to 31 March); closed holiday and Sunday afternoons, 1 January, 1 May, 15 August, Easter and Christmas; 500 lire.*

This was built in the 15C for the money changers. From the vestibule, adorned with 17C woodwork, you pass into the council chamber, which contains an inlaid stall, a statue of Justice by Benedetto da Maiano (15C) and the famous **frescoes★★** of Perugino and his pupils. These frescoes display the humanist spirit of the age, which sought to combine ancient culture and Christian feeling. On the left wall, above, are the Virtues, and below them, persons who displayed them. On the dividing pilaster is a self-portrait of Perugino. The Transfiguration and a Nativity are painted on the end wall. The composition of the Eternal Father, the Prophets and the Sibyls on the right wall is attributed to Raphaël; his own likeness appears in the prophet Daniel, and he is said to have portrayed the woman he loved as the Tiburtine Sibyl.

Cathedral★ (Duomo). — The cathedral is Gothic, but the façade to the Piazza Danti was completed with a Baroque doorway. The first two chapels to right and left as you enter are enclosed by curious wrought iron grilles (15 and 16C). The right hand chapel contains a Descent from the Cross by Barocchio (1569) which inspired Rubens in his Antwerp Descent. The first chapel on the left contains a ring said to be the Virgin's wedding ring.

In the Chapterhouse Museum *(open 9 am to noon and 3 to 6 pm; closed Mondays; 200 lire)* is a Madonna (1484) by Luca Signorelli.

Oratory of St. Bernardino★★ (San Bernardino) (AY D). — Walk to the church from the Corso Vannucci, along the picturesque **Via dei Priori★**. This Renaissance jewel by Agostino di Duccio (1461) is exquisite in its harmonious lines, the delicacy of its multicoloured marbles and its sculptures. The bas-reliefs on the façade in a pure style display, on the tympanum, St. Bernardino in glory, the life of the saint on the lintel and delightful angel musicians on the pedestals.

Via delle Volte della Pace★. — This is one of the most mysterious of the mediaeval streets of Perugia. Formed by a long 14C Gothic portico, it follows the Etruscan town wall.

Etruscan Arch★ (Arco Etrusco). — This imposing Etruscan structure is built of huge stone blocks. The small loggia surmounting the tower on the left is 16C. Alongside is the majestic 18C **Palazzo Gallenga**, now a university for foreign students.

Carducci Gardens (Giardini Carducci). — There is a superb **view★★** from these gardens, laid out on a terrace built on the foundations of the Rocca Paolina and overlooking the San Pietro quarter *(viewing table below the gardens, on the other side of the Viale Indipendenza)*.

■ ADDITIONAL SIGHTS

St. Peter's Church★★ (San Pietro) (BZ A). — To reach the church, go through the **Porta San Pietro★** (1475), a majestic but unfinished work of the Florentine, Agostino di Duccio.

The church was built at the end of the 10C, and remodelled several times, principally at the Renaissance. The portico and the curious tower, with a watch balcony supported on brackets halfway up, date from the 16C. The interior, with a nave and two aisles, contains, in the nave, eleven excellent canvases of the late 16C by Vassilacchi, *alias* Aliense, a Greek contemporary of El Greco and, like him, a disciple of Tintoretto. In the last chapel in the north aisle is a carved tabernacle by Mino da Fiesole. At the end of this aisle is a *Pietà* attributed to Benedetto Bonfighi. The chancel is furnished with 16C **stalls★★** marvellously adorned with statuettes of saints, Renaissance designs and encrustations. Ask for the end door to be opened; a loggia affords a **view★★** of the Tiber Valley and Assisi.

St. Dominic's Church★ (San Domenico) (BZ F). — An impressive Gothic church. The interior, with 17C additions, has frescoes and Gothic windows. There are fine 15C windows at the end of the chancel. In the north transept is the 14C funerary monument of Benedict XI.

The monastery houses the **National Archaeological Museum of Umbria★** (Museo Nazionale Archeologico dell'Umbria — *open 9 am to 1.30 pm and 9 am to 1 pm Sundays and holidays; closed Mondays, 1 January, 1 May, 2 June, 15 August, Easter and Christmas)* in which are Etruscan (urns, sarcophagi) and Roman Antiquities and a large prehistory collection.

Porta Marzia★ (BZ E). — This Etruscan gateway of the 2C BC gives access to the curious **Via Bagliona Sotterranea★** *(open 1 April to 30 September, 8 am to 2 pm and 3 to 7 pm; 8 am to 2 pm the rest of the year; closed Mondays, 1 January, 25 April, 1 May, 15 August, 25 and 31 December)*, which runs underground and is lined with 15C houses. The road and the gateway were part of the **Rocca Paolina**, which has largely been destroyed.

Church of St. Angelo★ (Sant'Angelo) (AY B). — This small church, in a peaceful quarter, is circular in shape and dates from the 5-6C. The interior includes sixteen ancient columns.

EXCURSIONS

Hypogeum★ (Ipogeo dei Volumni). — *Southeast, 6 km — 4 miles. Open 9 am to 2 pm (1 pm Sundays and holidays). Closed Mondays, Tuesday after Easter, 25 April and 1 May; 500 lire.* Go out by ②, the road to Foligno. To the left, a little before a level crossing, is the Hypogeum, an Etruscan cemetery hewn in the rock and comprising an *atrium* and nine funeral chambers. The Volumnian tomb is the largest; it contains six *cippi*, the biggest being that of the head of the family (2C BC).

Torgiano. — *Southeast, 16 km - 10 miles.* Leave by ②, road S 75 to Foligno and at the interchange *(7 km - 4 miles)*, take road S 3 *bis* to Todi and Rome. After 6 km - 4 miles — turn left. The village in the heart of a wine-growing region dominates the valley of the Tiber.

Its **wine museum★** tastefully presents the exhibits placed in context with the help of documents and photographs. In Room I note Etruscan funerary objects (5C BC) and Roman glassware. Ancient documents (Room II), tools (Rooms III, IV) illustrate the traditional Umbrian techniques. The room containing a large 7C press and that devoted to activities related to wine-growing (VII) are particularly interesting. But the museum's treasures comprise mainly ceramics (Rooms IX to XIII) from famous Italian factories arranged into three sections: wine for drinking at table, wine for pharmaceutical uses, wine and mythology. Pots from the Middle Ages (Room XI), items from Gubbio and Deruta dating from the 16C, pharmaceutical containers (Room XII) are of special interest; similarly in Room XIII, the Bacchus medallion by G. della Robbia and a round plate decorated with a scene from the Education of Bacchus by Mastro Giorgio (Gubbio, 1528), the inventor of the famous metallic lustre, the secret of which is now lost.

PESARO★ Marches _____

Michelin map 🔲🔲🔲 16 — pop 90 413
Town plan in Michelin Red Guide Italia (hotels and restaurants).

Pesaro is on the Adriatic seashore at the mouth of the smiling Foglia Valley, which is terraced with vineyards, orchards and Italian poplars. The town was the birthplace of the composer Rossini (1792-1868) whose house (No. 34 Via Rossini) is now a museum.

Municipal Museum★ (Musei Civici). — *Open: weekdays, 9.30 am to 12.30 pm and 4 to 7 pm (8.30 am to 1.30 pm only 1 October to 31 March); Sundays and holidays, 9.30 am to 12.30 pm throughout the year. Closed Mondays, 1 January, 1 May, 15 August, Easter and Christmas; 500 lire, free on Sundays.* From the Piazza del Popolo, in the centre of the town, where the Ducal Palace *(see below)* stands, follow the Via Rossini and the first street to the left.

The **picture gallery** contains mainly Primitives, among which the famous Pala di Pesaro (1475 — first room after the entrance) by Giovanni Bellini, luminous and colourful, stands out. This is an immense altarpiece representing the Virgin being crowned on the central panel, and, on the predella, St. George and the Dragon, the Conversion of St. Pául, the Crucifixion of St. Peter, the Nativity, St. Jerome, St. Francis receiving the Stigmata, and St. Terenzio, the patron saint of Pesaro. In the same room, also by Bellini, are two small panels of the Crucifixion and, a Head of St. John the Baptist and a polyptych by the Venetian Iacobello del Fiore (1370-1439).

The **ceramics section★★** is well displayed; the cases in the centre generally contain the finest pieces. The Umbrian potteries are well represented. Among them Deruta and Gubbio hold pride of place, followed by Castel Durante, Urbino and Pesaro which were at their peak in the 16C.

The most interesting works are those of Mastro Giorgio da Gubbio (case in the centre of Room 9), famous as the inventor of metallic lustre, and those of Niccolò Pellipario (central case in Room 10), for remarkable variety and grading of colour (Apollo and Marsyas, Dante and Virgil in Limbo, etc.). Finally, in the last room, note an expressive medallion of a *condottiere* (leader) by Andrea della Robbia (early 16C).

Ducal Palace (Palazzo Ducale). — The palace, built for a Sforza in the 15C, overlooks the Piazza del Popolo. The windows were adorned with festoons and *putti* (cherubs) at the beginning of the 17C; the court of honour was given a central doorway and windows in the 16C.

EXCURSION

Gabicce Mare Corniche Road★. — *Northwest, 27 km — 17 miles.* The road rises to a height above Pesaro and affords good views of the town. It touches the old and lonely villages of Fiorenzuola di Focara, lying within ramparts and overlooked by a graceful belfry, then Castel di Mezzo, before dropping gradually to Gabicce Mare. The road, at this point, goes from hill to hill, providing magnificent **views★** alternately of the sea and the surrounding countryside, Far away on the left is the Rocca di Gradara *(description p 120)*.

PESCARA Abruzzi _____

Michelin map 🔲🔲🔲 27 — Pop 136 921
Town plan in Michelin Red Guide Italia (hotels and restaurants).

Created in 1927 by the joining of Castellammare Adriatico and Pescara, this town has retained the name of the locality where Gabriele d'Annunzio was born in 1863. D'Annunzio was one of the greatest contemporary Italian writers *(see also p 131)*. The house in which he was born stands in the Corso Gabriele Manthoné.

The town straddles the river Pescara, and is encircled by hills. The pinewood, praised by D'Annunzio, is a most evocative setting. An extensive beach and modern facilities make this, the chief town of the province, a renowned resort of the Adriatic coast. A modern town with important industrial and commercial activities, Pescara is also one of the most active fishing ports of Abruzzi, thanks to a well built canal port.

Piacenza, originally built by the Romans at the end of the Via Emilia, was destroyed by the Barbarians. It flourished in the Middle Ages and in the 12C set up a communal government, later placed under an overlordship. In 1545 Pope Paul III Farnese gave Piacenza to his debauched and tyrannical son Pier Luigi, who was murdered in the town by a party of noblemen. After this its destiny was linked with that of Parma.

Piacenza, the first town to join Piedmont in forming the Italian Union in 1848, is an agricultural, business and industrial centre (nearby methane deposits).

The centre of the old town, surrounded by brick ramparts, is traversed by picturesque old and narrow streets; note especially the busy Via 20 Settembre, which links the Piazza dei Cavalli and the cathedral. A few fine mansions can be seen.

■ MAIN SIGHTS time : 3/4 hour

Town Hall★★ (Palazzo del Comune). — A Lombard Gothic building (1281) with arcades, large brick window openings under semicircular arches of elegant design and Ghibelline merlons, the hall has a severe but harmonious appearance. The marbles of the lower part and the brick of the upper storeys make a curious contrast. The gable on the left side is adorned with a rose window, while the façade of the right is pierced in its upper part with a rectangular window with graceful columns. A Romanesque Madonna, in a niche, overlooks the town.

In the square are remarkable equestrian statues, made at the beginning of the 17C, of Alessandro Farnese (on the left) and Ranuce I Farnese (on the right).

The 18C Governor's Palace — opposite the town hall — is surmounted by statues. The 13C Church of St. Francis (San Francesco), farther back, has been restored.

Cathedral★ (Duomo). — This church was built in the Lombard style (p 26) from 1122 to 1233, but was later restored. It now marks the transition from the Romanesque to the Gothic style. The façade is pierced with three doorways preceded by a porch and surmounted by a small loggia, and is adorned with a rose window. The massive Romanesque campanile to the left of the cathedral has on one of its faces an iron cage, the *gabbia,* in which wrongdoers were exposed, naked, to the mockery of the people. Go round the cathedral through the cloisters or canons' quarters to see the apse which has contorted architectural lines.

The interior on the plan of a Latin cross and with three aisles, is simple and forceful. A Lombard master craftsman, influenced by French Gothic architecture, designed the sextuple vaulting. Some of the dome frescoes are by Guercino. There are fine capitals in the crypt.

■ ADDITIONAL SIGHTS

Church of St. Sixtus (San Sisto) (B). — 16C. The architecture is curious. The façade is preceded by an atrium and a gateway with embossing and medallions. The interior has Renaissance decorations and domes at the entrance to the nave and in the aisles.

In the north arm of the transept is the tomb of Margaret of Parma, Duchess of Piacenza.

Church of St. Savin (San Savino) (A). — This 12C basilica has an 18C façade. The interior has pure lines and well proportioned barrel vaulting. In the crypt is a magnificent 12C mosaic pavement adorned with signs of the zodiac (apply to the sacristan).

Municipal Museum (Museo Civico). — *Provisionally closed. Temporary exhibitions of the works are held at the Farnese Palace from mid-September to mid-October.* The museum contains archaeological specimens among which is the famous Piacenza Liver, an Etruscan bronze

PIACENZA

PIACENZA*

covered with inscriptions which enabled diviners to interpret the entrails of sacrificial victims. Note also a Virgin by Botticelli, the 17 and 18C canvases and rich arms collection.

Madonna di Campagna (C). — This 16C church contains interesting frescoes and pictures, notably by the Venetian, Pordenone (16C), on the left as you enter.

Alberoni Gallery (Galleria Alberoni). — Leave by ②. Apply to No. 77, Via Emilia. *Open Sundays, 3 to 6 pm (5 pm in winter); at other times apply the Gallery Director, ☎ 63198; closed during July, August and September.* On view are eighteen Flemish, Italian and German tapestries of the 16 and 17C, an admirable Christ of the Column (1473) by Antonello da Messina, a Holy Family by Raphaël, a Holy Family by Signorelli, works by Rubens, Correggio, Caravaggio, Ribera, G. Reni, S. Rosa, Ludovico Carracci, Veronese, a Crucifix by Giovanni da Bologna and one by Bernini.

PIENZA * Tuscany _____

Michelin map **988** 15 — 52 km - 32 miles — southeast of Siena — Pop 2 622

Pienza is a charming little art centre showing great unity of style. It is also a curious example of Renaissance town planning.

A Humanist Pope. — Æneas Silvius Piccolomini (1405-1464) had undertaken many diplomatic missions before he became Pope in 1458 under the name of Pius II. His learning and his writings had made him famous, and in 1442 he had been nominated Poet Laureate by the Emperor Frederick III. As a lover of the arts, he released Filippo Lippi and Lucrezia Buti from their vows. Later the Florentine architect-sculptor Bernardino Rossellino transformed his native village of Corsignano into a town which took the name of Pienza in memory of its founder, Pope Pius.

■ **PIAZZA PIO II**★ (Pius II Square) *time: 1 1/4 hours*

This beautiful small Renaissance square is surrounded by buildings designed by Rossellino. A pretty Renaissance well, in front of the Palazzo Piccolomini, bears the coat of arms of that family. On walking round the cathedral you will find a pleasant **view**★ of the Val d'Orcia.

Cathedral★ (Duomo). — The cathedral, which was completed in 1462, has a Renaissance façade of noble simplicity. The interior (recently restored), shows Gothic tendencies. Several important paintings of the 15C Sienese school will be found there: a Madonna and Saints by Sano di Pietro and Vecchietta's masterpiece, an Assumption viewed by St. Agatha (holding a cup containing her breasts, which have been torn off by the executioner), Pope Pius I and Calixtus, and St. Catherine of Siena, remarkable for its gilded background, the charm of its colour and accuracy of the drawing. In the chancel the Gothic stalls bear the Piccolomini arms.

Palazzo Piccolomini★. — *Guided tours 10 am to 12.30 pm and 4 to 7 pm (3 to 6 pm 1 October to 31 March); closed Mondays and 15 January to 15 February; 1 000 lire.* This was designed by Rossellino and is characterised by the low relief of its embossing and pilasters. The court owes its grace to its slim Corinthian columns. From the two-storey loggia and the roof garden there is a view of the Val d'Orcia.

Museum★. — *Open 10 am to 12.30 pm and 3 to 6 pm (5 pm in winter); 500 lire.* The museum contains pictures of the 14 and 15C Sienese school, 15 and 16C Flemish tapestries and a remarkable 14C historiated cope made in England and presented to the cathedral by Pius II.

PIEVE DI CADORE * Venetia _____

Michelin map **988** 5 — 30 km - 19 miles — southeast of Cortina d'Ampezzo — *Local map p 93* — Alt 900 m - 2 953 ft — Pop 4 162

Pieve di Cadore, capital of the Cadore district, was the birthplace of the great painter **Titian** (1490-1576), whose lively, powerful and wilful genius was greatly influenced by the spirit and landscape of the mountains, for which, even in Venice, he did not cease to yearn. He several times depicted the Dolomite ranges in his pictures. The **house** in which he was born is now a museum *(open 1 June to 30 September, 9.30 am to 12.30 pm and 4 to 7 pm; 300 lire).*

His Madonna between Two Saints hangs in the **archidiaconal church** (third chapel on the left). The figure on the left is Titian himself.

Lake★. — The lake, 9 km - 5 1/2 miles — long and with an island at its centre, was formed by a dam. A pretty view of it can be had from the northern exit from Pieve on the national road.

PISA ** Tuscany _____

Michelin map **988** 14 — Pop 103 849

Pisa has the air of a capital city from which life has departed. Splendid buildings recall the past grandeur of the Pisan Republic.

A wide shopping street crossing Pisa from north to south is formed by the Via Oberdan, the Borgo Stretto and the Corso Italia, which ends in the Piazza Vittoria Emanuele II. Between the Borgo Stretto and the Via Curtatone e Montanara are many alleys and little squares where fish and vegetable markets are held. The quays of the Arno, lined with palaces, are severe and majestic. No. 17 Lungarno Mediceo is the 16C palace in which Byron wrote *Don Juan.*

HISTORICAL NOTES

In the 11C, Pisa was a busy commercial port and a rival of Genoa and Venice. In alliance with the Genoese, the Pisans waged victorious war against the Saracens and captured Sardinia, Corsica and the Balearic Islands. In 1099 they took part in the First Crusade. Pisan power and prosperity reached their zenith in the 12 and 13C, being marked by the development of the arts and the foundation of an important university.

Galileo (1564-1642). — The astronomer and physicist Galileo used the cathedral of his native town in his study of the movement of the pendulum; he used the Leaning Tower to work out the laws of gravity and the acceleration of falling bodies due to their weight. He quarrelled with scholars over his theory of the rotation of the universe and when compelled to renounce his theory by the Inquisition he whispered in despair, "nevertheless it does turn".

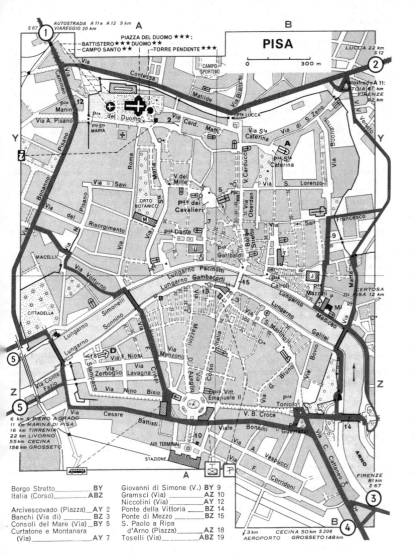

PISA

PIAZZA DEL DUOMO ★★★:
— BATTISTERO ★★★ DUOMO ★★
— CAMPO SANTO ★★ | ┌TORRE PENDENTE ★★★

0   300 m

Borgo Stretto_____BY
Italia (Corso)_____ABZ

Arcivescovado (Piazza)__AY 2
Banchi (Via di)_____BZ 3
Consoli del Mare (Via)__BY 5
Curtatone e Montanara
   (Via)_____AY 7

Giovanni di Simone (V.) BY 9
Gramsci (Via) _____AZ 10
Niccolini (Via) _____AY 12
Ponte della Vittoria ____BZ 14
Ponte di Mezzo _____BZ 15
S. Paolo a Ripa
   d'Arno (Piazza)_____AZ 18
Toselli (Via)_____ABZ 19

FINE ARTS

Pisan Religious Architecture (12 and 13C). — This may be seen not only in Pisa itself but all over the archbishopric of which it was the capital (Lucca, Pistoia, Prato and Arezzo) and even in Sardinia and Corsica, which were then Pisan territory. The gabled front is faced with white and green marble. At ground level, blind arches are decorated with a pattern of circles and lozenges; above are several storeys of loggias with small columns decorated with geometrical designs and animals. The arcades, loggias and arches are repeated on the sides of the apse.

A Dynasty of Artists. — The Pisan school of sculpture is noted for its sober style; it was especially distinguished by the work of the **Pisano** family of architect-sculptors. Nicolò Pisano, who died in 1280, studied ancient sculpture and developed a degree of realism which is also found in his contemporaries Duccio and Giotto. His chief works are: the pulpit in the Baptistry of Pisa and that in the Cathedral of Siena; the tomb of St. Dominic at Bologna, and the fountain at Perugia on which he worked with his son, Giovanni. The latter (c. 1250-1331), inspired by Parisian ivories, had a more supple technique than his father's. He sought to give dramatic expression to feeling and passion. His outstanding works are the pulpits in the Cathedral of Pisa and the Church of St. Andrew's in Pistoia and the façade of the Cathedral of Siena. Andrea Pisano (c. 1270-1348) did most of his work in Florence, where his refined manner may be observed in the south door of the Baptistry. Finally, Nino, Andrea's son (died 1365), had a keen sense of grace and modelling and worked in high relief. The museum and churches of Pisa contain several of his statues.

■ **PIAZZA DEL DUOMO★★★** (Cathedral Square) *time: 2 hours*

Enter on foot the Piazza del Duomo from the west, through the Porta Santa Maria (better known as the Porta Nuova), from which there is a remarkable view of the buildings in the square. Its south side is bounded by the 13C Hospital of Santa Chiara (St. Clara).

Visits to buildings on the Piazza. — *Open: Cathedral 7.45 am; Baptistry, Tower and Cemetery 9 am. Closed: 4.30 pm in January, 5 pm in February, 5.30 pm 1 to 15 March, 6 pm 16 to 31 March, 6.30 pm in April, 7 pm in May, 7.30 pm June to 15 August, 7 pm 16 August to 19 September, 6 pm 20 to 30 September, 5.30 pm 1 to 15 October, 5 pm 16 to 31 October, 4.45 pm in November and December.*

In addition, the Cathedral and Baptistry are closed from 1 to 3 pm.

Cathedral★★ (Duomo). — This structure in the Pisan Romanesque style (1068-1118) is of marble of alternating colours. Its architects were Buscheto, whose tomb is on the façade (left), and Rainaldo, the designer of that façade. The front elevation is light and graceful, with blind arches, a frieze carved with animals and fifty-four small marble columns arranged in four tiers. The bronze doors, made from designs by Giovanni da Bologna (1602), depict the Virgin in the centre and the Life of Christ at the sides. The transept door facing the Leaning Tower has remarkable highly stylised Romanesque bronze **panels★★★**, by Bonanno Pisano, depicting the Life of Christ.

The interior, with its nave and four aisles, is impressive. It is 100 m long and 30 m wide — 380 × 114 ft — and contains sixty-eight single columns. The coffered ceiling was rebuilt after the fire of 1596 which damaged part of the building. The transept has three aisles.

The beautiful **pulpit★★★** of Giovanni Pisano, which was damaged in the fire, was reconstructed with fragments of the original in 1926. The basin is supported by six porphyry columns and five pillars decorated with statues. Faith, Hope and Charity appear on the central pillar, whose base is adorned with the seven Liberal Arts. At the sides are St. Michael, the Evangelists supporting Christ, the Cardinal Virtues supporting the Church, which nourishes the Two Testaments, and Hercules and the Lion of Nemea. The panels on the basin are remarkably lifelike and depict the birth of St. John the Baptist, the Visitation and the Life of Christ.

The 17C bronze lamp of Galileo hangs opposite the pulpit. It was when the sacristan set this lamp swinging that Galileo conceived his theory of the movement of the pendulum.

The Crucifix on the high altar is the work of Giovanni da Bologna. Behind the high altar, note a fine Descent from the Cross painted by the Sienese, Il Sodoma (16C). A picture by Andrea del Sarto on a pillar to the right of the chancel, representing St. Agnes, faces a Madonna by Sogliani (16C). The inlaid stalls are 17C.

Baptistry★★★ (Battistero). — The baptistry is of marble. It was begun in 1153 and completed early in the 14C. The two first storeys are Romanesque, with added 14C gables. The plan is circular, roofed with a dome of unusual appearance, surmounted by a lantern turret, and a statue of St. John the Baptist. The main doorway, which is 13C, is framed between columns adorned with carvings: the life of St. John the Baptist on the lintel; on the uprights, the Work of the Months and the Apostles.

The impressive dome interior is 35 m - 115 ft — in diameter and has a remarkable echo. The marble font dates from 1246. The **pulpit★★** (1260) was designed by Nicolò Pisano; its sculptures, inspired by Roman art (the sarcophagi of the Campo Santo), depict the Nativity, the Adoration of the Magi, the Presentation in the Temple, the Crucifixion and the Last Judgment.

Leaning Tower★★★ (Torre Pendente). — *Admission: 1 000 lire.* The tower serves as a campanile or belfry; generally speaking, it is in the Romanesque style. It is built in white marble and was begun in 1174 by Bonanno Pisano and completed in 1350. Its leaning is caused by settling of the subsoil or a defect in the foundations, unless, as some hold, the architect sought thereby to prove his skill. The climb up 294 steps gives a curious sensation of being drawn towards the lower side. A panorama of the town can be seen from the top.

Cemetery★★ (Campo Santo). — *Admission: 1 000 lire.* This burial ground, which was founded in the 13C, is surrounded with ossuaries. The *Campo Santo* proper (Sacred Field), formed of earth from the Hill of Calvary brought by the Crusaders, is surmounted by Gothic galleries paved with 600 tombstones. The chapel on the east side is crowned with a dome. A bomb damaged some of the galleries in 1944.

The famous frescoes in the galleries date from the 14 and 15C. Several have been wiped out; others have been restored and may be seen in a special room. Greco-Roman sarcophagi, tombs and sculptures are arranged along the walls.

East Gallery: in the chapel opening off the gallery: 14C frescoes.

South Gallery: sketches found under the frescoes cover part of the wall.

West Gallery: from left to right, frescoes depict the Story of Esther (1591) and the Story of Judith (1607). In the centre are the chains of the old Port of Pisa.

North Gallery: the walls were painted with twenty-three admirable frescoes of scenes from the Old Testament (1468-1484) by the Florentine, Benozzo Gozzoli. These were partly destroyed and have been restored (in the chapel).

Pass into a room off the north gallery to see the **Triumph of Death**, an immense and celebrated fresco attributed to the Florentine artist Bonamico Buffalmacco (early 14C), depicting the brevity and vanity of worldly pleasures. Opposite are the Last Judgment and Hell.

■ ADDITIONAL SIGHTS

National Museum★★ (Museo Nazionale) (BZ M¹). — *Open 9 am to 2 pm (1 pm Sundays and holidays); closed Mondays, 1 January, 25 April, 1 May, first Sunday in June, 15 August and 25 December; 500 lire.* This museum has been well arranged in the Monastery of St. Matthew (San Matteo), where the rooms are situated round the 15C cloisters. The first rooms on the ground floor contain mediaeval sculptures of the Pisan school; the room devoted to Giovanni Pisano is outstanding. In the next room is the wonderful wooden statue of the Virgin of the Annunciation by Andrea Pisano.

A fragment of a rare polyptych by Masaccio and the paintings are on the first floor. Moving and hieratical Crucifixes of the Pisan school precede two Pisan masterpieces: a delightful Nursing Madonna, carved by Nino Pisano and the celebrated polyptych of Simone Martini, remarkable for the gentle sadness of the figures.

Piazza dei Cavalieri★ (AY). — This square displays the old setting of the 16 and 17C. It gets its name from the Cavalieri di Santo Stefano (Knights of St. Stephen), a military order which specialised in the struggle against the infidels. The Church and Campanile of St. Stephen (Santo Stefano) were built in 1569 to the plans of Vasari.

The Palazzo dei Cavalieri, left of the church, has a façade decorated by Vasari in 1562.

The same architect designed the Palazzo Gherardesca *(restoration work in progress).* In 1288, Ugolino della Gherardesca and his sons and grandsons were condemned to die by starvation in the former prison to the right of the entrance. Dante describes this episode in the *Divine Comedy.*

Church of St. Mary of the Thorn★ (Santa Maria della Spina) (AZ B). — To visit apply to the Tourist Office, Piazza del Duomo, ℡ 23535. This early 14C church stands alone on the quays of the Arno. It is adorned with statues and statuettes of the school of the Pisanos.

St. Paul on the Arno (San Paolo a Ripa d'Arno) (AZ D). — A Pisan Romanesque-Gothic façade.

St. Catherine's Church (Santa Caterina) (BY A). — The church has a graceful Pisan Gothic façade. In the nave, on the left, are an Apotheosis of St. Thomas by Traini (14C), a Holy Sepulchre and delicate statues by Nino Pisano, notably an Annunciation.

EXCURSIONS

Marina di Pisa★. — *West, 11 km - 7 miles.* Go out by ⑤, which follows the Arno. Marina is a popular seaside resort at the mouth of the Arno where elvers are caught in huge, fine-meshed nets. There is a view of Leghorn and walks to be enjoyed in the pinewoods. The great San Rossore pinewood is nearby, once the property of the Medicis and then the House of Savoy, it now belongs to the Presidency of the Republic.

Tirrenia★. — *Southwest, 16 km - 10 miles.* Leave by ⑤. Tirrenia, built beside thick pinewoods, has a fashionable beach; the local film studios have made the place famous.

San Piero a Grado. — *West, 6 km - 4 miles.* Go out by ⑤. The Romanesque **basilica★** of St. Peter on the Quay, built of a fine golden stone, stands on a quay of the ancient port of Pisa on which St. Peter is said to have landed when he came from Antioch. The apse, with three apsidal chapels adorned with alternating lozenges and circles, is remarkable. The campanile was destroyed in 1944. Inside, 14C frescoes depict the lives of St. Peter and St. Paul.

Carthusian Monastery of Pisa (Certosa di Pisa). — *East, 12 km - 7 miles. Open 8.30 am to 12.30 pm; closed Mondays, 1 January, 25 April, 1 May, first Sunday in June, 15 August and 25 December.* Go out by the Via Santa Marta, from which the road to Caprona branches off to the right. Just before the village turn left. The monastery is a fine group of 17-18C buildings with the Baroque church projecting from the centre of a huge façade. In the monastery are small 15C cloisters and large Classical **cloisters★** with a quaint fountain. There is a view of encircling mountains and the 13C fortress of La Verruca.

*To find a hotel or restaurant look in the current **Michelin Red Guide Italia**.*

PISTOIA ★ Tuscany ————————————————————————
Michelin map 〚988〛 14 — Pop 94 637
Town plan in Michelin Red Guide Italia (hotels and restaurants).

Pistoia, girdled by ramparts enclosing interesting buildings, is a town full of character. Ornamental flowers and plants are grown in the neighbourhood. The Via degli Orafi (Street of the Goldsmiths), a narrow shopping street, bustles with activity.

■ MAIN SIGHTS *time: 2 hours*

Piazza del Duomo★. — The cathedral and its campanile, the baptistry, the law courts and the town hall stand round this pretty square.

Cathedral (Duomo). — A large and impressive building in the Pisan Romanesque style *(p 26-27)*, though the Renaissance porch, which is adorned on the tympanum with a terracotta by Andrea della Robbia, shows Florentine influence. The campanile, 67 m - 220 ft — high (left of the façade), is most attractive with twin windows and three tiers of colonnaded galleries. The interior was greatly modified in the 16 and 17C.

Recent restoration work has revealed 13C frescoes in the lunettes above the doorways. A chapel in the south aisle, in which stands the tomb of Cino da Pistoia, a 14C writer contemporary with Dante, contains a splendid silver **altar★★** partly completed in the late 13C and later modified and extended in the 14 and 15C *(apply to the sacristan)*. The central portion shows St. James, in a niche, surrounded by saints and surmounted by Christ the King; scenes from the Old and New Testaments complete the decoration and include 628 characters. Go through the sacristy (on the right at the far end of the south aisle) to the **chapter museum** which contains a rich treasure (precious gold plate). In the chapel to the left of the high altar is a 'Virgin between St. John the Baptist and St. Zeno (1485), a serene picture remarkable for its subtle harmony of colours by Lorenzo di Credi probably from a composition by Verrocchio. The fonts (1499) on the reverse of the façade are by Andrea Ferrucci da Fiesole to a design by Benedetto da Maiano.

The **baptistry**, facing the cathedral, is a 14C structure built of white and green marble to the plans of Andrea Pisano, with an outside pulpit. The tympanum of the central doorway bears a statue of the Virgin and Child between St. Peter and St. John the Baptist, surmounting bas-reliefs depicting the martyrdom of St. John. A graceful basin in coloured marble by Lanfranco da Como (1226) has been recovered inside the baptistry.

The **Law Courts** (Palazzo Pretorio), formerly the governor's palace, are 14C. The courtyard is curiously decorated with frescoes and the painted or carved coats of arms of the governors.

The 14C **town hall** or Palazzo del Comune, which is symmetrical with the Palazzo Pretorio, has a severe but graceful façade over arcades, joined to the cathedral by an arch in 1637. The large council chamber has finely carved 16C walnut stalls.

Hospital (Ospedale del Ceppo). — The hospital was begun in 1277 and is named after the *ceppo*, a box in which offerings for the poor were collected. The portico (1514) on the façade was decorated by Giovanni della Robbia and his school with medallions (Life of the Virgin) and an admirable **frieze★★★** in terracotta, brightly coloured and expressive, showing the Seven Works of Mercy; from left to right: clothing the naked; welcoming strangers and pilgrims; caring for the sick; visiting prisoners; burying the dead; feeding the hungry and giving water to the thirsty. Between the scenes are statues of the Virtues.

St. Andrew's Church (Sant'Andrea). — This church in the pure Pisan Romanesque style (the interior is one of the best examples of this style) has a particularly curious but unfinished **façade★**. The lintel of the central doorway is adorned with a bas-relief in the Byzantine manner depicting the Journey of the Magi, the Announcement to Herod of the Birth of the Saviour, and the Adoration of the Magi. On the base, the author has signed his work in Latin.

Inside the church are two Crucifixes, one in gilded wood by Giovanni Pisano (placed inside a 15C tabernacle next to the first altar on the right), and the other in painted and gilded wood (first altar on the left), also attributed to the artist. The famous **pulpit★★** was executed (1298-1301) by this same Pisano in his dramatic, rather confused but intensely living manner. The platform is supported by six red porphyry columns and has bas-reliefs of the Annunciation and the Nativity, the Adoration of the Magi, the Massacre of the Innocents and the Crucifixion. At the corners are the Prophets and Sibyls who announced the coming of the Messiah.

■ ADDITIONAL SIGHTS

Church of St. John outside the City (San Giovanni Fuorcivitas). — This church, built from the 12 and the 14C and restored after the 1939-1945 War, has a long and spectacular **north façade★** in the Pisan Romanesque style. The doorway lintel was carved about 1162 by a certain Gruamons, also, perhaps, church architect.

In the nave, an impressive stoup is attributed to Giovanni Pisano: the three religious Virtues (Faith, Hope and Charity) form the pedestal and the four cardinal Virtues adorn the basin.

The **pulpit★** (1270) is the delicate work of Fra Guglielmo da Pisa, a pupil of Nicolò Pisano; it has carved panels depicting the Lives of Jesus and the Virgin, separated by the symbols of the Evangelists and two groups of three Prophets. Behind the high altar a gentle polyptych by the Florentine, Taddeo Gaddi (14C) represents the Virgin between St. James, St. Paul, St. Peter and St. John the Baptist. A predella (1370) on the left wall illustrates the life of St. John the Baptist *(to have the polyptych lit, apply to the sacristan)*. On the altar to the left is a glazed terracotta of the **Visitation★** attributed to Luca or Andrea della Robbia.

The entrance to a small Romanesque cloister is at No. 2, Via Francesco Crispi.

St. Bartholomew's Church (San Bartolomeo in Pantano). — This restored church, in the Pisan Romanesque style, with a sculptured doorway, has a lintel bearing pleasantly simple, even rustic figures of Christ and the Apostles. The church contains the oldest **pulpit★** in Pistoia, the work of Guido da Como (1250). It is adorned with Lombard sculptures in low relief depicting scenes from the Life of Christ. Note the curious subjects on the base of the pulpit.

St. Peter's (San Pietro). — *Piazza San Pietro.* This church in the Pisan Romanesque style is relieved with a doorway ornamented with statues of Christ handing the Keys to St. Peter.

St. Francis' Church (San Francesco). — *Piazza San Francesco d'Assisi.* This 13C church has 17C windows and altars. Dante and Petrarch are shown in one of the 14-15C frescoes in the chancel.

■ POLICASTRO, Gulf of ★★
Michelin map **988** 38

This great gulf which extends from the tip of Infreschi to Praia a Mare, its waters bathing the shores of Campania, Basilicata and Calabria, is hemmed in between high mountains whose peaks soar intermittently. The lower slopes carry meagre crops and plantations of cereals and olive trees, while clumps of chestnuts grow above. Clear skies, limpid blue sea, a coastline honeycombed with grottoes, fine beaches with small, active tourist resorts and admirable landscapes make the Gulf of Policastro one of the most attractive and popular coasts in southern Italy.

Tour. — The most spectacular run is that between Sapri and Praia a Mare. The road is a high *corniche* lined with oleanders and provided with belvederes. It overlooks the sea, whose intensely blue waves wash against fine rocks overhanging lonely creeks. Ruined watch towers crown the promontories. The small villages of **Maratea** (Acquafredda, Cersuta, Fiumicello, Maratea Porto, Marina di Maratea, Castrocucco) succeed one another along approximately 25 km - 15 1/2 miles — in an enchanting setting.

■ POMPEII ★★★ Campania
Michelin map **988** 27 — *Local map p 162* — Pop 22 260

Pompeii, the sumptuous town which was buried in one of the most disastrous volcanic eruptions in history, provides first class evidence of the ancient way of life. The ruins of the dead city are deeply moving, for the Romans seem still to people it in the deep silence.

The heart of the modern town is the **shrine of the Madonna del Rosario,** a splendid basilica built at the end of the 19C, which has become an important pilgrimage centre. You can see the treasury and the small **Vesuvian Museum** *(open 9 am to 12.30 pm, entrance on the left of the sanctuary):* samples of the volcanic matter ejected from Vesuvius, with drawings, lithographs and photographs tracing the various eruptions; drawings depicting scenes from the life of ancient Pompeii. From the bell-tower *(by lift: 8 am to 1 pm and 2 to 5 pm except in bad weather; 200 lire, on foot 100 lire)* there is a **view★** of the dead city.

HISTORICAL NOTES

Pompeii was founded about the 8C BC by the Oscans, a tribe of peasants and shepherds, from the Sarno valley. But, the traces of the most ancient buildings that have been discovered there date back to only the 6C BC. At that time, Greek influence was already prevalent in the city through Cumae which was then a powerful Greek colony.

At the end of the 5C BC, the Samnites, an inland tribe, conquered Campania, and Pompeii became a Samnite town for more than three centuries and knew great prosperity. During that period, it still remained under Greek influence and town planning and art flourished.

In the year 80 BC, the town fell under Roman domination and it then became a favourite resort of rich Romans. Roman families settled there. Pompeii adopted Roman organisation, language, life style, building methods and decoration.

On the Eve of the Cataclysm. — When the eruption of Vesuvius struck, Pompeii was a booming town with a population of about 25 000. As it was situated in a fertile region (the slopes of Mount Vesuvius were covered with woods and vineyards), its traditional activity was agriculture. Trade also flourished. Its wide streets and the deep ruts left in the huge cobblestones by chariot wheels are indications of the intense activity that reigned. The town was closer to the sea than at the present day and its port was probably located at the mouth of the Sarno which was then navigable. There were numerous shops. Pompeii had also developed its industrial activity, and several workshops were in operation. The people had a lively interest in spectacles and games, active politics, keen electoral competition as evidenced by the numerous inscriptions on the walls, equivalent to present-day election hoardings.

In the year 62 AD, an earthquake damaged the town extensively. This was quickly put right but several projects were in hand when the eruption of Vesuvius occurred and many buildings still bore traces of the former disaster. This explains why several columns were completely or nearly razed to the ground, and in some houses, objects were collected in one room.

The Eruption. — The terrible eruption of Vesuvius, which also destroyed Herculaneum and Stabiae (p 78) occurred in August 79. The younger Pliny, appalled, watched the cataclysm from Cape Miseno and gave a description of the scene which has become classic. There had been a strong earth tremor in the morning, and a layer of cinder, soon over one metre - 3 ft — deep, covered the ground. Some of the inhabitants fled, while others took cover indoors. But a second rain of molten lava and cinders fell, lasting a whole day and burying the town under a layer 6-7 m - 20-23 ft — deep. Bulwer-Lytton describes these events in his novel *The Last Days of Pompeii*.

Excavations. — Pompeii was rediscovered at the end of the 16C by the architect Fontana, when engaged in roadworks. But it was only in 1748, under the reign of Charles of Bourbon, that systematic excavation began. The finds had a tremendous effect in Europe, causing a tendency towards the revival of the antique in art and the development of a so-called Pompeiian style.

The excavations at Pompeii have proved less arduous than at Herculaneum as the layer of volcanic matter here was not as hard or deep. Two-thirds of the city have now been laid bare. Excavations continue to the east of the town, along Via dell'Abbondanza (restoration of the house of Julius Polybius). The Sarno Gate at the far end of the street and the northeast section of the wall have been uncovered recently. The necropolis beyond the Nuceria Gate in the southeast area, and the house of Marcus Fabius Rufus to the west have been excavated.

The original aim of the excavations has evolved considerably. Instead of just extracting from the ground any interesting items and removing objects and works of art from their setting, the idea is now to excavate and restore the buildings, and to replace decorative elements and objects in context so as to recreate as closely as possible the scene as it stood prior to the destruction of the town.

Casts made by pouring plaster into cavities left by bodies, roots, parts built in wood which were consumed by the volcanic ejections, conjure up a vivid picture of Pompeii's last moments. Consequently, this has made it possible to build new frames, doors, balconies, and to reconstruct the gardens. Roofs had collapsed under the weight of the cinders; some of them have been rebuilt.

ARCHITECTURE AND DECORATION

Building Methods. — Pompeii was destroyed before a degree of uniformity in building methods had been achieved and it presents diversity in the methods and materials used.

The severe and sturdy **Opus quadratum**, in large blocks of freestone piled on top of one another, can be seen in the most ancient parts of its wall built in the Pre-Samnite period, in the Greek tradition. The **Opus incertum**, popular with the Samnites, is made up of irregularly-shaped, smaller blocks of pumice-stone or lava bonded with mortar and is very common. The Romans introduced the **Opus reticulatum** to Pompeii, which consists of small light-coloured blocks of pumice-stone and darker ones of limestone arranged diagonally and sometimes used as a decorative motif: these walls are often strengthened at the angles by rows of freestone and bricks placed horizontally.

Fired bricks, the use of which became more frequent during the Empire, were used for the **Opus testaceum**: the walls are faced with triangular bricks laid flat with the pointed end turned inwards; sometimes for the purpose of strengthening the facing, the bricks alternate with a course made up of large rectangular bricks. The **Opus mixtum**, a later method, consists of alternate layers of brick and stone at regular intervals, making a pretty pattern in red and grey on the walls.

With the exception of the Opus quadratum, as from the 2C BC, the stonework consists generally of fragments of all sorts (stone, brick, pumice-stone...) mixed with mortar (Opus caementicium). The walls were often given an additional facing in plaster or marble.

The Pompeiian House. — (See plan and details of Roman house, p 23). There are several types of dwellings in Pompeii.

Besides the severe and sober Italic house with a single atrium dating from the early years of the Samnite era, of which many examples remain, there is a type of dwelling inspired by Greek designs, of much larger size and more richly decorated, with a larger number of rooms for seasonal use arranged around several atriums and a more spacious peristyle. With the arrival of the Romans and the problems arising from a growing population, a new kind of house evolved in which limited space is compensated for by richness of decoration, numerous ornaments and more refinement in garden lay-out.

The development of trade brought further change to the town: shops and workshops were integrated in large dwellings, storeys were added on. But, generally, the Pompeiian house remained an elegant, comfortable villa, always occupied by members of one family.

Pompeiian Painting. — A large number of paintings which adorned the walls of the dwellings have been transferred to the Archaeological Museum in Naples. However, a visit to the dead city gives a good idea of the pictorial decoration. There are four different styles.

The **1st style** which dates from the later part of the Samnite period (from the 2C BC), but caught on again towards the end of the era, is strictly speaking a style more suitable for decoration than painting: stucco facing in relief and with light touches of colour to look like marble.

With the Roman colonization, a **2nd style** evolved which, for thirty odd years, was adopted for the interior wall decoration. The raised design was abandoned in favour of painting with perspective created by strong lines and shading. Then the design takes on an architectural dimension: walls are divided into large panels by fake pillars surmounted by pediments or crowned by a small shrine, and they rest on a plinth in the centre. Between the fake pillars are false doors. The flat wall surface is replaced by perspectives with porticoes and deep gardens. Small motifs (vases, animals, statuettes) fill empty spaces, as if poised in the decor. It is the heyday of *trompe-l'œil* (false relief). For bare surfaces, the artists show a partiality for the famous **Pompeiian red**, cinnabar obtained from mercury sulphide. The walls are also adorned with large compositions including motifs and figures. The finest example is the famous fresco of the Villa of the Mysteries.

The **3rd style** which is in a different vein, developed in the early years of the Empire but did not last beyond 62 AD. False-relief is abandoned in favour of ornamentation. This flat style from which is excluded true or false relief, gained ground under the influence of Egypt. It is characterised by lightness, fine design and colour harmony. Within multiple panels with a frame of garlands and delicate pillars rendered more ethereal by the use of white paint, small, finely drawn motifs, airy silhouettes, scenes or landscapes in subtle colours with touches of brown, green and blue, stand out against a vast expanse in light yellow or clear red.

187

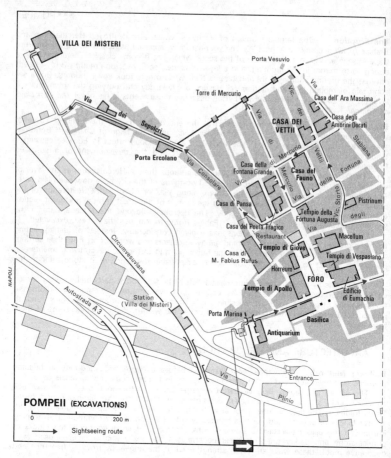

POMPEII (EXCAVATIONS)

0   200 m

→ Sightseeing route

Most of the frescoes uncovered at Pompeii belong to the **4th style**. It was popular in the latter years and it combines certain elements from the 2nd style (bright, contrasting colours, strong black, architectonic perspectives) and aspects inspired from the 3rd style (importance of purely decorative elements, miniatures). One of the most striking aspects of this style is the increased number of small pictures with heroic and mythological themes which cover whole panels. The decoration of the House of the Vettii is the best example of the richness of this style which, with its taste for extravagant ornamentation, conveys the opulence of the town in its final years.

TOUR *1 day*

Follow the route marked on the map above. Open 9 am to 1 hour before sunset (tickets sold up to one hour before closing time). Closed Mondays, 1 January, 25 April, 1 May, first Sunday in June, 15 August, Christmas; 750 lire. Apply to keepers to visit houses that may be closed.

Porta Marina. — This was the gateway through which the road passed to go down to the sea. There are separate gates for animals and pedestrians.

Antiquarium★★. — This contains historical records, objects in daily use and reconstructions of mills. There are mouldings of human beings and animals in the attitudes in which they died. There is a view of the Bay of Naples from the terrace.

The Streets. — The streets are straight and intersect at right angles. They are sunk between raised pavements and are interrupted at intervals by blocks of stone to enable pedestrians to cross without getting down from the pavement. This was particularly useful on rainy days when the roadway turned into a stream; these stepping stones were positioned so as to leave enough space for chariots.

Fountains, of simple design, adorned square basins all similar.

Forum★★★ (Foro). — This was the centre of the town, where are grouped most large buildings. In this area, religious ceremonies were held, trade was carried out and justice was dispensed. It was also the public meeting-place where speakers harangued the people, where official notices were proclaimed and elections were held. The immense square was paved with broad marble flagstones and adorned with statues of emperors. A portico surmounted by a terrace enclosed it on three sides.

The **Basilica★★**, the largest building in Pompeii, measures 67 m by 25 m - 220 × 82 ft. Judicial affairs and business were conducted there (the Law Courts were at the back of the building).

The **Temple of Apollo★★** (Tempio di Apollo), built before the Roman occupation, stood against the majestic background of Vesuvius. The altar was placed in front of the steps leading to the *cella* (shrine). Facing each other are copies of the statues of Apollo and Diana found on the spot (the originals are in the Naples Museum).

In the **Horreum**, a shop probably used for the sale of cereals, is exhibited archaeological equipment.

The **Temple of Jupiter★★** (Tempio di Giove), in the place of honour, is flanked by two triumphal arches, formerly faced with marble. It was badly damaged by the earthquake in 62 AD.

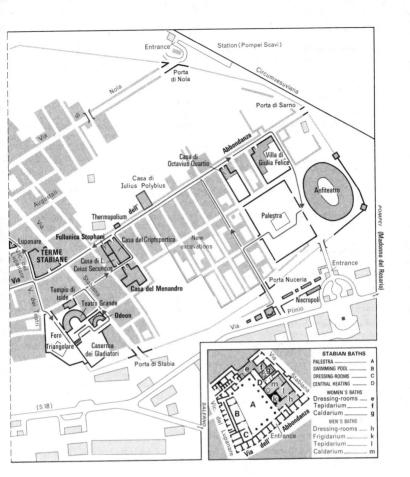

The **Macellum** was a large covered market. It was lined on two sides by shops giving on to the square and the street, and on the third side by shops opening on to an inner portico. In the centre, a kiosk surrounded by pillars crowned by a dome contained a basin where a large quantity of fish scales were recovered.

The **Temple of Vespasian** (Tempio di Vespasiano) contained a marble altar adorned with a sacrificial scene.

A fine doorway with a marble frame decorated with carvings of plants gave access to the **Building of Eumachia** (Edificio di Eumachia) built by the priestess for the powerful guild of the *fullones (p 190)* of which she was the patron. The building served as a wool market and was dedicated to the Empress Livia.

Triangular Forum★ (Foro Triangolare). — A majestic propylaeum, of which several Ionic columns remain, preceded the forum. Its small **Doric temple**, a few vestiges of which subsist, is rare evidence of the town's existence in the 6C BC.

Great Theatre★ (Teatro Grande). — The theatre was built in the Hellenistic period (5C BC) and remodelled by the Romans in the 1C AD. It was an open theatre which could be covered by a canopy. It could accommodate 5 000 spectators.

Gladiators' Barracks (Caserma dei Gladiatori). — This has a large esplanade bounded by a gateway, originally used as a foyer for the theatres.

Odeon★★. — Odeons, or covered theatres, were used for concerts, oratorical displays and ballets. This held only 800 spectators. It had a wooden roof and it dates from the early days of the Roman colonisation. Few modifications were made to the building.

Temple of Isis★ (Tempio di Iside). — This small temple is dedicated to the Egyptian goddess Isis, adopted by the Romans, who were very liberal in their choice of gods. It was completely rebuilt after the earthquake.

Casa di Lucius Ceius Secundus. — This is an interesting house with its façade faced with stucco made to look like marble as in the 1st style, and with its pretty little *atrium.*

Casa del Menandro★★. — This large patrician villa richly decorated with paintings (4th style) and mosaics, had its own baths. Part of the building was reserved for the servants' quarters. There is a Tuscan *atrium (p 24)* with a *lararium* arranged as a small shrine in one corner. It has a remarkable peristyle with Doric columns faced with stucco between which stands a low wall adorned with plants and animals. In one of the cellars has been found a splendid set of silverware (Naples Archaeological Museum). One room contains objects discovered in the house.

The house opens on to **Via dell'Abbondanza★★**, a commercial street lined with shops and houses. It is now most evocative as with the new excavation methods, the façades have been restored with overhangs, tiled canopies, doors, bronze wall brackets and inscriptions.

Casa del Criptoportico. — *No. 2, Via dell'Abbondanza.* After passing through the peristyle (note the painting in the *lararium:* Mercury with a peacock, snakes and foliage), go down to the Criptoportico, a wide underground passage surmounted by a fine barrel vault and with small windows. This type of corridor, which was very popular in Roman villas during the Empire, was used as a passage and for strolls as it was sheltered from the sun and from bad weather. There are also casts of bodies.

Fullonica Stephani★★. — *No. 7, Via dell'Abbondanza.* This was an example of a dwelling-house converted into workshops. The clothing industry was flourishing in Roman times as the full, draped costume required a lot of material. In the *fullonicae,* new fabrics were finished and used clothing was laundered. Several of these workshops have been uncovered in Pompeii. The **fullones** (fullers) cleaned the cloths by trampling them underfoot in vats filled with a mixture of water and soda or urine, dipped them in fuller's earth, brushed them outside on the terraces, washed them or touched up the colours with sulphurous steam.

Thermopolium★ (Termopolio). — This was a bar which also sold pre-cooked dishes. A stonework counter which gave directly on to the street formed the shop front; jars embedded in the counter contained the food for sale. Some were kept over a small fire to keep the food or drink hot.

Casa di Octavius Quartio★. — This was a rich dwelling judging from the fine marble *impluvium,* the *triclinium* adorned with frescoes (scenes from the *Iliad* on the left) and the **decoration★** against a white background of one of the rooms (beyond the peristyle) which is among the best examples of the 4th Pompeiian style. But its most luxurious feature was the loggia with a portico and the splendid garden; this **section★** was laid out for water displays.

Villa di Giulia Felice★. — Built just within the town boundary, it has three main parts: the dwelling, the baths which the owner opened to the public, and a section for letting including an inn and shops. The large garden is bounded by a fine portico.

Amphitheatre★ (Anfiteatro). — This is the oldest Roman amphitheatre known (80 BC). Alongside is the great *palestra* which was used as a training ground for athletes.

Necropolis at the Nuceria Gate★. — According to custom, tombs line one of the roads leading out of town. You can see the tomb of Eumachia (inscription), a small semicircular monument with the burial chamber built on to it.

Return to Via dell'Abbondanza and keep to the left to reach the baths.

Stabian Baths★★★ (Terme Stabiane). — *See plan p 189 and details of Roman baths p 24. Some sections are open only on request. Apply to the keeper.* These baths, the best preserved and most complete in Pompeii, are divided into sections for men and women. You enter through the *palestra* (A) for athletic games, to the left of which is a swimming pool, *piscina* (B) with adjacent dressing-rooms, *spogliatoio* (C). The **women's baths** begin at the far end, on the right, with dressing-rooms (e) fitted with wardrobes, a *tepidarium* (lukewarm, f) and a *caldarium* (hot, g). The central heating apparatus (D) is between the men's and women's baths. The **men's baths** have large, well preserved dressing-rooms (h), a *frigidarium* (cold, k), a *tepidarium* (I) and a *caldarium* (m). There is a fine stucco decoration on the coffered ceiling.

Lupanare. — The decorations are licentious.

Pistrinum★ — Baker's oven and flour-mills.

Casa degli Amorini Dorati★. — This house shows the refinement of the owner who probably lived during the reign of Nero, and his taste for the theatre. Medallions in glass and gilt depicting cupids have deteriorated. But the building as a whole, with a remarkable peristyle with one wing raised like a stage, is well preserved. Between the columns hang masks and *oscilla,* small discs in carved marble that move with the wind to ward off fate. Note the obsidian mirror set in the wall near the passage between the peristyle and *atrium.*

Casa dell'Ara Massima. — Well preserved **paintings★** (one in *trompe-l'œil*).

House of the Vettii★★★ (Casa dei Vettii). — The Vettii brothers were rich merchants. Their dwelling, the most lavishly decorated in the town, is the finest example of a house and garden that have been faithfully restored. The *atrium* with the roof rebuilt, opens directly on to the peristyle surrounding a garden. The frescoes in the *triclinium,* on the right of the peristyle, depicting mythological scenes and friezes of cupids are among the finest of Antiquity. Together with those in the two living-rooms on the main side of the peristyle, they make up a splendid set of paintings in the 4th Pompeiian style. Pots stand on the hearth in the kitchen.

Tower of the God Mercury★ (Torre di Mercurio). — A tower on the town wall arranged as a belvedere now affords an interesting **view★★** of the excavations.

Casa della Fontana Grande. — Its main feature is the large **fountain★** shaped as a niche decorated with mosaics and fragments of coloured glass in the Egyptian style.

Temple to Augustus' Spirit (Tempio della Fortuna Augusta). — This temple was dedicated to the cult of the Emperor Augustus.

House of the Faun★★ (Casa del Fauno). — This vast, luxurious house had two atriums, two peristyles and dining-rooms for all seasons. Italic and Hellenistic architecture coexist as can be seen from the two atriums (one is in the Tuscan style and the other in the 3rd Pompeiian style — *see p 187).* The bronze original of the famous statuette of the faun that adorned one of the impluviums is in the Naples Museum. The rooms contained admirable mosaics including the famous Battle of Alexander (Naples Museum).

Casa del Poeta Tragico★. — This house owes its name to a mosaic which is now in the Naples Museum. A watchdog in mosaic at the threshold bears the inscription *Cave Canem.*

Casa di Pansa. — A very spacious house partly converted for letting.

Herculaneum Gate★★ (Porta Ercolano). — This is the main gateway of Pompeii, having two gates for pedestrians and one for vehicles. It led to the road to Herculaneum.

Via dei Sepolcri★★. — A great melancholy pervades this street lined with monumental tombs and cypresses. There are examples of all forms of Greco-Roman funerary architecture: tombs with niches, small round or square temples, altars resting on a plinth, drum-shaped mausoleums, simple semicircular seats or exedrae (round niches with a semicircular seat)...

Villa of the Mysteries★★★ (Villa dei Misteri). — This was a former patrician villa. Near the present entrance were the out-buildings (partly excavated). In the main dwelling, the room on the right contains the splendid **fresco★** for which the villa is famous. This vast composition which fills the whole room, depicts against a background in Pompeiian red, the initiation of a young bride to the mysteries of the cult of Dionysius (Child reading the rites; scenes of offerings and sacrifices; flagellation; nuptials of Ariadne and Dionysius; dancing Bacchante; dressing of the bride). The lady of the house seems to have been a priestess of Dionysius. There is a fine peristyle and an underground passage *(cryptoportico).*

POMPOSA Abbey ★★ Emilia-Romagna

Michelin map **988** 15 — 49 km - 30 miles - east of Ferrara

Pomposa is the name of a Benedictine Abbey, founded in the 6C. It enjoyed great fame in the Middle Ages, especially from the 10 to the 12C, when it was distinguished by its Abbot, St. Guy (Guido) of Ravenna, and by Guido d'Arezzo, the inventor of the musical scale.

Open 1 May to 1 September: weekdays, 7.30 am to noon and 2 to 7 pm; Sundays and holidays, 6.30 am to 12.30 pm and 2.30 to 7.30 pm.

The fine Pre-Romanesque **church★★** in the style of Ravenna is preceded by a narthex whose decoration exemplifies the Byzantine style, consisting of symbolical creatures such as peacocks, lambs and eagles. To its left, an admirable Romanesque campanile (1063), massive and distinguished, rises heavenwards: note on the one hand the progression in the number and size of its windows, on the other the elegant simplicity of the Lombard bands and arches adorning its nine storeys; and finally, the variety of geometrical decoration obtained by the use of bricks. There is a fine view from the top.

The nave has kept some of its magnificent mosaic paving and two Romanesque stoups, one in the Byzantine style. The walls bear an exceptional series of 14C frescoes based on the illuminator's art. They should be viewed starting from the right hand wall, and from right to left. The upper band is devoted to the Old Testament, the lower to the Life of Christ; the corner pieces of the arches depict the Apocalypse. On the reverse of the façade are a Last Judgment and, in the apsidal chapel, Christ in Majesty.

Opposite stand the Law Courts where the abbot dispensed justice.

POPPI ★ Tuscany

Michelin map **988** 15 — 38 km - 24 miles — north of Arezzo — Pop 5 790

Poppi, a quiet, proud, picturesque little town, formerly the capital of the Casentino, overlooks the Arno Valley and is itself dominated by the lofty **castle** (now the town hall) of the Guidi Counts. This 13C Gothic palace, preceded by a shady esplanade, has trilobar windows, a gatehouse, a keep and merlons. It also has a curious **court★** decorated with coats of arms. From the top of the keep *(access: 8 am to 2 pm; closed Sundays and holidays)* there is a fine view of the valley and the mountains towards Camaldoli and La Verna.

PORDENONE Friuli-Venezia Giulia

Michelin map **988** 5 — Pop 52 284

Pordenone, an industrial town and provincial city, has an old quarter the heart of which is formed by the charming Piazza San Marco, where the cathedral and the town hall stand.

Pordenone was the birthplace of the painter Giovanni Antonio di Santis, known as Pordenone (1483-1539), who worked in Rome and in several towns of northern Italy.

Cathedral (Duomo). — This is dominated by a superb and unusual square **campanile★** with an octagonal crown. The apse dates from the 13C. A finely carved 16C doorway leads to the interior which has been remodelled in the 18C. On the first altar on the right as you come in is a Madonna of Pity (1515), masterpiece of the local painter Pordenone.

The **town hall** (1291), nearby, has a quaint façade adorned with a 16C loggia-tower. It proudly displays a clock and jack (a mechanical figure that strikes the hours).

Opposite, the **Palazzo Ricchieri** (17C), recently restored, houses the **Municipal Museum** (Museo Civico): works by Pordenone and by many artists from the Friuli district.

PORTOFINO Peninsula ★★★ Liguria

Michelin map **988** 13 — Local map p 200

This rocky, rugged promontory, overlooked by Monte Portofino (alt 610 m - 2 001 ft), forms one of the most attractive landscapes on the Italian Riviera.

Portofino★★★. — A favourite haunt of artists, this little fishing port lies at the head of a perfectly sheltered natural creek. Amidst the greenery, gaily coloured houses stand out clearly against the limpid blue sea.

The **Walk to the Lighthouse★★★** *(1 hour on foot Rtn)* is beautiful, especially in the evening, when the setting sun shines on the Gulf of Rapallo. After climbing the steps from the port you reach the little Church of St. George (San Giorgio — magnificent view from the terrace). Leaving this on your right, continue towards the lighthouse. Wonderful views unfold, first from above, of Portofino, and then of creeks full of clear, blue water among olive trees, yews and sea pines. Later the view opens out over the Gulf of Rapallo. From the lighthouse you can see right along the coast to La Spezia.

The hillside brick path between Paraggi and Portofino also affords beautiful views.

Near Paraggi, to the north, the old Benedictine Monastery of St. Jerome of Cervera (now private property), has received famous people, including popes and princes, who were driven to take shelter in Portofino by storms at sea. Richard Lionheart stopped there on his way to Syria.

Santa Margherita Ligure★. — This fashionable seaside and climatic resort is also a good excursion centre for the Portofino Peninsula. The **corniche★★** road makes a fine run.

San Lorenzo. — The church contains a **triptych★** by a master of Bruges (1499) depicting the Resurrection of Lazarus, the Martyrdom of St. Andrew and the Wedding Feast at Cana. After comparing this with the Wedding Feast in the Louvre, it seems possible to attribute the painting to the Flemish, Gerard David (Gheeraert Davit), who sent several of his pictures to Genoa and also lived there for a time.

Portofino Vetta (alt 450 m - 1476 ft). — Reached from the Via Aurelia by a toll road *(2 km - 1 1/4 miles; 500 lire per car plus 100 lire per person other than the driver)* starting near the Ruta tunnel from which there are good views of Camogli, San Rocco and the coast. An excellent **view★★** of the coast may be had from the promontory. The south end of the promontory has been enclosed as a nature reserve. A path leads from Portofino Vetta to San Fruttuoso *(3 hours on foot Rtn)*. The final stages are difficult.

Camogli. — *The approach road is narrow and difficult.* Tall houses crowded round a small, old-fashioned **port★**, form the setting for Camogli. Its attractions are a popular little beach, hills clothed in pine and olive groves, and varied excursions to the Portofino Peninsula. A path branching off a road that starts at Ruta, leads via San Rocco to the Chiappa Point.

PORTOFINO Peninsula★★★

San Fruttuoso★★. — This beautiful fishing village is at the head of a narrow bay under Monte Portofino. No road fit for cars leads to it, and to reach it you must take, at Rapallo, Santa Margherita, Portofino or Camogli, one of the boats which ply along the coast. It can be reached from Portofino by a pretty path marked with signposts *(4 1/2 hours on foot Rtn).*

Fishing boats are assembled in the slipway in front of the abbey founded by the Benedictines of Monte Cassino which shows the transition from Romanesque to Gothic architecture. Small cloisters shelter the tombs of the Dorias.

PORTOVENERE ★★ Liguria

Michelin map **988** 13 — 12 km - 7 miles — south of La Spezia — *Local map p 200* — Pop 5 081

From La Spezia a pretty **corniche road★** leads to Portovenere through olive groves along the shores of the gulf, where mussel-beds can be seen.

Portovenere is dominated by a 12-16C citadel. Ancient houses, some dating from the 12C, line the port and the main street; some were once fortified by the Genoese, who attached strategic importance to the site. The church of St. Lawrence (San Lorenzo), halfway up the slope, dates from the 12C; the tympanum depicts the martyrdom of St. Lawrence.

Continuing towards the end of the promontory, descend at the cave known as Byron's Grotto, to see a beautiful view of a creek surrounded by superb stratified rocks, surmounted by the ancient fortress. Byron found in these surroundings the inspiration for his poem the *Corsair.* The walled **Church of St. Peter** (San Pietro), at the tip of the promontory, is a Genoese building with 6C vestiges such as the marble paving near the entrance. From the roof of a small castle near the church there is an attractive **view★★** of the Gulf of La Spezia, the Cinqueterre *(p 83),* the Palmaria and Tino Islands where quarries of black, gold-veined marble are worked. *By boat to Palmaria: 8 and 10 am, noon and 5.30 pm; Rtn fare: 1 000 lire. In addition 3/4 hour tour including visit to the Palmaria, Tino and Tinetto Islands and the Blue Grotto — 19 March to end of September. Boats leave every 1/2 hour from 9.30 am; 2 000 lire.*

POTENZA Basilicata

Michelin map **988** 28 — Alt 823 m - 2 701 ft — Pop 63 797
Town plan in Michelin Red Guide Italia (hotels and restaurants)

Potenza overlooks the Basento Valley with wide mountain views. The ancient town of Potentia, founded by the Romans, flourished during the Empire. Today it is an active town, the principal town of Basilicata and a business centre. Its expansion, based largely on industries set up in the Betlemme and Gallitello plain, has been facilitated by the development of communication routes in the region. It is a rail and road junction.

Its tall, modern buildings, curiously terraced, make an unusual sight which is quite dazzling by night.

From Potenza the tourist can make excursions in **Lucania**, an indescribably wild region ravaged by erosion.

Excursion to the Monticchio Lakes. — *Northwest, 58 km - 36 miles.* Take road S 93 to Rionero in Vulture, then bear left. The two small, silvery lakes in Monticchio in a lovely **setting★** framed by a large forest are dominated by the slopes of the Vulture volcano.

POZZUOLI ★ Campania

Michelin map **988** 27 — 16 km - 10 miles west of Naples — *Local map p 164* — Pop 69 451

Pozzuoli is of Greek origin — its name evokes the **solfatara** *(p 163).* Under the Romans it became the chief port in the Mediterranean until the opening of Ostia.

Amphitheatre★★ (Anfiteatro) (a). — *By road S 7 Quater. Coming from Naples, turn right past the railway bridge. Open 9 am to one hour before sunset; closed Mondays (Tuesday when Monday is a holiday), 1 January, 25 April, 1 May, first Sunday in June, 15 August, 25 December; 1/4 hour; 500 lire.*

This amphitheatre is the third in size in Italy after the Coliseum in Rome and Santa Maria Capua Vetere. It could accommodate 40 000 spectators. Fairly well preserved, it is built of brick with stone basements, and dates from the reign of Vespasian (late IC).

The amphitheatre still has three tiers of seats and four main entrances. In the arena is a longitudinal trench connected with pits from which properties kept in the basements were raised (scenery and accessories) and the caged wild beasts were hoisted up by means of pulleys. The basements are well preserved; two ramps led down to them. The plan includes three main corridors, two of which follow the axes of the amphitheatre with the elliptical outer corridor adjoining two tiers of cells. The upper tier was formed into dens for the wild beasts. An aqueduct brought the water required for *naumachiæ* (naval battles) which were held there before the underground passages and pits were dug.

Temple of Serapis★ (Tempio di Serapide) (b). — The temple stands near the sea and was formerly a market, lined with shops opening into a portico. There is a sort of apse in the end wall in which was the statue of Serapis, the protecting god of traders. A circular edifice in the centre is supported by sixteen columns. The structure shows the effects of variations in ground level under the influence of volcanic action; the columns are encrusted up to a height of nearly 5.70 m -19 ft — by marine molluscs.

Temple of Augustus★ (Tempio di Augusto) (c). — *At the Cathedral, in the upper part of the old town (walk up).* On top of a hill where the Acropolis of ancient Puteoli stood, was a temple built by the Roman architect Cocceius in the early days of the Empire. It was converted into a Christian church and then into a Cathedral; the interior was remodelled in the Baroque style in the 17C. The destruction of this facing by fire in 1964 has revealed an imposing marble colonnade with its entablature. *Restoration in progress.*

Necropolis at Via Campana. — *North, 5 km - 3 miles.* On leaving town, make for Piazza Generale Capomazza, at the Annunziata junction (quadrivio). Small road signposted "Qualiano-Necropoli Romana". The ancient Roman way that linked Capua and Naples is lined with hypogea, mausoleums and columbariums. At the small church of St. Vito, there is a large mausoleum on a square plan surmounted by a tower in the middle of the road.

Bear left, after a humpback bridge turn left into the main road leading to Pozzuoli.

PRATO Tuscany

Michelin map **988** 14 — 20 km - 12 miles — northwest of Florence — Pop 156 955
Town plan in Michelin Red Guide Italia (hotels and restaurants).

Thanks to its textile industries, Prato has been called the Manchester of Italy. But it is also an art centre which has played a part in the history of Tuscany.

Legend of the Holy Girdle. — The Apostle Thomas, who did not believe in the Resurrection of Christ, refused to credit the Assumption of the Virgin, for he was away at the time. He asked that the tomb of the Mother of God should be opened; it was found to be full of lilies and roses. Raising his eyes to Heaven, Thomas saw the Virgin in Glory, loosening her girdle to give to him. This girdle is venerated at Prato.

An Artistic and Libertine Monk. — Fra Filippo Lippi (1406-1469) was ordained at fifteen but soon began to lead a dissolute life. Having fled from his monastery he was captured by Barbary pirates and sold as a slave in Africa, where his pictorial talents so amazed the Saracens that they set him free. On his return to the cloisters, Lippi met the blonde Lucrezia Buti, a beautiful nun at the convent of which Lippi was chaplain. Little Filippino was born the next year. There was a great scandal, but Cosimo de' Medici had the monk released from his vows and Lippi married Lucrezia, whose smooth, oval face he often reproduced in his Madonnas and Salomes. Finally he was poisoned by a jealous husband.

None the less, the art of this libertine monk remained religious; his drawing is pure, natural and simple and his finely graded colour is pleasantly fresh.

Filippino Lippi (1457-1504) continued to paint in his father's manner.

■ **MAIN SIGHTS** time: 2 hours

Cathedral★ (Duomo). — The cathedral was begun in the Romanesque (south side) and continued in the Gothic style for the transept, chancel and façade. The doorway is ornamented with a terracotta lunette by Andrea della Robbia.

The interior of the church, sober in style, has three aisles supported by massive columns of green marble. The pulpit (1473), original in design, by Mino da Fiesole and Antonio Rossellino, is adorned with skilfully carved scenes: the Martyrdom of St. John the Baptist, the Stoning of St. Stephen, the Assumption, etc. On the high altar is a Christ by Tacca (17C).

The **frescoes★★** by Filippo Lippi in the chancel form a striking picture of the lives of St. Stephen and St. John the Baptist. The most famous scene shows the banquet of Herod and Salome's dance. In this Filippo Lippi used all his knowledge of light and perspective *(to illuminate the frescoes, apply to the sacristy)*. The Bocchineri chapel in the south transept is decorated with frescoes by Paolo Ucello and Andrea di Giusto.

The **Chapel of the Holy Girdle★** (Capella del Sacro Cingolo 1385 - 1395), enclosed by a 15C grille, contains the precious relic, the story of which is told in frescoes by Agnolo Gaddi and his pupils (1392-1395). The Virgin and Child on the altar (1317) is by the sculptor Giovanni Pisano.

Next to the Cathedral is the **Chapter Museum** which contains a **pulpit** from which the Holy Girdle used to be shown. This pulpit designed by Michelozzo and Donatello was to the right of the Cathedral façade (it has been replaced by a copy). Note the Annunciation by Filippo Lippi and a fresco depicting Jacopone da Todi by P. Ucello.

Piazza del Comune★. — This square looks very well with its orange trees, its quaint fountain representing Bacchus as a child, its arcades and its buildings.

In the Law Courts (Palazzo Pretorio), a curious structure, rough and massive, the Romanesque and Gothic styles are mixed and represented by paired trilobar windows. The **Municipal Gallery** is on the first floor. *Open 9 am to 7 pm weekdays and 9 am to noon Sundays and holidays; closed Mondays and during exhibitions; 100 lire, free on Sundays and holidays.* There is a quaint Baroque statue of Bacchus as a child by Tacca and among the paintings a 14C predella by Bernardo Daddi relating the story of the Holy Girdle, a Virgin with Four Saints, by Lorenzo Monaco, and compositions of Filippo Lippi (Madonna, Nativity) and Filippino Lippi (Madonna Standing).

Imperial Castle★ (Castello dell'Imperatore). — *Open 9 am to noon and 4 to 7 pm; closed Wednesdays.* This castle which has been extensively restored recently, was built in the 13C on the site of a former residence of the Counts of Prato by order of Frederick II to strengthen the position of the Ghibellines *(p 18)*.

This imposing and balanced structure on a square plan with enormous towers jutting far out and crowned with cleft Ghibelline merlons, is a remarkable example of Swabian architecture which brings to mind the Castel del Monte *(p 77)*. You can visit the inner court and the towers and go round the parapet walk.

PROCIDA, Island of ★ Campania

Michelin map **988** 27 — *Local map p 162* — pop 10 233

Access. — Car ferries from **Naples** *(apply to CAREMAR, Mole Beverello, ☎ 315384; or to Società Navigazione LAURO, Mole Beverello, ☎ 313236)*. **Pozzuoli** *(apply in Pozzuoli to CAREMAR, ☎ 8671335; or to Società Navi Traghetto Pozzuoli, 3 Via C. Colombo, ☎ 8672124; or to AS, ☎ 8672419)*. **Ischia** *(apply to CAREMAR, ☎ 991781 in Ischia; or to Società Navi Traghetto Pozzuoli, address above; or to AS in Pozzuoli, address above)*.

*Hydrofoil (aliscafi) service from **Naples** (apply to Società ALILAURO, Port Sannazzaro, 13 Via Caracciolo, ☎ 681041; or to CAREMAR, Mole Beverello, ☎ 315384, in Naples — Information 313882)*.

Procida is formed of four craters levelled by erosion and partly submerged. This is the wildest island in the Bay of Naples. Fishermen, gardeners and wine-growers live there in delightful houses with domes, arcades and terraces, washed in white, yellow, ochre and pink.

Good **viewpoints★** are plentiful: the panoramic terrace of the castle, now a prison, on the Punta di Serra, and the Benedictine monastery ruins at Santa Margherita Vecchia. The trip round the island by boat *(about 3 hours)* is also recommended.

Graziella. — This was the first name of the pure and gentle island maiden, a daughter of poor fisher-folk, who fell in love with the young Alphonse de Lamartine when he took shelter from a storm on the island. Unfortunately the French poet left for Paris and forgot his promise to return, and sad Graziella died of a broken heart. Lamartine related this touching affair in a short novel, *Graziella,* and in one of the finest poems in his *Harmonies*.

RAPALLO * Liguria _____

Michelin map **988** 13 — *Local map p 200* — Pop 29 667

Town plan in Michelin Red Guide Italia (hotels and restaurants).

Rapallo, a resort with an international reputation has an ideal situation and enjoys a mild climate. Many walks can be taken in the nearby hills and towards the fishing village of San Michele di Pagana and the Portofino promontory *(p 191)*. A boat service links Rapallo with Portofino daily in summer *(1 500 lire single, 2 500 lire Rtn)* and in fine weather, with San Fruttuoso *(2 500 lire single, 4 000 lire Rtn)*. There are also boat trips to the Cinqueterre *(p 83)*: *5 000 lire single; 8 500 lire Rtn.*

Madonna di Montallegro (alt 612 m - 2 008 ft). — *Northeast, 11 km - 7 miles. Bus service, 900 lire Rtn.* There is a splendid **view★★** from the church of the Gulf of Rapallo. A winding path leads to a grassy hillock, on the left, from which there is a good view of the opposite slopes.

RAVELLO ★★★ Campania _____

Michelin map **988** 27 — *Local map p 45* — Pop. 2 375

Ravello, the Gateway to the East, with its alleys, stairways and roofed passages clings to the steep slopes of the Dragon Hill. The **site★★★**, suspended above the sea, is unforgettable.

Access. — The **panoramic road★★★** coming from Amalfi and Atrani climbs in hairpin bends up the narrow Dragon Valley (Valle del Dragone), planted with vines, fruit trees and olives. It affords several bird's-eye views of Atrani, the coast and the sea. The white walls and pink tiled roofs of monasteries, chapels and dwelling houses are scattered over the slopes.

Villa Rufolo★★★. — *Open 1 June to 30 September, 9.30 am to 1.30 pm and 3 to 7.40 pm; the rest of the year, 9.30 am to 1 pm and 2 to 6.40 pm. Closed Thursdays; 250 lire. Enter from the Piazza Vescovado.* The villa was built in the 11C by the rich Rufoli family of Ravello and was the residence of several popes, of Charles of Anjou and, more recently, of the German composer Wagner. The 11 and 12C architecture and the gardens make a picture of truly Oriental beauty in which sunlight shimmers, tea-roses bloom and fountains play.

The square court, planted with hydrangeas, with sharply pointed arches in the Sicilian-Norman style *(p 27)* surmounted by interlacing, is a little old cloister which has been restored.

A massive 11C tower overlooks the richly flowered gardens. There is a splendid **view★★★** over the jagged peaks and the distant Maiori Bay.

The winding **Via Annunziata★★**, passing to the left of the Villa Rufolo, beneath some arching and descending finally down some steps, possesses little known and attractive corners. It is lined by old churches and monasteries and affords lovely glimpses of the coast.

Villa Cimbrone★★★. — *Open 9 am to 7 pm; 250 lire.* The road leading to it from the Piazza Vescovado will please the stroller. There are views of the Dragon Valley and the Monasteries of Sant'Antonio (Gothic porch and small Romanesque cloisters) and Santa Chiara. Entering the villa enclosure first, on the left, are charming cloisters and a fine hall with ogive vaulting (curious grilles). At the garden entrance, bear right and walk along to the belvedere, from which there is an immense **panorama★★★** of the Gulf of Salerno as far as Paestum.

Cathedral (**Duomo**). — Founded in 1086, the church was transformed in the 18C. The campanile is 13C. In the centre of the façade is a fine bronze **door★**, cast by Barisano da Trani (1179). The Baroque nave, of which the antique columns have been uncovered, is adorned on the left with a Byzantine ambo (pulpit) and mosaics representing Jonah and the Whale, and on the right with a magnificent **pulpit★★** bearing a remarkable variety of fantastic animals (1272).

Church of St. John of the Bull★ (**San Giovanni del Toro**). — Climb the steps to the left of the cathedral and turn left to reach this little 11C church, restored in the 18C. It has antique columns and contains a 12C ambo.

RAVENNA ★★★ Emilia-Romagna _____

Michelin map **988** 15 — Pop 139 226

A former Imperial city, the Byzantium of the West, Ravenna is wrapped in nostalgic charm and contains the finest and richest evidences of early Christian art: its mosaics alone are worth a journey. The centre of the town is the **Piazza del Popolo**, embellished with two Venetian columns (1483) and the fine arcades of the town hall (15 and 16C).

HISTORICAL NOTES

Imperial Ravenna. — In AD 402 Honorius abandoned Rome and made Ravenna the capital of the Roman Empire. The town, built on piles, was more or less safe from the Barbarians and could use the port of Classis, founded by Augustus, to the south, which could accommodate up to 250 ships. Galla Placidia, the sister of Honorius a pious but adventurous woman of dazzling beauty, lavishly but rashly governed the Western Empire in the place of her son Valentinian. The spreading Barbarian invasions brought the Ostrogoth Kings Odoacer (476-493) and Theodoric (493-526) to Ravenna. Both embellished the town, and Theodoric became a Christian.

Then, in 540, Ravenna was conquered by the Byzantine Emperors. The town was administered by governors called Éxarchs and was loaded with favours by the Emperor Justinian and the Empress Theodora. Christianity spread quickly at this time; outstanding events were the martyrdom of St. Apollinaris, the preaching of St. Peter Chrysologus, and the proselytism of bishops. Two Christian sects, the Latin Arians and the Orthodox Greeks co-existed more or less successfully.

The Mosaics. — The Ravenna mosaics are the finest in Europe surpassing even those of Constantinople, Palermo and Venice. Dante, in the *Divine Comedy*, described them as a "symphony of colour", their chief characteristics being clarity, harmony, bright colours and decorative rhythm of design. The figures, with dark eyes, ringed with black, have a strange, distant expression. The mosaics are made up of small cubes called *tesserae*, laid irregularly in order to catch the light. The spirit they express is both realistic and mystical, with a symbolic meaning: doves drink from the Fountain of Life, peacocks symbolise immortality and stags represent souls.

The present-day School of Mosaicists at Ravenna has carried on the Byzantine tradition.

★★ MAUSOLEO DI GALLA PLACIDIA
★★ SAN VITALE
SEPOLCRO DI DANTE

★ BATTISTERO DEGLI ORTODOSSI
★ BASILICA S. APOLLINARE NUOVO

RAVENNA

0 ——————— 400 m

■ **MAIN SIGHTS** *time: 4 hours*

The oldest mosaics are in the Orthodox Baptistry and the Galla Placidia Tomb; next in chronological order are those adorning the Arians' Baptistry, St Apollinaris the New, St. Vitalis and, finally, St. Apollinaris in Classe.

Tomb of Galla Placidia★★ (Mausoleo di Galla Placidia). — *Enter through the grille in front of the church, Via San Vitale. Same times of opening as St. Vitalis. For illumination see automatic machine outside the tomb; 100 lire.* This mid-5C mausoleum in the form of a Latin cross, of Roman inspiration, is believed to have been built by the Empress Galla Placidia who wished to be buried there. Its wonderful **mosaics★★★** are famous for the range of their colours, notably the deep blues, and for their adaptation of decoration to the object decorated. The tympanum on the reverse of the entrance bears a mosaic of the Good Shepherd; opposite is St. Lawrence walking to the gridiron on which he was martyred by being roasted alive; to the left, an open book-case contains the Gospels; on the tympana of the transepts, stags (representing souls) drink from the Fountain of Life; on the dome are a Cross and evangelical symbols, and on either side of the windows are alabaster decorations showing the Apostles in white. Geometrical designs, animals and foliage are used as decoration.

The sarcophagus at the far end is supposed to contain the body of Galla Placidia.

Church of St. Vitalis★★ (San Vitale). — *Open 8.30 am to 7.30 pm (5 pm 1 October to 31 May, closed 1 January, 1 May, 15 August and 25 December).* This Byzantine church was consecrated in 547 by Archbishop Maximian. The brick exterior is plain but the interior is dazzling. The church has an octagonal plan, with a projecting chancel, an ambulatory roofed with ribbed vaulting, a dome and concentric galleries (the *matroneae*) reserved for the use of women during the services. The whole is a marvel of architectural originality, with its precious marbles, its Byzantine capitals and especially the admirable **mosaics★★★** in the chancel, divinely coloured, with blue, green and gold predominating. The mosaics on the sides and end wall of the chancel represent scenes from the Old Testament: on the left, Abraham and the three Angels and the Sacrifice of Isaac; on the right, the Death of Abel and the Offering of Melchizedek.

On the side walls inside the chancel are wonderful groups representing the Empress Theodora, with her suite, offering the Wine of the Sacrifice (note the Gifts of the Magi on her cloak), and the Emperor Justinian, attended by his court and by Maximian, offering the Bread of the Eucharist in surroundings of truly Byzantine splendour and solemnity enriched with gold. On the ceiling Christ the King is enthroned beside two angels, St. Vitalis, to whom he offers the crown of eternal glory, and Bishop Ecclesio, the founder of the church, who displays a model of the building.

Each year from the beginning of July to the beginning of August the church of St. Vitalis is the setting for an international festival of organ music.

To the left of the entrance to St. Vitalis is the former monastery of the same name. A **Museum of Antiquities** (Museo Nazionale) is housed in the cloisters and monastic buildings. It contains collections of tombstones and Roman sculptures, oriental fabrics, Byzantine bas-reliefs, panels painted in the Veneto-Cretan period and ivories; also an Apollo and Daphne, the so-called Diptych of Murano, and a head carved by Tullio Lombardo (16C), believed to be that of Gaston de Foix. *Open 8.30 am to 1.30 pm (noon Sundays and holidays); closed Mondays, 1 January, 1 May, 15 August and 25 December; 750 lire.*

Orthodox Baptistry★ (Battistero degli Ortodossi). — *Open weekdays, 9 am to noon and 2.30,to 6 pm (5 pm 1 October to 31 March); Sundays and holidays, 9 am to 1 pm only; 100 lire.* Known generally as the **Neoni Baptistry**, this contains superb **mosaics★★★** in brilliant and violently contrasting colours. The Byzantine bas-reliefs over the arches of the rotunda represent the prophets. The main arches over the bays are adorned with mosaics forming several different designs. The scene at the summit of the dome shows the Baptism of Christ and the Twelve Apostles.

The 18C cathedral, adjacent to the baptistry, is dominated by a rounded campanile of the 10-11C. It contains a 6C marble ambo (pulpit) adorned with symbolic animals.

Basilica of St. Apollinaris the New★ (Sant'Apollinare Nuovo). — *Open 8 am to noon and 2 to 7 pm (5 pm 1 October to 31 May).* The basilica was erected by Theodoric in the 6C. For long the basilica bore the name of San Martino in Ciel d'Oro (St. Martin in the Golden Sky). The beautiful rounded campanile dates from the 10C, but the portico is 16C. The spacious, well lit interior, with its twenty-four Greek marble columns, is adorned with brilliant **mosaics★★★**.

The left side of the basilica was reserved for women; the left frieze depicts twenty-two holy virgins leaving the town and port of Classis. Wearing Phrygian caps, they follow the Magi to offer crowns to the Crowned Virgin, surrounded by angels.

In the right frieze you will see a procession of twenty-six martyrs leaving the palace of Theodoric with an air of saintly simplicity, robed in white linen and also carrying crowns. They move solemnly towards Christ the King, who is surrounded by angels. Above both friezes are pictures of saints and prophets and, on the upper walls, scenes from the Life of Christ.

Dante's Tomb (Sepolcro di Dante). — Dante was exiled from Florence and took refuge first at Verona and then at Ravenna, where he died in 1321. His remains were laid near the Church of St. Francis (San Francesco). The Classical building in which the tomb now stands was erected in 1780.

■ ADDITIONAL SIGHTS

Theodoric's Tomb★ (Mausoleo di Teodorico) (Y A). — *Same times of opening as San Vitale. Apply to the Soprintendenza No. 17 Via San Vitale.* This curious monument, erected by Theodoric around AD 520 is built in huge blocks of free stone assembled without mortar, and is covered by a remarkable monolithic dome 11 m - 36 ft in diameter.

The decoration is sober and austere. Inside a Romanesque porphyry basin is used as a sarcophagus. Beside the mausoleum is a shady park.

Museum of the Archbishop's Palace (Museo dell'Arcivescovado) (Z M[1]). — *Weekdays, 16 March to 14 October, 9 am to noon and 2.30 to 6 pm; the rest of the year, (except Tuesday) 9 am to noon and 2.30 to 5 pm; Sundays and holidays (throughout the year), 9 am to 1 pm. Closed 1 January, Epiphany, Easter, 23 July, 2 November, Christmas and 31 December; 200 lire.* The museum is in the palace and contains the **pulpit★★** of Archbishop Maximian (6C), a masterpiece of carving in ivory with panels devoted to the Story of Joseph, the Life of Christ, and St. John the Baptist surrounded by the Evangelists.

The **Archiepiscopal Chapel★★**, known as the Oratory of St. Andrew, was built in the time of Bishop Peter II (494-519). It contains remarkable mosaics: medallions of apostles and of the first martyrs, and, in the atrium, a beautiful representation of Christ Militant. The cross of Agnellus, sheathed in silver plates depicting the Resurrection and the first Bishops of Ravenna, is 6C.

Arians' Baptistry (Battistero degli Ariani) (Y B). — *Open 8.30 am to 12.30 pm and 2.30 pm to sunset; closed 1 January, 1 May, 15 August and 25 December.* The baptistry which is thought to have been built by Theodoric at the beginning of the 6C, was consecrated to the Catholic form of worship in 558 AD. The dome is decorated with fine **mosaics★** also dating from the 6C. Note in the centre, the Baptism of Christ with St. John the Baptist, and in the surrounding band, the twelve Apostles and a throne adorned with a cross.

Public Gardens (Giardino Pubblico). — The apse of Santa Maria del Porto and the elegant Loggia del Giardino, built by Lombard craftsmen in 1508, give on this pleasant garden.

Picture Gallery (Pinacoteca Comunale) (Z M). — *Open 9 am to 1 pm and 2.30 to 5.30 pm; closed Mondays, 1 January, Easter, 25 April, 1 May, 15 August, 25 and 26 December; 200 lire (300 lire for exhibitions), free on Sundays and holidays.* The first room to the left of the entrance contains a masterpiece (1526) by Tullio Lombardo, the touching recumbent figure of a young knight, Guidarello Guidarelli, who was killed at Imola in 1501.

EXCURSIONS

Basilica of St. Apollinaris in Classe★★ (Sant'Apollinare in Classe). — *South, 5 km - 3 miles.* Leave by ③. Standing in open country where Classis once swarmed with ships and sailors, this is by far the most attractive of Ravenna's churches. It is also one of the most perfect.

The Church of St. Apollinaris was begun in AD 534 on the spot where the saint, who was the first martyr and Bishop of Ravenna, was buried. It was consecrated in 549 by Archbishop Maximian. The cylindrical tower dates only from the 11C. Its bays grow larger towards the summit.

The majestic **interior** *(same times of opening as St. Apollinaris the New)* comprises twelve great arches supported by Cipolin marble columns. In the side aisles lie superb early Christian sarcophagi carved with symbols (5-8C). Under the altar in the chancel lie the bones of St. Apollinaris.

The triumphal arch and the chancel are adorned with magnificent 6-7C **mosaics★★★**. They no longer have the savage brilliance of those of St. Vitalis or the Galla Placidia Mausoleum, but the freedom and simplicity of their composition are more marked. At the top of the arch, Christ is surrounded by the evangelical symbols and twelve lambs representing the Apostles; the Archangels Michael and Gabriel appear on the pedestals on either side, and below them, St. Matthew and St. Luke. The Transfiguration is depicted on the oven-vaulting of the apse: a great Latin cross, the *Salus Mundi* (Salvation of the World), is surrounded by a glory of stars between Moses and Elias and three lambs representing the Apostles, Peter, James and John, who witnessed the Mystery. Above the Cross can be seen the hand of the Eternal Father. Below, St. Apollinaris, the bishop, is seen among lambs representing the Elect in a beautiful landscape of flowers and rocks, including quaint details such as birds perching on trees.

Classe Pinewood★ (Pineta di Classe). — *South, 17 km - 11 miles.* Leave by ③. About 4 km - 2 1/2 miles — beyond the Basilica of St. Apollinaris and just before a bridge, bear left to take the road beside the Ghiaia Canal. Shortly after crossing over a rail track, you cross the canal by a metal bridge. From this point on signposts indicate the way. The majestic and lonely clumps of trees in the Classe Pinewood were praised by Dante, Byron and André Suarès.

REGGIO DI CALABRIA Calabria

Michelin map **988** 39 — Pop 180 298
Town plan in Michelin Red Guide Italia (hotels and restaurants).

Reggio, which stands close against the Aspromonte *(see below)*, is a pleasant town of modern appearance, rebuilt after the earthquake of 1908 along the Straits of Messina. Its beautifully coloured and changing waters have earned them the name of Rainbow of Italy. In calm weather, at dawn, the town of Messina is sometimes reflected on the surface by a phenomenon known as the "mirage of the fairy Morgana".

Reggio is surrounded with rich plantations of olives, vines (Moscato), orange and lemon trees and flowers used for making perfume. Half the world production of bergamot (a citrus fruit), most of which is exported to France, comes from Reggio.

There are boat (car ferry) and hydrofoil services to Sicily with frequent crossings.

Lungomare★★. — An elegant marine promenade affords views of the remarkable picture formed by Sicily, Messina, and the Straits, in which ships sail.

National Museum★ (Museo Nazionale). — *Open weekdays, 1 May to 30 September, 9 am to 2 pm and 5 to 7 pm; the rest of the year, 9 am to 4 pm; Sundays and holidays (throughout the year) 9 am to 1 pm. Closed Mondays, 1 January, 25 April, 1 May, first Sunday in June, 15 August and 25 December.* The collections are rich in antiques including an equestrian group in marble from the Temple of Locri, a Dioscurean group, Castor and Pollux (5C BC), a combat between Achilles and Memnon (6C BC), votive tablets illustrating the legend of Persephone and several bronze statues (5C BC). Note also two remarkable works by Antonello da Messina, a St. Jerome and Three Angels.

EXCURSION

Aspromonte★ — The massif is composed of towering heights culminating in the Montalto (1956 m - 6 417 ft). It displays a fine forest landscape of pine, beech and chestnut, with panoramas over the Tyrrhenian Sea. State road S 183 crosses the massif from north to south, passing through Gambarie. There is a view over the Straits of Messina.

REGGIO NELL'EMILIA Emilia-Romagna

Michelin map **988** 14 — Pop 130 031
Town plan in Michelin Red Guide Italia (hotels and restaurants).

Reggio is a rich industrial and commercial centre; it is also the birthplace of Ariosto *(p 100)*. Like Modena and Ferrara, it belonged to the Este family *(p 100)* from 1409 to 1776.

Parmeggiani Gallery★ (Galleria Parmeggiani). — *Closed temporarily.* The gallery has a gateway in the Hispano-Moorish style which was brought from Valencia and rebuilt here. The collections comprise gold plate and fabrics (14-18C), costumes, arms, furniture and paintings : Spanish and Flemish works (an El Greco of rare quality, a painting by Ribera, a 15C triptych of the Bruges school) as well as paintings by Italian artists (Moses saved from the Waters by A. Celesti, and Parnassus, a painting characteristic of late Mannerism in Florence).

RIETI Latium

Michelin map **988** 26 — 37 km - 23 miles — Southeast of Terni — Pop 43 296

Rieti lies at a meeting-place of valleys in the heart of a cultivated basin, and is the geographical centre of Italy. The town still shows the northern section of its 13C walls.

Piazza Cesare Battisti. — This is the architectural centre of the town. Through the 16-17C Palazzo del Governo and its elegant loggia you enter the **public garden★** with its box hedges. The cathedral has a 15C porch and a fine Romanesque campanile dating from 1252. Inside (first chapel on the left) is a fresco of the Madonna (1494). The crypt dates from 1157 *(apply to the sacristan)*.

Episcopal Palace (Palazzo Vescovile). — This stands to the right and rear of the cathedral and was built in the 13C. The **volte★**, heavily ribbed ogive arches bounding two large naves, are impressive. The late 13C Bishop's Arch spans the Via Cintia.

EXCURSIONS

The monasteries and landscape beloved by St. Francis are the main interest of the area.

Fonte Colombo Monastery★ (Convento di Fonte Colombo). — *Southwest, 5 km - 3 miles.* Go out by the Porta Romana and take the road on the right towards Contigliano which you follow for 3 km - 2 miles — among wheat fields and vines with giant stems. Bear left. In the old monastery, St. Francis underwent an operation which cured him of eye trouble. He dictated the Franciscan Rules in the grotto, after having fasted for forty days.

You will see the 12C Chapel of St. Mary Magdalen adorned with frescoes with the "T", the emblem of the Cross designed by St. Francis, the St. Michael Chapel and the grotto where St. Francis fasted; the tree-trunk in which Jesus appeared to him; the monastery, and the 15C church. There are pretty views of Rieti and Monte Terminillo.

Greccio Monastery* (Convento di Greccio). — *Northwest, 15 km - 9 miles*. Take the same route as above as far as the fork at Fonte Colombo; then continue on the Contigliano road and through the town, then 2 1/2 km - 1 1/2 miles — further in the Spinacceto district, turn left and go up to the esplanade; go through Greccio and after 2 1/2 km - 1 1/2 miles — you will reach a small esplanade in front of the monastery steps, where you leave the car.

The monastery clings at an altitude of 638 m - 2 093 ft — to a rock, which is on top of a vertical cliff; a remarkable view of Rieti and its basin is revealed. The buildings were erected partly at the time of St. Francis and partly in 1260 on the spot where St. Francis, celebrating Christmas in 1223, said mass at a manger *(presepio)* between an ox and an ass; thus started the custom of making cribs at Christmas.

A Franciscan will show you the Chapel of the Crib (frescoes by the school of Giotto) and where St. Francis and his companions lived. On the upper floor are the original church built in honour of St. Francis and the famous portrait of St. Francis when blind. Alongside is the cell of St. Bonaventura.

Monte Terminillo*. — *Northeast, 22 km - 14 miles*. Take the L'Aquila-Ascoli road; after 2 km - 1 1/4 miles — turn left. The road, climbing through meadows and beech woods, gives glimpses of the Rieti Basin and the Velino Valley. Monte Terminillo (2 213 m - 7 257 ft) is the "Mountain of Rome". A winter sports centre, **Rieti-Terminillo**, has been established at a place called Campoforogna (1 701 m - 5 580 ft) and also at Pian dei Valli (1 600 m - 5 250 ft).

RIMINI ** Emilia-Romagna
Michelin map **988** 15 - Pop 127 352
Town plan in Michelin Red Guide Italia (hotels and restaurants)

Like Janus, Rimini has two faces: that of an ancient city rich in history with its Roman and Renaissance monuments, and that of an international ultra-modern seaside resort with its small marina, airport and, in particular, a great beach of fine sand.

HISTORICAL NOTES

The fame of Rimini dates from the Roman occupation, when it became a stronghold at the junction of the Via Emilia and the Via Flaminia. But it was from the 13C onwards that the Malatesta family raised the prestige of the city, guarded as it was by a powerful citadel, to its greatest heights. After the fall of this family Rimini became a papal town.

The Malatestas. — Just as their coat of arms included the elephant and the rose, so they themselves combined extreme refinement with savagery and obstinacy. Already in the 13C this family figured in the chronicles of romance with the tragic lovers, Paolo Malatesta and Francesca da Rimini, who were murdered by the deformed and vicious Gianni Malatesta, the brother of Paolo and the husband of Francesca. Dante immortalised this episode in his *Inferno*. Sigismondo I Malatesta, a military leader who died in 1467, was full of charm and intelligence but ruthless none the less. He repudiated his first wife, poisoned his second, and strangled his third, and then made an irregular marriage with his favourite mistress, Isotta. Yet he was a cultured patron of the arts and protected painters like Piero della Francesca, Ghirlandaio and Pisanello.

■ SIGHTS *time: 1 hour*

Malatesta Temple* (Tempio Malatestiano). — The building was erected to shelter the tomb of Isotta. Sigismondo Malatesta entrusted the Florentine architect Alberti with the task of building the *tempio* in the Renaissance style. The unfinished façade in some respects recalls the Arch of Augustus : it had fluted columns with Corinthian capitals and medallions, and a frieze bearing the rose of the Malatestas and the intertwined initials of Sigismondo and Isotta encircles its base. Remarkable sculptured foliage and fascines frame the central doorway.

The spacious and imposing interior includes an allegorical decoration of exquisite grace and subtlety, due in large part to Agostino di Duccio. The details as seen in the chapels are described below. The first chapel on the right, with pilasters supported by elephants, is adorned with bas-reliefs of the Virtues; in the adjacent reliquary chapel, Piero della Francesca painted the portrait of Sigismondo Malatesta kneeling before St. Sigismund. The second chapel contains the tomb of Isotta, facing an admirable painted 14C Crucifix of the Rimini school. The bas-reliefs on the pillars of the third chapel symbolise the planets and the Signs of the Zodiac. The Arts and Sciences are represented in the third chapel on the left, and children at play in the second. The first chapel contains the cenotaph of Sigismondo's ancestors, adorned with bas-reliefs depicting a Roman Triumph and the Temple of Minerva.

The tomb of Sigismondo stands against the reverse of the entrance façade.

Bridge of Tiberius (Ponte di Tiberio). — The bridge was begun under Augustus and completed under Tiberius in AD 21, as an inscription states. The structure is of massive Istrian stones. The pilasters and frontons were restored during the Renaissance.

Arch of Augustus (Arco d'Augusto). — The arch was built in 27 BC and has a majestic appearance, with fine fluted columns and Corinthian capitals.

RIVA DEL GARDA * Trentino-Alto Adige
Michelin map **988** 4 — 50 km - 31 miles southwest of Trent — *Local map p 130* — Pop 13 202

The attractive little town of Riva, overlooked from the west by Monte Rocchetta, which is clothed in fir woods, lies in a pretty **setting**** at the northern extremity of Lake Garda and is one of its main tourist resorts.

The old town, near the harbour, is particularly charming; the Piazza 3 Novembre is dominated by the 13C Aponale Tower. The Rocca, a castle dating from 1124 and converted into barracks by the Austrians, is surrounded by moats forming moorings. It contains a museum and art galleries.

To the east of the town are magnificent gardens with a splendid avenue of magnolias.

Three kilometres - 2 miles — north of Riva, at Varone is an impressive **waterfall***.

The enchanting Italian or Ligurian Riviera is, like the French Riviera, a tourists' paradise. Washed by the blue waters of the Mediterranean, it offers all the spell of colour and beauty under skies which are always clear. From Ventimiglia to the Gulf of La Spezia the coast describes an arc backed by the attractive slopes of the Ligurian Apennines. The Riviera di Ponente lies west of Genoa, and the Riviera di Levante east of that great port.

History. — The Ligurians, who were not Latins, occupied these shores as early as the 7C BC and today many of the natives are characteristically Nordic, and blue-eyed.

Next came the Roman colonisation, which has left many traces, such as the Via Aurelia, antique monuments and marine salvage (amphorae at Albenga). Roman towns were built along the seashore. When the Barbarians invaded the country they were razed, their inhabitants moving to defensible sites in inland valleys. This happened, among other places, to Ventimiglia, Taggia and San Remo.

From the Middle Ages local history is identical with that of the Republic of Genoa.

Climate and Vegetation. — The Riviera became famous because of its permanently mild climate. The mountain barrier formed by the Apennines cuts off the north winds, while the coast lies open to warm sunshine (mean temperature for January is 9°C. — 48.2° F.). In summer a sea breeze tempers the burning sun.

Vegetation is to match: the countryside is clothed in pines, cypress, olive trees, orange and lemon trees. The scent of fields of flowers rises between Ventimiglia and Alassio; the supporting walls and the terraced gardens are covered with bougainvillaeas and roses. Vines garnish slopes cut into terraces in the Roja Valley, the environs of Genoa (Coronata) and the Cinqueterre *(p 83)*.

The fruits of the earth are used by the local oil mills, the candied-fruit factories and the scent distilleries. Those of the sea provide a livelihood for small, picturesque fishing ports.

(After photo by Arthaud)

A scene on the Riviera

TOUR

The main road artery of the Riviera is the spectacular Via Aurelia, of Roman origin — difficult, for it is winding and narrow, and carries dense traffic; it is duplicated by a motorway slightly inland. The Via Aurelia, often a *corniche* road, affords fine views when it crosses capes or promontories or runs close to the blue waters of the Ligurian Sea.

RIVIERA DI PONENTE (Western Riviera)

From Ventimiglia to Genoa — *180 km - 112 miles — about 5 hours.*

The road is much frequented by tourists. Many resorts and villas form an almost continuous chain of dwellings which often hide the view of the sea. The coastal plain is sometimes spacious and the adjacent valleys are cultivated in terraces.

Mortola Inferiore. — *Description p 152.*

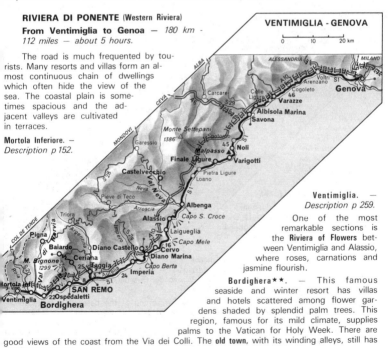

Ventimiglia. — *Description p 259.*

One of the most remarkable sections is the **Riviera of Flowers** between Ventimiglia and Alassio, where roses, carnations and jasmine flourish.

Bordighera★★. — This famous seaside and winter resort has villas and hotels scattered among flower gardens shaded by splendid palm trees. This region, famous for its mild climate, supplies palms to the Vatican for Holy Week. There are good views of the coast from the Via dei Colli. The **old town**, with its winding alleys, still has fortified gateways.

Ospedaletti★. — This very pretty winter resort lies at the head of a bay. Its name is derived from a hospital *(ospedale)* founded by the Knights of Rhodes.

Pines, eucalyptus, orange trees and splendid palm trees line the Corso Regina Margherita.

San Remo★★★ and Excursion to Baiardo★★. – *Description p 222.*

The *corniche* road between San Remo and Imperia is particularly remarkable.

Taggia★. — *Description p 233.*

RIVIERA, The Italian★★★

Imperia. — A provincial town formed by the merger of **Oneglia** — a small, active trading centre (oil) — and **Porto Maurizio** — whose harbour is dominated by the old town built on a promontory —, Imperia is also a health and tourist resort. Olive groves abound inland.

Diano Marina. — Its origin was a wood consecrated to the Ligurian god Bormanus, who was later assimilated with the goddess Diana by the Romans.

Diano Castello, a fortified village with a few monumental buildings, notably the 12C Chapel of the Knights of Malta, which has a multicoloured wooden roof.

Cervo. — Cervo clings to the rock and is one of the most picturesque villages on the Riviera. From the San Giovanni Battista esplanade there is a **view★** of a village and the sea.
Before reaching Alassio, the road passes Cape Mele, a good viewpoint, and then Laigueglia whose inhabitants used to dive for coral.

Alassio★. — This resort with its long beach lies along the shore of a great bay sheltered from cold winds by an amphitheatre of mountains (January temperature: 11°C. = 51.8°F.).
The view from Cape Santa Croce, just beyond Alassio, is one of the attractions of the journey.

Albenga. — *Description p 43.*

Finale Ligure. — Four villages, three linked by a splendid *corniche* road, form the large resort of Finale Ligure. **Finale Borgo,** 2 km - 1 1/2 miles — inland, is the former capital of the marquisate, with its town walls and its Gothic Collegiate Church of St. Blaise (San Biagio), built on a tower in the walls and flanked by a graceful campanile. **Finale Marina** has a fanciful Baroque façade to its basilica. **Finale Pia** has an abbey church with an elegant late 13C campanile.

Varigotti. — This town, built on the side of a promontory, boasts a fine sandy beach.

Malpasso★. — This stretch of country, once difficult and with a reputation for banditry, lies between Noli and Varigotti. A magnificent *corniche* road passes through it today.

Noli. — This fishing village still has ancient houses, three 13C towers of nobility and a Romanesque church. The apricots grown here are famous.

Savona. — *Description p 224.*

Albisola Marina. — The place is known for the skilled production of ceramics, carrying on a tradition of high quality dating from the 13C. At the end of the 16C a Duke of Nevers, a member of the Italian Gonzaga family, summoned the Conrade brothers from Albisola to Nevers to found a faïence factory. Ceramic exhibitions are held in the 17C **Villa Faraggiana.** *Open: 1 June to 30 September, 9 to 11.30 am and 3.30 to 5 pm; 1 October to 31 May, 9 to 11.30 am and 2.30 to 5.30 pm; closed Saturday and Sunday mornings and Tuesday; 500 lire.*
The 17-18C **Villa Gavotti** at Albisola Superiore belonged to the Della Roveres, the family of Popes Julius II and Sixtus IV. This luxurious mansion is surrounded by a magnificent garden.

Varazze. — A great beach stretches before this pleasant town, the birthplace of Jacobus de Voragine (1230-1298), author of the *Golden Legend,* the miraculous history of the saints.
The balcony-road overlooking the sea, from Varazze to Cogoleto, traverses a countryside of pinewoods before reaching Genoa *(p 117).*

GENOVA - LA SPEZIA
0   10   20 km

RIVIERA DI LEVANTE (Eastern Riviera)
From Genoa to La Spezia - *151 km - 94 miles — about 3 1/2 hours*

The Eastern Riviera extends from Genoa to La Spezia and the mouth of the Magra River. It has more character and is wilder than the Western Riviera. Sharp promontories, little sheltered coves or wide, sunny bays, cliffs, pinewoods and tiny fishing ports lend it charm.

The road is often winding and hilly but less often a *corniche* than west of Genoa.

Portofino Peninsula★★★.
— *Description p 191.*

Rapallo★. — *Description p 194.*

Chiavari. — Chiavari, an industrial town (slates and chair-making), is linked with **Lavagna** which is prolonged by Cavi. It has an extensive beach and a fine **park** in the centre of the town.

San Salvatore, 2 km - 1 1/4 miles — northeast from the coast, is known for its 13C Basilica dei Fieschi in a pure early Gothic style. The Palazzo dei Fieschi, opposite is a graceful Pisan Gothic building.

Sestri Levante★. — A seaside resort in an admirable setting at the base of a rocky peninsula on the Gulf of Rapallo. The praises of Sestri Levante were sung by Dante and Petrarch.
The road affords pretty views between Sestri Levante and La Spezia and especially from the Bracco Pass (**passo**) towards the Gulf of Moneglia.

Bonassola. — This is a small town set at the back of a cove, amid smiling hills covered with olives and pines.

Levanto. — *There are boat trips starting from Levanto to the Cinqueterre coast, Portovenere and Portofino. Apply to the Rossignoli Company,* ☎ *817582, or to Società Navigazione Monterosso,* ☎ *817545, in Monterosso al Mare.* In winter as in summer it is pleasant to stay at this little town buried in foliage and overlooked by a castle which is a relic of the Genoese Republic.
The road reaches La Spezia *(p 230).*

Michelin map 988 26 — Pop 2 914 640
Town plans in Michelin Red Guide Italia (hotels and restaurants)

Capital of an Empire to which it gave its name and the seat of Christianity after the collapse of ancient civilisations, Rome is rich in relics of its past and was for a long time the first museum-city in the world.

It is today no longer the marble city created by Augustus and the Emperors, nor the most brilliant court in Europe as during Papal rule. Since 1870 when it became the capital of Italy, Rome has undergone extensive urban development. The Roman landscape with its cypresses and umbrella pines under a sky of admirable purity and bathed in a lovely, golden light, remains a setting of unforgettable majesty; but its charms are nowadays marred by the bustle that characterizes a modern city and by the passion of the Romans for cars.

HISTORICAL NOTES

Ancient Rome. — Romulus, the legendary Latin founder of Rome on the Palatine Hill in 753 BC headed the **Reign of the Kings**. Three Sabine kings succeeded him, followed by three Etruscan kings; they governed Rome until 509 BC when the **Republic** was founded. This period was marked by violent struggles between the Patricians and the Plebeians and the conquest of the peninsula and of the Mediterranean basin. Octavius heralded the institution of the **Empire** when in 27 BC the Senate conferred on him the title of Augustus. In the 3C the Empire split in-to two parts, the Eastern and Western Empires. Power was shared by four emperors (tetrarchy). Rome, under siege, sought shelter behind high walls built by Aurelius (270-275). Pagan gods were renounced while Christianity expanded to such an extent that it became the state religion under the Emperor Constantine (306-337). During the 5 and 6C Rome yielded to the onslaughts of the Barbarians. Placed under the rule of Byzantium after the abolition of the Eastern Empire (476), Rome was in effect saved by its bishop, the Pope.

Papal Rome. — In 756 Pepin the Short took over the territories of the peninsula occupied by the Lombards and returned them not to the Byzantine Emperor but to the Pope, thus initiating the creation of the Papal States. In the Middle Ages Rome was poverty-stricken as it was torn by the conflicts between the Papacy and the Holy Roman Empire.

After the Renaissance, the Papacy reacted against the Protestant Reformation with the Counter-Reformation or Catholic Reformation laid down by the Council of Trent (1545-1563).

The Capital of Italy. — Following the Risorgimento, the states of the peninsula agreed to the unification of Italy under King Victor Emmanuel II (1861), but Rome and the Papal States re-mained aloof. In 1870 Rome was proclaimed capital of the kingdom. The Pope retired to the Vatican and the Roman Question was settled in 1929 by the Lateran Agreements.

ART IN ROME

In Antiquity. — The Romans, a nation of peasants and warriors, developed an interest in Art only after discovering Etruscan and Greek art. The ancient monuments of Rome which are dilapidated, are of interest mainly because of their historical value. In the museums, note in par-ticular Roman portraits, decorative objects and bas-reliefs.

In the Middle Ages. — In these poverty-stricken times, art is characterized by simplicity. Churches are soberly built in brick and adorned with elements taken from ancient monuments (pillars, capitals, cornices, etc.).

Civil architecture consisted mainly of palaces and villas built for patrician families.

Special mention must be made of the decorations created by the **Cosmati**, a guild of marble masons (12-13C) who specialized in assembling coloured marble fragments (pavements, episcopal thrones, ambos or pulpits, paschal candelabra), and in inlay with blue, red and gold enamel of pillars and friezes in cloisters.

During the Renaissance. — Martin V marked the beginning of this period by reinstating Rome as capital after the Great Schism. The Renaissance movement after the splendour it achieved in Florence, manifested itself in sober style in Rome. Church façades, smooth and flat, are simply adorned with flat pilasters. Palaces retain an austere look. The Renaissance came to an abrupt end in 1527 with the sacking of Rome by the army of Charles V.

During the Counter-Reformation. — During this period, art had to promote the principles of the Council of Trent. A typical church of the Counter-Reformation is that of Gesù *(p 204)*. Painting and sculpture declined into **Mannerism** *(see p 30)*.

Baroque Art. — From the reign of Urban VIII, movement spread to architecture. Church faça-des were enlivened with free-standing columns, niches and overhangs, the design of buildings became more sweeping, with rounded or curved lines according to Baroque inspiration.

Sculpture delighted in flowing draperies and cherubs perching on cornices and pediments. Painters aimed at visual effects with diagonal or spiral compositions.

From the 18C to the Present Day. — After Baroque exuberance, Neo-Classicism (mid 18C to early 19C) reverted to purity and symmetry of line.

The evolution of the major contemporary trends is traced in the **National Gallery of Modern Art (CV M12)** situated in the fine park of the Villa Borghese.

VISIT

Visitors will find in the next pages a selection of the most important sights of the capital. For practical purposes, we have grouped together those situated in the same area, linked by public transport or easily reached by car.

Plan your own itinerary with the help of the map on p 206-207 which indicates the sights listed and the roads to take.

Fashionable Quarters. — Luxury shops are to be found around the **Piazza del Popolo (BV)**, **Via del Corso (BCX)**, **Via del Babuino (BX)**, and **Via della Mercede (CX 41)**.

Via Veneto (CX), lined with cafes and luxurious hotels, is a fashionable international tourist centre which offers a lively night life.

Piazza Navona (BX) is a fashionable meeting-place where Romans, foreigners, tourists and globe-trotters foregather. The little streets of the **Trastevere (BY)** are dotted with restaurants embellished with arbours. In the **Via dei Coronari (BX 25)**, antique shops abound.

■ CAPITOL, ROMAN FORUM AND PALATINE plan p 203

PIAZZA VENEZIA★ (CY 82)

The Piazza in the centre of Rome is lined with palaces (Palazzo Venezia, Palazzo Bonaparte - CX D — and the 20C Palazzo delle Assicurazioni Generali di Venezia - CY F).

Palazzo Venezia★ (CY A). — This palace, built by Pope Paul II (1464-1471), is one of the first Renaissance buildings. The museum *(open 9 am to 1.30 pm; 1 pm Sundays and holidays; closed Mondays, 1 January, 25 April, 1 May, 1st Sunday in June, 15 August and Christmas; 1 000 lire)* on the first floor contains ceramics, a collection of 13-15C statues and tapestries (15-17C) and arms (15-18C) arranged in the three rooms of Paul II's apartment. The **Basilica of St. Mark** (San Marco), installed in the palace in the 15C, has a fine Renaissance façade★.

Memorial to Victor Emmanuel II (Vittoriano) **(CY B).** — This memorial by Giuseppe Sacconi (1885) dominates the Piazza Venezia and overshadows the other monuments of Rome by its size and harsh white colour. In its plinth is a **Risorgimento Museum★** *(entrance in Via di San Pietro in Carcere* - **CY 62**; *closed for restoration work).*

CAPITOL (Campidoglio) (CY)

On the hill which symbolized the power of ancient Rome, there now stands the city administrative offices, also the church of Santa Maria d'Aracoeli, the Piazza del Campidoglio and its palaces, and pleasant gardens.

Santa Maria d'Aracoeli★★ (CY C). — The church has a beautiful staircase built as an ex-voto after the plague of 1346, and a flat, austere façade characteristic of mediaeval architecture. It was built in 1250 on the spot where the Sibyl of theTiber announced the coming of Christ to Augustus. In the first chapel on the right are **frescoes★** by Pinturicchio (c. 1485).

Piazza del Campidoglio★★★ (CY 17). — This square was designed and partly laid out by Michelangelo from 1536 onwards. It is framed by three palaces and a balustrade with statues of the Heavenly Twins or Dioscuri; the **equestrian statue of Marcus Aurelius★★** (late 2C) in the centre was installed and restored by Michelangelo. The **Palazzo dei Conservatori★★★ (CY M1)**, built in the 15C and remodelled in 1568 by Giacomo della Porta, houses a **museum★★★** of antique art which includes the **She-Wolf★★★** (6-5C BC), the **Boy Extracting a Thorn★★★**, a Greek original or a very good copy dating back to the first century BC, a **Bust of Junius Brutus★★**, a remarkable head dating from the third century BC placed on a bust in the Renaissance period. *Open 9 am to 2 pm — 1 pm Sundays; also 5 to 8 pm Tuesdays and Thursdays, 8.30 to 11 pm Saturdays. Closed Mondays, 1 January, 1 May, 15 August, Easter and Christmas. 400 lire; 500 lire evenings.* The **picture gallery★** *(2nd floor)* contains mainly 17C paintings; on the landing are two 4C Roman pictures in inlaid marble.

The **New Palace★★★** (Palazzo Nuovo) **(CY M²)**, built in 1665 by Girolamo Rainaldi, houses the **Capitoline Museum★★** *(same visiting times and ticket as the museum in Palazzo dei Conservatori)* where you will see the **Dying Gaul★★★**, a Roman sculpture based on a bronze of the Pergamo school (3-2C BC); the **Emperors' Room★★** with portraits of all the emperors; the **Venus of the Capitol★★**, a Roman work inspired by the Venus of Cnidus by Praxiteles; and the **Mosaic of the Doves★★** from Hadrian's villa at Tivoli.

The **Senators' Palace★★★** (Palazzo Senatorio) **(CY H** — *not open)* is a 12C structure, remodelled between 1582 and 1602 by Giacomo della Porta and Girolamo Rainaldi.

ROMAN FORUM (Foro Romano)★★★ plan p 203

From Via del Campidoglio there is a beautiful **view★★★** of the ruins. The remains of the Roman Forum, the religious, political and commercial centre of ancient Rome, reflect the twelve centuries of history which created Roman civilisation. The Forum was excavated in the 19 and 20C.

Going down from the Capitol by the Via del Campidoglio, then by the Via del Foro Romano which form the ancient Clivus Capitolinus, you will see the **portico "degli Dei Consenti★"**, a colonnade of pillars with Corinthian capitals dating back to restoration work of AD 367; the portico was dedicated to the twelve principal Roman deities. Next comes the **Temple of Vespasian★★** (Tempio di Vespasiano — end of 1C) of which three elegant Corinthian columns remain.

Farther on, on the left, stands the **Mamertine Prison★** (Carcere Mamertino), State prison in Antiquity in which Jugurtha (105 BC) and Vercingetorix (52 BC) both died. According to legend, St. Peter and St. Paul caused a spring to gush forth in order to baptise their gaolers. Opposite is the **church of St. Luca and St. Martina★**, built in the 17C by Pietro da Cortona.

Continue to the Forum entrance: *open 9 am to 1 hour before sunset (1 pm Sundays and holidays). Closed Tuesdays, 1 January, Easter, 1 May, 15 August, 25 December; 1 000 lire.*

The **Basilica Emilia** was the second basilica erected in Rome (179 BC); fine remains of the architrave and pillars have been unearthed on the north side.

Take **Via Sacra★★** along which victorious generals marched in triumph, to the **Curia★★**, rebuilt in the 3C by Diocletian. In this building were held meetings of the Senate; nowadays it houses the **Plutea of Trajan★★★**, panels carved in the 2C with bas-reliefs depicting scenes from the life of the Emperor, and sacrificial animals.

The tribune for public speakers was called **Rostrum★ (a)** because it was adorned with *rostra* (beaks or rams) of galleys captured at Antium in 338 BC.

Nearby, the imposing **Triumphal Arch of Septimus Severus★★** (Arco di Settimio Severo) was built in AD 203 to commemorate this Emperor's victories over the Parthians. There remain only eight 4C columns of the **Temple of Saturn★★★** (Tempio di Saturno). The **Column of Phocas★** (Colonna di Foca) was erected in AD 608 in honour of the Byzantine Emperor Phocas who presented the Pantheon to Boniface IV. The **Basilica Giulia★★** which has five aisles, was built by Julius Caesar and completed by Augustus. It served as law court and exchange. The historical interest of the **Temple of Caesar** (Tempio di Cesare) **(b)** dedicated by Octavius in 29 BC and of which little now remains, is that it marked the institution in Rome of the cult of the Emperor as a deity. Three beautiful columns remain of the **Temple of Castor and Pollux★★★** (Tempio di Castore e Polluce), dedicated to the Heavenly Twins or Dioscuri, deities who helped the Romans defeat the Italic cities at Lake Regilus in about 496 BC. The circular **Temple of Vesta★★★** (Tempio di Vesta) stands near the **House of the Vestal Virgins★★★** (Casa delle Vestali), virgins whose duty it was to tend the Sacred Flame. The **Regia (c)**, although completely in ruins (relics protected by a roof), is of particular interest as it is thought to have been the house of Numa Pompilius, King of Rome and successor to Romulus. The **Temple of Antoninus and Faustina★★**

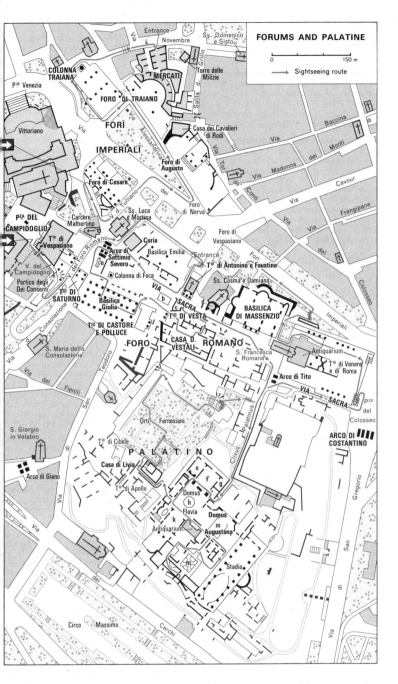

FORUMS AND PALATINE

0   150 m

→ Sightseeing route

(Tempio di Antonino e Faustina) dedicated to the Emperor Antoninus the Pius and his wife and decorated with a beautiful sculptured frieze of griffins and candelabra, is now occupied by the church of San Lorenzo in Miranda (17C). The **Temple of Romulus** (Tempio di Romolo-**d**) (the son of Maxentius, who died in 307) retains its concave façade with, between two porphyry columns, a door with two bronze panels dating from the 4C. The **Basilica of St. Maxentius**★★★ (Basilica di Massenzio) was completed by the Emperor Constantine. The **Arch of Titus**★★ (Arco di Tito), erected in 81 commemorates the capture of Jerusalem by the Emperor.

To visit the Temple of Venus and Rome and the Church of Sts. Cosmas and Damian, leave by the door near the Arch of Titus (see above).

PALATINE★★★ (Palatino) *(plan above)*

Same visiting times as the Roman Forum.

The Palatine Hill, where Romulus and Remus were discovered, was chosen by Domitian as the site for the Imperial Palace. This considerable building includes three principal areas: the **Domus Flavia**★ or official state apartments, the **Domus Augustana**★★ or private imperial apartments arranged on two levels around two peristyles, and the **Stadium**★ for athletic contests and entertainments. The Domus Flavia comprised three principal chambers: a basilica **(e)** where the Emperor dispensed justice, a throne-room **(f)** and a *lararium* **(g)** or private imperial chapel, and in addition, a peristyle **(h)** and an official dining-hall or *triclinium* **(k)** which opened on to two nymphea. The **House of Livia**★★ (Casa di Livia) probably belonged to Augustus (fine vestiges of paintings). The **Farnese Gardens** (Orti Farnesiani), laid out in 16C on the site of the palace of Tiberius, afford **views**★★ of the Forum and town.

Leave the Palatine by the Clivus Palatinus and take the Via Sacra by the Arch of Titus.

ROME★★★

Temple of Venus and Rome★ (Tempio di Venere e di Roma). — The temple built between 121 and 136 by Hadrian was the biggest in the city; its special feature is the twin *cellae* with apses built back to back.

Church of Sts. Cosmas and Damian (Santi Cosma e Damiano). — *Entrance in Via dei Fori Imperiali.* Built in the 6C on the ruins of the Temple of Romulus *(p 203)* and of the Forum of Vespasian *(p 211),* the church was remodelled in the 16 and 17C. Note the 17C **ceiling★**; **mosaics★** (late 7C on the arch; 6C in the apse); 18C **Neapolitan crib★** *(being restored).*

COLISEUM★★★ (Colosseo) (CY)

This amphitheatre, inaugurated in AD 80, and also known as the Flavian Amphitheatre after its initiator, Vespasian, first of the Flavian emperors, was given the name *Colosseo* perhaps because of the colossal statue of Nero, the Colosseum, which stood near by; perhaps also on account of its colossal dimensions (527 m - 1729 ft — in circumference and 57 m - 187 ft — high). With its three superimposed classical orders (Doric, Ionic and Corinthian), it is a masterpiece of the architecture of Antiquity. Brackets supported the bases of poles that fitted into holes in the upper cornice. This made it possible to stretch the linen awning *(velum)* to protect spectators from the sun and rain. Total capacity was 50 000.

Fights between men and beasts, gladiatorial contests, races and simulated naval battles took place in the arena. Excavations have brought to light "wings", located below the arena from where the wild beasts were brought up by a system of ramps and hoists.

ARCH OF CONSTANTINE★★★ (Arco di Constantino) (CY E)

The arch was erected to commemorate Constantine's victory over Maxentius in AD 315. Some of the bas-reliefs were removed from 2C monuments erected in honour of Trajan, Hadrian and Marcus Aurelius.

■ **PAPAL ROME** plan p 206

ENVIRONS OF THE PANTHEON

Pantheon★★★ (BX). — *Open 9 am to 1 hour before sunset. Closed 1 January, Easter Sunday and Monday, 1 May, 15 August, Christmas and 26 December.* The Pantheon, an ancient building perfectly preserved, founded by Agrippa in 27 BC and rebuilt by Hadrian (AD 117-125), was a temple which was converted into a church in the 7C. Access is through a portico supported by sixteen single granite columns, all ancient except for three on the left. The doors are original.

The **interior★★★**, a masterpiece of harmony and majesty, is dominated by a dome, the diameter of which is equal to its height. The side chapels, adorned with alternate curved and triangular pediments, contain the tombs of the kings of Italy and that of Raphaël (on the left).

St. Mary over Minerva Church★ (Santa Maria sopra Minerva) (BX A). — Founded in the 8C on the remains of a temple dedicated to Minerva, the church was rebuilt in 1280 in the Gothic style and remodelled in the 15C (doorways) and 17C (façade). The interior (pillars faced with grey marble in the 19C) is rich in **works of art★**: **frescoes★** by Filippino Lippi (south transept); statue of Christ (in front of the chancel, on the left) rough-hewn by Michelangelo and completed by his pupils; **tombs★** (chapel on the left of the chancel) from the Gothic period, the 15C and the Baroque era; at floor level, the tomb of Fra Angelico, Dominican painter who died in 1455.

In front of the church, there is a pretty square adorned with a small elephant (designed by Ercole Ferrata, pupil of Bernini, 1667) supporting an Egyptian obelisk.

Gesù★★★ (BY). — The mother-church of the Jesuits in Rome, built by Vignola in 1568, is a typical building of the Counter-Reformation. On the outside, the engaged pillars replace the flat pilasters of the Renaissance, with light and shade effects and recesses. The interior, which is vast to facilitate preaching, is lavishly decorated in the Baroque style: on the dome, the **Baciccia frescoes★★** illustrate the Triumph of the Name of Jesus (1679); the **St. Ignatius Chapel★★★** *(north transept)* where St. Ignatius of Loyola is buried, is the work of the Jesuit Brother Andrea Pozzo (1696-1700) and is sumptuously decorated.

Palazzo Doria Pamphili★ (CX M³). — One of the largest palaces in Rome, it has an 18C Baroque façade on the Via del Corso, a façade built in 1643 facing the via del Plebiscito, a 19C façade overlooking the Via della Gatta, and a fourth the Piazza del Collegio Romano.

Doria Pamphili Gallery★. — *Entrance in Piazza del Collegio Romano. On the first floor. Open 10 am to 1 pm; 1 000 lire; plus 1 000 lire for the private apartments. Closed Mondays, Wednesdays and Thursdays, 1 January, 1 May and 25 December.* Rich collections of paintings and sculptures including: **Rest on the Flight into Egypt★★★** by Caravaggio, a **bust of Olimpia Maidalchini Pamphili★★** by Algardi (Gallery 1); a **portrait of Innocent X★★★**, a masterpiece by Velasquez (Gallery 3); and **works★★** by Annibale Carracci (pictures in a semi-circle; Gallery 4).

The **private apartments★** *(guided tour)* were in use in the 16-18C.

St. Ignatius★ (Sant'Ignazio) (BX G). — The dome of this edifice of the Counter-Reformation (1626) is decorated with a Triumph of St. Ignatius, an amazing **fresco★★** in trompe-l'œil by Brother Andrea Pozzo (1684). Note also, by the same artist, the "Cupola", a simple canvas painted in *trompe-l'œil.*

The **Piazza Sant'Ignazio★** is like a stage set with characters entering from the alley-wings.

Piazza Colonna★ (BX). — An important centre of Roman life. The **column★** in the square was erected in the 2C to commemorate the wars of Marcus Aurelius.

On one side of the square, the **Palazzo Chigi** (BX C) (15-16C) is occupied by the Presidency of the Council of Ministers. Close by, the **Palazzo di Montecitorio** (BX D), started by Bernini in 1650 and completed by Carlo Fontana in 1697, is used as the Chamber of Deputies; in the square of the same name stands a 6C BC obelisk, brought back from Heliopolis (Egypt) by Augustus. The façade overlooking the Piazza del Parlamento (BX 47) dates from 1903-1925.

St. Augustine★ (Sant'Agostino) (BX E). — The late 15C church has a characteristic Renaissance façade. In the interior (remodelled in the 18 and 19C) note in particular the **Madonna del Parto★** by Jacopo Sansovino (1521) by the main door; the **prophet Isaiah★** (1512), a fresco by Raphaël *(third pillar on the left of the nave);* and the **Madonna of the Pilgrims★★★** by Caravaggio (1605) in the first chapel on the left.

St. Louis of the French★★ (San Luigi dei Francesi) (BX L). — *Closed Monday and Thursday afternoons.* This is the French church in Rome. Its façade, probably designed by Giacomo della Porta, heralds Baroque art with its projecting columns.

In the second chapel on the right are **frescoes by Domenichino★** illustrating the legend of St. Cecilia. In the fifth chapel on the left, note **paintings by Caravaggio★★★**, which illustrate his realism with strong *chiaroscuro* (scenes from the life of St. Matthew).

Palazzo Madama (BX F). — The palace, now the seat of the Senate, was built by the Medicis in the 16C. It is named after Princess Margaret of Austria, wife of Alessandro de' Medici. The Baroque façade overlooks Corso del Rinascimento (1649).

Palazzo della Sapienza (BX K). — Behind a plain façade (begun in 1575 from designs by Giacomo della Porta), the palace contains an elegant inner court and the church of **Sant'Ivo alla Sapienza★**, an example of the unorthodox style of architecture of Borromini, the rival of Bernini.

PIAZZA NAVONA QUARTER

Piazza Navona★★ (BX). — The square built on the site of Domitian's Stadium, retains its shape. A pleasant and lively pedestrian precinct, it is adorned at the centre by the Baroque masterpiece, Bernini's **Fountain of the Four Rivers★★★** completed in 1651. The statues represent the four rivers symbolising the four corners of the earth.

Among the churches and palaces surrounding the square, note **Sant'Agnese in Agone** (BX N) with a Baroque façade by Borromini (attractive **interior★** on the plan of a Greek cross), and the adjoining **Palazzo Pamphili** (17C).

Palazzo Braschi★ (BX M⁴). — Neo-Classical building dating from late 18C. In the northwest corner of the palace stands the statue of Pasquino, the most famous of the "talking statues" of Rome; in Papal Rome, the statue was plastered with lampoons criticising the political scene or denouncing moral standards.

The palace houses the **Museum of Rome★** which evokes the story of Rome since the Middle Ages. *(Open 9 am to 1.30 pm; 1 pm Sundays and holidays; Tuesdays and Thursdays 5.30 to 7.30 pm; closed Mondays, 1 January, 1 May, 15 August, Easter and Christmas; 1 200 lire.)*

Chiesa Nuova★ (BX Q). — This church which dates from the Counter-Reformation was rebuilt by St. Philip Neri (it was completed in 1605). The Baroque decoration (17C) of the interior is by Pietro da Cortona (dome supported by pendentives, apse and ceiling). In the chancel hang paintings by Rubens. The chapel on the left of the chancel contains the tomb of St. Philip.

To the left is the **Oratory of the Filippini**: elegant **façade★** by Borromini.

Via dei Coronari★ (BX 25). — Lined with antique shops and palaces in warm ochre and brown colours, it is one of the most pleasant streets in Rome. It derives its name from the sellers of rosaries and other religious items exhibiting their wares to pilgrims arriving from Porta del Popolo on their way to the Vatican.

St. Mary of Peace★ (Santa Maria della Pace) (BX X). — *Open 10.15 to 11.30 am Sundays and holidays.* The church was rebuilt in the 15C and was given a fine Baroque façade by Pietro da Cortona. The interior is on an original plan and has a short rectangular nave and an octagonal section with a dome and frescoes by Raphaël representing the four **Sibyls★**.

The cloisters are an early work by Bramante (1504).

Santa Maria dell' Anima (BX Y). — This is the church of German speaking Catholics, built in the 16C as a hall-church with three aisles of equal height.

CAMPO DEI FIORI QUARTER

Piazza Campo dei Fiori★ (BY). — A popular square of Rome which is the scene of a picturesque market daily. Note the statue of Giordano Bruno commemorating the execution of this heretical monk on 17 February 1600. Near Campo dei Fiori stand the finest Roman palaces.

Chancellery★★ (Palazzo della Cancelleria) (BXY S). — The palace built from 1483 to 1513, is an elegant Renaissance edifice with a plain façade with flat pilasters, pure lines and a harmonious inner court and was probably designed, in part, by Bramante.

The palace houses the Chancellery which has the task of drafting pontifical decrees.

Palazzo Farnese★★★ (BY). — *Inner court and gardens only open Sundays 11 am to noon.* The palace was built from 1515 by Cardinal Alessandro Farnese, who reigned as pope under the name of Paul III (1534-1549). He employed several architects: Antonio da Sangallo the Younger, Michelangelo (who designed the upper cornice of the façade, the Farnese coat of arms above the central balcony, and the second floor of the inner court), Vignola who collaborated on the inner court and built the palace's rear façade, and Giacomo della Porta who designed the loggia in that same façade.

The **frescoes★★★** in the Great Gallery are by Annibale Carracci and his school.

Palazzo Spada★ (BY M⁵). — The palace is occupied by the Council of State. It was built around 1540 probably by an architect of Sangallo's circle and illustrates the Mannerist fantasy that succeeded the austere majesty of the Renaissance (statues, stucco garlands, medallions and cartouches on the façade). The palace houses the **Spada gallery★** *(open 9 am to 1.30 pm; closed Mondays, 1 January, 25 April, 1 May, first Sunday in June, 15 August and Christmas; 500 lire);* which contains the paintings collected by Cardinal Spada and conveys the atmosphere of the private collection of a 17C patrician (works by Guido Reni, Guercino, etc.).

Area Sacra del Largo Argentina★★ (BY B). — *To be seen from Via S. Nicola de'Cesarini* (BY 61). These ruins excavated from 1926 to 1929 consisting of remains dating from the Republic are among the most ancient to have been found in Rome. The Area Sacra comprises mainly four temples facing east (towards Via S. Nicola de'Cesarini). The temple situated along Largo di Torre Argentina was converted into a church in the Middle Ages (remains of the apses); nearby is a circular temple; next to it is the most ancient of the group (6-5C BC); the fourth is partly hidden below Via Florida. These buildings were all rebuilt or remodelled several times before the beginning of the Empire.

Sant'Andrea della Valle★ (BY C). — This church was built from 1591 to 1665. The elegant Baroque **façade★★** is by Carlo Maderno and Carlo Rainaldi (1655-1665).

The sober interior is characteristic of the Counter-Reformation (the decorations of the vaults of the nave and of the north transept were added in the 20C). The **dome★★** designed by Carlo Maderno, is the second in size in the city after St. Peter's. Lanfranco painted the Glory of Paradise in rich colours; on the pendentives, the Evangelists are by Domenichino. In the **apse★**, the paintings by Domenichino are separated by ribs in white and gilded stucco.

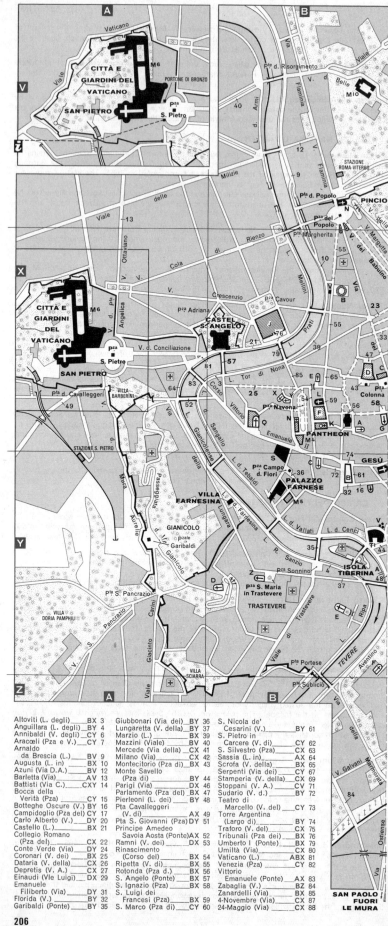

206

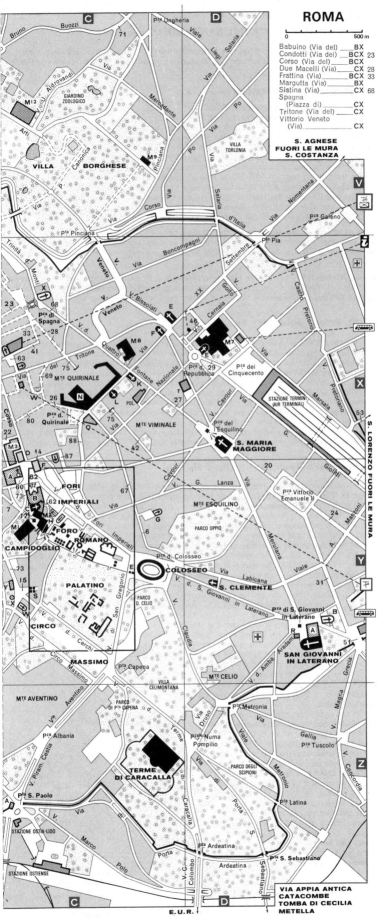

■ THE VATICAN — CASTEL SANT'ANGELO *plan p 206*

In view of their opening times, the Vatican museums and the Castel Sant'Angelo must be visited in the morning. The afternoon can be spent on a visit to St. Peter's Square and Basilica, ending at the Janiculum.

THE VATICAN CITY (Città del Vaticano) (AV)

The Vatican City is bounded by a wall built in the 9C by Leo IV and strengthened in the 16C, and to the east by the colonnade of St. Peter's Square. It makes up the greater part of the Vatican state as laid down in 1929 in the Lateran Agreements. The Vatican City, now only 44 hectares - 109 acres — and with less than one thousand inhabitants stems from the Papal States, a donation made in 8C by Pepin the Short to Pope Stephen II and lost in 1870 when Italy was united into one Kingdom with Rome as its capital. The Vatican State, with the pope as ruler, has its own flag and hymn; it prints stamps and mints its own coinage which is legal tender throughout Italy. In 1970, Pope Paul VI dissolved the armed forces retaining only the Swiss Guard who wear a colourful uniform said to have been designed by Michelangelo.

The Pope, who is the Head of State, is also the supreme head of the Universal Church, and from this very small state, the spiritual influence of the church radiates throughout the world through the person of the sovereign pontiff.

Visit of the City and Gardens of the Vatican★★★. — *St. Peter's Basilica and the Vatican museums may be visited freely, but guided tours only are allowed for the rest of the city and the gardens; 2 500 lire. Apply to the Ufficio Informazioni Pellegrini e Turisti, situated under the colonnade in St. Peter's Square.*

Public Audiences. — When the Pope is in residence in Rome, he grants a public audience on Wednesdays. Apply in advance from 9 am to 1 pm to the *Prefettura della Casa Pontificia (Portone di bronzo).* It is advisable to have a written recommendation from your parish priest.

St. Peter's Square★★★ (Piazza San Pietro)

This architectural masterpiece was created between 1656 and 1667 by Bernini. The two semicircles of the colonnade which adorn the square and frame the façade of the basilica, each composed of four rows of columns and surmounted by statues of saints and the coats of arms of Alessandro VII, form an ensemble of remarkable sobriety and majesty.

At the centre of the square stands an obelisk (1C BC) brought from Heliopolis (Egypt) to Rome in 37 by order of Caligula. It was erected here in 1585 on the initiative of Sixtus V by Domenico Fontana; at the top is a relic of the Holy Cross.

Between the two 17C fountains and the obelisk, two circular paving-stones mark the focal points of the ellipse formed by the Piazza. From these paving-stones, the colonnade appears to consist only of a single row of columns. Bernini achieved this perspective by keeping equidistant intervals between the columns whose diameter increases as they extend outwards.

St. Peter's Basilica★★★ (Basilica di San Pietro)

Constantine, the first Christian Emperor, decided in AD 324 to build a basilica on the site where St. Peter was buried after he had been martyred in Nero's circus. In the 15C rebuilding of the edifice proved necessary. For two centuries, the plan of the new basilica was constantly revised. The plan of a Greek cross surmounted by a dome drawn by Bramante and adopted by Michelangelo, was altered to a Latin cross at the behest of Paul V in 1606 when he instructed Carlo Maderna to add two bays and a façade to Michelangelo's square plan. From 1629 onwards, the basilica was decorated in sumptuous Baroque style by Bernini.

The **façade** which was completed in 1614 by C. Maderna is 115 m long and 45 m high (377 × 151 ft) and masks the dome. In the centre is the balcony from which the Pope gives his benediction *Urbi et Orbi* (to the City and the World).

Under the **portico**, note the first door on the left which has bronze panels carved by Giacomo Manzù (1964); the bronze central door which dates from the Renaissance (1455); and the door on the right or Holy Door which is opened and closed by the Pope to mark the beginning and end of a Jubilee Year.

Inside, it is customary to approach the stoups in the central nave which at first glance, appear of normal size but are in fact huge. Such size emphasises the gigantic dimensions of the basilica otherwise not apparent because of the harmony of its proportions. The length of St. Peter's can be compared to that of other great basilicas throughout the world by means of markers inserted in the pavement of the nave.

The first chapel on the right contains the **Pietà★★★**, the masterpiece carved by Michelangelo in 1499-1500, which shows his creative genius.

In the right aisle, adjoining the Chapel of the Blessed Sacrament, the **funerary monument of Gregory XIII★** is adorned with a bas-relief depicting the institution of the Gregorian calendar devised by that pope. Immediately past the right transept, the Neo-Classical **tomb of Clement XIII★★★** is by Canova (1792). The apse is dominated by **St. Peter's pulpit★★★** by Bernini (1666), a great carved throne in bronze encasing a 4C episcopal chair but symbolically attributed to St. Peter, and surmounted by a glory in gilded stucco. In the chancel on the right is a **monument to Urban VIII★★★** by Bernini (1647), a masterpiece of funerary art; on the left stands a **monument to Paul III★★★** by Guglielmo della Porta (16C), a disciple of Michelangelo.

At the **altar of St. Leo the Great** (chapel on the left of the chancel), there is a fine Baroque **altarpiece★** carved in high relief by Algardi. Nearby, **a monument to Alexander VII★**

(After photo by Gab. Fot. Naz., Rome)

Michelangelo—Pietà

characterised by extreme exuberance, is a late work of Bernini (1678) assisted by his pupils. The **baldaquin★★★** which crowns the pontifical altar which is 29 m - 95 ft — tall and stands as high as the Farnese Palace, brought strong criticism of Bernini; it is made from bronze taken from the Roman Parthenon and was described as theatrical.

The **dome★★★** designed by Michelangelo, which he himself built as far as the lantern, was completed in 1593 by Giacomo della Porta and Domenico Fontana. From the summit there is a **view★★★** of St. Peter's Square, the Vatican City and Rome from the Janiculum to Monte Mario *(access to the dome by the left aisle opposite the pillar between the first and second bays; open 8 am to 6 pm; 5.30 pm 1 October to 31 March, except when religious ceremonies and papal audiences are in progress; 1 000 lire).*

The 13C bronze **statue of St. Peter★★** overlooking the nave is attributed to Arnolfo di Cambio and is greatly venerated by pilgrims who come to kiss his feet. The **monument to Innocent VIII★★★** *(between the second and third bays in the left aisle)* dates from the Renaissance and is by Antonio del Pollaiuolo (1498). The **Stuart monument** *(between the first and second bays in the left aisle)* carved by Canova is adorned by beautiful **angels★** in bas-relief.

The **Museum of Art and History★★** *(entrance in the left aisle, opposite the Stuart monument; open 9 am to 12.30 pm and 3 to 6 pm, 4.30 pm 1 October to 31 March, except when religious ceremonies and papal audiences are in progress; 1 000 lire)* contains St. Peter's treasure.

Vatican Grottoes. — *Access by one of the pillars supporting the dome; open 8 am to 6 pm; 5 pm 1 October to 31 March.* The grottoes open to the public extend under the present basilica with a semi-circular section which follows the form of the apse of Constantine's basilica, extended to the east by three aisles. The grottoes contain items from the ancient basilica and the tombs of the great popes. In the centre of the apse on the left is the tomb of Pius XII and on the right the "ad caput" chapel near the tomb of St. Peter.

Vatican Museums★★★ (AV M⁶)

Open 9 am to 2 pm (tickets issued until 1 pm). In July, August and September 9 am to 5 pm (tickets issued until 4 pm) also during Holy and Easter weeks. Open also on last Sunday in the month from 9 am to 2 pm (access up to 1 pm) except when this coincides with one of the holidays given below. Closed on all remaining Sundays, 1 January, 11 February, 19 March, Easter Monday, 1 May, Ascension Day, Corpus Christi, 29 June, 14 and 15 August, 1 November, 8, 25 and 26 December. Entrance: Viale Vaticano; 2 000 lire.

The museums of the Vatican occupy part of the palaces built by the popes from the 13C onwards who have extended and embellished them to the present day. They include:

Pio-Clementino Museum★★★. — *First floor. Access by Cortile delle Corazze then left by the Simonetti staircase.* The museum is in the 15C Belvedere Palace built by Innocent VIII.

Room of the Greek Cross. — Two fine porphyry **sarcophagi★** dating from the 4C.

Round Room★. — This room is a fine architectural creation by Simonetti (18C). Note the **bust of Jupiter★** (a Roman work inspired by a 4C BC Greek original).

Room of the Muses. — The **Torso of the Belvedere★★★**, an extraordinary work dating from the 1C BC, greatly admired by Michelangelo.

Animals' Room. — **Statue of Meleager★**, a 2C Roman work copied from a bronze by Scopas.

Gallery of Statues. — This gallery contains a statue of **Ariadne Asleep★** flanked by two Roman candelabra and that of **Apollo watching a Lizard★** *(on the right as you enter, in the centre of the gallery)*, a replica after Praxiteles.

Busts' Room. — *In the extension to the Gallery of Statues.* **Busts of Cato and Portia★** (1C BC) illustrating the sobriety of early Roman art.

Cabinet of Masks. — *Facing the entrance to the Gallery of Statues.* **Venus of Cnidus★★**, a Roman copy of Praxiteles' Venus.

Octagonal Court★. — This inner courtyard, remodelled in the shape of an octagon in the 18C by Simonetti is studded with masterpieces. Particularly noteworthy are the **Laocoon Group★★★** depicting Laocoon, priest to Apollo, and his two sons choked to death by serpents: Greek art work dating from 1C BC in an extremely "Baroque" style; **Apollo★★★** (2C) probably a copy of a 4C BC Greek original, a picture of serenity; **Perseus★★**, a Neo-Classical work, by Canova (19C) bought by Pius VII; **Hermes★★★**, a 2C Roman work inspired from the Greek figures of Praxiteles; the **Athlete★★★** (1C) from an original by Lysippus.

Caesar

Etruscan Museum★. — Note in particular the remarkable 7C BC gold **fibula★★** adorned with lions and ducklings in high relief *(Room II)* and the **Mars★★** by Todi, a rare bronze statue from the 5C BC *(Room III).*

Room of the Chariot. — *2nd floor.* The room derives its name from the **chariot drawn by two horses★★** *(biga)*, a 1C Roman work reassembled in the 18C.

Passing along the long galleries linking the Belvedere Palace and the palaces erected by Nicholas V, Sixtus IV, Alexander VI and Julius II, pause awhile in the **Map Gallery★** whose walls were painted in the 16C by Father Ignazio Danti.

Raphaël Rooms★★★. — The rooms were built under Nicholas V (15C) and occupied again by Julius II who converted them into his private apartments. The pope entrusted the decoration to Il Sodoma, Perugino and Raphaël. The result is a pure Renaissance masterpiece.

Room of the Fire of the Borgo. — This was the last room to be decorated (1514-1517). Raphaël designed the frescoes but practically all were painted by his pupils. Note the Coronation of Charlemagne *(wall to the right of the entrance)*; the Fire of the Borgo, the Battle of Ostia and the Justification of Leo III.

Room of the Signature. — This room was painted between 1508 to 1511 by Raphaël. The Dispute of the Holy Sacrament *(wall to the right of the entrance)* represents the triumph of Religion; among the representatives of the terrestrial Church note Dante wearing a laurel crown.

In the School of Athens *(opposite the Dispute)*, Raphaël painted the exponents of human knowledge; in the centre are Plato and Aristotle; Archimedes, drawing geometrical figures on a slate, is drawn with the features of Bramante; Raphaël portrayed himself with a black beret standing next to Il Sodoma wearing a white one; when the painting was nearly complete, Raphaël added in the foreground, a solitary and melancholy Michelangelo.

On the other walls are depicted the Cardinal Virtues and Parnassus.

The vault is decorated with allegories relating to theology (above The Dispute), philosophy (above the School of Athens), justice and poetry.

Room of Heliodorus. — Opposite the entrance, you can see the Expulsion of Heliodorus from the Temple (note on the left, Julius II on the pontifical throne, the pope who drove the invaders out of Italy). The Miracle of Bolsena (see p 65) showing Julius II kneeling. The Deliverance of St. Peter, a painting famous for its light effects and Attila defeated by St. Leo the Great.

Room of Constantine. — This room was completed in 1525, five years after the death of Raphaël. The Vision of the Cross (wall facing the entrance) and the Victory of Constantine over Maxentius are by Guilio Romano, a disciple of Raphaël; the Baptism of Constantine was painted by another disciple, Francesco Penni; the Donation of Constantine was worked in collaboration by two artists who were among the main exponents of Mannerism (see p 30).

Raphaël's Loggia★★ (Loggia di Raffaelo). — Provisionally for specialists only. A long vaulted gallery decorated by Raphaël and his disciples. The vaulting is ornamented with scenes from the Old and New Testaments, and the walls and arches with stuccos and grotesques. The loggia, sometimes designated as the "Bible of Raphaël" is remarkable for its fantasy and freshness.

Grisaille Room and Chapel of Nicholas V★. — The former derives its name from the chiaroscuro paintings executed by Raphaël in 1517.

The **Chapel of Nicholas V★**, one of the oldest parts of the palaces (12-13C), was adorned with frescoes by Fra Angelico (stories of St. Stephen and St. Lawrence).

Borgia Apartment★ (Appartamento Borgia). — 1st floor. Rooms of the apartment of Pope Alexander VI decorated by Pinturicchio. Modern art exhibition.

Collection of Modern Religious Art★★. — A rich display of more than 500 paintings and sculptures presented by artists and collectors.

Sistine Chapel★★★ (Cappella Sistina). — A masterpiece of Renaissance art. The Sistine Chapel is the place where the conclave meets and the scene of the most solemn ceremonies of the Holy See. It was built between 1475 to 1481 by Sixtus IV who commissioned Umbrian and Florentine painters for the decoration of the side walls (1481-1483). Michelangelo was entrusted with the decoration of the ceiling (1508-1512) and wall above the altar (1535-41).

Left wall: Life of Moses. — Moses in Egypt (Perugino and Pinturicchio); Moses as a youth (Botticelli); Crossing of the Red Sea and Moses on Mount Sinai (Cosimo Rosselli); Punishment of Korah, Dathan and Abiram (Botticelli); Testament and Death of Moses (Luca Signorelli).

Right wall: Life of Christ. — Baptism of Jesus (Perugino and Pinturicchio); Temptation of Christ and Cleansing of the Leper (Botticelli); Calling of Sts. Peter and Andrew (Ghirlandaio); Sermon on the Mount and Healing the Leper (Cosimo Rosselli and Piero di Cosimo); Christ giving the Keys to St. Peter (Perugino); Last Supper (Cosimo Rosselli).

Vault. — This is covered with frescoes of admirable power, relief and colour by Michelangelo. At the summit of the arch, he painted nine panels illustrating the Creation of the world (start from the panel nearest the altar). At the panels' outer edges are the famous ignudi (nudes) typical of the power of Michelangelo's genius. Below, the Prophets' and Sibyls' portraits are remarkable for their expressiveness and diversity. At the angles of the vault, Michelangelo has depicted heroes of the people of Israël (David, Judith, Esther, Moses), and in the triangles, the forebears of Christ whose names appear in the cartouches above the windows.

The Last Judgment. — Wall above the altar. Michelangelo worked on this amazing composition from 1535 to 1541. At the summit are Christ in Judgment and the Virgin surrounded by Prophets and Saints carrying the instruments of their torture. At the call of the angels, the chosen go up to heaven (left) while the damned are hurled into hell (right).

Apostolic Library★ (Biblioteca Apostolica). — Go up some steps from the Sistine Chapel. A suite of rooms opening on to the west gallery of the palaces. At right angles to the gallery is the **Sistine Great Hall★** built in 1587 by Sixtus V who housed part of the Vatican Library there. The decoration is in the Mannerist style and it contains 17C cupboards painted in the 19C.

Braccio Nuovo. — Gallery parallel to the Sistine Great Hall. Note the **statue of Augustus★★**, a fine example of official Roman art (detailed decoration of the Emperor's armour).

Picture Gallery★★★ (Pinacoteca). — Works by Italian Primitives (Room I), by Florentine painters (Fra Angelico, Benozzo Gozzoli, Filippo Lippi) (Room III), by Melozzo da Forli (Angel Musicians) (Room IV), and by 15C Umbrian artists (Perugino, Pinturicchio) (Room VII). **Room VIII★★★** contains paintings by Raphaël (Coronation of the Virgin, Madonna di Foligno, Transfiguration). In Room IX is displayed the painting of **St. Jerome★★** by Leonardo da Vinci, the master of light effects, anatomy and expressiveness. The **Descent from the Cross★★** by Caravaggio (Room XII) expresses clearly the artist's reaction against Mannerism (Room XI).

Museums of Secular and Christian Art★. — Antique and Christian works of art (fine sarcophagi) displayed in a modern setting.

From the staircase leading to the Christian Museum, note the **mosaics from Caracalla's baths★** (3C) depicting athletes, gladiators and their trainers.

CASTEL SANT'ANGELO★★★ (ABX)

Open 9 am to 1 pm (noon Sundays and holidays). Closed Mondays, 1 January, 25 April, 1 May, 15 August and 25 December. 1 000 lire. This imposing fortress was built in AD 135 as a mausoleum for the Emperor Hadrian and his family. In the 6C Gregory the Great erected a chapel on top of the mausoleum to commemorate the apparition of an angel who by putting his sword back into its sheath, announced the end of a plague. In the 15C Nicholas V crowned the ancient building with a brick structure and the wall with corner watch towers. Alexander VI (1492-1503) added the octagonal bastions.

In 1527, during the sack of Rome, Clement VII took refuge in the castle and installed an apartment there which was later embellished by Paul III; the **Popes' Apartment★** stands isolated at the summit of the fortress and testifies to the graciousness of the popes' life style.

A long passageway (the Passetto) connects the fortress to the Vatican palaces.

A fine spiral ramp dating from Antiquity leads to the castle. From a terrace at the summit there is a splendid **panorama★★★** of the whole town.

The Castel Sant'Angelo is linked to the left bank of the Tiber by the graceful **Ponte Sant' Angelo★ (BX 57)** which is ornamented with Baroque angels carved by Bernini and with statues of Sts. Peter and Paul (16C).

JANICULUM★ (Gianicolo) (AY)

A long road running along the summit of the hill affords views★★★ of the town and of its domes. In Piazzale Garibaldi which is a belvedere, a monument has been erected to the defender of the Roman Republic (1849) against the papal troops.

■ FROM THE IMPERIAL FORUMS TO THE CATACOMBS *plan p 207*

Imperial Forums★★★ (Fori Imperiali) *plan p 203*

These were built by Caesar, Augustus, Trajan, Nerva and Vespasian to supplement the Roman Forum *(p 202)* which was found to be too small. There are hardly any remains of the forums of Nerva and of Vespasian. The Via dei Fori Imperiali (1932) divides the imperial forums.

Caesar's Forum★★ (Foro di Cesare). — *View from Via del Tulliano.* There remain some columns from the temple of Venus Genitrix erected by Caesar after a victory at Pharsal in AD 48.

Augustan Forum★★ (Foro di Augusto). — *View from Via Alessandrina.* Only a few columns of the temple of Mars the Avenger (Mars Ultor), where Caesar's sword was kept as a relic, remain standing. There are also vestiges of the temple's stairway and of the wall separating the forum from the popular quarter of Suburra. The forum is dominated by the House of the Knights of Rhodes (Casa di Cavalieri di Rodi) built in the 15C amidst the ancient ruins.

Trajan's Forum★★★ (Foro di Traiano). — This was the largest, indeed the finest, of the imperial forums. All that remains is essentially Trajan's column★★★ (Colonna Traiana) which depicts in over 100 scenes, episodes of the war waged by Trajan against the Dacians; the accuracy and delicacy of the design make this an unequalled masterpiece. A statue of St. Peter has been substituted for the Emperor's statue on the summit.

The markets★★★ (mercati) *(entrance in Via 4 Novembre; open 9 am to 1 pm and 3 to 6 pm; from 1 October to 31 May: 10 am to 5 pm; Sundays and holidays 9 am to 1 pm; closed Mondays, 1 January, 1 May, 15 August, Easter and Christmas; 200 lire)*, a supply and distribution centre for products, have kept their semicircular façade. This is an example of the genius of Apollodorus of Damascus who created a monumental design for this functional building.

Tower of the Militia★ (Torre delle Milizie). — *If it cannot be reached from Trajan's Markets, view from the steps of the church of Sts. Dominic and Sixtus.* This keep of a fortress built in the 13C by Gregory IX is one of the better preserved vestiges from mediaeval Rome. As it started to lean slightly following an earthquake in the 14C, one storey was lopped off and merlons added.

St. Peter in Chains★ (San Pietro in Vincoli) (CY G)

This church dates back to the reign of Pope Sixtus III (5C) and was remodelled between the 15 and 18C. Tourists come to admire Michelangelo's Moses★★★, a statue belonging to the mausoleum of Julius II *(at the far end of the south aisle)* and pilgrims to venerate the fetters of St. Peter on display in the confessional.

St. Clement★★ (San Clemente) (DY)

Founded in the 4C this is one of the most ancient Roman basilicas. Destroyed in 1084 during the Quarrel of the Church and the Empire, it was rebuilt in the 12C on the ruins of the former basilica.

Interior. — *Access often from the north aisle.* The interior retains its 12C basilical plan and is divided into three aisles by ancient columns. But its unity has been impaired by Baroque stucco decorations and modifications made in the 18C. There are remarkable 12C marble furnishings (ambos, paschal candelabrum), a 6C chancel screen and a 12C pavement by the Cosmati. The apse is decorated with a splendid 12C mosaic★★★ (note the colours, diversity of themes, fine style and

(After photo by Gab. Fot. Naz., Rome)

Michelangelo — Moses

rich symbolism). The Chapel of St. Catherine *(at the entrance of the north aisle)* is adorned with frescoes★ by Masolino da Panicale (1383-1447).

Lower Church. — *Open 9 am to noon and 3.30 to 6.30 pm (from 10 am to noon Sundays and holidays); 500 lire.* A stairway leads down to the level of the 4C basilica where fragments of 9, 11 and 12C frescoes can be seen.

This church stands on the site of a 3C temple dedicated to Mithras (Mithraeum). An ancient stairway gives access to the temple.

St. John Lateran★★★ (San Giovanni in Laterano) (DY)

St. John Lateran, the cathedral of Rome, is among the four major basilicas in Rome. The first basilica was founded by Constantine prior to St. Peter in the Vatican. It was rebuilt in the Baroque era by Borromini and in the 18C.

The main façade by Alessandro Galilei dates from the 18C and the central door has bronze panels that originally belonged to the Curia in the Roman Forum (modified in the 17C). The vast and grandiose interior has a 16C ceiling★★ which was restored in the 18C. In the nave, the statues of the Apostles★ by pupils of Bernini stand in niches built by Borromini. The elegant Corsini Chapel★ *(first in the north aisle)* was designed by Alessandro Galilei (18C). The transept ceiling★★ dates from the end of the 16C. The Chapel of the Blessed Sacrament *(north transept)* has fine ancient columns★ in gilded bronze. The pretty cloister★ is the work of the Vassalletto (13C), marble-masons who were associates of the Cosmati.

The baptistry★ (DY R) built in the 4C, is decorated with beautiful 5 and 7C mosaics.

In **Piazza di San Giovanni in Laterano** rises the tallest obelisk in Rome (15C BC Egyptian obelisk). The **Lateran Palace (DY A)** rebuilt in 1586 was the palace of the popes until their return from Avignon. The small edifice of the **"Scala Sancta" (DY B)** was erected in the 16C to house two precious vestiges from the mediaeval papal palace: the papal chapel (Sancta Sanctorum) and the staircase (Scala Sancta) traditionally identified as the one in the palace of Pontius Pilate that Christ walked up. Worshippers climb the stairs on their knees.

Caracalla's Baths★★ (Terme di Caracalla) (CZ)

Open 9 am to one hour before sunset. Closed Mondays, 1 January, 25 April, 1 May, 15 August and 25 December; 500 lire.

These baths *(see general information p 24)* built by Caracalla in AD 212 extend over more than 11 hectares - 27 acres — and could take 1 600 bathers at a time.

The main rooms *(caldarium, tepidarium and frigidarium)* were in the middle of the central building; the secondary rooms (changing-rooms, gymnasiums and dry-steam rooms or *laconicum*) were located on either side symmetrically.

A porticoed wall surrounded the central building. Amid the ruins of the *caldarium,* a circular room, 34 m - 112 ft — in diameter and originally covered by a dome is the setting for operatic performances in summer.

Porta San Sebastiano★ (DZ)

From this gate there is a remarkable view of the Aurelian Wall in which it was pierced in the 3C. Remodelled several times, in particular by Honorius in the 5C, it is a spectacular structure with tall bases in white marble and crenellated towers.

Via Appia Antica★★★ (DZ)

Opened in 312 BC, Via Appia Antica which linked Rome to Capua, Benevento and Brindisi, is one of main centres of Christian Rome with typical Christian cemeteries (catacombs).

The Catacombs★★★ (DZ). — These were underground cemeteries used from the 2C by the Christians. The catacombs were rediscovered in the 16 and 19C. They consist of long galleries dug on several levels radiating from a *hypogeum* or underground burial chamber belonging to a noble family converted to Christianity who also accommodated fellow Christians. The decorations of the catacombs (carvings or paintings of symbolic motifs) are precious examples of early Christian art. The most remarkable are:

The **Catacombs of St. Callistus★★★**, situated in Via Appia: *guided tour 8.30 am to noon and 2.30 to 6 pm (5 pm 1 October to 30 April); closed Wednesdays, 1 January, Easter and Christmas; 1 000 lire; time: 1/2 hour.*

The **Catacombs of St. Sebastian★★★**, also in Via Appia: *same opening times as St. Callistus but closed Thursdays.* The **Catacombs of Domitilla★★★** situated at 282 Via delle Sette Chiese: *same opening times as St. Callistus but closed Tuesdays.*

Tomb of Cecilia Metella★ (DZ). — This is an example of a 1C BC patrician tomb. Cecilia Metella was the wife of Crassus, son of the Crassus who together with Caesar and Pompey formed the first triumvirate. On the left of the entrance, access can be gained to the burial chamber which is conical in shape.

Via Appia Antica, like all major roads leading to Rome, was lined with tombs of which there are moving remains (tomb of Cecilia Metella at Casale Rotondo).

St. Paul without the Walls★★★ (San Paolo Fuori le Mura) (BZ)

One of the four major basilicas. It was built by Constantine in the 4C on the site of St. Paul's tomb. It was rebuilt in the 19C after it had been wholly destroyed by fire in 1823, on the original basilical plan of early Christian churches. The impressive **interior★★★** contains: an 11C bronze door made in Constantinople *(at the entrance of the first south aisle);* a Gothic **ciborium★★** by Arnolfo di Cambio (1285) placed on the high altar which stands above a marble plaque inscribed with the name Paul and dated 4C. In the **Chapel of the Blessed Sacrament★** *(on the right of the chancel),* note a 14C wooden figure of Christ on the cross attributed to Pietro Cavallini, a statue of St. Brigitta kneeling by Stefano Maderno (17C), a wooden statue of St. Paul (14 or 15C); and the paschal **candelabrum★★**, a Romanesque work of art by the Vassalletto (12C) to whom is also attributed, at least in part, the decoration of the **cloister★**.

■ FROM THE JANICULUM TO THE PORTA SAN PAOLO
plan p 206

Janiculum★ — *see p 211.*

San Pietro in Montorio★ (BY D)

This church was built at the end of the 15C and dedicated to St. Peter as according to legend, this was the site where the Apostle was crucified.

It has a Renaissance façade and plan (single nave lined with chapels shaped like apses). In the first chapel on the right, note a **Flagellation★** by Sebastiano del Piombo.

Tempietto★. — *Access: from the outside, by the door to the right of the church; or through the fourth chapel on the right inside the church.* This lovely, beautifully proportioned small temple is one of Bramante's early works in Rome where he arrived in 1499.

(After photo by Gab. Fot. Naz., Rome)

Bramante's Tempietto

View★★★ of Rome. — *From the esplanade in front of the church.* The view takes in the whole town dotted with domes of different shapes, from Monte Mario and the Castel Sant'Angelo to St. John Lateran with its pediment crowned with statues and, beyond the Aventine, to the Alban Hills.

Villa Farnesina★★ (BY)

Open 9 am to 1 pm. Closed Sundays and holidays.
An elegant country mansion built between 1508 and 1511 for the banker Agostino Chigi. Decorated with paintings, it is a Renaissance jewel. The vault of the gallery is adorned with the legend of Psyche and of Love by Raphaël assisted by Giulio Romano, Francesco Penni and Giovanni da Udine.

At the east end of the gallery opens a room where Raphaël painted Galatea (1511) *(on the right as you enter)*.

On the first floor are a drawing-room decorated in *trompe l'œil* by Baldassare Peruzzi and a bedroom with a harmonious and well balanced composition by Il Sodoma depicting the Marriage of Alexander and Roxana *(c 1509)*.

Santa Maria in Trastevere★ (BY Z)

This church stands in **Piazza Santa Maria in Trastevere★**, in the heart of one of the liveliest quarters of Rome. The fountain in the square was remodelled by Bernini in 1659.

The basilica, a 12C building altered in the 17, 18 and 19C contains remarkable **mosaics★★**: those on the triumphal arch and the apse dome are 12C; further down between the windows and the base of the triumphal arch, Pietro Cavallini (late 13C) depicted the life of the Virgin, a delicate masterpiece (Birth, Annunciation, Nativity, Epiphany, Presentation at the Temple, Dormition). The ceiling is decorated with the Assumption of the Virgin by Domenichino (17C).

Santa Cecilia in Trastevere★ (BY E)

The church built in the 9C on the site of a sanctuary dedicated to St. Cecilia was extensively remodelled in the 16, 18 and 19C. A small room *(access at the entrance of the south aisle)* is venerated as the site of the martyrdom of St. Cecilia. Under the altar is a **statue★ of St. Cecilia**, carved by Stefano Maderno in the attitude in which her remains were found after being transferred there in the 9C from a catacomb in Via Appia Antica.

Crypt. — *Open 9 am to noon and 4 to 7 pm; 6 pm October to May; 250 lire.*
This stands in the midst of the ruins of ancient houses which probably included the first shrine dedicated to St. Cecilia.

The Last Judgment by Pietro Cavallini★★★. — *Open Sundays at noon. Closed August. Apply to the Benedictine convent in the courtyard.*
This masterpiece of Roman art from the Middle Ages which was formerly on the reverse of the church façade, was damaged in the 16C. All that remains of this work by Pietro Cavallini *(c 1293)* is Christ in Judgment surrounded by angels with their wings in full spread between the Virgin and the imploring St. John The Baptist, the Apostles and, at the bottom of the picture, angels sounding the trumpet. Note the perfect distribution of light and shade, the nuances of expression of the characters and the subtle harmony of colours.

Island in the Tiber★ (Isola Tiberina) (BY)

The island, the subject of numerous legends, is said to be shaped like the boat that brought Aesculapius, the god of medicine to Rome. Downstream, Ponte Rotto, vestige of a 16C bridge, stands on the site of the ancient Ponte Emilius (2C BC).

Marcellus Theatre★★ (Teatro di Marcello) (BY T1)

The theatre was begun by Caesar and completed by Augustus around 13 BC. The latter dedicated it to his nephew. In the 16C, the Savelli family remodelled the theatre into a palace, of which there are some vestiges above the ancient arches; the palace then became the property of the Orsinis. The three fine **columns★★** nearby belonged to the **temple of Apollo Sosianus★★** (BY V) (1C BC).

Piazza Bocca della Verità★ (CY 15)

This is a pretty example of a Roman landscape with monuments from different eras studded in a setting of umbrella pines and pink and white oleanders.

Santa Maria in Cosmedin★ (CY W). — This church was originally a chapel installed in the 6C in an ancient building used to accommodate the town's supplies. In the 8C the chapel was enlarged into a church to which around 1120 were added a portico and a graceful **campanile★**.

Under the portico stands a huge mascaron known as Bocca della Verità (Mouth of Truth) from a legend that it bites the hand of anyone who has a lie on his conscience.

The interior, on the basilical plan, is divided into three aisles by ancient columns of varied origins. In the north aisle, by the door and in the sacristy, there remain several Corinthian columns from the ancient building.

Piazza della Bocca della Verità

The marble pavement and furnishings (ambos, paschal candelabrum, ciborium and episcopal throne) are the work of the Cosmati.

In the sacristy, there is an 8C mosaic originating from St. Peter's Basilica.

Arch of Janus (Arco di Giano) (CY S). — This massive 4C structure was the public gateway through which passed the busiest roads.

Temple of Vesta★ (Tempio di Vesta) (CY X). — This elegant little building, so-called because of its circular shape, dates from the 1C BC.

Temple of Manly Fortune★ (Tempio della Fortuna Virile) (CY Y). — Its austere appearance is characteristic of the discipline of the ancient Republic (2C BC).

Circus Maximus (CY)

A long esplanade planted with flowers has replaced the huge circus between the Palatine and Aventine, where up to 250 000 spectators gathered during the reign of Trajan.

Santa Sabina★★ (BY F)

This church dates from the 5C. Remodelled several times, after extensive restoration work it has regained its original aspect of a fine mediaeval church. The main **doorway★★** in cypress wood dates back to the 5C and has remarkable panels carved in low-relief (scenes from the Old and New Testament).

The **interior★★** of harmonious dimensions, is on the basilical plan (the two side chapels added in the 16 and 17C have been retained) with three aisles divided by columns with Corinthian capitals (note the delicate arches resting directly on the columns).

Above the doorway, there is a 5C mosaic. A 14C tomb decorated with mosaics stands in the nave and at the top of the south aisle is a fine Renaissance tomb.

Porta San Paolo★ (CZ)

From this gate starts the Via Ostiense that leads to the Basilica of St. Paul without the Walls (p 212). It was pierced in the Aurelian wall (3C, remodelled in the 4, 15 and 18C).

Pyramid of Caius Cestius★ (Piramide di Caio Cestio) (CZ A)

This pyramid faced with marble was the unusual tomb of the magistrate Caius Cestius who died in 12 BC.

■ FROM ST. MARY MAJOR TO THE TREVI FOUNTAIN

St. Mary Major★★★ (Santa Maria Maggiore) (DX)

One of the 4 major basilicas in Rome built by Sixtus III (AD 432-440) and remodelled several times. The campanile, the tallest in Rome, was erected in 1377. The façade is by Ferdinando Fuga (1743-1750). The original façade of the building on to which was added the loggia (closed), has kept its **mosaic★** decoration by Filippo Rusuti (end 13C) which has been extensively restored in the 19C.

The impressive **interior★★★** contains remarkable **mosaics★★★**: in the nave; those above the entablature are among the most ancient Christian mosaics in Rome and depict scenes from the Old Testament; on the 5C triumphal arch are scenes from the New Testament; in the apse, the main theme is the Coronation of the Virgin; it is composed of 5C elements but was completely repainted in the 13C by Jacopo Torriti.

The coffered **ceiling★** was said to have been gilded with the first gold brought from Peru. The **pavement** by the Cosmati (12C) was extensively restored in the 18C. The **chapel of Sixtus V** (in the south aisle) and the **Pauline chapel** (north aisle) were both built on the plan of a Greek cross, surmounted by a dome. One was added at the end of the 16C and the other at the beginning of the 17C and they are superbly decorated in the Baroque style.

Leave the church by the door at the bottom of the south aisle.

From Piazza dell'Esquilino where stands an Egyptian obelisk from the mausoleum of Augustus, there is a **view★★** of the imposing 17C chevet.

National Museum of Rome★★★ (Museo Nazionale Romano) (DX M7)
(or **Museum of the Baths**) (Museo delle Terme)

Open 9.30 am to 2 pm (1 pm Sundays and holidays). Closed Mondays, 1 January, Easter, 1 May, 15 August and 25 December; 1 000 lire.

The museum is housed in the ruins of Diocletian's Baths and in the Great cloisters of the Carthusian monastery which used to be attached to St. Mary of the Angels, and contains exceptional collections of antique sculptures and paintings.

Particulary noteworthy are: the **Ludovisi Throne★★★** (Room 2), a 5C BC classical Greek original depicting the Birth of Aphrodite; the head of the **Dying Persian★** (Room 4) a Greek work in the Hellenistic style; two delicately carved 1C **altars★** (Room V); the **statue of Augustus★★★** and amongst the other **works★** several fine Roman portraits (Room VII); the museum's **masterpieces★★★** (Room III); the late 6C and early 5C BC **works★★** : the Apollo of the Tiber, a copy of the Greek original and three incomplete, Greek, statues of women.

On the first floor are exhibited admirable 1C **frescoes★★★** from Livia's villa at Prima Porta, and **stuccoes and paintings★★★** found in a building dating from the reign of Augustus near Villa Farnesina (paintings in the 2nd and 3rd styles).

St. Mary of the Angels★★ (Santa Maria degli Angeli) (DX E)

The church was built in the 16C amid the ruins of Diocletian's Baths and was remodelled in the 18C by Vanvitelli.

The majestic **transept★** occupies the main room of the baths and it contains 8 ancient monolithic columns in red granite; for the sake of uniformity, Vanvitelli added columns in plain painted stonework in the two passages separating the transept from the chancel and vestibule.

In the transept are several paintings, dating mainly from the 18C.

St. Mary Victorious★★ (Santa Maria della Vittoria) (CX E)

The church was erected in 1608 by Carlo Maderna. However, its façade with flat pilasters designed by G.B. Soria and built in the Baroque era (1624-1626), is closer to the style of the Counter-Reformation. The interior★★★ which has a sumptuous Baroque decoration, contains the **Ecstasy of St. Theresa★★★** *(north transept)* by Bernini who also designed the chapel in which it stands.

Santa Susanna★★ (CX F)

Its **façade★★★** by Carlo Maderna (1603) has an impressive unity: note the harmony of the two storeys with twin superimposed pediments.

Palazzo Barberini★★ (CX M⁸)

Entrance in Via delle Quattro Fontane.
This palace built for the family of Pope Urban VIII is the realisation of the most famous Baroque architects: it was started in 1625 by Carlo Maderno, continued by Borromini in 1629, and finished by Bernini in 1633.

(After photo by Gab. Fot. Naz., Rome)

Bernini — The Ecstasy of St. Theresa

Picture gallery★★. — *Open 9 am to 2 pm (1 pm Sundays and holidays). Closed Mondays; 750 lire.* The monumental staircase leading to the gallery *(on the left under the portico)* was designed by Bernini. The works displayed are mainly from the 13 to 16C. Note the **triptych by Fra Angelico★★★** (Last Judgment, Ascension and Pentecost) (Room 3) remarkable for the serenity of expression; the **Fornarina★★★** by Raphaël thought to be a portrait of the painter's mistress (Room 8); a very expressive **portrait of Erasmus★★★** by Quentin Metsys (1517) (Room 12) and in the next room, a **portrait of Henry VIII★★★** by Hans Holbein the Younger ((1540). The last room open to visitors is the **drawing room★★★** of the palace with a vaulted ceiling painted between 1633 and 1639, a major work by Pietro da Cortona which illustrates the glory of the Barberini family from which was descended Pope Urban VIII: coat of arms with bees set in a laurel crown borne by Allegorical figures representing the Virtues; on the left, Divine Providence holding a sceptre; the scenes are skilfully divided by sections painted in *grisaille*.

St. Charles with the Four Fountains★★ (San Carlo alle Quattro Fontane) (CX K)

This church probably represents the finest expression of Borromini's Baroque genius; his art which reflects his troubled mind, expresses itself in undulating (sweep of the façade and of the cornices) and contrasting lines (on the upper floor, Borromini placed a convex niche below the medallion, in the concave central part). The façade was completed after Borromini's death (1667).
The **interior★★** is designed along the greater axis of an ellipse and the sense of movement is achieved by the alternate use of rounded and curved walls.
The pretty **cloisters★** are beautifully proportioned.

St. Andrew at the Quirinal★★ (Sant'Andrea al Quirinale) (CX L)

Built by Bernini from 1658 onwards, the church has a rounded porch. The **interior★★** designed on an elliptical plan, surrounded by vast side chapels, and with a chancel preceded by a false portico which gives an impression of depth, makes up for the small dimensions of the building. It is richly decorated with marble, gilt and stuccowork.

Piazza del Quirinale★★ (CX)

Lined with the noble façades of the palaces, adorned with antique statues and an obelisk, and ornamented with a fountain, this is an elegant square, typically Roman. The obelisk marked the entrance to Augustus' mausoleum; the statues of the Dioscuri flanking it belonged to the Baths of Constantine; the setting is completed by an antique basin from the Roman forum.

Palazzo del Quirinale★★ (CX N). — The official residence of the President of the Republic. Formerly the pope's summer residence, it was designed by 16, 17 and 18C architects (Flaminio Ponzio, Domenico Fontana, Carlo Maderna, Bernini, Ferdinando Fuga). *The interior can be visited only by applying to the palace's administrative offices (Via della Dataria — CX 26).*

Palazzo della Consulta (CX Q). — The Baroque **façade★** is by Ferdinando Fuga (18C).

Trevi Fountain★★★ (Fontana di Trevi) (CX W)

This grandiose late Baroque monument by Nicolò Salvi (1762) is one of the most famous sights of Rome; in the centre towers a statue of Neptune in a chariot drawn by two sea-horses and two tritons. It is the custom to throw two coins into the fountain, standing with one's back to it: one for a happy return to Rome, the second for the fulfilment of a wish.

■ THE FOREIGNERS' QUARTER

This is the name sometimes given to the area around the Piazza del Popolo where many foreigners took up residence after entering Rome through the Porta del Popolo.

Borghese Museum★★★ (Museo Borghese) (CV M⁹)

Open 9 am to 2 pm (1 pm Sundays and holidays). Closed Mondays, 1 January, Easter, 1 May, 15 August and 25 December; 1 000 lire weekdays.
The museum is housed in a small palace built in the 17C by Vasanzio for Cardinal Scipione Borghese in the setting of **Villa Borghese★★**, the biggest public park in Rome also created for the cardinal. The palace and gardens were remodelled in the 18C. Note on the ground floor: a

215

statue of **Pauline Bonaparte★★★**, a Neo-Classical masterpiece by Canova; the **Bernini sculptures★★★**, by the master of Roman Baroque art (David, Apollo and Daphne, the Rape of Proserpine, Aeneas and Anchises, Truth).

On the first floor: the **Deposition★★★** by Raphaël *(Rooms IX)*; **Diana the Huntress★★★** by Domenichino, and the **Madonna dei Palafrenieri★★★** (the Virgin, Jesus and St. Anne) by Caravaggio *(Room XIV)*; also sculptures by Bernini: two busts of Cardinal Scipione Borghese, Jupiter and the goat Amalthea, a terracotta model for the equestrian statue of Louis XIV destined for the park at Versailles; **Danae★★★** by Correggio *(Room XIX)*; **Sacred and Profane Love★★★** by Titian and the **portrait of a man★★★** by Antonello da Messina *(Room XX)*.

National Museum of the Villa Giulia★★★ (Museo Nazionale di Villa Giulia) (BV M 10)

Open 9 am to 2 pm (1 pm Sundays and holidays). Closed Mondays, 1 January, 25 April, 1 May, first Sunday in June, 15 August and Christmas; 500 lire.

This museum which is devoted to the Etruscan civilisation, is housed in **Villa Giulia★**, the country residence of Pope Julius III (1550-1555) built by Vignola and B. Ammanati.

The Etruscans *(see also p 22)*, a people of obscure origin, made their appearance in the Italian peninsula by the end of the 8C BC. They governed Rome between the 6 and 5C BC and were finally conquered by the Romans in the 1C BC. Knowledge of their civilisation was gained mainly from objects found in tombs. Note on the ground floor: the **Veii sculptures★★★** *(Room 7)*, rare vestiges of sculpture in the round, from a temple in the Etruscan city of Veii; the **Married Couple's Sarcophagus★★★** *(Room 6)* in terracotta like all Etruscan sarcophagi, from Cerveteri. On the first floor are small **bronzes★**, typically Etruscan; an **œnochoe★★** *(Room 15)*, a wine pitcher, a fine example of proto-Corinthian Greek art imported by the Etruscans and decorated with small designs; **vases★** in bucchero, black terracotta Etruscan pottery; the **Castellani collection★** *(Room 19)* of Greek and Etruscan ceramics; **jewels from the Castellani collection★** *(to visit, apply to the ticket office)*: antique jewellery and copies (8-7C BC). Returning to the ground floor, you will see vestiges

(After photo by Gab. Fot. Naz., Rome)

Married Couple's Sarcophagus

of the **temples of Falerii Veteres★ (bust of Apollo★)** *(Room 29)*; and the **Ficoroni cist★★★** *(Room 33)*, an Etruscan bronze casket decorated with engravings and carvings.

Piazza del Popolo★★ (BV)

This square, one of the largest in Rome, was designed by Giuseppe Valadier (1762-1839). Whilst retaining the Porta del Popolo, the Egyptian obelisk placed there in the 16C and the two Baroque churches marking the access to Via del Corso, the architect added two semicircles adorned with fountains and Neo-Classical allegorical statues and linked the east side to the terrace of the Pincio by a monumental complex of terraces and arcades.

Porta del Popolo★ (BV). — Pierced in the Aurelian wall in the 3C, it was adorned with an external façade in the 16C and an internal façade in the 17C (designed by Bernini).

Santa Maria del Popolo★★ (BV N). — This Renaissance church was remodelled in the Baroque era. It contains a splendid collection of **works of art★**: a delicate **fresco★** of the Adoration of the Magi by Pinturicchio (15C) *(first chapel on the right)*; a **tomb★** by Andrea Sansovino (c 1505) *(in the chancel)*; two **paintings by Caravaggio★★★** *(first chapel to the left of the chancel)*: the Conversion of St. Paul with superb light effects and the Crucifixion of St. Peter (a remarkable composition on a diagonal plan). The **Chigi Chapel★** *(2nd chapel on the left)* was built to Raphaël's harmonious design for the rich banker Agostino Chigi. Raphaël also designed the decorations on the cupola (worked in mosaic) and the statue of Jonas. In the Baroque period, Bernini carved the statues of Daniel and the Lion and Abakuk and the angel, and faced with marble the base of the pyramid shaped tombs of Agostino and Sigismondo Chigi.

Pincio (BV)

This fine public park laid out in the 19C by Giuseppe Valadier and linked to the park of the Villa Borghese, affords a **view★★★** which is particularly grandiose at dusk when the golden light of Rome is enhanced.

Piazza di Spagna★★ (CX)

This square, a popular tourist attraction, was so named in the 17C after the Spanish Embassy occupied the Palazzo di Spagna. It is dominated by the majestic **stairway of the Trinity of the Mountains★★** (Spanish Steps), built in the 18C by the architects de Sanctis and Specchi who adopted the Baroque style of perspective and *trompe-l'œil*; at the foot of the stairway is the **fountain of the Barcaccia** designed by Pietro Bernini (17C), and on the right is the house in which Keats dies in 1821; Shelley and Byron lived nearby. At the summit, the **Church of the Trinity of the Mountains★ (CX X)** is a French church built in the 16C and restored in the 19C. It contains a **Deposition from the Cross★** by Daniele da Volterra, an admirer of Michelangelo (1541) *(2nd chapel on the left)*.

Via dei Condotti (BCX 23)

Lined with elegant shops, Via dei Condotti was renowned throughout the world for the **Caffè Greco** which opened there in 1760. Nowadays, visitors come to muse amidst the portraits of the famous who frequented the establishment (Goethe, Berlioz, Wagner, Leopardi, d'Annunzio, Anderson, Stendhal etc.).

Via del Corso★★ (BCX)

Via del Corso, the main street in the centre of Rome, that attracts lively crowds with its numerous shops and cafés, runs on a straight line linking Piazza del Popolo and Piazza Venezia.

Lined with grandiose palaces dating from the Renaissance onwards, it became a centre for festivities as from the 15C and was the scene of famous horse races (corse) and carnival attractions.

Ara Pacis Augustae★★ (BX V)

Open 1 June to 30 September, 10 am to 1 pm and 3 to 6 pm; the rest of the year, 10 am to 4 pm. Closed Mondays, 1 January, Easter, 21 April, 1 May, 15 August and Christmas; 200 lire, free on Sundays and holidays. Placed in a modern building, this monumental altar surrounded by a wall was inaugurated in the year 9 BC to commemorate peace restored in Rome and the Empire by Augustus. The Augustan altar, with the base of the wall decorated with deli-

(After photo by Gab. Fot. Naz., Rome)

Ara Pacis—Imperial Procession

cate acanthus foliage and swans, and the sides adorned (facing Via di Ripetta) with a procession led by the Emperor and his family, and (facing the Tiber) with a procession of the Sacred Colleges, is a major work of the Golden Age, marking the zenith of Roman creative genius.

In the vicinity of the Augustan altar are vestiges of the **mausoleum of Augustus (BX B)** and of the Julio-Claudian family.

■ OTHER SIGHTS AWAY FROM THE CENTRE

E.U.R.★★ (DZ)

These initials, an abbreviation of "Esposizione Universale di Roma", indicate a modern quarter spreading to the south of Rome. Its origin goes back to 1937 when the government adopted the grandiose plan of a universal exhibition set for 1942 (the area was also named E 42). Work under the direction of the architect Marcello Piacentini started in 1939, was interrupted after the fall of the Fascist government but resumed on the occasion of the Holy Year of 1950 and the Olympic Games of 1960.

Inspired by an obsession with grandeur, and comprising massive buildings in white marble, the E.U.R. conforms to the plans laid down under Fascist rule.

The most remarkable monuments include:

The **Museo della Civiltà Romana★★** *(open Tuesdays and Thursdays 9 am to 5 pm; Wednesdays, Fridays and weekends 9 am to 1 pm; closed Mondays, 1 January, 21 April, 1 May, 15 August, Easter and Christmas; 200 lire)* presents a complete documentation, consisting solely of reproductions, on ancient Rome, from its origins to the end of the Empire.

The **Palazzo della Civiltà del Lavoro★** was built in 1938 by the architects Guerrini, La Padula and Romano. This massive and austere structure that exalts the glory of Rome (allegorical statues of the arts on the ground floor) is one of the most characteristic buildings of the E.U.R.

The **Church of Sts. Peter and Paul★** (1937-1941) in white travertine stone dominates the whole quarter.

St. Lawrence outside the Walls★ (San Lorenzo Fuori le Mura (DXY)

The basilica was originally a shrine built by Constantine to mark the tomb of St. Lawrence. The present building combines a 6C church (now the chancel) and a 13C church (the three aisles). It regained its mediaeval appearance following restoration work undertaken to repair the damage caused by bombs in 1943.

The elegant portico was reconstructed with 13C elements: graceful columns, beautiful frieze ornamented with mosaics, delicately carved cornice. Under the portico are **sarcophagi★** decorated with scenes of the grape harvest (5 or 6C).

Inside are **ambos★** (in the nave) and a **pontifical throne★** *(at the back of the chancel)* by the Cosmati. The two rows of columns in the chancel divided the 6C church into three aisles; the apse of that church occupied the site of the present triumphal arch.

St. Agnes outside the Walls★ and St. Constance★ (Sant'Agnese Fuori le Mura e Santa Costanza) (DV)

The **Church of St. Agnes outside the Walls★** was built in the 7C over the Saint's tomb. It was restored in the 19C (paintings added above the triumphal arch, between the tall windows and above the arches in the nave) and it has a fine basilical plan with galleries.

In the apse, there are 7C **mosaics★** which illustrate Byzantine influence on Roman art.

The **Church of St. Constance★** was the mausoleum of Constantine's daughters and was adjacent to a basilica which the Emperor built near the tomb of St. Agnes. This circular building is crowned by a cupola with a tall drum resting on a circle of twin columns linked by elegant arches. The surrounding barrel vaulted gallery is still decorated with 4C **mosaics★** (freshness and delicacy of the motifs against a light background).

A gourmet...?

If you are, look in the current Michelin Red Guide Italia for the establishment with stars.

ROVIGO Venetia

Michelin map **988** 15 — Pop 52 300

Town plan in Michelin Red Guide Italia (hotels and restaurants).

Rovigo is the capital of the **Polesina**, an agricultural province between the Adige and the Po. In the region of the Po Delta, with its wide and formerly deserted horizons — the setting of the film *Bitter Rice* — large-scale works of reclamation have been undertaken.

Picture Gallery (Pinacoteca). — *Open weekdays, 9 am to noon and 4.30 to 7 pm; Sundays and holidays, 10 am to noon. Closed Saturdays, 2 January and 24 December.* This is in the buildings of the Accademia dei Concordi under the arcades of the Piazza Vittoria Emanuele (No. 14), where the town hall also stands (Loggia dei Notai, 16C). The Venetian school is represented by Giovanni Bellini, Piazzetta (Celio Rodigino), Longhi (Giulio Contarini), Nicolò di Pietro, Tiepolo (Antonio Riccobono), and Rosalba Carriera (self-portrait); the foreign schools by Holbein, Gossaert, etc.

Our Lady of Succour (Madonna del Soccorso). — This late 16C octagonal church is adorned with paintings which make it look like a picture gallery.

SABBIONETA ★ Lombardy

Michelin map **988** 14 — 33 km - 21 miles — southwest of Mantua — Pop 4 961

This little town, still surrounded by its walls, was built on a regular plan and forms a curious example of 16C **town planning★**. Vespasiano (1531-1591), the youngest of the Gonzaga family, gathered a refined court here which earned Sabbioneta the nickname of Little Athens.
Guided tour of the principal monuments: 15 March to 30 October, 9.30 am to noon and 2.30 to 6 pm; the rest of the year, 10 am to noon and 2 to 3.30 pm; Sundays and holidays, closing time 1/2 hour later. Closed Mondays; 1 200 lire. Apply to the Ufficio Turistico, 15 Via Vespasiano Gonzaga or at the Ducale Bar.
The **Ducal Palace**, which contains interesting equestrian statues of the Gonzaga family, has two finely carved wooden coffered ceilings.
The **Olympic Theatre** was the masterpiece of Vicentino Scamozzi (1522-1616) and the first covered theatre in Europe. It has a ducal box adorned with colonnades, statues of gods and emperors and frescoes by the school of Veronese.
The former **Garden Palace** (Palazzo del Giardino — 1584) was designed for fêtes; the great **Gallery of Antiquities★**, was entirely painted with frescoes by Bernardino Campi.
Vespasiano Gonzaga is buried in the **Church of the Incoronata**, which contains his remarkable mausoleum by Leone Leoni (16C). The church has an octagonal plan, with circular galleries for the ducal family and court. The walls are adorned with paintings in *trompe-l'œil* (false relief).

SACRA DI SAN MICHELE ★★★ Piedmont

Michelin map **988** 12 — 37 km - 23 miles — west of Turin — Alt 962 m - 3 155 ft

Open 9 am to noon and 2 to 7 pm (at dusk in winter); time: 1 hour
This ancient Benedictine monastery, which dizzily overlooks the San Michele ravine, was built in 998 by Hugues de Montboissier, a member of a well known family of Auvergne.
When visiting the Sacra (or Sagra) di San Michele you may be struck by the similarity of its plan to that of the Mont-St-Michel in Normandy. It has a similar approach stairway, gatehouse and gates, esplanade and church, and the same arrangement of monastic buildings. It is known that a Piedmontese monk, Guglielmo da Volpiano (died 1031), who was a famous master builder, was taken to France by St. Mayeul, the Abbot of Cluny. He became Abbot of Fécamp and exercised a controlling influence over the development of Norman Benedictine monasteries, notably that of Mont-St-Michel, the building of which began in 1022.
The **abbey★★★**, which stands on a beautiful site, is perched high above the Dora Riparia Valley. In the 13C it housed more than 100 monks and controlled 140 monasteries.
After passing through the "iron gate" of the entrance gateway you climb the great stairway (or "staircase of the dead") leading to the Zodiac door, whose pilasters, columns and capitals were decorated by the famous Maestro Nicolò (1135) with sculptures depicting the Signs of the Zodiac, Cain and Abel, Samson and Delilah and other symbolic figures (women giving the breast to serpents). The Romanesque-Gothic church built at the top of the rocky point, has 16C frescoes (Christ's Tomb, the Death of the Virgin, the Assumption, on the left, the story and the legend of the foundation of the church on the right). The early 16C triptych on the high altar is by Defendente Ferrari; the carving on the capitals is outstanding.
From the esplanade there is a view of the Dora Valley, the Po Plain and the Turin Plain.

SALERNO ★ Campania

Michelin map **988** 28 — *Local map p 45* — Pop 162 780

Lying along the graceful curve of its Gulf, Salerno is divided into two quarters, one modern, by the sea, the other mediaeval, on the slopes of a hill crowned by a castle founded by the Lombard Prince Arechi in the 8C. Salerno possesses an active ceramic industry.
Salerno was at first Greek, then Roman. It became a principality under the Lombards. The Norman leader Robert Guiscard made it the capital of the Kingdom of Naples.
It was just south of Salerno that the 5th U.S. Army landed at dawn on 5 September 1943.

A Tooth to be Drawn. — In 1076 Robert Guiscard laid siege to Salerno, then held by his brother-in-law, Gisolf, who was obliged to surrender. Now Gisolf had a tooth of St. Matthew by which he set great store. When Guiscard demanded this relic, Gisolf did not haggle. He had a Jew's tooth pulled out and handed it over to his conqueror. But Guiscard discovered the fraud. He told Gisolf that unless he produced the apostle's tooth, all the teeth of its presumed owner would be pulled out. And Gisolf surrendered the real tooth.

Under the Sign of the Caduceus. — According to legend, the Four Masters, a Greek, a Latin, an Arab and a Hebrew, founded the School of Medicine of Salerno, which was the oldest in the western world. In fact, it would seem that the Benedictines presided over its growth from the 10C onwards. Its teaching became famous in the 11C, when teachers of all countries, even from Africa, imparted their knowledge to pupils from all over Europe. The school began to decline in the 14C.
The famous Code of Health, written in verse at Salerno by Giovanni da Milano in the 12C, was for long the standard text-book of pragmatic medicine.

■ SIGHTS *time: 2 hours*

Cathedral★★ (Duomo). — The cathedral is dedicated to St. Matthew, who is buried in the crypt. It was built at the order of Robert Guiscard and consecrated by Pope Gregory VII in 1085. Of Sicilian-Norman style, it was remodelled in the 18C.

A staircase leads to the 11C Lions' Door in the 18C façade, preceded by a graceful square atrium built of multicoloured stone, with ancient columns used again and overlapping arcades. A massive 12C square tower dominates the atrium.

The central doorway has 11C bronze doors cast in Constantinople.

The original antique columns have been unearthed in several places in the interior, and the mosaic representing St. Matthew on the reverse of the central doorway has been restored.

The impressive 12C **pulpit★★★** encrusted with decorative mosaics (doves pecking grapes) is supported by twelve columns with capitals adorned with fine carvings; with the paschal candelabrum and the ambo opposite, resting on four columns with wonderfully carved capitals, the furnishings form an outstanding group.

At the far end of the south aisle is a sarcophagus adorned with bas-reliefs depicting Bacchus and Ariadne. The Crusaders' Chapel, where the Crusaders had their arms blessed, opens into the south transept. Its paving and that of the chancel are 12C. Under the altar is the tomb of Pope Gregory VII, who died at Salerno in 1085 with the words: "I have loved justice and hated iniquity and I die in exile". It was he who sustained the controversy on investitures *(p 20)*. A mosaic in the oven-vault shows St. Matthew and St. Michael.

Behind the modern high altar stands the throne of Gregory VII. The Royal Chapel, which opens off the north transept, has as its ornament a composition made from fragments of an 11C mosaic incorporated in a fresco depicting a Baptism of Christ.

Passing to the nave, you will find in the first chapel the **tomb** of Marguerite of Durazzo, the wife of Charles II of Anjou, King of Naples; she died in 1412. Round the tomb the coloured bas-reliefs are of the arms of Anjou and the Queen among her family.

The Cathedral Museum *(entrance Via Monterisi; open 9.30 am to 2 pm; closed 21 September, 2 November, Easter and Christmas)*, contains the famous 12C Salerno **ivories★** depicting scenes from the Old and New Testaments.

Via Mercanti★. — This street, one of the most picturesque in old Salerno with its shops and ancient houses, buttresses and oratories, has as its east end an **Arechi Arch (A A)** built by the Lombards in the 8C and remodelled in the 12C (fine antique columns).

Lungomare Trieste★. — From this promenade there is a view of the Gulf of Salerno.

SAN CLEMENTE A CASAURIA Abbey ★★ Abruzzi

Michelin map **988** 27 — 40 km - 25 miles — southwest of Pescara.

Access : Leave Motorway A 25 by the exit road of the Torre de' Passeri interchange. Open 9 am to 1.30 pm; closed Mondays.

Originally situated on a small island in the Pescara River, the San Clemente Abbey was founded in 871 by the Emperor Ludovico II and was rebuilt in the 12C by the Cistercians in the transitional Romanesque-Gothic style. It is the finest building in the Abruzzi.

A deep portico, surmounted by a room in which the pilgrims used to leave their offerings, has three arches resting on remarkable capitals: the central arch is semicircular, the others pointed; the main doorway is decorated with exceptional sculpture: the uprights bear crowned figures of Byzantine origin; on the tympanum, Pope St. Clement is seated near the abbot, who is showing him a model of his abbey; the inscriptions and sculptures on the lintel refer to the foundation of the abbey and the transfer of the relics of St. Clement; the door was cast in 1191.

SAN CLEMENTE A CASAURIA Abbey★★

The interior comprises a nave and two aisles and a semicircular apse. It has typically Cistercian pointed arches with double mouldings, and the architectural simplicity dear to St. Bernard is noticeable. Halfway up the nave is a monumental 13C pulpit with decorative carvings in high relief; the paschal candelabrum of the same period, opposite, is no less magnificent. The high altar is surmounted by a Romanesque **ciborium★★★**, finely carved.

Two stairways at the ends of the side aisles lead to the 9C crypt, which has survived from the original structure and has vaulting supported by ancient columns.

The museum (museo Casàuriense) nearby consists of two rooms with works of art and some archaeological exhibits *(same opening times as the abbey)*.

SAN GIMIGNANO ★★★ Tuscany

Michelin map **988** 14 — Pop 7 501

The surprised and delighted stranger finds himself entering a small 14C town which has kept its mediaeval appearance unchanged. The city is encircled by ramparts bristling with fourteen tall towers of nobility, formerly seventy-two in number, which have earned it the nickname, San Gimignano of the Fine Towers. Stroll along the narrow streets lined with palaces and old houses (Via San Matteo, Via San Giovanni, etc.) which will delight lovers of the past.

The "Towers of Nobility". — Towers were built in towns in the Middle Ages by noble families who designed them for use as keeps during the struggle between the Guelphs and the Ghibellines, and later between local tyrants. For reasons of prestige, each lord built his tower as high as he could. These are frequently leaning towers: some say that this is due to subsidence caused by their size, others that they were designed that way by the architect to prove his skill.

Views of the Town. — Distant views can be obtained from Castel San Gimignano, to the south and from near Vico d'Elsa on the Certaldo-Poggibonsi road. A closer **view★** can be enjoyed from a by-road half a mile southeast of Piazzale Martiri di Montemaggio.

■ **SIGHTS** time : 2 hours

Museums and People's Palace: 1 April to 30 September 9 am to 12.30 pm and 3.30 to 6.30 pm except on Mondays; combined ticket: 1 000 lire.

Piazza della Cisterna★★. — The square is paved with bricks laid on their edges in a herring-bone pattern. It derives its name from a 13C cistern. All round, pell-mell are towers, mansions, and palaces built in a golden limestone in the 13 and 14C.

Piazza del Duomo★★. — The square is framed by several buildings and seven towers.

Cathedral★ (Duomo). — The façade was restored in 1818, but the interior is Romanesque. The reverse of the façade is adorned with frescoes *(lights by the second pillar on the left, 100 lire):* above, a Last Judgment (partly damaged) by Taddeo di Bartolo (1393) and below, a Martyrdom of St. Sebastian by Benozzo Gozzoli; the latter is framed by two painted wooden statues depicting the Annunciation by a Sienese sculptor, Jacopo della Quercia. The aisles are painted with 14C frescoes: in the south aisle, scenes from the Life of Christ by Barna da Siena: in the north aisle, Old Testament scenes by another Sienese, Bartolo di Fredi. At the far end of the north aisle, the Oratory of St John contains a beautiful fresco of the Annunciation by the local artist Sebastiano Mainardi, the

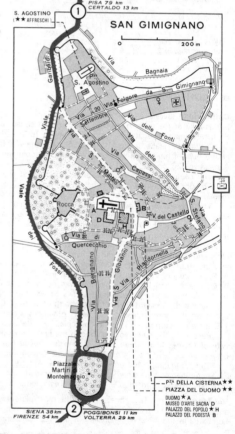

PISA 79 km
CERTALDO 13 km

S. AGOSTINO
(★★ AFFRESCHI)

SAN GIMIGNANO

0   200 m

SIENA 38 km
FIRENZE 54 km

POGGIBONSI 11 km
VOLTERRA 29 km

─ P^ZA DELLA CISTERNA ★★
─ PIAZZA DEL DUOMO ★★

DUOMO ★ A
MUSEO D'ARTE SACRA D
PALAZZO DEL POPOLO ★ H
PALAZZO DEL PODESTA B

son-in-law of Domenico Ghirlandaio. The chancel was remodelled in 1468 by Giuliano da Maiano.

The **Chapel of Santa Fina** *(ask for the lights to be switched on in the chapel or in the Oratory of St. John, 300 Lire; the combined ticket is valid)* at the far end of the south aisle, is dedicated to the local saint, who is known as the Saint of the Wallflowers because these flowers sprang up on her coffin, it is said, and on the towers of the town on the day of her death. The chapel, a graceful piece of architecture, was built in 1468 by Giuliano da Maiano. Later his nephew, Benedetto da Maiano, installed in it a finely carved marble and alabaster **altar★**. Ghirlandaio painted some admirable **frescoes★** there in 1470 relating the life of the saint.

Museum of Sacred Art and Etruscan Museum (D). — *Access through the vaulted passage to the left of the Cathedral; 500 lire.* The museums are in a 13C palace in the Piazza Pecori. On the ground and first floors are sculpture dating from the 10 to 15C (Crucifix carved in 1474 by Giuliano da Maiano) and 14C illuminated antiphonaries. Upstairs, are Etruscan and Roman exhibits.

People's Palace★ (Palazzo del Popolo). — *500 lire (tower only 300 lire).* The palace (late 13-early 14C) is dominated by a 54 m - 117 ft tall square tower from the top of which you can enjoy an unusual **view★★** over the brown roofs and towers of the town and of the Tuscan countryside. In the Council Chamber, adorned with frescoes by the Sienese school of the 14C depicting hunting scenes with Charles of Anjou, King of Naples, the Sienese Primitive artist, Lippo Memmi, painted in 1317, a masterly *Maestà* (Majesty), restored by Benozzo Gozzoli about 1467. Dante made a speech in this chamber in 1300.

The **Municipal Museum★** (Museo Civico) is on the second floor. Most of the paintings are of the 12 to 15C Sienese school. You will see: in Room 1, two paintings of the Madonna and Child with Saints (one is particularly luminous) by Benozzo Gozzoli, a great Virgin in Majesty by the Umbrian artist Pinturicchio (1512), a Madonna and Child by Pier Francesco Fiorentino, a Crucifix with Scenes of the Passion by Coppo di Marcovaldo, and a prized Annunciation in two round paintings by Filippino Lippi; in Room 2, panels depicting scenes from the life of Santa Fina by Lorenzo di Niccolò Gerini; in Room 3, two polyptychs by Taddeo di Bartolo (Madonna and Child, and scenes from the life of San Gimignano).

Governor's Palace (Palazzo del Podestà). — The palace dates from 1239. It includes a vast loggia on the ground floor surmounted by a great arch. It also comprises the impressive Rognosa Tower (51 m - 167 ft). Close by stands the 13C Chigi Palace flanked by its tower.

St. Augustine's Church (Sant'Agostino). — This is a 13C Romanesque-Gothic church. In the chancel are seventeen **frescoes★★** by Benozzo Gozzoli, a master of the Florentine Quattrocento (15C). The life of the famous theologian St. Augustine is depicted with the fresh colour, sense of perspective and love of intimate and familiar detail usual with this artist. The best scenes are Augustine Being Brought to School by his Mother, St. Monica, the Death of St. Monica, Augustine Teaching Philosophy in Rome, the Departure for Milan and his Funeral. A Coronation of the Virgin at the high altar is a graceful and delicate work by P. Pollaiuolo (1485).

Behind the façade, the Chapel of San Bartolo, paved with porcelain tiles from Valencia, contains an altar by Benedetto da Maiano (1494).

There are Renaissance cloisters on the left of the church *(access through the sacristy).*

SAN GIOVANNI IN VENERE Abruzzi

Michelin map 988 27 — 41 km - 25 miles — southeast of Pescara.

On reaching Fossacesia-Marina on road S 16, take the road towards Lanciano and, after 2 km - 1 1/2 miles — turn right. The Monastery of San Giovanni in Venere overlooks the Adriatic from a height of 107 m - 850 ft. It was built in the 12C over a former temple of Venus and has a magnificent church in the Cistercian style. You should see the fine sculptures of the main door, the pure semicircular apses and the crypt, adorned with 12C frescoes and whose marble columns were taken from ancient temples.

SAN GIOVANNI VALDARNO Tuscany

Michelin map 988 15 — 41 km - 25 miles — northwest of Arezzo — Pop 19 908

This industrial town still has a 13C town hall with arcades and loggias.

Montecarlo Monastery. — *3 km - 2 miles.* Turn to the right at the south gate of San Giovanni, and after the level crossing turn left into an uphill by-road. The Monastery of Montecarlo contains a jewel of Florentine painting: an **Annunciation★★** which is one of the greatest of Fra Angelico's paintings. The predella of the altarpiece depicts the Marriage of Mary and Joseph, the Visitation, the Epiphany, the Presentation of Jesus in the Temple and the Death of Mary. On the north wall is a pretty Coronation of the Virgin attributed to Neri di Bicci. The room preceding the sacristy contains a 15C Crucifixion attributed to Masaccio and his brother.

The elegant cloister dates from the 16C.

SAN MARINO ★★★

Michelin map 988 15 — 27 km - 17 miles — south of Rimini — Pop 20 968.

One of the smallest and most ancient states in the world (60 km² - 23 sq. miles) stands on an admirable **site★★★** on the slopes of Monte Titano. The Republic strikes its own coinage. It has a standing army normally engaged in ceremonial duties and its own police force.

San Marino is believed to have originated with the foundation of a hermitage by a pious mason named Marino, who was then seeking refuge from the persecutions of the Christians ordered by the Emperor Diocletian in the 4C AD. The first evidence of the independence of the Republic dates from 885, and the territory has remained sovereign since then, in spite of occasional difficulties. In the 15C San Marino took part with Urbino in the struggle against the Malatestas of Rimini. The Republic refused the offers of expansion made to it by Napoleon I. It gave asylum to Garibaldi in 1849; and again provided a refuge for many in the 1939-1945 War.

Customs and Economy. — The régime at San Marino has changed little in nine centuries, and the leading figures are still the two Captains Regent, who are chosen from among the sixty members of the Grand Council and installed every six months, on 1 April and 1 October, in a ceremony at which there is a display of picturesque uniforms and old costumes. The national festival, on 3 September, commemorates St. Marinus and the foundation of the Republic. Among other prerogatives, the Grand Council can confer titles of nobility.

The economy is based on agriculture, tourism, the sale of postage stamps, trade, minting and related activities and craft industries (ceramics).

The town looks mediaeval and offers admirable views and picturesque vistas. You reach it along the Rimini road and then the Strada Panoramica, which skirts the rocky spur and affords characteristic views of the sea and the Apennines.

■ **SIGHTS** *time: 3 hours*

Tour: 500 lire (ticket valid for all monuments and museums).

Government House (Palazzo del Governo). — Reconstructed in the Gothic style at the end of the 19C, this building contains a portrait of St. Marinus by Guercino. You can also visit the Great Council Chamber. There is a view of the Marecchia Valley from the Piazza della Libertà.

St. Marinus' Basilica (San Marino). — This contains the tomb of the saint (at the high altar). In the nearby Church of St. Peter (San Pietro) the sacristan shows two niches hewn in the rock which were used as beds by St. Marinus and his companion, St. Leo.

SAN MARINO

0 _____ 300 m

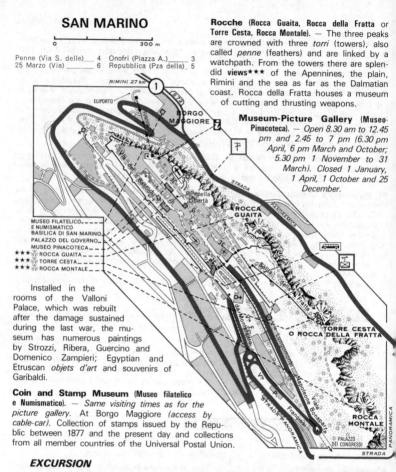

Rocche (Rocca Guaita, Rocca della Fratta or Torre Cesta, Rocca Montale). — The three peaks are crowned with three *torri* (towers), also called *penne* (feathers) and are linked by a watchpath. From the towers there are splendid views★★★ of the Apennines, the plain, Rimini and the sea as far as the Dalmatian coast. Rocca della Fratta houses a museum of cutting and thrusting weapons.

Museum-Picture Gallery (Museo-Pinacoteca). — *Open 8.30 am to 12.45 pm and 2.45 to 7 pm (6.30 pm April, 6 pm March and October; 5.30 pm 1 November to 31 March). Closed 1 January, 1 April, 1 October and 25 December.*

Installed in the rooms of the Valloni Palace, which was rebuilt after the damage sustained during the last war, the museum has numerous paintings by Strozzi, Ribera, Guercino and Domenico Zampieri; Egyptian and Etruscan *objets d'art* and souvenirs of Garibaldi.

Coin and Stamp Museum (Museo filatelico e Numismatico). — *Same visiting times as for the picture gallery.* At Borgo Maggiore *(access by cable-car)*. Collection of stamps issued by the Republic between 1877 and the present day and collections from all member countries of the Universal Postal Union.

EXCURSION

Verucchio. — *North.* Leave by ①. Either follow the road along the crest which offers the widest views *(9 km − 6 miles)* or the road that drops down into the Marecchia Valley *(15 km - 9 miles)*. Verucchio is a village guarding the Marecchia Valley. At the summit stands a massive castle which was the birthplace of the Malatestas *(p 198).* From the esplanade there is a fine view★★ of the Marecchia Valley and the Rimini Riviera.

SAN MINIATO ★ Tuscany

Michelin map 988 14 — 44 km - 27 miles — southwest of Florence — Pop 24 701

San Miniato lies along a hill crest forming an amphitheatre. It is a charming town which has kept its ancient appearance and affords pleasant views of the Arno Valley.

Cathedral (Duomo). — The cathedral originated in the 12C, when the battlemented campanile was built, but it was largely remodelled in the 15-16C. Opposite the cathedral is the episcopal palace in which the Countess Matilda of Tuscany was born in 1046. From behind the palace there is a view over the roofs of San Miniato and the Tuscan countryside; below is a square lined with old houses.

From the terrace to the left of the cathedral (view over the Arno Valley) walk up a steep path to the former Rocca (castle) of Frederick Barbarossa where there is a fine **panorama★**.

SAN REMO ★★★ Liguria

Michelin maps 988 12 or 195 20 — *Local map p 199* — Pop 63 867
Town plan in Michelin Red Guide Italia (hotels and restaurants).

The luxurious capital of the Riviera of Flowers enjoys a delightfully warm temperature and the highest average sunshine in Liguria. These advantages, together with its racecourse and its gay and brilliant festivals, make it a resort of worldwide repute. Near the Casino is the Corso dell'Imperatrice, famous for its Canary palms.

Flowers and Palms. — San Remo is the principal Italian flower market. In midwinter, from Ventimiglia to Alassio, carnations, roses, jasmine, hyacinths, narcisi, violets, tulips and mimosa cover about 8 650 acres of terraced fields, making them alive with scent and colour. From October to June the Mercato dei Fiori (Flower Market — which should be seen between 6 and 8 am) is one of the most characteristic sights on the Riviera: just under 20 000 tons of cut flowers are despatched to every part of Italy and abroad each year.

Old Town★ (Città Vecchia). — The Old Town, also called the *pigna* (beak) because of its pointed shape, is a maze of winding alleys and staircases. Walk down from the Piazza Castello to the Baroque Church of the Madonna della Costa; note the graceful façade. From the esplanade there is a pretty view of the town and the coast. Continue down to the lower town through the Gardens of Queen Helena, which occupy the site of the former castle.

Villa Ormond. — This is at the eastern exit from San Remo, surrounded by the tropical vegetation of a garden often used for flower shows.

EXCURSIONS

Monte Bignone (alt 1 299 m - 4 258 ft). — *1 1/2 hours Rtn by cable-car which leaves from the Via Isonzo; 1 500 lire Rtn.* A fine **panorama★** can be seen extending as far as Cannes in France.

Ceriana-Baiardo Road★★. — *25 km - 16 miles — about 1 hour.* Leave San Remo by the Corso Garibaldi and the Via Aurelia, road S 1 for Genoa, and after — 2 km - 1 1/2 miles — take the road to Poggio to the left. You follow, still to the left, a remarkable **road★★** affording impressive bird's-eye views of the sea and the Armea Valley. **Ceriana**, which is perched on a height, has a fine Romanesque church with a graceful porch. After Ceriana the winding road climbs to a narrow pass (alt 898 m - 2 946 ft), reached a little before **Baiardo**. From a point near the church a **panorama★** opens of the wild expanse of the Ligurian Alps.

SANSEPOLCRO ★ Tuscany

Michelin map **988** 15 — 38 km - 24 miles — northeast of Arezzo — Pop 15 695

Sansepolcro, a small industrial town (macaroni manufacture), lies in the centre of a cultivated basin. It still has ramparts and old houses.

It was in this town that the painter **Piero della Francesca** (*c.* 1416-1492), the son of a shoemaker, was born and lived. His austere and conscientious skill carried him to the summit of success; he was an original artist, seeking harmony in pale, sometimes rather neutral, colours, such as ash greys, light blues and cool browns. Skilful drawing makes his portraits true to life, while the noble serenity of his religious inspiration imparts life to his holy pictures.

An archery contest in mediaeval costume is held on the second Sunday in September.

Museum (Museo Civico). — *Open 9.30 to 1 pm and 3 to 6.30 pm (2.30 to 6 pm 1 October to 31 March). Closed 1 January, 1 May, 15 August and 25 December; 500 lire.* The museum occupies twelve rooms in the old town hall. It contains several leading **works★★** by Piero della Francesca: an impressive Resurrection showing his mature genius, an admirable polyptych of the Virgin of Pity, a St. Julian and a St. Ludovic. You will also see works by his pupil Luca Signorelli, by Pontormo, Bassano, Palma The Younger, Andrea and Giovanni della Robbia and other artists, all native of Sansepolcro (Raffaelino dal Colle, Santi di Tito, Giovanni Alberti...).

SANTA MARIA CAPUA VETERE Campania

Michelin map **988** 27 — 30 km - 19 miles — north of Naples — Pop 32 659

Santa Maria Capua Vetere is a busy agricultural market. It occupies the site of ancient Capua. After the Battle of Cannae (216 BC) Hannibal and his army grew soft here among the many pleasures and so came to be defeated by Scipio.

Amphitheatre★ (Anfiteatro). — *Open 9 am to 1 hour before sunset. Closed Mondays (Tuesday when Monday is a holiday), 1 January, 25 April, 1 May, first Sunday in June, 15 August and 25 December; 500 lire.* Built in the 1C AD on the outskirts of the Roman city, this was the largest amphitheatre in Italy after the Coliseum in Rome, measuring 170 m by 140 m - 558 × 459 ft. In the outer ring, formerly ornamented with statues, four tiers of galleries were surmounted by masts supporting a protective awning. Alongside the amphitheatre was a school for gladiators from which the slaves' revolt led by **Spartacus** started.

Basilica di Sant'Angelo in Formis★. — *North 5 km - 3 miles* — This church, an interesting building in the Romanesque style, was erected in the 11C by the Benedictines of Monte Cassino on the site of the Temple of Diana. Diana was worshipped here under the name of Tifatina. Remarkable Romanesque **frescoes★★** depict the Life of Jesus (nave); Christ giving His Blessing between the symbols of the Evangelists and of Abbot Didier, the builder of the church (central apse); and the Last Judgment (reverse of the façade).

SARONNO Lombardy

Michelin maps **988** 3 and **26** 18 — 26 km - 16 miles — northwest of Milan — Pop 36 632

The **Church of the Madonna dei Miracoli**, on the Milan-Varese road, was built in 1498 in the Renaissance style to commemorate a miraculous cure. The façade was added in 1578.

The remarkable **frescoes★** in the chancel are by Bernardino Luini and illustrate the Life of the Virgin. On the dome is the Concert of Angels (1536), a fresco by Gaudenzio Ferrari.

SARZANA ★ Liguria

Michelin map **988** 14 — 17 km - 11 miles — east of La Spezia — *Local map p 200* — Pop 19 497.

Busy Sarzana lies in the fertile plain of the Magra. The town was bought by the Bank of St. George *(p 117)* in 1496 and was an advanced base of the Republic of Genoa, a rival of Pisa. Its castles and 15C ramparts bear witness to its past military importance.

Cathedral (Duomo). — The cathedral has a 13C tower and a 14C doorway; nearly all the rest of the exterior is Renaissance. The interior was decorated in the 17C. A delicately sculptured marble **altarpiece★** in the north transept, representing the Coronation of the Virgin, is the work of Riccomanni (1432). The Chapel of the Precious Blood, to the right of the chancel, contains a phial in which the Blood of Christ is said to have been received. In the chapel to the left is a **Crucifixion★**, a Romanesque masterpiece for purity of line and grave serenity of expression. It was executed in 1138 by a certain Guglielmo, probably from Lucca.

Sarzanello Fortress★ (Fortezza di Sarzanello). — *1 km - 3/4 mile.* The approach is by way of a road, the Strada Panoramica which branches off the Viale Mazzini. The massive Sarzanello Citadel is also called the Castruccio Castracani Castle after the leader from Lucca who had it built in 1322. It stands on a height northeast of the town and is triangular in plan, with a detached bastion linked by a bridge to the main structure. The Sarzanello is a curious specimen of military architecture with deep moats and thick curtain walls reinforced with round towers. The square keep commanding the bridge leading to the bastion, the cellars and several rooms are open. The views are chiefly of the Apennine foothills.

SAVONA Liguria

Michelin map **988** 13 — *Local map p 199* — Pop 78 606

The fifth seaport in Italy, austere and sombre, Savona includes a modern quarter on a geometrical plan and an old town in which there are still Renaissance palaces. The most interesting streets are the Via Paleocapa, lined with shopping arcades, and the Via Pia, narrow and crowded. At the end of the latter, near the Torre Brandale, is a palace (2 Piazza del Brandale) which the future Pope Julius II had built by the Florentine architect, Sangallo. The nearby 16C cathedral with its 19C façade contains inlaid stalls presented by Julius II.

The Port. — The traffic handled by the Savona-Vado Ligure port (5 km - 3 miles — to the west) amounted to approximately 13 million metric tons in 1975. In addition to traditional freight (oil, coal, cellulose), Italian cars are exported in large numbers to the United States and to Britain. To the north of the port, a cable-way carries coal at the rate of 400 tons an hour to the San Giuseppe di Cairo depot, which can store 400 000 tons. Ironworks, chemical plants and shipyards contribute to the activities of the port. The Pancaldo Tower commemorates the sailor from Savona who was Magellan's pilot in his voyage round the world.

SCANNO ★★ Abruzzi

Michelin map **988** 27 — 31 km - 19 miles — south of Sulmona — *Local map p 42* — Alt 1 050 m - 3 445 ft — Pop 2 883

Scanno, in the heart of the Abruzzi, has preserved evidence of its past while equipping itself as a country resort, excursion and winter sports centre.

From a thrilling high mountain **site**★★ the town overlooks the Sagittario Valley and **Lake Scanno**★, formed by a landslide which blocked the river bed. Women, still wearing the dignified black local dress, probably of Oriental origin, walk the steep, narrow and vaulted streets, lined with picturesque houses and churches. To the right as you go up the main street, note a curious 14C fountain adorned with masks and bas-reliefs of the Annunciation.

From Scanno itself a chair-lift reaches *(14 minutes)* the **Colle Rotondo** (1 640 m - 5 380 ft): **panorama**★★ of the Abruzzi and, in the distance, the Gran Sasso d'Italia.

EXCURSION

Sagittario Gorges★★. — *Northwest, 16 km - 9 miles.* Between Villalago and Anversa degli Abruzzi, for a distance of 10 km - 6 miles — the Sagittario River has hollowed from the grey rock a series of impressive gorges, which the road follows with many twists and turns *(get out of the car to look into the depths)*. The gorges are partly filled by an elongated lake.

SERMONETA Latium

Michelin map **988** 26 — 20 km - 12 miles — northeast of Latina — Pop 6 174

This small mediaeval town, still encircled in part by ramparts, possesses an impressive 13-16C castle. *Guided tour: 11.30 am (10.30 am Sundays and holidays) to 12.30 pm and 3 to 6 pm (2 to 4 pm 1 October to 30 April). Closed 15 to 30 September, 23 December, 1 January and Thursdays; 1 000 lire; time 3/4 hour.*

The cathedral contains a delightful **panel**★ by Benozzo Gozzoli (15C): the Virgin, surrounded by angels, holds in her hands the town of Sermoneta, to which she had acted as protector.

SESTRIERE ★★ Piedmont

Michelin maps **988** 11 and **77** 9 — Alt 2 033 m - 6 670 ft — Pop 774

The winter sports resort has developed from the patronage of Turin industrialists. It possesses a well-known ski school, a skating rink, curling rinks, many mechanical hoists, including several cable-cars, to remarkable belvederes: the **Monte Fraitève** (alt 2 701 m - 8 862 ft) from which there is a magnificent **panorama**★★ *(access only from 15 November to 30 April and in August, time: 10 minutes by cable-car)*; the upper station at 2 600 m - 8 531 ft of the **Monte Sises** cable-car *(access only from 15 November to 30 April and in August, time: 10 minutes)* from which there is a **view**★★ over Sestrière and the valley; and the upper station at 2 555 m - 8 384 ft of the **Monte Banchetta** *(access only from 1 November to 30 April, time: 12 minutes)* from which there is a **view**★ towards the mountains on the French frontier.

SIENA ★★★ Tuscany

Michelin map **988** 15 — Pop 64 251

Town plan in Michelin Red Guide Italia (hotels and restaurants). Since the town centre is a traffic free zone, the location of car parks are shown on the plan opposite.

Siena "the beloved" is a mystical, gentle, passionate and generous art centre. It welcomes you with its motto: *Cor magis tibi Sena pandit* — Siena opens its heart to you — inscribed on the Camollia Gate (northwest).

The town invites a stroll through its narrow Gothic streets, lined with palaces and patrician mansions. Encircled by ramparts which seem too big for it, the town's plan extends over three converging red clay hills from which the colour burnt siena is named.

Siena is believed to have been founded at the beginning of the Roman era by Senius and Aschius, the sons of Remus, which explains why its coat of arms includes a she-wolf and twins (Romulus and Remus, according to legend, were nursed by a wolf).

Middle Ages (12-14C). — Siena became a republic and flourished on trade and banking. But dissension reigned. "The town", declared the historian Commines, "is all divided and is governed more madly than any town in Italy".

Siena fought with the Florentines, who in 1230 catapulted dead donkeys and excrement over its walls (to start a plague). In 1260 the Florentine troops again threatened the town. The Syndic (Mayor) and the people then dedicated Siena to the Virgin, seeking her protection. A few days later the Florentines were bloodily defeated at Montaperti.

An Admirer of the Sienese. — The admirer in question was a Gascon, **Blaise de Montluc**, who was sent by Henri II to help Siena to defend itself against the Emperor Charles V. The town resisted heroically from the beginning of 1554 to April 1555 with the help of its women, to whom Montluc said: "You deserve perpetual praise".

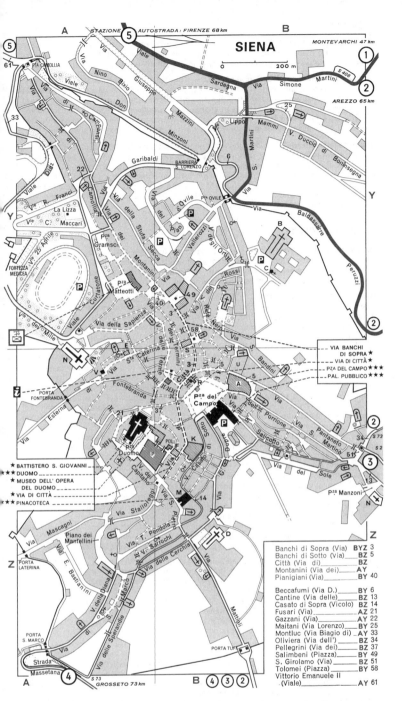

The Sienese School.

The Sienese School. — This included a few architect-sculptors: Tino di Camaino, Francesco di Giorgio and **Jacopo della Quercia** (1374-1438) with his own quiet, pure style.

But the artistic fame of Siena is due above all to its Primitive painters (late 12 - late 14C). They showed gentle, fervent piety and painted in the Byzantine manner, displaying religious feeling and using gilded or etched backgrounds. Their expression is full of beauty and tenderness. Their draughtsmanship, transparent colour and detail suggest miniature painting.

The 12-13C painted crucifixes still show a Byzantine stiffness from which **Duccio**, (died 1319) began to free himself with his exquisite sense of line and colour and his care for more expression. **Simone Martini** (died 1344) followed in his footsteps but imitated nature more closely; he was very famous in Europe and worked at the Papal Court in Avignon (France). His contemporaries Pietro and Ambrogio Lorenzetti had a taste for detail and a sense of colour.

These princes of Gothic painting were followed in the same spirit during the Quattrocento (15C) by attractive minor masters, not innovators, such as the delicate Lorenzo Monaco, the angelic Sassetta, the pure Sano di Pietro and the realistic Matteo di Giovanni.

A great artist, Il Sodoma, the pupil of Leonardo da Vinci, appeared in the 16C.

The Religious Past.

The Religious Past. — Great saints lived and worked in Siena.

St. Catherine (1347-1380) was the daughter of a dyer who had twenty-five children. She entered the Dominican Order at thirteen. Her golden legend is one of the richest in religious history. She had many visions and trances and received the Stigmata at Pisa in 1375. The mystic marriage of St. Catherine with Christ has been the favourite subject of many painters. Her political rôle was considerable: she wrote many letters and helped to bring the popes back from Avignon to Rome.

St. Bernardino (born 1380), is greatly venerated, in Siena, where he exercised a successful apostleship. He made the Basilica of the Observatory, to the north of the town, his main centre of teaching. He was an eloquent reformer whose sermons were caustic and humorous.

Mediaeval Administrative Organisation. — This has survived in part. Three quarters, the Città, Camollia and San Martino, correspond with the three hills on which the town was built. These *terzi* (thirds) were divided into fifty-nine *contrade* or parishes; only seventeen exist today. A *gonfaloniere* (standard-bearer) was in charge of the *gonfalone* (standard) of each *terzo*. The *carroccio* or Chariot of Liberty was the symbol of the commune and was taken into battle. A Council of the Bell, presided over by a *podestà* (governor) administered the town.

"Palio delle Contrade". — This, the most popular festival in Siena, is said to date back to the 13C and takes place on 2 July and on 16 August in the Piazza del Campo. It begins with a procession of the seventeen *contrade* in 15C costume carrying their emblems, while the *alfieri* brandish banners with extraordinary skill. The *carroccio* comes next, followed by the Municipal Guard, armed with halberds. The Corsa al Palio is a dangerous horse race round the square which is held in the late afternoon. The *palio,* a standard bearing the effigy of the Virgin to whom the race is dedicated, is awarded to the winner.

■ **MAIN SIGHTS** *time: 1 day*

Piazza del Campo★★★. — One could spend hours watching the play of light on the stones, for the square forms a monumental ensemble of almost matchless harmony. It is shaped like a scollop or a fan: eleven streets lead into it. The **Fonte Gaia** (Fountain of Joy) in the centre is a copy of the original by Jacopo della Quercia in the Palazzo Pubblico.

Town Hall★★★ (Palazzo Pubblico). — *Open 8.30 am to 7.30 pm; 1.30 pm 1 October to 31 March; closed Sunday afternoons and Easter and Christmas; 1 000 lire.* This sober and graceful Gothic structure (1288-1309) is one of the finest public buildings in Italy. The windows in the façade, with triple trilobar bays under supporting arches, are adorned with the coat of arms of Siena. The Torre del Mangia, a brick tower crowned with stone, is so named after a chief bellringer of the Middle Ages. It is 88 m - 286 1/2 ft — high (Canterbury, Bell Harry Tower: 71 m - 234 ft — to the pinnacles), and a superb **panorama★★** can be seen from the top *(access from inside the palace).* A 14-15C chapel with Renaissance decoration at the foot of the tower commemorates the gratitude of the Sienese, liberated from the plague in 1348. In 1425, St. Bernardino condemned the lustful habits of Sienese women from a wooden pulpit in front of the town hall. A doorway on the right of the chapel leads to a small inner courtyard.

On the first floor *(access by a doorway at the far end of the façade)* you can visit the apartments in which the governors and members of the council lived. In the Globe Room *(to the right as you enter)* are the admirable **Maestà★★** (1315) depicting the Virgin surrounded by Saints, and opposite, the **portrait★** of the Sienese general, Guidoriccio da Fogliano, on horseback, by Simone Martini. The next room on the right, known as the Hall of Peace, contains the famous **frescoes★** (1337-1339) of Ambrogio Lorenzetti, entitled Effects of Good (wall to the right and above the entrance) and Bad (facing the entrance) Government. Return by the Globe Room to reach, on the left, the **chapel★** with its frescoes by Taddeo di Bartolo (1408), its delicate chancel railing (1437), its magnificent **stalls★★** with early 15C inlaid back illustrating the Creed and, on the high altar, a fine picture by Il Sodoma. The Priors' Room on the right, which is adorned with a picturesque fresco by Spinello Aretino (1407) recalling the life of the Sienese Pope Alexander III, opens into the Cardinals' Room adjoining the chapel.

From the Risorgimento Room (on the opposite side of the passage) you can reach the tower. From the passage a stairway leads to the second floor where original fragments (extensively damaged) of the Fonte Gaia are kept in a loggia overlooking the countryside.

Cathedral★★★ (Duomo). — The cathedral stands in the Piazza del Duomo, as do the 18C Neo-Gothic Episcopal Palace on the right (facing away from the façade), the long façade of the Santa Maria della Scala Hospital, part of which dates from the 13C, opposite the cathedral, and the 16C Government Palace on the left.

The cathedral was begun during the late 12C and completed only in the 14C. The restored Romanesque-Gothic façade, richly decorated and faced with multicoloured marble, is the work of Giovanni Pisano, except for the upper part. The slim Romanesque campanile has a base of alternating white and black marble; the number of windows increases with the height.

Interior. — Romanesque pillars and walls faced with alternating bands in black and white marble, an imposing cupola, a deep chancel and a cornice frieze with the busts of the popes in terracotta above the main arches are the most characteristic features. Note at the entrance two 16C stoups, and on the façade a window dating from 1549.

The 15-16C **paving★★★** is unique. *(Parts of the paving are covered by floorboards which are removed only for a few days around 15 August.)* Several artists worked on it; of whom Beccafumi was one (died 1551). The mosaics and *graffiti* (niello-work) depict Allegories (allegory of Fortune in the middle of the nave), Virtues (at the far end of the chancel), Sibyls (in the aisles), and scenes from the Testaments (Massacre of the Innocents in the north transept).

In the south transept, in the Baroque Chapel of the Virgin of Siena are (on either side of the entrance) a St. Jerome and a Mary Magdalen in marble, the works of Bernini (17C).

The chancel, decorated with frescoes by Beccafumi (Paradise), has a high altar surmounted by an elegant bronze tabernacle by Vecchietta (15C) between two angels, one by Giovanni di Stefano and the other by Francesco di Giorgio Martini. A rose window contains stained glass (1288) depicting the Annunciation, the Coronation and Death of the Virgin. The stalls in the chancel form a remarkable collection of carved and inlaid **woodwork★★**: those at the far end are 16C, those on the sides date back to the 14C and were enriched with inlaid panels (1503) by Fra Giovanni da Verona. The 16C lectern was designed by Riccio.

Left of the apse the chapel of St. Ansan of Siena contains the tombstone of Bishop Pecci by Donatello. Beside the altar is the Gothic marble tombstone (1318) to the jurist, Cardinal Riccardo Petroni, by Tino di Camaino and his father Camaino di Crescentino.

The famous **pulpit★★** (1265-1268) at the entrance of the north transept was made by Nicolò Pisano, his son and Arnolfo di Cambio. The liberal arts are represented on the base of the central column and the Life of Jesus on the rostrum *(illumination: 100 lire).*

In a charming Renaissance chapel at the end of the transept is a forceful statue of St. John, in bronze, by Donatello (1457) and frescoes by Pinturicchio.

From the north aisle a charming doorway gives access to the famous **Libreria Piccolomini★**, built in 1495 by Cardinal Francesco Piccolomini, the future Pius III, to house the books of his uncle, AEneas Silvius Piccolomini (Pius II). The Umbrian painter Pinturicchio adorned it with ten

frescoes★★ (1509) depicting episodes in the life of the pontiff with remarkable charm and freshness. The most successful are those on the end wall showing the betrothal of the Emperor Frederick III and AEneas receiving the Cardinal's Hat. In the centre stands the famous marble statue of the Three Graces, a Roman sculpture showing Hellenistic influence. As you leave the Libreria, you will see, on the right, the imposing Piccolomini altar (late 15C) adorned with statues attributed to Michelangelo.

Cathedral Museum★ (Museo dell'Opera del Duomo). — *Open 9.30 am to 1 pm and 3 to 6 pm (9 am to 2 pm 1 October to 31 March). Closed 1 May, Easter and Christmas; 1 000 lire.* The museum is in the remains of a huge cathedral, the building of which began in 1339 but was interrupted by the plague of 1348. The present cathedral was to have been its transept; only the façade and part of the impressive arches in the nave remain of the original great enterprise.

On the ground floor of the museum note in the centre of the great hall, a very fine **sculpture★** of the Virgin, St. Anthony Abbot and a cardinal, made towards the end of his life (1438) by Jacopo della Quercia; along the walls are **statues★** of prophets, sages of Antiquity, and sibyls, by Giovanni Pisano, that originally adorned the cathedral façade. The famous **Maestà★★** (1308-1311) of Duccio is shown in a room on the first floor devoted to that master; it consists of a Crowned Virgin formerly placed on the high altar. Along the wall left of the entrance are displayed the fourteen panels depicting scenes from the Passion which were originally on the reverse side of the painting. On the right wall are a triptych of the **Birth of the Virgin★** (1342) by Pietro Lorenzetti and a **Virgin and Child★** by Duccio.

The rooms between the first and second floors house the Treasury: splendid **altar frontal★★** embroidered with gold and silver (Scenes from the Life of Christ). The rooms on the third floor contain fine paintings by Sienese Primitive artists (in the room opposite the stairway, a **Virgin with Large Eyes★** dating from the early 13C and the **Blessed Agostino Novello★** painted around 1330 by Simone Martini) and Renaissance painters (room to the right of the stairway).

There is a **view★** from the top of the unfinished façade.

Crypt. — *Open 9 am to 1 pm and 3 to 6 pm (5 pm holidays); closed November to end of February; 1 000 lire. Entrance on east side halfway up the stairway.* It contains statues by the school of Giovanni Pisano (Apostles) which adorned the cathedral façade.

Baptistry of St. John★ (San Giovanni). — This is below the cathedral and dates from the early 14C. Its Gothic façade was left unfinished. The interior is adorned with 15C frescoes. The **font★★** (in the centre) is also 15C *(ask for the lights to be turned on at the baptistry entrance).* The basin is adorned with bas-reliefs in gilded copper, relating the Life of St. John by Lorenzo Ghiberti (Baptism of Christ, St. John taken Prisoner), Donatello (the Feast of Herod), Jacopo della Quercia (Zacharia driven from the Temple), Turino da Siena (Birth of St. John the Baptist), Giovanni di Turino (St. John the Baptist Preaching). The statues of Faith and Hope are also by Donatello. The marble tabernacle in the centre is the work of Jacopo della Quercia.

Picture Gallery★★★ (Pinacoteca). — *Open 9 am to 2 pm (1 pm Sundays); closed Mondays, and holidays; 750 lire.* The extensive collection of 13-16C Sienese paintings is arranged in the 14C Palazzo Buonsignori.

On the second floor *(begin with the rooms on the right)* the most interesting works are the 12-13C painted Crucifixes (Room 1); the Virgin of the Franciscans, by Duccio (Room 4); the polyptychs of Segna di Bonaventura (Room 4) and Luca Thome (Room 5), a Madonna and Child by Simone Martini (Room 6) and a remarkable series of paintings by Ambrogio (Madonnas, an Annunciation and two charming scenes of a seaport and of a castle by a lake) and Pietro Lorenzetti (the Virgin of the Carmelites and a History of the Carmelites). Among other Primitives may be seen works by Simone Martini, Andrea and Taddeo di Bartolo (Room 11), Giovanni di Paolo (Room 13: a Virgin of Humility and a Last Judgment), Matteo di Giovanni (Rooms 14-15) and Sano di Pietro (Rooms 16-17).

On the first floor note Pinturicchio (Room 23: Holy Family), Beccafumi and Il Sodoma (Rooms 30-33). The latter painted a Christ of the Column of surprising plastic beauty.

Via di Città★, Via Banchi di Sopra★. — These narrow streets, with flagstones reaching to the walls of the remarkable palaces which line them, bustle with life.

Coming from Via San Pietro you will see in the Via di Città, on the left just before the turning, the 15C **Piccolomini delle Papesse Palace** (BZ F) with a façade embossed in the Florentine style. Practically opposite stands the long Gothic façade of the **Chigi-Saracini Palace** (BZ K), now the home of the Academy of Music. The sumptuous apartments include a **picture gallery★** *(to visit apply for an authorisation at the Accademia Musicale Chigiana,   46152).* There are works by Italian Flemish, Dutch and German masters.

Farther along, on the right, at the intersection formed by the Via di Città and the Banchi di Sotto and Banchi di Sopra streets, the **Loggia dei Mercanti** (BZ R), or Merchants' House, is in the transitional Gothic-Renaissance style; it used to house the commercial court. Unusual benches carry bas-reliefs depicting the philosophers and generals of Antiquity.

The Piazza Tolomei and on the left the 13C palace of the same name are elegant.

In the Piazza Salimbeni the 14C Salimbeni Palace at the end is Gothic, the 15C Spannocchi Palace on the right is Renaissance and the 16C Tantucci on the left is Baroque.

■ ADDITIONAL SIGHTS

St. Dominic's Church★ (San Domenico) (AYZ N). — St. Catherine had her trances in this 13-16C Gothic conventual church — an imposing building with a huge transept and a tiny chancel.

The Chapel "delle Volte" which occupies the whole width of the nave, on the right as you enter, contains the sole authentic portrait of the saint by Andrea Vanni (over the altar). Halfway along the nave, on the right, stands the Chapel of St. Catherine: the Renaissance **tabernacle★** carved in marble by Giovanni di Stefano, holds the head of the Saint. The end wall and the left wall are decorated with **frescoes★** by Il Sodoma, representing St. Catherine in Ecstasy receiving the Stigmata and assisting Nicolò di Tuldo, who had been sentenced to death. Further along, note an Adoration of the Shepherds by Francesco di Giorgio; on the high altar, a tabernacle with two angels carved by Benedetto da Maiano on either side of the high altar; in the first chapel on the right, a Madonna and Child and in the second chapel a St. Barbara with Mary Magdalen and St. Catherine of Alexandria by Matteo di Giovanni.

A stairway on the right in the nave leads to the 14C **crypt** with three aisles of noble dimensions. On the high altar is a great painting of Christ by Sano di Pietro (15C).

From the chevet of the church, there is a fine **view★** of old Sienna.

The **Branda fountain** (AZ V) below by the entrance in the Via Santa Caterina, dates from 1246.

Birthplace of St. Catherine (AYZ E). — *Open 9.30 am to 12.30 pm and 2.30 to 6.30 pm. Entrance in Via Santa Caterina.* The saint's house and the buildings erected around it have been turned into superimposed oratories. On the lower floor, you will see the cell where St. Catherine lived (relics). In one of the two oratories on the upper floor is a painted crucifix (13C) in front of which the saint is said to have received the Stigmata.

Piccolomini Palace★ (Palazzo Piccolomini) (BZ A). — *Open 9 am to 1.30 pm; closed Sundays and holidays. Entrance in Via Banchi di Sotto.* This palace is in the Florentine style. In it can be seen *(at the far end of the courtyard, stairs on the left; ring at the door marked "Archivo di Stato")* curious **tavolette★** or wooden tablets which were used as covers for public registers and were decorated with religious, allegorical or historical scenes, between 1258 and 1689.

St. Francis' Basilica (San Francesco) (BY B). — The Gothic church of the Franciscans was restored in the 19C. Note (first chapel on left of chancel) the frescoes of Pietro Lorenzetti, particularly a Crucifixion and those by Ambrogio Lorenzetti, in the third chapel, showing St. Louis of Toulouse before Boniface VIII and the Martyrdom of the Franciscans at Ceuta. The **St. Bernardino Oratory★** (Oratorio di S. Bernardino) (BY C), to the right of the square, contains frescoes by Il Sodoma (Life of the Virgin) and Beccafumi (Marriage of the Virgin), an agreeable Madonna by Sano di Pietro and some relics of St. Bernardino.

St. Augustine's Church (Sant'Agostino) (BZ D). — Dating from the 13C with a Baroque interior remodelled by Vanvitelli in the 18C. There is a remarkable **Adoration of the Crucifix★**, by Perugino, on the second altar on the right. The **Sacramento Chapel★** (or **Piccolomini**) *(door to the right in the nave)* contains **works★** by Ambrogio Lorenzetti including a fresco representing a Madonna with Saints; a highly expressionist Massacre of the Innocents by Matteo di Giovanni; and, on the altar, an Adoration of the Magi, by Il Sodoma.

Church of St. Mary of the Slaves (Santa Maria dei Servi) (BZ N). — (13C, remodelled in the 14-15C.) There are many **works of art★**: a Madonna (1261) by Coppo di Marcovaldo (first chapel, south aisle); a Massacre of the Innocents (1491), by Matteo di Giovanni (fourth chapel, south aisle). In the second chapel to the right in the chancel are a fresco by the school of Pietro Lorenzetti (Massacre of the Innocents) and a Virgin of the People (1317) by Lippo Memmi.

EXCURSIONS

Belcaro Castle★ (Castello di Belcaro). — *Southwest, 7 km - 4 miles.* Leave Siena by ④ and the road to Grosseto; pass the fork leading to Rome and take the second road to the right, towards Montalbuccio. At the top of a rise you skirt the castle grounds. Entrance on the right.

The mediaeval castle *(not open)* was remodelled in the 16C by Peruzzi, who adorned it with frescoes and grotesques. The parapet walk affords fine views of Siena.

Monteriggioni. — *Northwest, 10 km - 6 miles.* Leave Siena by ⑤ and road S 2. The village, which stands on a height, is girdled by a well preserved 13C **wall★**, reinforced by fourteen towers. This is the fortified site described by Dante in his *Inferno*.

SILA Massif ★★★ Calabria ────────────

Michelin map 988 39.

The Sila, whose name is derived from the Latin *sylva* (forest), has been called Italy's Little Switzerland. It is a great granite plateau with wide, gently undulating horizons. The highest point, the **Botte Donate**, accessible by the "Strada delle Vette" reaches 1 929 m - 6 332 ft (panorama). Magnificent forests of pine and evergreen oak and lonely, jade-green lakes make an unforgettable picture of snow-covered landscape until March or April (a winter sports centre).

The Sila, a Land of Other Times. — The region, which has remained wild, has preserved traditional ways and customs: the women still wear sober black costumes with pleated wool or velvet skirts.

Skilled trades flourish, notably at San Giovanni in Fiore, where potters, lacemakers, embroiderers and carpet weavers may be seen at work.

★★★FROM CATANZARO TO COSENZA *173 km - 107 miles — about 1 day*

On leaving Catanzaro *(p 80)* the road climbs the steep and deserted slopes of the fringes of the Sila Piccola, which is cleft with deep valleys planted with olive trees: **views★★** of Catanzaro and the sea. These follow one another up to the pass (alt 1 280 m - 4 099 ft) before Villaggio Mancuso, which is hidden in extensive pinewoods.

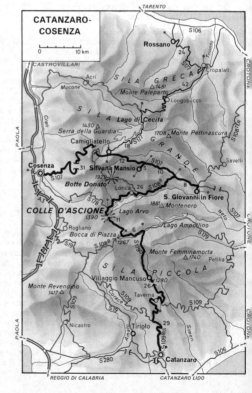

After this you descend gradually through parkland and mountain pastures on which brindle cows graze; the white houses of the smallholders, which were built after agrarian reforms in 1946, are surrounded by poor land.

Ascione Pass★★★ (Colle d'Ascione). — Affords an exceptional **view★★★** westwards to the Tyrrhenian Sea and eastwards over Lake Arvo. After the pass you skirt Lake Arvo before crossing the railway which is boldly sited.

San Giovanni in Fiore. — This town, the capital of the Sila, lies deep in the mountains. It was built round an abbey founded in the 12C.
Then, across a great plateau, undulating like a swell at sea, you reach Silvana Mansio.

Silvana Mansio. — The town lies in a lonely and picturesque forest setting.

Camigliatello. — From this little tourist centre (winter sports) you can take a trip on Lake Cecità, then on to Rossano passing through the Sila Greca (Greek Sila).

Lake Cecità (Lago di Cecità). — The lake's rugged shores resemble a lunar landscape.

Rossano. — This important Calabrian city still has a number of Byzantine buildings. The Church of St. Mark (San Marco) with its 11C dome is typical. The Diocesan Museum has a valuable 6C Greek Gospel.
Finally, you run down to Cosenza (p 88) through sometimes grim, sometimes smiling country.

SIRMIONE ★★ Lombardy

Michelin map **988** 4 — Local map p 130 — Pop 4 242

A narrow tongue of earth, ending in a rocky peninsula, juts out into the centre of a moraine which blocked the waters of the quaternary glacier and formed Lake Garda. Sirmione grew up at the base of this promontory. Its old houses huddle round the massive crenellated shape of the **Castle of the Scaligers** (open 9 am to 6 pm in summer and 9 am to 2 pm in winter; Sundays and holidays, 9 am to 1 pm throughout the year; closed Mondays unless a holiday, 1 January, 25 April, 1 May, first Sunday in June, 15 August and 25 December). There is a fine view from the keep. Outside the town, there is a spa with hot sulphur springs (69°C = 156.2°F). A road runs through the olive groves to the end of the rocky promontory where the famous **Grottoes of Catullus★★** (open 9 am to 7 pm in summer and 9 to 3 pm in winter; closed Mondays unless a holiday, 1 January, 25 April, 1 May, first Sunday in June, 15 August and 25 December; 500 lire), the remains of a Roman villa, will be found. In the holiday season an electrically powered truck and trailer runs between Sirmione and the caves. The setting is delightful with its olive trees, cypresses and aromatic plants, and with lovely **views★★** of Lake Garda. There is a antiquarium near the caves.

SORRENTO ★★ Campania

Michelin map **988** 27 — Local map p 45 — Pop 16 698

Sorrento stands overlooking the gulf of the same name, a town of beautiful gardens and sunsets, sung by poets and writers. This is where Ulysses resisted the call of the sirens, plugging his crew's ears with wax and making them lash him to the mast of his ship. It is also the birthplace of Tasso (1544), the author of Jerusalem Delivered (p 100).
Luxuriant plantations of orange and lemon trees are the pride of the people of Sorrento. In season daily boat and hydrofoil services run to Capri from Marina Piccola: p 73.

Villa Comunale. — From a terrace there is a magnificent **view★★** of the Bay of Naples: a little to the right Vesuvius is silhouetted against the sky; on the left the island of Procida and Cape Miseno are visible in the distance.

St. Francis' Church (San Francesco). — This Baroque church with a bulbous tower casts its shade over 13C **cloisters★** whose capitals support arches pointed in the Moorish style.

Correale Museum★ (Museo di Correale) (M). — Open 9.30 am to 12.30 pm and 4 to 7 pm (3 to 5 pm 1 October to 31 March). Closed Tuesdays, Sunday and holiday afternoons and February; 1 500 lire. The museum is housed in an 18C palace. On the ground floor, there is a small archaeological collection. Note also rare editions of the works of Tasso, autographed copies and the poet's death mask. Particularly noteworthy are the museum's collections of 17 and 18C furniture, mostly Neapolitan in style (Room 10, a beautiful ebony writing desk inlaid with ivory depicting Aesop's fables), and of china from Dresden, Vienna and Capodimonte (Naples). Among the paintings you will see a Deposition by A. Vaccaro (Room 8), portraits of the Apostles by Lanfranco (Room 9), and a Madonna by del Sarto (Room 16).

Belvedere. — Access, 100 lire for visitors without tickets for the Correale Museum. Beyond the Correale Museum, and a garden planted with orange and lemon trees, you reach a terrace jutting over the sea where you can admire the **view★★** of the sea and beautiful sunsets.

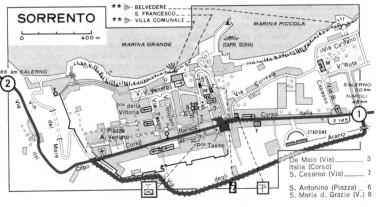

229

SORRENTO★★

EXCURSIONS *local map p 45*

Sorrento Point★★★ (Punta di Sorrento). — *2 km - 1 1/4 miles; plus 1/2 hour on foot Rtn.* Go out by ②. At a junction take the Sant'Agata road on the right. Leave the car in the piazza at Capo di Sorrento where the Villa Igea stands and take the road on the right and past the modern church, an alley going down through the gardens and olive groves. From the point you will get a superb **view★★★** of the Gulf of Sorrento and the Bay of Naples.

Tour round the Sorrento Peninsula★★★. — *42 km — 26 miles.* Leave Sorrento by ② and take the road on the right towards Massalubrense. Past this locality, the road climbs affording splendid views. A picturesque road leads to the pretty beach at Marina del Cantone. At **Sant' Agata sui Due Golfi,** a delightfully situated resort, take the road to the right, which rejoins the S 145 which you take towards Colli di San Petro. This road along the crests affords many bird's-eye views of the peninsula, the Gulf of Positano and Sorrento. Take road S 163 on the left to Sorrento by way of the picturesque descent to Meta.

SPELLO ★ Umbria

Michelin map **988** 16 — 12 km - 7 1/2 miles — southeast of Assisi — Pop 7 591

Spello is a picturesque little town with narrow streets, sometimes spanned by vaulting. It is built in terraces on the slopes of Monte Subasio and preserves some traces ot its rich Roman past. From the upper town there is a pretty **view★** over the valley.

St. Mary Major (Santa Maria Maggiore). — This is the first church on the right, going up the main street. It dates from the 12C, although the interior is Baroque.

In the Baglioni Chapel (north aisle), Pinturicchio painted in 1501, for the Baglioni family, overlords of Perugia, a series of splendid **frescoes★★** which display his narrative skill, sense of decoration, freshness and grace. Their themes are the Sibyls, on the vaulting, and, on the walls, the Annunciation, the Nativity and Jesus among the Doctors. Pinturicchio introduced his own portrait into the scene of the Annunciation in a little picture adorning the Virgin's room. The paving of the chapel is of Deruta faïence (1566).

SPERLONGA Latium

Michelin map **988** 26 — 18 km - 11 miles — east of Terracina — Pop 3 687

This village stands on a spur of the Aurunci Mountains which are holed by many caves.

Tiberius' Cave and the Archaeological Museum★ (Grotta di Tiberio e Museo Archeologico). — The **cave** *(to visit, apply to the Director's Office)* lies below the Gaetà-Terracina road. It was in this cave that the Emperor Tiberius narrowly escaped death when some blocks of stone fell from the roof when he was inside. In the **museum** *(open 9 am to 2 pm — 1 pm Sundays and holidays; closed Mondays, 1 January, 25 April, 1 May, 15 August and Christmas)* which is by the roadside, there are statues (4-2C BC), outstanding heads and busts (Ulysses, Athena) and some realistic theatrical masks.

La SPEZIA Liguria

Michelin map **988** 13 — *Local map p 200* — Pop 118 740
Town plan in Michelin Red Guide Italia (hotels and restaurants).

La Spezia is a naval base, a trading port and an important industrial (iron) and commercial centre with the largest naval dockyard in Italy. You can visit the **naval museum** *(open 9 am to noon and 3 to 6 pm; 50 lire; enter by the main gate of the Military Arsenal, Piazza Chiodo).*

From the Passeggiata al Mare there is a view of the gulf, the Apuan Alps and the marble quarries.

The environs of La Spezia are particularly pleasant, especially the Cinqueterre *(p 83)* Lerici *(p 132)* and Portovenere *(p 192)* on the **Gulf of La Spezia.** *The timetable and fares of the boat services are posted by the piers.*

SPOLETO ★ Umbria

Michelin map **988** 26 — 31 km - 19 miles — north of Terni — Pop 37 544

Spoleto, which was the capital of an important Lombard duchy from the 6 to 8C, lies in the heart of Umbria on the slopes of a hill crowned by the Rocca. The city was dear to St. Francis, who loved its austere character, tempered by the grace of streets and little squares.

The International Festival of the Two Worlds *(Dei Due Mondi)* when important theatrical, musical and choreographic performances are given and an exhibition of painting and sculpture is held, takes place annually from the last week in June to around 10 July.

The Stroller's Spoleto. — The Piazza del Mercato (Market Place) is filled in the morning, in fragrant disorder, with the gaily coloured produce of the vendors of vegetables, fruit and flowers. In the adjoining alleys the stroller will find many quaint vaulted passages and picturesque corners; the old shops in the Via Dei Duchi are interesting.

An alley and a stairway opposite the Palazzo Comunale (Town Hall) afford characteristic glimpses. Other old streets such as the Corso Garibaldi, the Via Porta Fuga, the Via di Fontesecca and the Via della Salara Vecchia are enlivened by the coming and going of passersby and artisans. The huge 20 m - 66 ft high statue adorning the Piazza della Stazione (Station Square) is by the American sculptor Alexander Calder.

■ **SIGHTS** *time : 3 hours*

Cathedral Square★★ (Piazza del Duomo). — The square is reached by a majestic stairway overlooked on the left by the three apses of the 10-12C **Church of Sant'Eufemia.**
The quiet square is lined with majestic palaces and hanging gardens.

Cathedral★ (Duomo). — The cathedral was consecrated in 1198 and remodelled in the 17C. The façade is fronted by a fine Renaissance porch; the central rose window is framed by the symbols of the Evangelists, with above, a famous mosaic by Solsterno (1207). The campanile is 11 and 12C, although its crown was added at the time of the Renaissance.

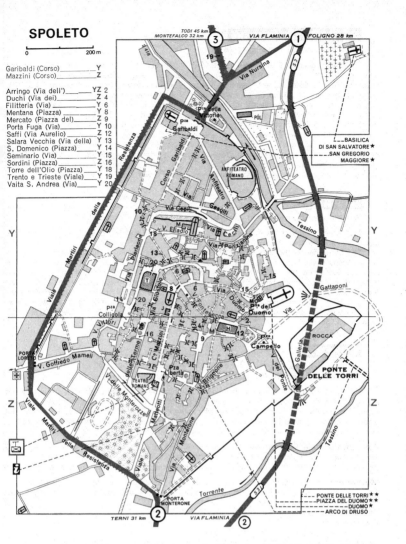

SPOLETO

The first chapel on the south side is decorated with frescoes by Pinturicchio *(to visit apply to the sacristan).* Lorenzo the Magnificent had the mausoleum of Fra Filippo Lippi built in the south transept. Filippino Lippi designed his father's tomb, including, in a medallion, a bust portraying him as the monk he had ceased to be *(see p 193).*

The apse contains **frescoes★★** (1467-1469) by Fra Filippo and his assistants, Fra Diamante and Pier Matteo d'Ameglia. From left to right they depict the Annunciation, the Nativity, the Death and the Coronation of the Virgin, the last having been restored. All are remarkable for softness and delicacy of atmosphere. The painter and his assistants, among them his son Filippino, included their own portraits on the right, in the scene of the Virgin's Death.

Bridge of Towers★★ (Ponte delle Torri). — Approach the bridge by the Via del Ponte. On the right, beyond the fortifications, a little belvedere affords a **view★** of the Monteluco cloaked in evergreen oaks, the olive wooded hillsides, the Tessino Valley and the Church of San Pietro.

The Ponte delle Torri, 230 m long and 80 m high - 755 × 262 ft — was built in the 14C over a Roman aqueduct which was used as a foundation. The bridge, used only by pedestrians, has ten Gothic arches and ends in a fort designed to guard its approaches. A balcony at its centre projects over the torrent.

St. Saviour's Basilica★ (San Salvatore). — This, one of the first Christian churches in Italy, was built by Oriental monks in the 4C and modified in the 9C. Many Roman materials, used again, can be distinguished. The façade includes a portico: note the brackets supporting the roof. The frames of doorways and window openings date from early Christian times. The Ionic and Corinthian columns in the interior are Roman.

St. Gregory Major's Church★ (San Gregorio Maggiore). — This is a Romanesque church of the 12C, modified in the 14C. The 14C Baptistry to the left of the entrance portico has walls covered with frescoes. The campanile is built of blocks from ancient buildings. Two dark, bare aisles and a nave rest on massive columns with canted capitals. In the chancel, which is supported by Roman columns of porphyry and marble, note on the right, a 15C fresco, and on the left, a 15C carved stone cupboard.

Arco di Druso (Arch of Drusus). — The Arch of Drusus was built in AD 23.

EXCURSION

St Peter's Church (San Pietro) and **Monteluco★★.** — *East, 8 km — 5 miles* — Go out by ② and turn into the first road to the left, towards Monteluco. St. Peter's has a curious Romanesque **façade★** of the 13C with realistic animal figures and sculptured scenes. The road climbs to the summit of Monteluco *(lucus = sacred grove),* the seat of an ancient cult. St. Francis and St. Bernardino of Siena came to live here as hermits in a monastery which still exists. A beautiful **panorama★★** of the Spoleto region can be seen.

STELVIO, Road to the ★★★

Michelin maps **988** 4 and **24** 17 18

The Passo dello Stelvio (2 757 m - 9 035 ft) connects the Val Venosta *(p 259)* with the Valtellina *(p 249)* and forms the language boundary between German, Italian and Romansh. From the **Pizzo Garibaldi** or the Dreisprachenspitze (Three Languages Peak — 2 843 m - 9 327 ft), north of the pass *(1/2 hour on foot Rtn),* there is a splendid **panorama★★** of the Ortlès Massif and the Eben Glacier. The Ortlès has over 100 glaciers covering an area of 190 km² - 73 sq. miles. It is also possible to reach the **Livrio refuge,** at an altitude of 3 174 m - 10 414 ft — from which there is an impressive **view★★** of the valley and the road with its many hairpin bends *(from June to October, 20 minutes by cable-car, 5 000 lire Rtn).*

The **road to the pass** is one of the most spectacular in the Alps — the east slope being the more remarkable: with forty-eight numbered bends, it affords magnificent views of the Ortlès glaciers, and particularly of the Eben Glacier. On the west side the road follows a torrent and makes an astonishing series of superimposed bends. Powerful waterfalls can be seen.

STRA Venetia

Michelin map **988** 5 — 12 km - 7 miles — east of Padua — Pop 6 027

This small town was for the Venetian nobility of the 17 and 18C one of the most desirable places in which to own a country villa.

The monumental 18C **Villa Nazionale★,** formerly the **Villa Pisani,** has huge rooms. It contains an **Apotheosis of the Pisani Family** in which Tiepolo showed extraordinary skill in the handling of perspectives. From the ballroom, there is a magnificent vista ornamented with a lake and bounded by the stable buildings (entertaining maze on the right). *Open 6 April to 30 September, villa: 9 am to 12.30 pm and 3 to 4.30 pm; park: 9 am to 6 pm; the rest of the year, villa and park: 9 am to 4 pm. The villa is closed at 12.30 pm on Sundays throughout the year. The villa and park are closed on Mondays and holidays. Admission: villa and park 200 lire; villa or park 150 lire.*

STRESA ★★ Piedmont

Michelin maps **988** 2 3 and **26** 7 — *Local map p 128* — Pop 5 156
Town plan in Michelin Red Guide Italia (hotels ands restaurants).

With first class hotel accommodation, parks and gardens, pleasant coolness in summer and a magnificent situation on the west bank of Lake Maggiore, at the foot of wooded hills and facing the Borromean Islands *(p 67)* of which there are fine **views★★,** Stresa is a delightful resort. It is also a good holiday centre with all the amenities including watersports, as well as skiing in winter at Mottarone. It is also a good centre for lake excursions.

Park of the Villa Pallavicino★. — *Open 8.30 am to 6.30 pm; closed 1 November to 18 March; 2 500 lire.* Under the age-old trees of the gardens live a great variety of animals in comparative freedom. Beautiful panorama over the lake and the surrounding mountains.

Mottarone★★★. — Reached either by the road to Armeno *(leave by ② of plan)* 29 km - 18 miles long, or by a scenic road 18 km - 11 miles long. It is a private toll road *(2 000 lire Rtn)* after Alpino. By cable-car from Stresa-Lido *(15 minutes Rtn, 4 000 lire Rtn).*

From the summit of the Mottarone (alt 1491 m - 4 892 ft) you can enjoy a remarkable **panorama★★★** of the Po Plain, the Lakes and the Alps from the Adamello to Monte Viso, with a superb view of the Monte Rosa Massif.

At Alpino, the **Alpine Garden★** (Giardino Alpinia — *open 8 am to 12.30 pm and 2.30 pm to 6 pm; closed Mondays and 1 October to 31 March)* where there are more than 2 000 Alpine plants, there is an excellent **view★★.**

(After photo by De Agostini)

Stresa—The Borromean Islands

SUBIACO Latium

Michelin map **988** 26 — Pop 8 860

The name of Subiaco, a small mediaeval town at the junction of the Acquaviva and Aniene Rivers, was made famous by St Benedict and his twin sister Scolastica, who, at the end of the 5C, retired there and built twelve little monasteries. There St. Benedict drew up the Benedictine Rule, based on two principles, *ora et labora* (pray and work), but was soon driven out by petty jealousies and withdrew to Monte Cassino, where he founded the famous monastery.

To get to the monasteries of Santa Scolastica and San Benedetto *(3 km - 2 miles)* take the Frosinone road and, shortly before the Aniene Bridge, turn left.

Convent of St. Scolastica (Monastero di Santa Scolastica). — *Open weekdays, 9 am to 12.15 pm and 4 to 7 pm (6 pm in winter); Sundays and holidays, 9 to 10 am and 5.30 to 8 pm (4.30 to 7 pm) except during services.* This convent, built on a fine site by St. Benedict, overlooks the Aniene Gorges. The majestic IIC Romanesque campanile is its oldest feature. The church, consecrated in 980, was remodelled in the 18C but still has a Gothic doorway. It is adjoined by three sets of cloisters: the first dating from 1580, the second Gothic and the third and finest with slender paired columns either straight or twisted, built by the Cosmati *(p 201)* in the 13C.

Monastery of St Benedict★ (Monastero di San Benedetto). — *Open 9 am to 12.30 pm, 3.15 to 7.30 pm (3 to 5.30 pm in winter).* A few hundred yards beyond the St. Scolastica Convent, leave the car on an esplanade and walk along a road lined with evergreen oaks to this monastery, which stands in a wild **setting★★** on the flank of a rock overhanging the gorge. Eight massive arches support the entire building, which is 13-14C.

The church is in two storeys. The upper storey has walls painted with frescoes of the 14C Sienese school (haloes in relief) and the 15C Umbrian school. The lower church, which is really a staircase punctuated with landings, is covered with frescoes by Magister Conxolus, an artist of the late 13C Roman school depicting scenes from the life of St. Benedict. On the end wall, on the left, a woman offers poisoned bread to the Saint; on the right, St Benedict orders a raven to carry off the poisoned bread. You now enter the **Sacred Grotto** (Sacro Speco), in which St. Benedict lived for three years.

Next, go up a winding staircase to the chapel of St. Gregory where is kept the first portrait of St. Francis (without stigmata or halo) painted by an unknown artist in 1224 to commemorate the Saint's visit to St. Benedict's grotto. The Scala Santa (Holy Staircase) leads down to the Lady chapel (frescoes by the Sienese school) and the Shepherds' Grotto. From there pass to a rose garden where St. Benedict threw himself into brambles to resist temptation. St. Francis is said to have grafted a rose bush on to the brambles as a tribute to St. Benedict. There is a view of the imposing buttresses supporting the monastery.

SULMONA ★ Abruzzi
Michelin map 988 27 — Local map p 42 — Pop 23 477

The market town of Sulmona lies on the floor of a fertile basin framed by majestic mountains. This old town was a dependency of the Kingdom of Naples until the Risorgimento (mid 19C). Earlier it was the birthplace of the poet Ovid, and it has kept its mediaeval character.

On Easter Sunday, the feast of the "Madonna che Scappa in piazza" is celebrated in Piazza Garibaldi: the statue of the Virgin is borne to a meeting with the Risen Christ; as she comes within sight of Him, she sheds her mourning clothes and appears in resplendent green.

Most of its sights are found along the main street which divides the town in two.

Palazzo dell'Annunziata★★. — The palace was built by a Brotherhood of Penitents; its sculptured façade is attractively original and harmonious in spite of varying styles. The admirable Gothic doorway on the left dates from 1415 as do the statues of the Virgin on the tympanum and St. Michael under the archivolt. It also displays a triple-arched window and four statues of Doctors of the Church (the first four starting from the left). The Renaissance central doorway and the window above it date from 1483. The south doorway and the last window were constructed in 1522. The sober and monumental façade of the adjacent church was built in 1710 to the design of the Milanese, Pietro Fontana.

Porta Napoli★. — This curious Gothic gate has historiated capitals. Note particularly the rare exterior with its arch, its bosses and, in the upper part, its rose decoration.

Piazza Garibaldi. — The piazza, which lies below the Corso Ovidio and which is reached down some steps, is the scene on Wednesdays and Fridays of a large and highly colourful market. Two sides of the square are bordered by a mediaeval aqueduct, while the east side remains open to the fine mountain setting. At the end of the square stands the great Gothic door of the Church of St. Martin. At one end of the aqueduct is the Renaissance **Fontana del Vecchio**.

On the other side of the Corso Ovidio, in the Piazza del Carmine, stood the Church of San Francesco della Scarpa — St. Francis with Shoes — so-called because the Franciscans who worshipped there wore shoes while others had only clogs. San Francesco has been wrecked by several earthquakes; the last was in 1933 and now only the Romanesque doorway remains.

SUSA Piedmont
Michelin maps 988 11 and 77 9 — Pop 7 141

Susa lies in a severe mountain setting commanding the roads to Montgenèvre and Mont Cenis. To reach Sestriere (description p 224) take the **road★** to the **Finestre Pass**, which runs through beautiful forests and affords ample views of the surrounding plateaux on the way up to the pass and deep vistas of the Chisone Valley on the far side.

The main street, narrow and picturesque, takes you to Susa's 11C **cathedral** which has a fine campanile in the Lombard Romanesque style. Go through the Savoy Gate built in the 3C by the Romans to the marble Arch of Augustus, erected in the 8C BC. The Roman arena to the south of the town has been excavated and restored.

TAGGIA ★ Liguria
Michelin map 988 12 — Local map p 199 — Pop 14 980

The partly fortified, little town of Taggia occupies a pleasant site commanding the Argentina Valley, which leads to the mediaeval village of Triora, perched on a spur.

In the 15 and 16C Taggia was an art centre possessing painters like Louis Bréa from Nice, the Piedmontese, Canavese and the Genoese, Perino del Vaga and Luca Cambiaso. Today the town hosts an Antique and Crafts Market which is held on the last Saturday and Sunday of each month. You will enjoy a stroll in the streets and squares, noting the oil-mills and the palaces. At the end of the valley a 15C bridge with a Pre-Romanesque arch spans the river.

St. Dominic's Church (San Domenico). — At the upper end of the town, and a little outside it, on the upper slopes, St. Dominic's adjoins peaceful cloisters enclosing a palm tree and monastic buildings of the 15C. In the church is a fine collection of **works★** by Louis Bréa, sober, sincere and of sometimes rather languid grace; among them, on the high altar, the Virgin of Pity, and on the left of the chancel, the Baptism of Christ.

TARANTO ★ Apulia
Michelin map 988 29 — Pop 246 828

Taranto is a well protected naval base at the end of a great roadstead, the Mare Grande. The town is actually situated on the strip of fortified islands and promontories which divide the Mare Grande from a further large inlet or inland sea, the Mare Piccolo. This inlet serves as a naval harbour. The encircling road affords good views.

The old quarter lies on an island linked with the modern town by a swing bridge guarded by a 15-16C castle. The new town has a cathedral built in 1971 by Gio Ponti.

Large iron foundries have been built just outside the town to the north. Choderlos de Laclos, author of "Les Liaisons Dangereuses", died at Taranto in 1803.

During Holy Week many processions — one lasting 12 hours and another 14 hours — take place in the town going from church to church at a very slow pace.

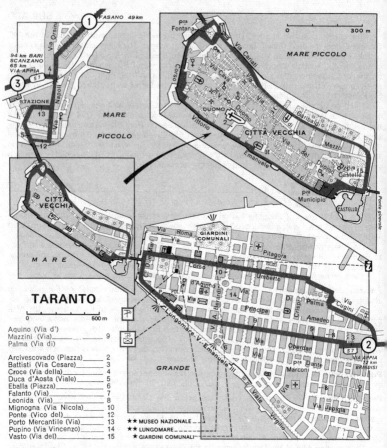

TARANTO

Aquino (Via d')	
Mazzini (Via)	9
Palma (Via di)	
Arcivescovado (Piazza)	2
Battisti (Via Cesare)	3
Croce (Via della)	4
Duca d'Aosta (Viale)	5
Eballa (Piazza)	6
Falanto (Via)	7
Leonida (Via)	8
Mignogna (Via Nicola)	10
Ponte (Vico del)	12
Porto Mercantile (Via)	13
Pupino (Via Vincenzo)	14
Vasto (Via del)	15

★★ MUSEO NAZIONALE
★★ LUNGOMARE
★ GIARDINI COMUNALI

Lungomare★★. — This long promenade, planted with palm trees and oleanders, affords an attractive view of the Taranto roadstead, which is one of the most majestic in Europe.

National Museum★★ (Museo Nazionale). — *Open 9 am to 2 pm (1 pm Sundays and holidays); closed Mondays, 1 January, 25 April, 1 May, Sunday after 2 June, 15 August, 25 December; time: 1/2 hour; 150 lire.* The first floor contains a collection of **Greek pottery★★★** of exceptional value, dating from the 7C BC to the Roman Era. Note the amphorae and the delightful terracotta statuettes representing dancers, musicians and fighting hoplites (Greek foot-soldiers). These archaeological specimens reveal the flourishing period of Magna Graecia, when Taranto belonged to the Spartans, who founded the city. A large collection of antique jewellery is shown in the Gold Room. There is also a prehistoric section in the museum.

Public Gardens★ (Giardini Comunali). — These gardens, laid out on a terrace, are embellished with exotic and luxuriant vegetation. There is a pretty view of the Mare Piccolo.

Cathedral (Duomo). — The 11-12C cathedral in the heart of the Old Town (Città Vecchia) has been much remodelled; it has a Baroque façade. The interior comprises a nave and two aisles supported by ancient columns with Roman or Byzantine capitals. The ceiling is 17C.

TARQUINIA ★ Latium

Michelin map **988** 25 — 21 km - 13 miles — northwest of Civitavecchia — Pop 13 289

The town of Tarquinia, crowning a rocky plateau, occupies a splendid **site★★** facing the sea. Towers and mediaeval palaces give it a picturesque appearance. Its worldwide fame is due to a magnificent Etruscan burial ground.

The Ancient City. — According to legend, the town was founded in the 12 or 13C BC. Archaeologists have found 9C BC vestiges of the Villanovian civilisation which derived its name from the village of Villanova near Bologna, and developed around the year 1000 BC in the Po Valley, in Tuscany and in the northern part of Latium, where the Etruscans later settled. Thanks to the Marta River, Tarquinia was a busy port. In the 6C AD it ruled the whole coast of Etruria. Under Roman rule, Tarquinia was decimated by malaria in the 4C BC and was sacked by the Lombards in the 7C. The inhabitants then moved to the present site, about 2 km -1 mile — northeast of the original position. In the 15C some tombs were discovered by chance, and by the end of the 19C, most had been excavated.

■ **SIGHTS** time: 2 1/2 hours

Necropolis★★ (Necropoli). — *Southeast, 4 km - 2 1/2 miles. Guided tour: about 1/2 hour; admission up to 1 hour before closing time of excavations. Apply to the museum (see p 235).* The burial ground is on a bare, wind swept ridge parallel with that on which the former Etruscan city stood. Only a few fragments and the foundations of a temple remain.

The necropolis extends for 5 km - 3 miles — and contains thousands of tombs dating from the 6-1C BC. It was at Tarquinia that archaeologists for the first time used a sort of drill with a photographic eye making it possible to judge the importance of a tomb without excavating.

The exterior of the tombs is of no architectural interest but there are remarkable **paintings★★★** on the walls of the burial chambers which are of the highest value in reconstructing the life and religion of the Etruscans. They include scenes of life on earth, such as festivals and dances, hunting and fishing, horse races, games and plays, and visions of life beyond the grave including pictures of the gods, funeral rites and religious symbols. Among the tombs left undisturbed, the keeper shows the following most frequently: the "**tomb of the Baron**" dating from late 6C; note the extreme refinement and realism of the designs. The **tomb of the Leopards** named after the two animals depicted on the end wall, dating back to the early 5C BC; the ceiling is decorated with motifs and the walls are adorned with a banquet scene including dancers and singers; the fresh colours and the lively and varied scenes make this one of the most beautiful tombs of the necropolis. The **tomb of the Lionesses** which dates from around 530-520 BC where you will see on the end wall, a man and a woman performing a wild dance and pictures of two lionesses (rather like panthers). The **tomb with Hunting and Fishing Scenes** consists of two chambers from the end of the 6C BC. *Several paintings are now in museum: see below.*

National Museum★ (Museo Nazionale Tarquiniese). — *Open 1 May to 30 September, 9 am to 1 pm and 4 to 7 pm; the rest of the year, 10 am to 4 pm (11 am to 4 pm Sundays and holidays). Closed Mondays and holidays; 500 lire.*

The museum is in the **Palazzo Vitelleschi★** which was built in 1439 for Cardinal Giovanni Vitelleschi and is an excellent example of early Renaissance architecture. Graceful windows, still Gothic in style, and a Renaissance loggia relieve the façade which bears the coat of arms of the Vitelleschis.

The inner court with its two tiers of tall Gothic arches, has pretty twin windows.

In the courtyard and ground floor rooms are curious Etruscan sarcophagi (6-5C BC).

On the first floor *(begin with the room at the far end)* note, among the pottery, ivories and ex-votos shaped like parts of the human body, the Attic bowls and amphorae of the 6C and especially two admirable **winged horses★★★** from the fronton of a temple at Tarquinia and dating from between the end of the 4C BC and the beginning of the 3C BC.

On the second floor, several **tombs★** have been reconstructed and decorated with paintings removed from their original site. These are the **tomb of the chariots**, in rather poor condition, dating from 500-490 BC; the **tomb with the Funeral Bed** (*c.* 460 BC); and the **tomb of the Triclinium**, one of the finest in the necropolis (480-470 BC) decorated with banqueting scenes.

From the terrace on the second floor, there is a pleasant view over the plain to the sea.

Church of St. Mary of the Citadel★ (Santa Maria in Castello). — *Access: take the Via Mazzini along the Vitelleschi Palace, then the Via di Porta Castello beyond the wall. To visit apply to the Bassi family at the house with stairs to the left of the church.*

The disused church stands near a tall tower built like a keep in the Middle Ages by a noble family. Formerly Tarquinia was dotted with such towers that were built as high as possible for prestige. Santa Maria is a fine Romanesque structure (1121-1208) with a gable-belfry, enclosed in a fortified citadel guarding the town. It has a fine doorway and an imposing interior.

Below the church there is a view of the ramparts and of the Latium countryside.

TARVISIO — Friuli-Venezia Giulia
Michelin map **988** 6 — Pop 6 057

Tarvisio is a charming small town of Roman origin and not far from the Austrian and Yugoslav frontiers. It is an important communications centre. Lying in the heart of dense pine forests, it has become a popular summer and winter sports resort.

EXCURSIONS

Fusine Lakes★★. — *East, 10 km - 6 miles.* The clear waters and the dark fir forests against the white slopes of Mount Mangart (2 678 m - 8 786 ft) are an unforgettable sight.

Monte Santo di Lussari. — *West, 5 km - 3 miles — plus 5 minutes by cable-car.* There are views, north over the Carnic Alps, west over the Dolomites and south over the Julian Alps.

TERAMO — Abruzzi
Michelin map **988** 26 — Pop 51 397

In the cathedral of this little town, at the high altar, is a superb 15C **altar front★** by Nicola di Guardiagrele in silver; also in the south aisle a fine **polyptych★** by Iacobello del Fiore.

TERNI — Umbria
Michelin map **988** 26 — Pop 113 147
Town plan in Michelin Red Guide Italia (hotels and restaurants).

Terni, an important industrial centre, has an old town with the Piazza della Repubblica as its centre and the Via Roma as its main street (Palazzo Spada, 16C, at No. 28).

EXCURSIONS

Marble Cascade★ (Cascata delle Marmore). — From Terni one can reach the cascade by the Rieti road (*east, 9 km - 6 miles — plus 1/2 hour on foot Rtn*), or by the Macerata road S 209 (*east, 7 km — 4 miles*). During the week the waters are tapped by nearby factories. *Open weekdays 5 to 6.30 pm 15 July to 31 August. Sundays and holidays : 10 am to noon and 3 to 9 pm 16 March to 30 April and 1 September to 30 October (also 6 pm to 9 pm on Saturdays during the same period); 10 am to 1 pm and 3 to 11 pm 1 May to 31 August (also on 22 May and 16 August same times — and 5 to 10 pm on Saturdays from 1 May to 14 July); 3 to 4 pm 1 November to 15 March.*

By the Rieti road: The *corniche* approach road overlooks the Velino Gorges, on the floor of which stand occasional factories. You will see picturesque views of the perched village of Papigno and a vista towards Piediluco and its lake.

On leaving Marmore, turn left just before a bridge, park the car in front of a cabaret and walk along the road. After 200 m - 200 yds — it reaches a belvedere overlooking the majestic cascade which drops a total of 160 m - 525 ft — in three successive falls down marble-lined clefts.

By the Macerata road: Fine view of the cascade from belvederes.

The Roman ruins at Carsulae. — *Northwest, 16 km - 10 miles.* Roman town destroyed in 9C.

Michelin map 988 26 — Pop 37 155

This smiling little town on a pleasant **site★** overlooking a pretty gulf has a curious nucleus of old buildings grouped round the Piazza del Municipio. Its canal-port is used by typical local fishing boats. In the Roman era Terracina was a fashionable country resort.

Terracina is linked with the **Island of Ponza★** *(description p 48). In summer, there are car ferry services (apply to Anxur Tours, 48 Viale della Vittoria, ☎ 74840 in Terracina).*

Piazza del Municipio. — The present square still has the paving of the Roman Forum.

The cathedral was built on the site of a former temple. It was consecrated in 1075 and is fronted by a portico on ancient columns which support an astonishing mosaic frieze of the 12C. The campanile is in the transitional Romanesque-Gothic style. In the interior, which forms a nave and two aisles on ancient columns, note the 13C paving and the fine **group★** consisting of the pulpit and the paschal candelabrum made by the Cosmati in the 13C *(p 201)*.

Temple of Jupiter (Tempio di Giove Anxur). — The colossal supporting arches of the temple (1C BC) which stand on the height overlooking Terracina can be seen from below.

EXCURSION

Circeo National Park. — The park covers Monte Circeo, the refuge of the wicked Circe, and it spreads to the north, on a narrow coastal strip which extends nearly as far as Foce Verde. Since 1961 the Island of Zannone has been included. From the coast road which runs along the **lake★** of Sabaudia which is 5 km - 3 miles — long, there is a characteristic view, on one hand of Monte Circeo, and on the other of Sabaudia, a town which only rose from the Pontine marshes in 1934.

Michelin map 988 26 — 31 km - 19 miles — east of Rome — Pop 45 705
Town plan in Michelin Red Guide Italia (hotels and restaurants).

Tivoli, the Tibur of the Romans, is a charming little town on the Aniene River, a tributary of the Tiber. Perched on an olive clad hill overlooking the Roman Campagna, its natural beauties, its well known wine and its villas attract many visitors.

■ VILLA ADRIANA★★★

4.5 km - 3 miles — before reaching Tivoli by road S 5, bear right; from the fork to the entrance of the excavations: 1.5 km - 1 mile.

Open 9 am to 1 hour before sunset. Closed Mondays (or Tuesday when Monday is a holiday), 1 January, 25 April, 1 May, 2 June, 15 August and Christmas; 750 lire.

Extending over a perimeter of approximatively 5 km - 3 miles — and comprising an imperial palace, baths, libraries, theatres and large gardens dotted with works of art, it was undoubtedly the most magnificent group of buildings in Antiquity designed by Hadrian inspired by his travels throughout the Empire. On his return from the eastern provinces in AD 126, he started work on his villa. As he was passionately interested in art and architecture, he wanted reproductions of the buildings and settings he had visited. In AD 134, the villa was nearly complete. Hadrian was then 58 years old. Afflicted by illness and the death of his young favourite Antinoüs, he died in Baia in AD 138. He was buried in his gigantic mausoleum in Rome. The emperors who succeeded him probably continued to visit Tivoli. Zenobia, Queen of Palmyra, spent the last days of her life there as a prisoner of Aurelius.

The estate then fell into ruin. Hadrian's villa was excavated between the 15 and 19C. Over 300 works of art have been brought to light and are now exhibited in museums in Rome, London, Berlin, Dresden, Stockholm and Leningrad or have been acquired for private collections.

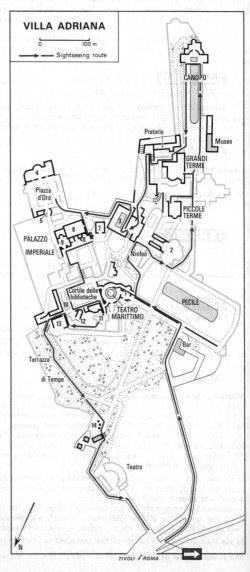

VILLA ADRIANA

In 1870, the estate passed into the hands of the Italian Government and excavation work was undertaken. Amazing vaults, walls, columns, and occasionally stuccoes and mosaics were laid bare after the vegetation had been cleared. Presumably the present entrance was not that used in the time of Hadrian. As the villa was a new concept, archaeologists have not been able to identify the buildings and their function precisely. Prior to the visit, you can see a model of the villa which is exhibited in a room next to the bar.

Pecile★★. — This is the name of a gateway in Athens which Hadrian wanted to reproduce. All that remains is mostly the North wall which leads to the excavation site proper. Note the opus reticulatum (small diamond-shaped tufa blocks arranged diagonally): Villa Adriana is one of the last examples of this building method which was becoming obsolete by the end of the 2C. The grooves along the wall were filled with bricks which were removed when the villa was plundered and reused for building, in particular of the Villa d'Este in Tivoli.

The Pecile was shaped like a large rectangle with the smaller sides rounded, lined with porticoes designed so that one side was always in the shade.

The room with an apse called the "**Philosophers' Hall**" (1) was probably used as a reading room.

Maritime Theatre★★★ (Teatro Marittimo). — This circular structure consisting of a portico and a central building on an island surrounded by a canal was a secluded spot undoubtedly favoured by Hadrian who had become a recluse. The island was reached by small movable bridges.

Walk in a southerly direction.

The esplanade bordered by high walls was first taken to be a stadium but was later identified as a nymphaeum *(ninfeo)*. Amidst the ruins you can see one of the cryptoporticoes of the villa; it is thought that there were so many of these semi-underground passages that one could go round the estate without emerging. The tall columns that remain standing belonged to a structure comprising three semicircular rooms opening on to a courtyard (2).

Baths★★ (Terme). — These include the Great Baths and the Small Baths. Their architecture illustrates the refinement lavished on the villa: rooms on a rectangular plan with concave walls, some on an octagonal plan with alternating concave and convex walls and others on a circular plan with niches alternating with doorways. One of the most impressive chambers is that of the Great Baths complete with recess and partly covered by vestiges of a splendid vault. The adjacent room still contains some stuccoes on the vault.

The tall structure known as the **Praetorium** (Pretorio) was probably a warehouse.

Museum (Museo). — The museum houses the more recent finds from Villa Adriana. The works of particular interest are Roman copies of the Amazon by Phidias and of the caryatids by Polyclitus, copies of the statues of the Erechteum at the Acropolis in Athens. These statues were placed around the Canopus.

Canopus★★★ (Canopo). — It was on a visit to Egypt that Hadrian conceived the idea of commemorating the town of Canopus famous for its Temple of Serapis. Canopus was reached from Alexandria by a canal lined with temples and gardens. Hadrian converted the site in that particular area to recreate the Egyptian setting including a canal. At the southern end, he built an edifice reminiscent of the Temple of Serapis; in addition to the cult of Serapis, Hadrian dedicated the temple to his young friend Antinoüs who drowned in the Nile.

Return to the Praetorium and Great Baths and continue to the vestiges overlooking the nymphaeum. Then bear right.

Walk alongside a large **fishpond** surrounded by portico (Quadriportico con peschiera) (3).

Imperial Palace (Palazzo Imperiale). — It extended from the Piazza d'Oro to the libraries.

Piazza d'Oro★★. — This was a rectangular piazza surrounded by a double portico. It is of no practical use and was created to satisfy the whim of an aesthete. At the far end of the piazza (south east), there are remains of an octagonal room (4): the eight sides, in an alternating concave and convex pattern, were preceded by a small portico (one of these has been restored).

On the opposite side of the square, a room (5) crowned by a cupola and with walls dotted with niches, was flanked by two smaller rooms: the one on the left still contains vestiges of its fine mosaic paving.

Room of the Doric Pilasters★★ (6). — The room is so-called as it is lined with a portico with pilasters adorned with Doric capitals and plinths supporting a Doric architrave (partially reconstructed in one corner). On the left is the **firemen's barracks** (Caserma dei Vigili) (7).

Adjacent to the room with Doric pilasters is a large section of a semicircular wall that probably belonged to a summer **dining-room** (triclinio estivo) (8); there are also remains of the oval basins of a **nymphaeum** (ninfeo di palazzo) (9). These constructions gave on to a courtyard separated by a cryptoportico from the **Court of the Libraries** (Cortile delle Biblioteche). One side of the latter is occupied by ten rooms facing each other used as an infirmary (10); each one of these could hold three beds; there is a fine mosaic **pavement★**.

From the area around the Court of the Libraries, there is a pleasant **view★** of the countryside with ruins, cypresses and umbrella pines in a harmonious setting.

Libraries. — There are some remains north west of the square; according to legend, a Greek library (11) and a Latin library (12) stood on the spot.

On the way to the Terrace of Tempe, you pass by several rooms with mosaic paving that were part of a **dining-room** (triclinio imperiale) (13).

Terrace of Tempe (Terrazza di Tempe). — This leafy grove overlooks the valley which the Emperor named after a Greek site in Thessaly. From the Terrace of Tempe, rejoin the road leading to Villa Adriana. You will see a small **round temple** (14) which has been restored and is attributed to the cult of Venus as a statue of the goddess has been found on the spot. Continue along the downward slope and note on the left traces of a **theatre**.

Go to Tivoli.

The Piazza Garibaldi affords a view of **Rocca Pia**, a fortress built by Pius II (1458-1464).

■ VILLA D'ESTE★★★

In 1550 Cardinal Ippolito II d'Este on whom François I conferred great honours but who fell into disgrace with his son Henri II, decided to retire to Tivoli. He then started work on a country villa on the site of a former Benedictine monastery. The Neapolitan architect Pirro Ligorio was engaged for the plans. The villa which has a plain exterior, is adorned with splendid gardens where fountains and statues create a graceful decor typical of the Mannerist era. The cardinal turned the slopes to the west of the town into terraced gardens extending over more than 3 hectares - 7 acres. Illustrious guests visited the villa: Popes Pius IV and Gregory III and after the death of the cardinal, Paul IV, Paul V, Pius IX as well as writers and artists, Benvenuto Cellini, Titian and Tasso. On Monday 3 April 1581, Montaigne paid a visit to the villa and was received by Cardinal Luigi d'Este who succeeded his uncle. In 1759 although the alleys had become overgrown and the fountains no longer sang, Fragonard and Hubert Robert who were then students at the French Academy in Rome, accompanied by their patron the Abbé de Saint Non spent the whole summer there and painted the views from every angle.

The villa has been restored following the bombing in 1944 that damaged the palace courtyard, part of the gardens and canals.

Church of St. Mary Major (Santa Maria Maggiore). — This is the old church of the Benedictine monastery. It has a lovely Gothic façade and a 17C bell tower. Inside, there are two 15C triptychs (in the chancel); above the one on the left is a painting of the Virgin by the artist Jacopo Torriti who worked mainly in mosaic at the end of the 13C.

Palaces and Gardens★★★. — *Open 9 am to 1 hour before sunset. Closed 1 January, 15 August, Easter and Christmas; 1 000 lire. Illumination of gardens Easter to 30 September.* Go into the inner courtyard, the former cloister of the Benedictine convent. Then descend to the ground floor.

Main Drawing Room. — This room is decorated with Mannerist paintings by pupils of Girolamo Muziano and Federico Zuccari. On the left wall are depicted the gardens as laid out in the 16C. The ceiling is adorned with the Banquet of the Gods; and on the right wall is a fountain in mosaic and rocaille.

From the loggia in front there is a pleasant view★ of the gardens and of Tivoli.

Take a staircase with twin ramps to the alley on the upper level of the gardens.

Bicchierone Fountain (Fontana del Bicchierone). — This fountain shaped like a shell with a large moss-covered basin from which water pours out, is sometimes attributed to Bernini.

"Rometta". — This means "Little Rome". The cardinal wanted to recreate some typical monuments of ancient Rome: a pond ornamented with a boat (Island in the Tiber) surmounted by an obelisk. Further up, next to fake ruins stands the allegorical statue of Rome and the She-Wolf.

Avenue of the Hundred Fountains★★★ (Viale delle Cento Fontane). — Along this straight alley-way, jets of water gush from small boats, obelisks, heads of animals, eagles and lilies recalling the Este coat of arms. It is one of the most agreeable spots in the gardens.

Ovato Fountain★★★ (Fontana dell'Ovato). — A statue of the Sibyl dominates it and allegorical statues of rivers are dotted around. On the sides of the basin surrounded by balustrades and rock gardens half-covered with moss, water from the Aniene gushes from statues of naiads. Note the pretty ceramic decoration on the front of the oval basin.

Organ Fountain★★★ (Fontana dell'Organo). — This was a musical fountain with an organ hidden in the upper part of the fountain activated by the force of the water. The inventor of this ingenious mechanism was the Frenchman Claude Venard (16C). Montaigne who viewed the fountain wrote in his Journal on his travels in Italy: "The organ music is produced by water falling with great force in a circular, vaulted cave thus stirring the trapped air and causing it to escape by the organ pipes. Another jet of water drives a wheel with cogs that plays the keys of the organ in a set order, thus simulating the sound of trumpets".

Fish-pools (Le Peschiere). — The three basins were formerly fish pools where swam fish destined for the Cardinal's table on days of abstinence. There is a fine view★★ of the water jets of the Organ fountain.

Nature fountain (Fontana della Natura). — It is adorned with a statue of Diana of Ephesus, the fertility goddess.

On the right was the main entrance to the villa, dominating the valley.

Dragon Fountain (Fontana dei Draghi). — This was created in honour of Pope Gregory XIII who visited the villa in September 1572 shortly before the Cardinal's demise. The dragons recall the coat of arms of the Buoncompagni family from which the Pope was descended.

Bird or Owl Fountain (Fontana della Civetta). — The fountain has been restored several times. It derives its name from a hydraulic mechanism placed in a niche, which produced bird songs. An owl appeared intermittently and gave out its baleful call.

On the left, the **fountain of Proserpina** abducted by Pluto has been modernised.

From Villa d'Este, you can reach Villa Gregoriana by the alleys of the old town.

The setting is pleasant and lively and there are still some vestiges of the past.

The **cathedral**, rebuilt in the 17C and flanked by a 12C Romanesque campanile, contains a fine set of 13C wooden statues depicting the **Descent from the Cross★**.

■ VILLA GREGORIANA★

Open 9.30 am to 1 hour before sunset; closed Mondays; 350 lire.

In a hilly setting, this wooded park criss-crossed by paths spans the Aniene at a point where the river flows into a narrow ravine and turns into a waterfall.

Go down the steps and then bear right towards the **Great Cascade★★**.

This leads to a terrace overlooking the cascade. Further down from a belvedere you can see the waters cascading into the ravine.

Retrace your steps and when you reach the sign "Grotte di Nettuno e Sirena, cascata Bernini" take the small stairway leading down to the bottom of the ravine.

You then reach the **Grotto of the Siren** where the waters of the Aniene surge into a cave with a great crash.

Return to the signpost "Grotte di Nettuno e tempio di Vesta", then take the path that climbs up the opposite slope. The path branches on the right towards the "Tempio di Vesta e Sibilla". Bear left in the direction of the Grotta di Nettuno. Pass through two tunnels in succession, before taking on the left a path that slopes down. At **Neptune's Grotto** a powerful waterfall gushes forth in fantastic rocky scenery.

Retrace your steps and as you come out of the tunnels take the climbing road on the left overlooking the ravine and several little cascades. You will emerge into a garden with an exit from Villa Gregoriana by the temple of the Sibyl.

Temple of the Sibyl. — This is also called the temple of Vesta as the shrines to the goddess were usually circular. This graceful Corinthian edifice dates from the end of the Republic. Next to it is another Ionic temple of the same period which is sometimes attributed also to the Sibyl. Both are built in travertine marble.

TODI ★★ Umbria

Michelin map **988** 25 26 — Pop 17 241

Todi, a charming little old town on a pretty site★, has preserved three sets of walls: the Etruscan (Marzia Gate), the Roman and the mediaeval. Its symbol is the eagle.

■ **SIGHTS** time: 4 hours

Piazza del Popolo★★. — This square in the centre of Todi is surrounded by buildings which illustrate the vigour of the town's commercial life in the Middle Ages.

In the centre, the Gothic **Priors' Palace★**, formerly the seat of the *podestà* (mayor or governor), is crowned with Guelph battlements; the windows were remodelled at the Renaissance. On the left is a curious 14C tower on a trapezoidal plan.

On the left, the **Palace of the Captain★** is linked with the **Palace of the People★**, which is also supported by massive pillars surmounted by semicircular arches. The latter, one of the oldest communal palaces in Italy, is in the Lombard style, crowned by Ghibelline merlons, and it has been extensively remodelled over the centuries. On the first floor is the large Council Chamber, now the **Lapidary Museum** *(restoration and reorganisation in progress; visits suspended)*.

On the top floor are housed the **picture gallery**, the **Etruscan and Roman Museum**, the Archives and the Municipal Library.

Cathedral★ (Duomo). — This is a great Romanesque building dating from early 12C. A majestic staircase, with balustrades bearing the fleur-de-lys blason and tiara of Pope Paul III Farnese (16C), leads to a majestic façade, all in white and pink marble, in the Romanesque-Gothic style. The doors of the central entrance were carved in the 17C; the great rose window is pierced and fretted in the Umbrian manner; the Gothic campanile dates from the 13C. Walk round the building to look at the Romanesque apse, with carved brackets, and to enjoy the quiet old streets with their glimpses of the countryside.

Inside the cathedral note the Gothic capitals adorned with figurines and the curious Renaissance font; also the inlaid stalls in the chancel (1530).

Piazza Garibaldi. — This square adjoining the Piazza del Popolo is graced with a fine palace with vermicular embossing of the Florentine Renaissance type. From the terrace there is a pretty view★★ of the valley and distant, softly rounded hills.

Church of St. Fortunatus★★ (San Fortunato). — The church stands in the Piazza della Repubblica. Building lasted from 1292 to 1460, so that Gothic features are mingled with the Renaissance style. A staircase and flowerbeds lead up to the façade, which was left unfinished. The **central doorway★★** catches the eye by the richness and delicacy of its decoration. Two statues, one on either side, represent the Virgin and the Angel of the Annunciation. Note also the uprights and embrasures carved with an amusingly naïve Sacrifice of Isaac.

The interior, which is well lit, sober and slenderly built, is designed in the Gothic style of a German hall church, which is characterised by a nave and aisles of equal height. In the fourth chapel on the right is a fine fresco, both delicate and firmly handled, painted by Masolino in 1432. In the crypt is the tomb of Jacopone da Todi (1230-1307), a Franciscan monk, a poet and the author of the *Stabat Mater*.

Castle (Rocca). — Passing to the right of San Fortunato, walk to the ruins of the 14C castle. View★★ of Santa Maria della Consolazione and, right, of the Tiber Valley.

Santa Maria della Consolazione Church★. — *1 km - 3/4 mile — west on the road to Orvieto.* This Renaissance church was built of pale stone between 1508 and 1609 by several architects who drew inspiration from the designs of Bramante. The plan is that of a Greek cross; four polygonal apses are reinforced by pilasters with composite capitals; the dome, whose drum is designed in accordance with Bramante's rhythmic principles *(see p 30)*, rises roundly from the flat terrace roof. The twelve statues of the Apostles are by Scalza (16C).

TRANI Apulia

Michelin map **988** 29 — Pop 42 595

Trani is an important market centre for the wines of Apulia. It also has a picturesque port surrounded by old houses.

Cathedral★ (Cattedrale). — The Cathedral of San Nicola Pellegrino is remarkable for the sweep of its vertical lines and the austere harmony of its façades. It was built in the 13C and has recently been restored. The main features outside are the imposing transept with its carved archivolt and the façade ornamented with blind arcades, bays and carved doorways; the unusual **bronze door★** was cast in 1179. Inside, the Romanesque style shows Norman influence in the tribunes, woodwork, twin pillars and triumphal arch.

Public Garden★ (Giardino Pubblico). — The public garden, on a shady, flower decked terrace to the right of the port, overlooks the sea and the old town.

TRASIMENO, Lake Umbria

Michelin map **988** 15 — 28 km - 17 miles — west of Perugia.

Lake Trasimeno attracts the traveller by the splendour of its light and the silvery hue of its waters. It is the largest lake in central and southern Italy, with an area of 128 km² - 50 sq. miles — a circumference of 45 km - 28 miles — and an average depth of 7 m - 23 ft.

A pretty overall view of it can be enjoyed from Monte del Lago, a small village built on a headland dominating the east bank. To the north, the fine road from Tuoro to Lisciano, climbing steeply above the lake affords splendid birds'-eye views★ of the lake as far as the small pass (about 7 km - 4 miles). Its banks are clothed with umbrella pines, cypresses, vineyards and olive groves which supply, it is said, the best oil in Italy.

A motor-boat service from Passignano goes to the Maggiore Island (single 800 lire; 1500 lire Rtn) and to Castiglione del Lago on the opposite side (single 1300 lire, 2500 lire Rtn).

The Battle of Trasimeno. — On 24 June 217 BC, in torrid heat, Hannibal the Carthaginian routed the Roman troops of the Consul Flaminius after a terrible slaughter that turned the rivers red with blood; 16 000 Romans died, among them the consul, who had given battle in spite of unfavourable omens.

The battlefield has been identified as part of the plain extending from Cortona to the lake.

■ TOWNS AND SIGHTS

Passignano sul Trasimeno*. — This pleasant town, frequented by walkers, lies opposite the wild and lonely Maggiore and Minore Islands.

Castiglione del Lago*. — This town on a chalky promontory dotted with olive trees still has a 14C mediaeval castle. Fine views from the promontory summit.

TRENT* (TRENTO) Trentino-Alto Adige

Michelin map 988 4 – *Local map p 68* – Pop 98 680

Trent is on the Adige River and the road to the Brenner Pass. It lies encircled by rocky heights, valleys and mountain pastures. Austrian and Italian influences meet here.

A good **view*** of the town can be obtained from the Dosso Trento, on which there is a Neo-Classical temple erected to the memory of Cesare Battisti, an Italian patriot hanged by the Austrians in 1916.

From 1027 to 1803, under the sway of bishops representing the Holy Roman Empire, Trent enjoyed a happy life. After the Napoleonic yoke came the rule of Austria which lay heavily on the town from 1814 to 1918, when it was liberated by the Italian Army. Since 1948 Trent has formed part of the autonomous area of Trentino-Alto Adige.

Council of Trent (1545-1563). — The Council, called by Pope Paul III to study methods of combating Protestantism, sat in the cathedral and in the Church of Santa Maria Maggiore. Several sessions were required, and Paul III found himself at variance with the Emperor Charles V who urged the council to treat the Protestants with consideration.

The main decisions taken had to do with the re-establishment of ecclesiastical authority, compulsory residence for bishops, limitation of plural livings and abolition of the sale of indulgences. The articles of faith were laid down in canons. These results marked the beginning of the Counter-Reformation which changed the character of the church.

■ MAIN SIGHTS *time: 2 hours*

Piazza del Duomo*. — This cobbled square crowded with pigeons is the centre of the town. Round it stand the Cathedral, the Law Courts, the Municipal Tower (belfry) and the Rella houses, painted with 16C allegorical frescoes. The Baroque Fountain of Neptune in the centre of the square is 18C.

Cathedral* (Duomo). — This majestic building is in the Lombard Romanesque style *(p 26)*.

The façade of the north transept is pierced with a window forming a Wheel of Fortune: Christ stands at the summit, the symbols of the Evangelists rise towards him.

Inside, note the unusual sweep of the stairway leading to the towers. To the right, in the 17C Chapel of the Crucifix, is a large wooden Crucifix in front of which the decrees of the Council were proclaimed. The high altar is crowned by a Baroque canopy; in the south transept is the tomb of the Venetian commander Sanseverino who died in 1486.

Diocesan Museum (Museo Diocesano) (AZ M). — *Open 1 April to 31 October, 9 am to noon and 2 to 6 pm; closed Wednesdays; 500 lire. Enter from the Piazza del Duomo.* The museum in the restored 13C Palazzo Pretorio, contains the best objects of the cathedral treasure, several paintings of the Council and seven very fine Renaissance **tapestries*** which were woven by Peter van Aelst from Brussels.

Via Belenzani (AZ 3). — This street is lined with palaces, in the Venetian style. Opposite the 16C town hall are the Salvadori and Geremia mansions, with walls painted with frescoes.

TRENTO

Battisti (Piazza Cesare)	BZ 2
Carducci (Largo)	BZ 5
Duomo (Piazza)	AZ 6
Garibaldi (Via)	ABZ 7
Manci (Via)	ABY
Mazzini (Via)	ABZ
Oriola (Via)	BZ 9
Oss. Mazzurana (Via)	BZ 10
S. Pietro (Via)	BYZ 15
S. Simonino (Via)	BZ 16
S. Vigilio (Via)	BZ 17
Belenzani (Via R.)	AZ 3
Cantone	BY 4
Giovanelli (Via)	BZ 8
Pio X (Via)	AZ 12
Prepositura (Via)	AZ 13
S. Lorenzo (Cavalcavia)	AY 14
Ventuno (Via dei)	BYZ 19

CASTELLO DEL BUON CONSIGLIO ★
VIA MANCI
Pza DEL DUOMO ★
DUOMO ★
MUSEO DIOCESANO

Via Manci (ABY). — No. 63, the Palazzo Galazzo (1602), with embossed stonework and huge pilasters, marks the transition between the Renaissance and Classical styles. The **Cantone**★, at the end of the Via Manci, is a picturesque and busy crossroads.

The Venetian and mountain styles are intermingled all along the street: Venetian loggias, frescoes in the Italian style and the wide, overhanging roofs of mountain regions.

Castle of Good Counsel★ (Castello del Buon Consiglio). — *Open 9 am to noon and 2 to 6 pm (4.30 pm 1 October to 30 April); closed Mondays and holidays.* This castle was formerly the residence of the prince-bishops and now houses the Provincial Museum of Art. On the left are the 13C Castelvecchio (Old Castle) and the Torre Grande known as the Tower of Augustus; in the centre is the 16C Renaissance Palazzo Magno, in which were the bishop's apartments; and on the extreme right the square Torre dell'Aquila (Eagle Tower).

The Castelvecchio has a beautiful court in the Venetian Gothic style with four tiers of galleries adorned with frescoes, including the portraits of the prince-bishops. The Palazzo Magno also has a remarkable court. The apartments of the prince-bishops, decorated with stucco and frescoes, house the museums of archaeology, ethnology and painting. There are rich collections of Renaissance bronzes, Faenza ceramics and Meissen statuettes. The fine frescoes in the loggia, together with those on the staircase and gallery leading to it, were painted about 1531 by Romanino da Brescia.

■ ADDITIONAL SIGHTS

Palazzo Tabarelli★ (BZ F). — A remarkable building in the Venetian Renaissance style with pilasters, pink marble columns and medallions.

St. Mary Major's Church (Santa Maria Maggiore) (AZ B). — Meetings of the Council of Trent were held in this Renaissance church with a Romanesque campanile. A marble organ loft by Vicenzo and Girolamo Grandi (1534) in the chancel has an attractive elegance. At the second altar on the right, in the nave, is a 16C altarpiece of the Madonna and saints by Moroni.

St. Apollinaris (Sant'Apollinare) (AY D). — Small church of Romanesque origin on the right bank of the Adige; a curious steep roof covers two rounded Gothic arches.

EXCURSION

Monte Bondone (alt 2 098 m - 6 884 ft). — *West, 24 km - 15 miles.* Leave by ⑤, road S 45 *bis,* and after 3 km - 2 miles — bear left. The road, twisting as it climbs, goes through hamlets which come to life during the winter sports season. It affords outstanding **views**★★, eastwards over Trent and the Adige Valley, then northwards towards Mount Paganella and finally, after Vason, of the Brenta Mountains in the west.

TREVISO ★ Venetia

Michelin map 988 5 — Pop 89 991
Town plan in Michelin Red Guide Italia (hotels and restaurants).

Treviso is surrounded by 15C ramparts and intersected by canals. It is an interesting old town where it is pleasant to stroll in streets lined with porticoes and corbelled houses painted with frescoes in the Venetian style. Treviso reached its zenith in the 13C under the overlordship of Gherardo da Camino; its fortunes were afterwards linked with those of Venice. Under the French Empire, Marshal Mortier was made Duke of Treviso and Napoleon I ordered the building of the magnificent Treviso-Venice road, which still has its original width.

■ OLD TOWN (Città Vecchia) *time: 2 hours*

The Old Town is picturesque. In Piazza dei Signori stands the municipal bell-tower. On this square is the Trecento Palace which is Romanesque; nearby is the Loggia dei Cavalieri, an interesting building, also Romanesque in style. The town pawn shop stands in the square of the same name, Piazza Monte di Pietà *(ring for caretaker):* the chapel has 16C gilded leatherwork. Further down, the 14C church of Santa Lucia is adorned with remarkable frescoes of the school of Tommaso da Modena.

On the opposite bank of the Botteniga River to the east you will see the Church of San Francesco, built in the transitional Romanesque-Gothic style. It has a fine keel-shaped wooden ceiling and contains the tombstone of Petrarch's daughter, Francesca Petrarca (fourth pillar) and the tomb of Pietro, the son of Dante Alighieri, in the north transept and frescoes by Tommaso da Modena (14C) in the first chapel on the left in the chancel. The Church of Santa Caterina is interesting with its chapel of the Innocents and frescoes by Tommaso da Modena and other 14 and 15C artists.

■ ADDITIONAL SIGHTS

L. Bailo Museum★. — *Open 9 am to noon and 2 to 6 pm (5 pm 1 October to 30 April). Closed Mondays, 1 January, 1 May, 15 August, 25 December and Sunday and holiday afternoons.* The picture gallery contains frescoes by Tommaso da Modena (the Life of St. Ursula) who was influenced by Giotto, and by Vitale da Bologna; pictures by Cima da Conegliano, Giovanni Bellini, Titian, Girolamo da Treviso, Pietro and Alessandro Longhi and Jacopo Bassano. There is a penetrating portrait of a Dominican by Lotto, works by Pâris Bordone and a St. John the Baptist Preaching by Tiepolo.

Cathedral (Duomo). — The 16C church has seven domes, a neo-Classical façade and a Romanesque crypt. Left of the cathedral is an 11-12C baptistry. In the Chapel of the Annunciation to the right of the chancel are mannered frescoes by Pordenone and on the altar piece is an Annunciation by Titian.

St. Nicholas' Church (San Nicolò). — The Romanesque-Gothic church contains frescoes by Tommaso da Modena (14C) and Lorenzo Lotto.

Nearby, the hall of the Dominican Chapter is adorned with portraits of illustrious ecclesiastics of that Order by Tommaso da Modena.

Ramparts' Promenade. — North of the town, these afford a good view of the Alps.

TRIESTE * Friuli-Venezia Giulia _____

Michelin map **988** 6 — Pop 262 929

Town plan in Michelin Red Guide Italia (hotels and restaurants).

Trieste, the largest seaport on the Adriatic, is the maritime outlet of Austria and it handles part of the traffic to and from Yugoslavia.

The origins of the town are very ancient; the Celts and the Illyrians disputed it before the Romans made it their important trading centre of Tergeste; its citadel guarded the eastern frontiers of the Empire; it came under the sway of the Patriarch of Aquileia and then, in the Middle Ages, under that of Venice; in 1382 it placed itself under the protection of Austria. In 1719 it became a free port and began to enjoy great prosperity. Trieste was often used as a refuge by political exiles. James Joyce lived here for some years until 1914.

In 1945 Trieste became an independent territory under United Nations control. It was returned to Italy only in November 1954 after much upheaval and following a plebiscite.

The Port and its Shipyards. — The port is large and equipped on an extensive scale (station, arsenal). Its traffic is furnished more by Austrian and Yugoslav than by Italian goods. An oil pipeline, with a diameter of 1 m - 3 ft — and an annual capacity of 50 million tons of oil, links the town with the refineries of Ingolstadt in southern Germany and Vienna. Port reconstructions now allow tankers of 160 000 tons to berth. A charming canal-port, made in 1756, forms an extension of the Porto Vecchio.

From Monfalcone in the north, which specialises in building large liners, to Muggia in the south, large shipyards contribute to local industry. In Bagnoli della Rosandra (South-East exit), there is a large factory producing turbine machinery. Among other industries, metal, cement and oil refining are important. Extension of the port is in progress: enlargement of the pleasure sailing area, modernisation of quays and basins, building of a graving dock for 250 000 ton vessels and quays reserved for various industrial establishments.

At the north end of the port stands a lighthouse built in 1927 to honour those who died at sea.

■ **SIGHTS** *time: 1 1/2 hours*

Piazza dell'Unità d'Italia*. — Three palaces dating from 1900 stand upon this square: the Government Palace, the City Hall and the offices of the Lloyd Triestino. The square opens onto the piers which make a pleasant promenade by the sea. From the jetty you can enjoy lovely views of the bay, the Piazza dell'Unità d'Italia, the town and the hills.

St. Justus Basilica* (Basilica di San Giusto). — The St. Justus Basilica on the top of the hill, where the ancient city used to be, was founded in the 5C on the site of a Roman temple. The façade is pierced with a fine Gothic rose window decorated with a Roman stele and bronze busts. The campanile, whose lowest storey includes Roman columns, bears a 14C statue of St. Justus. A panorama can be seen from its top.

TRIESTE

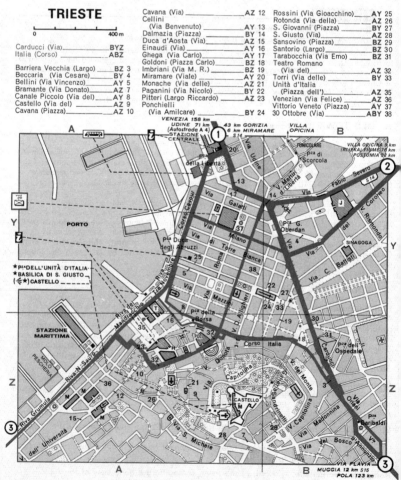

The interior comprises a nave and four aisles. The side aisles belonged to two separate 6 and 11C basilicas which were joined by the building of the central nave in the 14C. In the south apse of the completed building, 13C mosaics represent Christ between St. Justus and St. Servulus, and 11C frescoes depict the legend of St. Justus. A magnificent 12C mosaic in the north apse shows the Virgin in Majesty between the Archangels Michael and Gabriel, and, below, the Apostles.

The 15-16C castle, standing higher, houses a museum of weapons and furniture. There are **views★** of the town and the sea from the parapet walk.

EXCURSIONS

Villa Opicina. — *North, 9 km - 6 miles*. Leave by ②. After 4.5 km - 3 miles — turn left off road S 58. Villa Opicina, on the edge of the Carso High Plateau (alt 348 m - 1 128 ft) can also be reached by cable-car. Return down to the Piazzale Belvedere station, from near which you get a wide **panorama★★** of the town and the bay.

Miramare. — *Northwest, 6 km - 4 miles*. Leave by ①. This castle, high above the sea, was built for Archduke Maximilian of Austria, who was executed by shooting in Mexico in 1867, and his wife, Princess Charlotte, who died insane. It is surrounded by beautiful terraced **gardens★**.

The castle is open: 9 am to 2 pm (1 pm on Sundays and holidays); closed Mondays (Tuesday when Monday is a holiday), 1 January, 25 April, 1 May, 15 August and at Christmas; 500 lire. Gardens are open 9 am to 1 hour before sunset. A Son et Lumière *performance is given in summer.*

Grotta Gigante★. — *North, 13 km - 8 miles*. Leave by ②. Take the same route as for Villa Opicina. At Opicina bear left again towards the Borgo Grotta Gigante. A stairway leads down to a chamber of impressive size where one can walk among the splendid concretions. There is a speleological museum at the entrance to the cave. *Guided tours: January, February, November, December, 9.30 to 11.30 am and 2.30 to 4.30 pm (every hour); March and October, 9 am to noon and 2 to 5 pm (every 1/2 hour); April to end of September, 9 am to noon and 2 to 7 pm (every 1/2 hour). Closed Mondays unless a holiday; 2 000 lire.*

TROIA Apulia
Michelin map 988 28 — 17 km - 10 miles — southwest of Foggia — Pop 8 135

Troia is well sited on the lower slopes of the Apennines, overlooking the plain.

Cathedral★. — This remarkable Romanesque building happily combines Apulian influences and Norman features. The exterior is characterised by an imposing transept and a curious chevet with columns. The façade is pierced with a rose window which is unique in its lack of symmetry and its delicately fretted sculptures. The bronze doors in the Byzantine style were cast by Oderisio da Benevento in 1119 and 1127. Inside, the pulpit dates from 1169.

TROPEA ★ Calabria
Michelin map 988 39 — Pop 7 485

Tropea, a fishing port, is built into the cliff on which it stands. This ancient small town knew a time of glory under Angevin and Spanish rule. Its beaches of fine white sand washed by crystal clear water, its headlands and picturesque jagged rocks and a good view of the sea and Stromboli lend charm to its **site★**.

From a terrace at the end of the town you can look at the **Chapel of St. Mary of the Isle** (Santa Maria dell'Isola), a black-and-white stone building, a former Benedictine annexe built on a rocky islet. The Norman Romanesque **cathedral**, stands on the edge of the north ramparts.

TRULLI District ★★★ Apulia
Michelin map 988 29.

A district marked by very curious buildings extends between Monopoli, Castellana Grotte and Martina Franca. Its capital is Alberobello.

The *Trulli*. — In these strange white, dry-stone structures with domed roofs, standing in groups of three or four on ochre-coloured soil, can be seen traces of prehistoric Saracen and Christian civilisations, similar to the *nuraghi* of Sardinia. The *trulli* are whitewashed, except, sometimes, for the roofs, which are covered with stone tiles. The rooms are roofed with domes of different sizes, each having a central chimney. An outside staircase serves the attic; large jars to hold grain, oil and wine are placed at its foot. The *Trulli* are strangely decorated: the upper parts of the façades are often adorned with statues or crosses. The unwhitewashed domes bear crosses and painted signs that are perhaps survivals of mediaeval times when the mystical brotherhood of the Rosicrucians spread throughout the Mediterranean area.

■ TOWNS AND SIGHTS

Alberobello★★. — *Description p 43*.

Gioia del Colle. — Gioia has a fine **castle★** of Norman origin rebuilt by Frederick of Swabia in the 13C. The exterior is severe.

Castellana Caves★★★ (Grotta di Castellana). — *From 1 April to 30 September: short tours every hour 8.30 am to 12.30 pm and 2.30 to 7 pm (length: 500 m - 550 yds, 1 500 lire); complete tours every hour 8 am to noon and 2 to 6 pm (length: 3 km - 2 miles — 3 000 lire). From 1 October to 31 March (every hour): short tours 8.30 am to 12.30 pm and 3.30 to 5.30 pm — 1 500 lire); complete tours 9 am to noon and 2 to 5 pm — 3 500 lire.* These great caves contain a fine series of chambers with remarkable concretions; draperies, richly coloured stalactites and stalagmites — note particularly the greenish-yellow tints caused by sulphur deposits.

Martina Franca. — To the right from the road to Locorotondo you will find an overall **view★** of the Trulli region.

Putignano. — One kilometre from the cave, to the right, on the road to Turi, after a level crossing, is the entrance to a **cave★** containing pretty limestone concretions *(500 lire)*.

TURIN ★★ (TORINO)

Piedmont

Michelin map 988 12 — Pop 1 172 482.

Town plan in Michelin Red Guide Italia (hotels and restaurants).

Most of the capital of Piedmont was built on a regular plan in the 17 and 18C. It is a lively, prosperous town, with wide, arcaded avenues and spacious squares. Architecturally the main points of interest are the many rich churches and the decoration of the impressive palaces.

The **Mole Antonelliana (CX)**, a peculiar and daring structure, built from 1863 to 1890 by Antonelli, overlooks the town. A lift will take you up, 84 m - 275 ft — to the base of the spire *(open 1 May to 30 September, 10 am to noon, 2.30 to 7.30 pm and 9 to 11 pm; at other times of the year, 8.30 am to noon and 3 to 6 pm, closed on Mondays; 500 lire)* from where there is a good panoramic view of the town and the Alps.

There is another good view of Turin to be had from the **Capuchin Monastery (CZ)** on the right bank of the River Po.

LIFE IN TURIN

The life of the town is concentrated in the Via Roma, the Piazza San Carlo and the Via Po, which leads to the huge Piazza Vittorio Veneto, built in the Classical style.

The modern looking Via Roma is lined with arcades sheltering the windows of luxury shops. The Piazza San Carlo, halfway along the Via Roma, is the meeting-place of fashionable women, while connoisseurs linger in the antiquaries' and booksellers' shops. The large cafés built in the Neo-Classical style which open on the Via Po played a part in the politics of the 19C.

The courteous and refined atmosphere of Turin is that of a cultural centre distinguished by many bookshops, well known newspapers *(Stampa)* and a large university.

But the cult of the spirit does not compel neglect of the flesh, and the people of Turin, with appetites whetted by their famous Martini, Cinzano or Carpano Vermouths, do not disdain good cooking. *Cardi in bagna cauda* (cardoons in piquant sauce) and *tartufi bianchi* (white truffles) are specialities eaten with crisp rolls and accompanied by the delectable wines of the region. Sweetmeats, chocolates and stuffed pastries, are also excellent.

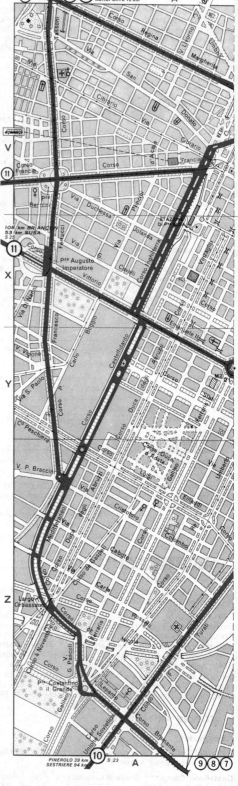

HISTORICAL NOTES

In the course of its history Turin had to withstand two severe sieges from the French. The first in 1640 ended after 5 months with the town being taken. In the second, in 1706, Turin held out against the troops of Louis XIV, thanks partly to the heroism of a soldier, Pietro Micca, who finally blew himself up at the same time as a gallery in the citadel.

Turin was the capital of the Po Department from 1800 until 1814. The town had previously been annexed to France by François I from 1536 to 1562.

The House of Savoy. — This dynasty, descended from Umberto (Humbert) the Whitehanded, who died in 1056, reigned over Savoy and Piedmont for nearly nine centuries. It became the reigning house of Sardinia from 1720 onwards and of all Italy from 1861 to 1945. From 1720 the royal family resided at Turin.

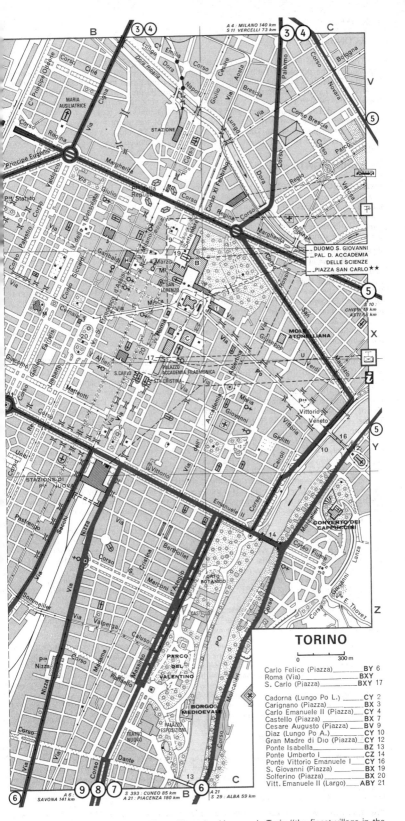

TORINO

0 — 300 m

Carlo Felice (Piazza)_____BY 6
Roma (Via)_____BXY
S. Carlo (Piazza)_____BXY 17

Cadorna (Lungo Po L.) _____CY 2
Carignano (Piazza)_____BX 3
Carlo Emanuele II (Piazza)__CY 4
Castello (Piazza) _____BX 7
Cesare Augusto (Piazza) ___BV 9
Diaz (Lungo Po A.)_____CY 10
Gran Madre di Dio (Piazza)__CY 12
Ponte Isabella_____BZ 13
Ponte Umberto I_____CZ 14
Ponte Vittorio Emanuele I __CY 16
S. Giovanni (Piazza) _____BX 19
Solferino (Piazza)_____BX 20
Vitt. Emanuele II (Largo)__ABY 21

DUOMO S. GIOVANNI
PAL. D. ACCADEMIA
DELLE SCIENZE
PIAZZA SAN CARLO ★★

Charles Emmanuel III (1732-1773), a philosopher-king, made Turin "the finest village in the world" in the words of Montesquieu.

Charles Albert (1830-1849) fought the Austrians, driving them back to Lombardy but was defeated by them at Novara. Victor Emmanuel II (1849-1878), a popular and intelligent man, encountered a man of destiny, the Piedmontese, Cavour. Between them they sealed the Franco-Piedmontese alliance which won the battles of Solferino and Magenta, and with the help of Garibaldi brought about Italian unity *(p 19)*.

St. John Bosco. — It was in Turin, in the 19C, that John Bosco founded the Salesian Order (St. Francis de Sales). Among the order's aims was the rescue of abandoned children and their training in a craft or trade. The saint's shrine is in the Basilica of Mary Auxiliary **(BV)**.

ECONOMY

Thanks to the intense activity of its suburban industries, Turin is the capital of Italian engineering. The people of Turin are born mechanics and most of the motor engineers come from the Politecnico of Turin University; it is here that the Italian motor industry, represented by FIAT and Lancia, was born. Turin is responsible for 85 per cent of Italian car production. Many of the modern FIAT works are established in the suburbs south of the town (Mirafiori).

Important tyre manufacturers and well known coachbuilders (one of the most famous having been Pinin Farina) contribute to the prosperity of the motor industry of Turin, whose products are displayed at the Turin Motor Show (1978, 1980, etc.).

The textile and clothing industries are also highly developed.

■ MAIN SIGHTS *time: 3 hours*

Piazza San Carlo★★. — This is a graceful piece of town planning. The Churches of San Carlo and Santa Cristina, symmetrically placed on the south side, frame the Via Roma. The curious façade of Santa Cristina, surmounted by candelabra, was designed by the famous Sicilio-Turinese architect Juvara. On the east side is the 17C palace which was the residence of the French Ambassadors from 1771 to 1789 and since 1838 is the home of the philharmonic academy. In the centre of the square stands the statue (1838) of Filiberto Emanuele.

Academy of Science (Palazzo dell'Accademia delle Scienze). — 17C palace by Guarini.

The **Museum of Antiquities** is on the ground floor with bronzes from Industria, Greek vases and ceramics.

The **Egyptian Museum★★** which is one of the richest in Europe (effigies of Rameses II and the kings of the New Empire, the temple of Thutmose III, dating from *c*. 1450 BC and transported from El-Elessiya, south of Aswan, funeral chambers, etc.) occupies part of the ground floor and all the first floor. *Open 9 am to 2 pm (1 pm Sundays and holidays); closed Mondays, 1 January, 25 April, 1 May, 15 August and Christmas; 750 lire.*

The **Galleria Sabauda★★** on the second floor *(same times and conditions as for the Egyptian museum)* comprises five sections.

The first includes a collection of works by 15-17C Piedmontese artists. Note a polyptych (1493) by Gandolfino da Roreto, a triptych by Gian Martino Spanzotti (*c*. 1455-1528), early works (Scenes from the Life of the Virgin) and mature (Deposition) paintings by Gaudenzio Ferrari, an altarpiece (1498) by Macrino d'Alba and works by Moncalvo and Guala (18C).

Among the pictures exhibited in the section devoted to other Italian schools are a Madonna by Barnaba da Modena (14C), a small painting by Bernardo Daddi (Coronation of the Virgin) and several remarkable 15C works by Tuscan painters: a Madonna by Fra Angelico, Tobias and the Archangel (Il Toblino) by Antonio and Piero Pollaiuolo, Eleanor of Toledo by Bronzino. An Annunciation by Orazio Gentileschi is outstanding among the works by the followers of Caravaggio *(p 31);* the 15-16C Lombard School is well represented. The paintings include a polyptych (1462), the only signed work by Paolo da Brescia, and the Adorations (Presepi) by Savoldo also from Brescia. Francesco del Cairo and Tanzio da Varallo illustrate the development of Mannerism *(p 30)* in Lombardy and Piedmont. Garofalo — with excellent works — and Mazzolino exemplify Emilian painting in the 16C, Albani and Guercino represent the 17C and the Bolognese Crespi the 18C. The Venetian school is represented by large canvasses by the Bassano family, a masterpiece by Veronese (The Feast in the House of Simon), views of Turin by B. Bellotto, the Triumph of Aurelian by G.B. Tiepolo and *"capriccios"* by Francesco Guardi.

The Dutch and Flemish collections are probably the richest in Italy. Among the most outstanding works are St. Francis receiving the Stigmata by Van Eyck, two small religious paintings by Rogier Van der Weyden, the Passion by Memling, an impressive group of official portraits including the famous Children of Charles I of England, by Van Dyck, and the celebrated Old Man asleep showing Rembrandt's brilliant technique.

The section devoted to French, German and Spanish artists displays portraits by François Clouet (Marguerite de Valois), a St. Jerome by Valentin de Boulogne, and the Knife-Grinder ("Arrotino") by Caspar Netscher.

The **Gualino Collection★** is an outstanding selection of paintings, sculptures, furnishings and gold and silver plate: note in particular the Oriental carvings, a set of small paintings on a gilded background, several Renaissance masterpieces and 18C pastels.

St. John's Cathedral (Duomo San Giovanni). — This Renaissance cathedral was built at the end of the 15C for Cardinal Della Rovere. The façade by Meo Del Caprino, has three delicately carved doorways while the crown of the campanile was designed by Juvara in 1720.

Inside, behind the aspe, the **Chapel of the Holy Shroud★** (Cappella della Santa Sindone) is the work of Guarini (17C), who designed the curious architecture of the bold dome (height 60 m - 197 ft). An urn on the altar contains the Holy Shroud (only occasionally shown to the faithful) in which Christ is said to have been wrapped after the descent from the Cross. The outline of his body is imprinted on the shroud, making it "the oldest photograph in the world".

■ ADDITIONAL SIGHTS

Valentino Park (Parco del Valentino) (BCZ). — The park extends along the Po for about 1.5 km - 1 mile — and contains the Castello del Valentino, built in 1688 for the Duchess Marie-Christine of France, the Exhibition Palace, the Teatro Nuovo (New Theatre — 2 000 seats), and the **Borgo Medioevale★** with its castle, a curious and faithful reconstruction of a mediaeval building. *Open 9.30 am to noon and 3 to 6 pm; closed Mondays and weekday holidays; 100 lire.*

Car Museum★ (Museo dell'Automobile Carlo Biscaretti di Ruffia). — *Open 9.30 to 12.30 pm and 3 to 7 pm; 16 November to 31 March, 10 am to 12.30 pm and 3 to 5.30 pm; closed Mondays, 15 August and between Christmas and Epiphany; 1 000 lire.* South of the town (road ⑧), at No. 40 Corso Unità d'Italia, within a vast modern building is an exhibition of cars, chassis and engines. A library of more than 8 000 volumes and historic archives complete the museum.

Palazzo Madama (BX A). — *Open 9 am to 7 pm; closed Mondays, 1 January, Easter and Christmas and weekday holidays; 200 lire.* The palace stands in the centre of the Piazza Castello. It was so-called because the mother of Charles Emmanuel II, "Madama Reale", Marie-Christine of France, lived there. The Porta Decumana, part of the old Augustinian ramparts, forms the original nucleus of the building. The eastern section, in brick, is late mediaeval (15C), but the west façade, in stone, was designed in the 18C by Juvara in a style full of nobility.

In the **museum of ancient art★** (Museo d'Arte Antica) on the ground floor are interesting Gothic carvings, such as those on the 15C stalls from the Abbey of Staffarda, and such remarkable paintings as a Madonna by Barnaba da Modena, a Trinity of the 15C French school, a Portrait of a Man by Antonello da Messina (15C) and several pictures of the Piedmontese school. In a large gallery where an 18C Venetian state barge that once belonged to the Kings of Sardinia is on show may also be seen 17 and 18C paintings by Italian (among them Piedmontese) and foreign artists.

Sumptuous 18C apartments complete with furniture and paintings of the period may be visited on the first floor.

On the second floor *(lift)* is a rich collection of faïence, porcelain, ivory, etc.

Royal Palace (Palazzo Reale) (BCX B). — The princes of the house of Savoy lived in this plain 17-18C building until 1865. The **Armeria Reale★** (Royal Armoury — *open 9 am to 2 pm (1 pm Sundays and holidays); closed Mondays, 1 January, 25 April, 1 May, 15 August, Christmas; 100 lire; free on Sundays and holidays)* contains a splendid collection of arms and armour and interesting military souvenirs.

Standing slightly back on the Piazza Castello is the Church of San Lorenzo which was adorned with a dome and a bold crown by Guarini in the 17C. Next door, in the Palazzo Chiablese a **Film Museum** (BX M1) has been installed *(entrance: No. 2 Piazza S. Giovanni). Open: 1 June — 31 October, 10 am to noon and 3 to 6 pm; 3 November — 30 April, 10 am to noon, 3 to 6.30 pm and 8.30 to 11 pm. Closed Mondays and holidays; 500 lire.*

Palazzo Carignano (BX C). — The palazzo has a fine Baroque façade by Guarini to the Piazza Carignano. Victor Emmanuel II was born in this palace in 1820.

Municipal Gallery of Modern Art (AY M2). — *Same times of opening as the Palazzo Madama (see p 246).* Paintings, sculpture, drawings, and engravings of the 19 and 20C are shown. The 19C collections are mainly Italian paintings, among which are several Piedmontese artists (Antonio Fontanesi and Lorenzo Delleani). The 20C is well represented (second floor).

The gallery has an Oriental department *(to visit apply to the caretaker)* with Buddhist sculpture, Islamic glass and Assyrian bas-reliefs dating from the reign of Sargo II.

EXCURSIONS

See the plan of Turin and its suburbs in Michelin Red Guide Italia (hotels and restaurants).

Tour to Superga and La Maddalena. — *East, 25 km - 15 1/2 miles.* The **basilica of Superga★**, a masterpiece by Juvara, stands on a summit at an altitude of 672 m - 2 205 ft. It was built between 1717 and 1731 to fulfil a vow made by Victor Amadeus II when praying for the defeat of the troops of Louis XIV, who were then besieging his capital. The monumental façade and its impressive columns and pilasters are its chief features. On the left of the chancel, the chapel dedicated to the Virgin is a pilgrimage centre. The basilica is the Pantheon of the Kings of Sardinia *(the tombs are open, 9.30 am to 12.30 pm and 2.30 to 6.30 pm from 1 April to 30 September; 10 am to 12.30 pm and 3 to 5 pm the rest of the year; closed Fridays and 8 september; apply at the door on the left of the basilica).* From the esplanade there is a fine **view★★★** of Turin, the Po Plain and the Alps.

From Superga, you can take a pretty road via Pino Torinese to Colle della Maddalena affording **views★** of Turin.

Colle della Maddalena. — This pass, at an altitude of 715 m - 2 346 ft — affords many **views** of Turin. The **Parco della Rimembranza** commemorates the men of Turin who died in the First World War *(viewing table).* At the highest point stands a lighthouse, the Faro della Vittoria.

The **Europa Park**, beautifully landscaped, overlooks part of the town.

Stupinigi Palace★ (Palazzina di caccia). — *Southwest, 11 km - 7 miles. Guided tours: 10 to 12.30 pm and 3 to 6 pm (2 to 5 pm in winter). Closed Mondays, Fridays, 1 January, 1 May, 15 August, 1 November, Easter and Christmas; 1 000 lire.* The huge building was a hunting lodge built by Juvara (early 18C) for Victor Amadeus II of Savoy. Napoleon lived there before assuming the crown of Italy. It houses a furniture museum. The apartments are richly decorated with stucco and paintings by Cignaroli and Van Loo and adorned with valuable furniture (P. Piffetti, L. Prinotto, G. Bonzanigo) and *objets d'art.*

A magnificent park surrounds the palazzina.

TUSCANIA ★ Latium

Michelin map 988 25 — 24 km - 15 miles — west of Viterbo — Pop 7 103

Tuscania was a powerful Etruscan town, a Roman municipality and an important mediaeval centre. It displays fragments of its walls and two superb churches, a little way out of town. The town's artistic heritage was considerably damaged by the earthquake of February 1971. A programme of restoration is now underway.

St. Peter's Church★★ (San Pietro). — The golden-hued façade of St. Peter's, which was built on the site of an Etruscan acropolis, stands at the end of a square, overgrown with weeds. To the left are two mediaeval towers and to the right the former bishop's palace.

The well balanced façade dates from the beginning of the 13C. The symbols of the Evangelists surround a rose window, probably of the Umbrian school (badly damaged, but now restored). Lower down, an atalanta (or a dancer?) and a man being choked by a snake have no doubt been taken from Etruscan buildings. Part of the apse collapsed during the tremor.

The interior was built by Lombard master masons in the 11C; massive columns with beautiful capitals support curious denticulated arches; the central nave has its original and highly decorative paving. *(The work of recovery and assembly of the fragments is in progress).*

The **crypt★★** contains a forest of little columns, all different and of various periods — Roman, Pre-Romanesque and Romanesque — supporting ribbed vaulting.

St. Mary Major's Church★ (Santa Maria Maggiore). — This late 12C church repeats the main features of St. Peter's. Also seriously damaged, this building will be rebuilt in its original form.

Note especially the 13C Romanesque **doorways★★** with their masterly scultpures. The central doorway, surmounted by a loggia and a rose window, has on its tympanum a curious Virgin between the Lamb and the Sacrifice of Isaac.

Inside is an ambo (small pulpit) built up of 8-9C and 12C fragments. There is a realistic 14C fresco over the triumphal arch of the Last Judgment.

UDINE ★ Friuli-Venezia Giulia

Michelin map 988 6 — Pop 103 051
Town plan in Michelin Red Guide Italia (hotels and restaurants).

This charming town of the Friuli was the seat of the Patriarchs of Aquilea from 1238 to 1420 when it passed under Venetian rule.

Udine nestles round a hill encircled by the picturesque alleyway, the Vicolo Sottomonte, with a **castle** *(restoration in progress)* on its summit. This impressive early 16C edifice, the seat of the representatives of the Most Serene Republic (Venice), was damaged by the 1976 earthquake. The esplanade in front of the castle, affords pretty views of the town and Friuli area.

Secluded squares and narrow streets, often lined with arcades, will please the stroller. In the centre, the Piazza Matteotti, where the market is held, is adorned with a fountain, a Virgin's Column and a graceful Baroque church of the 16C. Note also the Via Vittorio Veneto, where shops line a row of arches and the picturesque Via Mercato Vecchio.

Six kilometres from Udine is the market town of **Campo Formio,** famous for the treaty (1797) between France and Austria which marked the end of Napoleon's first campaign in Italy.

Piazza della Libertà★★. — The Piazza della Libertà has kept its Renaissance air, which makes it one of the most beautiful squares in Italy. Here you will see the former Gothic town hall (1457), also known as the Loggia del Lionello from the name of its architect. It is distinguished by the lightness and grace of its balconies and the white and rose stone used in its building. The 16C **Loggia di San Giovanni** is surmounted by the clock tower, with Moorish jacks (mechanical figures that strike the hours) known as the Mori and similar to those at Venice. A 16C fountain plays in the centre of the square, not far from statues of Hercules and Cacus (a fire-god) and the columns of Justice and St. Mark.

Cathedral (Duomo). — This Gothic building has good doorways. The massive campanile has, on one of its faces, a fine Annunciation and Archangel Gabriel dating from the 14C. Inside, the Baroque **decoration★** is curious: tombs, a pulpit, an organ, altarpieces and remarkable historiated stalls. Tiepolo painted amusing *trompe-l'œil* frescoes in the Chapel of the Holy Sacrament.

The Oratory of Purity, to the right of the cathedral, has a ceiling decorated with a remarkable Assumption in 1757 by Tiepolo. *Open 7.30 am to noon and 3.30 to 7.30 pm; ask for the key at the cathedral sacristy.*

Archbishop's Palace (Palazzo Arcivescovile). — *Open 9 am to noon except Saturdays, Sundays and holidays.* The 16-18C palace, which is flanked by its chapel, boasts **frescoes★** by Tiepolo decorating its grand staircase, the roof of which is painted with a Fall of the Rebel Angels. The apartments are adorned with an admirably composed Judgment of Solomon.

Church of Santa Maria del Castello. — *Below the castle.* The church is 13C with a 16C façade. The campanile of the same period has a figure of the Archangel Gabriel at its summit. Inside, in the south apse, is a 13C fresco of the Descent from the Cross.

URBINO ★★ Marches

Michelin map 988 15 16 — Pop 16 216

Urbino, proud and peaceful, is built on two hills overlooking undulating country side.

Life in Urbino. — The town, which is still girt with ramparts, is a quiet, artistic city, with steep, narrow streets lined with many palaces. As you stroll through the alleys and stairways of Urbino, you get amusing glimpses of little courts planted with bright geraniums and bird's eye views of the old roofs covered with Romanesque tiles, the belfries and the countryside.

A Humanist Court. — Urbino was ruled by the Montefeltro family from the 12C onwards and reached its zenith in the reign (1444-1482) of **Duke Federico da Montefeltro,** a wise leader who loved art and letters. Having had his nose broken and his right eye put out in a tournament, he would be portrayed only in profile, (e.g. Piero della Francesca's portrait, Uffizi Museum, Florence).

Federico, a pupil of Vittorino da Feltre *(p 137)* at Mantua, became Director of the Military College at Urbino and was nicknamed the "Light of Italy". Dressed in a simple red robe, he walked among his people, who knelt as he passed and said: "God keep you, lord!"

He was the patron of many artists, including the architects Luciano Laurana, Bramante and Francesco di Giorgio and the painters Piero della Francesca, Melozzo da Forlì and Paolo Uccello, the Spaniard, Berruguete, the Fleming, Just van Gand, and finally Giovanni Santi, the father of the great Raffaello d'Urbino (Raphaël).

Federico's son, Guidobaldo, continued his father's beneficence under the influence of his wife, Elizabeth Gonzaga, who was clever and gentle. The refined life of the Court of Urbino at the beginning of the 16C is described by Balthasar Castiglione, in a book entitled *Il Cortigiano* which became the gentleman's code.

The Principality passed to a Della Rovere in 1508 and was taken back by the church in 1626.

■ **MAIN SIGHTS** time: 2 1/2 hours

Ducal Palace★★★ (Palazzo Ducale). — *Open weekdays 9 am to 7 pm; Sundays and holidays 9 am to 1 pm. Closed Mondays, 1 January, 25 April, 1 May, first Sunday in June, 15 August and Christmas; 750 lire.* The palace was begun in 1444 on the orders of Federico, who from 1466 to 1472 entrusted the work to the Dalmatian architect Laurana. It was Laurana's task to unify old Gothic designs, the work of Tuscan master masons, and new Renaissance ideas. He created a masterpiece of balance and taste. The palace was completed in 1482 by Francesco di Giorgio Martini.

Overlooking the valley, to the west, the massive building resembles a fortress and presents loggias superimposed between two towers. To the east, the long wall pierced with elegant paired windows extends at one end into two wings at right angles bordering Piazza Duca Federico which is closed on the third side by the Cathedral. The windows and doors are adorned with the Montefeltro arms and mottoes as well as the initials F.D. (Federico Dux).

The court of honour in the centre of the buildings is well balanced and harmonious, with lines of Classical simplicity and bears a Latin inscription in praise of Federico I. A staircase on the left leads to the apartments, in which the National Gallery of the Marches is housed.

National Gallery of the Marches★★ (Galleria Nazionale delle Marche). — *Same conditions of opening as the Palazzo Ducale.* The pictures are soberly displayed in rooms which still have their original decoration: Montefeltro coats of arms, delicately carved chimney pieces and door frames, inlays after Botticelli, Martini, etc.

Enter the throne-room, where superb 17C Gobelins tapestries hang. They represent the Acts of the Apostles, after Raphaël, and bear the arms of Cardinal Mazarin and the signature of Jean Lefèvre. Next comes the Night Watch Room, so-called because the little court of Guidobaldo and Elizabeth, described by Castiglione, used to meet there late in the evening; it contains a polyptych by Vivarini and some paintings of the 15C Venetian school. The following rooms were the duchess's apartments.

In the duke's apartments are these masterpieces: a Madonna by Verrochio; the admirable **predella** of the Profanation of the Host (1465-1469) by Paolo Uccello; the Communion of the Apostles by Just van Gand; the Flagellation and the Madonna of Senigallia by Piero della Francesca and a portrait of a woman, known as The Mute, by Raphaël. The astonishing **studiolo★★★** (study) of the duke is furnished with remarkable inlays probably after Botticelli. These were sur-

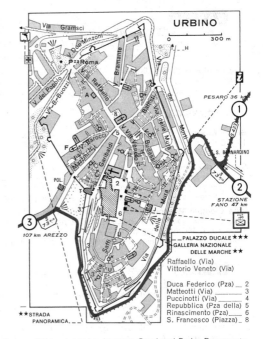

URBINO

PESARO 36 km
S. BERNARDINO
STAZIONE FANO 47 km

107 km AREZZO

★★STRADA PANORAMICA

■ PALAZZO DUCALE ★★★
GALLERIA NAZIONALE
DELLE MARCHE ★★

Raffaello (Via)
Vittorio Veneto (Via)

Duca Federico (Pza) __ 2
Matteotti (Via) _____ 3
Puccinotti (Via) _____ 4
Repubblica (Pza della) 5
Rinascimento (Pza) ___ 6
S. Francesco (Piazza) _ 8

mounted by panels representing Famous Men painted by Just van Gand and Pedro Berruguete.

Strada Panoramica★★. — This panoramic road starts from the **Piazza Roma** (view★★ from Monte Titano to Monte Catria) and follows the crest of a hill facing the town. It reveals admirable **views★★★** of the ramparts, the lower town, the ducal palace and the cathedral.

■ ADDITIONAL SIGHTS

St. John's Oratory (San Giovanni) (F). — *Walk down the Via Mazzini and take the Via Posta Vecchia on the right, then the Via Barocci on the left; open 10 am to noon and 3 to 5 pm closed on Sunday afternoons and holidays; 100 lire.* Inside it are curious **frescoes★★** by the Salimbene brothers (1416) depicting the life of St. John the Baptist.

Raphaël's House★ (Casa di Raffaello) (A). — *Open 1 April to 30 September, 9 am to 1 pm and 3 to 7 pm; 1 October to 31 May, 12.30, to 4.30 pm weekdays; Sundays and holidays, 9 am to 1 pm. Ring the bell. Closed Mondays; 500 lire.* Raphaël lived here up to the age of fourteen. In the room where he was born is a fresco of the Madonna, the first work of the young painter. The Virgin is a portrait of Raphaël's mother, and the Child one of Raphaël himself.

St. Bernardino's Church (San Bernardino). — *East, 3 km - 2 miles.* At the Pesaro-Fano crossroads, take the by-road on the left of the Calvary. The pretty church in the Classical style, attributed to Francesco di Giorgio or Bramante, contains the tombs of Federico and his son Guidobaldo, Dukes of Urbino, and their wives. From the esplanade there is a pretty **view★** of Urbino.

EXCURSION

Furlo Gorge★ (Gola del Furlo). — *Southeast, 17 km - 11 miles. Leave by* ②. This deep and narrow ravine has been cut out by the Candigliano. The Via Flaminia, built by the Romans in AD 76, follows its path. The lake has been formed by the construction of a dam.

VALTELLINA Lombardy _____

Michelin map **988** 3 4.

The Valtellina is a long Alpine valley extending for about 125 km - 75 miles — along the Adda River, between the Stelvio Pass *(p 232)* and Lake Como. Its capital is **Sondrio**, whose collegiate church possesses a Miracle of St. Gregory (1720) by Pietro Ligari, the greatest painter of the Valtellina. On the sunny slopes of the valley, vines grow and yield well known vintages.

Tirano is a pleasant little town of mountain houses, overlooked by several bell-towers. It is the starting point of the railway to St. Moritz through the Bernina Pass (2 323 m - 7 586 ft), the highest railway line in Europe without a cog-railway section.

One kilometre - 1/2 mile — to the west is the **Church of the Madonna di Tirano**, a popular place of pilgrimage. This is a graceful Renaissance building (1504) with fine doorways and an interior entirely covered with stucco and sculptures (1590-1608). The organ is interesting.

The road climbing from Tresenda *(10 km - 6 miles — southwest of Tirano)* to the **Passo d'Aprica** (1 172 m - 3 843 ft), to the south, affords a pretty view over the Valtellina.

VARALLO Piedmont _____

Michelin maps **988** 2 and **26** 5 6 — 59 km - 37 miles — northwest of Novara — *Local map p 128* — Pop 8 183

Varallo, in the Val Sesia and an excursion centre for the Alpine valleys, was the birthplace of the painter Gaudenzio Ferrari (*c.* 1480-1546), who was the pupil of Leonardo da Vinci but showed definite originality and picturesque realism. The Church of St. Mary of Grace (Santa Maria delle Grazie) bears beautiful **frescoes★** by this painter, depicting the Life of Jesus.

The **Church of the Sacro Monte★**, which is reached by road *(2.5 km - 1 1/2 miles — Rtn),* was built in the 15C. The building is vast; it contains forty-three chapels and was decorated with frescoes by great painters, among them Gaudenzio Ferrari and Il Morazzone.

VARESE Lombardy

Michelin maps **988** 3 and **26** 8 — *Local map p 128* — Pop 91 130
Town plan in Michelin Red Guide Italia (hotels and restaurants).

Varese is busy, airy and prosperous. Its centre is the modern Piazza Monte Grappa.

Este Gardens★ (Giardini Estensi). — The town hall, a palace built for Duke Francesco III d'Este between 1768 and 1780, is embellished by delightful gardens.

From the upper terrace there is a fine view of Varese and towards the Alps.

EXCURSIONS

Sacro Monte★★. — *North, 8 km - 5 miles.* The village of Santa Maria del Monte and the 16-17C Baroque pilgrimage Church of Sacro Monte stand at an altitude of 880 m - 2 887 ft. The **view★★** of Varese and the lakes is magnificent.

Campo dei Fiori. — *North, 10 km - 6 miles.* From the Sacro Monte the road climbs to the Campo dei Fiori, from which there is a panorama of four lakes. From there you can reach *(3/4 hour on foot Rtn)* the summit of **Monte Tre Croci** (Three Crosses Mountain — 1 111 m - 3 645 ft) from which a wide **panorama★★★**, embracing five lakes, can be seen.

Villa Cicogna-Mozzoni. — *At Bisuschio (northeast, 9 km - 6 miles — road S 344). Guided tours 9 am to noon and 2 to 6.30 pm (5.30 pm in autumn). Closed 5 November to 15 April; 1 500 lire.* A 16C residence with a lovely porticoed court decorated with frescoes by the Campi brothers. Inside are numerous frescoes and coffered ceilings. There is also a pleasant garden.

VENICE ★★★ (VENEZIA) Venetia

Michelin map **988** 5 — Pop 358 266
Town plan in Michelin Red Guide Italia (hotels and restaurants)

A fascinating city between sea and sky, like Venus rising from the waves, Venice welcomes tourists from the five continents drawn to her by the charm of her water and pellucid light, free from all dust and cooled by the sea breezes. She also offers the intellectual pleasures to be derived from her masterpieces which mark the meeting of East and West.

The vanished greatness of Venice accounts for the myth of an artificial, voluptuous and tragic city, the scene of intrigues plotted in an atmosphere of corruption where dreams became nightmares. The Romantics especially have described this atmosphere.

Today the exceptional position of Venice constitutes a threat to its very existence. The nature of the terrain on which it is built induces a sinking while the level of the surrounding waters is constantly rising. Various measures have already been taken and a plan to safeguard and remedy the position is under investigation.

The Marriage of Venice and the Sea. — Every year, from 1173 to 1797, a gorgeous ceremony perfectly expressed what used to be the greatness of Venice and is still its beauty. After the Venetian Republic supported Pope Alexander III in his struggle againsgt the Emperor Frederick Barbarossa, the Pontiff gave the Doge a ring as a symbol of his "rule of the sea". In memory of this, every year on Ascension Day, the Doge, dressed in cloth of gold, boarded *Bucentaur*, his gilded state galley, and sailed out to throw a ring into the sea with the words: "We wed thee, Sea, in token of our perpetual rule."

Access. — The classic approach route is through Mestre and the great road and railway bridge, 4 km - 3 miles — long. The trip across the lagoon is somewhat spoilt by the sight of the smoke from the port of Mestre, which is disfigured by oil refineries and engineering workshops. The bridge leads to the Piazzale Roma **(AX)**, where you must leave the car in one of the paying garages in the square or in the specially provided car parks on the artificial island of Tronchetto nearby *(July to mid-October, allow at least one hour's delay)*.

Transport. — The best way to make contact with Venice from the Piazzale Roma is to take the *vaporetto* (little steamer — *line No. 1 "accellerato", omnibus service)* that runs to St. Mark's *(1/2 hour)*, via the Grand Canal. The *motoscafi* (motor-boats) are quicker *(Line No. 2, direct service — 1/4 hour)*, taking a short-cut through the Rio Nuovo. The gondolas *(1 hour)* are delightful, but it is wise to agree in advance on the charge as one would with a *facchino* (porter). In town, the canals can be crossed in the gondolas and *traghetti* (ferries). *For the circular line* (linea circolare) *and other vaporetto routes* (servizi di vaporetti) *see the plan pp 252 and 253.*

Seasons. — The best are spring and autumn. The Venice "Season" is in summer, with Film Festivals at the Lido, the Royal Regatta on the Grand Canal, etc.

In even years from June to October, the Arts Bienniale brings together the works of the world's leading artists in the Giardini Pavilion *(access via Riva dei 7 Martiri — DZ).*

IDLING IN VENICE

Venice invites *farniente* (idleness) and strolling. Its silence is restful and its sundials are inscribed with the words: *Horas non numero nisi serenas* (I count only the happy hours).

Venice is built on 117 islands; it has 150 canals and 400 bridges. A canal is called a *rio,* a square a *campo,* a street a *calle* or *salizzada,* and a quay a *riva* or *fondamenta.* The narrow streets, with their historic names, are paved with flagstones but have no footpaths; men charge along them pushing barrows and shouting *"Le gambe!"* ("Legs!") by way of warning. They are lined with flower decked balconies, Madonnas, shop signs and lanterns. Artisans' stalls and palaces stand side by side. The squares are charming. The brick bridges, with white stone trimmings, are pitched high to allow barges to pass under them.

The **Frari** Quarter **(ABX)** and that of Santa Maria Formosa **(CX)** are the most characteristic.

The hub of public life is the Piazza San Marco (St. Mark's Square — CY), where tourists and citizens sit on the terraces of the famous Florian and Quadri cafés to listen to the music, dream and see the mosaics of St. Mark's glow under the rays of the setting sun. The Quadri is more popular but the Florian is the best-known café: founded in 1720 it has received Byron, Goethe, George Sand, Musset and Wagner within its mirrored and allegory-painted walls.

The **Marzarie** or **Mercerie** **(CXY 52, 54, 51, 53)** start from the square which has sumptuous window displays of lace, jewellery, looking-glasses and ebony-wood or Murano glass negroes serving as torch-holders. The Marzarie lead to the Rialto Bridge. On the far side of this are the displays of greengrocers' *(erberie)* and fishmongers' shops *(pescherie).*

Meals in the *trattorie* (restaurants) are among the attractions of Venice. The fare consists chiefly of sea-food, *baccala* (dried cod) with anchovies, *scampi* (prawns), *calamaretti* (squid), *cicale di mare* (crustaceans — squill-fish), but also calf's liver cooked in the Venetian way. These dishes are often accompanied by the pleasant wines grown in the neighbouring regions to Venice: Soave, Valpolicella, the Adige Valley wines, Prosecco, Cabernet and others.

Gondolas and Gondoliers. — Gondolas are inseparable from a mental picture of Venice: gondolas dancing over the ripples or moored to the tall posts called *pali* near the Paglia Bridge **(CY)**, where the gondoliers' Madonna stands; gondolas for serenades lit with lanterns, gliding on the small canals at night, police gondolas, refuse collecting gondolas, fire service gondolas, goods delivery gondolas and even funeral gondolas with black pompoms. As for the gondoliers, wearing sailors' jumpers and straw hats with coloured ribbons, they murmur *gondola, gondola* as they propel their craft with a single oar, humming their songs.

The Venetians. — Venetians have pale complexions and lisp slightly. The golden haired Venetian woman is rare today.

Their sense of intrigue and their subtlety were displayed equally in love and in politics: Venetian procuresses, spies and ambassadors used to be equally famous for their skill. The black velvet mask and domino, so often worn in Venice, added to the secrecy. Venetians love pomp. The people are fond of festivals and gorgeous processions: at one time the Carnival, now the Feast of the Redeemer at the *Giudecca* (night between the third Saturday and Sunday of July) and the Grand Canal Regattas (first Sunday in September).

HISTORICAL NOTES

Venice was founded in AD 811 by the inhabitants of Malamocco, near the Lido, fleeing from the Franks. Guided by pigeons carrying little crosses, we are told, they settled on the Rivo Alto, known today as the Rialto. In 823 the bones of St. Mark the Evangelist were brought from Alexandria; he became the protector of the town. The Republic was developed under the rule of a *doge,* a name derived from the Latin *dux* (leader).

The Venetian Empire. — From the 9 to the 13C, Venice grew steadily richer; for the Venetians, the Crusades were as much a commercial as a religious enterprise. Istria and Dalmatia were conquered at the end of the 10C. The Crusaders, led by Doge Dandolo, captured Constantinople in 1204. The products of its sack flowed to Venice, while trade in spices, fabrics and precious stones from markets established in the East grew apace. Marco Polo (1254-1324) became Governor of a province under Kubla Khan and returned with fabulous riches. When a prisoner of the Genoese, he related his adventures in French in his *Book of Marvels.* In the 14C, Venice was at war with and finally defeated the Genoese.

Zenith. — The 15C saw Venetian power at its zenith: the Turks were defeated at Gallipoli in 1416 and the Venetians held the kingdoms of Morea, Cyprus and Candia (Crete) in the Levant. In Italy, between 1414 and 1428, they captured Verona, Vicenza, Padua, Udine, and then Brescia and Bergamo. The Adriatic became the Venetian Sea from Corfu to the Po.

Council of Ten. — The Council of Ten was an offshoot of the Grand Council, which included the names of 297 families recorded in the famous Golden Book. The members of the Council of Ten, who wore dark clothing and were called the Black Councillors, held full powers, legislative, executive and judicial. The Council kept a network of secret police: its sentences, not subject to appeal, were rendered in the absence of the accused and carried out immediately.

Decline. — The decline of Venice coincided with its period of artistic development. The capture of Constantinople by the Turks in 1453 started the decadence. The discovery of America caused a shift in the currents of trade. Venice had to keep up an exhausting struggle with the Turks, who seized Cyprus in 1500 but were defeated in 1571 in the naval battle of **Lepanto**, in which the Venetians played an important part. Their decline, however, was confirmed in the 17C when the Turks captured Candia (Crete) after a twenty-five-year siege. The "Most Serene Republic" came to an end in 1797. The Council of Ten destroyed the constitution. Bonaparte fulminated "I shall be an Attila for Venice" and ordered the *Bucentaur* to be burnt.

Venetian painting. — The Venetian school of painting *(see table pp 28 and 29)* is characterised by the predominance of colour and an evident sense of light in landscapes full of poetry. Portraits are sensual and theatrical in execution. Defects peculiar to the school are a certain lack of idealism, and the relative neglect of form, which was cultivated by the Florentines.

There were few Primitive painters except Paolo and Lorenzo Veneziano and a few artists of the school of Murano (the Vivarinis). The real beginnings of Venetian painting are exemplified by the Bellini family: Jacopo, the father, and Gentile (1429-1507) and Giovanni (1430-1516), his sons. The first was a narrative painter and a shrewd portraitist; the second a painter of gentle Madonnas, was a great colourist. **Giorgione** (1475-1510) showed himself to be a poet and a dreamer in his mystical subjects. Lorenzo Lotto (1480-1556), a realist, was the only one of his successors who escaped his influence. With them we may note Alvise Vivarini and Carpaccio (1455-1525), who left an accurate record of Venetian life.

The Renaissance ended in splendour with three great artists: Titian (1490-1576), born at Pieve di Cadore, introduced movement into painting and was also a skilled colourist; **Veronese** (1528-1588), a specialist in the use of green and in large mural decoration, sought pretty and luminous colours in his religious scenes, which he used as pretexts for describing the luxurious lives of the patricians of the Most Serene Republic; and finally **Tintoretto** (1518-1594), the son of a dyer, a visionary whose dramatic technique is supported by the use of chiaroscuro and contrasting colour. In this he was imitated by his brilliant pupil, El Greco.

The artists of the 18C recalled Venice and its peculiar light, grey-blue, iridescent and slightly misty: Canaletto, his pupil Guardi (1712-1793), who painted in luminous touches, Longhi, the author of intimate scenes, and Tiepolo (1690-1770), a master decorator.

British and French painters have loved Venice and painted various aspects of it: among them are Turner (1775-1851), Corot, Boudin, Monet, Marquet, Van Dongen and Carzou.

Spontaneity and colour are also found in the musicians of Venice, of whom the best known is Vivaldi (1678-1743), *il prete rosso* (the red-haired priest).

Venetian Palaces. — These have kept their form through the centuries, in spite of changes in style. The architect in search of the picturesque gives great prominence to the façade, in coloured marble, with many windows grouped in the centre and loggias and balconies mounted on brackets. The inner court is adorned with marble, friezes and large heads above the windows. The kitchens (on the top floor) are surmounted by tall conical chimneys peculiar to Venice.

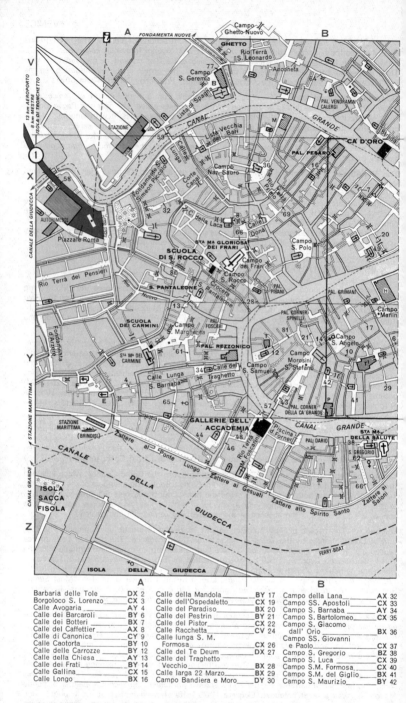

Literary Anthology. — Many, many writers have described Venice: Shakespeare in *Othello* and *The Merchant of Venice,* Byron, Keats, Goethe, Chateaubriand, Mme de Staël *(Corinne),* Musset and George Sand, Barrès, H. de Régnier *(Heures Incertaines),* Ruskin *(The Stones of Venice),* Suarès *(Voyage du Condottiere),* Giono *(Voyage en Italie),* Ben Jonson, Jules Romains *(Volpone),* James Morris *(Venice).*

Among the Italians, note Goldoni (the Italian Molière), Casanova and D'Annunzio.

■ MAIN SIGHTS *time: about 3 days*

ST. MARK'S SQUARE★★★ (Piazza San Marco) (CY)

St. Mark's Square is famous all over the world; it forms a great marble saloon, 175 m long by 80 m wide — 290 × 90 yds. All round, covered galleries shelter famous cafés and luxury shops. In front of the basilica are three flag-poles with bases which were carved in the 16C, symbolising the Venetian Kingdoms of Cyprus, Candia (Crete) and Morea.

The square opens on the Grand Canal through the delightful **Piazzetta★★★**, formerly called Il Broglio (Intrigue) because from 10 am to noon only the nobles were allowed to meet there and traffic in appointments and hatch their plots. The two granite columns surmounted by the Lion of St. Mark and the statue of St. Theodore were brought from Constantinople.

St. Mark's Basilica★★★ (Basilica San Marco). — The basilica was the State Church of the Republic, or more exactly the Chapel of the Doges, who attended ceremonies and made their public appearances in this building.

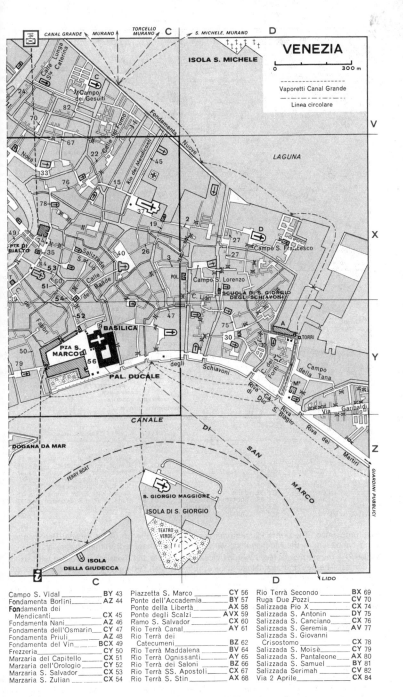

VENEZIA

0   300 m

- - - - - Vaporetti Canal Grande

——— Linea circolare

St. Mark's is a structure of mingled Byzantine and Western style, built from 1063 to 1073 to shelter the tomb of the Evangelist Mark. Changes were made at the time of the Renaissance and in the 17C. Despite the great variety of styles the outcome is a unified and harmonious ensemble. The rich decoration of marbles and mosaics on gilded backgrounds earned the basilica the name of the Chiesa d'Oro (golden church).

St. Mark's is built on the plan of a Greek Cross, 76 m long by 62 m wide - 250 × 202 ft; it is surmounted by a bulbous dome flanked by four smaller domes of unequal height placed on the arms of the cross; the narthex, at the west end of the church, opens on the square.

Façade. — This is pierced with five large doorways adorned with variegated marbles and sculptures. Between the doorway arches six curious bas-reliefs in the Primitive Christian style depict Hercules (at both ends), St. George, St. Demetrius, the Virgin Mary and the Archangel Gabriel.

The central doorway is surmounted by the four famous **bronze horses** (replaced by copies) dating from the Greco-Roman period, brought from Constantinople by Doge Dandolo in 1204. They were once alleged to be the work of Lysippus. In 1797, Napoleon I had them removed to Paris but they were returned to their original site at the fall of the French Empire. The vaulting and the archivolt of the central doorway are adorned with beautiful 13-14C sculptures illustrating symbolic animals, the Work of the Months, Virtues and Sibyls, and Trades and Prophets. 6C Byzantine bronze panels form the door.

At the lateral doorways, mosaics depict the Translation of the body of St. Mark. There is a picture of the basilica in its original form on the 13C door, last on the left.

The porphyry group, known as the **Tetrarchs** (4C), stands to the right of the façade, near the Doges' Palace. At the corner is the *pietra del bando* (proclamation stone), where laws

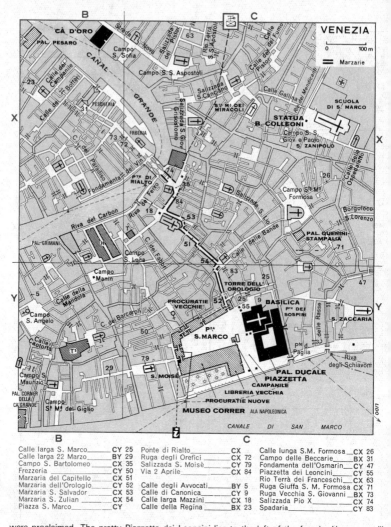

were proclaimed. The pretty Piazzetta dei Leoncini lies to the left of the façade. Here you will see a tympanum in the Moorish style with a Nativity and some Byzantine bas-reliefs.

Narthex. — The narthex is faced with multicoloured marble and mosaics and roofed with six little domes. The 13C mosaics depict scenes from the Old Testament. The fine Byzantine columns date from various periods, from the 6 to the 11C, and two of the three curious bronze doors, encrusted with silver, are 12C. The sarcophagi of the early doges were laid in the niches; two may still be seen in their original setting. One red marble flagstone marks the spot where the Emperor Frederick Barbarossa made obeisance to Pope Alexander III in 1177.

Interior. — The dazzling decoration is composed of rare marbles, porphyry and **mosaics★★★** of Byzantine (12-13C) and Renaissance (16C) inspiration. The 12C paving is highly decorative.

In the nave, on the reverse of the tympanum over the main doorway, a 13C mosaic portrays Christ, the Virgin and St. Mark. The Arch of Paradise over the narthex is adorned with 16C mosaics illustrating the Last Judgment based on cartoons by Tintoretto. The early 12C mosaic on the first dome above the nave, symbolises Pentecost: note the people about to be converted at the feet of the Apostles, and the angels on the squinches. Christ and the Virgin, surrounded by Prophets, are seen in the Byzantine mosaics on the walls, divided into ten panels, five on each side. On the arch dividing the dome above the nave from the central dome is a fine Crucifixion in the Byzantine style, also in mosaic (13C).

From the south aisle, where there is a porphyry stoup, you enter the baptistry, adorned with mosaics (14C) depicting the Life of Christ and that of St. John the Baptist. The Evangelical Mission of the Apostles is shown on the dome, while the Fathers of the Greek Church appear on the squinches. The baptistry contains the Sansovino Font (1545) and doges' tombs. The Chapel of St. Zeno, with interesting 13C mosaics of the life of St. Mark, is in the narthex.

In the north aisle stands the *capitello*, a small marble shrine topped by a large oriental agate. The north transept contains interesting mosaics: episodes in the life of St. John the Evangelist (on the dome); Last Supper and Miracles of Jesus after Veronese and Tintoretto (on the great arch between the dome of St. John the Evangelist and the central dome).

An Ascension, in mosaic, on the dome over the transept crossing, is 13C. It is flanked by the Evangelists (on the squinches of the dome) and, at the corners, by statues of angels in the Romanesque style. An iconostasis (stand for statues) in front of the chancel was made in 1394 and carries fine sculptures of Christ on the Cross, the Virgin and the Apostles.

The **chancel** *(open 10 am to 5 pm weekdays and 2 to 5 pm Sundays and holidays; tickets from a chapel on the right, valid also for the treasury: 300 lire)* is roofed with a dome whose Byzantine mosaics represent Christ and the Virgin among the Prophets. On the roof to the right another mosaic shows the Translation of the Relics of St. Mark. The Evangelist is entombed under the high altar, above which rises a green marble canopy supported by splendid oriental alabaster columns carved with scenes from the Gospels. The famous **Pala d'Oro★★★**, gold altarpiece, displays a wonderful assemblage of gold, silver, enamel and jewels. It was made at Constantinople in 976 and restored at Venice in 1105 and 1345.

Through the south transept you reach the rich **treasury★★★** *(same times of opening and ticket as for the chancel)*, partly formed in the 13C from booty from the pillage of Constantinople, by the Crusaders in 1204. It includes Byzantine gold work and enamels, the Pulpit of St. Mark, reliquaries, rare relics, a Thorn of the Crown, a Nail of the Cross, etc.

At the far end of the chancel are translucent alabaster columns and to the left a bronze door by Sansovino (16C) leading to the sacristy.

Before leaving the basilica, go up, through the narthex, to the galleries so as to get a good view of the mosaics and the domes. The **Marciano Museum** is in the galleries *(open 10 am to 5 pm; 300 lire)*. There is an attractive view from the Bronze Horses' platform.

Campanile★. — The straight lined simplicity of this 99 m - 324 ft high bell-tower makes a contrast with the riot of decoration on the basilica. From the summit *(access by lift: 10 am to 11 pm in summer; 10 am to 4 pm in winter; 800 lire)* there is a fine **panorama★★** of Venice.

The 10C campanile collapsed in 1902 and was rebuilt. In falling it damaged the *loggetta* (small loggia) built at its foot by Sansovino in 1549; this has since been skilfully repaired. The **loggetta** has very pure lines; note the fine 18C bronze doors and, in the niches, the statues by Sansovino. A delightful Madonna, also by Sansovino, will be found in the interior.

Clock Tower★ and Law Courts★ (Torre dell'Orologio e Procuratie). — With their galleries and columns these buildings make a graceful background for the square. The **Clock Tower★** dates from the end of the 15C. The dial bears the signs of the zodiac. On its summit are the famous *Mori* (Moors), a pair of giant bronze jacks which have been striking the hours for 500 years. Enter through the first door on the left in the Marzaria dell'Orologio; open 9 am to noon and 3 to 5 pm; closed Sunday afternoons and holidays; 1 000 lire. To the left of the Clock Tower, the **Procuratie Vecchie★** (Old Law Courts), built at the beginning of the 16C, served as a residence for the procurators attached to the building committee of the basilica, who were responsible for its upkeep. The **Procuratie Nuove★**, opposite, date from the 17C.

The **Ala Napoleonica**, which completes the square, was built by order of Napoleon in 1810. Under its arch is the entrance to the **Correr Museum★★** *(open 10 am to 4 pm weekdays, 9.30 am to 12.30 pm Sundays; closed Tuesdays and holidays; 500 lire)* which contains the historical and artistic collections of the city. In the *pinacoteca* (picture gallery), on the second floor, note the *pietà* by Antonello da Messina; the portrait of Doge Mocenigo by Gentile Bellini; a *pietà*, Madonna and Transfiguration by Giovanni Bellini; the famous Courtesans, by Carpaccio; a Madonna by Thierry Bouts, and a Crucifixion by Van der Goes.

Doges' Palace★★★ (Palazzo Ducale). — The palace was a symbol of Venetian power and glory and was both the residence of the doges and the seat of government. Built in the 12C in the place of an edifice dating from 825 AD, it was completely transformed in the 14, 15 and 16C.

A pretty geometrical pattern in white and pink marble lends great charm to the two façades. The ground floor gallery is supported by thirty-six columns with exquisite 14-15C historiated capitals representing Virtues, Vices, Months, Trades and Animals. The groups at the corners of the palace represent, from left to right, the Judgment of Solomon (attributed to Jacopo della Quercia), Adam and Eve, and Noah's Drunkenness (14-15C Gothic scultpures). The open upper gallery has seventy-one columns surmounted by quatrefoil oculi. The façades bear two loggias: one overlooking the Piazzetta built in 1536, and the other overlooking the jetty, in 1404.

The main entrance is the Porta della Carta, so-called because placards bearing decrees were posted on it. It is in the Flamboyant Gothic style (1442) and has on its tympanum a Lion of St. Mark before which Doge Foscari (copy made in the 19C — the doge's head only is kept in the palace) is kneeling. In the niches on the uprights are figures representing Strength and Prudence (right) and Temperance and Charity (left).

The Courtyard. — This is entered via the Porta della Carta and a covered passage which terminates in the Arco Foscari. On either side of this arch are replicas of statues of Adam and Eve by Rizzo (1476). The arch gives directly onto the famous Giants' Stairway (Scala dei Giganti) so called after the massive figures of Mars and Neptune by Sansovino (1554) at its summit.

The courtyard is a splendid example of Renaissance style, richly adorned with sculptures. The main façade is remarkable with its alternating rhythmic bays *(p 30)* and Venetian arches and its decoration of pilasters and friezes of oculi and lions' heads. The courtyard side of the covered passage includes the clock façade, dating from 1615 by B. Monopola. The wells with bronze copings date from the 16C. Doge Faliero, who was accused of conspiring against the Republic, was beheaded in this courtyard in 1355.

Interior. — Open 1 April to 15 October 8.30 am to 7 pm; the rest of the year 9.30 am to 4 pm. Closed 1 January, 1 May, 1, 21 November, 8, 25, 26 December; 1 500 lire. By way of the Scala d'Oro (Golden Stairway — Sansovino, 1558), which starts from the gallery on the first floor, one reaches the **doges' apartments** *(temporary exhibitions)*. These include the room of the Scarlatti (wearers of scarlet robes) and those of the Ducat, Grimani, Erizzo, the Stuccoes, the Pilosophers, etc., wherein are shown works by Bosch, Bellini and Tiepolo.

Continue once more up the Scala d'Oro to the floor above.

The square vestibule has a gilded ceiling with paintings by Tintoretto.

The elegant **Four Doors Room** is adorned with paintings by Tintoretto, who decorated the ceiling. There is also a picture of Doge Grimani adoring the Faith, painted partly by Titian.

The **Anticollegio** is a former waiting-room. It contains a fine chimney piece with atlantes (male figures used as columns). The Rape of Europa, on the wall, to the right, is a famous work by Veronese. On the other walls, Tintoretto painted an exceptional series of mythological subjects: the Marriage of Ariadne and Bacchus, Minerva repelling Mars, the Forge of Vulcan, Mercury and the Graces. On the ceiling is a painting of Venice bestowing honours and rewards by Veronese.

The **College Hall** used to be the ambassadors' audience room. The ceiling is decorated with eleven paintings by Veronese and his pupils (1677). Above the ducal throne Veronese painted the doge, Sebastiano Venier, giving thanks to Christ for the naval victory of Lepanto over the Turks. On the walls are allegories by Tintoretto with portraits of the doges.

The ceiling of the **Senate Chamber** is decorated with a remarkable Triumph of Venice by Tintoretto, who also painted the Descent from the Cross (above the ducal throne). After going back through the Four Doors Room, you enter the **meeting-chamber of the Council of Ten**, containing two paintings by Veronese (Old Oriental with a Young Woman and Juno offering the Doges' Headdress to Venice).

Go up to the four Armouries — one contains a suit of Henri IV — and on the landing you can see the *Bocca di Leone*, a model of a lion's head in which written denunciations were left.

Next is the **Grand Council Chamber★★★**, which is the finest room in the palace and measures 52 m by 23 m - 170 × 75 ft. The walls are adorned with paintings illustrating Venetian history. Over the doge's throne Tintoretto painted his masterpiece, **Paradise**, one of the largest composi-

tions in the world (22 m by 7 m - 72 × 23 ft). On the ceiling (near the throne) Veronese painted one of his masterpieces, the **Apotheosis of Venice**, while the cornice bears the portraits of
seventy-six Doges: one of the frames is empty — the missing one is Faliero the traitor.

The **Ballot Room★★★** is ornamented with paintings depicting Venetian naval victories. On
the cornice, the frieze continues the series of portraits of the Doges, the last one being that of
Ludovico Manin (1797). Next make for the Bridge of Sighs *(see below)* and the prisons, ending
the visit by the Censors' Room and the Avogaria.

Libreria Vecchia★ (Old Library). — A harmonious building designed by Sansovino in 1553.

The **Archaeological Museum** at No.17 *(open 9 am to 1.30 pm — 12.30 pm Sundays and
holidays; closed Mondays, 1 January, 25 April, 1 May, first Sunday in June, 15 August and
25 December; 500 lire)* contains Greco-Roman sculpture and Roman portraits.

The **Marciana Library** is housed in No.12 *(open 1 April to 30 September 10 am, 11 am and
noon. Closed Sundays and holidays, the week before Easter and fifteen days from end of
August to beginning of September)*. Through a door flanked by caryatids you enter the Sansovino Room, with a ceiling decorated by Veronese, Strozzi and others. The treasures of the
library are shown here, notably miniatures and especially the famous Grimani Breviary (Flemish
school, 15-16C).

To the left of the library, on the canal, are the 16C Zecca Mint, designed by Sansovino,
and the former royal gardens.

Bridge of Sighs★ (Ponte dei Sospiri). — The Bridge of Sighs connects the Doges' Palace with
the prisons, in which Casanova was incarcerated but from which he made a fantastic escape. It
dates from the 17C and owes its name to the lamentations of prisoners who were
conducted across it to their place of execution.

St. Moses' Church (San Moisè). — The church stands west of St. Mark's Square. Its curious
Baroque façade is dominated by the statue of the patriarch.

GRAND CANAL★★★ (Canal Grande)

The French writer Philippe de Commines wrote of the Grand Canal in the 15C: "I think it is
the finest street in all the world and has the finest houses." The canal is nearly 3 km - 2 miles
long and is lined with two hundred 12-18C marble palaces in which the patricians whose names
were in the Golden Book used to live.

Tour the Grand Canal in a steamer, or a gondola, starting from St. Mark's Square.

Right Bank (East). — Palazzo Corner della Ca' Grande, late Renaissance (Sansovino, 1537).
— Palazzo Corner-Spinelli, Renaissance (late 15 and early 16C).
— Palazzo Grimani, late Renaissance, the masterpiece of Sanmicheli (late 16C).
— Ca' d'Oro★★, the "golden house". This, the most elegant palace in Venice, is in the
   ornate Gothic style (1440). It used to be gilded all over.

   The Franchetti Gallery *(closed during reorganisation)* is housed in buildings round a
   pleasant court containing a well. It possesses tapestries and sculptures and a fine col-
   lection of pictures, including a St. Sebastian, by Mantegna; works by Carpaccio; a
   Venus with a Looking Glass, by Titian, a portrait by Van Dyck; two good Guardis; a
   Nativity by Filippino Lippi; a Venus Sleeping and a Young Faun by Bordone.
— Palazzo Vendramin-Calergi, Renaissance (1509), where Wagner died in 1883.

Left Bank (West). — Palazzo Dario, Gothic (1487), where Henri de Régnier lived.
— Palazzo Venier dei Leoni (18C) unfinished: **Peggy Guggenheim Gallery of Modern Art★.**
— **Palazzo Rezzonico★** *(same times of opening as the Museo Correr, p 255)* designed
   by Longhena (1680) and Massari (1745), imposing and well balanced. It houses a Set-
   tecento (18C) Museum; Venetian Baroque furniture, black and gold and heavily carved;
   ceilings and paintings by Gian-Battista Tiepolo; pastels by Rosalba Carriera (first floor);
   two masterpieces by Guardi (the Ridotto and the Nuns' Parlor); genre pictures by
   Longhi, and charming sketches by Gian-Domenico Tiepolo (second floor); porcelain and
   majolica; costumes (third floor — temporarily closed).
— Palazzo Foscari, 15C Gothic, brick. This was the residence of Doge Foscari, who was
   deposed by the Council of Ten in 1457 and died in this house next day.
— Palazzo Pisani: 15C, Gothic.
— **Palazzo Pesaro★,** open 10 am to 4 pm *(9.30 am to 12.30 pm Sundays and holidays); closed Mondays; 250 lire; free Sundays.* This is Longhena's Baroque masterpiece
   (1710): within is a gallery of modern art.

Rialto Bridge★ (Ponte di Rialto) (CX). — The graceful Rialto Bridge, built from 1588 to 1592 by
Antonio da Ponte, was designed to allow an armed galley to pass under it and has therefore, a
pronounced "hump". It is in the centre of the business quarter, is lined with shops and on the
outer sides, galleries affording views of the Grand Canal. The Fondaco dei Tedeschi, now a
Post Office, was used in the 12-14C as a warehouse by German merchants.

The lively Vegetable *(Erberia)* and Fish Markets *(Pescheria)* are on the west bank.

ACADEMY OF FINE ARTS★★★ (Gallerie dell'Accademia) (ABZ)

Open 9 am to 2 pm (1 pm on Sundays and holidays); closed Mondays; 1 000 lire.

The Academy is housed in the School and Church of St. Mary of Charity (Santa Maria
della Carità — 15C, with an 18C façade) and in the Lateran Canon's Convent. It displays a
complete review of Venetian painting from the 14 to the 18C.

The first room, a former chapterhall of the Brotherhood of Santa Maria with a 15C ceiling,
contains works by the few Venetian Primitives, notably Paolo and Lorenzo Veneziano (14C):
polyptychs of the Coronation of the Virgin, the Annunciation, etc.

In the following rooms you will see a **Sacra Conversazione,** Holy Conversation between the
Madonna and Saints, which is a majestic and decorative composition by Giovanni Bellini; pic-
tures by Carpaccio, a Madonna of the Orange Tree by Cima de Conegliano; a Madonna with
St. Mary Magdalen and St. Catherine by Giovanni Bellini; St. George, by the Paduan,
Mantegna; a St. Jerome, by the Tuscan, Piero della Francesca; a Madonna by the Ferrarian,
Cosimo Tura (1455), and a fine Portrait of a Young Man by Hans Memling, of Bruges. One of
the jewels of the collection, Giorgione's **Tempest** (painted *c.* 1505), is surrounded with works by
Giovanni Bellini. Pause before Tintoretto's famous Virgin of the Treasurers, full of ease and
dignity. There are also portraits by Lorenzo Lotto. Titian's last work, the **Pietà** (1576) is remarkable for its dramatic sense. In the **Meal in the House of Levi,** Veronese used all the magic of his
palette. There are also works by Tintoretto, notably his Miracles of St. Mark.

In the following rooms, the 17 and 18C are represented by paintings by Tiepolo, Piazzetta, Rosalba Carriera, Canaletto, Longhi and Guardi. Room XX contains the **Miracles of the Holy Cross**, a series of paintings of which three are by Gentile Bellini and one is by Carpaccio. Note especially a Gentile Bellini, the Procession of Relics in St. Mark's Square which is a faithful record of Venetian life in 1500.

The **Legend of St. Ursula** in the next room is a series of nine pictures (1490-c. 1500) by Carpaccio in which the painter displays an eye for picturesque detail.

Finally, the Presentation of the Virgin at the Temple, by Titian, is a picture full of charm.

PRINCIPAL CHURCHES

Church of St. Mary of Salvation★ (Santa Maria della Salute) (BZ). — The Salute was built at the entrance to the Grand Canal in the 17C by Longhena after an epidemic of plague, to fulfil a vow. It stands on an admirable site at the water's edge. The monumental interior is built on an octagonal plan and is surmounted by a dome. The sacristy *(open weekdays 9 am to noon and 3 to 6.30 pm — 5.30 pm 1 October to 31 March; 200 lire)* contains twelve paintings by Titian (altarpiece of St. Mark), and Tintoretto's **Marriage at Cana.**

Near Santa Maria are the charming **Campo San Gregorio** and a 15C Gothic church with a fine 15C doorway. At the end of the Punta della Salute (on the south side of the Grand Canal) is the **Dogana da Mar** (1677), or Maritime Customs Office. A revolving statue of Fortune, acting as a weather-vane, is mounted on a small tower.

Church of St. George Major★ (San Giorgio Maggiore) (CZ). — This church on the Island of San Giorgio, facing St. Mark's Square, was begun by Palladio in 1566 and completed in 1610 by Scamozzi, the designer of its noble façade. The interior is severe but of majestic proportions. Two paintings by Tintoretto hang in the chancel; they are the Harvest of Manna and the Last Supper, which is remarkable for its chiaroscuro. *The church is open from 9 am to 12.30 pm and 2 to 7 pm (5 pm November to March); the campanile is also open; ascent by lift (same times as the church in summer, by request in winter); 400 lire.*

See the cloisters by Palladio and the monumental staircase by Longhena (18C) in the monastery (now occupied by the Cini Foundation).

St. John and St. Paul's Church★ (Ss. Giovanni e Paolo or San Zanipolo) (CX). — This Gothic church (1234-1430), built by the Dominicans, stands in a spacious square. To the right of the church is a graceful 16C well; also a masterpiece by the Florentine, Verrocchio (1488), is the fine **equestrian statue★★**, full of power and energy, of the leader, Bartolomeo **Colleoni.**

This is the pantheon of Venice; it contains many tombs of doges and patricians. Among the paintings is a beautiful altarpiece by Giovanni Bellini (second altar in the south aisle) and an Assumption of the Virgin, an Adoration of the Shepherds and an Annunciation by Veronese on the ceiling of the Rosary Chapel *(entrance in the north transept).*

To the left of the church, in the square, is the **Scuola di San Marco** (St. Mark's School — CX), with a Renaissance **façade★** richly decorated with sculptures by Pietro and Tullio Lombardo. Note the doorway and its tympanum with a painting of St. Mark.

The **Rio dei Mendicanti** (Beggars' Canal), which runs beside the Scuola di San Marco, was frequently painted by Canaletto and Guardi.

St. Mary's Church★ (Santa Maria Gloriosa dei Frari) (AX). — *Open 9 am to noon and 3 to 6 pm; closed Sunday and holiday mornings; 200 lire.* This is a Franciscan Gothic church and the largest in Venice. Examine the magnificent painted altarpieces and particularly the **works of Titian★★**; the famous **Assumption** on the high altar, and, on the second altar in the north aisle, the admirable **Virgin of the Pesaro family.** A triptych of a **Madonna and Saints★** full of gentleness and feeling, by Giovanni Bellini, is shown in the sacristy.

St. Zachary's Church (San Zaccaria) (CY). — *Open 8.30 am to noon and 4 to 6 pm.* San Zaccaria, which dates from the Renaissance, stands in a pleasant square. It has a 13C campanile. In the north aisle (at the second altar) is an altarpiece of the **Madonna with Four Saints** *(illumination)* by Giovanni Bellini. In the San Tarasio Chapel there is a fresco by Andrea del Castagno (on the apse ceiling), and three splendid **altarpieces★★** by Antonio Vivarini (paintings) and Ludovico da Forli (sculpture).

SCHOOLS (Scuole)

The *Scuole,* typically Venetian institutions (there were 6 large ones) were confraternities which often assumed charitable roles. A *Scuola* usually included an assembly room, chapel and almshouse. Some undertook the education of poor or orphaned girls.

Scuola di San Rocco★★★ (AX). — *Open 9 am to 1 pm and 4 to 6.30 pm 1 March to 31 October; 10 am to 1 pm the rest of the year. Closed 1 January, Easter, Christmas and Sunday and holiday afternoons; 1 000 lire.* The 16C Renaissance building has a graceful façade of basket-handle arches and fluted Corinthian columns, with allegorical friezes and marble encrustations on the fronton. The great hall, with its ceilings, its strange Baroque woodwork and its paintings, is splendid. It contains an outstanding series of fifty-six canvases by Tintoretto, at which the painter worked for eighteen years. The best are: on the ground floor, an Annunciation and a Massacre of the Innocents; on the first floor, in the Great Hall, Manna Raining down from Heaven, the Miracle of the Brazen Serpent, Moses Drawing Water from the Rock (on ceiling), The Nativity, Ascension (on the walls); in the small Albergo Room, Christ before Pilate, the Ascent to Calvary and an immense dramatic Crucifixion which Tintoretto regarded as his best work. There are also paintings by Titian, Giorgione and Tiepolo (on the easels, first floor).

The **Church of San Pantaleon,** not far from the Scuola di San Rocco, has a magnificent 18C **ceiling★** painted in *trompe-l'œil* (false relief) by Fumiani, to the glory of St. Pantaleon.

Scuola di San Giorgio degli Schiavoni★ (DX — 1451). — *Open 9.30 am to 12.30 pm and 3.30 to 6.30 pm 1 April to 31 October; 10 am to 12.30 pm and 3 to 6 pm the rest of the year; closed on Mondays, 1 May, 15 August, Sunday and holiday afternoons; 500 lire.* This institution received natives of Esclavonia, now called Dalmatia, who were citizens of the Venetian Republic, and in particular old seamen. The Renaissance oratory is adorned with exquisite **paintings by Carpaccio★★** relating the Story of St. Jerome, the Legend of St. George and the Miracle of St. Tryphon.

Scuola dei Carmini★ (AY). — *Open 8 am (9 am in winter) to noon and 2 to 5 pm; closed Sunday and holiday afternoons; 500 lire.* Inside the ceiling is decorated with a masterly group of paintings by Tiepolo including a fresco depicting the **Virgin in Glory,** with the Child, presenting the scapulary to Blessed Simon Stock.

■ ADDITIONAL SIGHTS

Arsenal (DY A). — The Arsenal was founded in 1104 and rebuilt in the 15 and 16C. The entrance to the basin is guarded by two towers dating from 1574. The monumental gateway to their left (1460) is preceded by Baroque statues and lions of Greek origin. The Arsenal was famous throughout Europe. In its heyday it could build and equip a small galley in a single day.

Naval Museum (DY M1). — *Open 9 am to 1 pm; closed Sundays and holidays; 200 lire.* The museum near the Riva San Biagio, contains several models of 16-18C Venetian ships (galleys, barges, galleons...) and a small model of one of the doges' famous *Bucentaurs* (state barges).

Palazzo Labia (AV B). — *Radio and Television Centre (concerts); authorisation needed to visit.* This 18C palace contains a room completely covered in frescoes by Tiepolo depicting the story of Antony and Cleopatra. Several ceilings in the palace are also by the artist.

Giudecca Island (Isola della Giudecca) (CZ). — Quiet, picturesque quarters with small gardens surround the Church of the Redeemer, built after the plague of 1579. There is a Madonna and Child with Angel Musicians by Alvise Vivarini in the sacristy.

Ghetto (AV). — In the 16C the Jews were relegated to the Campo del Ghetto Nuovo.

Palazzo Querini-Stampalia (CX). — *Open 10 am to 4 pm (10 am to 3 pm 1 November to 1 March and Sundays and holidays throughout the year); closed Mondays, 1 January, 25 April, 1 May, 15 August, Easter and Christmas; 500 lire, free on Sundays.* Picture gallery containing a series of works by Donato and Caterino Veneziano (Coronation of The Virgin), the Florentine Lorenzo di Credi (Adoration of The Virgin), Giovanni Bellini (Presentation of Jesus in the Temple), Palma il Vecchio (Sacred Conversation), V. Catena (Judith), and Pietro Longhi (Scenes of Life in Venice in the 18C).

Churches. — There are approximately 200 churches in Venice, nearly all interesting. Among them are:

1. East of the Grand Canal: **Santa Maria dei Miracoli★ (CX)** *(to visit apply to the Rector of the church of San Camoiano ☏ 5390)*, built in 1489 by P. Lombardo the church is a jewel of Renaissance architecture adorned with multicoloured marbles; the **Gesuiti (CV C)**, in the Baroque style of the 18C, with a curious Martyrdom of St. Lawrence by Titian (first chapel on the left); **San Francesco della Vigna (DX D)**, designed by Sansovino (16C), with a façade by Palladio and Classical cloisters. Inside, note two remarkable paintings of the Virgin and Child by Br. Antonio da Negroponte, in the south transept, and Giovanni Bellini, in the Holy Chapel *(the chapel can be opened and lit from 9 am to noon and 4 to 7 pm; access through the north transept).*

2. West of the Grand Canal: **San Sebastiano (AY E)**, 16C, has interesting **interior decoration★** including paintings (Story of Queen Esther on the ceiling) by Veronese and a curious organ dating from the end of the 16C. The Church **dell'Angelo Raffaele (AY F)** contains seven delightful **paintings★** (Scenes from the Life of Tobias) of the 18C, attributed to one of the Guardis.

EXCURSIONS

The **Lagoon,** separated from the sea by a coastal strip known as the Lido is tidal and very pleasant to explore by *vaporetto.* In addition to the sailings mentioned below, excursions to the islands of the lagoon, leave from the Riva degli Schiavoni **(CDY)** and the station.

Burano★. — *From the Fondamenta Nuove* **(CV)**: *3/4 hour by steamer.* A fishing village known for its lace and its painted houses.

Chioggia★. — *Access via the Lido — Line No. 11: bus to Alberoni, ferry, bus to Pallestrina and motor-boat (about 2 hours).* Chioggia is an ancient seaside town engaged in fishing. Follow the two main canals lined with colourful fishing boats and spanned by hump-backed bridges. Large ships are berthed along the wide San Domenico Canal. The main street (Corso del Popolo) is lined with houses in the Venetian style of the 16 and 17C.

The Lido★★★. — *From San Zaccaria, direct boat service (1/4 hour). From Piazzale Roma, direct steamer service (40 minutes). From Tronchetto 35 minutes by ferry boat, and 1 hour to Punta Sabbioni.* The Lido is one of the most fashionable resorts on the Adriatic. The casino, designed on modern lines, is one of the few in Italy in which gambling is allowed. In winter it operates in Palazzo Vedramin in Venice. Another pleasant modern building is the marble palace in which the International Film Festival is held in August and September each year.

Lido di Iesolo★. — *By steamer to Punta Sabbioni and by motor coach to Iesolo.* This seaside resort was founded quite recently but is now much frequented.

Murano★. — *From the Fondamenta Nuove* **(CV)**; *1/4 hour by steamer.* This town on an island in the Lagoon, whose main street consists of a canal lined with Renaissance houses, has been a great glass-working centre since 1292. In the 15C it was also the headquarters of a school of painting founded by Antonio Vivarini. Continuing up the canal, to the left on the far bank is the **Glasswork Museum★** (Museo d'Arte Vetraria): *open weekdays 10 am to 4 pm; Sundays and holidays 9.30 am to 12.30 pm; closed Tuesdays; 500 lire.* The museum is in the 15-17C Palazzo Giustiniani and contains a unique collection of glassware from ancient to modern times, decorated, painted, engraved and in filigree. Note the lustres and Venetian looking-glasses.

A little farther on the right, the early 12C Church of **Santi Maria e Donato** *(restoration of the church interior in progress)* which is in the Veneto-Byzantine style, has a fine apse with galleries one above the other. The campanile is both slim and solid. At its base is the War Memorial.

San Francesco del Deserto. — *Reached by ship from Murano.* This is a Franciscan monastery. St. Francis landed on the island when returning from the Orient in 1220.

San Michele. — *From the Fondamenta Nuove: 5 minutes by steamer.* This is the burial ground of Venice and resting-place of Stravinsky. It contains a pretty 15C Renaissance church with 14C cloisters.

Torcello★★. — *From the Fondamenta Nuove* (CV); *3/4 hour by steamer.* This village was once an important town and the seat of a bishop; it began to decline in the 9C AD. The main **Piazza★**, where the chief buildings are, is now grass-grown. The Veneto-Byzantine Church of Santa Fosca, built at the beginning of the 11C on an octagonal plan, is surrounded by a peristyle with Byzantine capitals. To the left of Santa Fosca stands the 9-11C **cathedral★**. This has a fine 11C mosaic pavement, a nave and two aisles whose arches rest on Greek marble columns with 11C Corinthian capitals and an iconostasis closing the nave adorned with 11-12C Byzantine bas-reliefs (peacocks front to front, lions and foliage) and 15C paintings. To the left of the iconostasis is a curious pulpit. The cathedral contains several fine Byzantine **mosaics★★**: the most spectacular, on the back of the façade, is 12-13C and depicts the Last Judgment; a second, which is in the apse, dates from the 13C and, with admirable purity and nobility, pictures the Mother of God. A 7C baptistry stands next to the cathedral *(excavations in progress)*. There is also a small archaeological museum with finds from the excavations including Byzantine stone fragments from the 10-13C.

The Brenta Riviera★★. — *Description p 68.*

VENOSTA, Val ★ Trentino-Alto Adige
Michelin map 988 4.

The Val Venosta is a transverse furrow through which the Adige River flows. It is bounded on the north by the Venostan Alps, dominated by the glacier-covered mass of the Palla Bianca (alt 3 736 m - 12 258 ft), and on the south by the Rhaetic Alps and the Ortlès Cevedale Massif. The Upper Val Venosta, whose capital is **Malles Venosta** communicates with the Valtellina *(see p 249)*, which is the Upper Valley of the Adda, through the Stelvio Pass *(p 232)*.

When going through the Val Venosta you will see fruit trees (apples) covering the lower slopes, mountain style houses, castles (Sluderno, Castelbello) and several pleasant **country churches** in the Romanesque style, sometimes painted with frescoes.

VENTIMIGLIA Liguria
Michelin maps 988 12 — 195 29 — *Local map p 199* — Pop 27 226
Town plan in Michelin Red Guide Italia (hotels and restaurants).

Ventimiglia lies at the mouth of the Roya Valley. It has an old quarter in terraces on the hillside west of the valley, and a modern lower town to the east where a Flower Market is held in the Via Roma. The public gardens, shaded by palm trees, border the sea.

Old Town★ (Città Vecchia). — The entire old town is cut by steps and covered ways; follow the alleys, locally known as *scuri,* and you will discover one old house after another. From the end of the Via del Capo there is a wide view of the horizon from Bordighera to Cap Ferrat. Interesting buildings to visit: the cathedral much restored in the 11 and 12C; the baptistry, built in the 11C, still possesses its original 5C piscina and a baptismal font of 1100; the 17C "Neri" Oratory and the Church of San Michele, a former Benedictine priory dating from the 11 and 12C.

EXCURSIONS

Mortola Inferiore. — *West, 5 km - 3 miles. Description p 152.*

Val di Nervia★. — *North, 21 km - 13 miles.* From Ventimiglia to Pigna, passing through Dolceacqua, which is known for its wines, its hump-backed bridge and the ruins of the Doria family castle, you note the transition from Mediterranean to mountain vegetation.

Pigna★ seems strikingly foreign. The alleys, vaulted passages and arcades of this curious little town will surprise the visitor. In the 15C church is a polyptych by Giovanni Canavese.

VERCELLI Piedmont
Michelin maps 988 12 and 26 16 — Pop 54 543
Town plan in Michelin Red Guide Italia (hotels and restaurants).

Vercelli is an important rice market. It has picturesque, quiet old quarters, especially between the cathedral and the Piazza Cavour, which is the centre of the town.

Buildings. — The **Abbey Church of Sant'Andrea** (St. Andrew — *entrance in Via Galileo Ferraris),* near the station and the fine public garden southwest of the cathedral, is in 13C Cistercian Gothic style; the tympana of the doors bear sculptures by the school of the Parmesan, Antelami. Left of the church, the buildings of a former Cistercian monastery encircle a small cloister, part of which dates from the 15C. The arches are supported by groups of four small Romanesque columns; the group provides a sight rare in Italy of the transition from Romanesque to Gothic architecture.

The **Church of San Cristoforo,** behind Piazza Mazzini, has on its high altar a masterpiece by the 16C Piedmontese painter Gaudenzio Ferrari, the Madonna of the Orange Tree.

La VERNA Monastery ★★ Tuscany
Michelin map 988 15 — 45 km - 27 miles — north of Arezzo — Alt 1 128 m - 3 701 ft

A superb and impressive countryside is traversed by the roads leading to the Monastery of La Verna *(open 8 am to 7 pm; 8 am to noon and 1 to 6 pm in winter),* overlooking chalk cliffs and standing in grim solitude in an ancient clump of pines and beeches. The monastery was founded in 1214 by St. Francis of Assisi, who received the stigmata there on 14 September 1224. It afterwards became a popular place of pilgrimage.

You can see the Chapel of Santa Maria degli Angeli, the bed of St. Francis, the "Sasso Spicco", the Chapel of the Stigmata.

The basilica contains several terracottas by Andrea della Robbia, of which a remarkable pair represent the Annunciation and the Nativity, and an impressive organ.

VERONA ★★★ Venetia ___

Michelin map **988** 4 — Pop 270 868

Verona stands on the banks of the Adige in a setting of cypress covered hills. It is red and ochre coloured, and pink, too, thanks to its marble, and it is, after Venice, the finest art centre in Venetia. The fashionable Piazza Bra, with its garden shaded by great cedar trees and café terraces, is linked by the Via Mazzini to the heart of the old town.

The opera season at the Arena and the theatrical summer season *(June to September)* both draw large crowds. In the economic sphere, the International Agricultural and Livestock Fairs offer feasts of colour. The wines and fruits of the region are famous. The town possesses one of the largest fruit cold stores in Europe.

HISTORICAL NOTES

Enclosed in its 16C fortifications, Verona was regarded as the key to northern Italy. The town actually reached its zenith, however, under the Scaligers, Princes of the Scala, between 1260 and 1387. Then it passed to the Visconti of Milan before submitting to Venetian rule from 1405 to 1801.

Romeo and Juliet. — These two young people immortalised by Shakespeare, belonged to rival families: Romeo to the Montecchi (Montagues), who were Guelphs and supported the Pope, and Juliet to the Capuleti (Capulets), who were Ghibellines and supported the Emperor Frederick I. The scenes of the ball, the balcony, the secret marriage, the farewells, the suicide of Romeo and then of Juliet all set in Verona, took place about 1302.

Pisanello and the Veronese School. — Pisanello (1387-1451) was born and worked at Verona but also travelled to Venice, Florence, Ferrara, Mantua and Rimini. He was a draughtsman, painter and medal-maker who combined imagination and poetic fantasy with love of detail and of nature: he was both a good animal painter and a shrewd portraitist. His taste for the exotic was probably influenced by the active trade relations between Verona and the Orient.

The Veronese school (15 to 16C) is rich in landscape painters and portraitists. Note the names of Francesco Buonsignori, Liberale da Verona, Morone and Girolamo dai Libri, painter and miniaturist. Paolo Veronese was born at Verona but was Venetian by adoption.

The Congress of Verona. — In 1822 the Congress of Verona between members of the Holy Alliance gathered crowned heads who showed great diligence in attending social occasions. Chateaubriand, then France's Foreign Minister, maintained that France should intervene in Spain to re-establish order; this was done by the capture of the Trocadero in the Bay of Cadiz in the following year. Apart from this, no decision was reached. This Congress found a historian in Chateaubriand, who extracted material for three volumes from its record of nullity.

VERONA

0   300 m

★★SAN ZENO MAGGIORE

Anfiteatro (Via)	CY 2
Cappello (Via)	CY
Erbe (Piazza delle)	CY 6
Leoni (Via)	CY 8
Mazzini (Via)	CY
Porta Borsari (Corso)	CY
Roma (Via)	BYZ
S. Anastasia (Corso)	CY
Signori (Piazza dei)	CY 24
Stella (Via)	CY 25

■ MAIN SIGHTS time: 5 hours

Centre of the Town★★★ (Centro della Città). — The nucleus of the old town includes pleasant squares connected by alleys and arcaded passages or stairways.

Piazza delle Erbe★★. — This, the Square of Herbs, is the former Roman forum, round which chariot races used to be run. Today it is a lively and colourful spot, especially when the stalls and awnings of the flower, fruit and vegetable market are set up. In line, down the middle of the square, stands a column dating from 1401, the *capitello* of the *podesti*, 16C mayors or governors — a rostrum from which decrees and sentences were proclaimed — the fountain known as the Madonna of Verona, with a Roman statue and a Venetian column surmounted by the winged Lion of St. Mark (1523).

Palaces and old houses, some with pink marble columns, make an attractive framework round the square. Behind the lion, on the north side, are the Baroque Palazzo Maffei (1668) and, to the left of the palace, the Gardello Tower (1370); on the west, the Merchants' House (1301) crowned with battlements, and on the east, near the lion, those of the Mazzantis (16C) and the Scaligers, with traces of frescoes, and the tall Lamberti Tower.

In the Via Cappello (No. 23) is the 13C palace of the Capulets **(CY K)**, with Juliet's balcony *(open 9 am to noon and 2.30 to 6 pm; 5.30 pm in winter; closed Mondays; 300 lire)*. Go through the Arco della Costa to reach the Piazza dei Signori.

Piazza dei Signori★★. — This square, thronged with pigeons and children, looks like an open-air *salon* in its sober elegance. The statue of Dante stands in the centre.

The 12C town hall on the south side is dominated on its right by the Lamberti Tower *(same times as above, 300 lire or 500 lire by lift)*, built of brick and stone, with an octagonal summit. This building is connected by an arch with the 12-16C Law Courts.

The late 13C Governor's Palace on the east side, opposite, with a fine Classical doorway, was the residence of the Scaligers before it became that of the Venetian Governors. Giotto worked on its interior decoration.

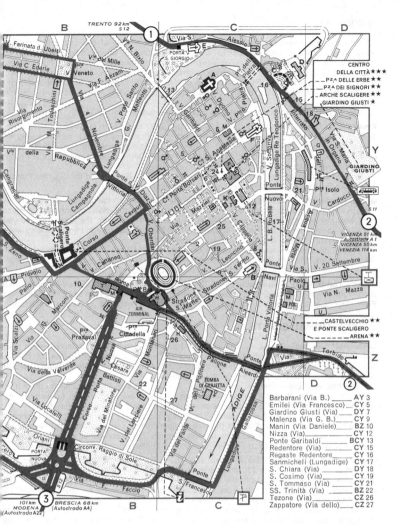

The **Loggia del Consiglio** on the north side is a light and graceful Renaissance building with refined decoration. To the west, up five pink marble steps and under an arch, you will reach the charming little Piazza Mazzanti, with a pink marble well and old houses with great balconies.

Tombs of the Scaligers★★ (Arche Scaligere). — The Scaligers had their tombs built between their palace and their church *(open 9 am to noon and 2.30 to 6 pm; 2.30 to 5.30 pm in winter; closed Mondays; 500 lire)*. The sarcophagi bear the arms of the family, with the symbolical *scala* (ladder). The largest tombs, those of Mastino II (died 1351) and Cansignorio (died about 1375), are Gothic mausolea surrounded by marble balustrades and 14C wrought iron grilles. They are decorated with sculptured religious scenes and statues of saints in niches.

Over the door of the Romanesque Church of **Santa Maria Antica** is the tomb of the popular Cangrande I (died 1329). On the summit he is shown mounted on a horse.

Old Castle and Bridge of the Scaligers★★ (Castelvecchio e Ponte Scaligero). — The Old Castle was built by Cangrande II Scaliger in 1354. It is in two parts, separated by a passage overlooked by the keep. The building has undergone considerable restoration in the last few years.

The castle contains an interesting **museum of art★** whose paintings, sculpture and collections of arms and jewellery are well displayed *(open 9 am to 7 pm in July and August; 9 am to noon and 2.30 to 6 pm the rest of the year; closed Mondays, 1 January, 25 April, 1 May, 15 August, 1 November, Easter and 8, 25 and 26 Christmas; 1 000 lire)*.

On the ground floor are Veronese statues and carvings of the 10 to the 15C.

In the original apartments can be seen 12 to 16C frescoes executed by local artists as well as canvases by Pisanello, Stefano da Verona, Giambono, Iacopo, Gentile and Giovanni Bellini, Mantegna and Carpaccio. The rooms known as the Galleria contain works by artists of the Veronese school, such as Morone, Cavazzola, Girolamo dai Libri and finally Veronese himself. The Venetian school is represented by Tintoretto, Guardi, Tiepolo and Longhi.

A 1C Roman arch has been reconstructed east of the palace.

The **Scaliger Bridge** links the castle with the north bank of the river, from which a pretty view of the fortified area can be enjoyed. The bridge itself, with its Ghibelline battlements, was built in 1354. It was destroyed by the Germans in 1945 but has been rebuilt.

St. Zeno Major★★ (Chiesa di San Zeno Maggiore). — St. Zeno is one of the finest Romanesque churches in northern Italy. It was built on the basilical plan and in the Lombard style *(see p 27)*.

Seen from the outside, its most remarkably sober and well proportioned features are the campanile, with its alternating courses, and the façade, which is pierced with a rose window. The 14C tower of the former abbey stands on the left.

The entrance porch, supported by two lions, shelters admirable 11-12C **doors★★★** sheathed in bronze plates on which scenes from the Old and New Testaments are depicted in an expressive and lively way. On either side are remarkable 12C bas-reliefs representing scenes from the Bible and the Golden Legend, by the master sculptors Nicolò and Guglielmo. On the tympanum of the doorway is a statue of St. Zeno.

The imposing interior has a keel-shaped roof. On the reverse of the façade is a processional cross painted in 1360 by Lorenzo Veneziano. At the high altar is a splendid **triptych★★** (1459) of the Madonna and Saints, in which Mantegna shows his mastery of drawing and perspective. This masterpiece, after being "borrowed" by Napoleon, was returned, in part, after the fall of the Emperor. The panels of the predella are still in the Louvre in Paris and in the museum at Tours. Note also, on the chancel barrier, the late 14C statues of Christ and the Apostles.

North of the church are Romanesque cloisters, remodelled in the 14C.

Arena★★. — *Open 9 am to noon and 2.30 to 6 pm (2.30 to 5.30 pm in winter); closed Mondays; 300 lire.* This amphitheatre, among the largest in the Roman world, is 152 m long by 128 m wide and 30 m high - 500 × 420 × 100 ft. It could accommodate nearly 25 000 spectators. Its origin is believed to date from the end of the 1C. Musical performances are still given in the theatre, which has perfect acoustics.

In the **Piazza Bra** are the Neo-Classical town hall (1838) by Barbieri and the dignified Palazzo delle Gran Guardia (1610), prolonged by 14C battlemented walls.

Giusti Gardens★ (Giardino Giusti). — *Apply to the caretaker at the palace; 800 lire.* These gardens of a palace dating from 1580 are laid out in terraces in the Italian manner with avenues lined with pruned cypress trees and grottoes. A shady path climbs to the summit where you can enjoy splendid views of Verona. It was here that Maffei (dramatist and archaeologist) used to hold meetings of the Arcadian Academy in the 18C.

A little distance to the west, **Santa Maria in Organo,** (DY G) the Renaissance church of the Olivetan monks, contains fine inlaid stalls (1499 — *ask the sacristan to light them).* The central dome and the transept vaults are adorned with frescoes by D. Morone (late 15C).

Juliet's Tomb (Tomba di Giulietta) (CZ). — The tomb is in the Capuchin cloisters *(entrance from the Via del Pontiere; same times of opening as for the Arena)* south of the town near the Adige River. The cloisters adjoin the little church in which Juliet's marriage to Romeo took place.

■ ADDITIONAL SIGHTS

Cathedral★★ (Duomo) (CY A). — The cathedral has a 12C Romanesque chancel, Gothic nave and Classical tower. The remarkable main doorway in the Lombard Romanesque style is adorned with figures of the prophets on the splayings and with bas-reliefs by Nicolò, two of which represent Roland and Oliver, on the uprights.

The interior displays fine red marble pillars. The altarpiece of the first altar on the left as you enter is decorated with a serene Assumption by Titian *(ask the sacristan to illuminate it).* The chancel is enclosed by a marble balustrade designed by Sanmicheli in the 16C.

To the left of the cathedral within Romanesque cloisters, the remains of the original basilica have been laid bare. Parts of the mosaic flooring and some columns can be seen.

The canons' quarters are pleasant to walk through. They consist of canons' houses, a bishop's palace and the Baptistry of San Giovanni in Fonte *(apply to the sacristan).*

Church of St. Anastasia★ (Sant'Anastasia) (CY F). — The church is Gothic; it was begun at the chevet at the end of the 13C and completed in the 15C. The campanile is remarkable; a good view of it can be had from the banks of the Adige. The façade is pierced with a 14C double doorway, adorned with frescoes and sculptures. To its left are a Gothic tomb and the Church of St. Peter the Martyr, in the Lombard Gothic style.

At the transept crossing, the pilasters at the entrance to the Pellegrini chapel (second from the right), bear four figures of the apostles painted by Michele da Verona. Inside, note the seventeen **terracottas★** (1435) depicting the Life of Jesus by Michele da Firenze.

In the Cavalli chapel (first on the right) there is a famous fresco by the Veronese, Altichero, a disciple of Giotto, showing Knights of the Cavalli family being presented to the Virgin by their patron saints. In the main chapel is the tomb of the mercenary leader Cortesia Serego.

Church of St. Firmanus Major★ (San Fermo Maggiore) (CYZ B). — This picturesque church was built in the 11-12C over an older church, which today serves as a crypt. The church was remodelled in the 14C; the Romanesque and Gothic styles are mingled in the façade. The interior, with its timberwork and 14C frescoes, has a curious appearance: it contains numerous works of art, including a pulpit dated 1396, the 16C tomb of the physicist Girolamo della Torre, and a **fresco★** of the Annunciation by Pisanello, surrounding the Brenzoni mausoleum (1430).

Roman Theatre★ (Teatro Romano) (CY C). — *Same times of opening as for the Arena.* The theatre dates from the time of Augustus. Theatrical performances are given here in summer. Within its walls stands the Church of Santa Libera, whose construction was begun in the 10C; it has a Gothic porch. Do not fail to go up to the left to the former monastery of San Girolamo *(lift — archaeological museum).* It has delightful little cloisters.

Castle of St. Peter (Castel San Pietro) (CY D). — Here the Romans built their fortifications, and here lived King Theodoric of the Ostrogoths and King Alboin of the Lombards (died AD 573). From the terraces there is a magnificent **view★★** of the town.

St. George's Church (San Giorgio in Braida) (CY E). — San Giorgio, standing on the bank of the Adige, is a fine 16C Renaissance church with a dome and a campanile designed by Sanmicheli. It contains valuable pictures, notably a Madonna by Girolamo dai Libri (fourth chapel on the left) and a Martyrdom of St. George by Paolo Veronese on the high altar.

Corso Cavour (BY). — This, formerly the main street of Verona, is lined with imposing palaces, the most remarkable being the Palazzo Bevilacqua, by Sanmicheli (1530).

██ VIAREGGIO ★★ Tuscany _____

Michelin map ▓▓▓ 14 — *Local map p 200* — Pop 59 460

This luxurious and fashionable seaside resort, the pearl of the Tyrrhenian coast, is full of life and gaiety in summer. Many amusements are available to holidaymakers and the Carnival includes a great masked procession. There is a picturesque canal-port.

The two **pinewoods,** the Western and the Eastern (Ponente and Levante), consisting of still, silent sea and umbrella pines, are divided by well kept rides.

Torre del Lago Puccini. — *Southeast, 5 km - 3 miles.* This is where the composer **Puccini,** born at Lucca (1858-1924), wrote *La Bohème, Tosca* and *Madame Butterfly.* Nearby lies **Lake Massaciuccoli,** on the shores of which are Puccini's tomb and villa with mementoes.

Michelin map **988** 4 5 — Pop 118 178

The proud and noble city of Vicenza lies in a pretty setting at the foot of the Berici Mountains. The rich men of the past built nearly one hundred palaces here, which give the town the air of a Venice on land.

Palladio. — Andrea di Pietro, known as Palladio, the last great architect of the Renaissance, was born at Padua in 1508 and died at Vicenza in 1580. His influence was great, both in Italy and abroad. After studying the monuments in Rome and the work of Vitruvius, a Roman architect, he perfected the Palladian style, characterised by pilasters and columns of composite structure on a colossal scale and an attic often surmounted by statues or trophies. The just proportions, noble design, architectural rhythm and logically vertical orders compel admiration. Palladio therefore quickly won great success; his treatise on architecture, in four volumes, is world famous. His pupil, Scamozzi (1552-1616), another native of Vicenza, carried on his style.

■ **MAIN SIGHTS** *time: 2 hours*

Piazza dei Signori★★. — Like St. Mark's Square in Venice, the square is an open-air meeting-place and a relic of the forum of antiquity. As in the Piazzetta in Venice, there are two columns; these bear effigies of the Lion of St. Mark and the Redeemer.

With the lofty **Torre Bissara**★, a 12C belfry, the **"basilica"**★★ (1549) occupies one whole side of the square. The elevation is one of Palladio's masterpieces, with two superimposed galleries in the Doric and Ionic orders, admirable for their power, proportion and purity. The great keel —shaped roof destroyed by bombing, has been rebuilt. The building was in no way religious but was a meeting-place for the Vicenzan notables.

The 15-16C **Monte di Pietà** opposite, with buildings framing the Baroque façade of the Church of St. Vincent, is adorned with frescoes. The **Loggia del Capitanio**, formerly the residence of the Venetian Governor, to the left, at the corner of the Via del Monte, was begun to the plans of Palladio in 1571 and left unfinished. It is characterised by its colossal orders with composite capitals and statues and stuccoes commemorating the naval victory of Lepanto *(p 251)*.

Corso Andrea Palladio★. — This, the main street of Vicenza, is embellished by many palaces designed by Palladio and his pupils. Starting from the Piazzale De Gasperi at the very beginning of the Corso, several fine Renaissance examples catch the eye. Next you reach the Corso Fogazzaro, where the Palazzo Valmarana, begun by Palladio in 1566, stands at No. 16. Farther along the Corso Palladio, on the right, the Town Hall (1592) is one of the most successful works of Scamozzi. In the Contrà Porti, at No. 12, is the Palazzo Thiene, and opposite, at No. 11, the Palazzo Barbarano Porto.

Return to the Corso Palladio. The rear façade of the Palazzo Thiene, which was built by Palladio, runs, on the left side, for nearly the entire length of the Via San Gaetano Thiene. The Palazzo Da Schio at No. 145 in the Corso Palladio in the Venetian Gothic style was formerly known as the "Ca d'Oro" because the frescoes that used to cover it were on a gold background. Destroyed in 1944, it was rebuilt in 1950. At the end is Palladio's own 16C house.

Olympic Theatre★ (Teatro Olimpico). — *Open 9.30 am to 12.30 pm and 3 to 5.30 pm (2 to 4 pm, 15 October to 15 March); closed Sundays afternoons and holidays; 600 lire*. This splendid building was designed by Palladio on the model of the theatres of antiquity. It was completed by Scamozzi and opened in 1583. The **stage**★★ is one of the finest in existence, with its superimposed niches, columns and statues and its streets painted in *trompe-l'œil* (false relief) by Scamozzi.

Municipal Museum★ (Museo Civico). — *Open 9.30 am to 12.30 pm and 2.30 to 4.30 pm (Sundays and holidays, 10 am to noon); closed Sundays afternoons and Mondays; 400 lire*. The museum is in the Palazzo Chiericati, one of Palladio's most original buildings. The collections of paintings are on the first floor: they include Venetian Primitives (Paolo Veneziano: The Dormition of the Virgin); a Crucifixion attributed to Memling; canvases by Bartolomeo Montagna, successor of Bellini, Mantegna and Carpaccio, and founder of the Vicenzan school of painting. This school is represented by a masterpiece of Buonconsiglio (16C) in the form of a dramatic *pietà*. See also the paintings of the Venetians and those of the Flemings.

■ **ADDITIONAL SIGHTS**

Church of the Holy Crown (Santa Corona) (BY C). — The church was built in the 13C in honour of a Holy Thorn presented by St. Louis, King of France. Inside it you will see two distinguished **pictures**★★: a Baptism of Christ by Giovanni Bellini (fifth altar on the left) and an Adoration of the Magi by Veronese (third chapel on the right).

Cathedral (Duomo) (AZ V). — The cathedral has a Renaissance apse and a Gothic façade and nave. In the fifth chapel on the right is a polyptych (1356) by Lorenzo Veneziano.

Salvi Garden (Giardino Salvi) (AZ). — It is overlooked by two 16-17C loggias.

EXCURSIONS

Monte Berico Basilica. — *South, 2 km - 1 1/4 miles. Access: see plan in Michelin Red Guide Italia.* The basilica in the form of a Greek Cross is Baroque in style (17C). From the esplanade a wide **panorama**★★ of Vicenza, the Venetian Plain and the Alps can be seen.

Villa Valmarana "ai Nani". — *South, 2 km - 1 1/4 miles.* Go out by ④ and turn into the first road to the right. The villa dates from the 17C and was adorned in 1757 with splendid **frescoes**★ by Giovanni Battista Tiepolo and his son, Domenico. *Open Mondays to Saturdays 3 to 6.30 pm (5.30 pm in winter); Thursdays, weekends and holidays 10 am to noon; closed 15 November to 15 March; 1 000 lire.*

Rotonda★★. — *Southeast, 2 km - 1 1/4 miles.* Go out by ④ and turn into the second road to the right. The Villa Capra or Rotonda, is one of Palladio's most famous creations — the plan of Chiswick House in London was inspired by it *(the park only may be visited from 9 am to noon and 3 to 6 pm; 5 pm in winter; 500 lire)*.

Montecchio Maggiore. — *Southwest, 13 km -8 miles.* Leave by ⑤, road S 11. The ruins of the two perched castles remind one of Romeo and Juliet. There are good **views**★ of the Po Plain and Vicenza.

Monti Berici. — Go out by ④. These volcanic hills south of Vicenza make a setting for many patrician villas, some of which have been transformed into farms.

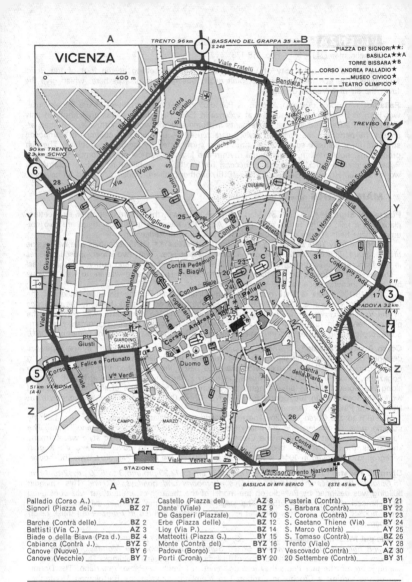

VICENZA

TRENTO 96 km — BASSANO DEL GRAPPA 35 km — S 248

TREVISO 51 km

PIAZZA DEI SIGNORI★★:
BASILICA★★A
TORRE BISSARA★B
CORSO ANDREA PALLADIO★
MUSEO CIVICO★
TEATRO OLIMPICO★

0 — 400 m

90 km TRENTO — 23 km SCHIO

51 km VERONA (A 4)

PADOVA 32 km (A 4) — S 11

STAZIONE

BASILICA DI Mte BERICO — ESTE 45 km

Palladio (Corso A.)	**ABYZ**	Castello (Piazza del)	**AZ** 8	Pusteria (Contrà)	**BY** 21
Signori (Piazza dei)	**BZ** 27	Dante (Viale)	**BZ** 9	S. Barbara (Contrà)	**BY** 22
		De Gasperi (Piazzale)	**AZ** 10	S. Corona (Contrà)	**BY** 23
Barche (Contrà delle)	**BZ** 2	Erbe (Piazza delle)	**BZ** 12	S. Gaetano Thiene (Via)	**BY** 24
Battisti (Via C.)	**AZ** 3	Lioy (Via P.)	**BZ** 14	S. Marco (Contrà)	**AY** 25
Biade o della Biava (Pza d.)	**BZ** 4	Matteotti (Piazza G.)	**BY** 15	S. Tomaso (Contrà)	**BZ** 26
Cabianca (Contrà J.)	**BYZ** 5	Monte (Contrà del)	**BYZ** 16	Trento (Viale)	**AY** 28
Canove (Nuove)	**BY** 6	Padova (Borgo)	**BY** 17	Vescovado (Contrà)	**AZ** 30
Canove (Vecchie)	**BY** 7	Porti (Cronà)	**BY** 20	20 Settembre (Contrà)	**BY** 31

VINCI ★ Tuscany

Michelin map 988 14 — 24 km - 15 miles — south of Pistoia — Pop 13 412

Near this town built on the slopes of Monte Albano, the great **Leonardo da Vinci** was born in 1452 (he died in Amboise in France in 1519). The 11C castle contains the **Museo Vinciano** and the **Biblioteca Leonardiana**. *Open: 2 May to 30 September, 9 am to noon and 2.30 to 6.30 pm (Sundays and holidays, 10 am to noon and 3 to 7 pm); 1 October to 31 April, 9 am to noon and 2 to 6 pm (Sundays and holidays, 10 am to noon and 2.30 to 6.30 pm). Closed Wednesdays, 1 January, 1 May, 15 August, Easter and Christmas; 500 lire.*

The house in which the artist was born lies 2 km - one mile — to the north on the Anchiano road, in a gentle **setting★★**. Pellucid light, silver leaved olive trees, terraced fields enclosed by low walls and a horizon of low hills make a restful scene.

VIPITENO (STERZING) Trentino-Alto Adige

Michelin map 988 4 — 69 km - 43 miles — north of Bolzano — Pop 5 176

Vipiteno is a picturesque little town and a popular resort both in winter and in summer. The **main street★**, barred at one end by the Torre di Città (1468), is lined with 15-16C Tyrolean houses with arcades, oriel windows and wrought iron signs. The **town hall** on the right is late Gothic in style. The **Multscher Museum** at No. 112 in the Piazza Mitra, contains four beautiful panels (1458) painted by Hans Multscher for the parish church altarpiece.

VITERBO ★ Latium

Michelin map 988 25 — Pop 58 013

Viterbo, still encircled by its **walls**, has kept a mediaeval air which is accentuated by the number of its artisans: carpenters, blacksmiths, locksmiths, gilders, etc.

Mediaeval City★★ (Città Medioevale). — *Follow the route shown on the plan: 1 hour on foot.* Start from the Piazza Plebiscito, where stand the 16C town hall and the 13C Governor's Palace topped by a 15C tower. Take the Via San Lorenzo, which skirts the charming little Piazza Gesù (market), then make for the Piazza della Morte, which is quiet and shady. The Via San Lorenzo ends at the superb **Piazza San Lorenzo★★**. This square, which occupies the site of the former Etruscan acropolis, transports you back to the Middle Ages with its old houses on Etruscan foundations, its cathedral dating from 1192 and adorned with a fine Gothic campanile and its 13C **Papal Palace**★★ — one of the most interesting examples of Gothic civil architecture in Latium. An outside staircase gives access to the great hall in which several popes were elected.

To the right a vast arch, upheld by an enormous column, supports a delightful loggia. Its slender columns and delicate arches stand in silhouette against the sky.

Returning to the Piazza della Morte, enter the **San Pellegrino quarter**★★. This is populous, working-class and extremely typical with arches, towers, outside staircases and fountains. Its centre is the delightful little Piazza San Pellegrino, with a church of the same name and the 13C Palazzo degli Alessandri.

Farther north, in a square, stands the **Fontana Grande**★, a curious 13C fountain fed by a Roman aqueduct.

The Via Saffi (pretty 14C house at No. 13) leads to the small Piazza delle Erbe (Square of Herbs).

Municipal Museum★ (Museo Civico). — *Open weekdays, 8.30 am to 2 pm; Sundays and holidays, 9 am to 1 pm. Closed Mondays, 1 January, 25 April, 1 May, first Sunday in June, 15 August, Christmas; 100 lire.* The museum is housed in the ancient monastery of Santa Maria della Verità and contains collections of Etruscan and Roman objects brought to light

VITERBO

Italia (Corso)		
Marconi (Via)		7
Matteotti (Via)		8
Caduti (Piazza dei)		2
Cardinale La Fontaine (Via)		3
Erbe (Piazza delle)		4
Fabbriche (Via delle)		5
Garibaldi (Via)		6

Morte (Piazza della)	9
Pace (Via)	10
Plebiscito (Piazza del)	12
Rocca (Piazza della)	13
Roma (Via)	14
Rosselli (Via F.)	15
S. Lorenzo (Via)	17
S. Pellegrino (Via)	18
S. Pellegrino (Piazza)	19
Saffi (Via Aurelio)	22
Verità (Via della)	23

★★CITTÀ MEDIOEVALE
★★PIAZZA SAN LORENZO
★★PALAZZO DEI PAPI (C)
★★QUARTIERE S. PELLEGRINO
★FONTANA GRANDE

in the area. The fine Gothic cloister is lined with sarcophagi from the burial grounds at Riello, Acquarossa, Norchia and Castel d'Asso. In the gallery on the ground floor are exhibited funerary ornaments most of which are also from the burial grounds.

In the picture gallery on the first floor, you will see a terracotta by the della Robbias, a large canvas by Salvator Rosa (Incredulity of St. Thomas), two masterpieces by Sebastiano del Piombo (Pietà, Flagellation) and an Adoration by the local painter Pastura (15-16C).

EXCURSIONS

Church of the Madonna of the Oak (Madonna della Quercia). — *3 km - 2 miles.* Go out by ①. The church is in the Tuscan Renaissance style, with an embossed façade and tympana by Andrea della Robbia. To the right are fine cloisters, half Gothic, half Renaissance.

Villa Lante★★. — *5 km - 3 miles. Open 9 am to 1 hour before sunset. Park open but to visit the villa apply in writing to Signora M. Lucidi, Administrator, Villa Lante. Closed Mondays, 1 January, 25 April, 1 May, first Sunday in June, 15 August and Christmas.* Two kilometres-one mile — beyond the Church of the Madonna della Quercia on the Orte road, you come to Bagnaia crowned by the Villa Lante, the country house of several popes. This majestic Renaissance building was erected in the 16C to the designs of Vignola. A lovely Italian garden adorned with fountains rises up the hillside beside the villa which is further surrounded by parkland *(open 10.30 am daily, identification necessary)*. The large square basin and the two pavilions opposite the entrance are open only on demand *(apply to the caretaker)*. The two pavilions are decorated inside with 16 and 17C frescoes. "The palace is small but pretty and pleasant", wrote Montaigne in his *Diary of a Voyage to Italy*. A plaque on the left pavilion recalls the visit of the illustrious traveller.

Lake Vico★ (Lago di Vico). — *Southeast, 18 km - 11 miles.* Leave by ②. *Description p 73.*

Bomarzo. — *Northeast, 21 km - 13 miles.* Leave by ①. The park of the 16C Villa Orsini is decorated with **fantastic sculptures**★ *(500 lire)*.

VITTORIO VENETO — Venetia

Michelin map 988 5 — 41 km - 25 miles — north of Treviso — Pop 31 021

This town, which gave its name to the great victory of the Italians over the Austrians (October-November 1918), is divided into two quarters: industrial **Ceneda**, to the south which has an ancient town hall (now the War Museum) with a loggia attributed to Sansovino, and **Serravalle** to the north. Serravalle has kept its ancient look. The main square, in which a "Venetian column" (symbol of conquest) stands, is lined with attractive Gothic or Renaissance houses, some of them painted with frescoes, and a graceful little town hall in the 14-15C Decorated Gothic style. The cathedral, on the far side of the river, contains a good canvas by Titian: Madonna and Saints.

The Tuscan hills, a commanding position and well preserved walls make up a severe but harmonious **setting★★** for the Etruscan, Roman and mediaeval town of Volterra. Its austerity is tempered by the sunny sky and the golden tinge of the building stone. The Volterrans turn and polish alabaster ornaments which can be bought in many shops and at the showrooms of the co-operative *(Consorzio Produttori dell'Alabastro)*.

Large salt-pans west of the town are used in the manufacture of fine salt and soda.

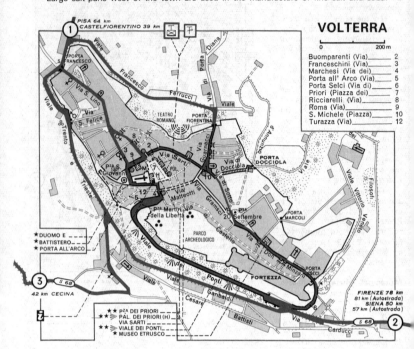

VOLTERRA

Buomparenti (Via)	2
Franceschini (Via)	3
Marchesi (Via dei)	4
Porta all' Arco (Via)	5
Porta Selci (Via di)	6
Priori (Piazza dei)	7
Ricciarelli (Via)	8
Roma (Via)	9
S. Michele (Piazza)	10
Turazza (Via)	12

Piazza dei Priori★★. — The Piazza is surrounded by grim palaces. The 13C **Palazzo Pretorio**, on the right, is pierced with twin windows and linked with the Torre del Porcellino, so-called because of the wild boar depicted in bas-relief on the upper part of the tower.

The 13C **Palazzo dei Priori** *(admission: 300 lire)* opposite is adorned with the emblems of the Florentine Governors. Inside the palace you can visit the council chamber (fresco by Orcagna) and a small picture gallery containing the works of Tuscan artists. Note an altarpiece and a predella by the Sienese, Taddeo di Bartolo and Benedetto di Giovanni; an Annunciation (1491) by Luca Signorelli; and a Descent from the Cross with stylised figures by Il Rosso. From the top of the tower there is a **panorama★★** of the roofs of Volterra, the metal-bearing mountains and smoke of Larderello to the south and the salt heaps and Val Cecina to the west.

To the left of the Palazzo dei Priori take the Via Turazza.

Cathedral and Baptistry★ (Duomo e Battistero). — In the picturesque Piazza San Giovanni stands the cathedral, in the Pisan Romanesque style, which has been remodelled several times. The interior comprises a nave and two aisles with monolithic columns and 16C capitals. In the Chapel of the Madonna, on the left as you enter, are frescoes by Benozzo Gozzoli, a Madonna of wonderful grace and purity and, opposite, an Epiphany. The transept, which is lit by alabaster paned windows, contains, in the second chapel in the north arm, a Virgin of the 15C Sienese school, and in the second chapel in the south arm, a 13C painted wooden sculpture, Descent from the Cross. The octagonal baptistry dates from 1283.

Porta all' Arco★. — The Etruscan Gate of the Bow is built of colossal stone blocks.

Go back to Piazza San Giovanni; take Via Roma, passing the bishop's palace and the Buomparenti Arch.

Via Sarti. — This street is lined with palaces with rings in the walls for tying up horses. Note No.1, the Solaïni Palace attributed to Antonio da Sangallo, and at No. 37, the Incontri Palace with a superb Renaissance façade designed by Ammannati.

In the Piazza San Michele are the church of the same name with a Romanesque façade, and a curious tower-house.

Beyond Porta Fiorentina, you will see 1C Roman ruins. Go back to Piazza San Michele and then make for **Porta Docciola**, a fortified gate near which is a curious mediaeval washtub. Then take Via Gransci.

Etruscan Museum★ (Museo Etrusco Guarnacci). — *Open 9.30 am to 1 pm and 2.30 to 6 pm (9 am to 1 pm and 2.30 am to 4.30 pm 1 October to 31 March). Closed Mondays, Sunday and holiday afternoons (1 October to 31 March), 1 January, Easter and Christmas; 1 000 lire.* Ceramics and more than 600 funeral urns, some of which are cleverly carved with reclining figures and domestic scenes, make up the exhibition.

Viale dei Ponti. — The Viale is a favourite walk of the Volterrans. It affords splendid **views★★** of the metal-bearing mountains. Above it stands the Fortezza, now used as a prison, an impressive mass of military architecture formed by the 14C Rocca Vecchia and the Rocca Nuova, built in 1472, with a keep and four corner towers.

Balze★. — *Northwest, 1 km - 3/4 mile.* Go out by ① and turn to the left after the Church of San Giusto and to the right after the Volterra signboard. The *Balze* (slopes) are due to erosion, which has caused great, tumbled landslides. There is a view over the countryside.

SARDINIA

With its area of 24 089 km² — 9 300 sq miles — wild Sardinia is the largest island in the Mediterranean, after Sicily. The population exceeds 1 592 000 (N. Ireland: area, 5 452 sq miles; population, 1 485 500). The Punta la Marmora in the Gennargentu Range is its highest peak with an altitude of 1 834 m — 6 017 ft. The mountains are covered with brushwood which gives out a strong scent in spring: it is composed of eucalyptus, euphorbia, asphodel, arbutus, lentisk, myrtle, cactus, fig trees, medlars and wild roses.

The Sardinians have the inherited virtues of shepherds and mountaineers, a keen sense of honour and hospitality. They still wear their magnificent costumes on feast days in the mountains or in the towns for the main religious or folk events (festival of St. Efisio in Cagliari, Sagra del Redentore in Nuoro, Cavalcata Sarda in Sassari). Handicrafts are still practised by the women, who make baskets and weave carpets, tapestries and fabrics.

Historical Notes. — Sardinia has an ancient history. The *nuraghi* or fortress houses date from the earliest times. They are strange conical structures, built with huge blocks of stone laid on one another without mortar. It is in these and in the tombs that the remarkable bronze statues, of which Cagliari Museum has a collection, were found. The island is said to have been colonised by the Cretans. Phoenicians, Carthaginians, Romans, Pisans and Genoese occupied it in succession before the Spaniards displaced them in 1718, when the island passed under the rule of the Dukes of Savoy, who took the title of Kings of Sardinia. The various occupants left few artistic traces. However, the Romanesque or Gothic churches underwent the influence of the Pisan style; the Baroque churches are decorated in Spanish taste.

Sardinia today. — The economy of Sardinia was for a very long period based on agriculture and sheep rearing. Nowadays tourism and industry are being developed. Sardinia is now an autonomous region and enjoys a special status which gives it a large measure of administrative freedom and the power to adopt special legislation, particularly in relation to tourism which is booming with the building of hotel complexes, the most spectacular of which are the luxury developments of the **Costa Smeralda** or northeast coast.

After concentrating on the improvement of the land, the modernisation of the coal mines (Carbonia) and lead and zinc mines (Iglesias), the intensive exploitation of the salt-pans at Cagliari, Sardinia has embarked on an industrialization programme. In the north, south and centre of the island large petrochemical plants and chemical processing industries have been established and this has led to the setting up of manufacturing industries. In the interior, the industrial zone of Ottana, southwest of Nuoro, boasts one of the largest factories of synthetic textiles in Europe. In the south, there is a huge aluminium plant.

The sudden transition from a traditional economy has disturbed the balance and attempts are being made to remedy this by a revival of agriculture and cattle rearing with the emphasis on meat, butter and cheese production.

In view of its rapid development, Sardinia has adopted strict measures to preserve its beautiful landscape, fine beaches and clear waters against pollution.

Access. – By air: air services link Cagliari, Alghero, Sassari (Alghero airport) and Olbia with most large Italian cities and with Nice and Paris.

Apply for information to ALITALIA, ATI, ALISARDA *and* ITAVIA.

By sea: ships (some take cars) leave Civitavecchia for Cagliari, Olbia and Porto Torres *(apply to the Tirrenia Company, Stazione Marittima, Civitavecchia, ☏ 28801 and for the Golfo Aranci (Turlazio Agency, 42 Viale Garibaldi, Civitavecchia, ☏ 21326);* leave Naples *(Tirrenia Company, Stazione Marittima, ☏ 312181)* for Cagliari; leave Genoa for Cagliari, Olbia and Porto Torres *(Tirrenia Company, Pontile Colombo, Genoa, ☏ 26981);* leave Leghorn for Olbia (TRANS-TIRRENO EXPRESS, 10 Via Pieroni, Leghorn, ☏ 422373); leave Palermo for Cagliari *(Tirrenia Company, Via Roma 385, Palermo, ☏ 588215);* leave Trapani for Cagliari *(Salvo Agency, 52, Corso Italia, Trapani, 27480).*

Tour of the Island. A quick tour can be made by car in 5-6 days, following the route Cagliari — Oristano — Sassari and environs — Alghero and environs — Castelsardo —

La Maddalena — Olbia — Nuoro — Dorgali — Arbatax — Muravera — Cagliari.
There are few petrol pumps along the roads on the east side of the island.

ABBASANTA

Michelin map 988 33 — Pop 2 241

This is the most important livestock market on the island.

Nuraghe Losa★. — *2 km — 1 1/2 miles — to the southwest, near the road to Cagliari.* This fortified house is built of huge stone blocks and has three floors and several rooms, niches, cells, winding corridors and domes.

ALGHERO ★

Michelin map 988 33 — Pop 37 654

The early history of this pleasant little port set amid olive trees, eucalyptus and parasol pines is unknown; its present history is that it is becoming more and more popular as a seaside resort. In 1354 Alghero was occupied by the Catalans and its Spanish air has gained it the nickname of the Barcelonetta of Sardinia. The people still wear Catalan costume and speak Catalan. The beach, 5 km — 3 miles — long, extends northwards from the village.

Città Vecchia★ (Old Town). — Narrow streets crowd the centre of a small peninsula encircled by fortifications. The cathedral has a remarkable doorway and a campanile in the Catalan Gothic style.

From the quay at the foot of the ramparts you can watch the picturesque coming and going of the fishing-boats, some of which are still used for coral fishing.

EXCURSIONS

Porto Conte and Neptune's Grotto★★★. — *14 km — 9 miles. Description p 270.*

ARBATAX ★

Michelin map 988 34.

This picturesque little **port★** has a name of Arab origin. It is isolated in a beautiful mountain setting on the Tyrrhenian Sea and is used by cargo ships carrying wood and cork.

The coast is lined with porphyry rocks whose red colour makes a vivid contrast with the blue sea. A spacious, gently sloping beach lies at the head of the bay.

EXCURSION

Dorgali road★★★. — For an almost uninhabited stretch of more than 70 km - 40 miles — the road skirts impressive gorges and affords distant views of an empty sea.

BARUMINI

Michelin map 988 33 — Pop 1 573

Barumini contains substantial traces of the earliest period of Sardinian history.

Nuraghe su Nuraxi★. — A massive fortress formed of several towers connected by galleries, an armoury and courtyards with wells.

To the west are the remains of a village, possibly dating from the Bronze Age, recently laid bare.

BOSA

Michelin map 988 33 — Pop 8 990

The Castle of Serravalle dominates this small town, which has preserved the Church of Sant'Antonio, in the Catalan Gothic style. The Church of San Pietro Extramuros, 1 km - 3/4 mile — from the town, is an 11C building with a 14C façade.

CAGLIARI

Michelin map 988 33 — Pop 241 720

Cagliari is the capital of the island. It is a modern looking town with an old nucleus surrounded by fortifications built by the Pisans in the 13C. Built on a hill overlooking the bay, it is a busy seaport, and was once a flourishing Carthaginian city.

The festival of Sant'Efisio (an officer in Diocletian's army who converted to Christianity and became the patron Saint of Sardinia), from 1 to 4 May, includes several processions.

■ MAIN SIGHTS *time: 2 hours*

Terrazza Umberto I. — This terrace is laid out on the site of a 16C Spanish bastion. It affords a remarkable **view★★** of the lower town, the harbour, the lagoon and the pinewoods. The glittering expanses of the salt-pans lie on the horizon.

Cathedral (Cattedrale). — The cathedral, which stands in the characteristic old quarter, was built in the transitional Romanesque-Gothic style of Pisa, in the 13C. It was remodelled in the 17C. The façade is a modern imitation.

Enter the building by the graceful Gothic doorway in the south side. Inside are magnificent **pulpits★★** executed by Guglielmo for the Cathedral of Pisa in 1162.

In the second chapel on the right, note a curious 13C Madonna in gilded wood in the Franco-Spanish style, and in the north transept, the Baroque tomb of King Martin I of Aragon (1395-1410), also in the Gothic chapel to the left, a triptych by Michele Cavaro, a Sardinian painter of the Renaissance.

Through a little door on the right of the chancel go down to the **Santuario,** a crypt with 17C decoration in relief, stucco and marble. Note the reliquaries on all sides of the Christian martyrs of Cagliari; a door opens on the right into a chapel containing the tomb of Marie-Louise of Savoy, the wife of King Louis XVIII of France.

In a room over the chapterhouse is a rich treasury containing a triptych attributed to Van der Weyden; it was originally in the apartments of Pope Clement VII, which were pillaged in the sack of Rome by the imperial army in 1527.

National Archaeological Museum★ (Museo Archeologico Nazionale). — *Open 9 am to 2 pm (1 pm Sundays and holidays); closed Mondays, 1 January, 25 April, 1 May, 15 August and 25 December; 500 lire; ticket also valid for the St. Pancras Tower.*

The museum has a large collection of weapons, pottery and especially **sculptures★★★** of the earliest period of Sardinian history. Punic, Greek and Roman art are represented in the other rooms.

The first floor houses a picture gallery devoted chiefly to paintings of the Sardinian school.

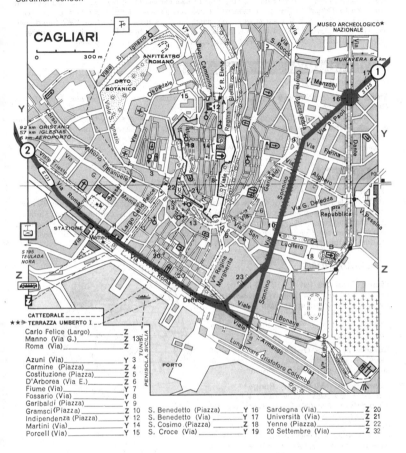

■ ADDITIONAL SIGHTS

Tower of St. Pancras★ (Torre di San Pancrazio) (Y A). — *Restoration work is currently in progress.* The square, massive Tower of St Pancras, built in 1304, is a vestige of the Pisan fortifications.

Roman Amphitheatre (Anfiteatro Romano) (Y). — Lying to the north of the town, the theatre is the largest Roman monument in Sardinia.

Botanical Garden (Orto Botanico) (Y). — *Open 8 am to 2 pm; closed Sundays and holidays.* This displays luxuriant Mediterranean and tropical vegetation.

St. Saturninus' Basilica (San Saturnino) (Z B). — The building, which is in the form of a Greek cross, dates in the main from the 5C. The centre of the basilica is believed to be one of the oldest Christian churches of the Mediterranean region.

EXCURSIONS

Muravera Road★★★. — *Northeast, 64 km - 40 miles.* Twenty-five kilometres - 15 1/2 miles — past Cagliari the road is beautiful, hugging the cliffs and dizzily overlooking wild gorges.

Nora. — *Southwest, 33 km - 21 miles.* Take the road S 195. Nora was founded in 700 BC by the Phoenicians in a beautiful setting near Cape Pula. The city then fell under Carthaginian and later Roman rule.

The remains of houses, a Punic temple, a well preserved Roman theatre, baths and roads have been excavated.

The Church of Sant'Efisio built in the 11C (partly restored), on the site of the martyrdom of the Saint is the goal of a procession in traditional costume that sets out annually between 1 and 4 May.

CASTELSARDO

Michelin map 988 23 — Pop 5 173

Castelsardo occupies a pretty **site★** on a promontory overlooking the sea and is joined to the coast by a small isthmus. Its women make wickerwork.

In the cathedral is a remarkable Madonna by the 15C Master of Castelsardo.

DORGALI

Michelin map 988 34 — Pop 7 538

Dorgali, a former Saracen colony, is a traditional Sardinian village, where the inhabitants are essentially engaged in agriculture, stock-rearing and production of handicrafts.

EXCURSION

Through a tunnel under Monte Bardia, from the exit of which there is a **view★★** of the coast, make *(9 km - 6 miles)* for the little port of **Cala Gonone**. From here you can sail *(apply to Pro Loco in Dorgali)* anywhere between Arbatax and Orosei, along a coastline pierced with marine caves, in which the last seals in the island, survivals from the Ice Age, have found shelter. The finest cave is that of the Bue Marino (Sea Ox) which has 5 km - 3 miles — of galleries *(motor-boat tours from April to September; apply to the Pro Loco in Dorgali).*

The MADDALENA Archipelago ★★

Michelin map 988 23.

Access. — *Car ferry services link La Maddalena with Palau (time: 1/4 hour) and Santa Teresa Gallura (time : 1 hour).*
The Maddalena Archipelago consists of fourteen islands and islets whose charm, for tourists, lies in their wild state. The largest, the Island of La Maddalena, has become a favourite seaside centre. It is linked by a causeway with the Island of **Caprera** where the house and tomb of Garibaldi, which are carefully preserved, attract many visitors.

NUORO

Michelin map 988 33 — Pop 36 148

Nuoro lies at the foot of Monte Ortobene, at the boundary of Barbagia and the Gennargentu Range. The most typical people of the island live in this central part of Sardinia. Customs, traditions, folklore and dress have remained unchanged since ancient times. The feast of the Redeemer *(Sagra del Redentore)* celebrated on 29 August includes a procession in regional costumes through the town. There is also a Folk Festival.

EXCURSIONS

Monte Ortobene (alt 955 m - 3 133 ft). — *East, 9 km - 6 miles.* This is a pleasant site for excursions in summer. From the summit, there is a **panorama★** (Mount Albo to the northeast and the Gennargentu Mountain Range to the south).

Nuraghi di Serra Orrios★. — *23 km - 14 miles — east, near the Dorgali road.* A curious group of prehistoric structures.

Gennargentu Mountain Range★★★. — *295 km - 183 miles — by roads which are often difficult. Leave early in the morning and be prepared for a long day.* Follow the Nuoro road to Fonni, the highest village in the island, through Lanusei where you will see a wide panorama, Seui-Aritzo, where chestnut

(After photo by T.C.I.)

A nuraghe

trousseau-chests are made, **Sorgono**, known for its site, its wine and its cork, and Desulo, with its local costumes, to Fonni and Nuoro. This magnificent run, during which you will see many *nuraghi,* affords scenes of unforgettable wildness on a lonely massif whose slopes are covered with groves of cork oaks and chestnut trees.

OLBIA

Michelin map 988 23 24 — Pop 30 716

Olbia is a busy port, the terminal of the Civitavecchia steamship lines and a port of call for merchant ships carrying cargoes of cork and shellfish caught in the bay.
From the port there is an attractive **view★** of the bay, dotted with reefs and enclosed by the rocky Islands of Molara and Tavolara, on which wild goats live.

PORTO CONTE

Michelin map 988 33 — 13 km - 8 miles — northeast of Alghero

This, the ancient Portus Nympharum or Port of Nymphs, lies on the shores of a beautiful **bay★★** whose blue, clear waters are bounded by an impressive rocky coast.

Neptune's Grotto★★★ (Grotta di Nettuno). — In the rocky wall of Cape Caccia the sea has formed this amazing cave, comprising an entrance vestibule, an inner lake and great chambers lined with the most variegated stalactites. *Reached either by the coast road and the stairway (654 steps) or by boat starting from Alghero; from the last two weeks in April to mid-October boats leave Alghero at 9 am and 3 pm; in July and August also at 10 am and 4 pm; time 3 hours.*

PORTO TORRES

Michelin map 988 23 33 — Pop 20 850

At the head of a great gulf bounded on the north by the Island of Asinara (a convict settlement), Porto Torres serves as the port of Sassari.

San Gavino Basilica★. — The basilica is very long, with bare sober lines, and is a fine example of Sardinian mediaeval art. It was built at the end of the 11C by the Pisans and enlarged by the Lombard master builders. Note the two apses and the ancient columns in the nave, and a fine sarcophagus in the crypt *(apply to the priest at Casa No. 5).*

SANTA GIUSTA

Michelin map 988 33 — Pop 3 051

Near the road through the village is a **Romanesque basilica★** of the 12C with graceful and delicate lines and a remarkable unity of design, in which the Pisan and Lombard styles are happily combined. The nave and two aisles are supported by Roman columns taken from an earlier building. The raised chancel is built over a crypt.

SASSARI

Michelin map 988 33 — Pop 118 384

Sassari is the second town in Sardinia. It offers the tourist a contrast between its spacious, airy modern quarters and its mediaeval nucleus, nestling round the cathedral. In the centre of the town is the pleasant Piazza Cavallino, planted with palm trees.

Festivals. — The famous *Cavalcata Sarda* takes place on the last but one Sunday in May. It is a colourful procession of people from nearly all the various provinces of Sardinia in their local costumes. The procession ends with a frenetic race in which several horsemen take part.

The *Festa dei Candelieri* (Feast of Candles), celebrated on 14 August, includes processions in which men in Spanish dress carry huge wooden candles, gilded or silver painted.

Cathedral (Duomo). — The cathedral is built in many styles and has its original 13C campanile with a 17C crown, a Gothic interior and a curious late 17C Spanish Baroque **façade★**.

St. Mary of Bethlehem Church (Santa Maria di Betlem). — A 13C Romanesque façade.

Sanna National Museum. — *Open 9 am to 2 pm (1 pm Sundays and holidays); closed Mondays, 1 January, 25 April, 1 May, first Sunday in June, 15 August and 25 December; 500 lire.* The museum is in the Via Roma and contains rich archaeological collections including a section devoted to Sardinian ethnography. In the small picture gallery are a fine Madonna (1473) by the Venetian, Bartolomeo Vivarini and a few works of the Flemish school (Gossaert).

EXCURSION

Holy Trinity Church★ (Santissima Trinità di Saccargia). — *Southeast, 17 km - 11 miles.* On the road to Cagliari, turn left 15 km - 9 miles — from Sassari. This ancient and lonely Camaldulian abbey was founded in the 12C. The church, in the Pisan-Romanesque style, is built in decorative courses of black and white stone. The elegant façade includes a porch supported on columns carved with monsters and animals. Above are two fake galleries. A slender **campanile★★** dominates the whole.

Inside, the apse is adorned with fine 13C frescoes representing Christ the King, the Virgin with the Apostles and scenes of the Passion.

TEMPIO PAUSANIA

Michelin map 988 23 — Pop 14 599

Tempio is the centre of the cork industry and the capital of Gallura, an extremely wild province covering the north of the island. Only the cork woods break up the *macchia* (heathland), a mass of scented flowers in spring.

Tempio is also known for the mineral springs which flow at the "Fonte Rinaggiu".

SICILY

Sicily, the largest of the Mediterranean islands, has an area of 25 709 km² - 10 027 sq. miles. It is triangular in shape and was named Trinacria (Greek for triangle) by the Ancients. Nearly 5 million people live on its soil, which is generally mountainous and reaches at its highest point, Mount Etna, an altitude of 3 340 m - 10 959 ft. The 1908 earthquake almost entirely destroyed Messina and the 1968 one affected the western part of the island.

HISTORICAL AND GEOGRAPHICAL NOTES

The history of Sicily is rather complicated. The island was part of Magna Graecia (Greater Greece) from the 8C BC, when Syracuse became the rival of Athens. After the First Punic War (against Carthage) the Romans seized it and exploited its resources to the full with the help of more or less dishonest pro-consuls such as Gaius Verres, whom Cicero denounced. Then it was invaded by the Barbarians, who were followed in the 9C and 10C by the Saracens.

The Normans under Roger de Hauteville, coming from Calabria, drove out the Saracens in the 11 and 12C but were themselves eliminated by the descendants of Frederick Barbarossa, Holy Roman Emperor (c. 1123-1190). At the death of the last Hohenstaufen, the pope invested Charles of Anjou king of Naples but he was driven out after the bloody massacre known as the Sicilian Vespers at Palermo in 1282 (see p 279).

The House of Aragon then took the place of that of Anjou, and later Sicily was returned by marriage to the Bourbon Kings of Naples, who, in their turn were displaced by the troops of Garibaldi in 1860. The Anglo-American landings between Licata and Syracuse in 1943 ended in the Germans abandoning the island after more than a month of heavy fighting. Since 1948 the island, designated as a region, enjoys a certain degree of autonomy, with a Parliament at Palermo.

Many Sicilians are close to the land: they cultivate vines and almond trees and grow mainly citrus fruit and cotton in the southwest; some re-afforestation has been undertaken (Piazza Armerina area) and also irrigation (around Regalbuto). Among the important industries on the island are sulphur mining between Caltanissetta and Agrigento, the complex of chemical industries in Priolo, northwest of Syracuse, the fertiliser factory at Porto Empedocle which uses the potassium found at San Cataldo, the oil resources discovered near Gela and Ragusa and the refinery at Augusta.

Sicily, however, also remains the archaeological museum of Europe with temples, theatres and citadels of Magna Graecia, Roman bridges and aqueducts, Saracen mosques, houses and towers and Norman churches, castles and palaces. As for the Sicilians, they still show the Arab physical type with occasional Norman characteristics in some of the women who have fair hair and blue eyes. A few peasants still go about in the famous Sicilian carriages, drawn by little horses bedecked with plumes, tassels and bells, and painted with scenes from Ariosto's romance, Orlando Furioso (see p 100).

Access. — **By air:** air services link Palermo, Catania and Trapani with most large Italian cities. Apply to ALITALIA, ATI and ITAVIA.

By sea: ships (car ferries) leave Villa San Giovanni and Reggio di Calabria for Messina (apply at the station: Stazione Ferrovie dello Stato, Villa San Giovanni, ℡ 775201 and Reggio di Calabria, ℡ 99940); leave Naples for Messina (Agenzia Genovese, 78 Via Depretis, Naples, ℡ 312109) and for Palermo, Catania and Syracuse (Tirrenia Company, Stazione Marittima, Naples, ℡ 312181); leave Cagliari for Palermo and Trapani (AGENAVE, 11 Piazza Deffenu, Cagliari, ℡ 663205); leave Genoa for Palermo (Grandi Traghetti Company, 10 Via Ravasco, Genoa, ℡ 567051); leave Leghorn for Palermo (Agenzia Marittima L.V. Ghiande — Sicilferry GT — 24 Via Vittorio Veneto, Leghorn, ℡ 28314).

Hydrofoils (aliscafi) link Messina to Reggio di Calabria (apply to the SNAV, Stazione Marittima, Reggio di Calabria, ℡ 29568).

Tour of the Island. — The itinerary indicated on the map below enables the visitor to tour the island in 15 days following the coastline in an anti-clockwise direction and to climb Etna (from Catania or Fiumefreddo). We recommend also making a detour inland along the route Agrigento — Enna — Piazza Armerina — Gela, which would require approximately an extra day.

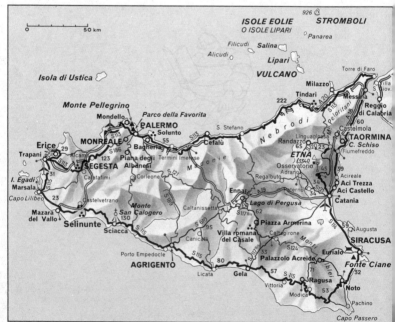

Michelin map **988** 36 — Pop 51 058
Town plan in Michelin Red Guide Italia (hotels and restaurants).

Agrigento, the Greek Akragas, is beautifully situated on a hill. It includes an ancient section where impressive ruins are strung out along the Valley of Temples, and also a mediaeval quarter of steep, narrow alleys, lying behind the shady, bird thronged Piazza Roma.

Until 1927 Agrigento was known by the Saracen name Girgenti. It was the birthplace of the famous dramatist Pirandello (1867-1936) and the Greek philosopher Empedocles.

■ VALLEY OF TEMPLES★★★ (Valle dei Templi)

tour : 1 day — buildings floodlit in the season

Tour the temples, if possible, early in the morning or at sunset. By following the panoramic road, Strada Panoramica *(marked on the map below)*, you will get a good view of these magnificent Doric temples *(see p 22)* whose stone, in the brilliant light, takes on the warm colour of honey. The destruction of the temples, long supposed to be due to earthquakes, is now also thought to have been the result of anti-pagan activities by the early Christians, who, however, spared the Temple of Concord and turned it into a church.

Temple of Juno★★ (Tempio di Giunone Lacinia). — This temple, which dates from the middle of the 5C BC, is improperly so-called in memory of the Temple of Hera (the Greek Juno) which stands on the Lacinian Hill at Crotone. On the east side you will see the sacrificial altar.

Temple of Concord★★★ (Tempio della Concordia). — This temple was built between 450 and 440 BC, it is the most massive, the most majestic and the best-preserved of the Doric temples in Sicily. It resembles the Temple of Theseus in Athens, but it is not known to what deity it was dedicated. Its present name is taken from a Roman inscription found nearby.

The temple is built of volcanic rock; the stucco that covered it has disappeared. It is surrounded by thirty-four columns and is 42 m long by 19.5 m wide — 138 × 65 ft. Its size is best appreciated from a distance.

A little to the west, in the beautiful flower garden of the Villa Aurea, are interesting catacombs and underground tombs dating from the Christian period.

Temple of Hercules★★ (Tempio di Ercole). — The Temple of Hercules, dating from the 6C BC, is believed to be the oldest of the Agrigento temples. Eight of its columns have been raised and the others make an impressive jumble of ruins. Note the holes in the column centres to insert the tenons.

Temple of Jupiter★★ (Tempio di Giove). — The Temple of Olympian Jupiter, huge but ruined, dates from the 5C BC. Its entablature was supported by telemones (columns in the form of male figures), colossal statues, one of which, the **Gigante**, a giant 7.5 m tall — 25 ft — has been reconstructed and is now on view in the Archaeological Museum. A reproduction, lying on the ground, gives an idea of the enormous scale of the building.

Temple of the Dioscuri — Heavenly Twins★★ (Tempio dei Dioscuri). — This 5C temple is usually known as the Dioscuri, although it is possible that it was dedicated to Demeter and Persephone. Only four of the columns supporting the entablature remain.

Across the ravines may be seen the columns of a temple to Vulcan.

Tero's Tomb★ (Tomba di Terone). — The tomb, said to be of Tero, Tyrant of Agrigento, stands amidst olive trees. The tomb is 9 m - 30 ft — high and really dates from the Roman era.

Oratory of Phalaris★ (Oratorio di Falaride). — At the back of the Church of St. Nicholas (San Nicola), which was constructed from material taken from the old temples, stands a little temple, built in the 1C BC, and transformed, in the Middle Ages, into a Christian chapel. The temple is said to have been the Oratory of Phalaris, the first "Tyrant" of Agrigento. It houses *(temporarily)* a Roman **sarcophagus★** which depicts the story of Phaedra and which was so beloved by Goethe. Nearby is an amphitheatre dating from Greek times.

Graeco-Roman Quarter★ (Quartiere Ellenistico Romano). — *Open 9 am to one hour before sunset. Closed Sundays, 1 January, 25 April, 1 May, first Sunday in June, 15 August and Christmas.* The houses that have recently been uncovered show how the Romans planted their town within the existing Greek one.

■ ADDITIONAL SIGHTS

Church of St. Blaise (San Biagio). — *1/4 hour on foot Rtn from the platform beyond the cemetery.* This small Norman-style 12C Romanesque church was built in golden stone on the foundations of a temple to Demeter dating from the 5C BC.

There is a most attractive **view★★** from the church of the San Biagio Valley, the temples and the sea.

National Archaeological Museum (Museo Archeologico Nazionale). — *Open 9 am to 2 pm (1 pm Sundays and holidays). Tickets issued up to 1/2 hour before closing time. Closed Mondays, 1 January, 25 April, 1 May, first Sunday in June, 15 August and Christmas.*

The museum, which is near the Romanesque-Gothic Church of St. Nicholas, contains a giant head of the god Telamon as well as three more heads of the god from the Temple of Jupiter, a valuable collection of Greek vases, the Agrigento Ephebus and numerous archaeological specimens recovered from the excavations made at Agrigento and at Caltanissetta.

The Diocesan Museum exhibits are provisionally on display in the Archaeological Museum. Note the two fine caskets in 12C Limoges enamelware and 17 and 18C sacerdotal vestments.

Diocesan Museum. — *Restoration work in progress. To visit, apply to the Curia in Agrigento. See opening times of the National Archaeological Museum.*

Municipal Museum (Museo Civico). — *Open 8.30 am to 2 pm; closed Sundays and holidays.* Mediaeval and modern art collections (Sicilian landscape paintings).

CATANIA★

Michelin map 988 37 — Pop 400 130

Catania is a busy seaport and the second town in Sicily after Palermo, though it has been destroyed several times by the eruptions of Mount Etna. It is a fine city with wide, regular streets, laid out by the 18C architect Vaccarini. It holds the heat record for all Italy, above 40° C. (104° F) in the shade. The town's heraldic animal is the elephant, emblem of Minerva.

Bellini Gardens★★ (Giardino Bellini). — These pleasant gardens recall the memory of the musician Vincenzo Bellini, who was born at Catania in 1801. They spread over two hills covered with flowers and tropical vegetation. From them you will see a fine panorama of the town and Mount Etna. Public story-tellers may sometimes be seen in the gardens.

Via Etnea★. — This famous straight street is over 3 km - 2 miles — long; it is lined with the chief shops in Catania. From south to north the Via Etnea crosses the Piazza del Duomo, then the great Piazza dell'Università with its palace built by Vaccarini, and finally the Piazza Stesicoro before skirting the Bellini Gardens.

Piazza del Duomo★. — This, the monumental centre of the town, is a Baroque ensemble designed by Vaccarini and includes the Elephant Fountain, the town hall and the façade of the cathedral. Left of the cathedral is a garden with tropical plants and oleanders.

The cathedral, built at the end of the 11C by the Norman King, Roger I, has been remodelled several times. Go round the building to the left and into a court where the original apse built of volcanic rock may be seen. Inside, glance at the columns and Romanesque capitals of the Norman building, recently uncovered, and the carved 16C stalls in the chancel.

Ursino Castle★ (Castello Ursino). — *Open 9 am to 2 pm (noon Sundays and holidays). Closed weekday holidays.* This bare, grim castle was built in the 13C by Frederick II of Hohenstaufen at the water's edge, from which it was separated by lava deposits in the 1669 eruption. It contains the municipal museum.

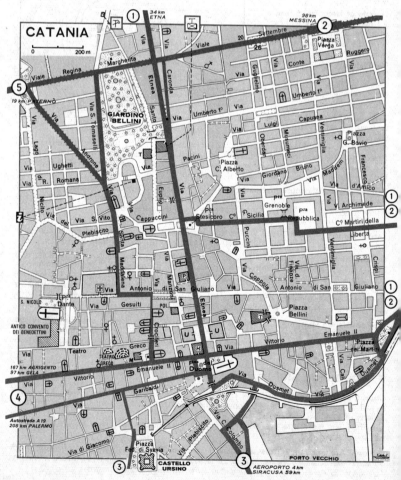

Greek Theatre (Teatro Greco). — *Open 9 am to 1 hour before sunset; closed Mondays and on some public holidays.* The Greek theatre, which had been incorporated into some neighbouring houses, was rebuilt of volcanic rock in the Roman era near the Odeon, itself a small theatre.

St. Nicholas' Church (San Niccolò). — A great 18C church (organ by Donato del Piano) adjoining a huge Benedictine monastery in the Baroque style.

EXCURSIONS

Mount Etna★★★ (by the south slope) and **Tour of Etna★★**. — *Descriptions p 276.*

Aci Castello★. — *Northeast, 9 km - 6 miles.* Go out by ②. Aci Castello is a small fishing centre, pleasantly situated on a rocky coast within view of the Scogli dei Ciclopi. The triangular black volcanic rock **castle★** is sited on the point of a rock.

Aci Trezza★. — *North, 11 km - 7 miles.* Go out by ②. A country resort and curious fishing village. The strange shaped **Scogli dei Ciclopi★**, Cyclops' Reefs, emerge from the sea at the harbour entrance. These are supposed to be the rocks hurled by the Cyclops Polyphemus after Ulysses had blinded him by thrusting a blazing stake into his single eye.

CEFALÙ ★

Michelin map **988** 36 — Pop 13 523

Cefalù is a small fishing town in a fine **setting★★**, hemmed in between the sea and a rocky promontory. It boasts a splendid Romanesque cathedral.

Cathedral★★. — *Time : 1/2 hour.* Built of golden tinted stone which stands out against the rocky background of the cliff, the cathedral was erected to fulfil a vow made by the Norman King, Roger II (12C), when in danger of shipwreck. The church, erected between 1133 and 1148, therefore has well marked Norman features in its three apses, its transept pierced at the base with large *oculi* (round openings) and especially its façade, flanked by two square towers. The emblasoned portico was rebuilt by a Lombard master in the 15C.

The timbers roofing two aisles and the great triumphal archway leading to the chancel are also Norman. Columns supporting the splendid **capitals★★** in the Sicilian-Norman style *(see p 27)* separate pointed arches. At the beginning of the nave is a 12C font. The oven vault of the central apse is covered with beautiful **mosaics★★** on a gilded background displaying a surprising variety of colour and forming an admirable expression of Byzantine art in its decline (12C).

Mandralisca Museum (Museo Mandralisca). — *Open weekdays, 9.30 am to noon and 3.30 to 6 pm; Sundays and holidays, 9.30 to 12.30 pm April to end of October; 1 000 lire.* The museum possesses a remarkable Portrait of a Man (1470) by Antonello da Messina.

ENNA ★

Michelin map **988** 36 — Alt 942 m - 3 091 ft — Pop 29 428

Enna lies in an isolated position in the centre of the island. Its panoramic **site★★** on the edge of a plateau has earned it the nickname of the Belvedere of Sicily.

Castle★ (Castello). — *Open 9 am to 1 pm and 3 to 7 pm.* This mediaeval castle on the top of the hill still has six of its original twenty towers. From the top of the Pisan Tower there is an exceptional **panorama★★★** embracing most of the Sicilian mountain chains, Etna, Lake Pergusa and the sea, looking south. The terraces afford good views.

Panoramic Promenade★ (Passeggiata Panoramica). — A pleasant promenade on the north front of the town between the castle and the Piazza Crispi affords many views.

Cathedral (Duomo). — This was rebuilt in the Baroque style in the 16 and 17C but still has its 14C Gothic apses. It has a curious **façade★** to the square in the form of a tower.

Near the cathedral, note the Gothic or Baroque churches and palaces showing Catalan influences, including windows with convex Spanish gratings known as *rejats*.

Public Garden and Tower★ (Giardino Pubblico e Torre di Federico). — From the top of the octagonal tower *(open 9 am to 1 pm and 3 to 7 pm)* there is a good view.

EXCURSION

Lake Pergusa (Lago di Pergusa). — *10 km — 6 miles — south.* Take the road to Piazza Armerina. A mysterious atmosphere broods over this oval lake, which is fringed with eucalyptus and aquatic plants. On its shores, according to legend, Pluto carried off the youthful Proserpine, daughter of Ceres and future Queen of the Infernal Regions.

A speed-track for racing cars has been laid out in this once sacred spot.

ERICE ★★

Michelin map **988** 35 — 14 km - 9 miles — northeast of Trapani — Alt 751 m - 2 464 ft — Pop 25 719

An unforgettably beautiful **setting★★★** characterises Erice, the Greek and Phoenician Eryx. Today it is a pleasant country resort with a mediaeval air. The Sicilian-Norman *(p 27)* houses cluster within the town walls, almost vertically above the sea.

This summer resort is known for its cool air, pinewoods, tranquillity and many walks.

Erice is reached by two splendid roads offering many views of the country and the sea, or by cable-car from Trapani *(8 am to 2 pm, every hour; additional trips in summer at 5, 6, 7 and 8 pm; fare: 500 lire single, 800 lire Rtn).*

Castle (Castello). — This romantic castle, dating from the Norman period, crowns Monte Erice on the site of the Temple of Venus the Mother (Ericina), who was deeply venerated by ancient mariners. In the nearby gardens are several belvederes from which there are admirable **views★★★** of Trapani, the coast, the sea, the Egadi Islands, the Island of Pantelleria and, in clear weather, Cape Bon in Tunisia.

Church of the Mother of God (Chiesa Matrice). — The church, which has taken the place of the Temple of Venus the Mother (Ericina), was built in the 14C on foundations made of stones taken from the temples. The square campanile with twin Gothic windows is remarkable.

Michelin map 988 37 — Alt approx. 3 340 m - 10 959 ft

Etna is the highest point in the island and is snow capped for most of the year. It is still active and is the largest and one of the most famous volcanoes in Europe.

Etna was born of undersea eruptions which also formed the Plain of Catania, formerly covered by the sea. Its eruptions were frequent in ancient times: we know of 135. In the Middle Ages the volcano erupted in 1329 and 1381. But the greatest disaster occurred in 1669, when the flow of lava reached the sea, largely devastating Catania as it passed.

The outstanding eruptions in our time were those of 1910, when twenty-three new craters appeared, of 1917, when a jet of lava squirted up to 800 m - 2 500 ft — above its base, and of 1923, when the lava ejected remained hot eighteen months after the eruption. In 1928 the town of Mascali was completely destroyed by a flow of lava. The last stirrings of Etna took place in 1947, 1949, 1950-1951, 1954, 1964, 1971 and 1974; the volcano still smokes and may erupt at any time.

The mountain has the appearance of a huge, black, distorted cone which can be seen from a distance of 250 km - 155 miles. On its lower slopes, which are extremely fertile, orange, mandarin and lemon trees, olives, agaves and fig trees flourish, as well as banana, eucalyptus, palm and umbrella pine trees. There are also vines which produce the delicious Etna wine. Chestnut trees grow above the 500 m - 1 500 ft — level and give way higher up to oak, beech, birch and pine. Above 2 100 m - 6 500 ft — is the barren zone, where only a few clumps of *Astralagus Aetnensis* (a kind of vetch) will be seen scattered on the slopes of secondary craters, among the clinker and volcanic rock. With a view to the future use of this land arboreal broom is being planted. It has exceptionally powerful roots which penetrate into the subsoil and break up the lava. Almonds, ground-nuts and finally olives will be grown in alternation. It may be hoped that vines will appear in their turn.

On the north and south faces of the volcano, there are winter sports resorts.

■ THE ASCENT OF ETNA★★★

The ascent of Etna can be made by the south face from Catania *(April to November),* or by the northeast face from Fiumefreddo *(mid-May to mid-October).* Wear warm clothing and strong shoes.

Ascent by the South Face. — *From Catania 68 km - 42 miles* — *Rtn, plus 16 minutes by cable-car and 1 hour by Land-Rover Rtn. Fare: 12 000 lire including guide.* Leave Catania by ①. At Barriera del Bosco, take the road to Nicolosi affording splendid views over Catania and its bay, to the **Sapienza Refuge** (alt 1 910 m — 6 266 ft). From the refuge, a cable-car *(8.30 am to sunset all the year round)* climbs to an altitude of 2 500 m - 8 202 ft — *(self-service restaurant near the upper station)* from where all purpose vehicles take tourists to about one hundred metres from the central crater and to the craters on the northeast side at an altitude of about 2 900 m - 9 515 ft — *(guides from the Alpine Club accompany the tour).* The excursion affords unforgettable views. The central crater with its smoking sides and the active craters and explosions on the northeast side are very impressive.

From the **Torre del Filosofo Refuge** (hotel), you can make a short descent on the eastern face to the Giannicola Rocks, a massif overlooking the grandiose Bove Valley which is bounded by lava walls more than 1 200 m - 3 900 ft — high pierced with numerous pot-holes and crevasses.

Excursions can be made at night (apply in advance): you will see a Dantesque spectacle made by molten lava at the bottom of the crater and an impressive sunrise with a view of the Lipari Isles and the Bove Valley. *Apply to S.I.T.A.S., 45 Piazza Vittorio Emanuele, Nicolosi, ☎ 911158.*

Ascent by the Northeast Face. — *From Fiumefreddo, 46 km - 29 miles* — *Rtn, plus 2 hours by minibus Rtn. Fare: about 12 000 lire, including guide.* Take road S 120 to Linguaglossa, then bear left. The road goes through the Linguaglossa pinewoods; after 14 1/2 km - 9 miles — leave your car in the village of Mareneve and take the minibus *(daily 8.30 am to 6 pm)* which takes you to within 200 m - 656 ft — of the central crater. The visit *(time : 1 hour; guides from the Alpine Club)* is a memorable experience.

Excursions can be made at night *(apply in advance)* which afford impressive views from the crater's edge. *Enquiries to S.T.A.R. Society, 233 Via Roma, Linguaglossa, ☎ 643180.*

■ TOUR OF ETNA★★ *138 km — 86 miles — about half a day*

This beautiful tour, which goes through Fiumefreddo, Linguaglossa, Randazzo (cathedral with three fine apses dating from the 13C) and Adrano, surprises by the contrast between lush vegetation and the desolate appearance of the lava fields. Groves of almond trees, olives, oranges and mandarins alternate with vineyards. The spectacular sections of the run are the coast between Catania and Fiumefreddo, with pretty views of the Rocks of Aci Trezza *(p 275)* and Aci Castello *(p 275);* the road between Adrano and Randazzo, with glimpses of the Simeto Valley; and finally Paternò, well sited on a basalt knoll crowned with a Norman castle and surrounded by orange groves which produce the best oranges in Italy.

Alternative route from Catania to Linguaglossa. — By way of Nicolosi, the Sapienza Refuge *(see above),* Zafferana, Fornazzo and the Citelli Refuge *(increased distance: 63 km - 39 miles):* particularly picturesque road which winds around the sides of the volcano.

GELA

Michelin map 988 36 — Pop 74 570

Gela, founded in 688 BC by islanders from Crete and Rhodes, was once an important Greek colony. The town was destroyed and restored several times and it was completely rebuilt in 1230 by Frederick of Swabia. It was in the plain of Gela, among the most fertile areas on the island, that the U.S. troops landed in July 1943. The discovery of oil near the resort has caused a new, industrial town to be built along the coast and has brought both economic and industrial prosperity to the region. Gela is also a resort and an interesting archaeological centre.

Ancient Memories. — Lovers of archaeology will find good specimens in the **National Museum★** *(open 9 am to 2 pm — 1 pm Sundays and holidays; tickets issued up to 1/2 hour before closing-time; closed Tuesdays, 1 January, 25 April, 1 May, first Sunday in June, 15 August and Christmas):* pottery, vases and medals. Also to be seen are the ruins of Doric temples (6C BC) and Greek dwellings in the Parco della Rimembranza. To the west of the town, at Caposoprano, excavation work has revealed 4C BC Greek fortifications .

LIPARI Islands ★★★ or AEOLIAN ISLANDS

Michelin map **988** 37 — Pop 12 445

The Lipari Islands are also called the **AEolian Islands** because the Ancients thought AEolus, the God of the Winds, lived there. The archipelago comprises seven main islands. Lipari, Vulcano, Alicudi, Salina, Filicudi, Panarea and Stromboli, all of exceptional interest for their volcanic nature, their beauty, their light and their climate.

A deep blue, warm, clear sea, ideal for underwater fishing, peculiar marine creatures including flying-fish, sword-fish, turtles, sea-horses and hammer-fish, make the Lipari Islands a refuge for those who like to live close to nature. The inhabitants fish, grow vines and quarry pumice-stone. Tourists can spend one day visiting the islands by boat and make excursions to Lipari, Vulcano or Stromboli.

Access. — Boats leave from <u>Messina</u> *(apply to SI.RE.MAR., 7 Via M. Aspa,* ☏ *53460);* <u>Milazzo</u> *(Alliatour, Via dei Mille, Palazzo S. Rita,* ☏ *923242);* <u>Naples</u> *(C. Genovese Agency, 78 Via Depretis,* ☏ *312109).*

Hydrofoils *(aliscafi)* leave from <u>Messina</u> *(Aliscafi SNAV Company, Cortina del Porto, Messina* ☏ *364044);* Milazzo *(Aliscafi — Sud Company, 14 Via Rizzo,* <u>Milazzo</u>, ☏ *921820 or Alliatour, address as above — for car ferries: S. Nav. Generale Insulare, 12 Via L. Rizzo,* ☏ *923415);* <u>Palermo</u> *(Cosulich Agency, 41 Via E. Amari, Palermo,* ☏ *588297);* <u>Cefalù</u> *(Barbaro Agency, 76 Corso Ruggero, Cefalù,* ☏ *21595);* <u>Naples</u> *(Aliscafi SNAV Company, 10 Via Caracciolo, Naples,* ☏ *660444),* and <u>Reggio di Calabria</u> *(Aliscafi SNAV Company,* ☏ *29568).*

■ LIPARI★★

This, the largest island in the archipelago, is formed of volcanic rock dipping vertically into the sea. On the slopes, note two curious strata of obsidian, a glazed black volcanic stone.

Two beaches, Marina Lunga (port) and Marina Corta, frame the town of Lipari, which is encircled by 13-14C walls and dominated by a 16C Norman castle which houses an archaeological museum *(open 9 am to 2 pm; 1 pm Sundays and holidays; closed Mondays, 1 January, 15 August, Easter and Christmas).* Nearby there is a pretty view of the bay.

Excursions can be made to Quattrocchi and Piano Conte (panoramas), and to Cannetto (pumice-stone quarries and strata of obsidian). Between the islands of Lipari and Vulcano, in the **Bocche di Vulcano** (Mouths of Vulcan), stand picturesque rocks resembling Druidical stones, among them the Pietralunga, a basalt needle nearly 72 m - 240 ft — high.

■ VULCANO★★★

According to mythology, AEolus, the God of the Winds, lived on this island. It has a wild and desolate appearance and rocky, rugged shores riven with crevasses from which hot water springs and hot mud flows.

Excursions to the large Vulcano crater *(approx. 2 1/2 hours on foot Rtn)* and to the Vulcanello *(approx. 1 hour on foot Rtn)* are very interesting for the impressive views they afford of the craters and of the archipelago. *Excursions should be made in the early morning.* From Capo Grillo there is a view of all the islands.

On the other hand, if you have time, make a tour of the island by boat to see the many curious views, especially on the northwest coast, which is fringed with impressive basalt reefs.

■ STROMBOLI★★★

The volcano of Stromboli, with its plume of smoke, has a sombre beauty, forming a wild island on which such soil as can be cultivated is covered with vines yielding an exquisite Malvasia wine. The little square white houses are markedly Moorish in style.

The crater, in the form of a cone, 926 m - 3 038 ft — high, has frequent minor eruptions with ejections of lava and explosions. You can see the spectacle by climbing to the crater with a guide *(7 hours on foot Rtn, difficult climb),* or watch from a boat the fall of lava and incandescent stones into the sea along a *serra* or crevasse named the Sciara del Fuoco (Pit of Fire). At night the scene becomes both beautiful and terrifying.

Strombolicchio, near Stromboli, is a picturesque rocky islet whose summit can be reached by a steep stairway. It affords a splendid view of Stromboli, the Lipari Archipelago and the coasts of Calabria and Sicily.

■ SALINA★

The island is formed from six extinct volcanoes of which two have retained their characteristic outline. You can climb up to the highest crater, Monte Fossa delle Felci, (962 m - 3 156 ft), which dominates the archipelago. There is a pleasant panoramic road round the island. The vines grown on the terraced lower slopes yield the delicious golden Malvasia wine.

MARSALA

Michelin map **988** 35 — Pop 85 446

Marsala, the ancient Lilybaeum, on Cape Lilibeo, is an African looking town. The Saracens first destroyed then rebuilt it and called it Marsah el Allah (Port of God). It is known for its richly coloured and strong tasting wines. It was at Marsala that Garibaldi landed at the start of the Expedition of the Thousand, which freed Sicily and southern Italy from the sway of the Bourbons. The **Cavallotti Gardens,** at the northern boundary of Marsala, are overlooked by a belvedere giving a view of Trapani, Erice and the Egadi Islands.

MAZARA DEL VALLO

Michelin map **988** 35 — Pop 43 259

The many domes and bell-towers of this pretty town give it a picturesque appearance.

Piazza della Repubblica. — A square surrounded by graceful buildings: the Palazzo del Seminario (Seminary), an 18C bishop's palace with a 16C loggia, and a Baroque cathedral. The statue of St. Vito, the patron saint of the town, stands in front of the seminary.

Gardens (Giardini). — The public gardens beside the Piazza della Repubblica overlook the sea. Note the ruins of the Norman castle.

MESSINA *

Michelin map **988** 37 — Pop 269 414

Town plan in Michelin Red Guide Italia (hotels and restaurants).

Messina lies at the entrance to the Straits of Messina and at the foot of the Peloritani Mountains. Its straight streets run parallel with the deep blue sea.

The town has often suffered from earthquakes, especially that of 1908, which destroyed 90 per cent of it. Since then Messina has been rebuilt and with its perfectly sheltered harbour and its International Fair in August, has again become a busy trading centre.

Museum* (Museo). — *At the end of the Viale della Libertà, on the way out of the town to the north, near the sea. Open 9 am to 2 pm (1 pm Sundays and holidays); closed Mondays, 1 January, 25 April, 1 May, first Sunday in June, 15 August, Easter and Christmas; 500 lire.* The museum is arranged in quite good taste and has some pleasant surprises for the art lover: a polyptych (1473) by Antonello da Messina, Virgin and Child with Saints, full of calm gentleness and tender melancholy; a sombre Adoration of the Shepherds and a dramatic Resurrection of Lazarus, both by Caravaggio; a 14C wooden Crucifix and a bronze pelican of the 13C; two sculptures by Montorsoli (16C) representing Neptune and Scylla, the monster of antiquity who devoured sailors *(p 71)*; a St. Catherine in the ancient style by A. Gagini (16C), and finally a remarkable Descent from the Cross painted by the Fleming, Colin van Coter (late 15C).

Cathedral (Duomo). — The cathedral, almost entirely rebuilt after the earthquake of 1908, still displays main features in the Norman-Romanesque style. Note an interesting 15-16C central **doorway***, finely carved, and a bell-tower 60 m - 196 ft — high, fitted with a curious **astronomical clock*** believed to be the world's largest.

In the Piazza del Duomo is the graceful 16C Baroque Fountain of Orion.

Church of the Annunciation (Annunziata dei Catalani). — A small Romanesque church, half-Norman (apses), half-Moorish, near the cathedral at the end of the Via Cesare Battisti.

MILAZZO

Michelin map **988** 37 — Pop 30 344

This is the starting point for excursions by boat *(see p 277)* to the Lipari Islands. It stands at the root of the Milazzo Peninsula and is dominated by a 13C castle.

Milazzo boasts a spacious and agreeable **lungomare*** or seashore promenade.

MONREALE ***

Michelin map **988** 35 — Pop 25 297

The present town overlooking the Conca d'Oro (Golden Conch Shell) of Palermo has grown up round the famous Benedictine **abbey** of the same name.

The Abbey of Monreale (Mount Royal) was founded by the Norman King, William II and shows a remarkable combination of Norman architecture and Sicilian-Arab decoration. *Time: 1 1/2 hours.*

Cathedral*** (Duomo). — *Open 7 am to 12.30 pm and 3 to 6 pm*

The fine central carved doorway in the façade has beautiful bronze doors made in the 12C by Bonanno Pisano, who also worked on those of the Cathedral at Pisa. The north door is the work of Barisano da Trani (12C). The coloured stonework of the apses makes a remarkable decoration. From the court of the nearby palace there is a pretty view of the Conca d'Oro.

The interior decoration of the building, in multicoloured marble, betrays Arab inspiration. But it is the dazzling 12C **mosaics***** that are outstanding. They represent the complete cycle of the Old and New Testaments (view them from right to left and from top to bottom). A gigantic Christ conferring His Blessing is enthroned in the central apse.

Above the episcopal throne, on the right in the chancel, a mosaic represents King William II offering the cathedral to the Virgin. Another mosaic opposite, over the royal throne, shows the same King William receiving his crown from the hands of Christ.

You will also see the treasury to the left of the chancel *(500 lire)*. From the terraces *(500 lire)* near the basilica there is a view of the Conca d'Oro.

Cloisters*** (Chiostro). — *Open in summer, weekdays: 9 am to 12.30 pm and 3 to 5.30 pm. In winter, weekdays: 9 am to 2.30 pm. Sundays and holidays : 9 am to 12.30 pm all the year round. Closed Tuesdays, 1 January, 3 May, 15 August, Easter and Christmas; 500 lire, free on Sundays and holidays.*

The cloisters to the right of the church are as famous as the mosaics. They offer characteristic views of the abbey church. On the south side is a curious fountain that was used as a lavabo by the monks. The galleries, with sharply pointed arches, are supported by twin columns whose sculptured capitals, remarkably free in execution, should be examined in detail.

NOTO *

Michelin map **988** 37 — 32 km - 20 miles — southwest of Syracuse — Pop 24 541

Noto lies in a district rich in olive and almond groves enclosed by low walls. It was rebuilt after the earthquake of 1693.

Corso*. — This street is a remarkable example of 18C town planning. Palaces and a church in the Spanish inspired Baroque style are grouped along it, forming majestic vistas.

PALAZZOLO ACREIDE

Michelin map **988** 37 — 37 km - 23 miles — northeast of Ragusa — Pop 9 862

Palazzolo Acreide is the successor of the ancient Syracusan colony of Akrai.

Archaeological Area* (Zona Archeologica). — *Open 9 am to 1 hour before sunset. Closed Mondays, 1 and 6 January, 1 May, 15 August, 8, 25 and 26 December.* At the top of the hill may be seen a Greek theatre, the *agora* (forum) and *latomies* (stone quarries). The *Santoni,* a little farther on, are statues carved in the rock.

PALERMO ★★★

Michelin map **988** 35 — Pop 687 587
Town plan in Michelin Red Guide Italia (hotels and restaurants).

This, the capital and the chief seaport of Sicily, is built at the head of a wide bay enclosed on the north by Monte Pellegrino and on the south by Cape Zafferano. It lies on the edge of a wonderfully fertile plain bounded by hills and nicknamed the Conca d'Oro (Golden Conch Shell), on which palm and orange groves flourish.

Life in Palermo. — The **Quattro Canti** (Four Corners) form a busy crossroads in the centre of Palermo where two main streets intersect. Popular Palermo, that of the fishermen and artisans, is crowded into picturesque alleys festooned with washing hung out to dry, round a basin which formed the nucleus of the harbour. The fashionable quarters are near the Via della Libertà, a wide thoroughfare between side streets planted with trees and houses with fine palm planted gardens. The **Piazza Castelnuovo** is, with the Via Ruggero Settimo, the smart quarter of Palermo; at nightfall, under the trees, well dressed tourists and Palermans gather in the quarter to enjoy cream puffs, fruit sherbets, melon ices and the real Sicilian *cassata*, made of cake, liqueur flavoured ice cream and candied fruits.

HISTORICAL NOTES

Crossroads of Civilisations. — Palermo was founded by the Phoenicians and conquered by the Romans. From 831 to 1072 it was under the sway of the Saracens, who gave it the peculiar atmosphere suggested today by the luxuriance of its gardens, the shape of the domes on some buildings and the physical type and mentality of the people.

The Norman descendants of the Hautevilles and the Guiscards made Palermo their capital from 1072 to 1194, Roger II taking the title of King of the Two Sicilies. They were great builders and succeeded in blending Norman architectural styles with the decorative traditions of the Saracens and Byzantines: their reign was the golden age of art in Palermo.

Later, the Hohenstaufen and Angevin kings introduced the Gothic style (13C). From 1300 to 1647 the Spaniards gave preeminence to the Baroque style as understood in their country, but their successors, the Bourbons of Naples, had no influence on the life of Palermo.

The Sicilian Vespers. — Since 1266 the brother of St. Louis, Charles I of Anjou, supported by the pope, had held the town. But his rule was unpopular. The Sicilians had nicknamed the French, who spoke Italian badly, the *tartaglioni* or stammerers. On the Tuesday after Easter 1282, as the bells were ringing for vespers, some Frenchmen insulted a young woman of Palermo in the Church of Santo Spirito. Insurrection broke out, and all Frenchmen who could not pronounce the word *cicero* (chick-pea) correctly were massacred.

MAIN SIGHTS *time: 1 day*

Town centre★★★ (Centro della Città). — Three pretty squares gracefully recall the atmosphere of old-time Palermo: the Quattro Canti, the Piazza Pretoria and the Piazza Bellini. Their charm is enhanced by flood-lighting in the evening.

Quattro Canti★★. — The Quattro Canti, Four Corners, with their canted walls, form a fine ensemble in the Spanish Baroque style. The statues in the niches represent the protecting saints of the town and the kings of Spain; those on the fountains, the seasons.

The Baroque Church of San Giuseppe is astonishingly decorative, especially inside.

Piazza Pretoria★. — The square is reached by stairs. Note the town hall and a spectacular fountain★★ surmounted with many statues, the work of 16C Florentine sculptors.

Piazza Bellini★★. — This delightful square contains two buildings typical of Palermo: the Martorana and the San Cataldo.

The **Martorana★★** is also called Santa Maria dell'Ammiraglio (St. Mary of the Admiral) because it was founded in 1143 by George of Antioch, Admiral of the Fleet to King Roger. A Baroque façade has been added on the north side. Pass under the elegant 12C belfry-porch, with storeys rising out of one another, and cross two bays added in the 17C to enter the original church. This is decorated with beautiful Byzantine mosaics. On the façade of the original church, two panels depict Roger I crowned by Christ and George of Antioch kneeling before the Virgin. *Open 8 am to 1 pm and 4 to 8 pm (3.30 to 5 pm 2 October to 30 April); closed Sunday and holiday afternoons.*

The 12C Church of **San Cataldo★★** *(it is only possible to visit when the Martorana is open, apply to the caretaker of the Martorana)* has fully preserved its Moorish appearance, with its domes and geometrical decoration. The Church of St. Catherine, on the other side of the square, a fine example of Sicilian Baroque, was built in the 17C.

Church of St. John of the Hermits★★ (San Giovanni degli Eremiti). — *Open 1 May to 30 September, weekdays: 9 am to 1 pm and 3.30-6.30 pm 1 October to 30 April, weekdays: 9 am to 3 pm; Sundays and holidays: 9 am to 1 pm throughout the year. Closed Mondays, 1 January, 25 April, 1 May, 15 August, Easter and Christmas.* The church, which Arab architects helped to construct, was built in 1132 at the request of King Roger II and is picturesquely crowned with pink domes. Beside it is a garden of tropical plants with pleasant 13C cloisters of small twin columns, now profusely overgrown with flowers, palms and orange trees.

Palace of the Normans★★ (Palazzo di Normanni). — *Open Mondays, Fridays and Saturdays 9 am to 12.30 pm. The Palatine Chapel is open everyday from 9 am to 1 pm and also from 3 to 4 pm weekdays only except Wednesday.* This immense palace which has been remodelled several times, is today the seat of the Sicilian Parliament. Only the central section and the Pisan Tower are of the Norman period.

The **Palatine Chapel★★★** on the first floor *(stairs on the left in the courtyard)* was built in the reign of Roger II, between 1130 and 1140. It is a wonderful specimen of Arab-Norman decoration. Ten ancient columns support a nave and two aisles; the nave has a magnificent ceiling *(illuminated by request)* with alveoli in the Moorish style. The marble paving is relieved with mosaics. Dazzling mosaics with gilded backgrounds cover the upper walls, the dome and the apses. Note also the chancel barrier, pulpit, paschal candelabrum and the royal throne. The rooms on the second floor, including the **King Roger's Room★★**, may be visited. The room is 12C, with highly stylised mosaics of the chase.

The **garden★** of the Villa Bonanno, opposite the palace, boasts superb palms and plane trees. To the right of the palace the majestic **Porta Nuova** (New Gate) shows a Renaissance style in transition towards Baroque (atlantes).

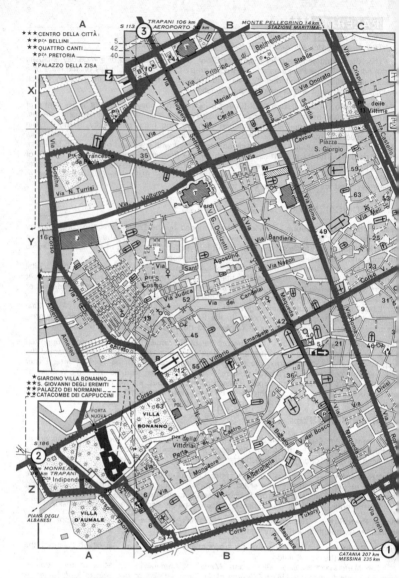

Botanical Garden★★ (Orto Botanico). — *Open 1 June to 30 September, 8 am to 2 pm; the rest of the year, 9 am to noon and 2 to 4 pm; closed Sundays and holidays.* The garden covers 10 ha - 25 acres —, is quiet and secluded and contains curious tropical plants and trees including a magnificent magnolia fig tree.

Palazzo Abbatellis★. — In this 15C palace, which has pretty Gothic windows and an elegant doorway, is the **National Gallery of Sicily★★**, including a museum of mediaeval art and a picture gallery. *Open 9 am to 2 pm (1 pm Sundays and holidays); tickets issued up to 1/2 hour before closing-time; closed Mondays, 1 January, 25 April, 1 May, 2 June, 15 August and Christmas. 750 lire.*

There is an amazing and dramatic 15C **fresco of Death Triumphant★★★**, a picture of merciless realism; the bust of Eleonora of Aragon by Francesco Laurana (15C), admirable in its pure modelling; and the Annunciation by Antonello da Messina (15C).

Palazzo Chiaramonte★. — A fine Gothic palace (1307) which served as a model for many buildings in Sicily and southern Italy.

Garibaldi Gardens (Giardino Garibaldi). — This garden in front of the Palazzo Chiaramonte contains two huge **ficus★★** (magnolia fig trees) whose trunks resemble columns.

Palazzo della Zisa★. — A magnificent pleasure palace in the Arab-Norman style built from 1160 onwards by William I *(temporarily closed for restoration work)*.

■ ADDITIONAL SIGHTS

Capuchin Catacombs★★ (Catacombe dei Cappuccini). — *Guided tours 9 am to noon and 3.30 to 5 pm; closed Sundays; donation.* These catacombs are an impressive sight. About 8 000 corpses, including those of babies, children, adults and old men and women, often clothed, are lined up in various attitudes. The very dry air preserves them.

Archaeological Museum★ (Museo Archeologico) (BY M). — *Open 9 am to 2 pm (1 pm on Sundays and holidays); closed Mondays, 1 January, 25 April, 1 May, 15 August and 25 December. 750 lire.*

The museum, which is housed in a 16C monastery, contains the products of excavations. Note on the ground floor, anthropoid sarcophagi (6-5C BC), an Egyptian inscription known as the Palermo Stone, the cyma decorated with lions' heads for draining rain water from the roof of the Temple of Himera *(circa* 480 BC) and especially remarkable **metopes★★** from

PALERMO

```
0                    300 m
```

temples at Selinus (6-5C BC). On the first floor are exhibited objects recovered in recent excavations at Himera, Palermo, Marsala, Poggioreale, Selinus... On the second floor *(temporarily closed for reorganisation)*, a fine collection of Greek vases, Roman mosaics and a prehistoric collection are on display.

Cathedral★ (BZ B). — The cathedral, which was founded at the end of the 12C, is built in the Sicilian-Norman style *(see p 27)* but has often been restored and modified; the chevet and the great 15C south porch, with its fine carved wooden doors, are the most interesting features. The cathedral is joined to its 12C campanile by two arches and is crowned with an 18C dome. In the interior, which was reconstructed in the 18C, see on the right the chapel of the Hohenstaufens containing the tombs of that family including that of the Emperor Frederick II.

St. Lawrence Oratory★ (Oratorio di San Lorenzo) (CY C). — The Oratory, No. 5 in the Via Immacolatella, is decorated inside with curious Baroque plaster mouldings by Serpotta (17C). These mouldings illustrate the lives of St. Francis and St. Lawrence. On the altar is a Nativity by Caravaggio. The carved wood supports, inlaid with mother of pearl, of the marble benches lining the oratory, are remarkable.

St. Mary of the Chain★ (Santa Maria della Catena) (DY D). — This late 15C church in the transitional Gothic-Renaissance style has a fine interior with low, graceful arches. The church stands near the chain with which the Old Port used to be closed.

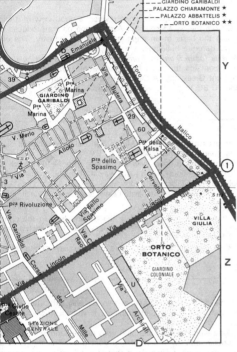

Villa Giulia (DZ). — A pretty 18C **garden★** *(open 9 am to 8 pm)* with tropical plants, ponds and rare trees, where Goethe used to come.

Villa d'Aumale (AZ). — Only the garden (enquire about opening times) and the museum (apply to Prof. Ventimiglia, ☎ 664618) may be visited. The villa was built in the 18C and is surrounded by a fine **garden★** laid out in the Italian manner. King Louis-Philippe of France lived here in exile. A museum of Sicilian carts is housed in one wing of the Villa d'Aumale.

EXCURSIONS

Monreale★★★. – *8 km - 5 miles.* Leave by ②. Description p 278.

Park of the Favourite★ (Parco della Favorita). — *3 km - 2 miles.* Leave by ③. This beautiful landscape park at the foot of Monte Pellegrino was finished in 1799 by the Bourbons, who had the Palazzina Cinese (Chinese villa) built there.

Monte Pellegrino★★. — *14 km — 9 miles.* The winding Via P. Bonanno affords repeated views of Palermo and the Conca d'Oro. As you climb you will leave on your left the road to the Castle of Utveggio. (From the terraces there is a fine panorama). You arrive at the 17C **Church of St. Rosalia**, built on the site of the cave to which this saint, Patron of Palermo, had retired. From the church a road leads to a platform affording a fine **view★★** of the coast; the road goes down to the beach at Mondello and along the coast back to Palermo.

Mondello. — *North, 11 km - 7 miles.* Start from the Parco della Favorita and return by the coast road. The Lido di Mondello is the beach of Palermo. The little fishermen's village which has given it its name is charming.

Bagheria. — *East, 16 km - 10 miles.* Leave by ①. The town is built in terraces on a small hill. It is known for its Baroque villas, and especially for the Villa Palagonia, which has **sculptures★** of grotesques and monsters. The ruins of Soluntum *(p 282)* are 4 km - 2 miles — from Bagheria.

Piana degli Albanesi. — *South, 23.5 km - 14 1/2 miles.* This picturesque town, which is reached from Palermo by a panoramic road, is the settlement of an Albanian colony founded in 1488. The inhabitants have preserved their dialect and their traditional dress. On feast days (Epiphany, Easter), you can attend services celebrated in the Greek Orthodox ritual before a congregation wearing rich costumes.

PIAZZA ARMERINA

Michelin map **988** 36 — Alt 731 m - 2 398 ft — Pop 22 499

Piazza stands on a peculiar site with its grey houses huddled on a hill topped by a Baroque cathedral. From the Garibaldi Gardens (Enna road) there is a characteristic view of the town.

Roman Villa of Casale★ (Villa Romana del Casale). — *Southwest, 6 km - 4 miles. Open 9 am to 2 hours before sunset; closed 1 January, 25 April, 1 May, first Sunday in June, 15 August and Christmas; 500 lire.*

Tarred approach road; signboard. Superb **mosaics★★** have been unearthed in the foundations of this villa, dating from the 3 or 4C. The chief qualities of these mosaics are their wide range of colour and easy, natural posing. Note in the *triclinium* (common-room) the Labours of Hercules, the Fall of the Giants and the Child Grape Harvesters.

RAGUSA

Michelin map **988** 37 — Pop 65 998

Ragusa lies in a typical **setting★** on a plateau between deep ravines; a good view of it can be had at the entrance to the town, from the Syracuse road. Asphalt and oil are produced in the immediate neighbourhood, forming the basis of an important chemical industry. The old town of Ragusa Ibla has majestic 18C Baroque buildings.

The small **Ibleo Archaeological Museum** *(open 9 am to 2 pm — 1 pm Sundays and holidays; closed Mondays and public holidays)* contains the finds from excavations undertaken in the area: funerary materials from the ancient Greek city of Camarina, and from burial grounds at Caucana and Castiglione; remarkable 4C BC terracotta ware and Roman mosaics.

SCIACCA

Michelin map **988** 35 — Pop 35 792

Sciacca, all white and built in terraces on the slope of Monte San Calogero where it dips to the sea, has a Moorish look. It is a large thermal resort.

The **Villa Comunale** (public garden) provides a good view of the sea. The 14-16C **Church of St. Margaret** (Santa Margherita) is at the town boundary on the way to Trapani. It has on its north side an interesting transitional Gothic-Renaissance doorway.

A short way up the Via Pietro Gerardi stands the **Steripinto Palace**, built in the Catalan style of the 15C with diamond shaped bosses.

Monte San Calogero★. — *8 km - 5 miles.* Go out by road S 188 *ter* and turn to the right, some 500 m - 547 yds — after leaving the town. The memorial you pass is to the French airship Dixmude, which was lost at sea off Sciacca in 1923.

From the summit (386 m - 1 266 ft), beside the church, there is a fine view of the coast.

SEGESTA Ruins ★★★

Michelin map **988** 35.

Segesta was the great rival of Selinus in the 5C AD, and in its war with that city it appealed for help to the Athenians and then to the Carthaginians. It was destroyed by the Saracens about AD 1000.

The **Temple** of Segesta stands alone among mountains cleft with ravines and scorched by the sun. The impressive silence is broken only by the wind and goat bells. The temple is a Doric building (430 BC), pure and graceful, with a peristyle of thirty-six columns. From points near it there are wonderful views of the mountains and gorges.

The approach road to the semicircular theatre, with a diameter of 63 m - 207 ft — branches off to the left opposite a small inn. There is a fine view over the Gulf of Castellammare.

SELINUS ★★ (SELINUNTE)

Michelin map **988** 35.

Selinus was founded in the middle of the 7C BC and was destroyed in 409 BC by the Carthaginians. The huge ruins of the Selinus temples with their enormous foundations, perhaps wrecked by earthquakes, will impress the visitor, as will the silence of this solitary spot, broken only by the swish of a wave on the seashore. The admirable metopes which adorned these temples are in the Archaeological Museum at Palermo *(p 280)*. Visit to the archaeological site *(reorganisation in progress): 9 am to one hour before sunset; closed Mondays, 1 January, 25 April, 1 May, 15 August and 25 December; 100 lire weekdays.*

Oriental Temples★★. — Coming from the east, you reach an esplanade where stand the remains of three temples. The first **(E)** has recently been reconstructed. It is thought that the largest **(G)**, to the right of the road, was dedicated to Apollo: the columns, over 16 m - 50 ft — high, were built of blocks each weighing several tons.

Acropolis★★. — This stood on the other side of the depression called Gorgo Cottone. It was surrounded by a wall. There rose several temples **(A, O, C, D, B)** and the residential quarter of a Carthaginian city (4-3C BC) which have recently been excavated.

To the north, part of the ancient city has been laid bare. Westwards, on the opposite bank of the Modione stand the remains of the Sanctuary of Demeter Malophoros (the dispenser of fruits) and of another temple **(M)**.

SOLUNTUM (SOLUNTO)

Michelin map **988** 36.

Soluntum stands on the summit of a promontory overlooking Cape Zafferano. It was a Phoenician village but passed under Roman influence in the 3C BC.

Ruins★. — *17 km - 10 miles* — from Palermo, take the road to Cape Zafferano, and directly afterwards the road on the left to the excavations *(reorganisation in progress — open 9 am to 1 hour before sunset; closed Mondays, 1 January, 25 April, 1 May, 15 August and 25 December; 100 lire weekdays, 70 lire holidays (weekdays), free on Sundays).* Soluntum has kept traces of its ancient forum, streets, houses, drainage, etc.

From Soluntum take the **road to Cape Zafferano** lined with eucalyptus trees, passing through Porticello, a curious fishing village (Sicilian carts).

SYRACUSE ★★★ (SIRACUSA)

Michelin map **988** 37 — Pop 124 111

The name of Syracuse suggests a warm climate, blue skies, a beautiful bay and the ancient ruins of a Greek city which was the rival of Athens. This is one of the high spots for tourists.

Syracuse was colonised in 734 BC by Greeks from Corinth who peopled the Island of Ortygia. It soon fell under the yoke of the Tyrants. In the time of its splendour the town had 300 000 inhabitants and ruled all Sicily. Captured by the Romans in 212 BC, it was occupied successively by the Barbarians, the Byzantines (6C AD), the Arabs (9C) and by the Normans.

The Tyrants of Syracuse. — In the Greek world, dictators called Tyrants (from the Greek word *turannos*) exercised unlimited power over certain cities, especially Syracuse. Already in 485 BC Gelon, the Tyrant of Gela, had become master of Syracuse and, with the help of the Tyrant of Agrigento, Thero, had defeated the Carthaginians at Imera. After a brief period of democracy Gelon was succeeded by the famous Denys the Elder. Denys (430-368 BC) lived in constant fear. This is symbolised by the sword which he had suspended by a horsehair above the head of Damocles, a jealous courtier. The Tyrant of Syracuse wore a shirt of mail under his clothing, changed his room every night and, not daring to be attended by a barber, had his beard singed by his daughters.

The Forgetfulness of Archimedes. — Archimedes, the famous geometrician born at Syracuse in 287 BC, was so absent-minded that he would forget to eat and drink. His servants would drag him to his bath, and there he continued to draw geometrical figures with his finger in the ashes of the wood fire. It was in his bath that he discovered his principle: any body immersed in water loses weight equivalent to that of the water it displaces. Delighted, he jumped out of the bath and ran naked through the streets shouting: "Eureka!" (I have it!).

When defending Syracuse against the Romans, Archimedes set fire to the enemy fleet by focusing the sun's rays with a system of mirrors and lenses. But when the Romans succeeded in entering the town by surprise, Archimedes, deep in his calculations, did not hear them, and a Roman soldier ran him through with his sword.

■ ARCHAEOLOGICAL AREA★★★ (Zona Archaeologica) *time: 2 1/2 hours*

Open 9 am to 1 hour before sunset; closed Mondays, 1 and 6 January, 1 May, 15 August and 8, 25 and 26 December; 500 lire.

The area extends over the ancient quarter of Neapolis, on a site overlooking the Ionian Sea.

Viale Rizzo★★. — This is a panoramic road, which affords remarkable overall views of the ancient ruins, the city of Syracuse and the sea.

Greek Theatre★★★ (Teatro Greco). — The theatre dates from the 5C BC and is one of the largest (134 m - 440 ft — across) and best preserved theatres of the ancient world. The first performance of *The Persians* of AEschylus was given in it. There is a view of Syracuse from the upper tier of seats. You can also see the remains of the porticoes and the Muses' Cave, with a fountain. A little farther on is the **road to the tombs**, which is hewn out of the rock.

The monumental **Altar of Hiero II** was built by that Tyrant for public sacrifices.

Paradise Quarry★★★ (Latomia del Paradiso). — This former quarry in the chalk, which is surmounted by a belvedere, was so-named in the 17C by the painter Caravaggio. Part of the roof has fallen but the natural pillars exist in a pretty orange garden.

The **Ear of Denys★★★** (Orecchio di Dionisio) is an artificial grotto in the form of an ear-lobe, 65 m long and 25 m high — 213 × 76 ft. It is famous for its exceptional echo, which enabled the Tyrant Denys to overhear the talk of the prisoners he confined in a lower room.

The **Cordmakers' Cave★★** (Grotta dei Cordari) gets its name from the cord makers who worked there, being able, thanks to the humid air, to spin and plait their hemp.

Roman Amphitheatre★ (Anfiteatro Romano). — The 2C AD amphitheatre is hewn out of the rock. The entrance and gangways for animals and gladiators can still be seen.

Catacombs of St. John★★ (Catacombe di San Giovanni). — A monk will show you through these 5-6C catacombs, consisting of a main gallery from which secondary galleries radiate. These end in chapels, some of them painted with frescoes. When leaving the catacombs, pay a visit to the 4C crypt of St. Marziano. This was the first Christian church in Sicily.

■ OLD TOWN★★ (Città vecchia)

On the Island of Ortygia the streets are rich in mediaeval or Baroque palaces, oratories, wrought iron balconies and small, secluded squares open to the Ionian Sea.

Arethusa Fountain★ (Fonte Aretusa). — This is the legendary cradle of the city. The nymph Arethusa, pursued by the river-god Alpheus, took refuge in the Island of Ortygia and changed into a spring. Though near the sea, the fountain, built with a wall, runs with fresh water. From the nearby platform there is a view of the beautiful Bay of Syracuse.

Cathedral★ (Duomo). — The cathedral was built in the 7C on the foundations of the former Temple of Minerva, using the nine columns which can be seen on the north side and the nineteen columns of the nave. The monumental Baroque façade stands in a fine square lined with oleanders and Baroque palaces. Inside, note the 13C font (first chapel on the right) and the St. Lucy Chapel (Santa Lucia — second on the right).

■ ADDITIONAL SIGHTS

National Archaeological Museum★★ (Museo Archeologico Nazionale) (BZ M). — *Open 9 am to 2 pm; closed Mondays, 1 and 6 January, 1 May, 15 August and 8, 25 and 26 Christmas; 500 lire.* The museum is important for those wishing to know about Greek civilisation in Sicily. There is a marvellous collection of 5 and 4C BC vases. Outstanding items are the famous **Venus Anadyomene**, a Roman copy of an original Greek statue and a remarkable small Heracles, dating from the 4C AD. Two other exhibits are a reconstruction of the temple roofs and the curious early Christian sarcophagus of Valerius and Adelphia.

Capuchins' Quarry★★ (Latomia dei Cappuccini) (BY B). — *Provisionally closed.* Fine vegetation; 7 000 Athenians, made prisoner by Denys of Syracuse in 414 BC, were interned in the quarries.

Foro Italico (BZ). — A favourite walk for the Syracusans, it affords a superb **view★★** of the Bay of Syracuse.

SIRACUSA

0   400 m

St. Lucy's Church (Santa Lucia) **(BY C)**. — Burial of St. Lucy, by Caravaggio, in chancel.

Palazzo Bellomo(BZ G). — Built in the 13C and remodelled in the 15C, the palace houses the **National Museum** *(open 9 am to 2 pm; closed Mondays, 1 January, 25 April, 1 May, 15 August and 25 December; 100 lire),* in which you will see a fine Annunciation by Antonello da Messina and works by Venetian Mannerist painters; sacerdotal vestments, furniture and ceramics.

EXCURSIONS

Cyane Fountain★★ (Fonte Ciane). — *About 4 hours west by boat Rtn; fare by arrangement with the boatman.* Start from Porto Grande. You reach the fountain by going up the Cyane River, along which there are papyrus beds. According to legend, the nymph Cyane, wife of Anapo, was changed into a spring because she opposed the abduction of Proserpine by Pluto.

Castle of Euryalus★ (Castello Eurialo). — *Northwest, 9 km - 6 miles.* This, one of the greatest fortresses of the Greek era, was built by Denys the Elder. Fine panorama.

TAORMINA ★★★

Michelin map 988 37 — Pop 10 054

Taormina stands on a wonderful **site**★★★ at an altitude of 206 m - 675 ft. It forms a balcony overlooking the sea, facing Etna, and is a climatic resort of worldwide repute. Tourists can enjoy its peaceful atmosphere and its beautiful monuments, views and gardens.

Greek Theatre★★ (Teatro Greco). — *Open 9 am to 1 hour before sunset; closed Mondays, 1 and 6 January, 1 May, 15 August and Christmas; 750 lire.* The theatre dates from the Hellenic period — 3C BC — but was remodelled by the Romans. It measures 109 m - 358 ft — across. Performances of Classical plays are given in summer. From the upper tiers there is a **view**★★★, between the stage columns, of the littoral and Etna — best at sunrise and sunset.

Public Gardens★★ (Giardino Pubblico). — The gardens are decked with flowers and exotic plants. The view from the terraces commands the coast and Sicilian Sea.

Piazza 9 Aprile★. — A terrace giving a fine panoramic **view**★★ over the Gulf of Taormina.

Corso Umberto★. — This, the main street of Taormina, is bounded by the Porta Catania, Porta del Centro, Torre dell'Orologio (Clock Tower) and the Porta Messina.

The Cathedral with its Gothic façade stands in the Piazza del Duomo. The Palazzo Corvaia in the Piazza Vittorio Emanuele (formerly the Forum) dates from the 15C.

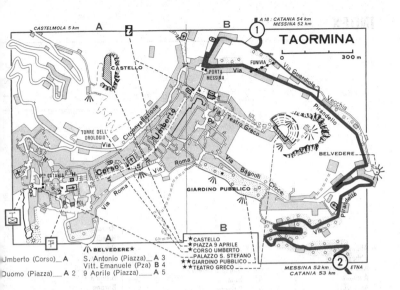

TAORMINA

Umberto (Corso)__ **A**	S. Antonio (Piazza)__ **A 3**	
Duomo (Piazza)__ **A 2**	Vitt. Emanuele (Pza) **B 4**	
	9 Aprile (Piazza)____ **A 5**	

★ CASTELLO
★ PIAZZA 9 APRILE
★ CORSO UMBERTO
★★ PALAZZO S. STEFANO
★★ GIARDINO PUBBLICO
★★ TEATRO GRECO

Castle★ (Castello). — The castle is built on the summit of Monte Tauro (390 m — 1 279 ft), on the remains of the former acropolis. There is a **panorama★★** of Taormina, the coast and Etna.

Belvedere★. — A balcony view of the Aspromonte in Calabria, the Sicilian coast and Etna.

St. Stephen's Palace (Palazzo Santo Stefano). — Fine 15C building.

EXCURSIONS

Castelmola★. — *Northwest, 5 km - 3 miles.* This village, once the rival of Taormina, is surmounted by castle walls. There is a wide view of Sicily and the sea.

Cape Schisò. — *South, 7 km - 4 miles.* Leave by ②, the road to Catania. Remains of ancient Naxos, a Greek colony founded in 735 BC and destroyed by the tyrants of Syracuse *(p 283).*

TINDARI

Michelin map 988 37.

The ancient Greek Tyndaris, founded in 396 BC, is perched on the summit of the cape of the same name and overlooks the whole Gulf of Patti.

Belvedere. — The belvedere is near a church which is a place of pilgrimage. There are interesting **views★★** of the Gulf of Patti, the Peloritani Mountains and Nebrodi.

Ruins. — By following the remains of the city walls you will reach the theatre on a fine site facing the sea. From the theatre the Decumanus (main street of the town) leads to the basilica and the forum and runs beside quarters recently uncovered.

TRAPANI

Michelin map 988 35 — Pop 70 308

Trapani, has a sheltered port (salt trade) within sight of the Egadi Isles.

A pretty road, running beside the sea, links the centre of the town with San Giuliano beach. The **Villa Margherita** is a pleasant public park in the centre of the town.

Church of the Annunciation (Santuario dell'Annunziata). — The church was built early in the 14C and remodelled and enlarged in the 17C. The 16C Renaissance Sailors' Chapel on the north side is crowned with a dome. The **Chapel of the Madonna★**, behind the high altar, contains a Renaissance arch carved in the 16C, a bronze grille dated 1591 and a graceful statue of the Virgin attributed to Nino Pisano (14C).

The **Pepoli Museum**, in the conventual buildings *(open 9 am to 1.30 pm; in addition 3 to 6 pm on Wednesday (5.30 pm in winter); closed on Mondays; 500 lire),* has a picture gallery in which there are a polyptych by the 15C Sienese school; a St. Francis by Titian and a Pietà by Roberto di Oderisio (14C). Local crafts are also on display.

Egadi Isles★ (Isole Egadi). — *Daily car ferry service from Trapani to Favignana, Levanzo and Marettimo (apply to the Salvo Agency, Molo Sanità, ☎ 40515); aliscafi (hydrofoils) provide swift crossings to the three islands (apply to Salvo Agency, address as above, or to Aliscafi — Sud Company, 9 Via Eurialo, Trapani, ☎ 22803).* The islands attract with their wild aspect, transparent blue sea and the beauty of the shores. The port of Favignana, the main town of the group of islands, is guarded from above by old forts which were used as prisons by the Bourbons. A factory for canning the tunny captured in *tonnara,* or nets, and killed by harpoon *(mattanza)* stands in the town; the fishing takes place in May and June.

USTICA Island ★★

Michelin map 988 35 — Pop 1 104

Access. — *From Palermo, boat service (some boats take cars) — apply to SIREMAR, 120 Via F. Crispi, Palermo, ☎ 582403. Hydrofoil service 1 May to 15 October (apply to Pietro Barbaro, 51 Via Principe di Belmonte, ☎ 586533).*

This volcanic island is picturesque with black lava soil reaching down to the water's edge, a coastline indented with creeks and hollowed with caves, white houses and terraced croplands. An ancient fortress dominates all.

When walking you get **views★★** of the sea and different parts of the island. The **Blue Grotto★** (Grotta Azzurra) can only be reached by boat.

INDEX

MANUFACTURE FRANÇAISE DES PNEUMATIQUES MICHELIN

© Michelin et Cᵢₑ, propriétaires-éditeurs, 1981

Société en commandite par actions au capital de 700 millions de francs

R.C. Clermont-Fd B 855 200 507 - Siège Social Clermont-Fd (France)

ISBN 2 06 015 330 - 1

Photocompo. : Ateliers Typographiques à Châtillon-sous-Bagneux — Imp. ISTRA, Strasbourg

Printed in France 4-81-60 — Dépôt légal 2ᵉ trim. 1981